Table of Contents

*This book is made to be read in order. Skipping ahead may phrasing.

Introduction

Part 1 – Blocks & Deflections

Part 2 – Head Movement

How To Best Use This Book and Make Progress

The purpose of this book is not to start you off from scratch, nor is it to have you master every style and technique explained within. Instead, it is to introduce you to a wide range of concepts, styles and techniques so that you may use them to help build upon your own style. For instance, even if you never again try to use the High Guard, the principles explained in that section could still help you to absorb and deflect the impact of punches in your own chosen style. Nearly every technique explained in this book is possible in any Stance or any Guard. Always practice under the eyes of a qualified, professional coach.

Many of these principles build upon each other, so it is highly recommended that your read this book in order. Much of the crucial information lies within the drills, so it is best to read them even if you do not have a chance to practice them. At the end of each chapter (and sometimes mid chapter) a list of fighters who use the techniques explained, and when they used them, has been provided. There are a lot of strange and untested techniques out there, so I figured it best to hold this book to the same standards as any other work of non-fiction and provide references.

As always with martial arts, learning these principles will take a lot of hard work. Remember to have fun; after all there is nothing more satisfying than the feeling of finally pulling off that perfect counter.

Basic Principles

Head Movement In A Wide vs Narrow Stance

Having a wide, squared up stance and posture (Pic A) verses a more narrow, sideways stance (Pic B) comes with a lot of benefits and downsides. But one thing that's vital to understand is how each affects head movement.

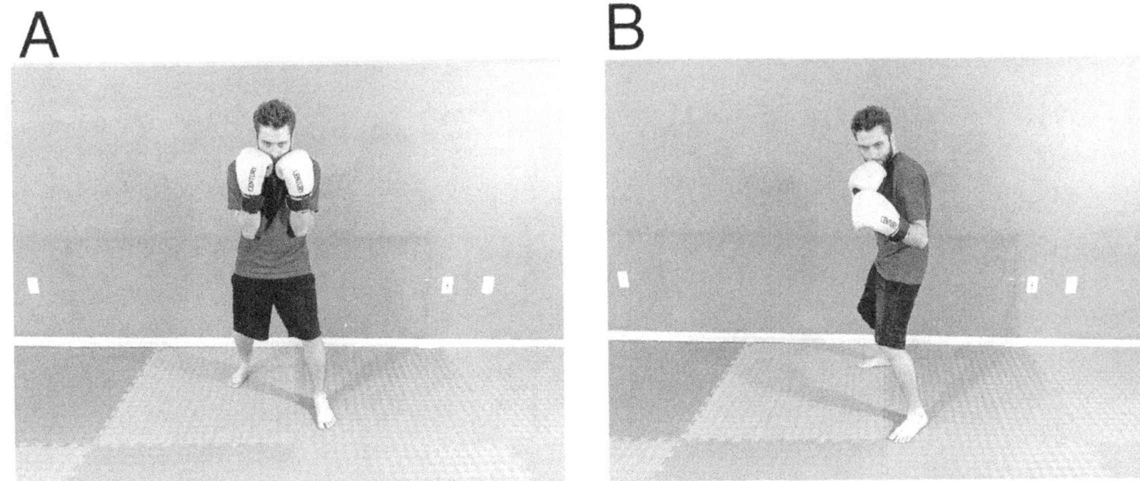

A more forward stance limits how far you can Pull back (Pic A), but it also allows you more lateral (side to side) movement. In other words, you can Duck, Slip or Weave much further to the left and right (Pics B to D). *Keep in mind that these pictures are only meant to display the full range of motion possible, and most fighters would not over extend their torso this much (although some great fighters have and do).*

In contrast, a more narrow stance only allows for lateral head movement to the Inside (Pics A to B). You are able to Pull back much further (Pic C) but will be very limited in how far you can Slip, Duck or Weave to the Outside (Pic D).

Returning With A Counter vs Intercepting With A Counter

Most counters are Return Counters, where you perform a defensive movement to avoid a strike (Pics A to B) and then Return a strike of your own once you are safe (Pic C). A more dangerous, but effective, method is to Intercept an opponent's strike by throwing a strike of your own at the same time (Pics D to E).

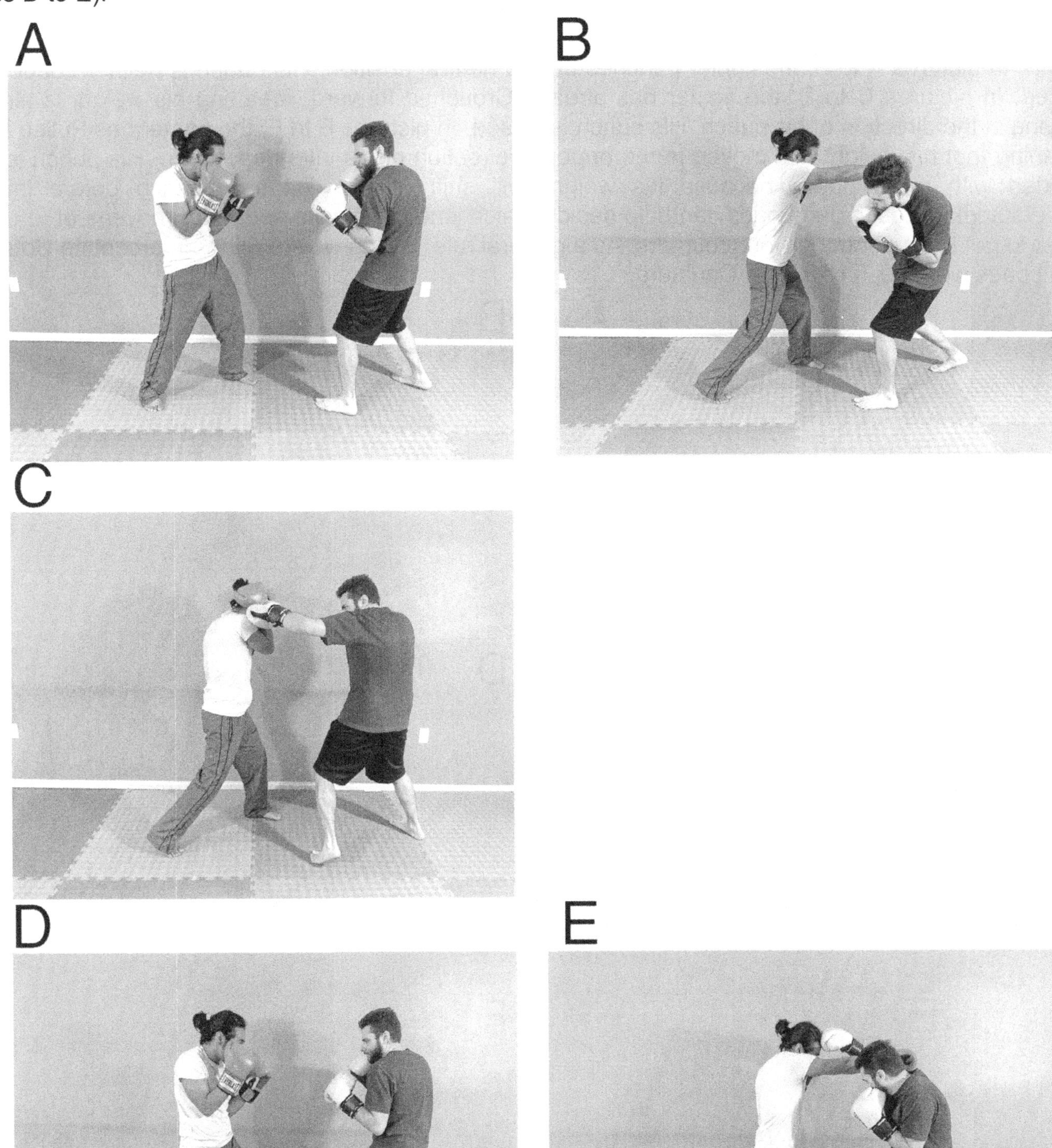

Loaded Strikes vs Eased Strikes

A Loaded strike means that the strike has weight behind it because your weight is Loaded in the opposite way that the strike is travelling. For instance, you may have your weight on your Rear Foot and punch forward, Loading the strike. Or you may have your weight on your Right Foot and strike to the left. An Eased strike means that throwing the strike will be easier, as you have already positioned your weight toward the direction of your strike. For instance, you place your weight on your Lead Foot and then move forward.

In pictures A to B, the fighter punches from a neutral position. His punch is neither Loaded nor Eased. In pictures C to D, the fighter has already Crouched forward, meaning his weight is already moving in the direction of his punch. His punch is Eased. In pictures E to F, the fighter has Pulled back, meaning that his weight has moved in the opposite direction of his intended punch. His punch is now Loaded with more power because his weight will shift over a longer distance before impact. Understanding Eases and Loads can help decide which kinds of blocks and head movement to use in order to get the most out of your counters. As a general rule, Eases work best for Intercepting Counters and Loads work best for Return Counters.

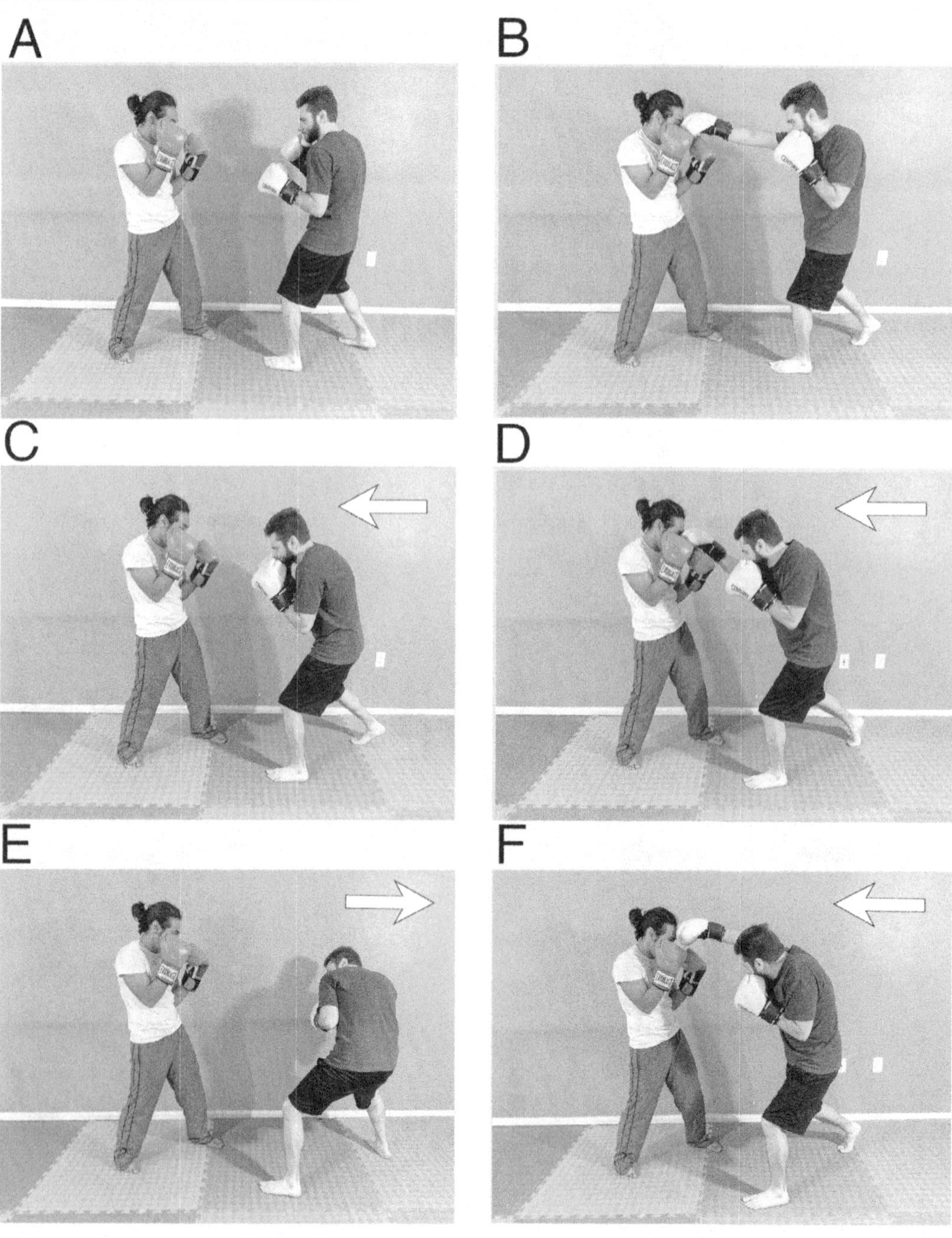

Orthodox vs Southpaw

It is called an Orthodox stance when you have your left foot forward (Pic A) and a Southpaw Stance if you have your right foot forward (Pic B). This holds true regardless of if you are in an Open or Closed stance with your opponent.

A

B

Open vs Closed Stance

A Closed Stance is one where you and your opponent both have the same foot forward (Pic A). You either both have your left foot forward or both have your right foot forward. An Open Stance is one where you and your opponent have opposite feet forward (Pic B). Either you have your right foot forward and your opponent has their left foot forward, or you have your left foot forward and your opponent has their right foot forward.

A

B

A Closed Stance makes it harder for you and your opponent to attack with their Rear Side. This is because your Lead Side will obstruct Rear Side attacks. In this way it may be considered a safer stance. However, in a Closed Stance you will be more susceptible to Lead Side attacks like the Jab (Pic A). Notice in Pic A how the fighters Lead Hand and Lead Shoulder are in position to obstruct a Cross, but a Jab may get through.

In contrast, in an Open Stance your Lead Side and your opponent's Lead Side will get in each other's way (Pic B). However, this makes it easier to attack with your Rear Side. This is because your Lead Side is no longer in the way to obstruct Rear Side attacks (Pic C & D).

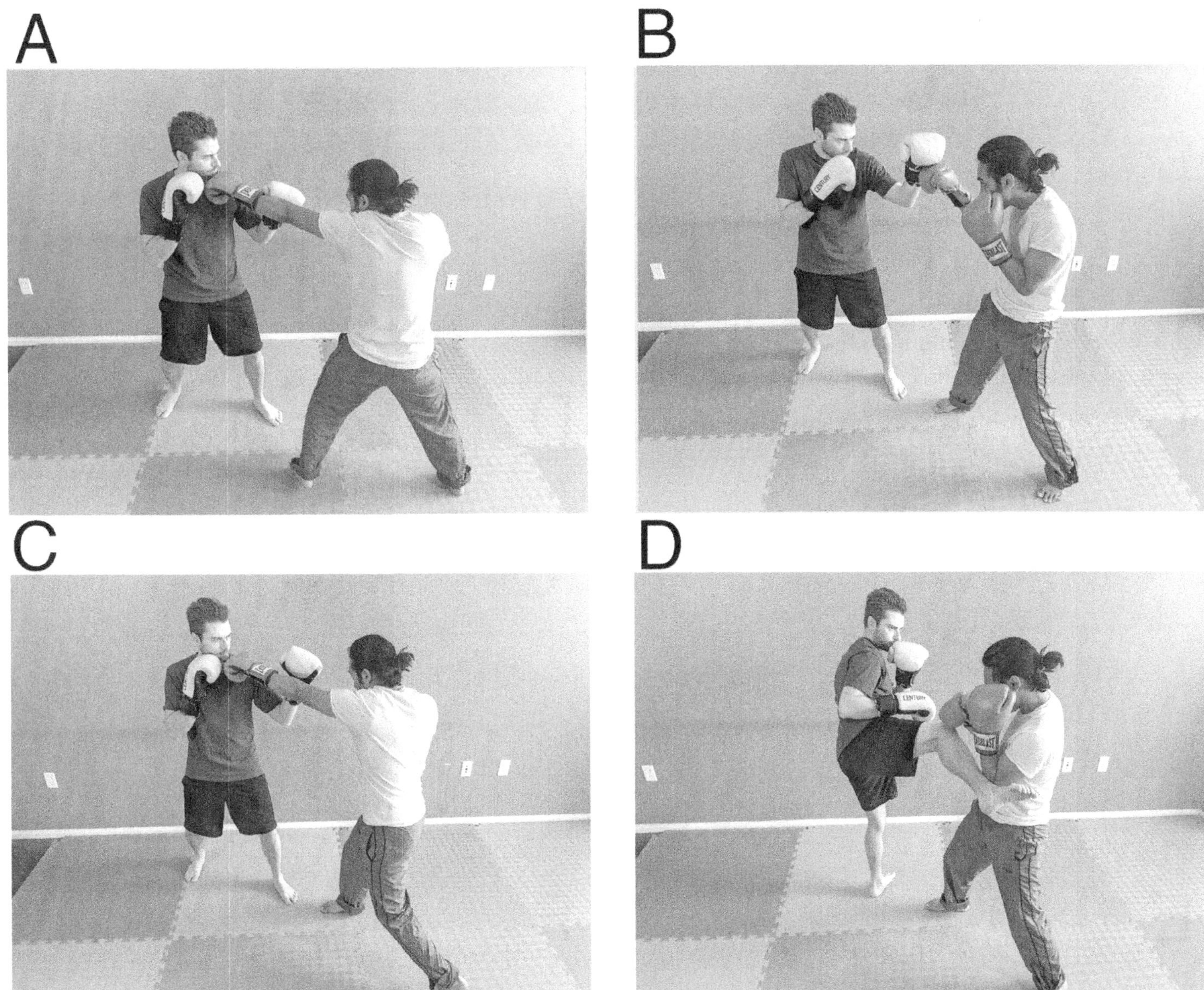

From a grappling perspective, it is easier to go after the opponents Rear Leg in a Closed Stance (Pics A to C). This makes techniques like the Double Leg Takedown easier to pull off. In contrast, an Open Stance moves a fighter's Rear Leg further away, especially if they stand in a bladed, narrow stance (Pics D to F). This will make Double Legs more difficult, as it will be harder to grab the Rear Leg.

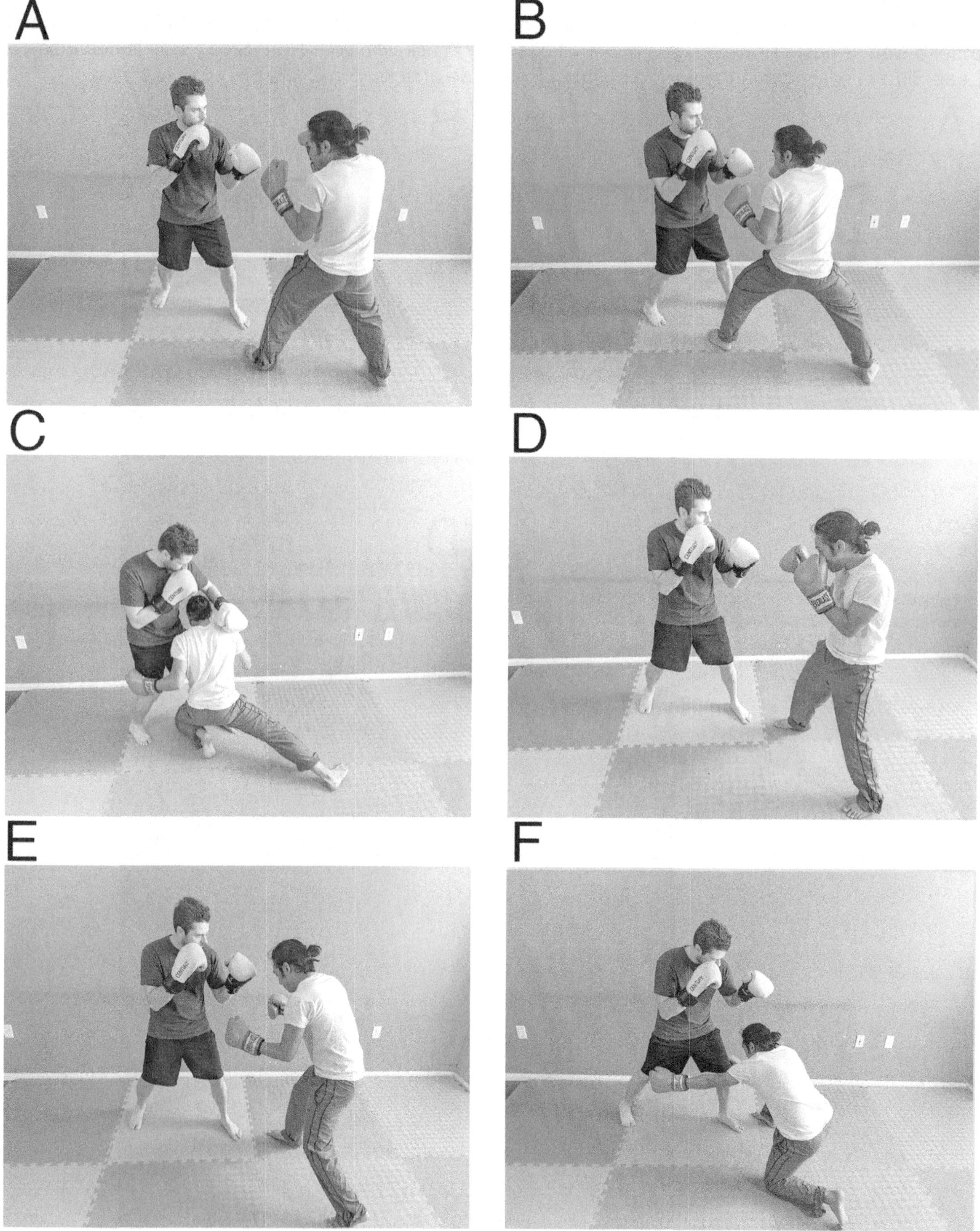

While an Open Stance may make Double Legs and certain other takedowns more difficult, it will also make it easier to secure a Single Leg or any other techniques that involve controlling a fighters Lead Leg (Pics A to C). This is because the front foot of both fighters are closer to each other and therefore it is easier to take an Outside Position with your Lead Foot.

A

B

C

Inside vs Outside

To step Inside is to move towards your opponent's chest (Pics A to B). To step Outside is to move towards their back (Pics C to D). This holds true when in a Closed or an Open Stance, if you are in Orthodox or Southpaw. Moving Outside is generally a superior position, as your opponent has less chances to hit you as you are behind them. However, look out for spinning attacks if your style allows them.

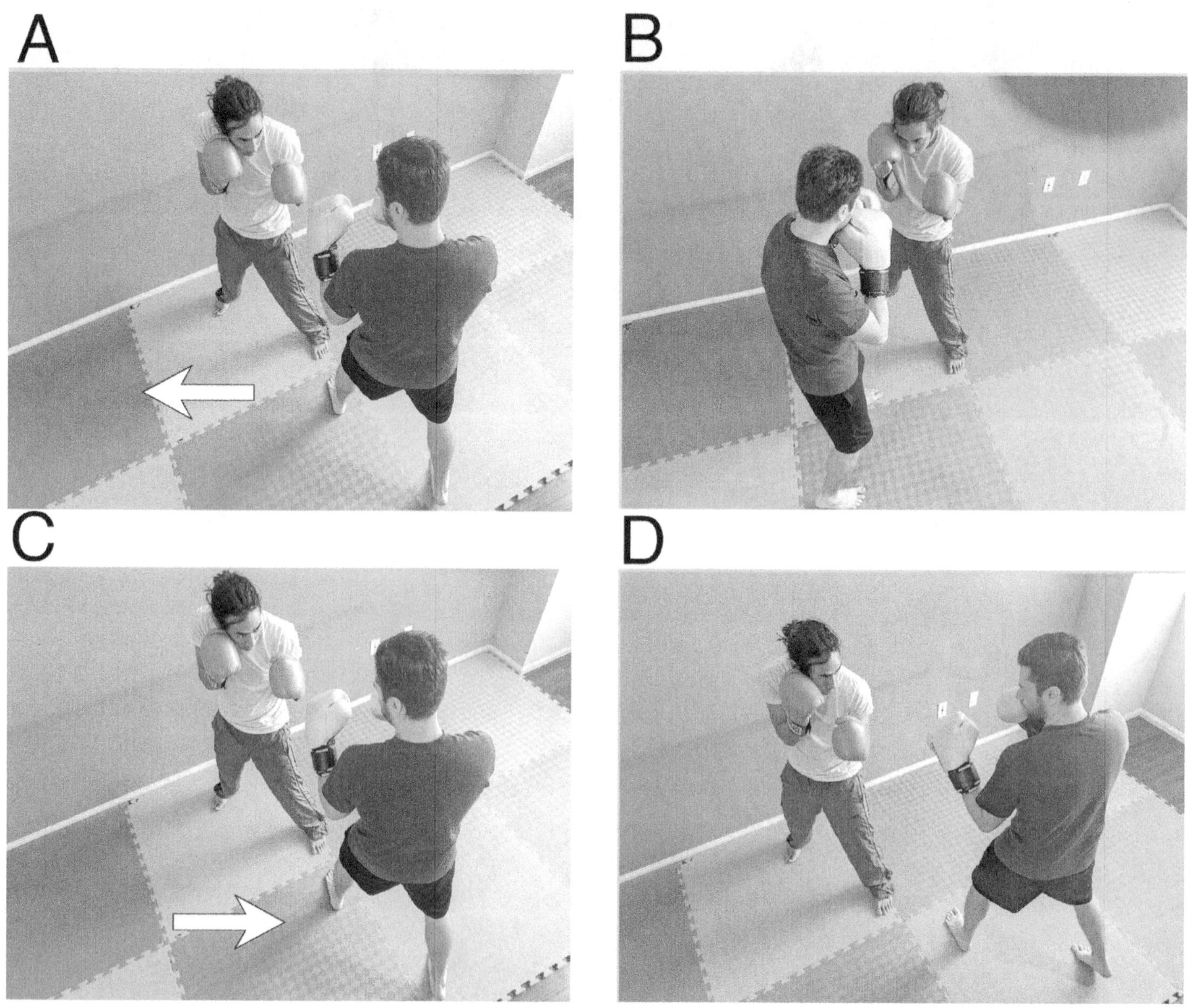

Taking a dominant Outside Foot Position is especially important in an Open Stance (Pics A to B). As mentioned before, the Lead Foot and Hands of both competitors tend to get in each other's way in an Open Stance. You can help your chances of defending or landing by adjusting your position. But keep in mind, there are times when it is favorable to move Inside as well (Pics C to D).

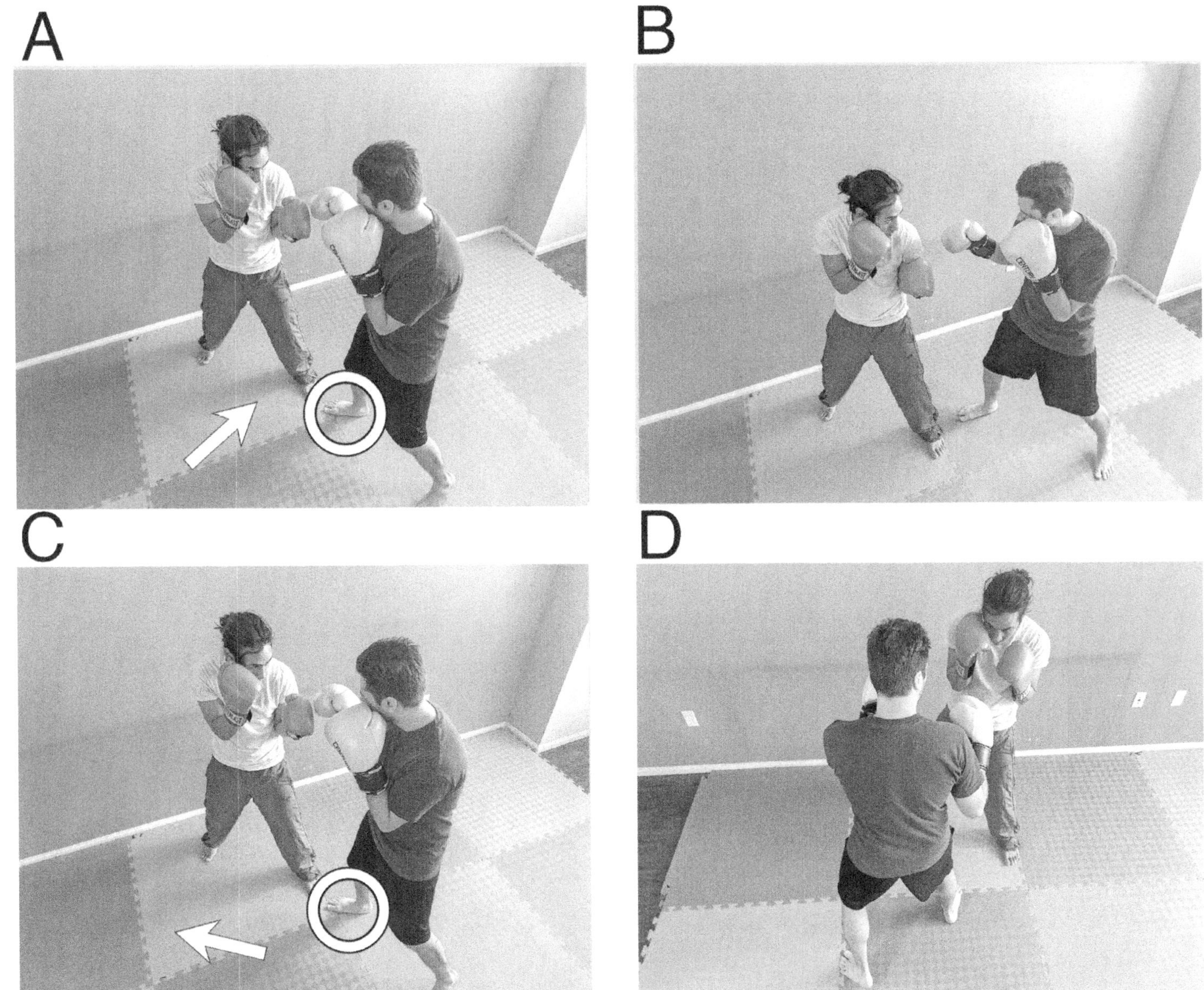

Stepping Outside will tend to give a better angle with which you can land your Rear Side attacks (Pics A to B). In particular, your Rear Straight will be nicely aligned right down the center. Rarer is to step Inside to align your Lead Hand down the center (Pics C to D). This can come with the downside of lining up your opponent's Rear Hand for them. However, if you fire off a Jab as you step Inside you will be in position to beat any of your opponent's attacks by taking a straighter path (Pics E & F).

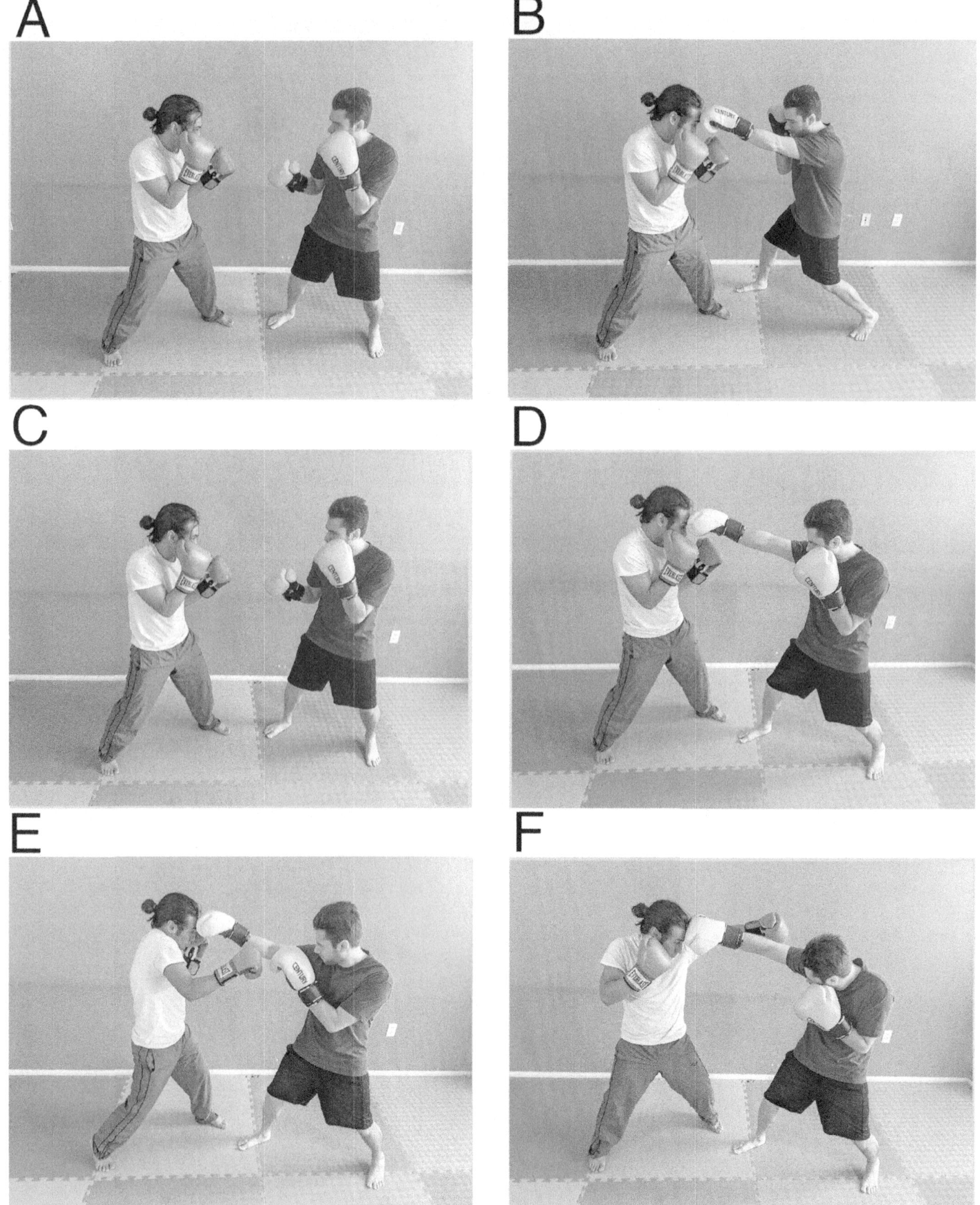

How To Drill

This book offers a number of drills to accompany the techniques. Some of the drills are more basic, but most are about mastering a specific concept. If you need some ideas on how to drill the specific techniques in this book, then I would recommend using the sequence below. Always go light until a competent coach advises you it is safe to go harder.

Steps

1. Practice in the air with a coach checking your form
2. Practice in the mirror
3. Practice the sequence on a bag or mitts
4. Practice low impact with a partner, trying to hit each other
5. Have partner mix in other attacks and other combinations you are already familiar with
6. Practice during light sparring

After this stage the technique should be perfected. It should come instinctually during moderate to hard sparring and even during real competitions or street fights. In the same way that your foot now instinctually presses the brake without you needing to consciously tell it to do so when seeing an obstruction in the road, so too will these counters come to you if the correct stimuli is presented.

Side Note: When drilling head movement with your partner, make sure to hit where their head just was rather than trying to follow it. Following head movement mid-strike is impressive during actual sparring or in a fight, but is pointless if you already know beforehand where your partners head will end up during that drill. In other words, if the drill is for your partner to evade a Jab by Slipping left, do not throw your punch to the left to catch them anyways. During a real fight you would have no way of knowing they would Slip left; they may instead Slip right, Duck, Parry, Cover Block, or simply step back. Catching your partner by following their head mid punch not only sets them up for failure, but also gives you a false sense of confidence. Be an excellent partner and find partners who are there to learn as well.

Part 1 – Blocks & Deflections

Catches, Parries & Traps

Catches

Catches are somewhere between a Block and a Parry. They do fight force with more force by stopping the impact of the strike, but at the same time they also allow for a bit more nuance. For instance, when Catching a punch you may be able to throw it off course; something that could not be done with most blocks. At the same time, you will be opening up your guard by extending your hand forward (Pics A to B). Catches can create opportunities for very fast counters, but will also leave you more vulnerable to Hooks on the side which you Catch. Overall, you will find that Catches are a reliable and simple method of defense. They are only useful against certain strikes like the Jab, but of course, negating an opponent's Jab is no small thing.

Rear Catch Against Jabs

Catch your opponent's strike by extending your Rear hand forward from your Guard. Try to do this at the last possible second (Pics A to B). Make sure to apply force, or your opponent will easily break through your Catch. At the same time, do not overextend. After all, one major benefit of the Catch is that it does not disturb your posture and requires little effort. After a successful catch, your hand should return immediately to Guard. Be especially wary of a follow up Lead Hook (Pic C).

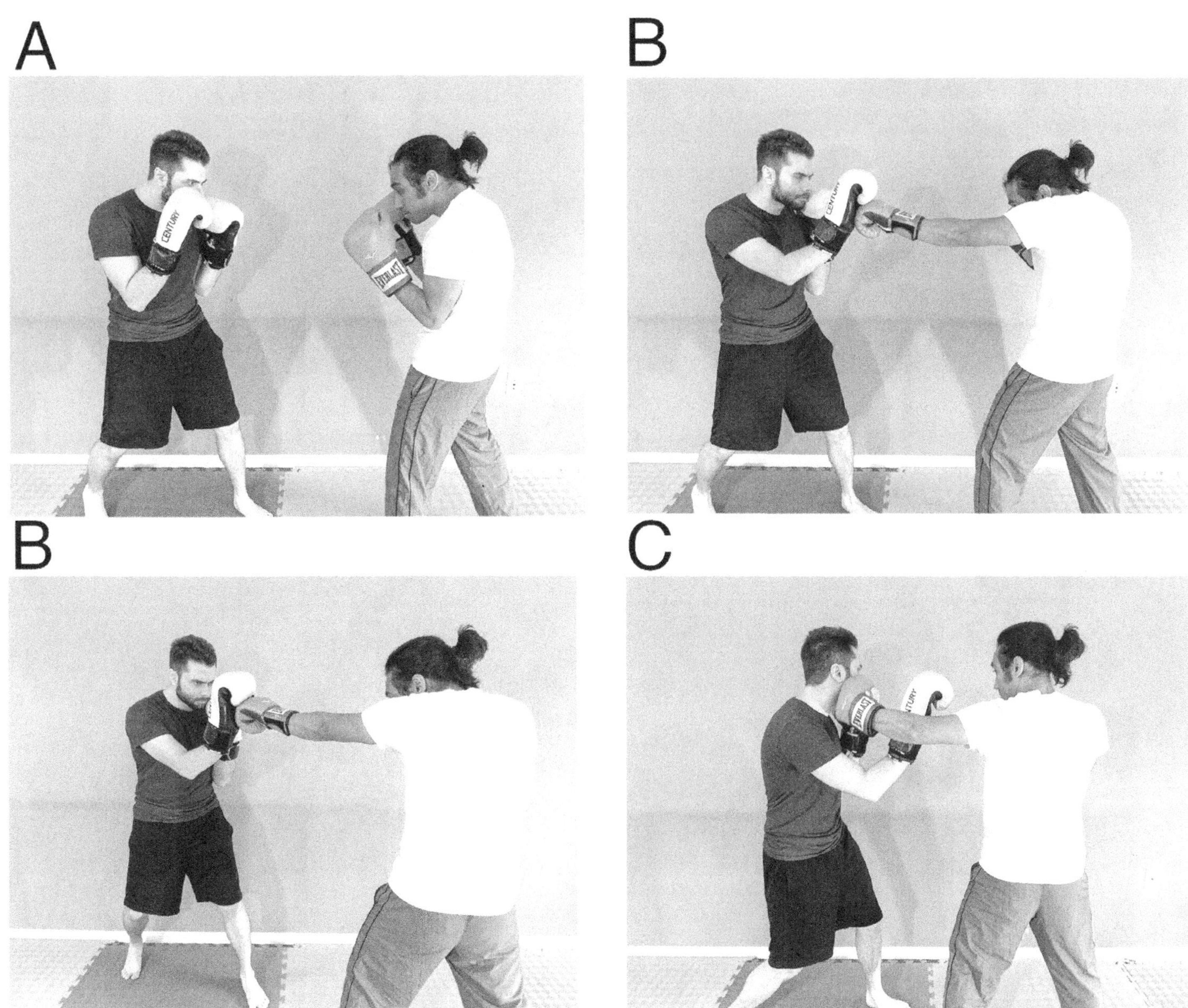

The Rear Catch is a specific defense used mostly for one attack (the Jab), but it is also a viable option against long Hooks (PIC A) that don't have too much of a curve. Or against Crosses when used in combination with a Shoulder Roll (Pic B) or an Elbow Block (Pic C).

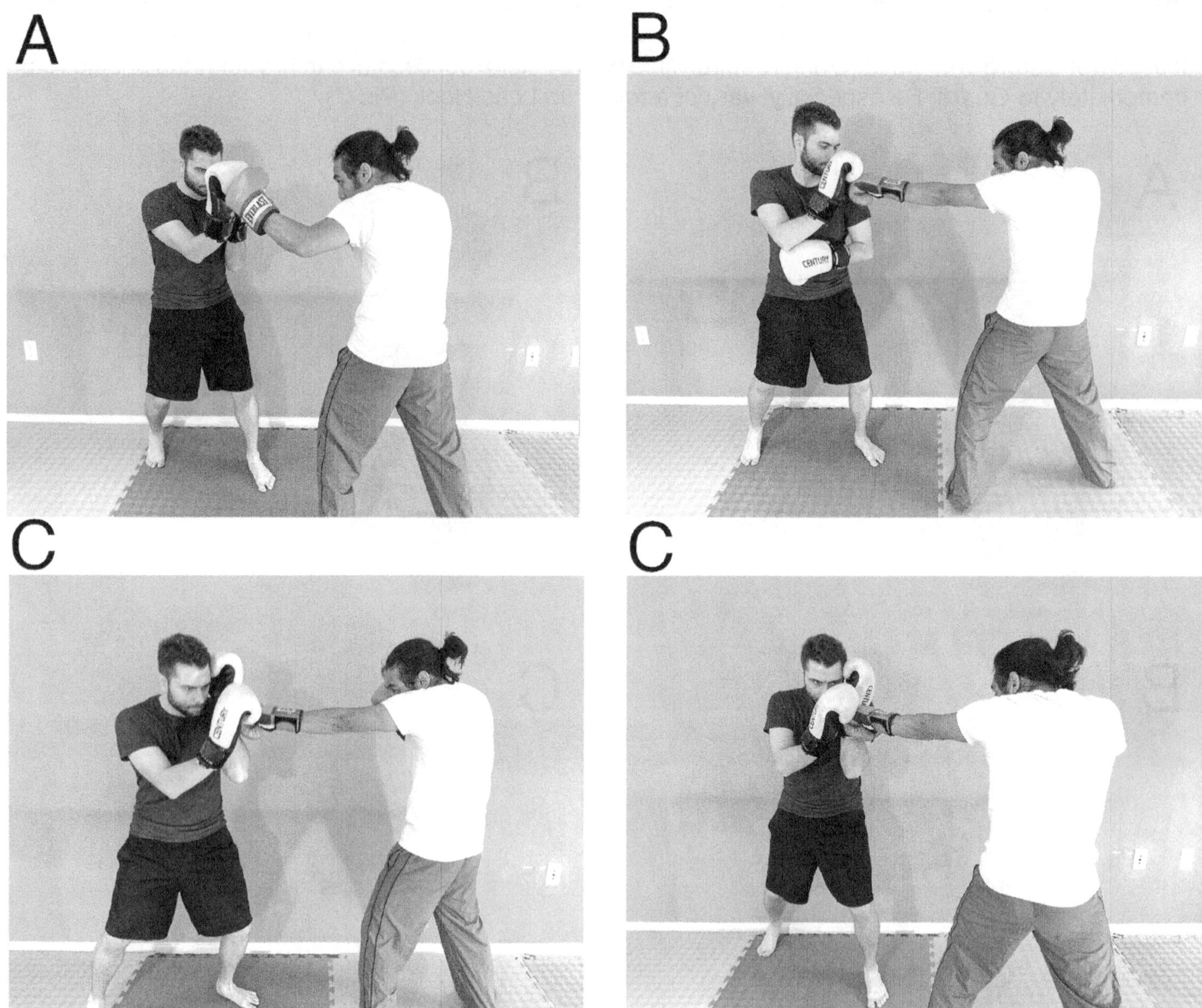

Lead Catch Against Crosses

Catch your opponent's strike by extending your Lead Hand forward from Guard at the last possible second. (Pics A to B).

The Lead Catch is a far riskier venture. Not only do you need to apply much more force by stopping your opponent's power hand with your weaker hand, you are also in a much more compromising position if you happened to predict the wrong punch. For instance, you may think you are Catching a Cross while actually opening yourself to a Rear Hook. That's not to say it can't be done. Canelo Alvarez and George Foreman are fighters who have made good use of the Lead Catch.

A

B

B

Catch & Redirect High

There are two ways to perform the Upward Catch, also known as a Bump. The first is to Catch your opponent's hand and then push it upwards, opening up their midsection to attack. (Pics A to C). The second is to target their wrist or forearm, coming up from underneath. (Pics D to F). This is especially useful if your hand is in a lower position than your opponent's before beginning the movement. For instance, if they keep a High Guard.

This is a very subtle movement with little movement or effort required to work. The main purpose of this defense is to knock the opponent's punch high in order to create openings. Although kickboxers and MMA fighters have occasionally sent opponents to the canvas by pushing up their kick, it is very hard to pull off. Great fighters who relied on this technique include Sugar Ray Robinson (who paired it with Catches, Inside Parries and Leverage Blocks), and Floyd Mayweather (who paired it with his Philly Shell defenses). Remember that you can look up who used these techniques and when in the Reference section at the end of each chapter.

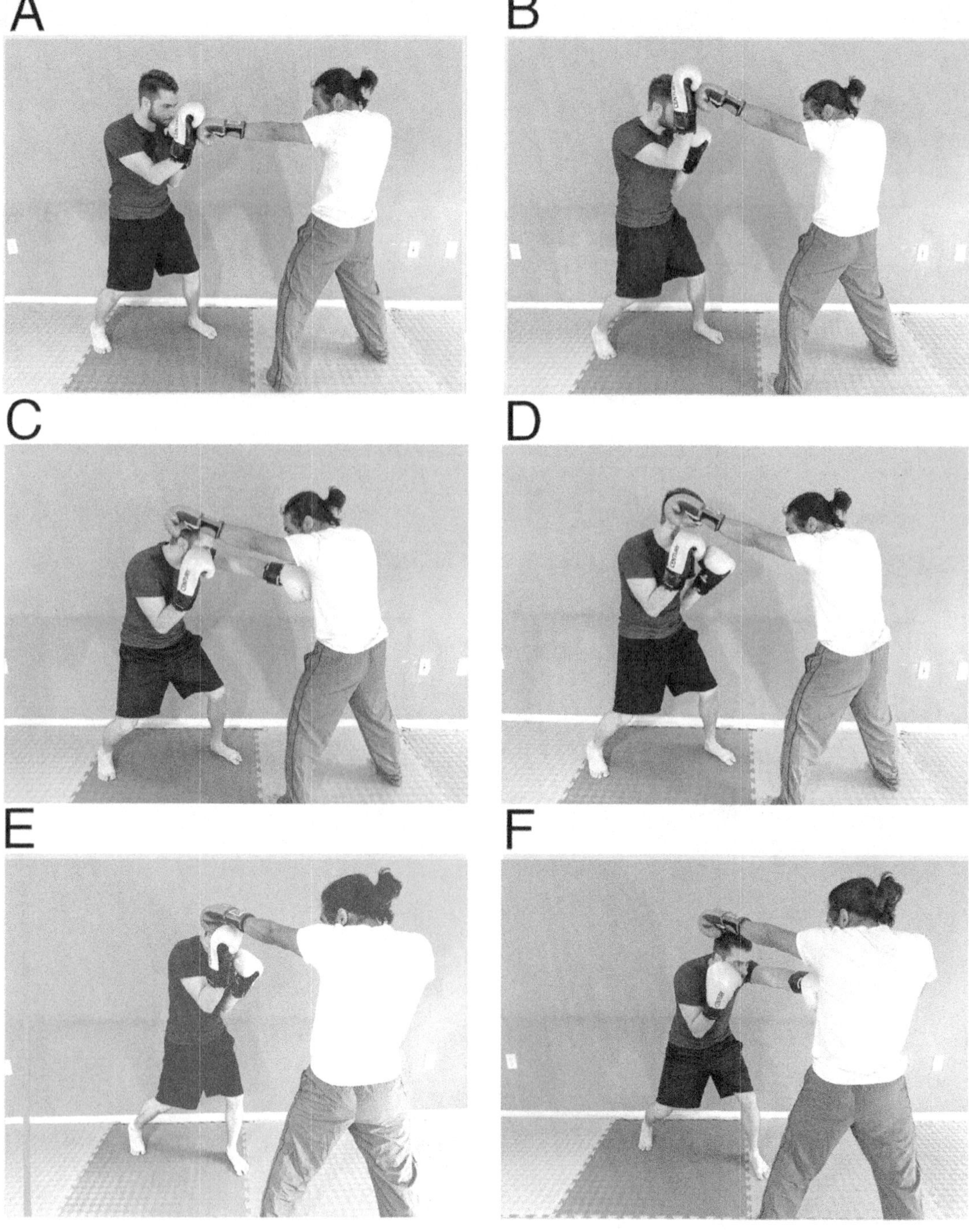

Catch & Redirect Low

Catch your opponent's hand and then push it downwards, opening up their chin to attack by clearing away their hand. (Pics A to B). Only a small amount of force is needed. If your hand travels too far down, you may end up exposing yourself instead. A counter will work very well off of the same hand that caught your opponent's punch. For instance, use a Rear Catch to swipe an opponent's Jab down and then counter with a cross off the same hand. (Pic C).

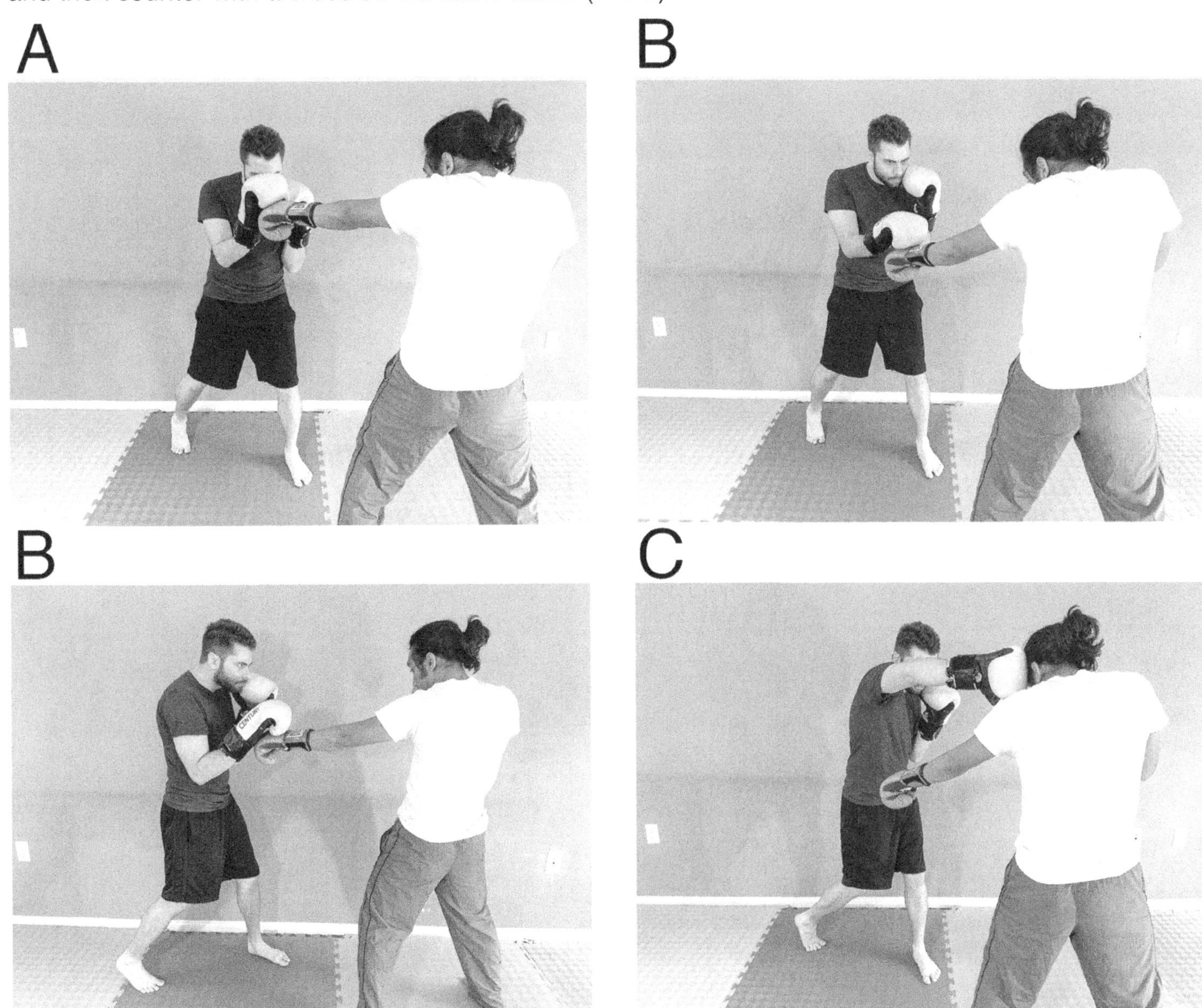

Open Stance Considerations

In an Open Stance, you and your opponent's Lead Hand and Lead Leg tend to get in each other's way. This means that Redirecting your opponent's Lead Hand is a highly valuable tool for a Southpaw fighter or an Orthodox fighter going up against one. Redirecting your opponent's Jab after you Catch it can create openings for your own Lead Hand (Pics A to D & E to F). This is an important concept to understand.

Catching Straights To The Body

Catch your opponent's low strike by extending your hand forward and down from guard at the last possible second. (Pic A). Keep your elbow as close to your ribs as possible, trying your best to only move your hand. Make sure to apply force, or your opponent will easily break through your Catch. You may also Duck as you Catch to lower your level to that of your opponent. That way you do not need to open up your Guard so much.

The upside of a Rear Low Catch is that is allows you to defend a Body Jab *and* fire out your own Lead Hand without disturbing your balance. In contrast, blocking may have required turning or tilting to take the force on your elbow or forearm.

While this same principle can apply for defending a Cross to the body(Pic B), it is usually best to simply Cover Block with your elbow (Pic C), as lowering and extending your Lead Hand will always leave your chin vulnerable to an opponent's power side (Pic B).

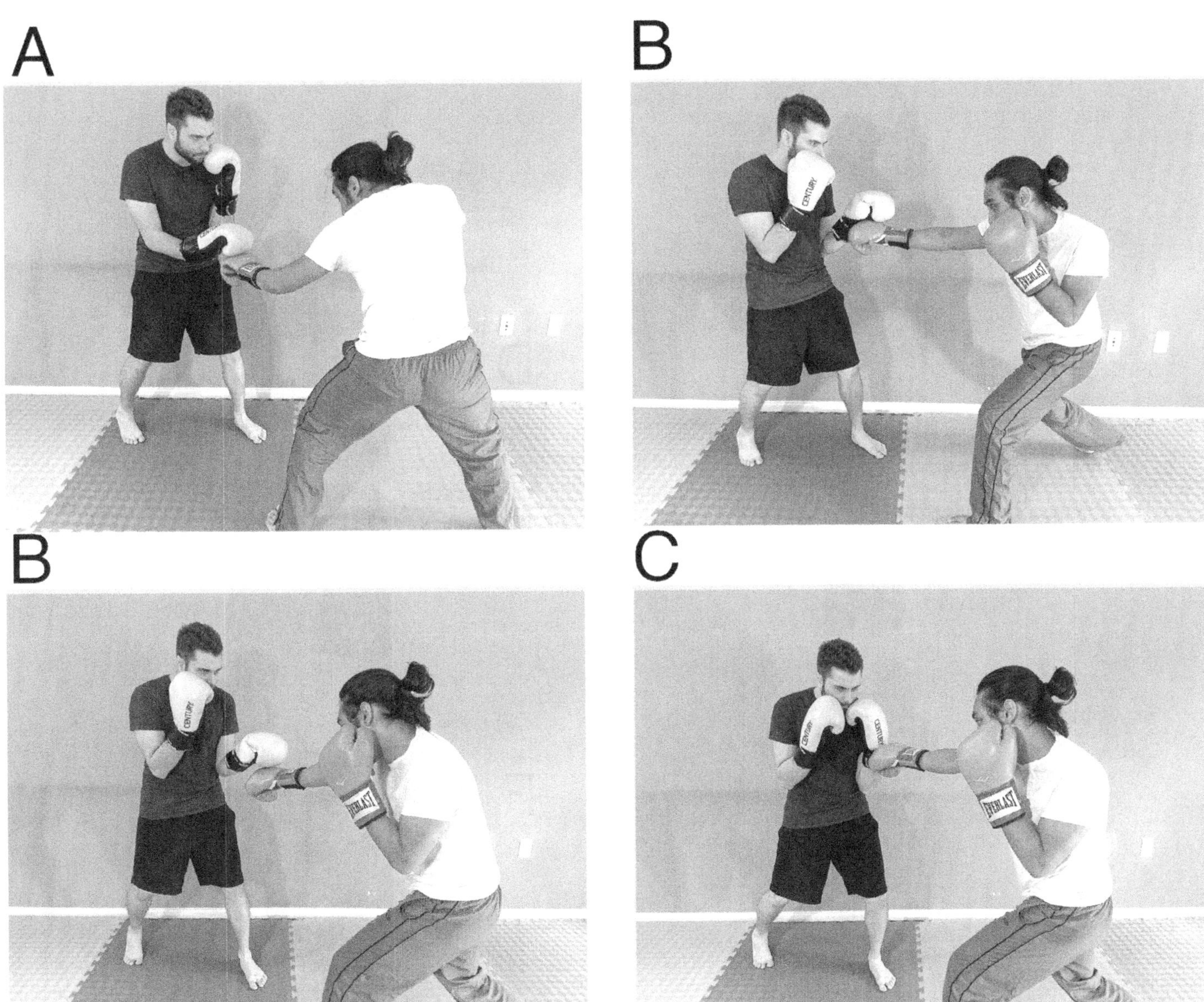

Catching Uppercuts

Most fighters either overreact or underreact to Uppercuts. Those that underreact usually pinch their arms together tightly to stop the punch coming up the middle. Not only does this often fail, it also opens them up to Hooks. Those that overreact use their entire arm to block the punch or jump and lean back like they just stepped on a land mine. While both methods can have merits in certain circumstances, a simple Catch is all that is required to stop an Uppercut. Catch the punch on your palm, as close to your guard as possible (Pics A to C). You may only need to move your hand a few inches. As always, you must be careful not to use too little force, or your hand will come flying back into your face (Pic D). At the same time, you need not drop your hand to meet the punch to early, exposing yourself to follow up attacks (Pics E to F).

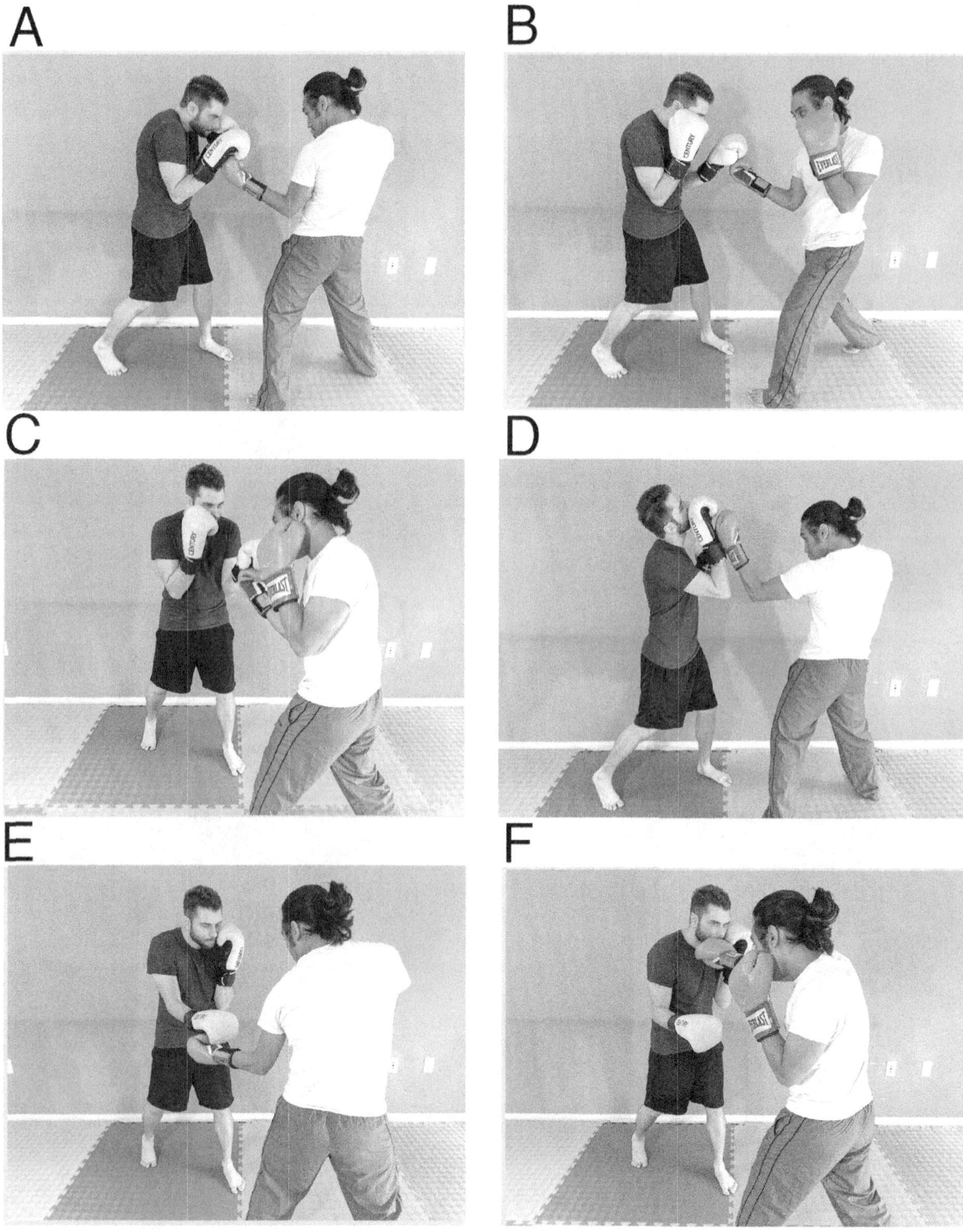

Drills

Drill 1 A

The drills in this section are simplistic, but will familiarize you with important concepts that are built upon throughout the book. It is best to take your time with them. To begin, Catch your partner's Jab(Pics A to B). Then, return a Jab of your own. Your partner will Catch your Jab as well (Pic C).

Now it's your turn to attack. Repeat the drill, switching which partner is attacking, and which is defending and countering. As always, begin by standing in place. Go slow and pause between attacks. As you both improve, up the speed, adding in footwork and feints. Try to actually hit your partner. Remember, this should be a light tap. Refer to the section on How To Drill to learn how to progress to using more power safely. If unsure, always ask your teacher or coach.

If in an Open Stance, you will be both Catching and Jabbing with your Lead Hand.

A

B

C

Drill 1 B

In the last drill you defended with a Return Counter, only firing back after you had defended your partners attack. Now it is time to try an Intercepting Counter. As your partner throws a Jab, Catch it and ***at the same time*** Intercept his attack with a Jab of your own. Your partner must then Catch your Intercepting Counter with his other hand (Pics A to B).

If in an Open Stance, you will Intercept with a Cross instead. (Pics C & D)

Once both partners have mastered this drill, you may combine this drill with the previous one. In other words, you may alternate using either a Return or an Intercepting Jab. This will force you and your partner to get used to defending both.

Drill 2 A

Catch your partners Jab and then Return a Cross (Pics A to B). Switch off each time.

Next perform the same drill with a Jab-Cross combination, defending the Jab–Cross with Catches and then Returning with a Jab-Cross combo of your own (Pics C to F). You may keep one partner as the attacker or switch off each time. If in an Open Stance, pay close attention to where you place your Lead Foot and how this helps or hinders your attacks.

Once you are comfortable with both of these sequences, it's time for the fun to begin. Your partner now alternates between attacks, throwing either a Jab *or* a Jab-Cross combination. You will again counter his Jab with a Cross, and his 1-2 with your own 1-2. You will notice, however, that it is far harder to safely throw your own Return Cross against your partners Jab when there is the possibility that he may follow up his Jab with a Cross of his own. Fights are messy things, and you must always be ready to counter or defend in any eventuality. This drill is a great lesson on how to balance risk vs reward.

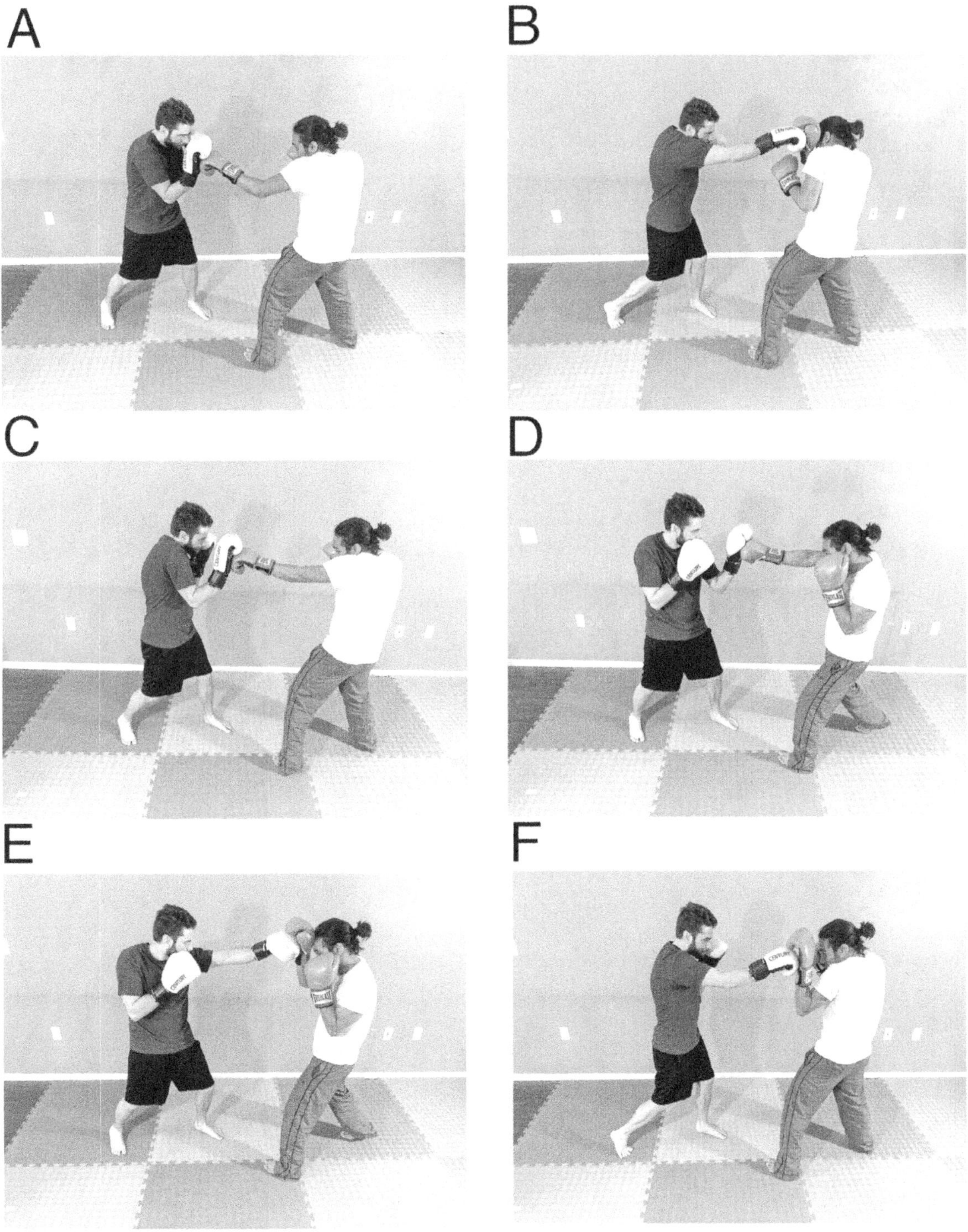

Drill 2 B

Have your partner throw a Jab-Cross combination, switching up aiming for your head or your body with each punch (Pics A to B). Try to use every combination of high and low. (Jab high-Cross low, Jab low-Cross high, Jab low-Cross low, etc.). Next, try to follow up with a Return Jab or Cross (Pic C). Once you are comfortable, try the drill again with Intercepting Counters. You may notice that it is fairly easy to Intercept your partners body punches with a punch to their head.

B

C

Drill 3

Take turns with your partner throwing and defending either a Jab-Lead Uppercut Combination (Pics A to C) or Jab-Rear Uppercut combination(Pics D to F). This will help teach you to inherently know which side your opponent is going to throw with, even at close range. When you are both comfortable, you may add onto the drill by Returning an Uppercut after defending.

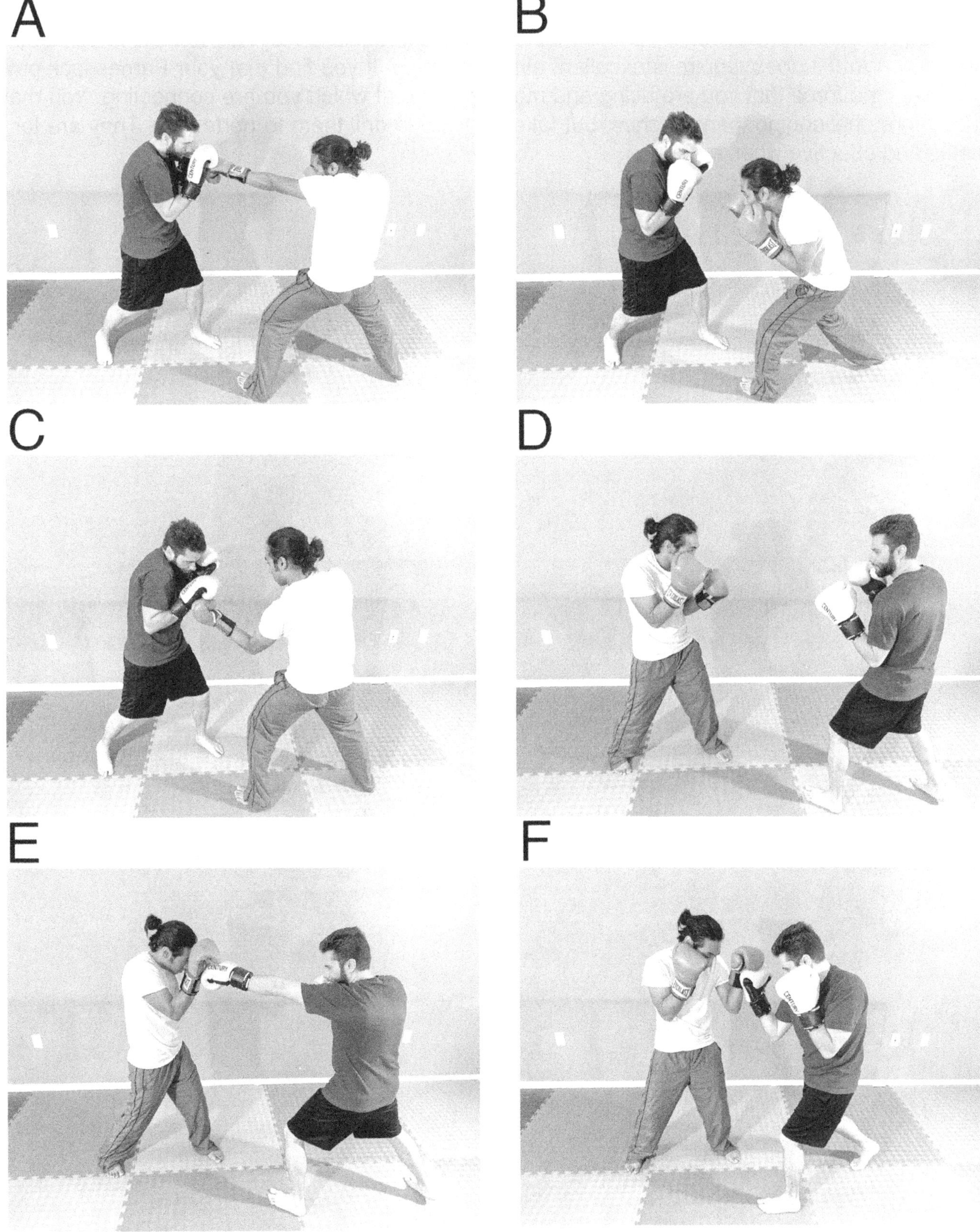

Parries

Parries are the go-to tool of the nuanced fighter. While many would argue that head movement is the highest form of defense because it leaves both hands free to attack, Parries provide some things that head movement just doesn't. Parries can ruin the retraction of an opponent's strike, destroy their ability to set up another attack, and throw them off balance. If done right it can even create new openings to exploit.

Keep in mind that above all, Parries must be subtle. It requires very little force to knock a powerful strike away. What it does require is excellent aim and timing. If you find that your Parries lack power, it may be less the force that you are using and more the time at which you are connecting. You may find Parries more challenging than Catches, but take the time to drill them to perfection. They are far more versatile and effective when mastered.

Outside Parry

Move your Hand from the Outside to the Inside, towards the center of your body (Pics A to B). Usually, your right hand will be used to Parry your opponent's left, and vice versa (Pics C to D). Unlike the Catch, it is not necessary to use too much force with Parries. Keep your movement as small as possible and try to connect near the end of your opponent's attack. Try to throw the opponent's strike off course, ruining their retraction and opening them up to attack. A good range of motion for beginners is to end with your hand by your opposite shoulder, ensuring that your opponent's punch goes over or past that same shoulder. You may find it possible to minimize the motion over time, especially in combination with head movement. For instance, Slipping and Parrying simultaneously can help to condense the motion of both.

The Outside Parry is a valuable tool for those with forward facing, squared up guards, as it works well to defend the center. As with the Lead Catch, it is usually best to avoid using a Lead Outside Parry. However, diverting an opponent's Cross can lead to some high risk/high reward counter opportunities.

Specialty Counter: Rear Outside Parry to Double Leg Takedown

GSP often used a Rear Outside Parry to clear his opponents arm out of the way before shooting for a takedown(Pics A to F). This prevented the opponent from immediately framing off of GSP's head or shoulder, or securing an Under Hook with the Lead Hand. At times he even pinned his opponent's lead arm, rendering it completely useless for takedown defense(Pic D).

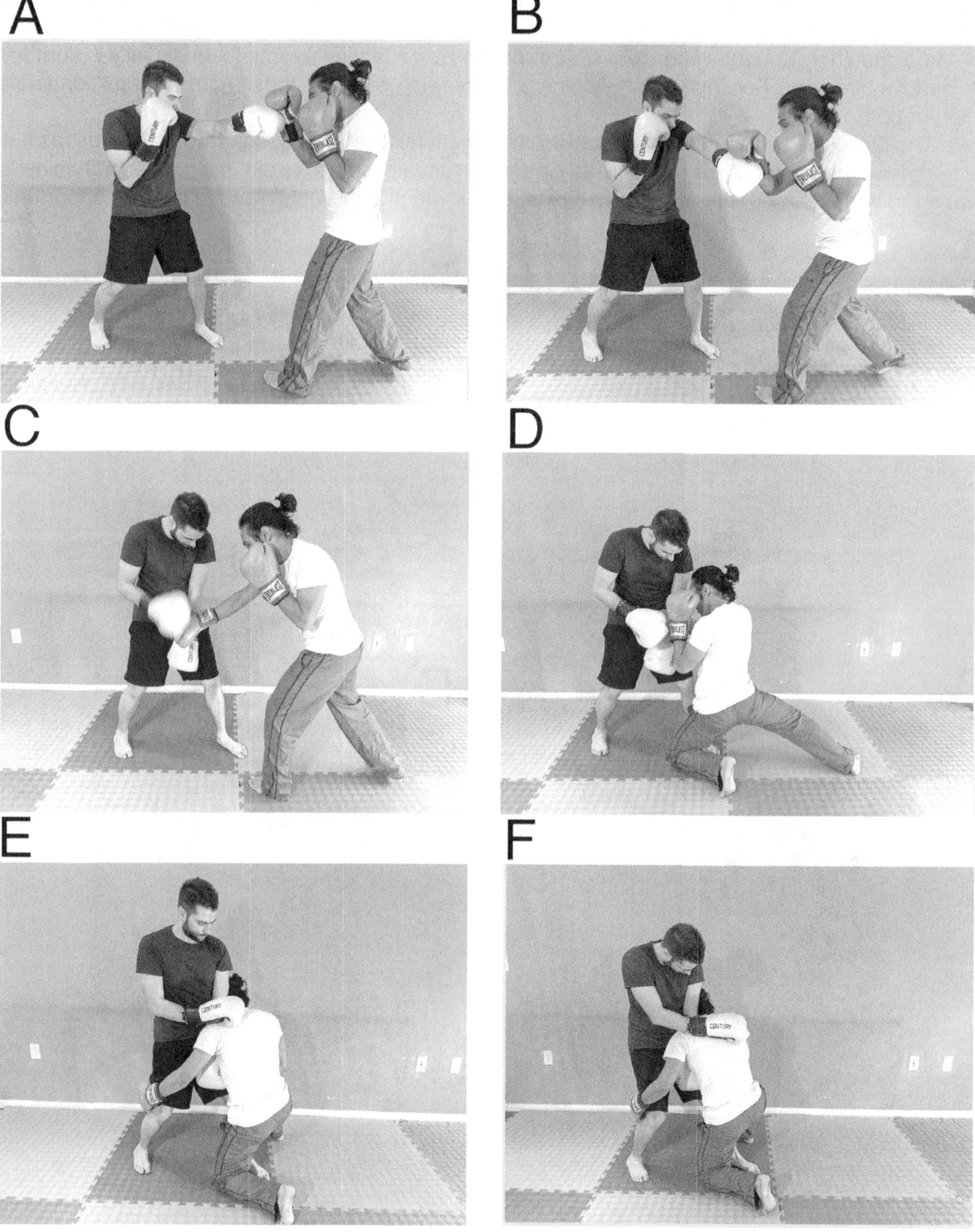

Trap & Redirect Across

If your reflexes are lightning fast, then you may be able to turn an Outside Parry into a Trap by closing your hand around your opponent's wrist and pulling his arm across his body (Pics A to C). This pull can greatly destabilize your opponent, and may even be used as an arm drag (as seen by Mighty Mouse Johnson.) Primarily though, it ensures that your opponent is left with several openings on the side of the trapped hand. While difficult to pull off in boxing gloves, it is still a very potent move in many forms of combat sports.

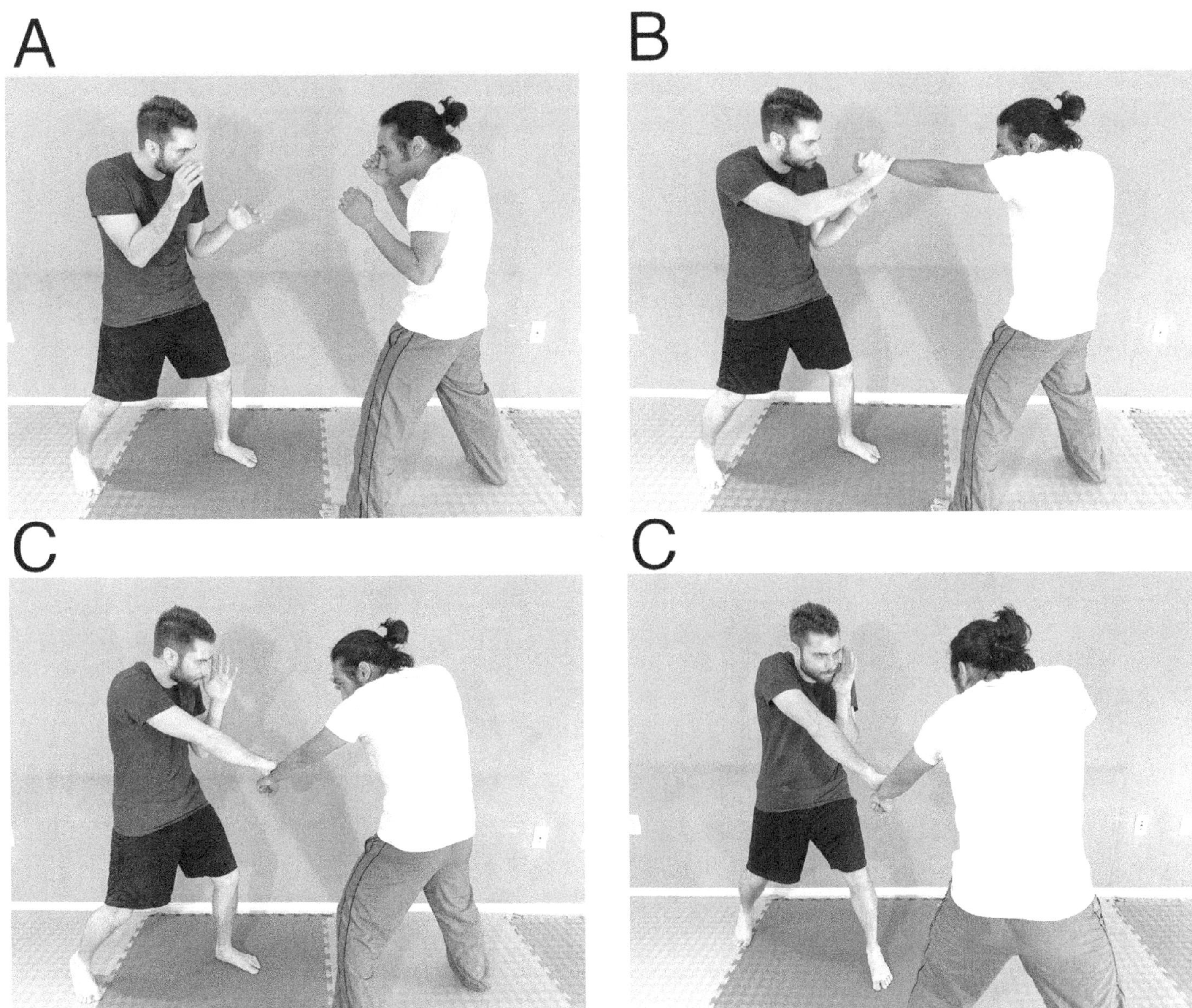

Specialty Counter: Trap Opponent's Jab & Elbow

If your style or sport allows elbows, then this counter may be right up your alley. Catch an opponent's Jab, and then step in close. At the same time, pull down on your opponent's wrist and flare your elbow. Release at the last instance, slamming an elbow into their exposed chin. (Pics A to D). If you find that someone has Trapped your wrist, then you can do what Ferguson did to Cerrone and step in first to Intercept your opponent's Trap with an Elbow of your own (Pics E to F).

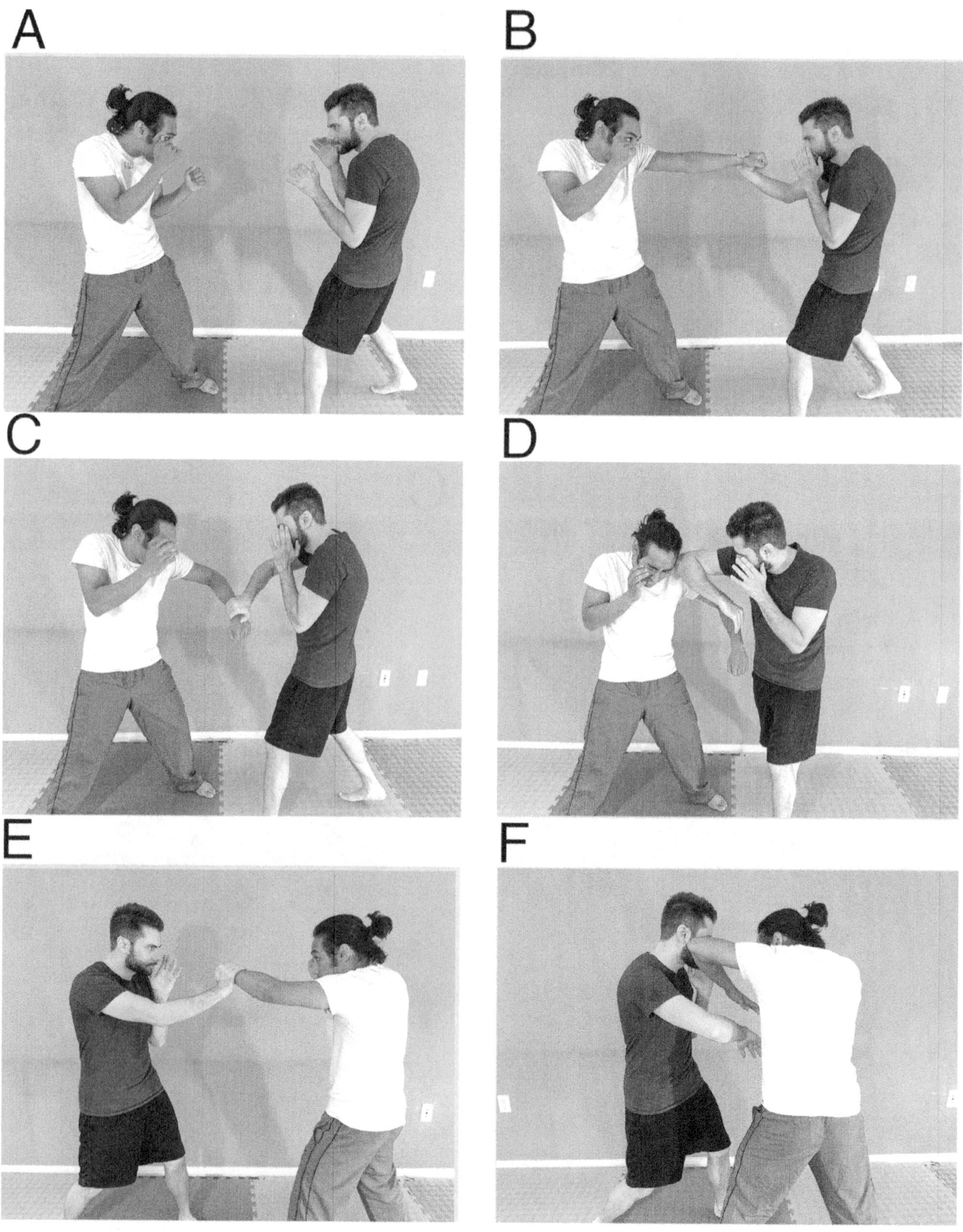

Inside Parry/Glance Off

Extend your hand, moving it from the Inside to the Outside, away from the center of your body (Pics A to B). The Inside Parry can at times have a far more "forward" feel to it, similar to a Leverage Block. Think of those scenes in a movie where two swordsmen clash and one shears his blade down the length of the others until the hilts are touching. Your extended arm can do the same to your opponent's punch.

Other times, the Inside Parry can be used with a more sideways force, swiping away your opponent's attack in the exact opposite way of the Outside Parry. Or it may feel more like a Catch against an opponent's long Hook. Timed correctly, the Inside Parry can throw your opponent off balance and disturb the retraction of their punch.

The Rear Inside Parry/Glance Off is great for fighters who use a narrow stance, as their rear hand is closer to their Center Line. This puts them in a more advantageous position to catch their opponents punch from the Inside (Pics C to D). It also couples very well with Catches and Bumps, as the movements are very similar and it is easy to turn one into another. The major benefit of the Inside Parry is that it allows you to split your opponent's Guard, taking an inside position to establish a hold or shoot a strike down the middle (Pics E to F).

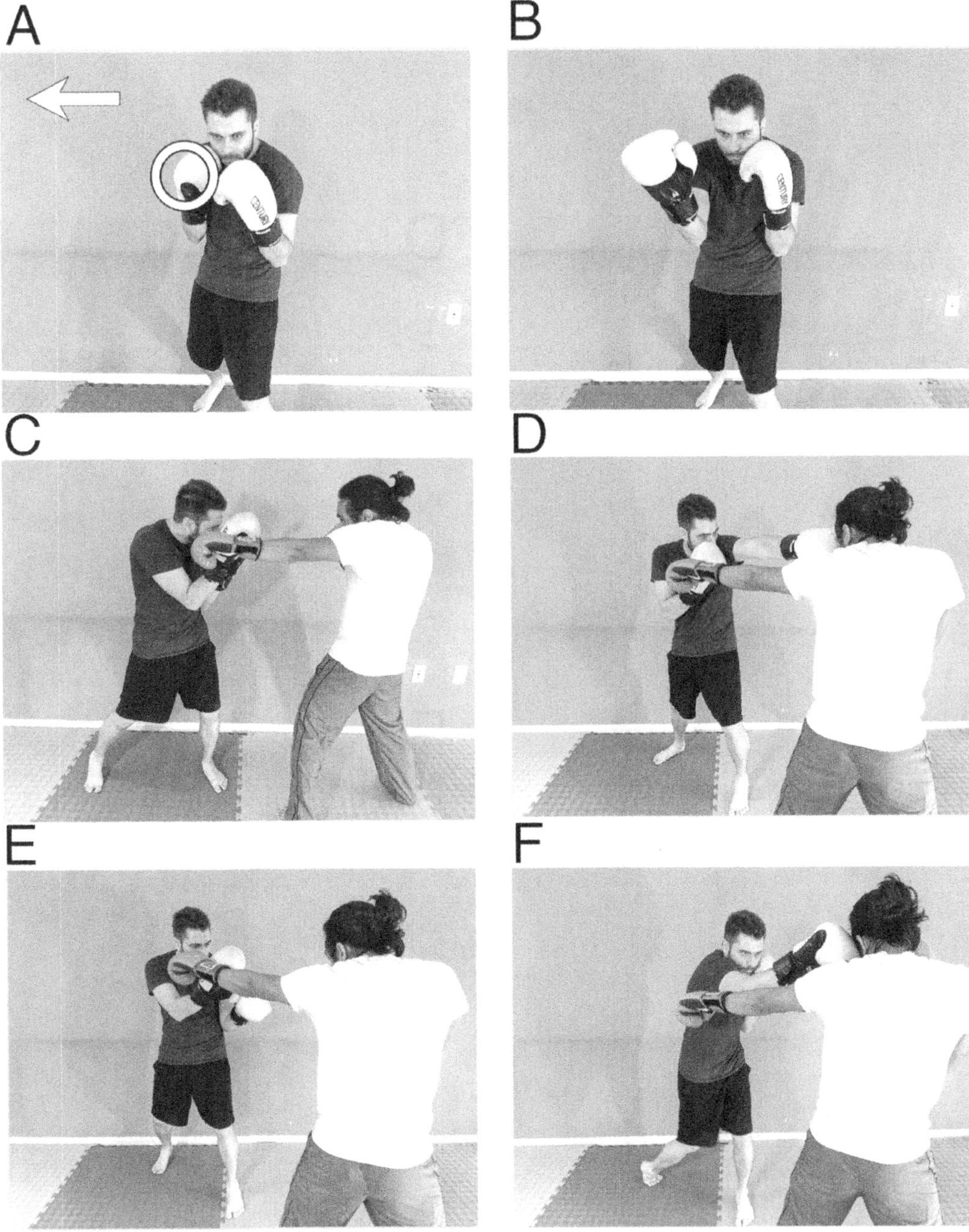

Drills

Drill 1 A

Have your partner throw 1-2 combinations at your head. Try to defend them with both Inside Parries and Outside Parries. You may notice that if you have a more forward, squared up stance, you are far better able to use Outside Parries (Pics A to C). Those with a narrow, sideways stance may find it easier to use Inside Parries (Pics D to F). However, everyone is different, and the point of this book is to find what works well for you.

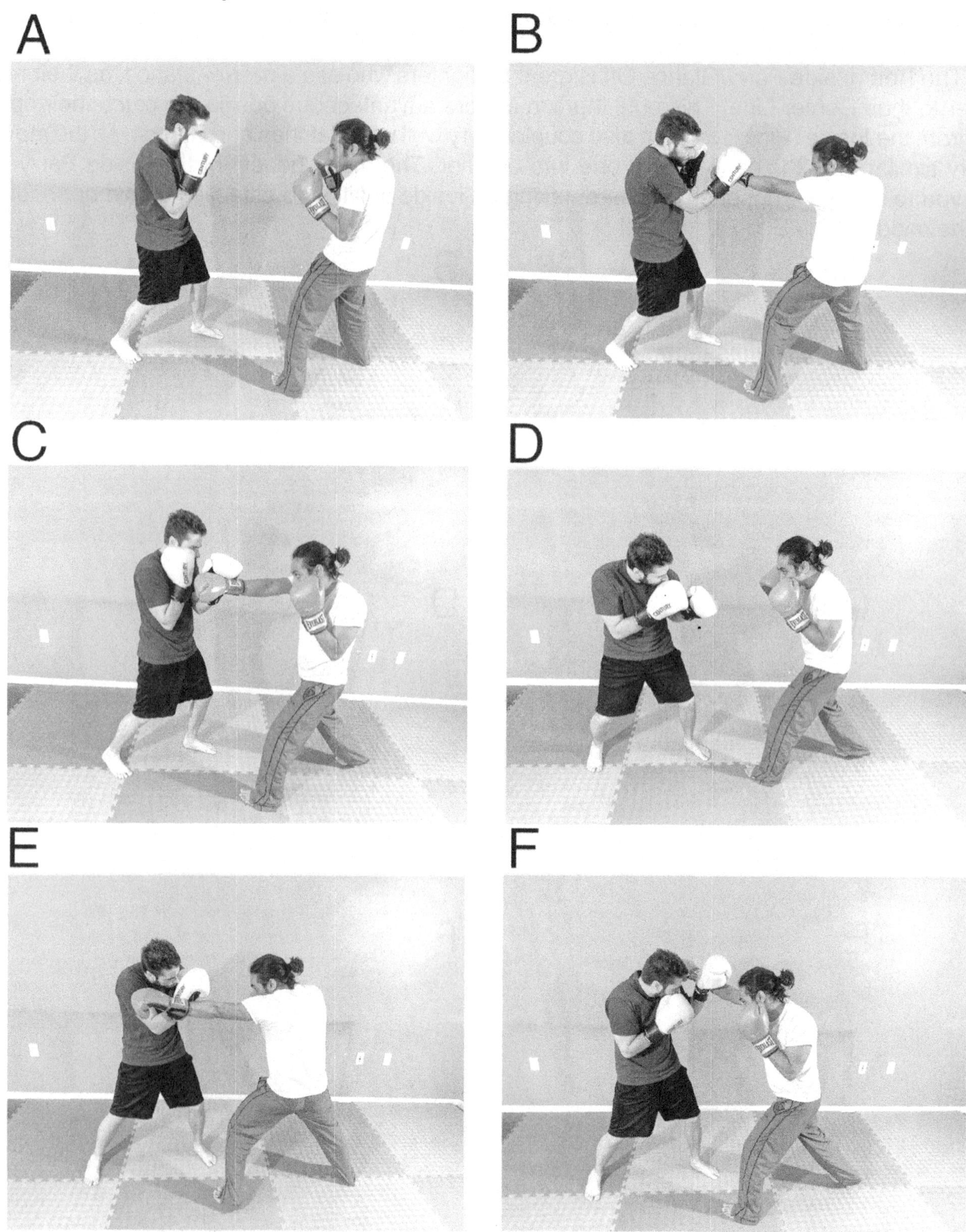

Drill 1 B

Now perform the same drill, but this time circle either Inside or Outside. You will probably find that you are better aligned to use Outside Parries while stepping Outside (Pics A to B), and better aligned to use Inside Parries while stepping Inside (Pics C to D).

Drill 2

Now that you have found a personal preference, it's time to put it to use. Have your partner throw either Double Jabs (Pics A to B) or Jab-Cross (Pics C to F) combinations at you. You may Return or Intercept their second attack with either a Jab or a Cross (Pics A to B & C to F). The key thing to take away is how to use your Parries and Catches against multiple attacks. Pay attention to which sequences work well together for defending (Catch & Inside Parry, Outside Parry to Catch, etc...), and take note of which techniques work best to set up counters. For this drill, switch who is defending and who is attacking every round rather than going back and forth, so that you have the time to really get the feel of it.

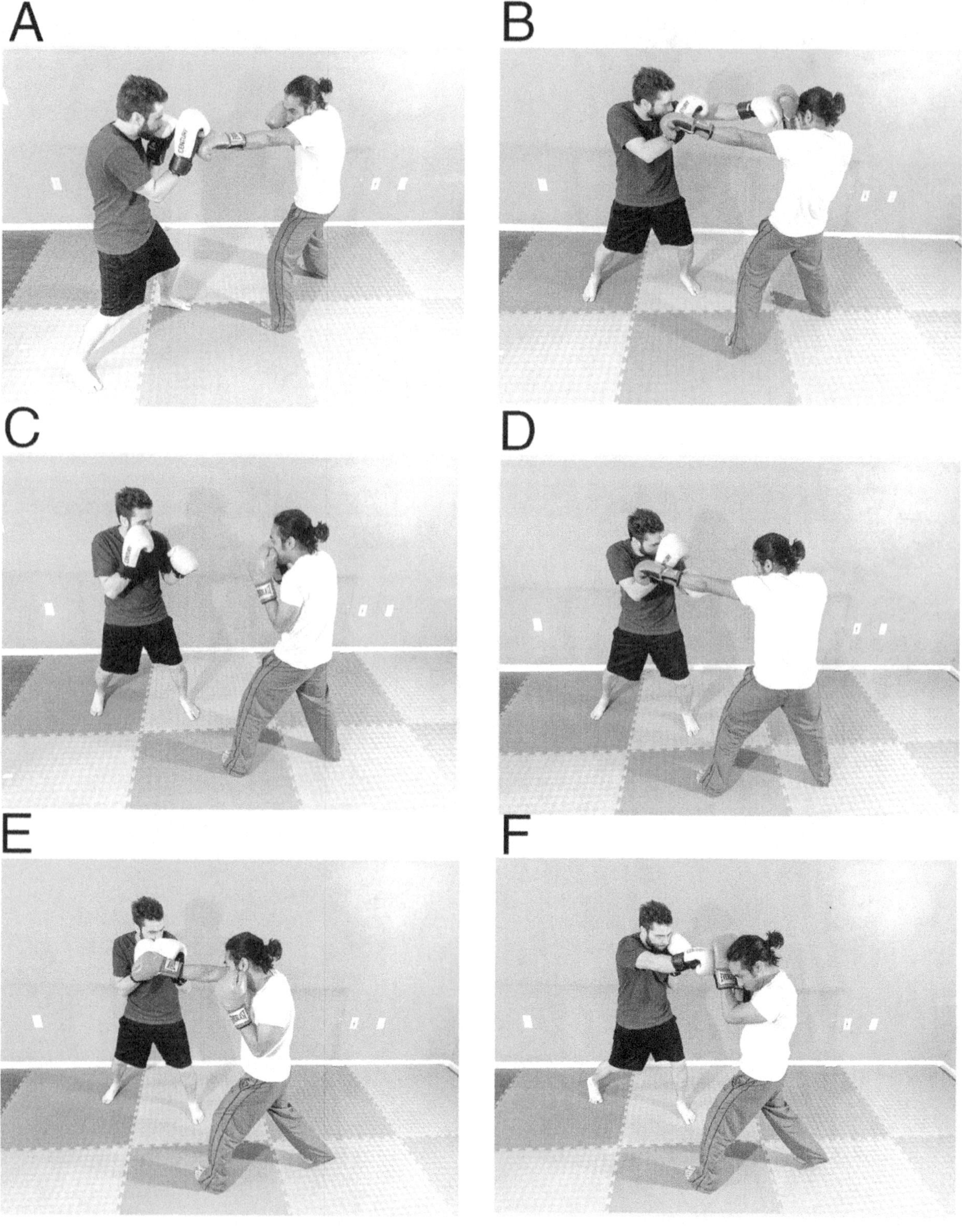

Brush Away/ Downward Inside Parry

Lower your hand and sweep it down and out, away from your body. Keep your elbow in tight and retract your hand back to guard as quickly as possible. This movement should be used from Long Range only, otherwise you will open yourself up to damaging counters.

The "Brush Away" as Dempsey called it is mainly used at long range against body shots (Pics A to C). It is useful in that it is multipurpose, low risk, and makes the opponent pay by disturbing their balance and retraction. It may be especially useful against body snatchers like Inoue, who specialize in finding and targeting the smallest holes in their opponent's guard. If you find that body punches are sneaking through your Cover Blocks, then the Brush Away may provide you with an effective response. Watch Sugar Ray Leonard's fights against Tommy The Hitman Hearns if you want to see two fighters both using the Brush Away to great effect. It is also highly useful against Teeps and Sidekicks, as you can throw your opponent's kick off course to set up an off-angle counter (Pics D to E) or attack their Standing Leg (Pic F). Do not use against Roundhouses.

Drill 1 A

This drill is for after you have practiced Brush Aways back and forth and have the hang of them.

Have your opponent throw Double Jabs at you, alternating between high and low combinations (Pics A to B). Do not counter, but pick your moments to attack with Jab-Cross combinations (alternating high and low as well). Neither partner needs to wait or take turns. Switch which partner does which combinations every round.

Cross Parrying/Catching Punches

To perform the Cross Parry, move your Lead Hand from the Outside to the Inside, towards the center of your body. Reach past your Center Line and make contact with the opponent's hand or arm on the opposite side, Parrying their Left Hand or Left Leg with your Left Hand (or vice versa).

Rear Cross Parries are usually a terrible idea, but Lead Cross Parries are useful under certain circumstances (Pics A to B). For instance, if you are particularly worried about attacks from your opponent's Power/Rear Side, then you may wish to step Outside and use Lead Hand Parries/Catches against your opponent's Jab (Pics C to F). This is very viable from long range. It helps you stay more safely sideways (rather than squaring up to use your Rear Side to Block or Parry) and keeps you moving away from the opponent's Rear Side attacks. The Cinderella Man used this same tactic against Max Baer to negate his insanely powerful right hand.

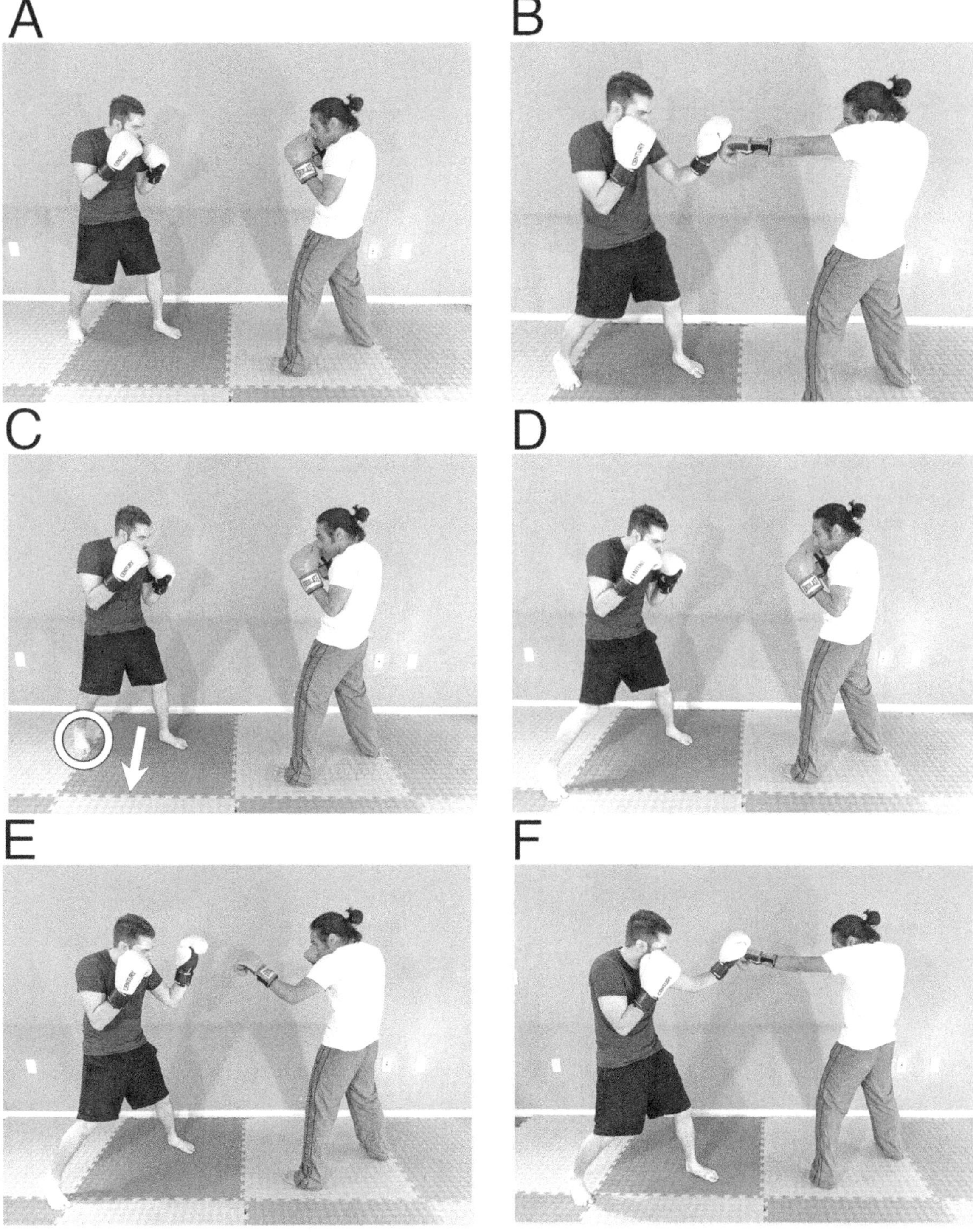

Open Stance Considerations

Cross Parries are much more viable in an Open Stance. If you step Outside your opponent's Lead Foot, you can easily use your Rear Hand to Catch or Parry your opponent's Lead Hand attacks (Pics A to B).

You can also Parry your opponent's Rear Side attacks with you Lead Hand. However, this should be used rarely, and usually while moving to the Inside (Pics C to D).

Drills

Moving to the Outside, practice Cross Parrying or Cross Catching your opponent's Jab, then Return a Cross (Pics A to C). If kicks are allowed in your sport, then this a simple but powerful setup to land a Rear Leg Roundhouse to your opponent's Lead Leg (Pics D to F). You should be at an angle to easily land, while your opponent will be out of position to offer a counter. To add difficulty, your opponent may occasionally add on Crosses or a Rear Leg Roundhouse to their Jab. *As a quick aside, some fighters do like to Cross Catch Uppercuts, which you can experiment with if you like. However, this does open up your chin to an immediate Hook off your opponent's opposite hand.*

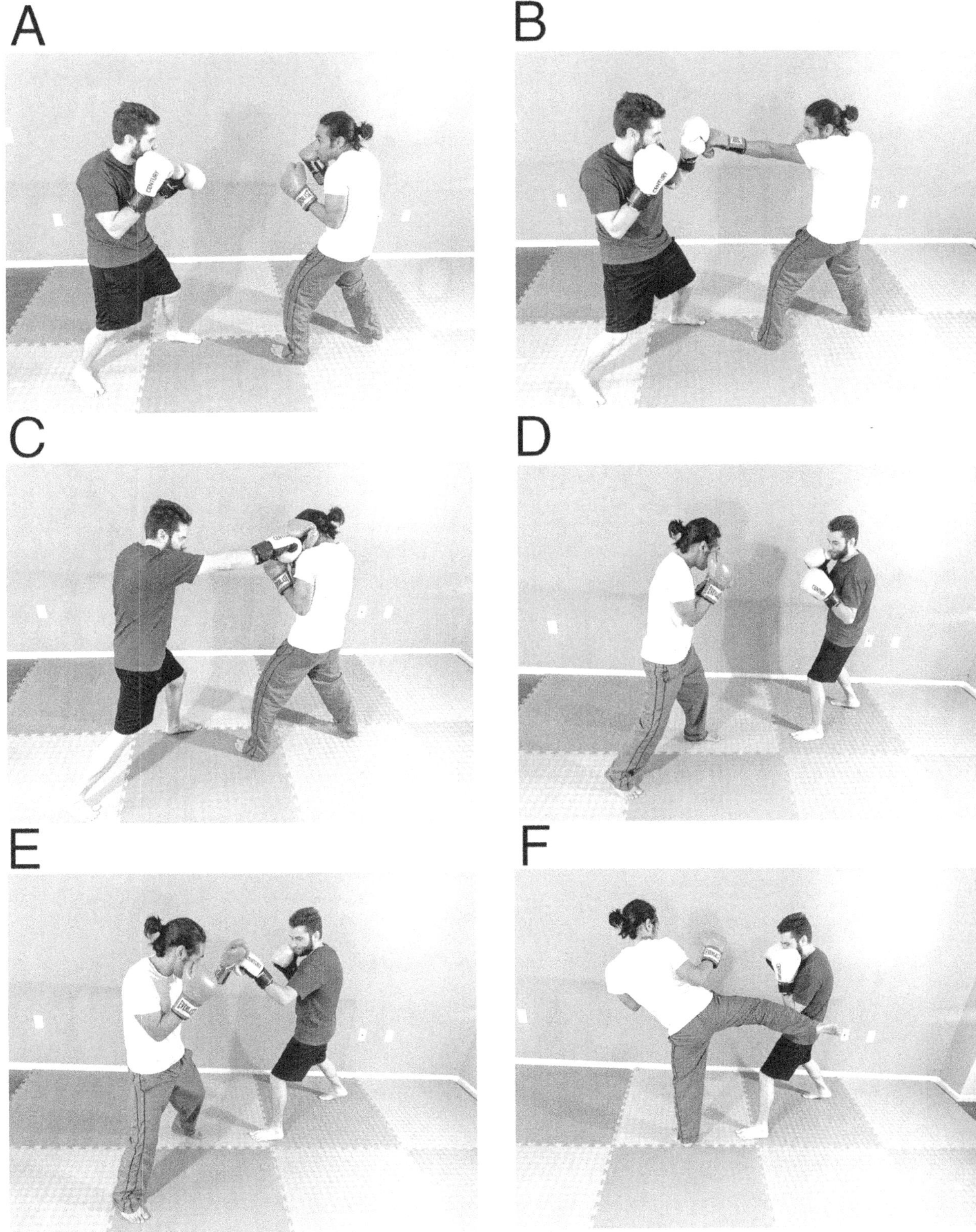

If in an Open Stance, practice using both hands to Catch or Parry while moving Outside. You may also try countering with either hand or foot (Pics A to B & C to D).

Cross Parrying & Sweeping Kicks & Knees

This is the gold standard for blocking kicks in modern combat. Although it may seem counterintuitive, it is far better to deflect Roundhouse Kicks with the arm from the opposite side from which your opponent's kick is coming. In other words, if your opponent is throwing a Roundhouse Kick with their right leg to your left side, then you will parry it with your right hand (Pics A to B). The reason for this is that trying to directly block a powerful kick can end up badly damaging your arm (arms have been broken in high level competitions this way before). Furthermore, blocking on the same side often has insufficient force to fully stop the kick anyways. So, keep one arm covering your body and use the other to Cross Catch/Parry the kick.

Once you have made contact, push the kick away and *down* (Pic B). It is crucial when Cross Parrying a kick to always move your hand in a diagonal motion, across *and* down. This helps to throw the kick off target and drains a lot of the force from the kick by altering its trajectory (rather than trying to meet it head-on and taking the impact directly). It can also be effective to make contact with your forearm rather than your hand, especially when your opponent it closer.

Cross Parries also work well for Front Kicks/Teeps (Pics C to D), and can be used like the Brush Away to throw opponent's off balance.

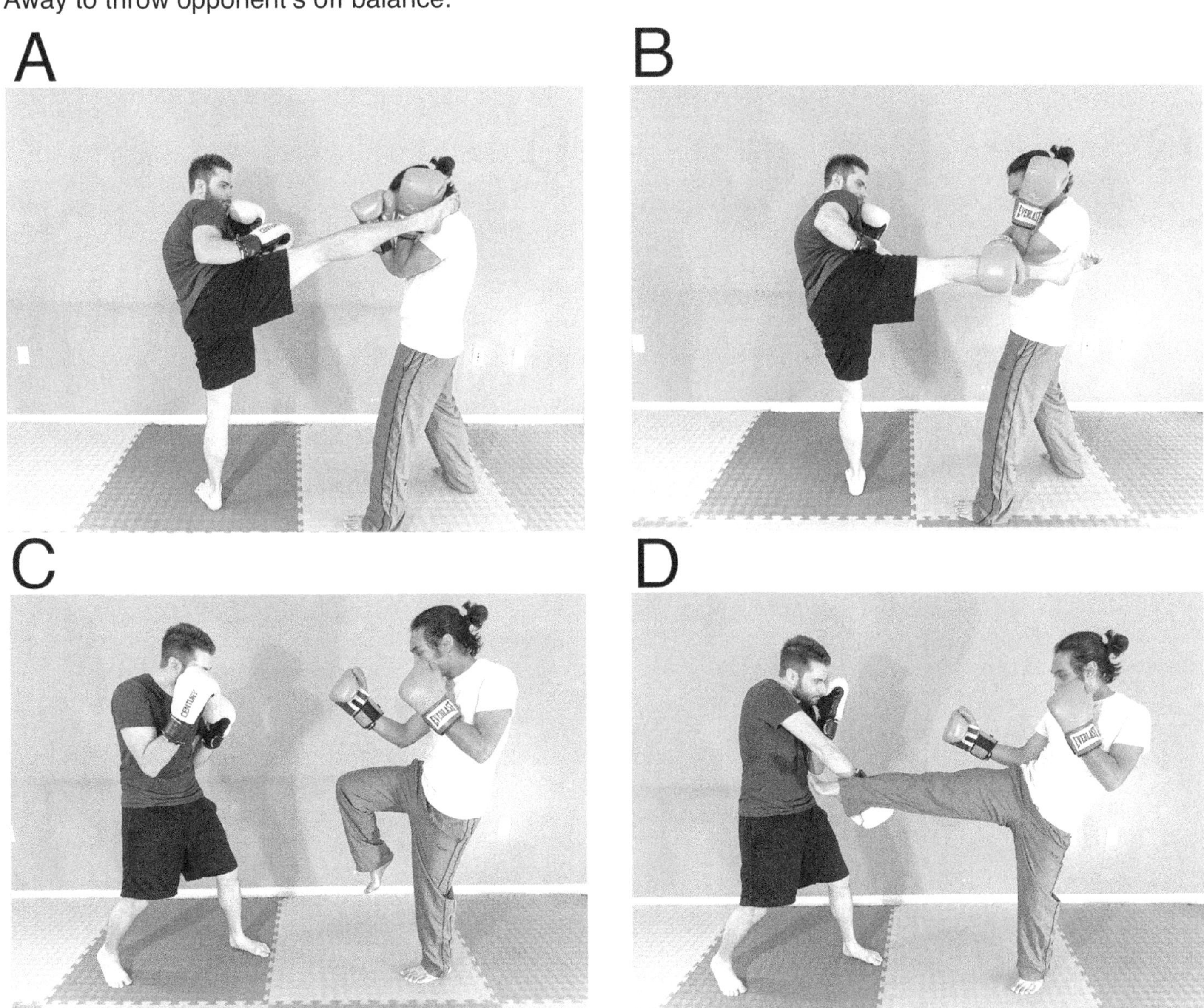

Throwing your opponent's leg off course works just as well for Roundhouse kicks. You can continue your Parry to sweep your opponent's leg, throwing them off line and attacking them from a superior angle (Pics A to d). This may require a slight step back or away to clear space. Experiment to find the ideal range and angle.

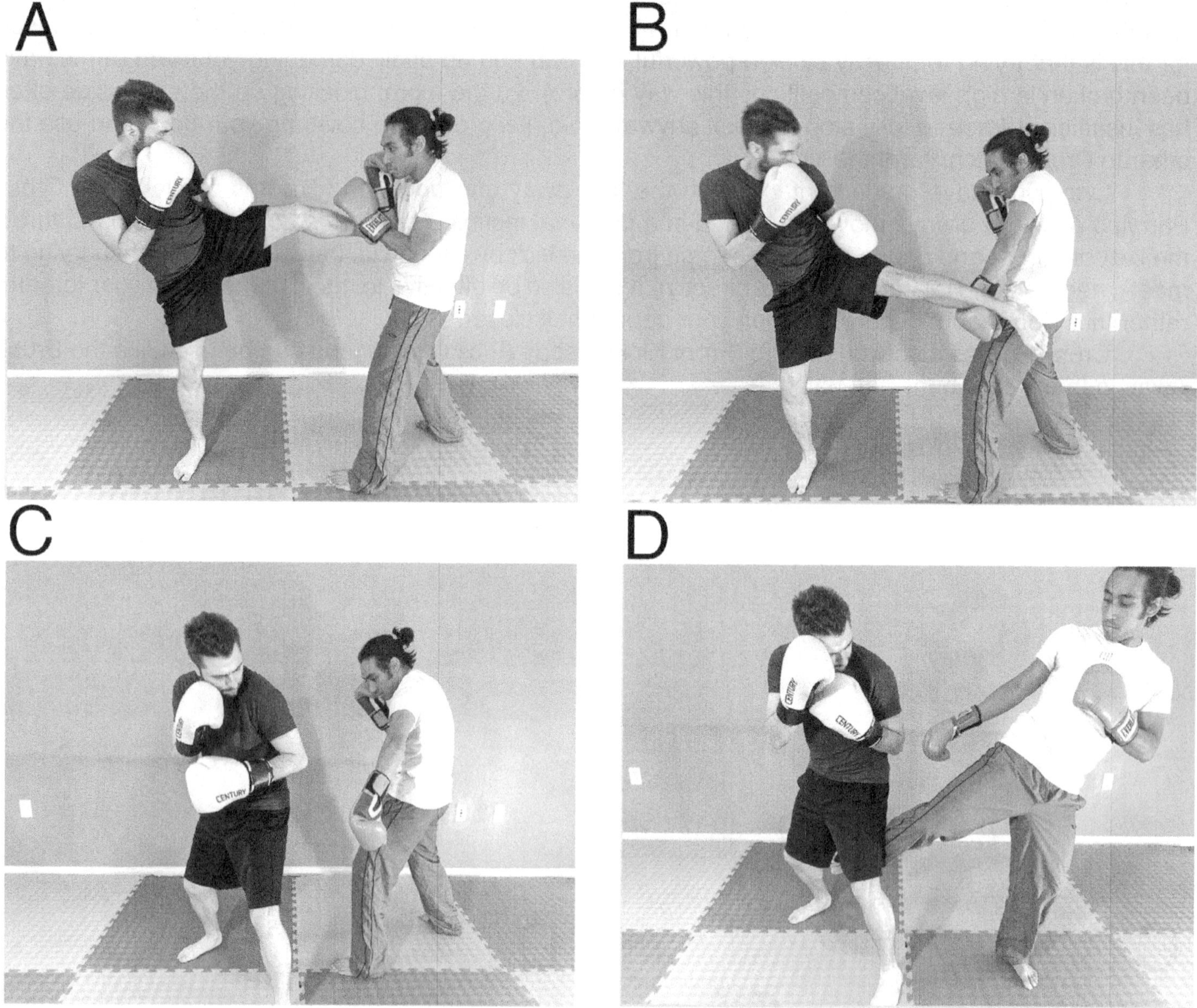

Drills

Drill 1 A

Both you and your partner try to tag the other with Lead Teeps, Rear Teeps and Roundhouse Kicks to the body or head. Do not leg kick except as a counter after throwing your partners leg off course, and go light! For Teeps, use either a Cross Parry to throw them off angle (Pics A to B), or a Brush Away to square them up (Pics C to D). Only use Cross Parries for Roundhouse Kicks (Pics E to F). *Keep in mind that in these pictures we are holding poses for the camera, and in reality the kick should already be thrown away before it reaches full extension.*

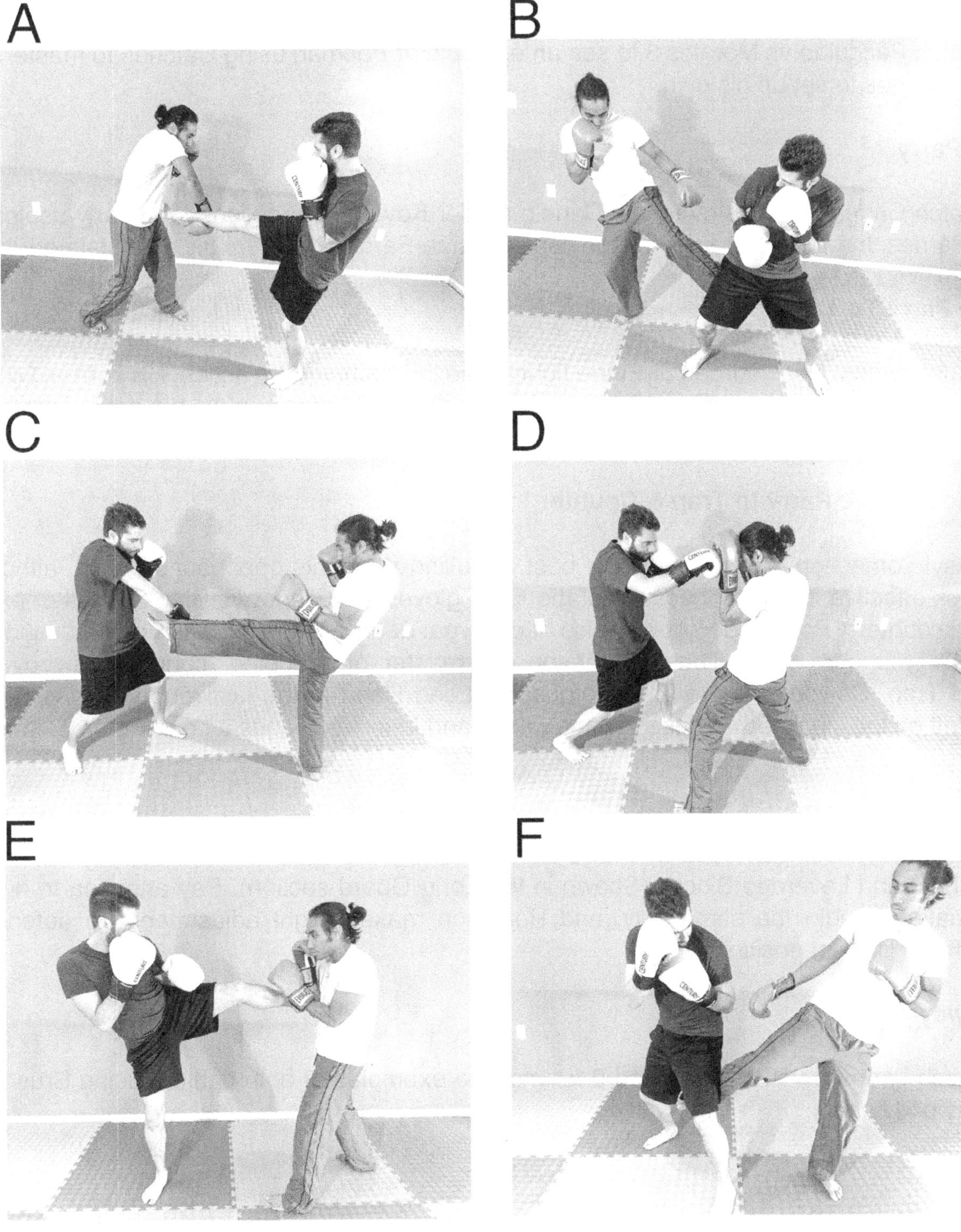

References – Catches & Parries

Catches

For an old school example of Rear Catches, watch Joe Louis use them against James Braddock. Note how he Jabs and Catches at the same time to intercept Braddock's punch. For a newer example, check out the MMA fight between GSP and Michael Bisping. GSP did an amazing job Catching punches with smaller MMA gloves. For Lead Catches, watch George Foreman. Foreman was big and strong enough to Catch Crosses with his Lead Hand. Foreman was also great at Redirecting his opponent's punches after he Caught them to clear space for a counter punch.

Catches – Open Stance Considerations

Watch Pacquiao vs Morales 3 to see an example of Pacman using Catches to masterfully Redirect punches to set up his own.

Outside Parry

Watch Canelo vs Kovalev to see Canelo render Kovalev's excellent Jab nearly useless through Outside Parries. In MMA, Toney Ferguson uses Outside Parries to set up his devastating Elbows.

*Outside Parry To Takedown

Watch almost any Georges St-Peirre fight to see this technique in action. His fight vs Diaz contains a great example in round 3 with 4:10 left on the clock. GSP actually pulls his arm down and pins it, rendering it useless to defend the takedown.

*Using An Outside Parry to Trap & Counter

Vasyl Lomachenko is probably the best at pulling down his opponent's punch, although it's of course less effective in boxing because of the large gloves. McGregor vs Diaz 2 is full of examples of Traps and counters. Poirier vs Holloway also had a great deal of Trapping, with counters landed by both fighters. Or you can watch Toney Ferguson, as master of Trapping, counter Cowboy Cerrone's attempted Trap. Cowboy tries to Trap Ferguson's Lead Hand in the last round of their fight with 23 seconds left on the clock. But Ferguson goes with in and lands and lands a Lead Elbow Return Counter.

Inside Parry

Sugar Ray Robinson used an Inside Parry far more than almost any other fighter. He paired it with Catches, and Leverage Blocks (Shown in the Long Guard section). Pay attention to how each of these variations begin the same way, and Robinson makes slight adjustments to defend different punches from different positions.

Brush Away

Watch Leonard vs Hearns 1 and 2 for multiple examples of both fighters using Brush Aways to clear away body shots.

Cross Parries

Check out Fury vs Wilder 2 to watch Fury control Wilder's Lead Hand (Which he uses to set up his terrifying Cross) by Cross Parrying with his Lead Hand. Fury would also step Outside away from Fury's right at the same time, and turn his Cross Parry into Cross Frames and Leverage Guards (Covered in the Long Guard section). Once again, McGregor vs Diaz 2 provides plenty of great examples in MMA. McGregor uses Cross Parries to land his left.

Cross Parries – Open Stance Considerations

Roy Jones Jr. used Rear Cross Parries to defend and counter with a Lead Hook, knocking down two of his opponents with this same tactic; Richard Frazier and Reggie Johnson.

Cross Parrying/Sweeping Kicks

Watch Anthony Pettis vs Wonderboy Thompson to see Pettis smoothly Cross Parry Thompson's Roundhouse Kick's from a High Guard. He also landed some nice Return Counters off of this defense. While Pettis had trouble dealing with Thompson's hand speed and Sidekicks, neutralizing Thompson's Round Kick (Thompson has maybe the best in the UFC) with such subtle, small movements is an impressive feat.

Blocks & Deflections

Lead Shoulder Roll/Block

Push your shoulder up high, pressing against your chin, and turn your body to narrow your posture. This will allow your shoulder to shield you (Pics A to B). You don't need to enter a Philly Shell Guard to Shoulder Roll, but your lead hand may move forward naturally as you hunch your shoulder (Pics C to D). You may either Block the punch with your arm or shoulder, or turn the punch off of your shoulder almost like a Parry. Many do not raise their shoulder high enough, so be sure to hunch it up as high as you can (Pics E to F). Watch Mayweather to see just how much of your face it is actually possible to cover by elevating your shoulder.

The Shoulder Roll is primarily used to defend against the Cross (read on to the Philly Shell section to learn how to alter the movement to defend against many different kinds of strikes).
It works incredibly well, but be careful not to let your arm or shoulder take too much punishment. Practice until you are able to deflect your opponent's punches away, as if they are sliding or gliding off of you. This will minimize impact.

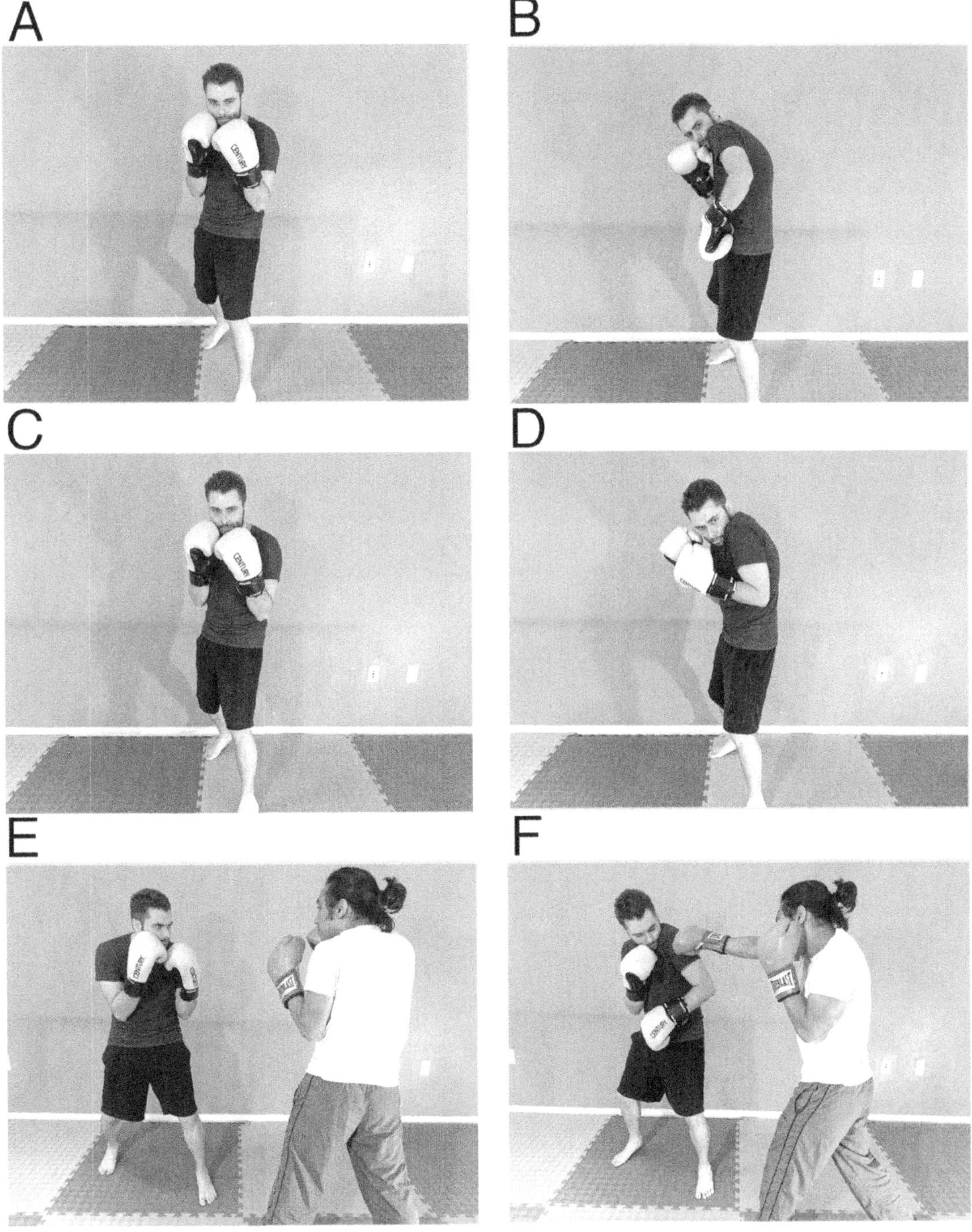

Open Stance Considerations

In an Open Stance, you will Shoulder Roll against your opponent's Lead Side instead. A Pivot will help you to dispel the force of the attack (Pics A to B). Or, if you get the correct angle, it's possible to block attacks rather than Roll by stepping Inside (Pics C to D). Fighters like James Tony have pulled this off many times over the course of their career. Pivoting Out can also work to Slip Rear Side attacks thrown as a follow up, making it a multipurpose defense (Pics E to F).

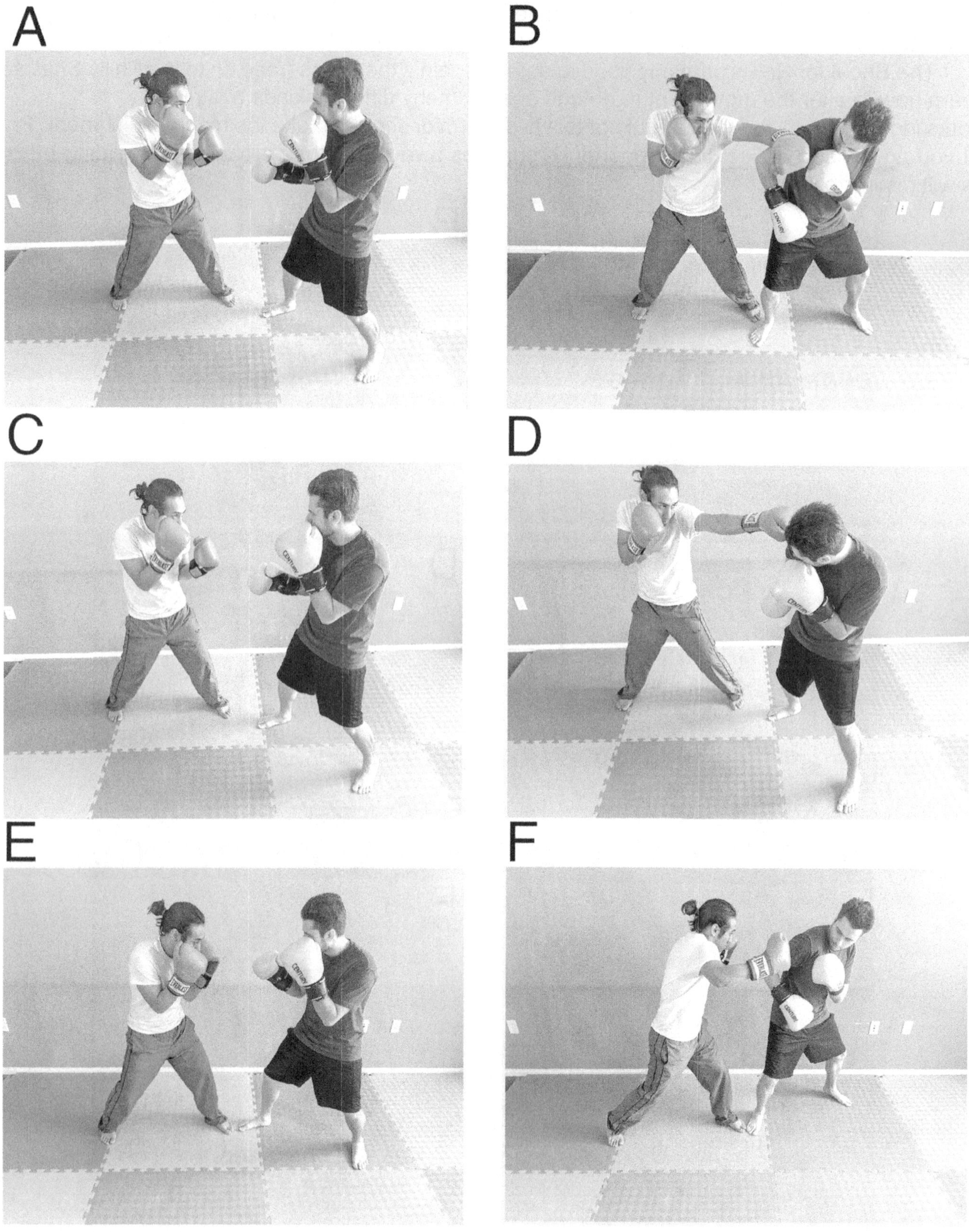

Drill

Have your partner throw Jabs at you and defend however you like (Pics A to D). Once in a while, they will surprise you by adding on a Cross. Be ready to Shoulder Roll and then immediately fire back a Cross of your own. If in an Open Stance, use the techniques outlined before.

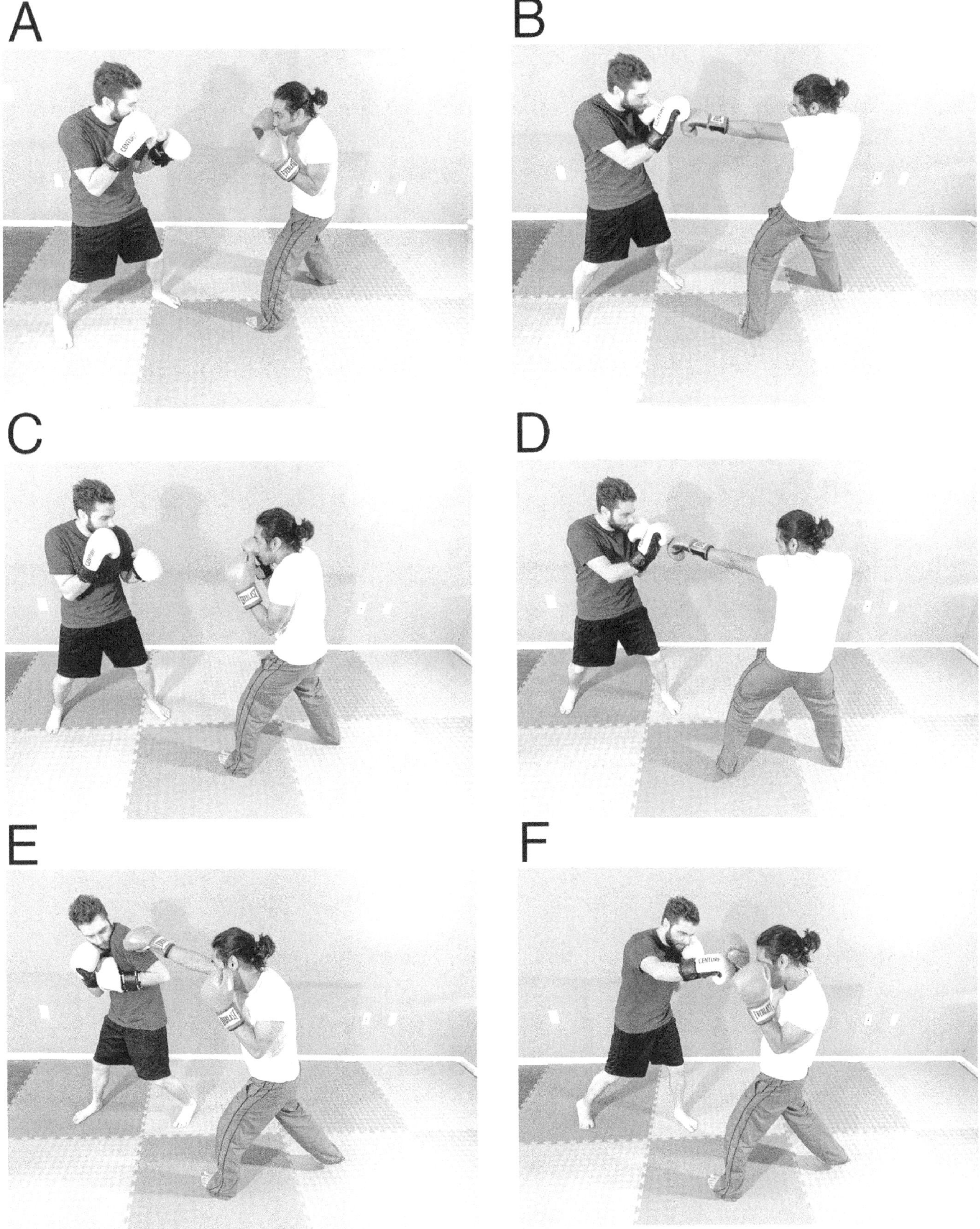

Cover Blocks

Cover Block High

Raise your Hand up until your palm is on your temple to block strikes to the head (Pics A to B). You may also hunch and tuck your chin to bring your temple to your hand (Pic C), or stay upright and simply raise your arm (Pic D). Do not make the mistake of keeping your head in line with the blow. This will not only hurt, but also obstruct your vision. Instead, turn your body very slightly to move your head out of the line of fire and position your guard in line with the incoming blow.

Raising your Guard will leave small openings below your elbows, so be vigilant. Keep your elbow tight against your ribs, pinned. Exhale and squeeze your muscles upon impact, then immediately relax so that you may freely move onto a fluid attack or another defensive technique. Try to time it to where your opponent connects just before you finish raising your arm into position. If your arm is still moving upon impact it will help to dispel the force of the blow. A slight bending and twisting of your arm and wrist at the last second can help with this too, as well as help to brace and harden the muscles in your arm.

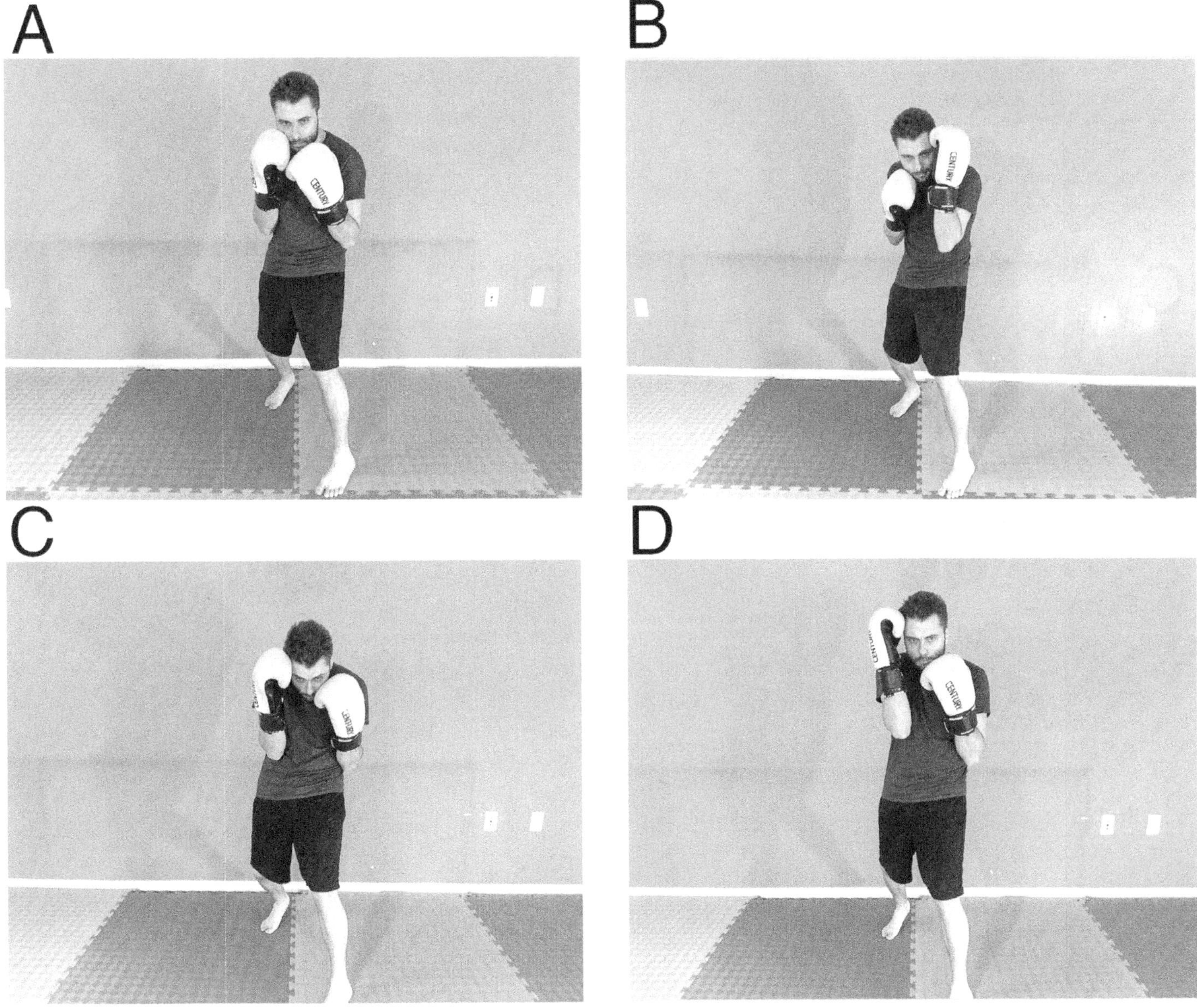

For straight on strikes like Jabs and Crosses, you can take the impact of the strike on your arm directly (Pics A to B), or "chop" the strike away with the motion of your body. This will deflect it off of your arm (Pics C to D). This can be thought of as an Outside Parry, but you are using your whole Guard instead of your hand. As mentioned before, try to move your head slightly off line so the impact does not travel through your arm into your head.

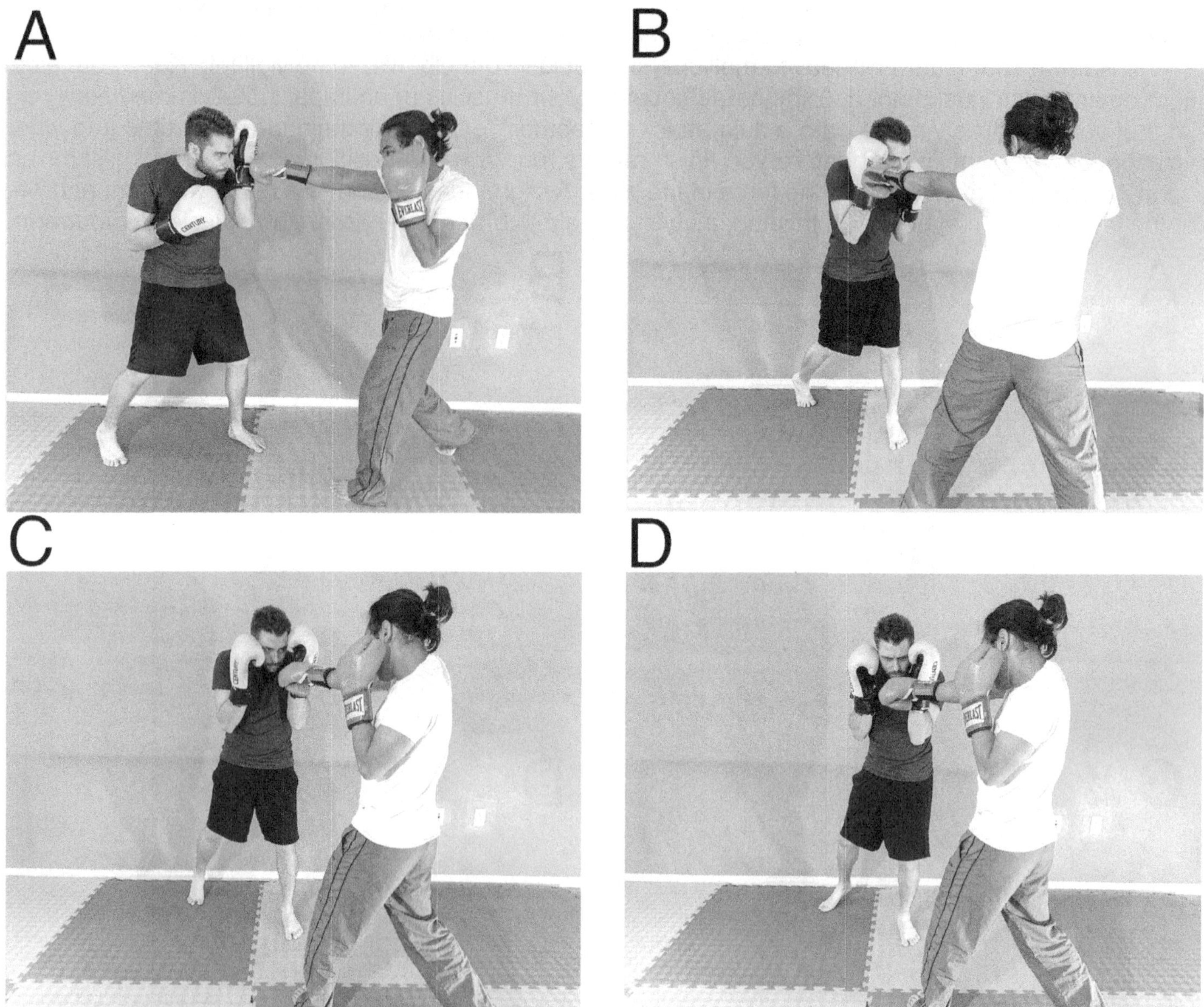

To defend against curved strikes like Hooks you must turn in to square up, hunch your shoulder, and then move your blocking hand further back as if combing your hair (Pics A to B). You may also choose to move in closer to your opponent, allowing their punch to wrap harmlessly around you (Pics C & D).

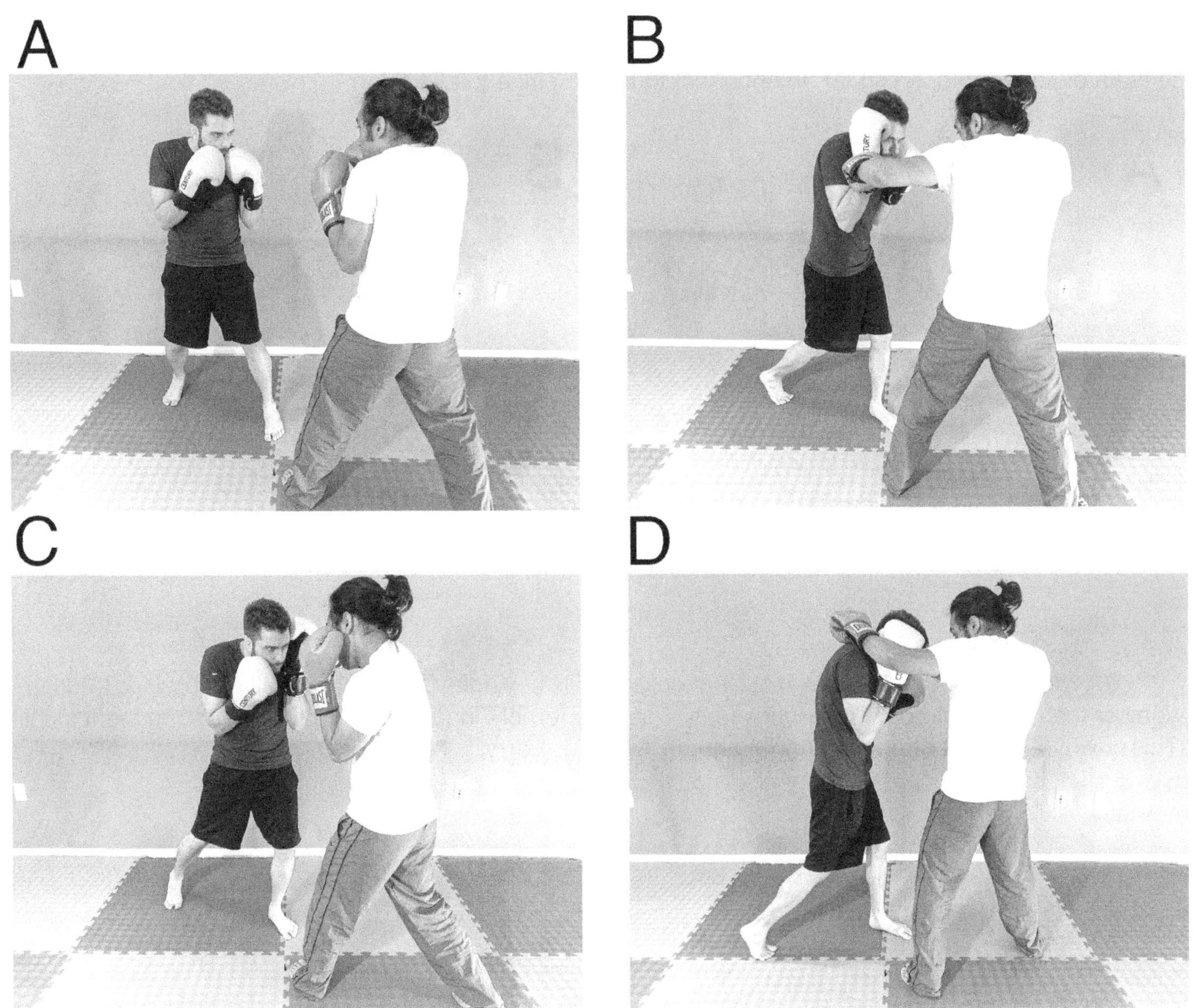

Cover blocks are multipurpose blocks. This means that they can defend against many different attacks with minimal movement. But this does not mean that slight adjustments should not be made depending on the incoming attack.

You need to be careful about the small openings you are leaving by Cover Blocking. For instance, moving your hand too far forward will open up the side of your head (Pic A), and moving it too far to the side will open you up to linear attacks (Pic B). Try not to overreact. By minimizing your movements your Guard should at least provide enough resistance to slow and dispel most attacks. In other words, never leave a big enough opening for an opponent to land a strike totally clean.

A

B

A quick note about Cover Blocking kicks: While a single Cover Block will often work to defend against the impact of your opponent's foot, it can be terribly inadequate against your opponent's shin. This is why it is most often paired with another block or Parry.

Cover Block Low

To defend a strike to the body, very slightly lower your elbow to protect your ribs (Pics A to B). Twisting and leaning with the strike may help to absorb some of the force of the blow. Rather than lower one of their arms, many fighters choose to keep their hands up high and either crouch or squat down lower to put their arms in position to block (Pics C to D). We will go more into this in the High Guard section. For now, keep in mind that using Low Cover Blocks and remaining more upright may temporarily open up your head(Pic B), but it will also keep you lighter on your feet. It's up to you to decide which works best for you.

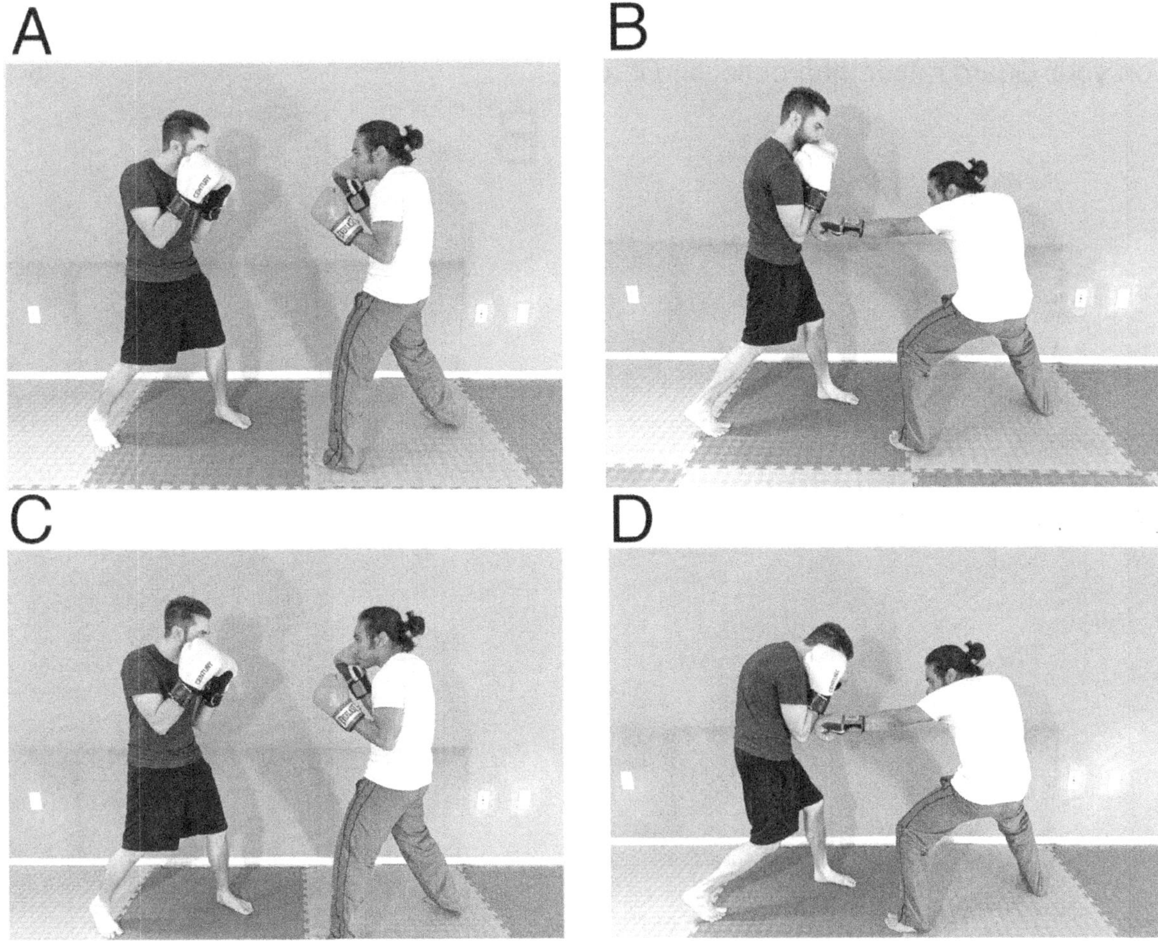

Be aware that you will need to move your elbow, either more forward (Pic A), or more to the side (Pics B), depending on which punch you opponent is throwing. Keep in mind that an opponent can target your liver just as well coming from the front (with a Shovel Hook or Uppercut), as they can by coming around the side.

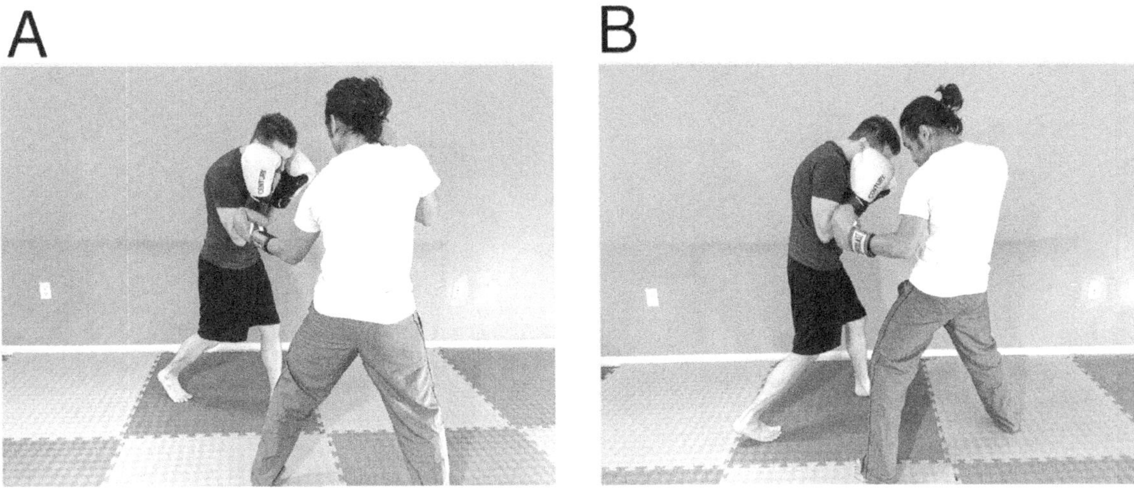

Reinforced Cover Block

Block a strike as you normally would, but reinforce your primary block with your opposite arm, crossing it over your centerline like a Cross Parry (Pics A to B). Make sure you have full visibility, or that at least one eye unobstructed. Any loss of vision should always be temporary and only partial.

Reinforcing your block can add additional stability. It helps you to continue aggressively chasing your opponent without taking the time to retreat, or stop and brace. GGG is a prime example of a fighter who knows how to keep moving forward through his opponent's punches without taking damage by expertly deflecting and absorbing punches on his Guard. Reinforced Blocks can be dangerous however, as they open up one side of your Guard in order to help reinforce the other side.

This block works for kicks as well, but unlike the Cross Parry, you will be taking the full impact of the blow on your Guard rather than deflecting it away.

B

Open Stance Considerations

In an Open Stance, it will be a little harder to defend your Rear Side as your opponent has more angles to try to sneak attacks through your Guard (in Pics A to B the punch finds a way through). The most common way to defend your Rear Side effectively is to step or even lean to the Outside as you Cover Block (Pics C to D). This angle will take away openings on the front of your Guard, which your opponent could have used to sneak through a Rear Side attack. In this way you need only worry about covering the side of your guard, which is much easier to do. This technique is favored by Lomachenko.

Another way is to step deep Inside and square up (Pics E to F). This angle will only let your opponent attack the front of your Guard, and limits the power he can generate by putting him at an awkward angle. This technique is favored by Manny Pacquiao.

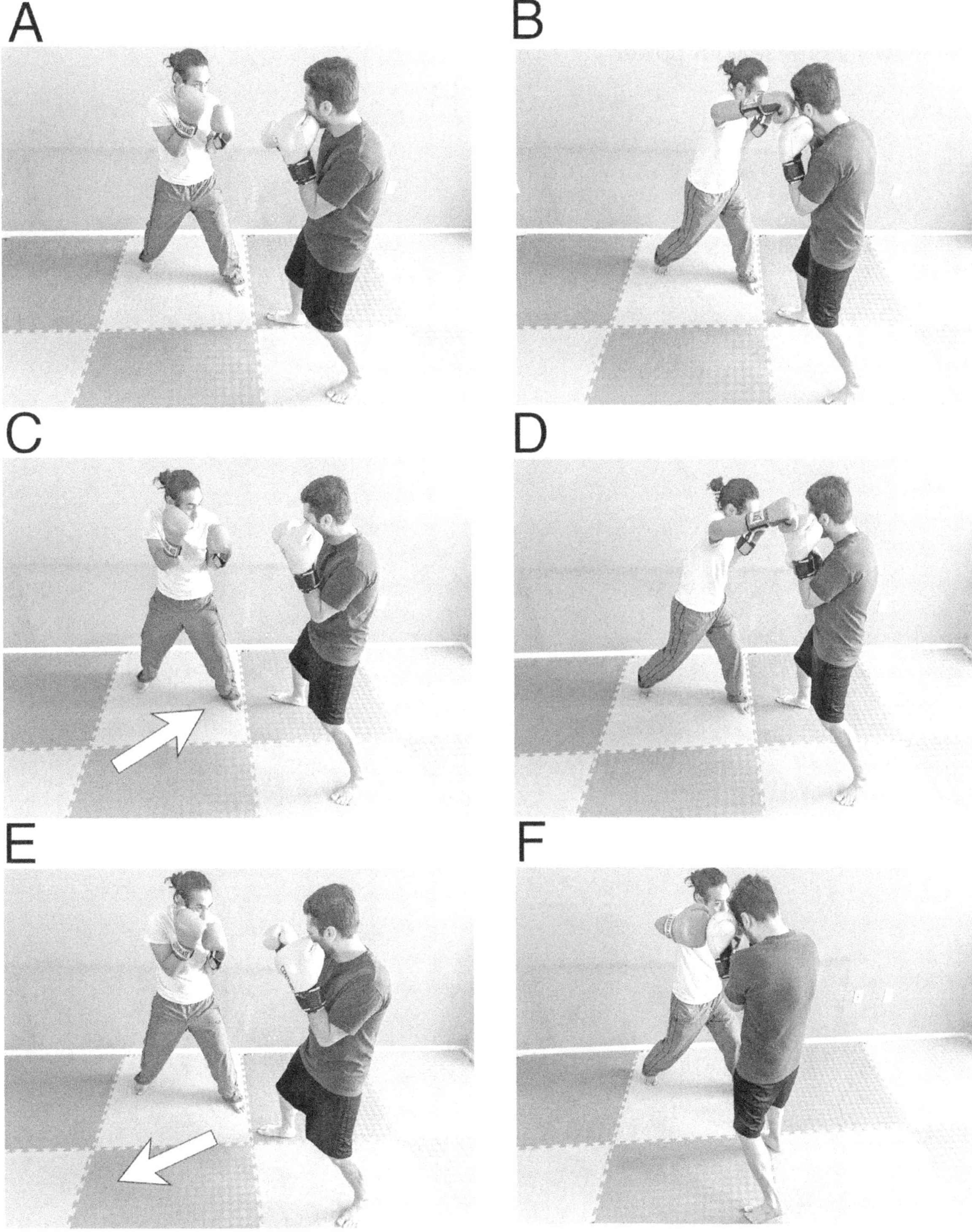

Drills

Drill 1 A

Have one person Double Jab and the other counter with a Jab-Cross (Pics A to F). Take turns attacking and defending. Either arm may be used to Cover Block Jabs. You will find that Blocking with your Rear Side loads up your jab with more power, but leaves you more open to follow up punches.

For this drill, focus on the timing of your Blocks. Your arm should still be moving as your opponent's punch makes contact, helping to dispel some of the force. Tighten your muscles and then immediately let go of the tension and relax. Breath out as you get hit, just like when you throw a strike. Your head should move slightly out of the way so as not to absorb as much impact through your Guard. By the end of the drill, you should feel much less impact from the strikes being thrown, even as you and your partner slowly increase your power.

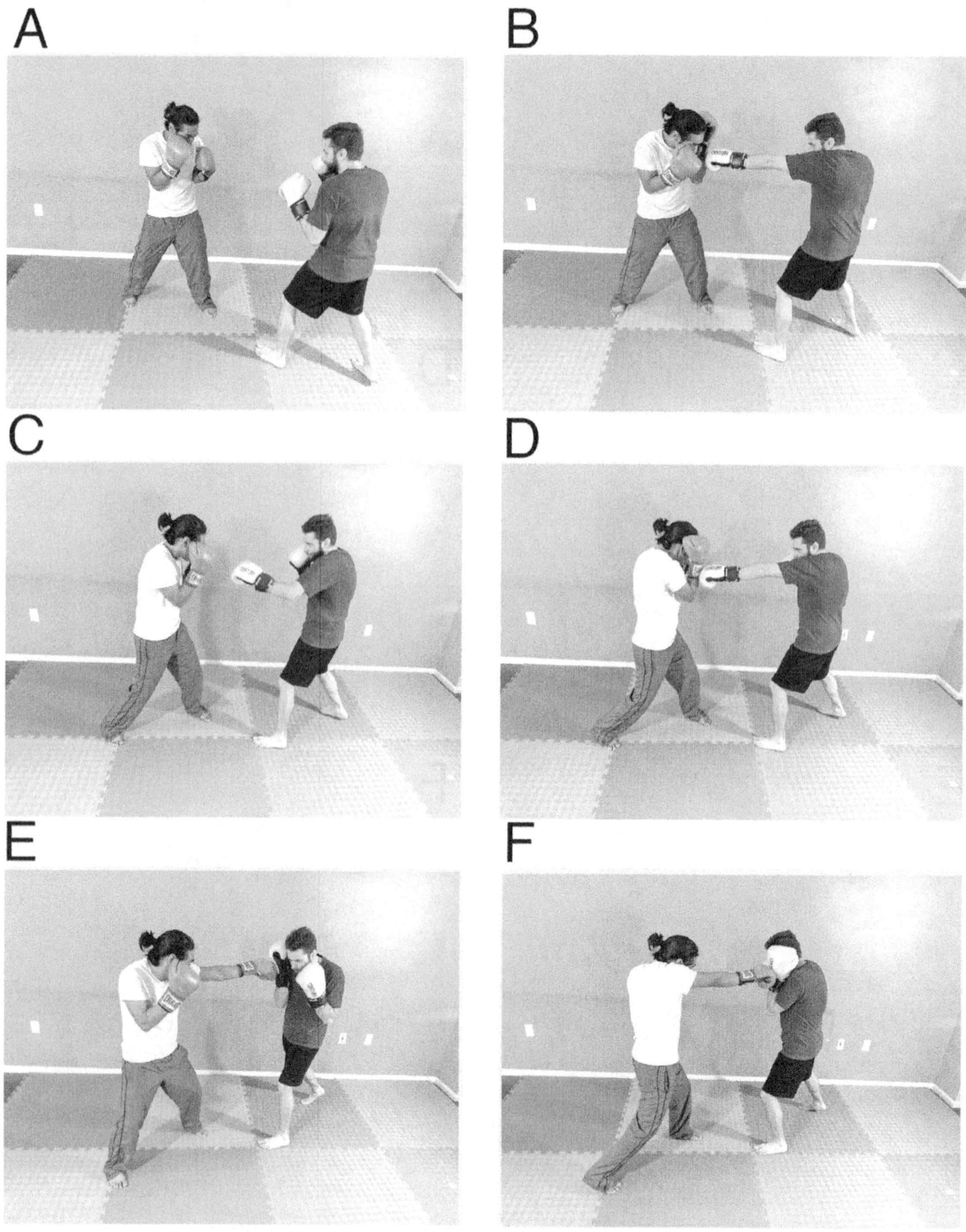

Drill 1 B

Have your partner throw a Jab-Body Hook combination to either side and then Return or Intercept with a Hook off the opposite side (Pics A to D).Take turns attacking and defending. Play close attention to how you adjust your Guard to block Straights vs Hooks and high vs low punches.

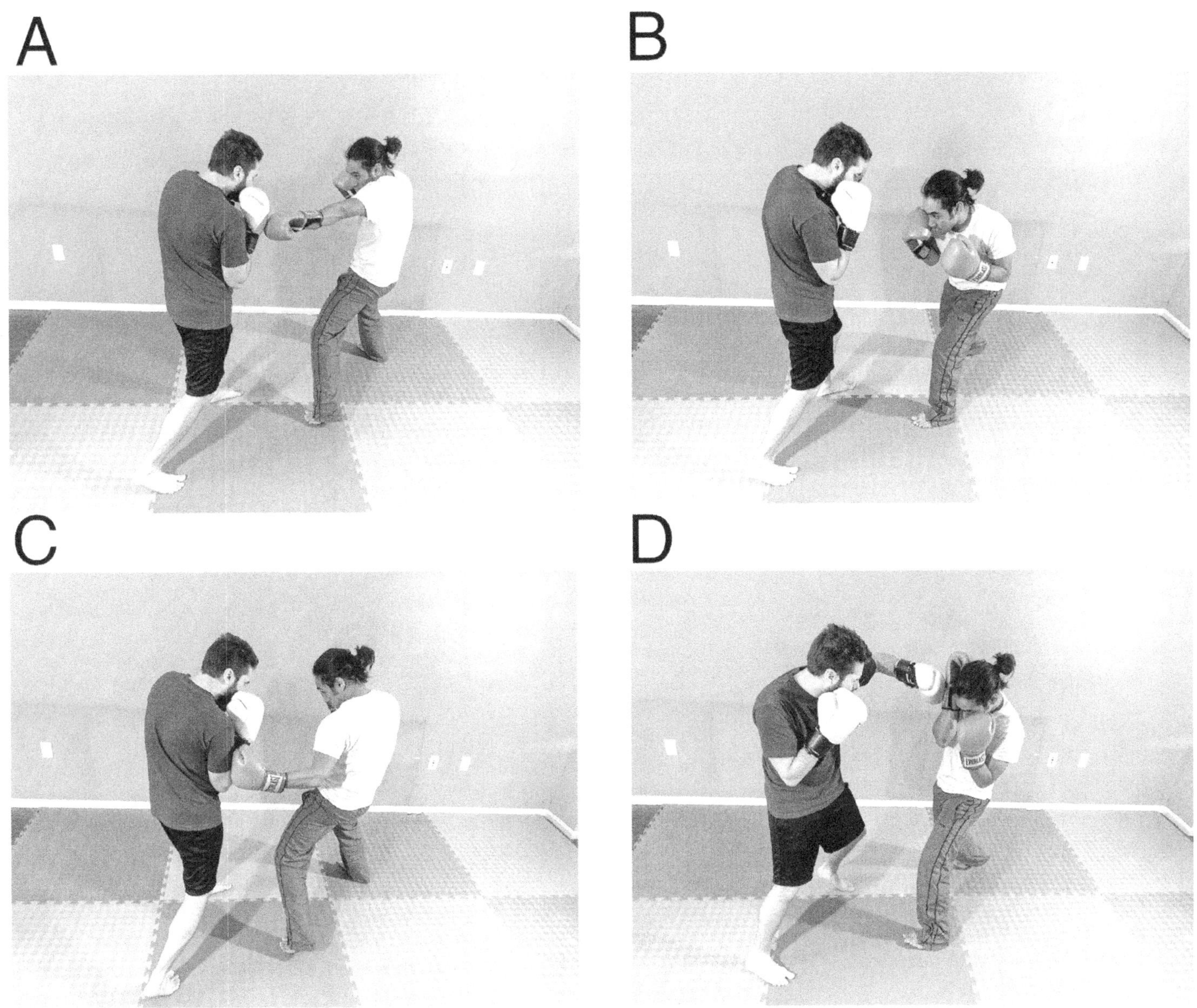

Drill 1 C

A great counter to a Body Hook is a Hook to the head off the same side, taking advantage of the temporary opening. Have your partner throw a Body Hook to either side and then Return a Hook of your own. Take turns attacking and defending with your partner, mixing up attacking their Lead Side (Pics A to C) and Rear Side (Pics E to F).

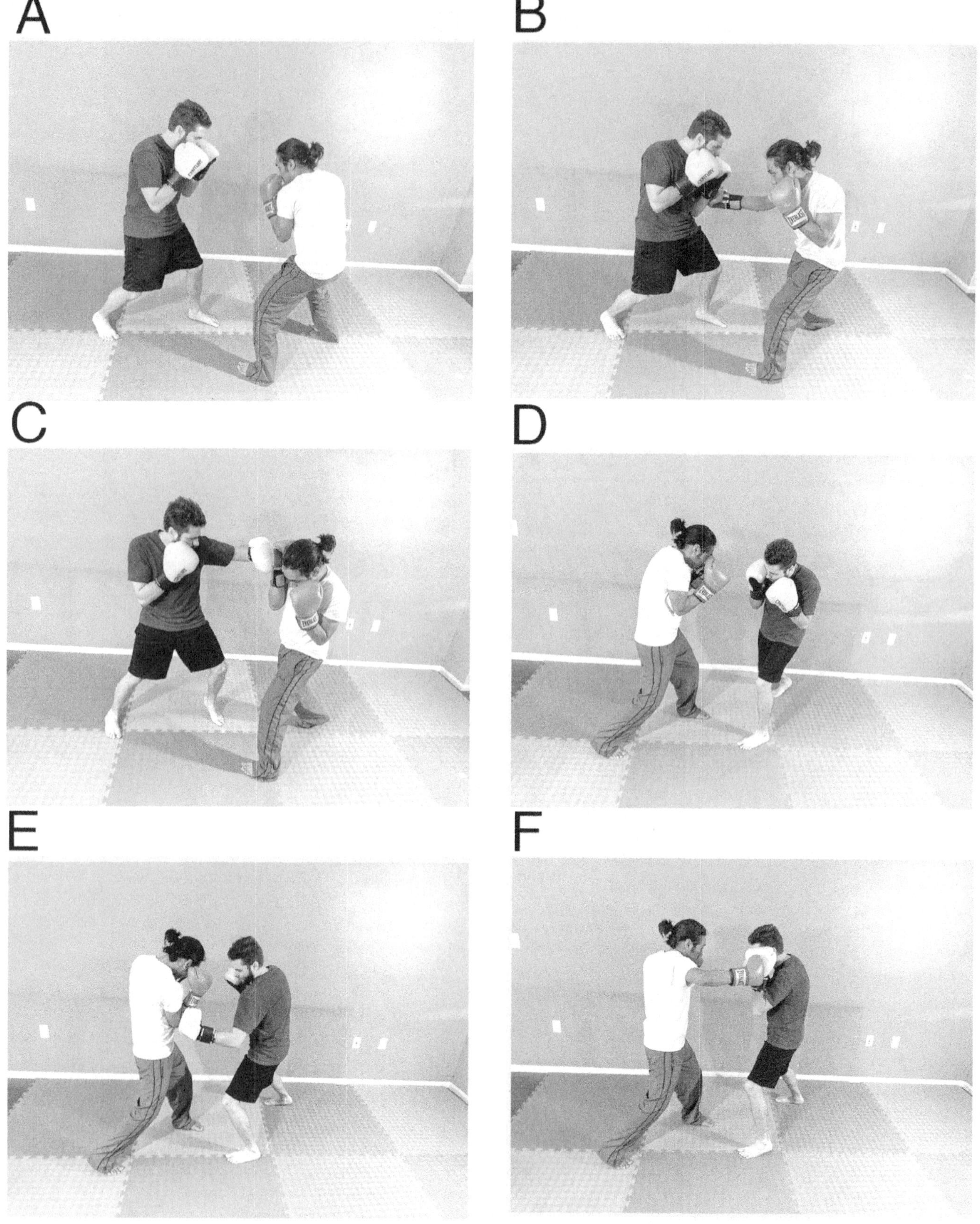

Drill 1 D

Have your partner double up on their Hook to the same side (Pics A to C). They may use any combination of high and low (High Hook-low Hook, low Hook-high Hook, both low, both high) and may attack either side. After Blocking, Return an Uppercut to their opposite side and then use that same hand to throw a Hook (Pics D to F). Take turns attacking and defending.

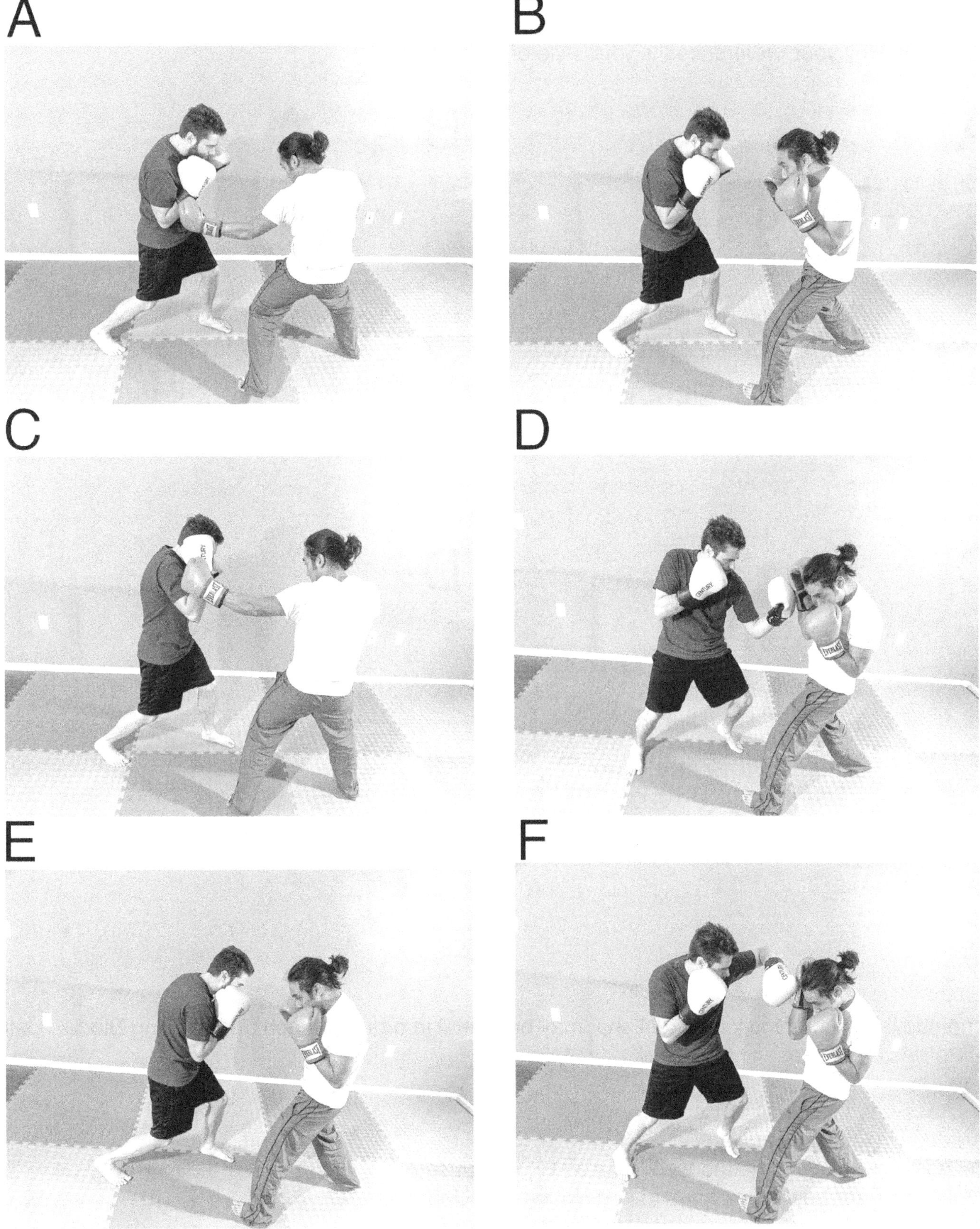

Drill 1 E

Now have your partner throw Straights and Hooks at you for one round. Use Catches and Parries to defend Straights and Cover Blocks to defend Hooks (Pics A to C). If your Catches and Parries have been overextended until now, this will expose that and teach you how to reach out just enough to bring your arm back and Cover Block in time. After a while, you may mix Cover Blocks back in to defend Straights (Pic D).. This will help you decide which defense you feel works best for you. Many like Rear Catches and Parries for Jabs but prefer Cover Blocks for Crosses (although many do not). Try to understand why your preference fits your style or inclination.

Some additional combinations to drill that may be useful in order to teach transitioning Blocks, Catches and Parries are:

Jab-Cross-Lead Hook-Rear Hook
Jab-Lead Uppercut-Rear Hook
Jab-Cross-Lead Leg Roundhouse-Rear Leg Roundhouse
Double Jab-Rear Leg Roundhouse-Lead Hook-Lead Uppercut

Forearm Block

Raise your hand high like a Cover Block, but allow your elbow to leave your side and your hand to extend past your face. Take the strike on your arm (Pics A to B).

A

B

Ideally your block will have enough power to stop your opponent's strike in its path, but there are times when the force of the blow may be too much. In this case, you may throw your opponent's punch off course by rolling the punch off your elbow, flaring it up after your forearm has already slowed the punch down. Keep your elbow in place until the last second (Pics A to C).

A

B

C

Or you can "glide" in, moving into your opponent's strike. This works very well against Hooks. Try to wedge your hand or arm in the crook or your opponent's elbow (Pics A to C). This may have a similar feel to it as an Inside Parry. If you want to you can step in closer to clinch.

A

B

C

Against body blows, you can lower your forearm to cut off Hooks or Uppercuts. Think of chopping down. This is an amazing multipurpose Block that can defend most of your body without requiring much nuance. Keep in mind however that your head will be left open.

The major advantage of Forearm Blocks are that your arm is detached from your head and body, so there is no chance that you take the impact of a blow through your Guard. It can also afford you clearer vision. On the other hand, this will leave many more openings for your opponent to sneak shots through. It is up to you how much you wish to open up your defenses.

Drill

Have your partner throw Hooks to your head from either side. Practice stepping away from their attack as you Forearm Block to dispel the force of the blow. Then Return a punch off the opposite side (Pics A to F). Stepping away like this also works well for Roundhouse Kicks, and you can try this as well. You may be surprised at just how much force is taken out of your partner's kicks by moving away from it as you Block.

Like Cover Blocks, Forearm Blocks can also be used to Block Straights. As with a Cover Block, you will take the impact on the back of your forearm. This technique is much rarer, but on the other hand it's also one of the top defenses used by Manny Pacquiao. Manny uses this block while stepping back before popping back in to counter. Just like stepping sideways to blunt the impact of hooks, dissipation of force is a big reason the technique works for him. You can try this too and see how it works for your style.

Concept – Smallest Opposing Force Necessary

After drilling Cover Blocks and Forearm Blocks, you may be wondering where one ends and one begins. Some practitioners prefer to keep their gloves stapled to their heads and their elbows glued to their ribs when blocking, simply tightening their arm upon impact. This is a fine option if that is all there is time for. Others may block far out from their bodies, though this is rarer. However, keeping your arm touching your head and body means you may feel a great deal of impact from your opponent's strike through your guard (Pics A to B), while blocking wide leaves you "wide open" for follow up shots (Pics C to D). Over time, most experienced fighters learn to find a middle ground. They open their Guard just enough to dispel the force of their opponent's blow and then return their hand back to position immediately. Read on to see how.

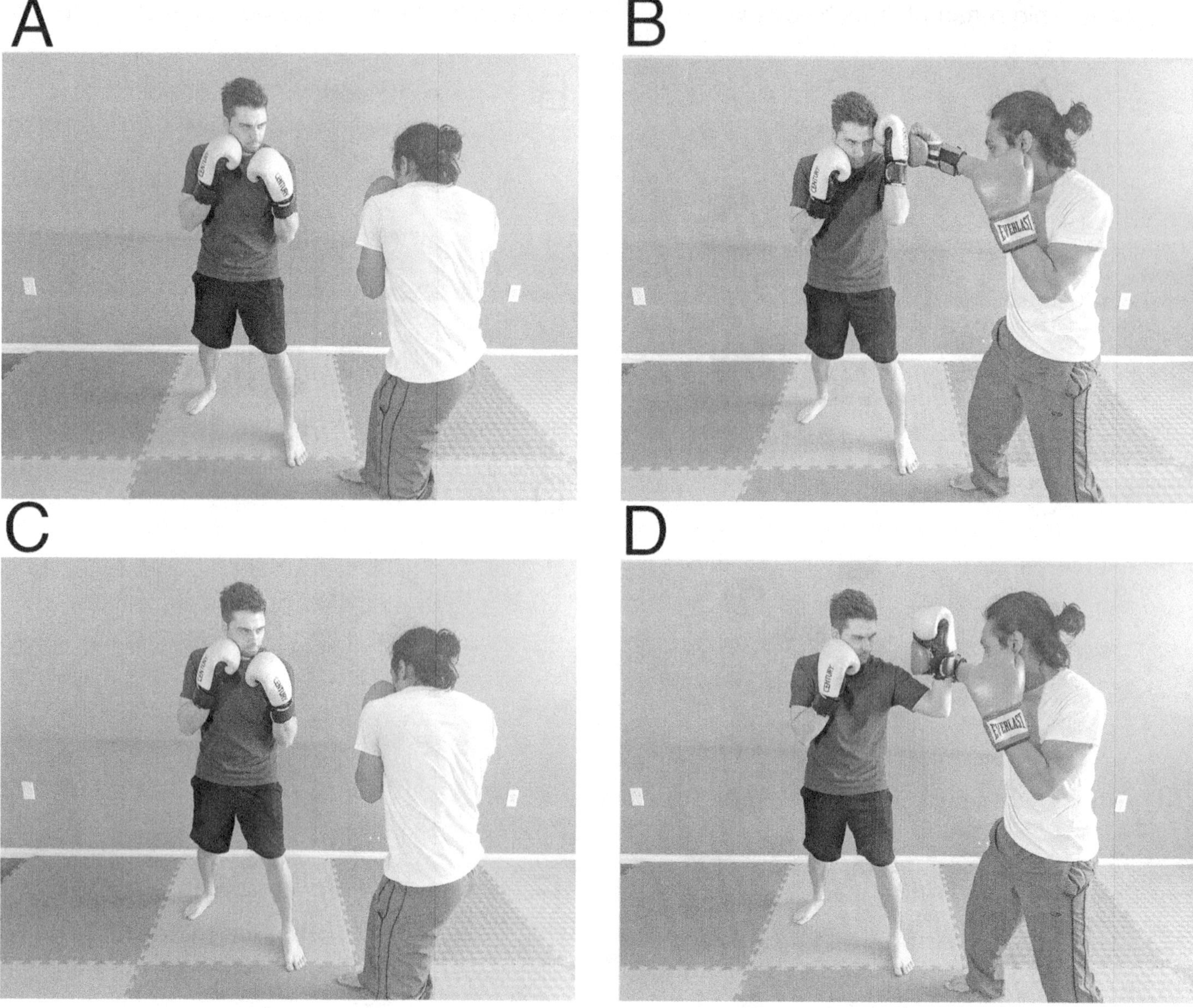

In picture A, the fighter has brought his hand straight up, keeping his glove on his temple. His Guard is secure, but he will feel a lot of the impact through his glove. If he is tired the strike may knock his glove aside and connect. In picture B, the fighter has opened his Guard by bringing his glove away from his temple by a quarter of an inch. This small movement leaves few openings but will shield him from a great deal of the impact.

A

B

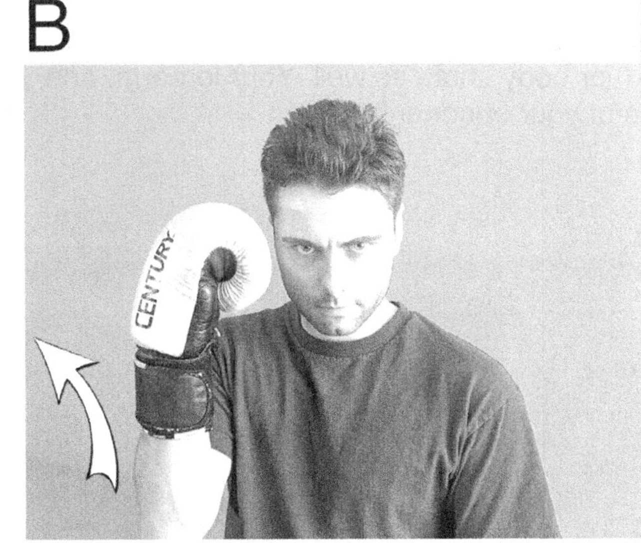

The motion should begin just before your opponent is about to connect. Your arm should make a small circle as you bring your glove up and out to catch the punch (Pics A to B) before quickly returning to a tight Guard (Pics C to D). This technique requires expert timing and should be practiced until it is second nature.

A

B

C

D

When using this technique against linear strikes, you will probably want to circle inward instead (Pics A to D). Think of Wax On, Wax Off from the Karate Kid (although as mentioned the movement will be much more subtle). Notice the very small gap between forehead and glove in picture B. This is due to the fighter slightly pushing his arm forward to meet force with force.

Although, if you truly master the spirit of this technique then your glove may not leave your head at all. This is because you will be using the perfect amount of opposing force against your opponent's strikes to negate their impact while not opening your Guard in the slightest. This same principle can be used for body shots as well. Your forearm, and your elbow with it, will make a small circle to dispel the force of your opponent's punch.

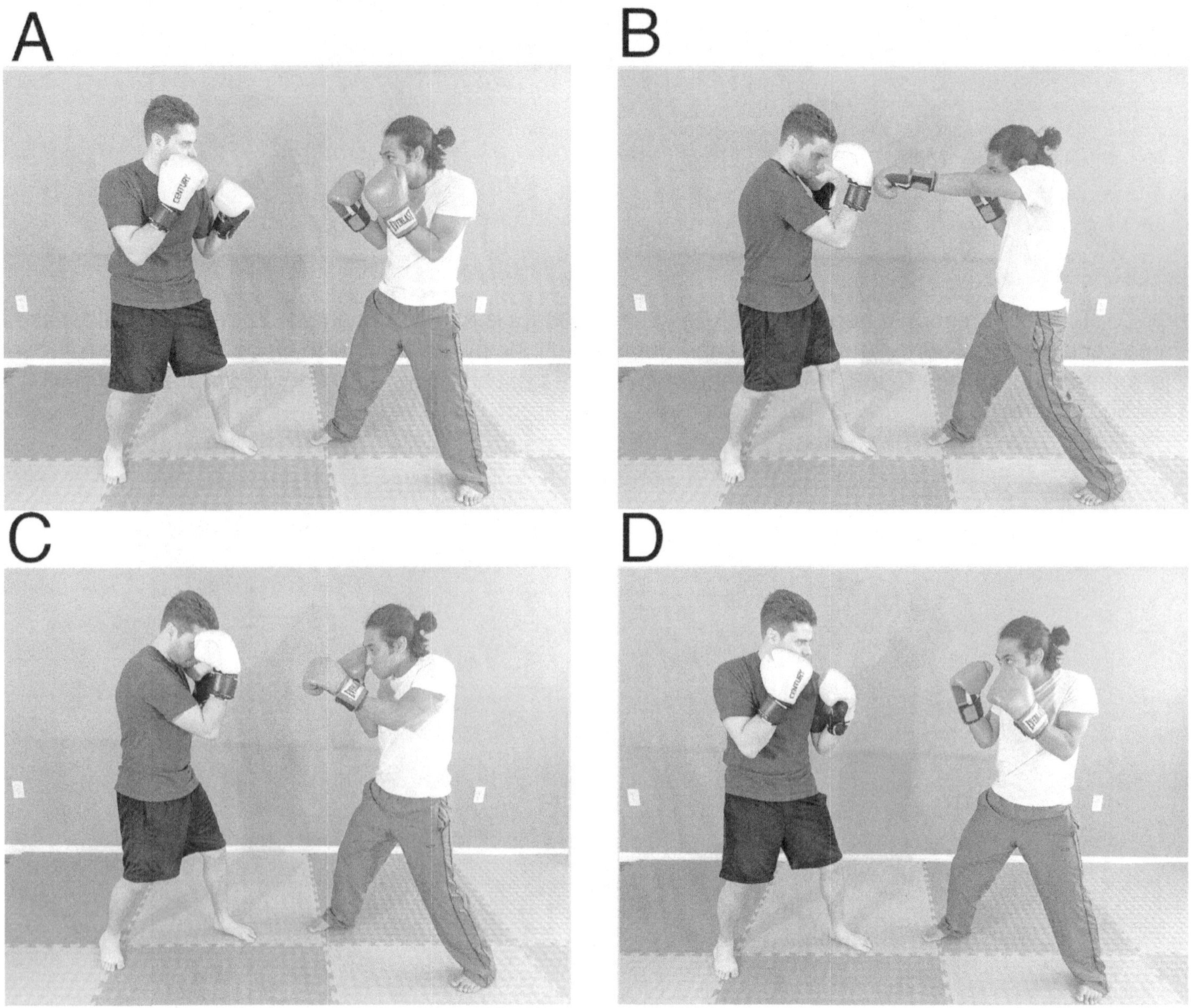

Low Block

Swipe your arm down to meet your opponent's kick (Pics A to D). As mentioned before, this is not your preferred block for dealing with kicks. It leaves your head vulnerable and taking the impact of a hard kick directly can damage your arm. That being said, it is a good one to know for a few reasons. First, it is fine against kicks at long range, especially if you know you will be blocking your opponent's instep or foot. If you keep getting hit with Roundhouse Kicks off angle from long range and cannot lift your knee in time, then a good Low Block can be a very simple life saver.

Or if you want to stay just a bit closer so it's easier to counter but keep your mobility, you can Low Block your opponent's kick without the need to Check and then move right in to attack. Mighty Mouse Johnson, one of the best there has ever been, does this on occasion.

If you're in a bad position and all out of options, it may be better to throw out the Low Block than to just take the hit. Then again, if you were wrong and your opponent was throwing a Head Kick, then it may not.

Finally, some infighters like Roberto Duran use a low block to stop body hooks at Close Range. If you want to do this make sure to hunch your shoulder to protect your chin.

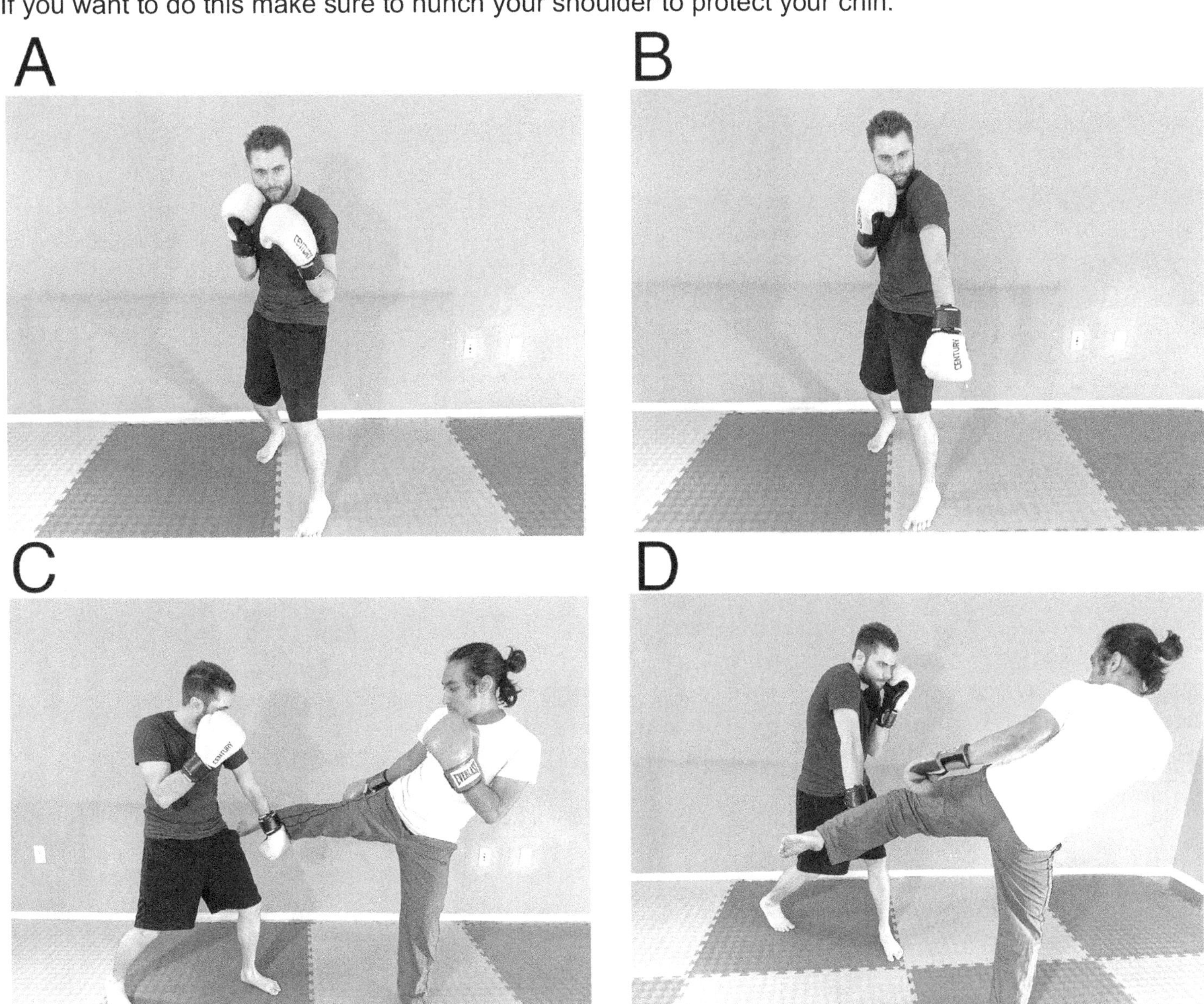

Elbow Block

Begin like a High Cover Block, but move your hand past your ear, as if combing your hair. Bend your arm and raise your Elbow to chest or chin level. Keep your Elbow tucked in tight towards your Center Line (Pics A to B & C to D).

Unlike the Cover Block or the Forearm Block, the Elbow Bock requires you to bend your arm almost completely. This exposes far more of your mid-section, but also provides a much sturdier point of impact that spares your head. While the Cover Block should use well-timed trunk movement to defuse the power of the strike, Elbow Blocks provide enough mass to absorb your opponent's blow without much upper body movement needed. This makes it ideal for kickboxing and MMA. That being said, certain boxers did use this block extensively (Salvador Sanchez being a great example). He would usually be Ducking down in a deep Crouch, meaning he did not have to worry about exposing his midsection by using this block.

To defend Linear strikes, such as the Jab or Cross, align your elbow to your opponent's strike. This is an absolutely devastating technique in combat sports with smaller gloves. Rumble Johnson and Randy Couture both relied on this technique in the earlier days of MMA. The goal is to let your opponent run their hand or foot into the point of your Elbow (Pics A to C).

The more common use is to defend against attacks from the side, such as the Hook or Roundhouse Kick (Pics D to F). Make sure that the meaty part of the outside of your forearm, triceps and shoulder make contact with the strike at around the same time. If the impact is great and you still need to dispel the force of the blow, you can reinforce the block, turn your upper body, or take a small step away.

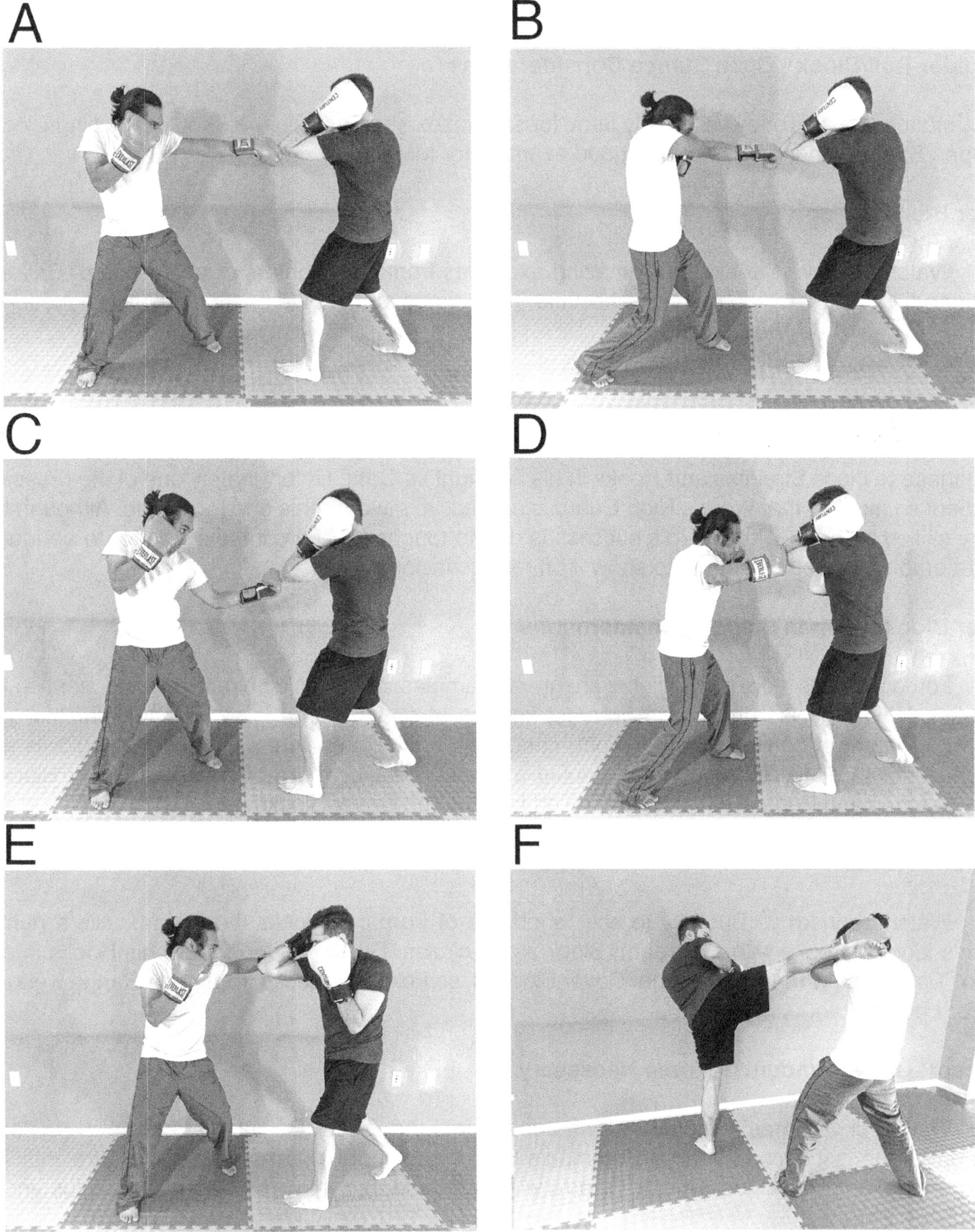

References – Arm Blocks

Shoulder Roll/Block

Shoulder Rolls will be covered in far more depth in the Philly Shell section, but for now check out the fights and highlight reels of George Benton. Benton is a great old school boxer to watch to see just how effective the Shoulder Roll can be, and how it can be used as both a block and a roll. Anderson Silva is one of the few to do it well in MMA. Many times he would use it in conjunction with a Leverage Block or Frame (covered in the Long Guard section).

Shoulder Roll/Block - Open Stance Considerations

Watch James Toney vs Vassily Jirov for several examples of Toney Shoulder Rolling/Blocking in an Open Stance. Anderson Silva is a good example for MMA.

Cover Blocks

Watch GGG vs Canelo 2 for amazing examples from both fighters of every kind of Cover Block mentioned. This fight will be mentioned several more times and should be studied in slow motion.

Reinforced Cover Blocks

In kickboxing and Muay Thai, Ramon Dekkers would often use Reinforced Blocks against Head Kicks. This left his hands in a better position to follow up with hard counter-punches. Ward can be seen using these to block Straights and Hooks in his first fight vs Gatti. Unfortunately one of the reasons they stand out so much is that Ward's High Guard is unreactive save for this one technique. Although he was a very skilled boxer, a lot of Ward's success is due to toughness. Of course it's better to be tough, but it's preferable that you only need to show it on rare occasions.

Cover Blocks – Open Stance Considerations

Lomachenko's more recent fights are great examples, but I would be remiss not to mention Pernell Whitaker. Whitaker was one of the greatest fighters of all time, and is a contender for the greatest Southpaw fighter of all time. It's well worth checking out all of his fights. Of course, Hagler is another contender for that title and should be studied as well. Whitaker more often mixed Cover Blocks with Rolls, Catches and Parries, while Hagler relied far more on Cover Blocks.

Forearm Blocks

Watch Leonard vs Duran 2 to see good use of Forearm Blocks. Leonard blocks a number of Duran's looping Hooks with a Forearm Block as he circles. Duran tended to turn his Hooks into some kind of Tie or Hold when his opponent Cover Blocked, so Forearm Blocks from Long-Range worked very well for Leonard.

Concept – Least Amount of Force Necessary

Watch Ali vs Foreman. While Ali was up against the ropes (Beginning in the 4th), he flared his arms out at the last second against Foreman's Hooks and shot his arms out against Straights. This is an extreme example and a downright bizarre way to defend, but Ali was a defensive genius and in the end it kept him safe. While you probably don't want to use these exact motions, it does work as a great example of the concept.

For a more conventional approach, watch Manny Pacquiao vs Margarito. While Margarito mostly just Shells up when defending (allowing Manny to punch through the consistent holes in his Guard), Manny varies the distance between his hands and his head. He alternates between Forearm Blocks, Cover Blocks and everything in between. The difference in technique is clearly shown on the fighter's faces at the end of the fight.

Elbow Blocks

In boxing, Salvador Sanchez often used Elbow Blocks while Ducking as an extra layer of protection. Mayweather also uses Rear Elbow Blocks from his Philly Shell Guard. In kickboxing and MMA Elbow Blocks are far more common, to the point where you can see it in almost any fight. Randy Couture and Rampage Jackson were some of the first to realize their potential in MMA. TJ Dillashaw vs Cody Garbrandt 1 and 2 are more modern fights with some good examples (but honestly there are a lot of fights with the same amount, I just think those are great fights everyone should watch if they can).

Lead Check/Knee Block

Raise your knee up high, aiming your shin towards your opponent's shin as they attempt to kick your leg or midsection (Pics A to B). Some believe that flexing your foot helps to brace your leg and harden the point of impact (Pics C to D). You can experiment with this for yourself and see which method you prefer.

A B

C 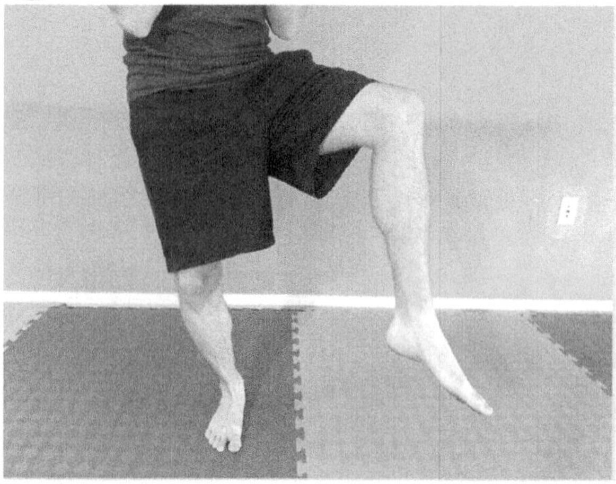 D

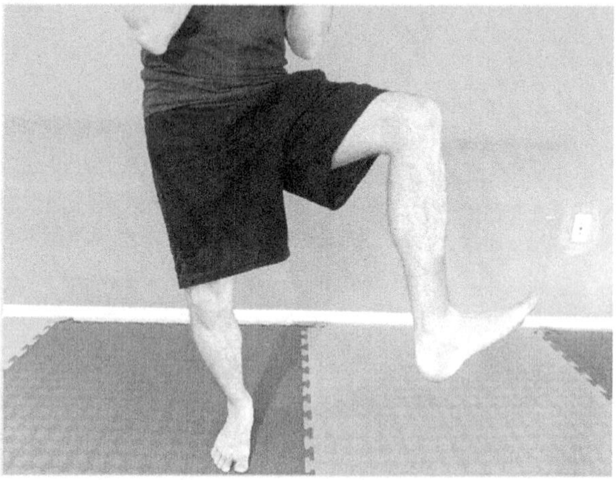

Some prominent fighters like Fedor Emelianenko prefer to limit how far they turn out their knee against Roundhouse Kicks. They instead take the impact on the edge of their shin (Pic A) rather than taking it straight on (Pic B). They feel that this limits the impact, saves time, and leaves them less exposed. This is something that you may wish to experiment with during the upcoming drills.

A B

If your opponent throws a Lead Leg Roundhouse, he will be aiming for the Inside of your leg. Raise your knee and turn your shin *Inside*, towards your opponent's kick (Pics A to B). Upon impact, think of "pushing" your opponent's leg away to step down and return to your normal stance. Alternatively, you can use the Check to move deeper into your opponent's space, crowding them and getting within punching or even clinching range.

If your opponent throws a Rear Leg Roundhouse, turn your knee *Outside* about 45 degrees, aiming the sharp part of your shin towards their kick (Pics C to D). Again, think of "pushing" your opponent's leg away to return to your normal stance. To defend against a Teep or Sidekick to the leg or midsection, you can simply raise your knee straight up, towards your opponent's foot(Pics E to F).

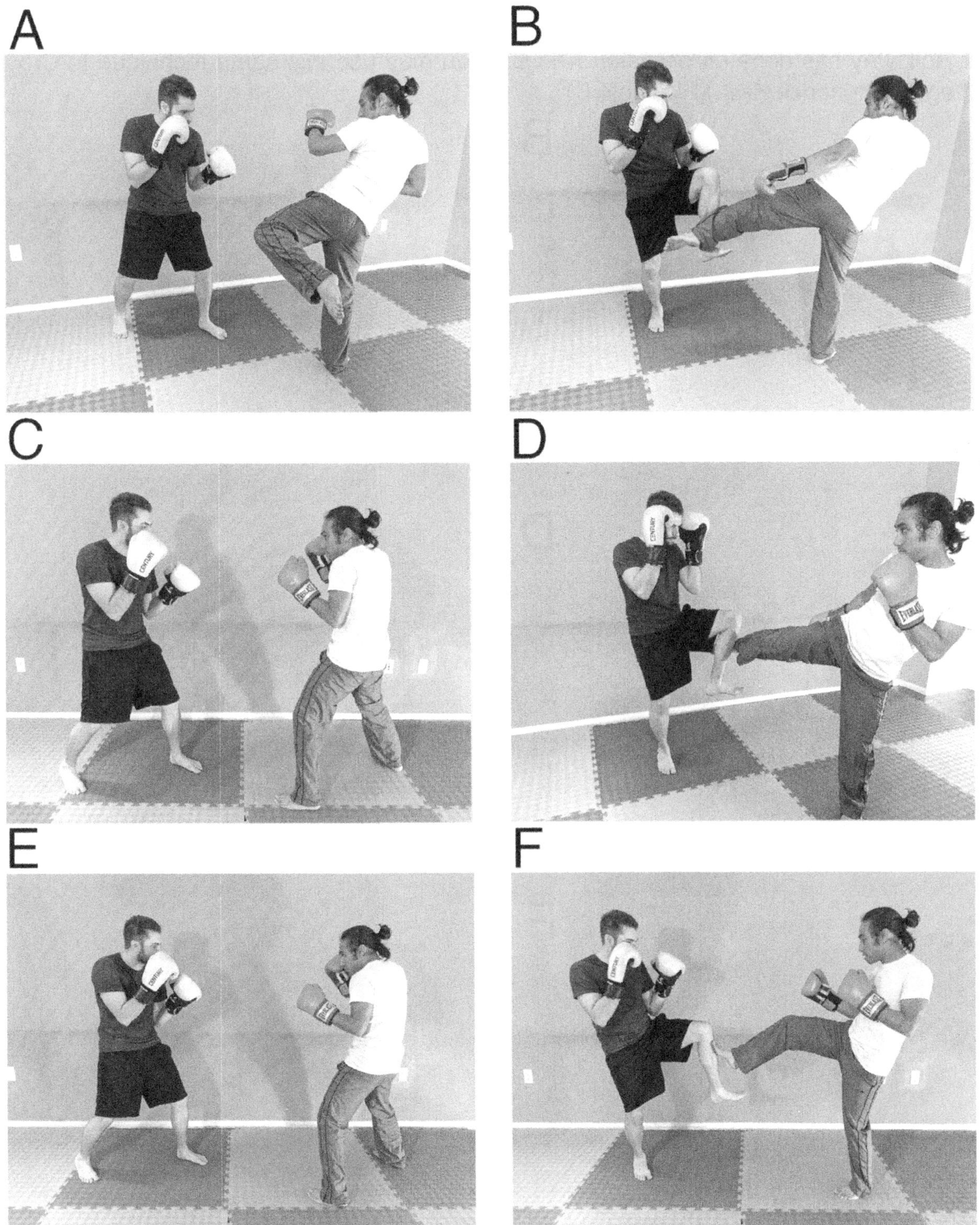

Rear Check/Knee Block

Raise your knee up high, aiming your shin towards your opponent's shin as they attempt to kick your leg or midsection (Pics A to B).

If your opponent throws a Lead Leg Roundhouse, he will most likely be aiming for the Inside of your Lead Leg. However, they may also get fancy and aim for your Rear Leg off of a feint or some tricky footwork. Either way, raise your Rear Knee and turn your knee out about 45 degrees. Upon impact, you may dull the damage taken by allowing your leg to bend in, and then think of "pushing" your opponent's leg away to help you stay balanced and return to your normal stance. This won't hurt them as bad, but the same goes for your own leg. Alternatively, you can step forward off of your Check into a Southpaw position, as Max Holloway has done on occasion (Pic C). You may use this same technique to Cross Check his Rear Leg Roundhouse Kick. (Pics D to F)

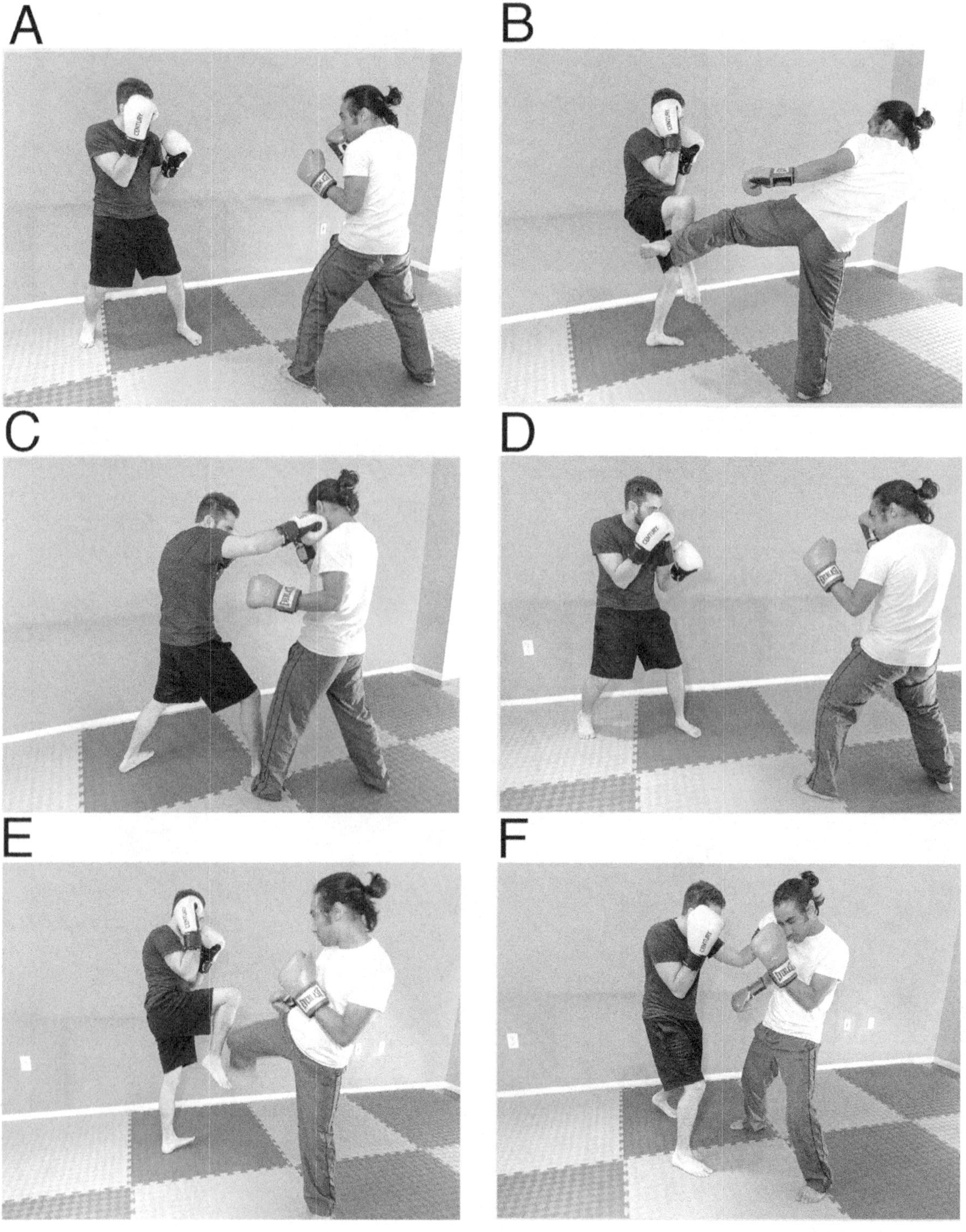

Open Stance Considerations

In an Open Stance, the main concern will be your opponent's Rear Leg attacking the inside of your Lead Leg (Pics A to B). If you keep your Lead Foot on the Outside of your opponent's, then it should make his Lead Roundhouse Kick difficult to land or too weak to do any damage (Pics C to D).

If you prefer a narrow, more sideways stance then you can Check your opponent's Rear Leg Roundhouse fairly easily with a Lead Leg Cross Check (Pics A to B). From a more forward stance a Rear Check will work nicely (Pic D). Some fighters tend to target an opponent's Rear Leg with their Rear Leg in an Open Stance (Pic C). This is a unique situation that only applies to fighters in an Open Stance, so be prepared.

A Lead Leg Roundhouse is still viable, but your opponent must step Outside to generate any power at all (Pics A to C). Once again, stepping Outside should take the attack away from him (Pics D to F).

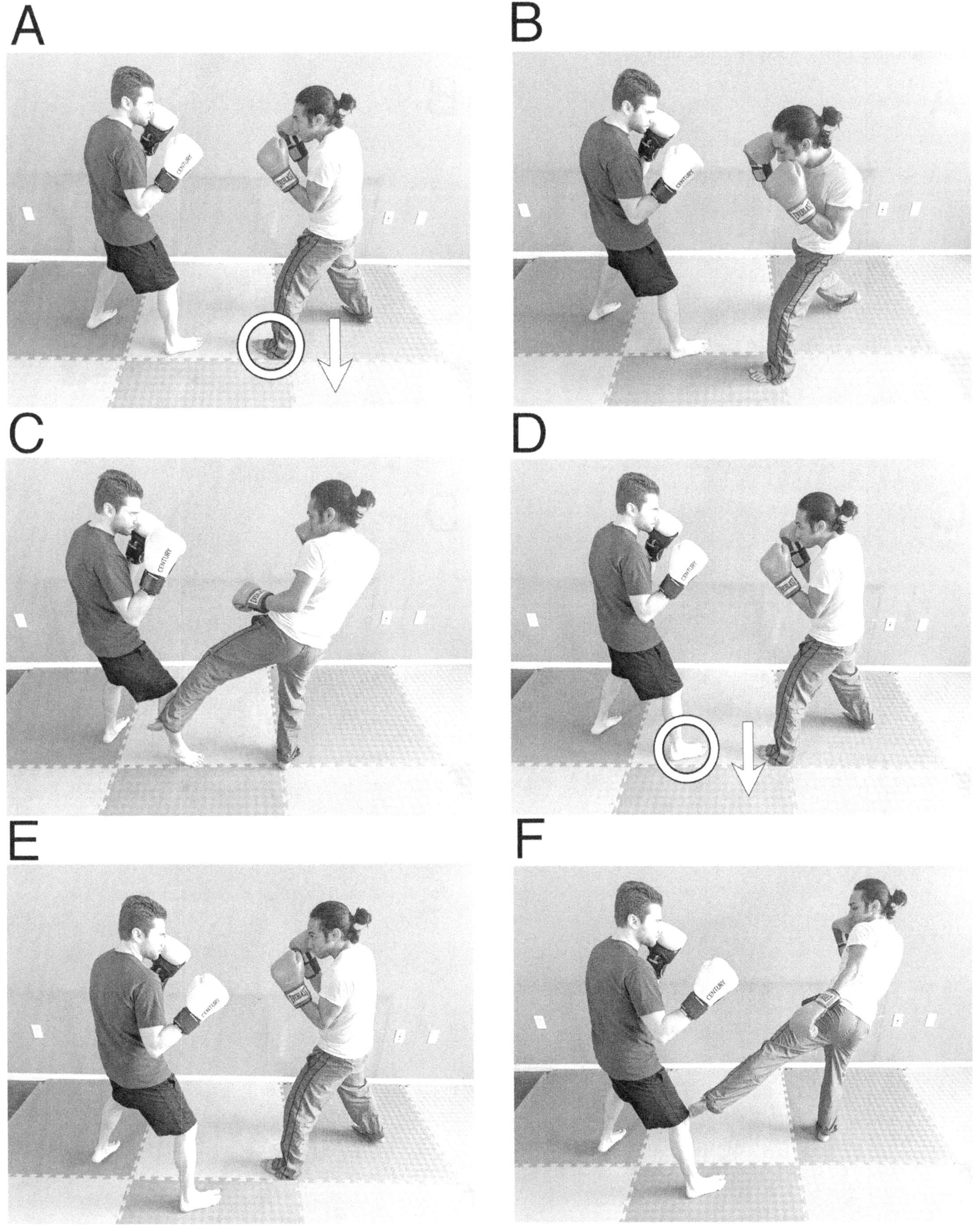

Open Stance Specialty Counter

A great counter in an Open Stance is to Intercept an opponent's Rear Leg Roundhouse kick with a Teep (Pics A to C) or Sidekick (Pic D). Wonderboy Thompson has made a career out of this. Since your Lead Leg is closer to your target and is taking a straighter path than your opponent's curving kick, it should be fairly easy to land first.

Step Checks - Checking Against Ankle/Calf Kicks

Raise your heel up towards your body to bend your knee, or lift your foot off the ground very slightly. Raising your heel will allow you to turn your shin towards your opponent's kick, taking the impact of the strike on the bone (Pics A to B). After the kick has connected, drop your weight down hard to reestablish your stance (Pics C to D). Sinking down like this helps to regain your stability and ads more weight to your Check. As such, this technique works nearly as well if your opponent catches you before or after you plant your foot.

Calf kicks have been dominating in MMA lately, and very few fighters know how to correctly defend them. The simple technique outlined above will go a long way to negate this popular attack. Watch Ernesto Hoost or early Conor McGregor to see how to pull off this defense effectively. You can step with this technique as well, meaning he can move to a better angle to counter (Pics E to F).

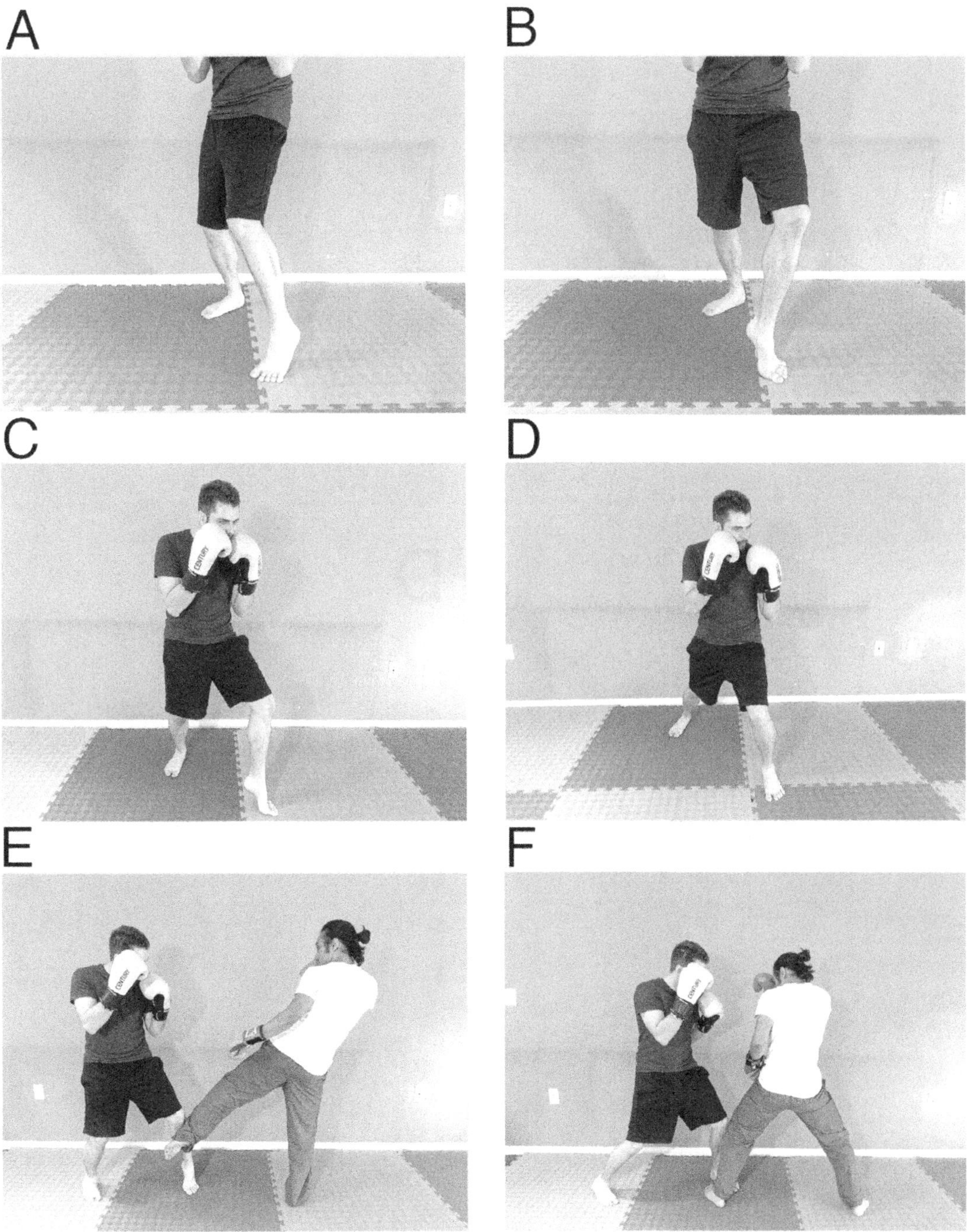

An alternative that some fighters are using to deal with Calf Kicks is to use the faster motion of lifting their heel to their butt rather than raising their knee up towards their chest. This is also covered over the next few pages.

Quick Check - Checking The Sidekick & Oblique Kick To The Knee

The Side Kick and Oblique Kick to the knee are very difficult to defend against for one simple reason: they are generally thrown as Intercepting Counters. The kick usually lands as you are stuck in place with most your weight on your Lead Leg, making it difficult to Check (Pics A to B & C to D).

You can try this yourself by leaning heavy on your Lead Foot and then Checking. You will find you need to take extra time to center yourself before you can begin to lift your foot off the ground. This is time that you may not have in a fight.

Pulling your leg back is a great defense if possible (covered in a later section) but once again, you may not have time. Believe it or not, the best alternative to pulling back is to simply lift your heel to your glute. This method of Checking was actually far more common in older versions of Muay Thai. Recently Robert Whitaker used it to stay safe and earn a victory against Yoel Romero.

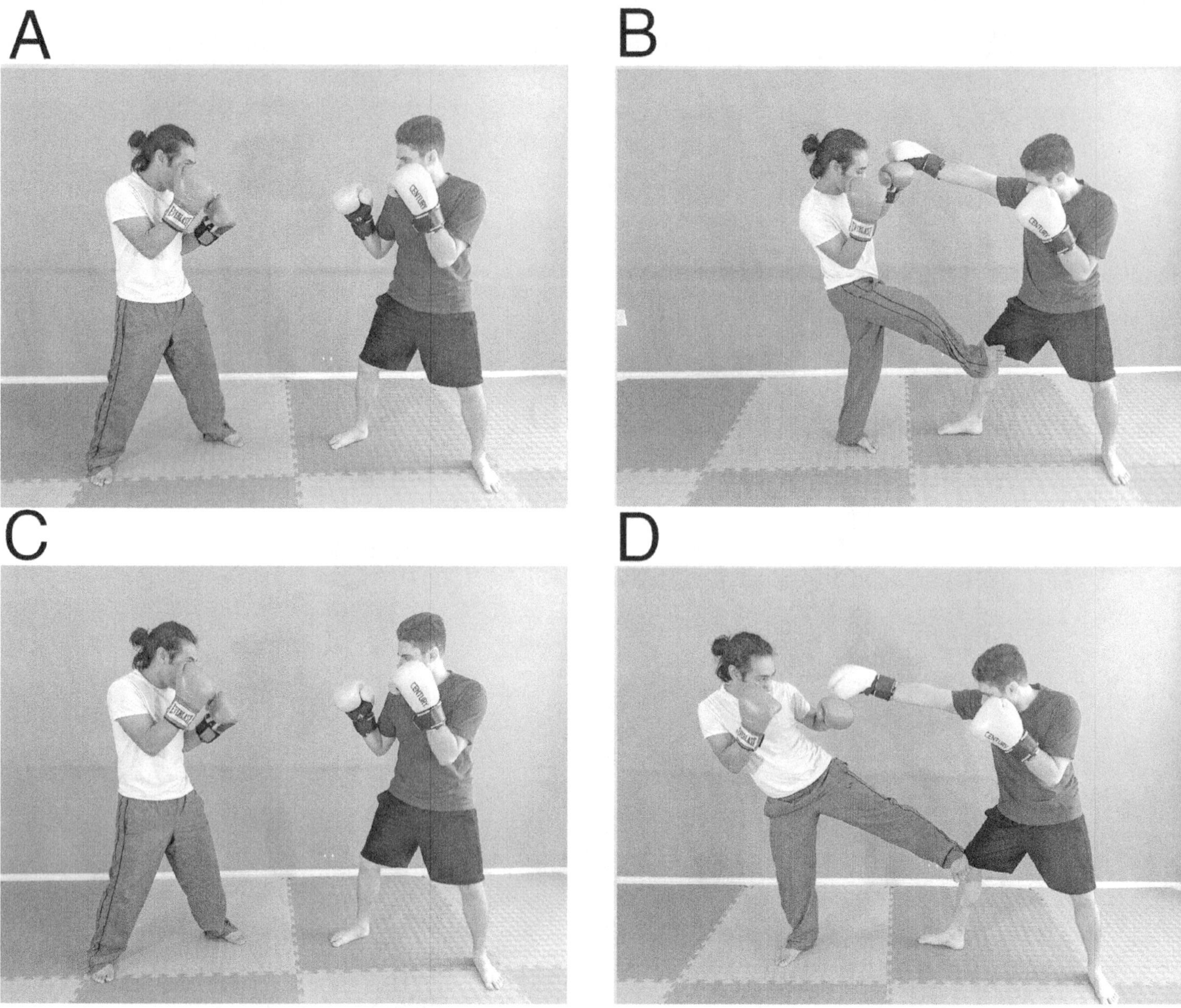

Because you don't need to lean back first as you would to lift up your knee, it is possible to block the kick in time by lifting your heel straight back instead (Pics A to D). This should be a very fast motion, quickly lifting your foot and then putting it right back down. It will work equally well against an Oblique Kick (Pic B) or a Sidekick (Pic C). Bending your leg in this way creates a hard target for your opponent, and will hopefully discourage them from attempting the technique again. Do not drill Side Kicks or Oblique Kicks to the leg or knee without a qualified professional coaching you through it. Damage is very possible and extreme caution is a necessity.

Drills

Drill 1 A

Have your partner throw a Lead Leg or Rear Leg Roundhouse Kick to your leg. Check the kick and then immediately Return a Rear Leg Roundhouse of your own. (Pics A to C & D to F) Try to catch them before they have finished retracting enough to check the kick, but keep it light! Take turns attacking and defending. Wear shin pads unless you want to hurt for days. The only reason we aren't is that we are not actually throwing, but rather holding the poses for these pictures.

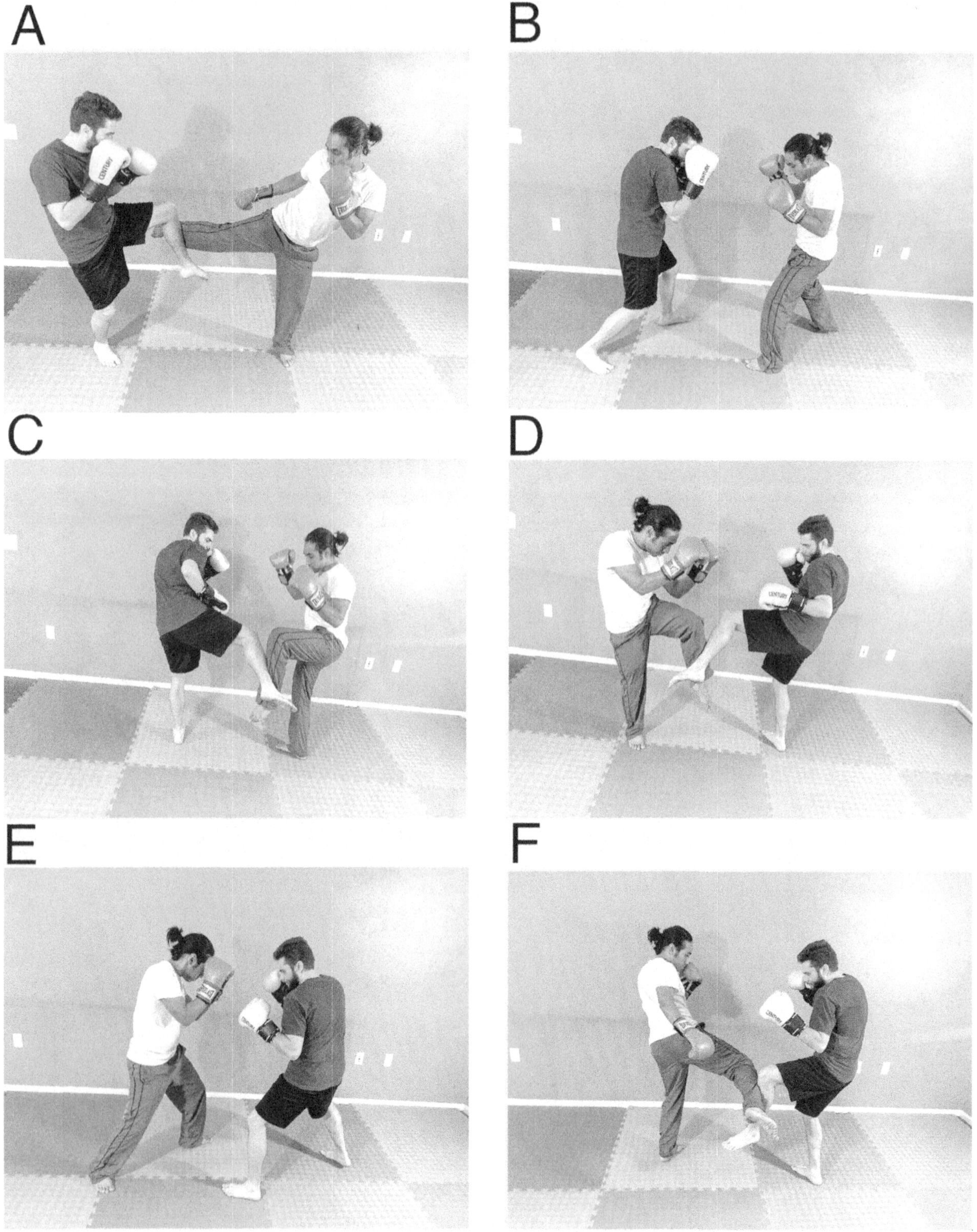

Drill 1 B

Have your partner throw a Jab (Pic A) and then follow up with a Roundhouse to your leg, calf, body or head (B Pics). After checking, it is now your turn to throw a Lead Leg Roundhouse to whichever target you wish (C Pics). Have your partner attack for one round and then it is your turn to attack while he defends and counters.

This drill will help you quickly distinguish exactly where your partner is aiming and use the correct method to defend it. Roundhouses are extremely difficult to gauge, and there have been many, many knockouts resulting from a fighter misjudging his opponent's target.

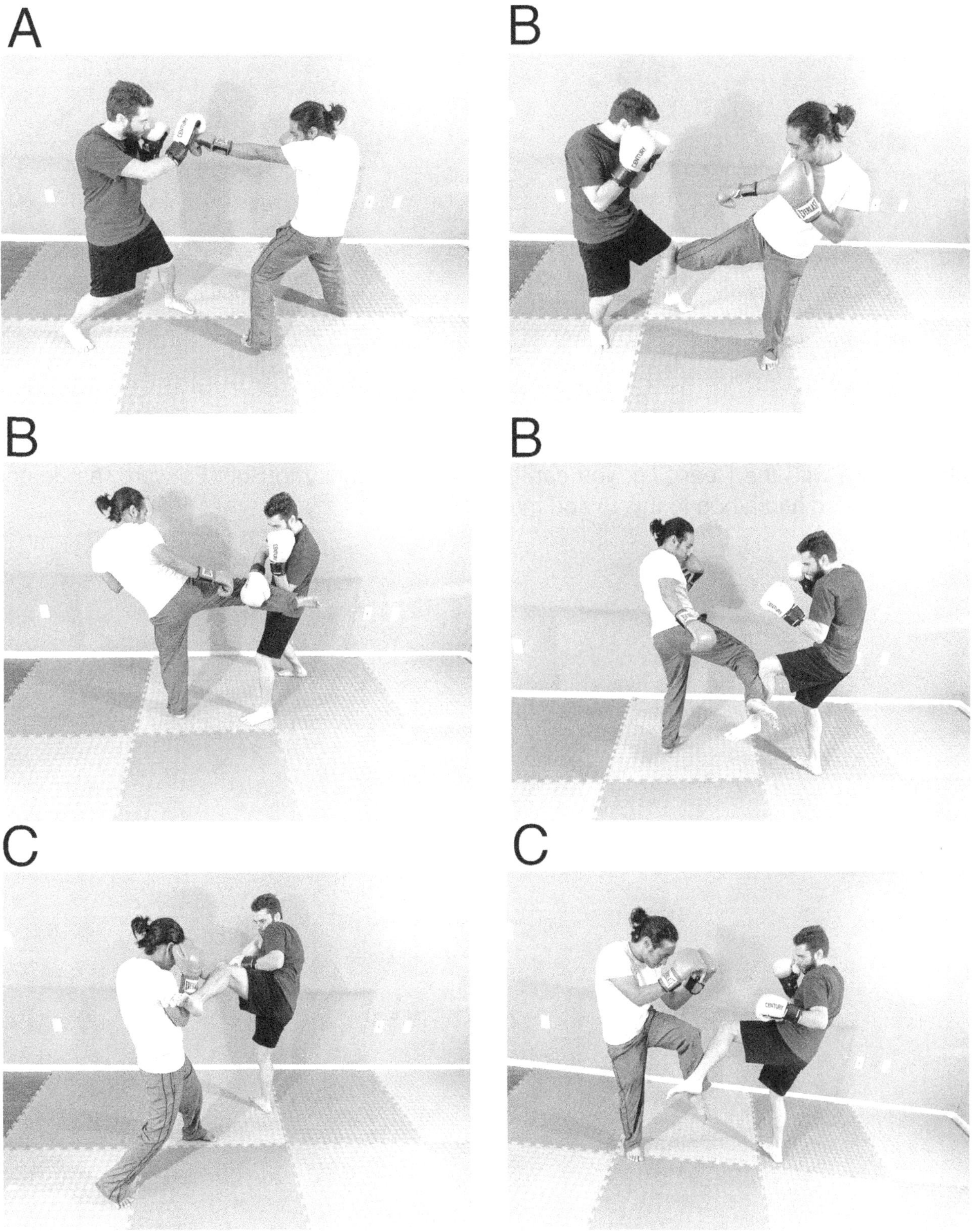

Drop Step Check & Hop Variation

One of the major downsides of a Leg Check it that is leaves you vulnerable by cementing you in place for a split second. A useful alternative is to use your Check to move forward, similar to the Drop Step outlined in Jack Dempsey's famous book on boxing, Championship Fighting. You may use a regular Check or a Quick Check for this technique. Lean forward into your Check and drop down into a punch, frame or a clinch (Pics A to B). To add extra distance, you can hop off of the back foot.

A

B

If Checking with the Rear Leg, you can use the opportunity to Shift Forward, as demonstrated before. You can also add a hop to this to add more distance.

Reinforced Check

Sometimes it is best not to gamble on exactly where a kick is going to land and just block the entirety of one side. This is done by combining an arm block with a Check on the same side (A to B & C).For instance, you can use a Cover Block, Forearm Block, or Elbow Block in conjunction with your Check on the same side. It is usually best to place your knee on the outside of your elbow, as the bigger bone can better take the impact of a kick.

The exemption to the same side rule is to block a Roundhouse coming to the Inside with a Lead Leg Inside Check, and at the same time protect your head and body with an arm block on the opposite side (Pic D). In all cases, you may wish to Double Reinforce your block by either supporting your Cover Block with another Cover Block, or Parrying to deflect the kick away (Pics E & F).

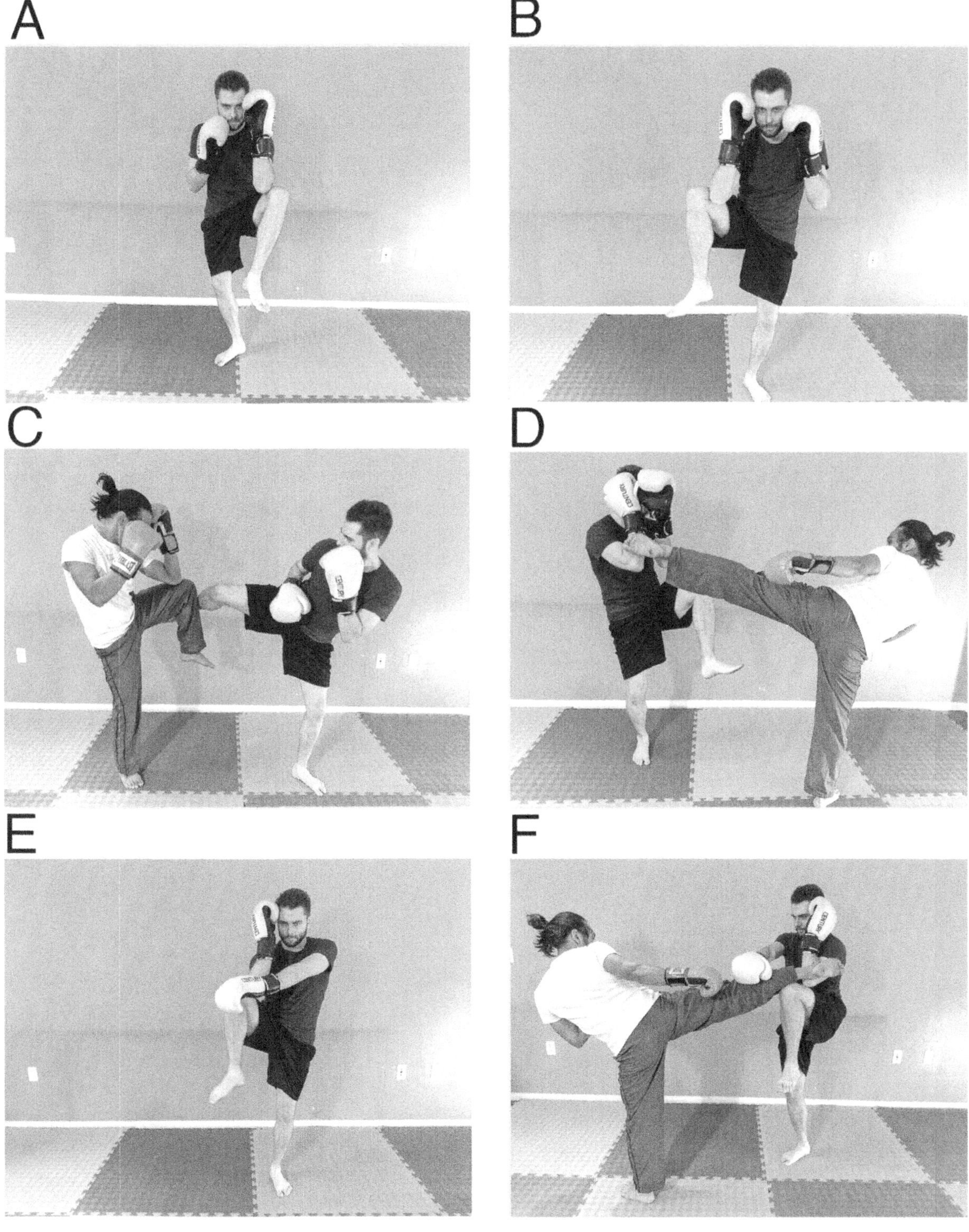

Open Stance Considerations

\

You are much more likely to Cover Block and Check with opposite sides in an Open Stance. This situation will occur when you Cross Check an opponent's Rear Leg Roundhouse with your Led Leg and Cover Block with your Rear Arm (Pics A to B). Cross Checking with your Lead Leg will let you immediately step down into a Return Counter with your Rear Side (Pics A to C). In contrast, Checking with your Rear Leg would require far more adjustments before countering, leaving you less able to follow your opponent and catch them with a counter if they move away (Pics D to E).

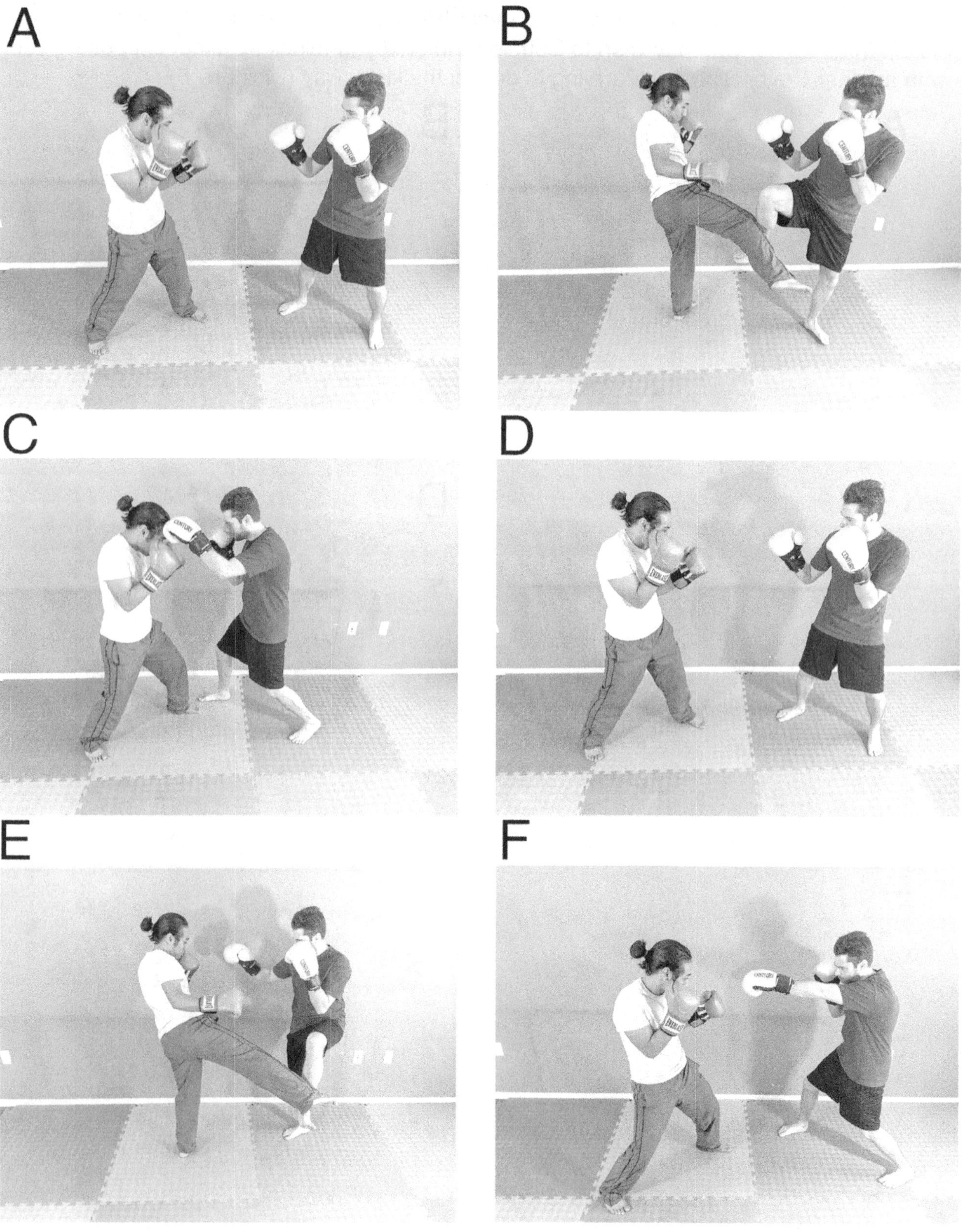

Leg Brace

Lean your knee forward over your toes and sink your weight down. Depending on the width of your stance, you may need to step out first (Pics A to B). Squeeze your leg and brace hard, thinking of moving forward into your opponent's kick.

Bracing is popular in MMA, as it allows you to keep your stability, unlike a Check. Whether in kickboxing or MMA, Bracing is useful if you do not want to lose your mobility by Checking, or as a way to stay in range while delivering an Intercepting punch or kick (Pics C to D).

Be warned that Leg Braces do not work near as well against Sidekicks or Oblique Kicks to the knee, especially if the opponent is skilled and knows how to angle in these kicks from the side (Pics E to F). If one of these kicks hits the side of your knee, it could cause some serious damage, and more so if your weight is fully planted. Use Quick Checks or Pull Backs against these attacks instead. Do not drill Side Kicks or Oblique Kicks to the leg or knee without a qualified professional coaching you through it. Damage is very possible and extreme caution is a necessity.

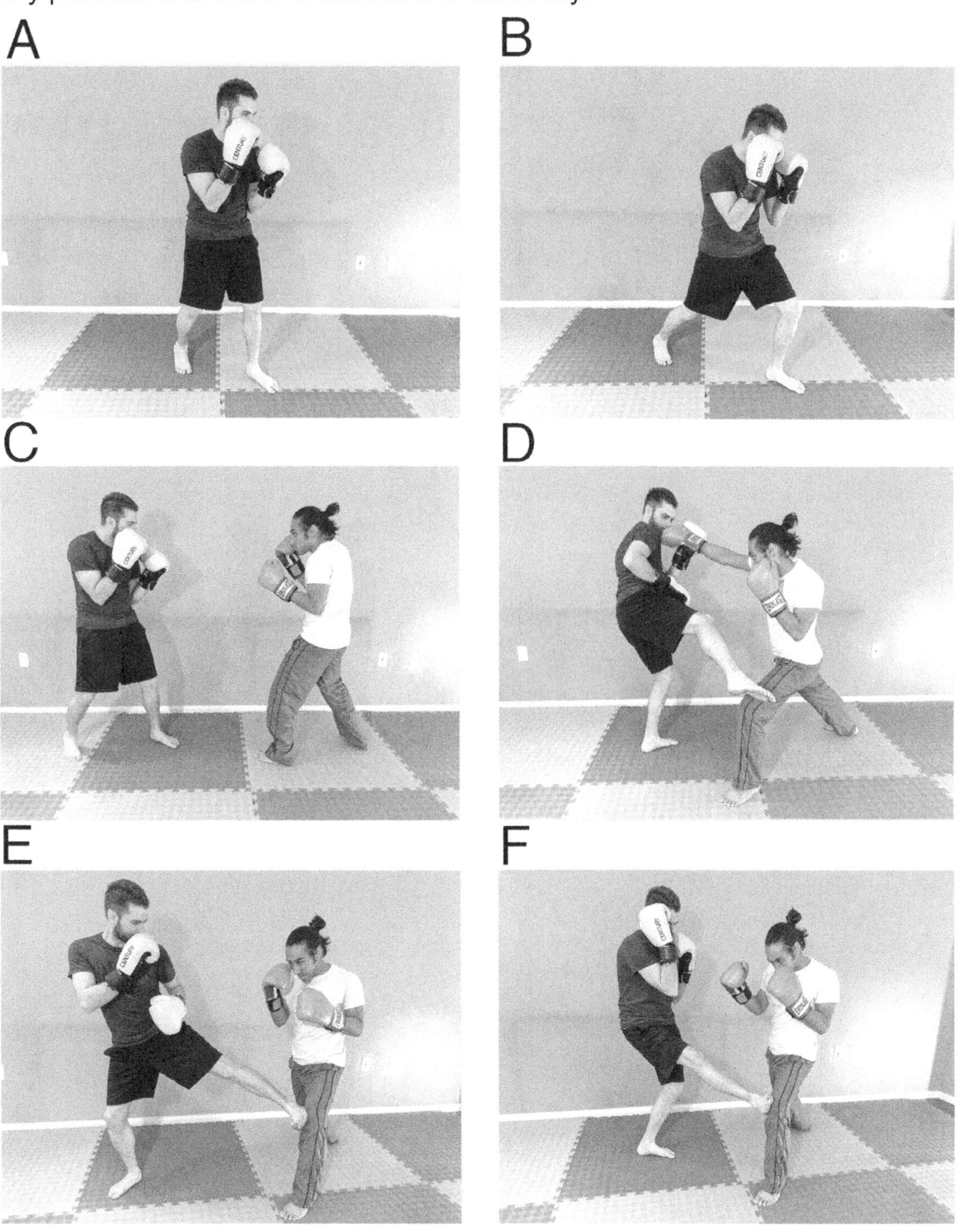

Open Stance Considerations

In an Open Stance it's may be better to Check or Pull Back (more on that in the Low Guard Section) than to Brace. Bracing against a Lead Leg kick is fine (Pics A to B), but Bracing against a Rear Roundhouse in an Open Stance leaves you far more open (Pic C). You are just as likely to get hit in the stomach or groin (Pic D). You have to be 100 percent sure that your opponent is targeting your leg and not your stomach or head. Even then, leg kicks in this situation have a tendency to slide up the thigh and connect with your cup. If you still want to Brace in an Open Stance, be careful and keep these considerations in mind.

References – Checks

Checks

Dieselnoi (one of the greatest Muay Thai fighters of all time) is a great example of a fighter who used Checks to enter into Close-Range. Recently a video of his fight with Samart (another GOAT with a completely opposite, movement based style) has surfaced. Watch it to see how Diselnoi used Checks to Shift forward, cut off the ring, and enter into Close-Range to drown Samart in the clinch.
Or you can watch Ernesto Hoost to see a great example of a fighter Checking Leg Kicks to Return Counter with a harder Leg Kick of his own. Hoost is another all-time-great with maybe the most terrifying Leg Kicks ever.

Checks – Open Stance Considerations

In their earlier fights, Cro Cop (who fights Southpaw) seemed to have no answer against Hoost's (who fights Orthodox) ridiculous Roundhouse Kicks. But in their 2000 fight, Cro Cop did an amazing job Checking almost every one of Hoost's kicks. Watch the fight to see how Cro Cop alternates which leg is Checking based on angles and distance. Although Cro Cop won the standard 3 rounds (in my opinion) the judges ruled it a draw and required an extra round. Hoost won the last round by switching strategies and clinching with Cro Cop, who had gassed by that point. Regardless of the decision, the fight stands out as a defensive master class by Cro Cop against one of the greatest kickers ever.

Angles – Open Stance Considerations

Watch Stephen Thompson vs Rory McDonald for a great example of how the Outside foot position can help to set up Lead Leg Roundhouse Kicks to the calf. Even though he keeps a sideways, narrow stance, Thompson is able to put power into his Lead Leg Roundhouse Kicks by positioning his Lead Foot Outside. Thompson notices he can land the kick with impunity near the end of the first round and never stop throwing them. By round 5 McDonalds leg is close to giving out and he wobbles when Thompson lands his kicks.

To see a great example of how an Inside Position in an Open Stance helps to land Rear Leg Roundhouses to your opponent's Rear Leg, check out nearly any Andy Hug fight. Hug was unusual in that he often targeted his opponent's Rear Leg, but it proved to be a highly effective tactic.

Step Checks - Checking Ankle Kicks

McGregor vs Max Holloway is a great one to watch to see this technique in action, as Holloway throws lots of Ankle Kicks with either leg. He even lands a few clean, so you can watch the vast different between how a correct Check leaves McGregor perfectly balanced while a kick that lands leaves him in a bad, unstable position. You can also compare the effectiveness of this technique against his altered defenses against Dustin Porier, where he switched to a deep lead-leg heavy stance and mostly Braced rather than Step Checked. Finally, Hoost vs Sefo is one instance of this kind of Check damaging the striker and leading to a knockdown.

Quick Check - Checking Oblique Kicks & Sidekicks

In Whitaker vs Romero 1 (An amazing fight!) Romero tore the tendons in Whitaker's knee with Sidekicks and Oblique Kicks, putting him out for a year. In their rematch (an ever more amazing fight and one of my favorites) Whitaker came prepared. He defending Romero's Sidekicks and Oblique Kicks by lifting his heel directly to his glute. Romero's technique was by no means new (Savate and old school

Muay Thai fighters had sometimes Checked in a similar way) but it was one of the first time the defense had been used against these kinds of kicks in a high profile MMA fight. When you watch the fight, note how Whitaker is able to keep his weight on his Lead Foot and still Check effectively.

For a quick example of this technique working against a Roundhouse Kick, check out Cejudo vs Dillashaw. Finding himself at Close-Range with a heavy Lead Foot, Cejudo simply lifts his heel to his glute and continues pressing forward. This takes places 5 seconds into the fight, after Cejudo evades Dillashaw's Rear Leg Roundhouse from Southpaw, he then uses a Quick Check to avoid Dillashaw's Rear Leg Roundhouse from Orthodox.

Drop Step Check & Hop

Benny the Jet Urquidez loved to enter exchanges with this technique. More recently, Max Holloway has used this technique in the same way. He would also sometimes turn the Check into a Sidekick to the leg or Shift forward into Southpaw. Holloway has recently turned into more of a boxer, so check out his fights before his bouts with Jose Aldo to see this tactic in action.

Reinforced Check

I've already mentioned how well Cro Cop did in his 2000 fight against Hoost's legendary Leg Kicks, but Cro Cop had legendary kicks himself. Cro Cop's Head Kicks were one of the most feared strikes in kickboxing and MMA history. He moved so fast that it often looked as if he kicked over his opponent's head. It was only after the slow motion replay that you could notice the opponent's head snap violently back and forth before they collapsed to the canvas. A big factor in Cro Cop's success was his ability to find the smallest cracks in his opponent's Guard, sneaking his Roundhouse Kicks under opponent's elbows to crack their ribs or over their Cover Block or Cross Parry to catch them on the temple.

That is why when he fought Fedor, Fedor decided to block everything at once. By Checking, Cover Blocking and Cross Blocking at the same time, Fedor defended every single vulnerability on one side of his body. Covering everything at the same time this way meant there was no need to guess and therefor no chance of a kick sneaking through the gaps in his defense. Using his knee to cover his body also meant that Fedor could flare his elbow out without worrying about Body Kicks sneaking underneath his arm. According to him, flaring his elbow angled his forearm in a way that deflected his opponent's kicks over his head. It's this attention to small details that helped put Fedor in contention for the title of greatest MMA fighter of all time.

Leg Brace

Maybe the best use of a Leg Brace is to Brace against an opponent's Rear Leg Roundhouse Kick while Intercepting with a Cross. This is fairly common, but I would recommend highlights of Tenshin Nasukawa to watch this technique result in a knockdown. Machida used the same tactic against Jon Jones and put him in deep trouble with it. Strange to think how MMA history would have changed if Machida had managed to finish Jones off then and win the fight. As mentioned before, Braces are tricky in an Open Stance. However, Poirier did stagger Gaethje by Bracing in an Open Stance and landing a hard Return Counter Cross (which lead to the end of the fight). That being said, he got his leg trashed every other time he had Braced during the fight. It's up to you.

High Guard

High Guard is unique in that it can be used effectively by both highly skilled defensive fighters and by those who lack any kind of defensive skills at all. Skillful boxers use it to add a base of protection from which they can pull off more subtle defense. In contrast, some power punching brawlers with good chins use it to take a hit so they can give a harder one back. In this book we will explore how the High Guard may be used to dispel some of the impact of the punch as you take it on your Guard. After drilling these techniques it is suggested that you explore ways to use the defense in the Basics section to supplement your High Guard. In this way your High Guard will can be a failsafe or a tactic rather than your one and only line of defense.

Absorbing Blows With Body Motion & Footwork

Show me a fighter who bites down on his mouthguard and moves forward to eat punches on his Guard and I will show you a fighter with a very short career. The truly talented fighters you see are not taking near as much damage as you may think. That is because they know how to move with punches and kicks to absorb and dispel their force.

The High Guard is a great Guard to choose for this style of fighting. For our purposes, High Guard means any Guard where the hands are kept on your cheeks (Pic A) to your temple (Pic B). Higher Guards are possible (some Muay Thai and MMA fighters put their hands near the top of their head), but rare. Remember, as with all the techniques in this book, the principles explored can be incorporated into any style.

In this section we will break down the different ways to move your feet and upper body to negate the impact of punches. It is rare that you will only be using one of these motions, but each should be understood individually if you hope to effectively negate the many different kinds of strikes that will inevitably be thrown at you in a fight. Also, getting used to the feeling of taking shots and learning how to dispel that force is useful no matter what your style is.

As an added bonus, learning these movement patterns will be a great precursor to learning head movement. It may also be argued that this is the safest way to learn how to Roll with punches. This is because the motion that you will practice as you dispel the impact of strikes on your Guard is the same that you use to Roll with punches that land.

GGG vs Canelo 2 is an amazing example of two fighters who use the techniques outlined in this chapter to great effect. I would recommend studying both of their fights in slow motion to supplement this book.

A

B

Shell

This is the most basic defense taught to many on their first day. It is best used with a squared up, forward facing stance. Used correctly, this technique is a nuanced and versatile tool for quickly closing the distance. However, it is also the go-to method taught by inept coaches who want their students to take shots so that they can get close enough to maybe give some back. So, let's look at a few ways to correctly use the Shell.

First, get into position by pinching your elbows together. Your hands must rest on your eyebrows, and you must be careful not to obscure your vision (Pics A to B). As is, this technique will cover Body Straights. However, Straights or Uppercuts to the head can easily slip through. From Mid to Close Range you will be open to Hooks. However, you can adjust by temporarily bringing one arm in front to defend your centerline (Pics C & D). When you do this, you must pull your other hand back so that you have full visibility out of one eye. Pulling back in this way will defend against Hooks. After the strike is defended, immediately return to Guard or adjust your Shell for the next attack.

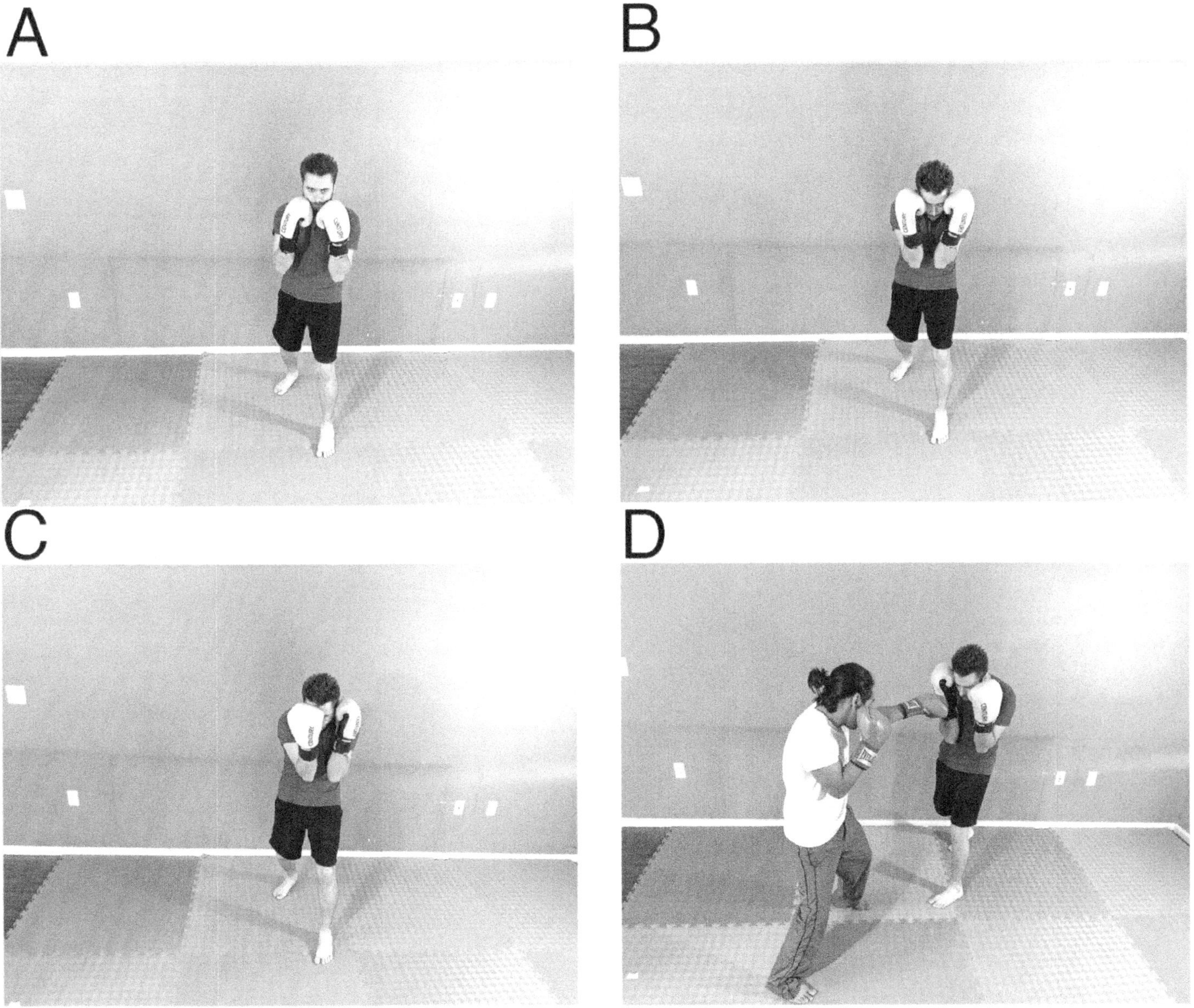

Another way to accomplish the same thing is to move your head offline but keep your guard pinched together (Pics E to F). It does not need to be as exaggerated as the pictures, but it can be. This not only gets your head out of the way, but also retains visibility.

These are the basics of how to use the Shell without stepping or using upper body movement. They will result in taking a lot of the impact our your opponent's strike. However, adjusting your Guard in these ways is preferable to simply squeezing your forearms tight, obstructing your vision, and hoping for the best. Read on for more advanced techniques.

E

F

Twist

The Shell is a great way to use the High Guard to directly absorb punches. Now let's take a look at how to use it in conjunction with body movement to help dispel and absorb the force of our opponent's punches.

The Twist is the same motion which most fighters use to Slip punches (and also to throw punches). Rotate on the ball of your front or back foot (or maybe front foot depending on your style or situation) in order to rotate your trunk (Pics A to D). If the strike lands on the front of your Guard or in between your arms, then the twisting motion will allow you to move forward, sliding past their punch (Pics E to F). Always sink your weight down upon impact to keep your balance.

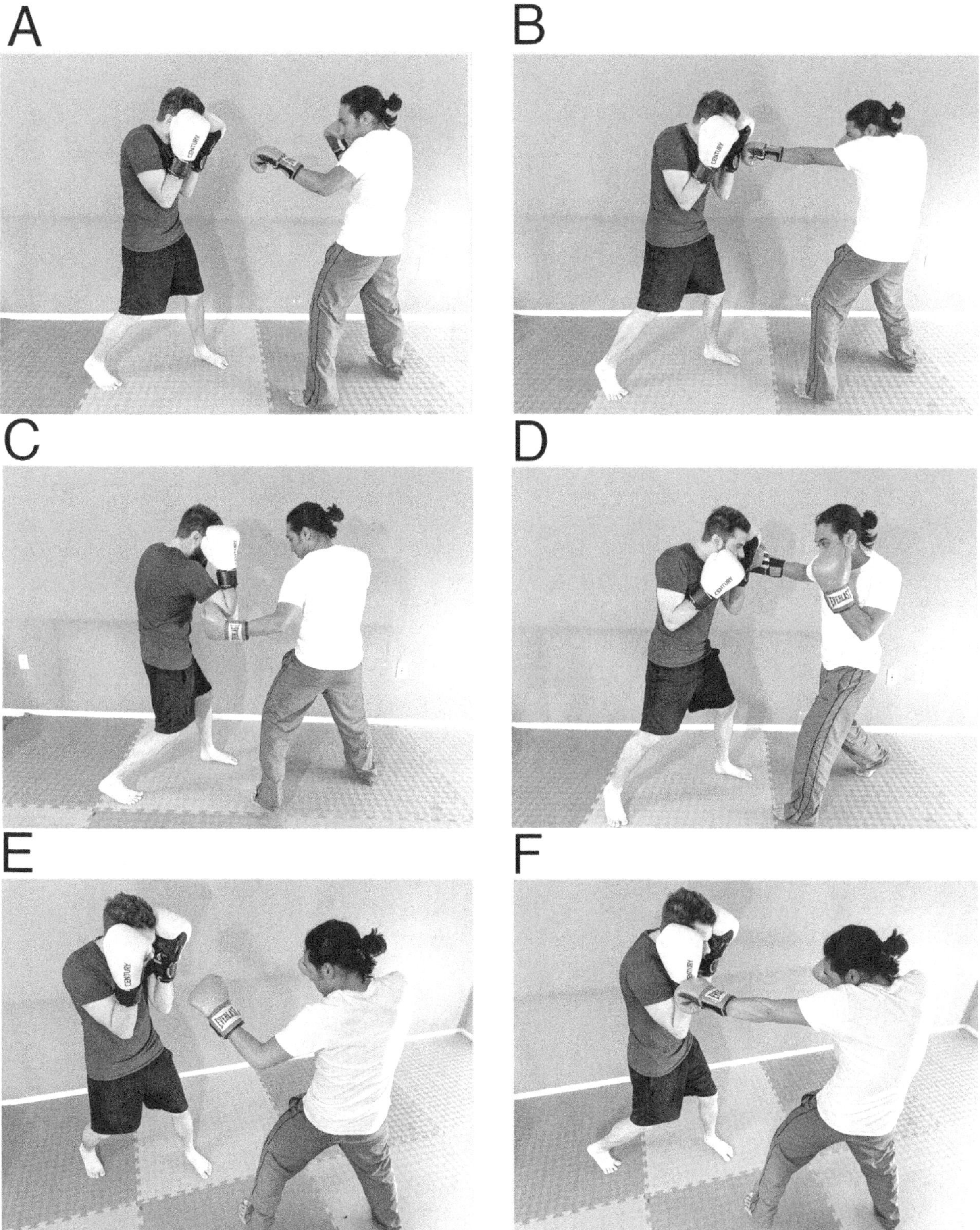

If the punch lands on the side of your Guard, then the rotation of your body will absorb some of the blow, allowing you to take the impact of the strike while moving forward (Pics A to B).

An important idea to master is stepping away from your opponent's strike to further negate the power of their blow. This can be used in tandem with any of the movements shown in this section. In Pics C to D, the fighter dispels the impact of the strike by stepping left. In Pics E to F he does the same by stepping right, but moves forward at the same time to close the distance.

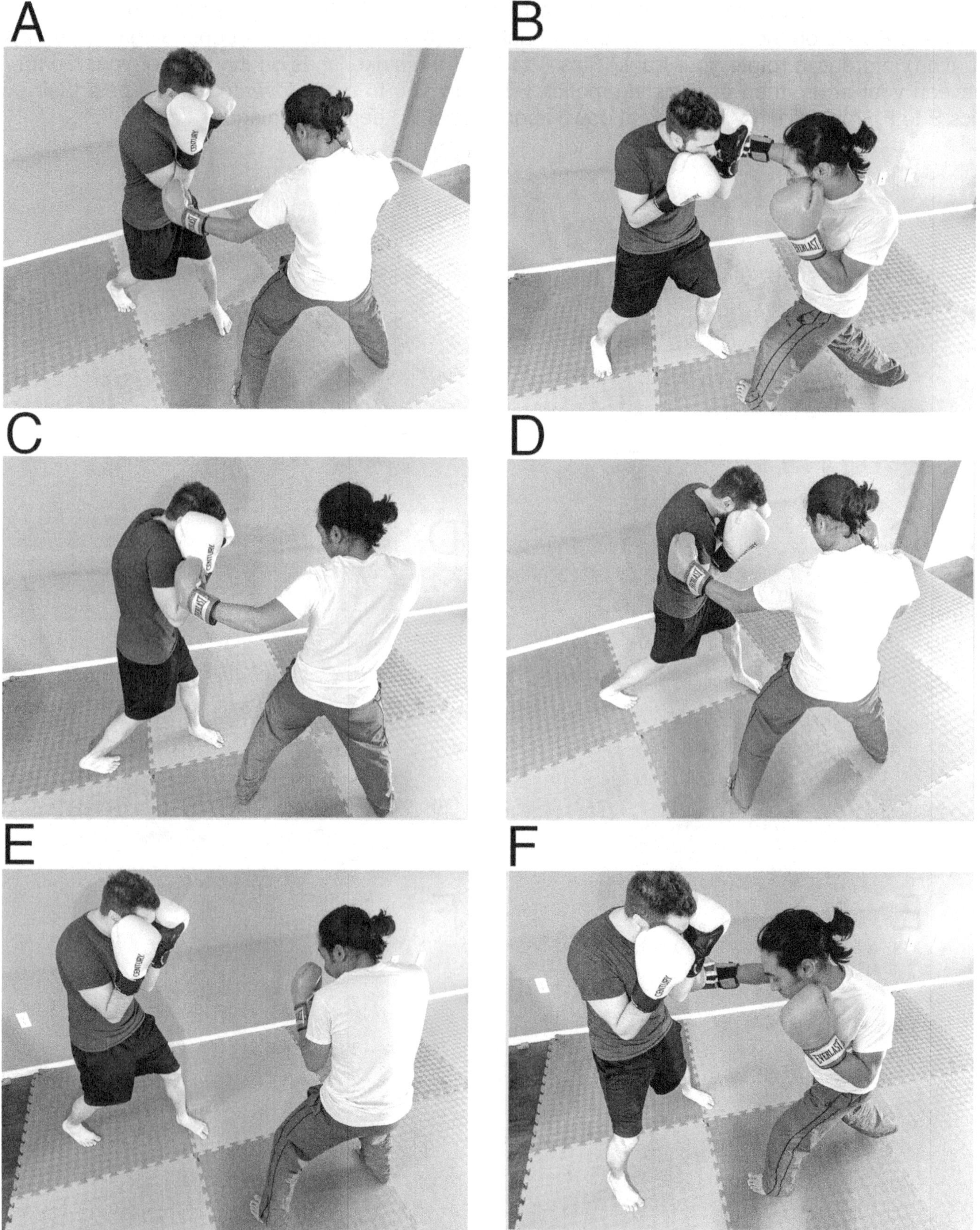

Tilt

This is the same motion that Tyson and other Peek-A-Boo fighters used to slip punches. Rather than Pivot (the conventional way to Slip or block strikes), you will instead stay more squared up and lean to the side (Pics A to B). Not only will this absorb the impact, but your opponent's punches will be more likely to slide harmlessly off your Guard as well. This motion will be explored more in the Peek-A-Boo section.

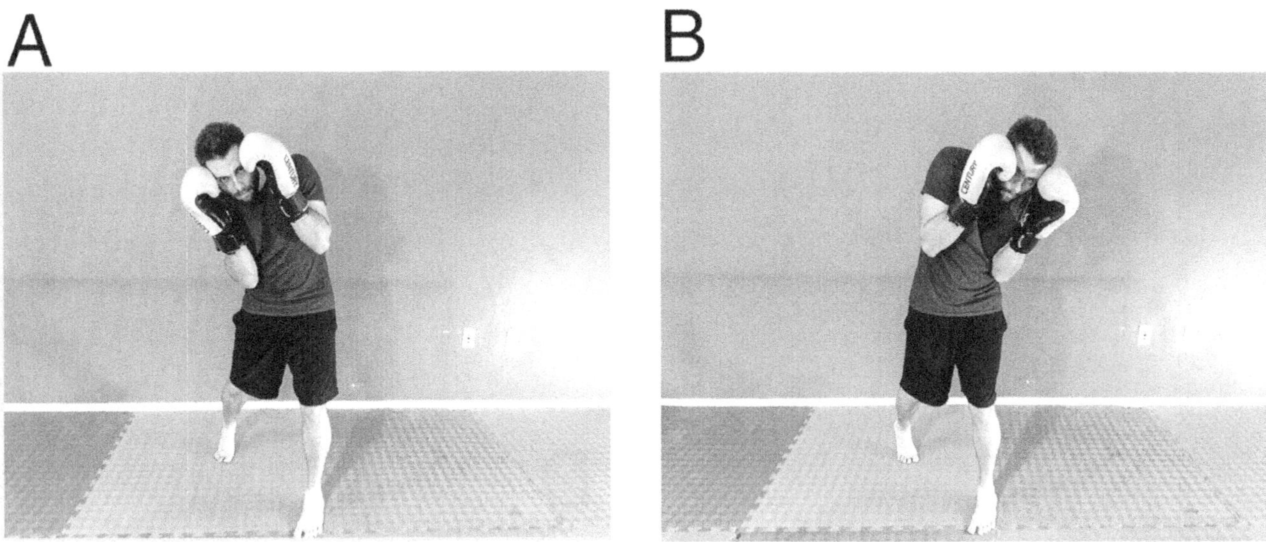

Against Hooks to the head, Tilt away from the strike so that it slides up and over your Guard. The motion should help Load up a counter strike (Pics A to D).

A B

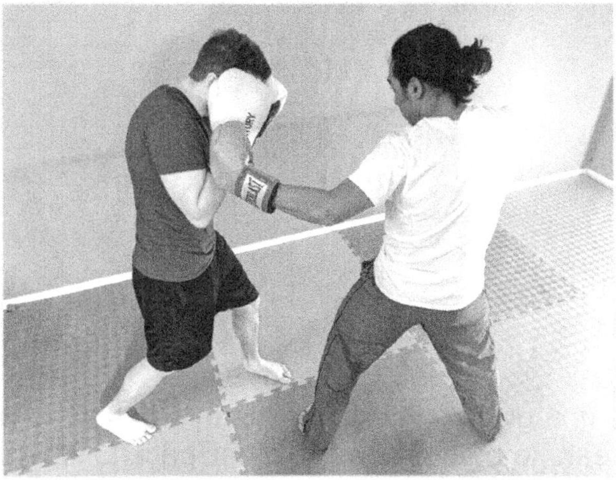

C  D

For body blows, you can keep your head protected (Pic A) and still cover one of the defensive holes in your midsection by leaning towards the punch (Pics B to D). This will even work for Uppercuts.

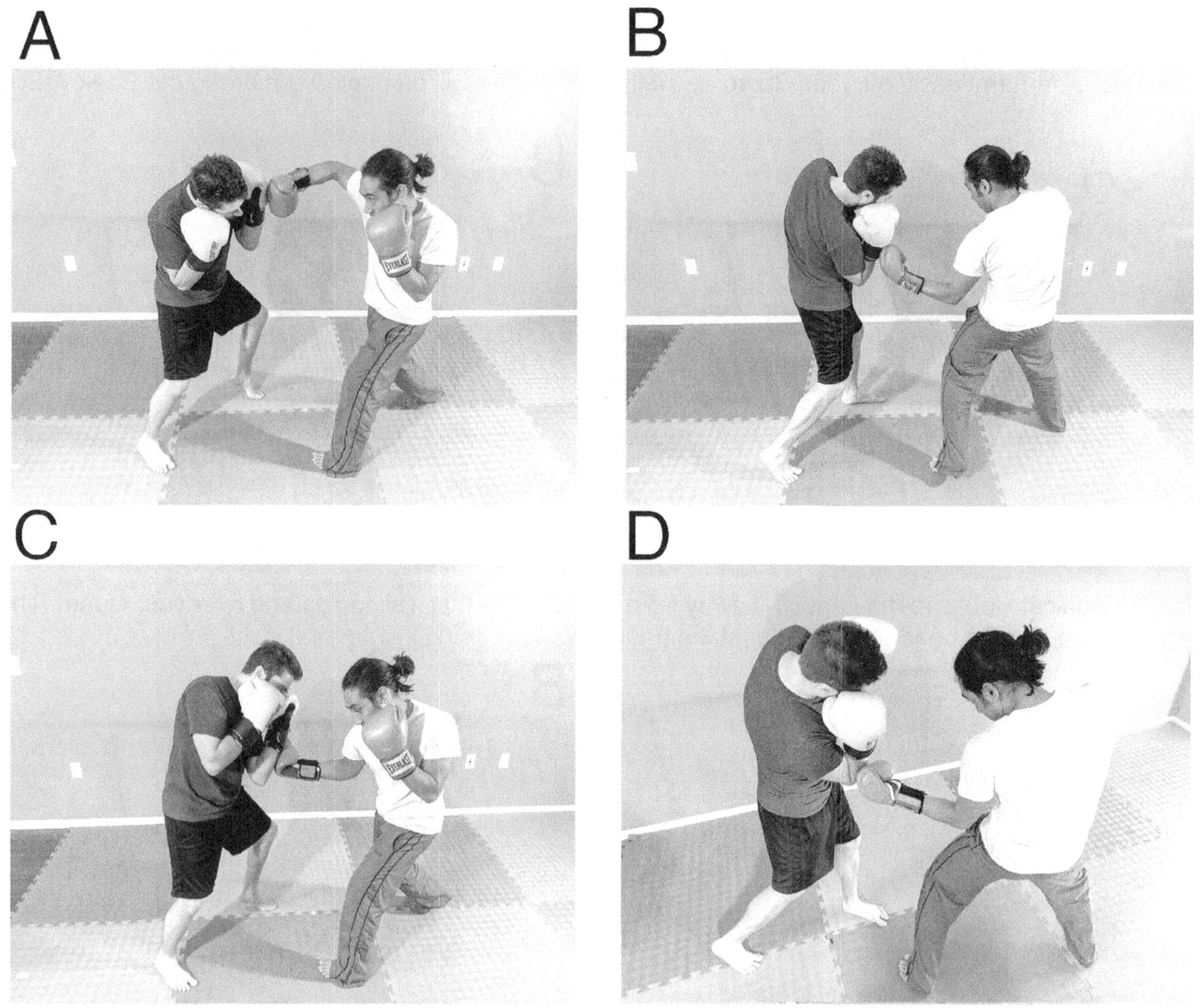

Inoue is a great fighter to watch to see how to perform this principle correctly. Lomachenko also uses this Lean to both side as he steps back to stay as safe as possible.

Open Stance Considerations – Specialty Counters

In an Open Stance, Tilting and stepping to the Outside is a great way to defend against a Rear Hook or Cross and take a superior angle at the same time (Pics A to B). From your new position, a Lead Hook is a great counter (Pic C).

Similarly, Tilting and stepping to the Inside is a great way to defend against a Lead Hook. This lines up your Rear Hand for a liver shot (Pics D to F). Liver shots are more devastating in an Open Stance since they are delivered with the more powerful Rear Side, sometimes called the Power Side.

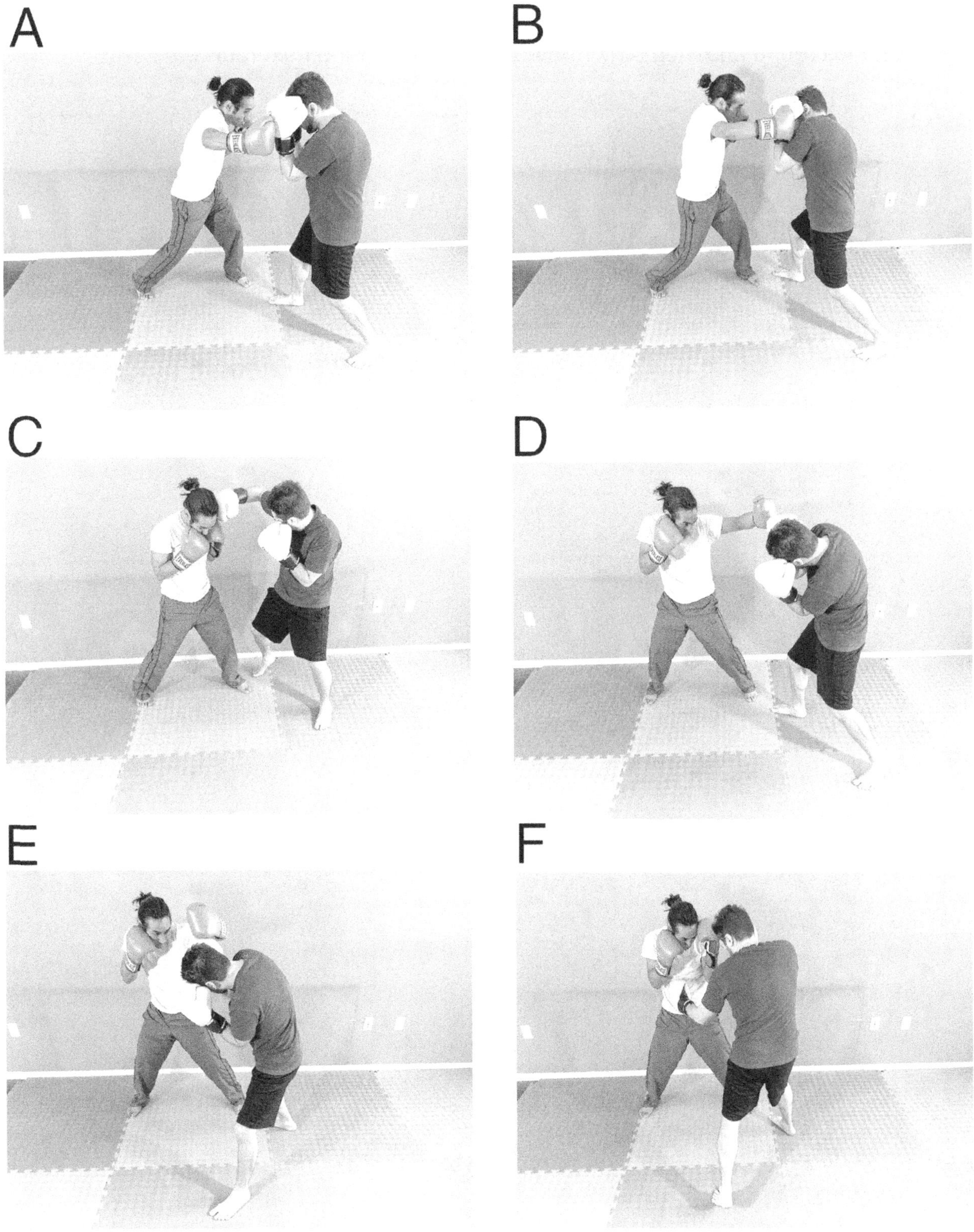

Drills

Drill 1 A

Have your partner throw all manner of punches at you and Tilt to avoid them. Begin slowly, taking very light punches and working your way up. Notices which punches are easy for you to take and which you are having difficulty with. Although it would be highly unrealistic to expect to only use this technique as your primary defense, it is very useful to figure out what does and does not work for you. Furthermore, developing these reactions as a fail-safe for when an opponent lands a hard shot could prove to be invaluable. Go a full round and then switch with you partner for the next round.

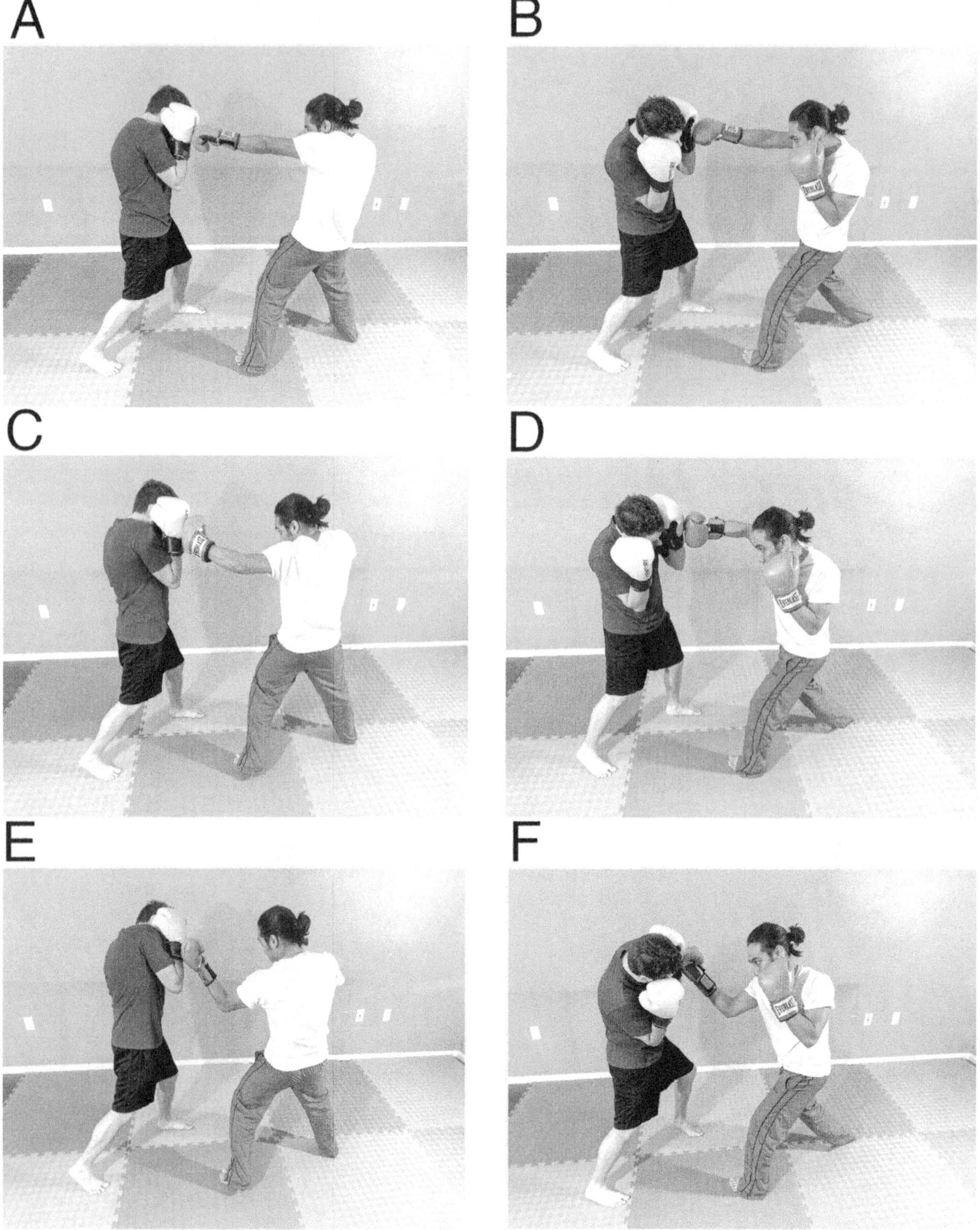

Drill 1 B

Now repeat the last drill using Twists. Try to move your arms as little as possible, using the movement of your body to dispel the force of your partner's punches. Pay close attention to what feels natural and what is not working so well. Go a full round and then switch who is attacking and who is defending for the next round.

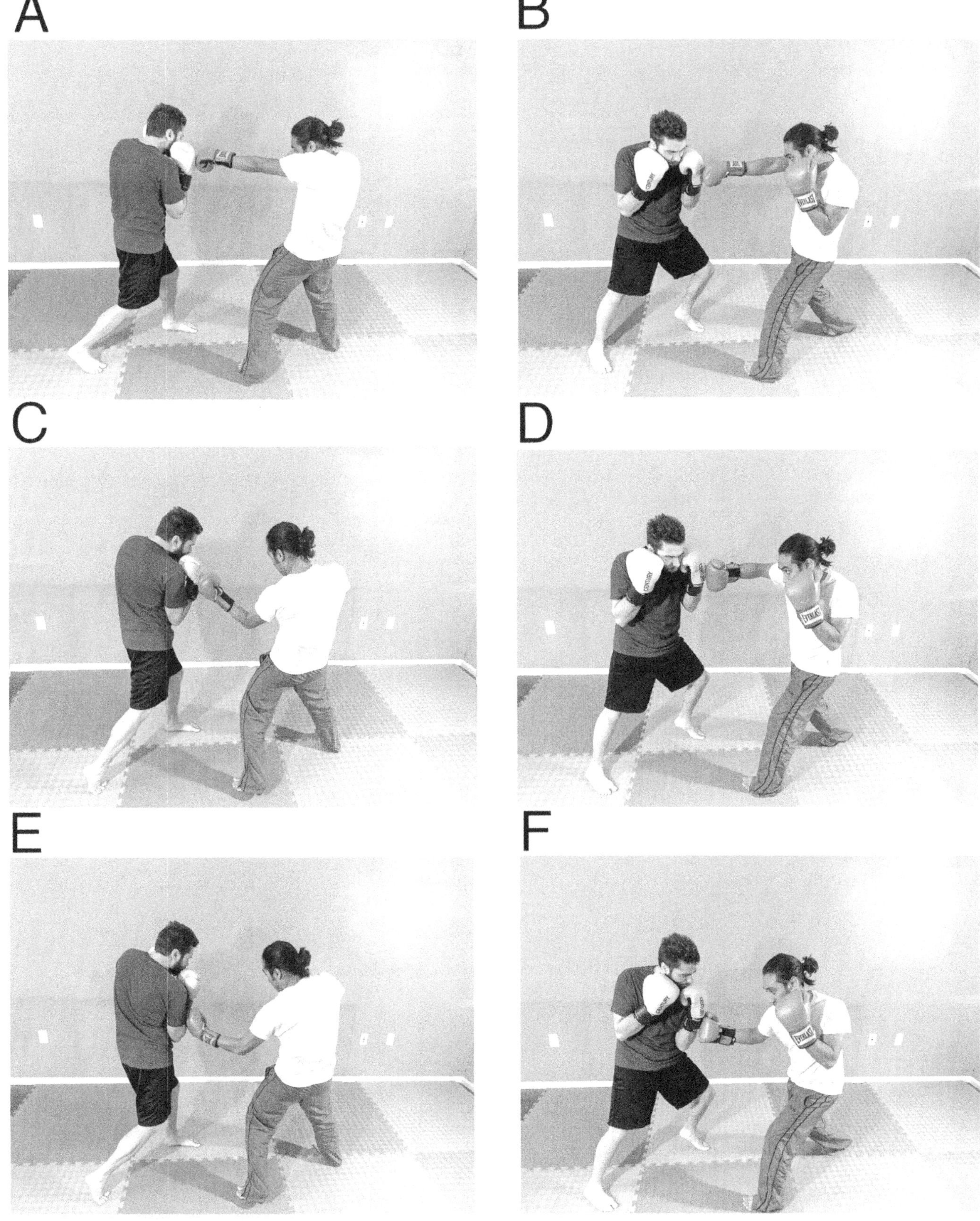

Drill 1 C

Now it's time to take the last two drills and combine them. Put the two motions together and use what has worked best for you to dispel the force of your partners punches. Using a Lean to begin the motion and then Twisting at the last moment usually works well. Go a full round and then switch who is attacking and who is defending for the next round. When it is your turn again, try countering your partners punches.

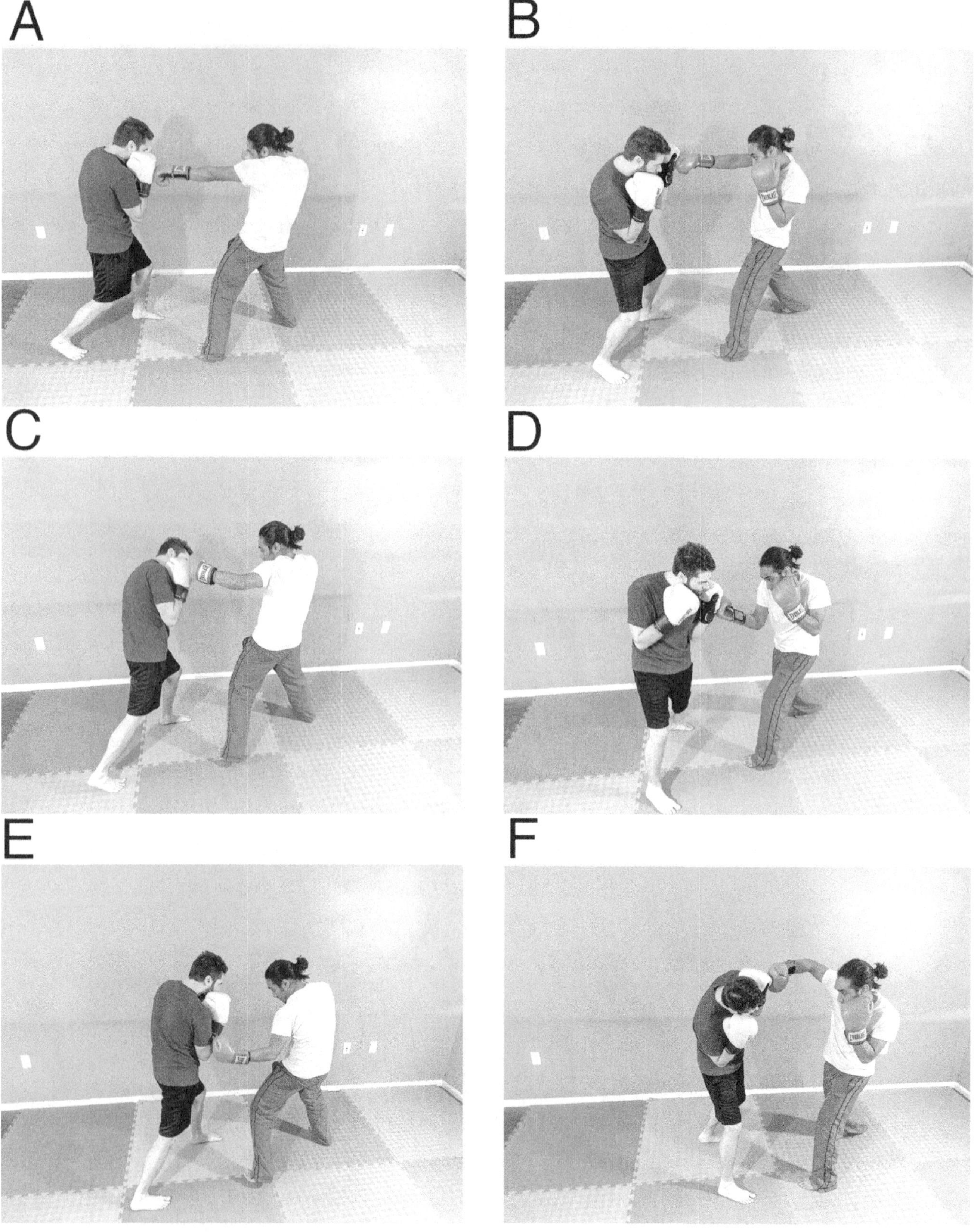

Pull

If your weight is already forward, then it is fairly easy to dispel the force of a Straight Punch by simply moving your weight backwards. You may also lean back and place more weight on your back foot if required. The point of this technique is to give up as little space as possible. The opponent is hoping that his punches will keep you away. By taking some of the force on your Guard you only need to take a small step back to stay safe and can immediately rebound back to recover your distance (Pics A to D). This, like all the techniques listed, is a matter of timing.

Roll

If your opponent is striking at you from the side, and especially if their strike is curving downward like an Overhand, then you may want to Roll out of the punch. To do this, hunch your shoulder, tuck your chin, and Tilt or Twist with the force of the punch (Pics A to B) as you Duck (Pic C). You should then reverse direction near the end of your Duck (Pic D), Weaving underneath the blow to come up back in position to counter (Pics E to F). In fact, a Roll is very similar to a Weave (covered in the Basic Head Movement section). The difference is that with a Roll you will first go with the motion of the punch before Ducking under and returning to your normal Posture. As always, a small step back or away may help to blunt the force of the blow.

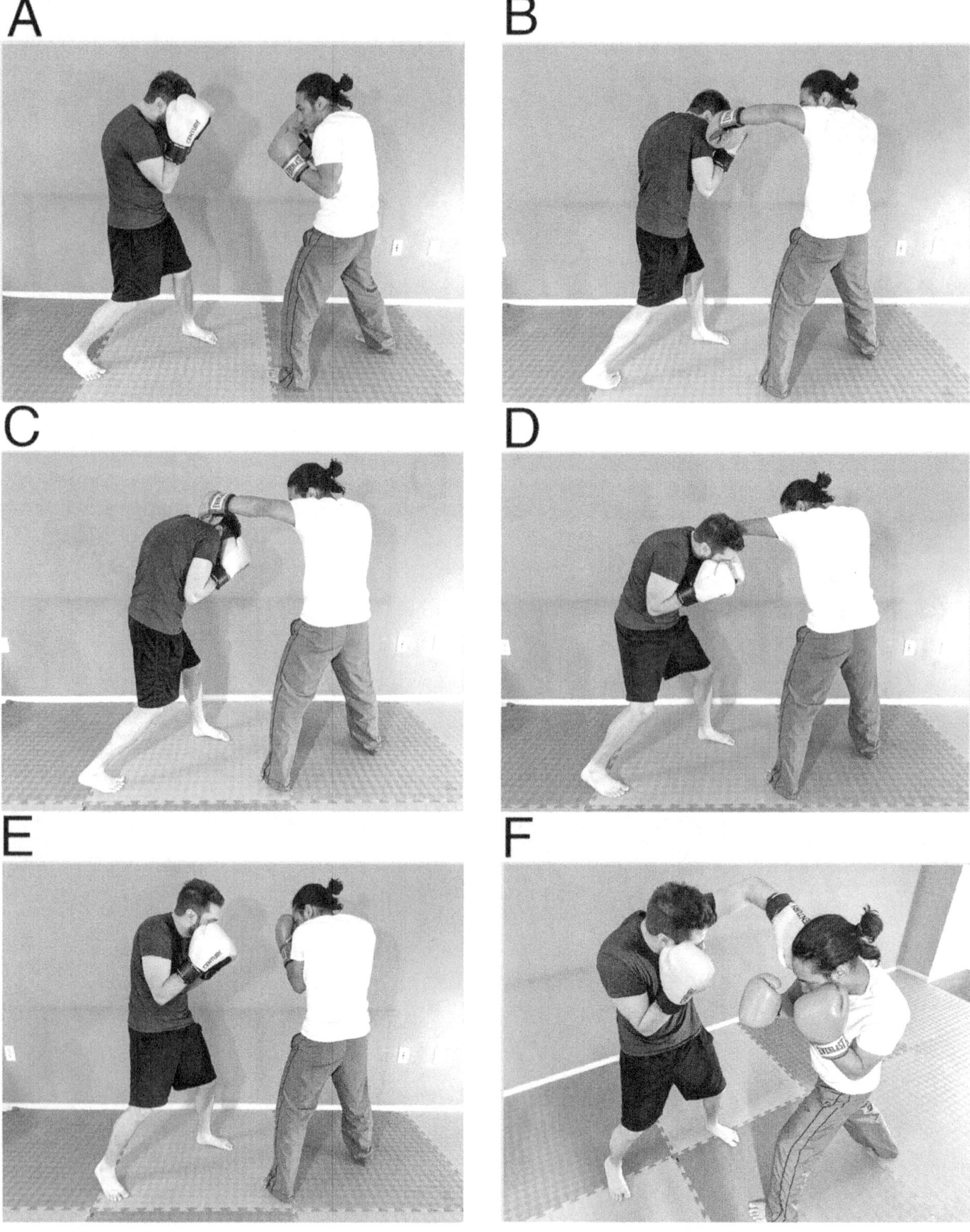

Smother

It may seem counterintuitive, but the best way to stop many strikes are to move into them (Pics A to B). The idea is to get your opponent to overshoot, or to stop their strike before it has had time to build power. This is mostly applicable for Hooks.

A

B

Drills

Drill 1

Move forward as quickly as you can while your partner throws light punches at you. Roll with your partner's punches (Pics A to D) and stop to reset when you feel you did not take the punch correctly. Once you close enough distance correctly, you will be in range to Smother rather than Roll. Once you get close enough to Smother your partner's Hooks (Pics E to F), allow him to move away. Then repeat the drill for the remainder of the round. Switch who is attacking and who is defending the next round.

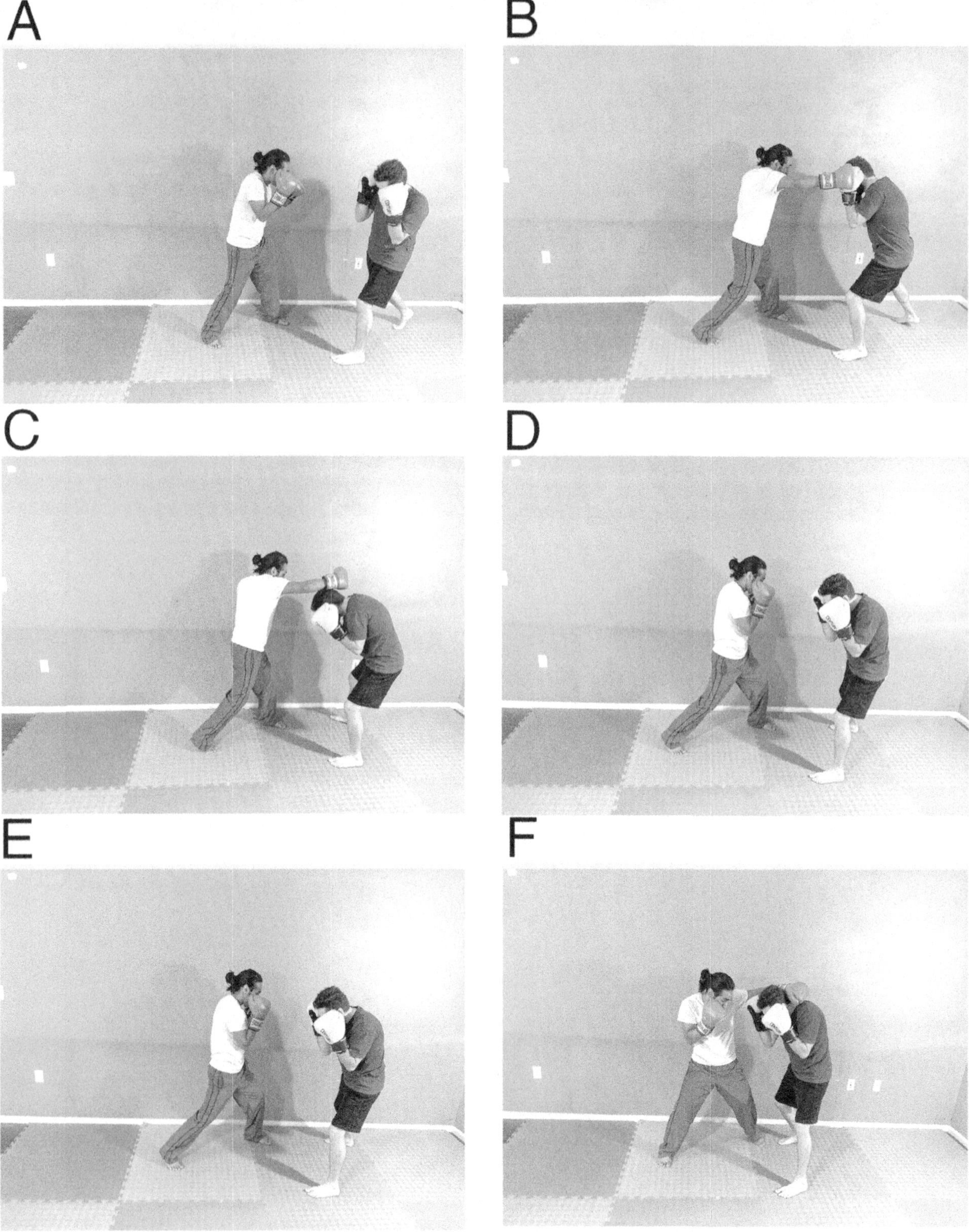

Drill 1 B

Now instead of only moving forward, try moving laterally to cut off the ring (Pics A to D). You may find yourself unintentionally Slipping, Ducking or Weaving punches. As mentioned before, these movements are a great precursor to becoming comfortable with head movement. When stepping laterally, make sure to maintain the stance you are most comfortable with and not to square up your body much more than usual (until you have your opponent close to the ropes that is).

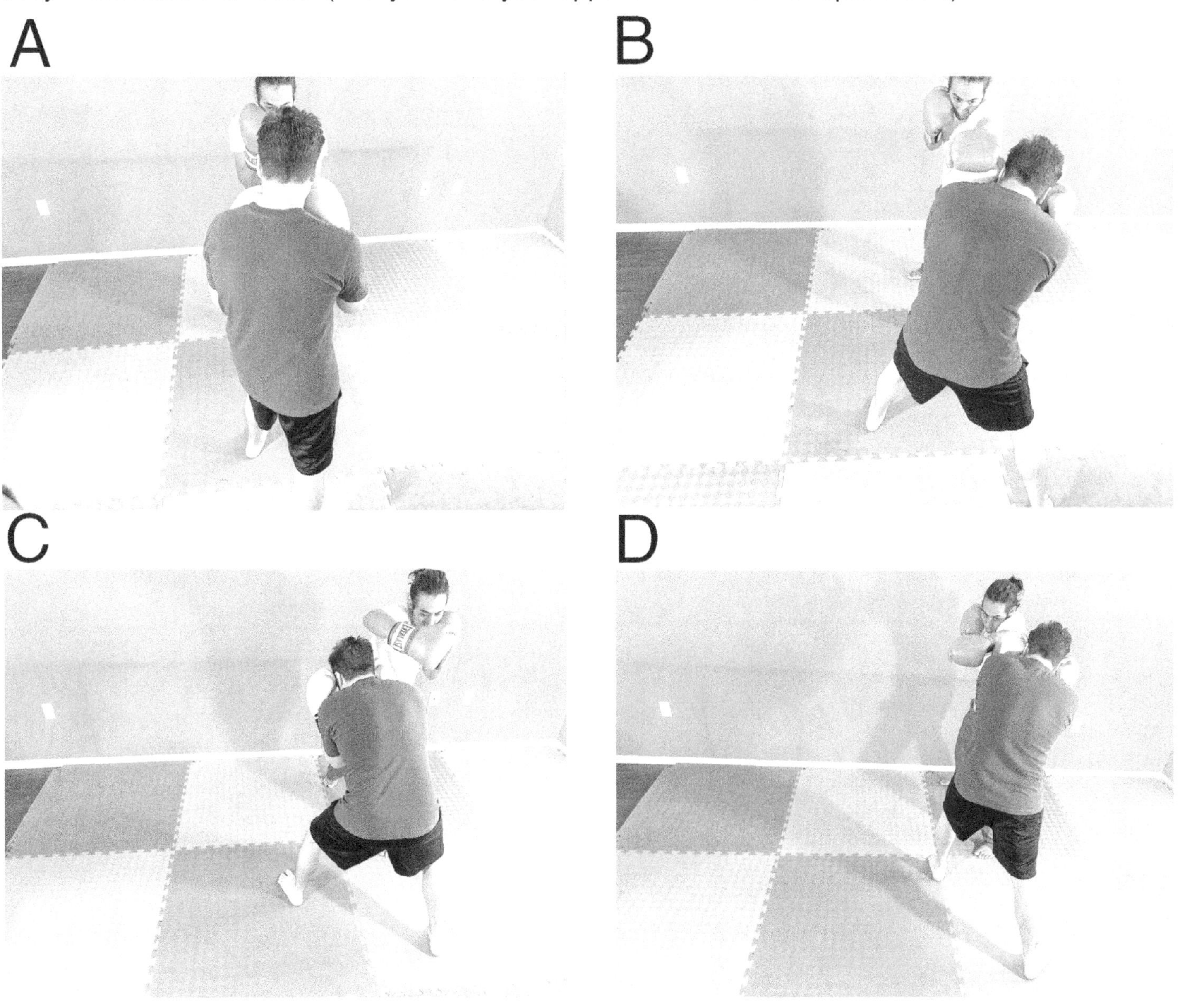

If in an Open Stance, try to keep your Lead Foot Outside of theirs, even if you are moving in the opposite direction. Keeping your Lead Foot on the Outside will help to cut off their escape (Pics A to D).

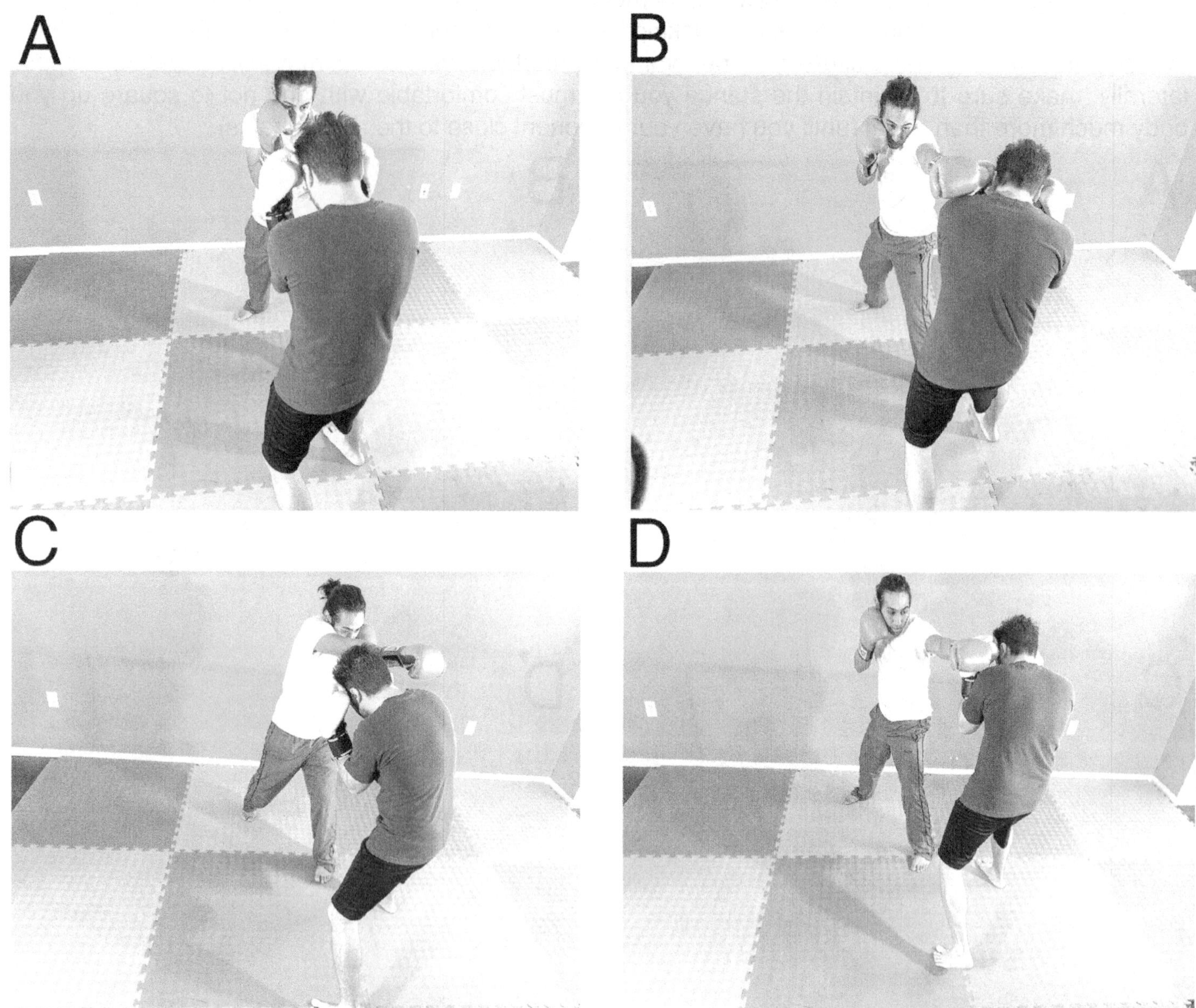

Drill 2

Now add back in the techniques you have been missing from the Basic Guard section, adding them to the High Guard tactics that help you close distance more quickly. You may wish to do what Canelo does and use Parries for Straight Punches (Pic A) and Forearm Blocks for Body Hooks and Uppercuts (Pic B). Or you may wish to follow Gaethje's lead and use Leg Checks (Pics C and D) and Reinforced Cover Blocks for Roundhouse kicks (Pic E). Or you may wish to go with what has worked best for you so far. Using a High Guard is a fine balance between closing distance and taking too much damage. Head movement (covered in Part 2) can also go a long way towards mitigating damage.

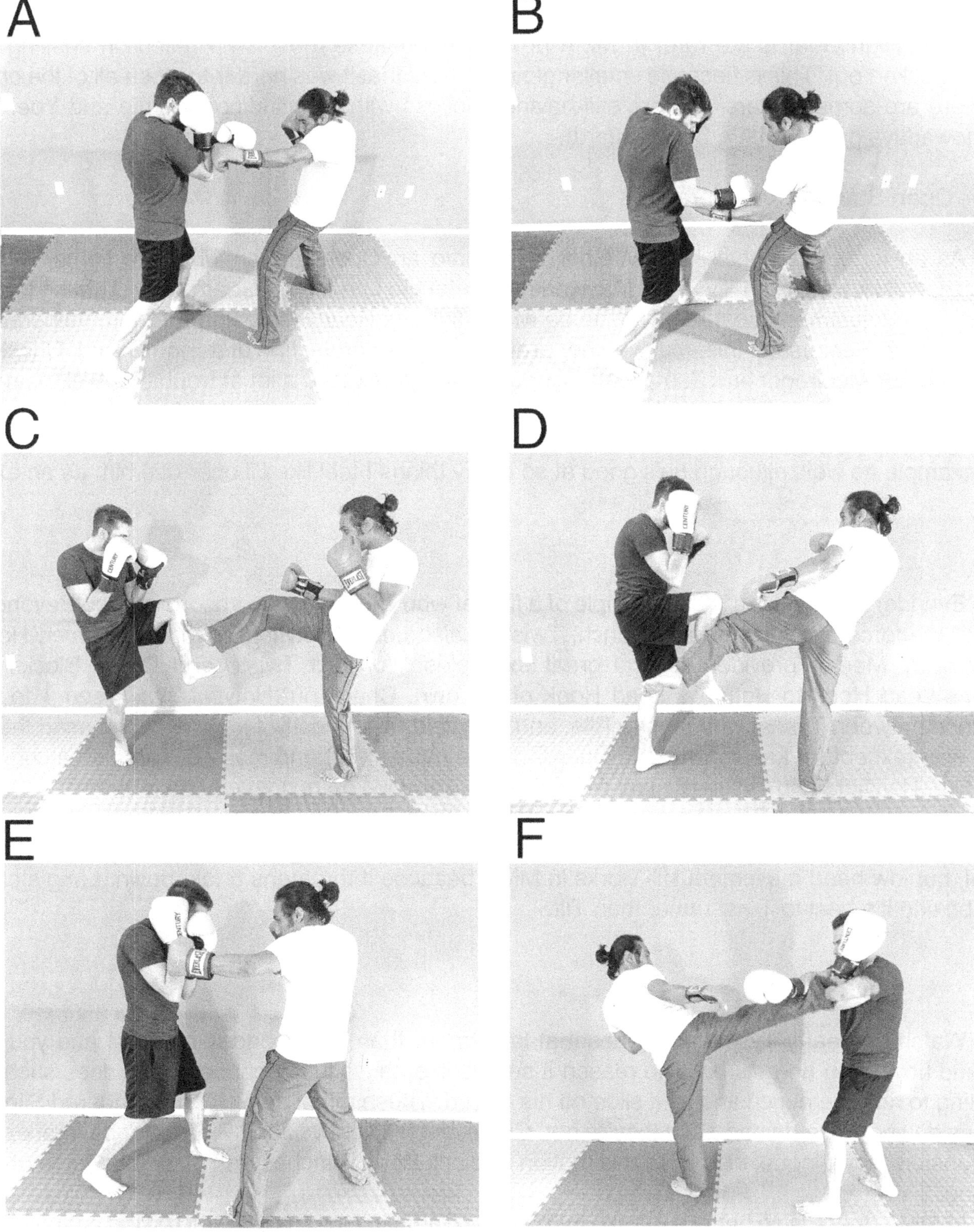

References – High Guard

Shell

In boxing there are few better to study when it comes to the High Guard than Canelo. His fight vs Kovalev was masterful and will probably be referenced again (and again.) You may notice that all of the techniques explained about the Shell in this book are present in that fight, and Canelo uses them to dominate a much bigger opponent.

In kickboxing, Bellator Champ Gabriel Varga has a simple but subtle High Guard. I had the chance to spar him and was even more impressed with his skills in person.

Tight High Guards are rarer in MMA nowadays because those who relied on shelling up kept getting knocked out. This is because smaller gloves meant that it was harder to close all of the openings. Still, there are some fighters who are still having success with it, including Gaethje and Yoel Romero (who nowadays pairs it with a Cross Guard).

Shell – Open Stance Considerations

As an Orthodox fighter, Mayweather is put into an Open Stance when he fights Southpaws. Rather than stick with his Philly Shell, Mayweather prefers to use a High Guard when fighting in an Open Stance. This adjustment most likely has to do with a fighters Rear Side being far more vulnerable in an Open Position. Because of this, Mayweather prefers the extra protection of a High Guard. Check out his fights vs Conor McGregor and Zab Judah (although Zab gave Floyd a lot of trouble at first, he made the right adjustments to win comfortably). As with Canelo, notice the small adjustments he makes with his forearms depending on the situation and how he moves his head behind his Guard. Lomachenko is a great example as well, although he's good at so many things I feel like I'll over-use him as an example.

Twist

Evander Holyfield is a great example of a fighter who Twists to help absorb impact. Beyond dulling some of the force of his opponent's punch, Twisting also Loads Holyfield's Return Counter. Holyfield's fight vs Ray Mercer provides several great examples. Holyfield Twists and Cover Blocks against Mercer's Lead Hook to Return a Lead Hook of his own. Check out Holyfield vs Tyson 1 to see the difference between Tyson, who mostly Tilts, and Holyfield, who mostly Twists. Keep in mind there is no wrong way (except for keeping a static Guard with no movement) and many boxers use a combination of the two. Holyfield and Tyson are just two extreme examples on opposite ends of the spectrum.

Keep in mind that Twisting is far more common than Titling in kickboxing compared to boxing and MMA. This is because Titling lowers your head, putting it closer to a kick or knee. This holds true in MMA as well, but low head movement still works in MMA because it threatens a takedown. Long story short, in kickboxing it's best to Twist rather than Tilt.

Tilt

Watch any early Tyson fight (ones that lasts more than 30 seconds anyways) and you may be surprised how often he gets hit. The reason it seems like he isn't is because Tyson does such a great job Tilting to ride the punch and let it slide off his Guard. These might as well be considered Slips as the punches do such little damage, but they're not. Check out his fight vs Jose Ribalta for several examples. The Monster, Inoya Inoue, also uses this motion to block Body Punches and dispel the force of shots to the head.

In MMA, there is no better example than Justin Gaethje. Gaethje did well relying entirely on Titling in a High Guard before he came to the UFC. Along with allowing him to take a tremendous amount of strikes by dispelling the force of the blows, Gaethje's movement also acted to discourage takedowns by keeping his head lower than his opponent's.

Once he entered the most elite MMA organization and fought the most elite fighters, he lost several close (and incredibly bloody) fights. However, he then adjusted by supplementing his High Guard with more head movement and footwork. This adjustment allowed him to beat several top ten competitors in a row. It's a great idea to watch his newer fights so you can see how a High Guard can work as a base to build other defenses around. However, it's also worth it to watch his first few UFC fights just to see how much damage it's possible to absorb with the High Guard alone.

Stepping With Punches

I said before that I would mention GGG vs Canelo 2 again, so here it is. GGG does a great job stepping away from Canelo's hardest punches to blunt the force of the blow. But honestly, nearly any GGG fights would work to see a demonstration of this technique. GGG would often step away and then counter from the new angle.

Pulls

Mikey Garcia is great at Pulling away behind his High Guard to dispel the force of the punch on his Guard, often adding a step back to it. You can check out any of his fights to see this, but I would actually recommend watching his fight vs Spence. Even though Garcia lost, he jumped up way past his weight class to go against one of the best boxers of our generation. As such, seeing him survive the last few rounds to end the fight on his feet may actually be more instructive than watching one of his many victories. I would recommend watching how he Smothers as well, as he alternates between Pulling and Smothering very well.

Smother

Roberto Duran usually entered with his own punches, but he had a number of ways to get inside by evading his opponent's punches as well. One of these ways was to move into his opponent's Hooks. Watch nearly any fight to see him do this,

Rolls

When it comes to Rolls, there are few better to watch than the Mexican fighters Salvador Sanchez and Julio Cesar Chavez. Sanchez's fight against Danny Lopez (either of them) has a lot of examples from great camera angles that really show off this technique. Of course, Tyson has a number of KO's landed off of Rolls as well.

Cross Guard

It's hard to believe now, but the Cross Guard used to be one of the more popular Guards in Boxing. There are a couple reasons for its past popularity as well as why it fell out of use. The main culprit for both, however, is most likely the evolution of the boxing glove. Back when fighters used no gloves and later on when they used very light gloves, it was seen as far riskier to aim for the head. This is because skulls are hard, and hands are full of weak, tiny bones prone to breaking. As such, most fighters spent the majority of their time endeavoring to knock out their opponent's with blows to the body.

A common defense against these body blows was to rest the arm across the midsection vertically, known as a "Fold." Seeing as it was difficult to defend both sides of the head when one hand is busy defending the entirety of the lower body, "folding" your other hand high to protect both sides of your head was a natural alteration to make. And by using the forearms and elbows to defend punches, you were adding even more hazards for your opponent's hands.

Lately there has been somewhat of a resurgence of the Cross Guard, but in truth it has never really left. Foreman used the Cross Guard to help him retake the title in the 90s; Manson Gibson used it to supplement his karate style to become one of the best kickboxers during the height of the K-1 era; Buakaw uses a hybrid Cross Guard with his Long Guard in modern day Muay Thai, and Yoel Romero has had great success with it in MMA. In other words, it's far from being a relic of times past. For many fighters the Cross Guard provides an edge over competitors.

The Cross Guard has rarely been used in MMA, so the best way to deal with kicks must be deduced from the few fighters who have used the system. That being said, the results so far look pretty promising. If anything, the arms already being half way to Cross Parrying seems to be an advantage, and having one hand low helps to prevent take downs by securing Under-hooks or Framing on the hips.

Rear Hand Defenses In The Cross Guard

In the Cross Guard, your Rear Hand is folded high around your body, protecting both sides of your head. If starting from a Basic Guard, you can begin this Block as if it were an Outside Parry, or even use it as such before settling into the correct position by crossing your Rear Hand over your Lead Shoulder (Pics A to B & C to D). Tuck your chin under your arm or into the crook of your elbow. If beginning in a Cross Guard, then this motion is unnecessary. Simply follow the defensives outlined below.

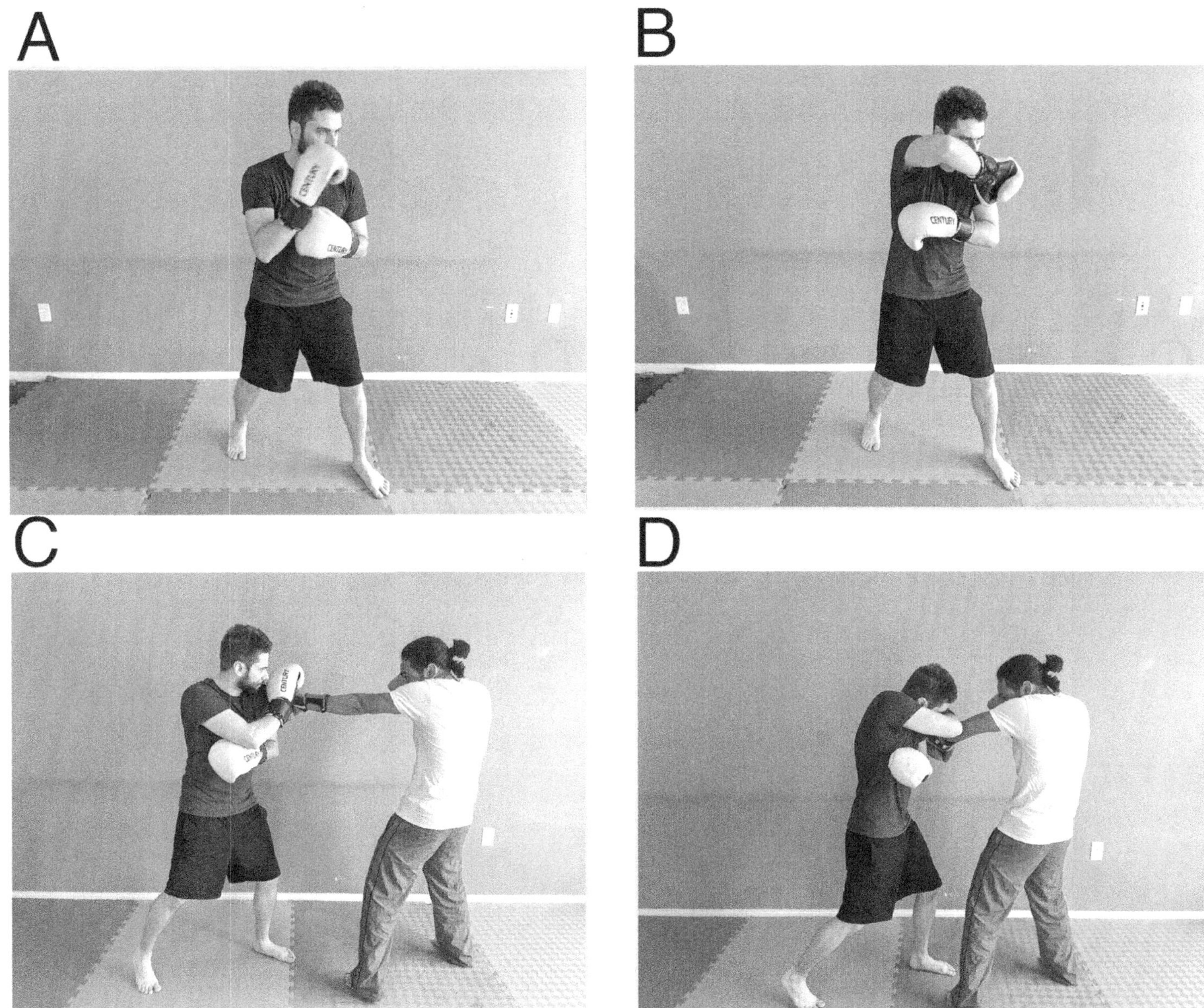

To block Linear Strikes, you may raise your elbow to take the impact on your forearm or elbow directly (Pics A & B), or you may deflect the punch upward by catching your opponent's strike from underneath as it extends (Pics C to D).

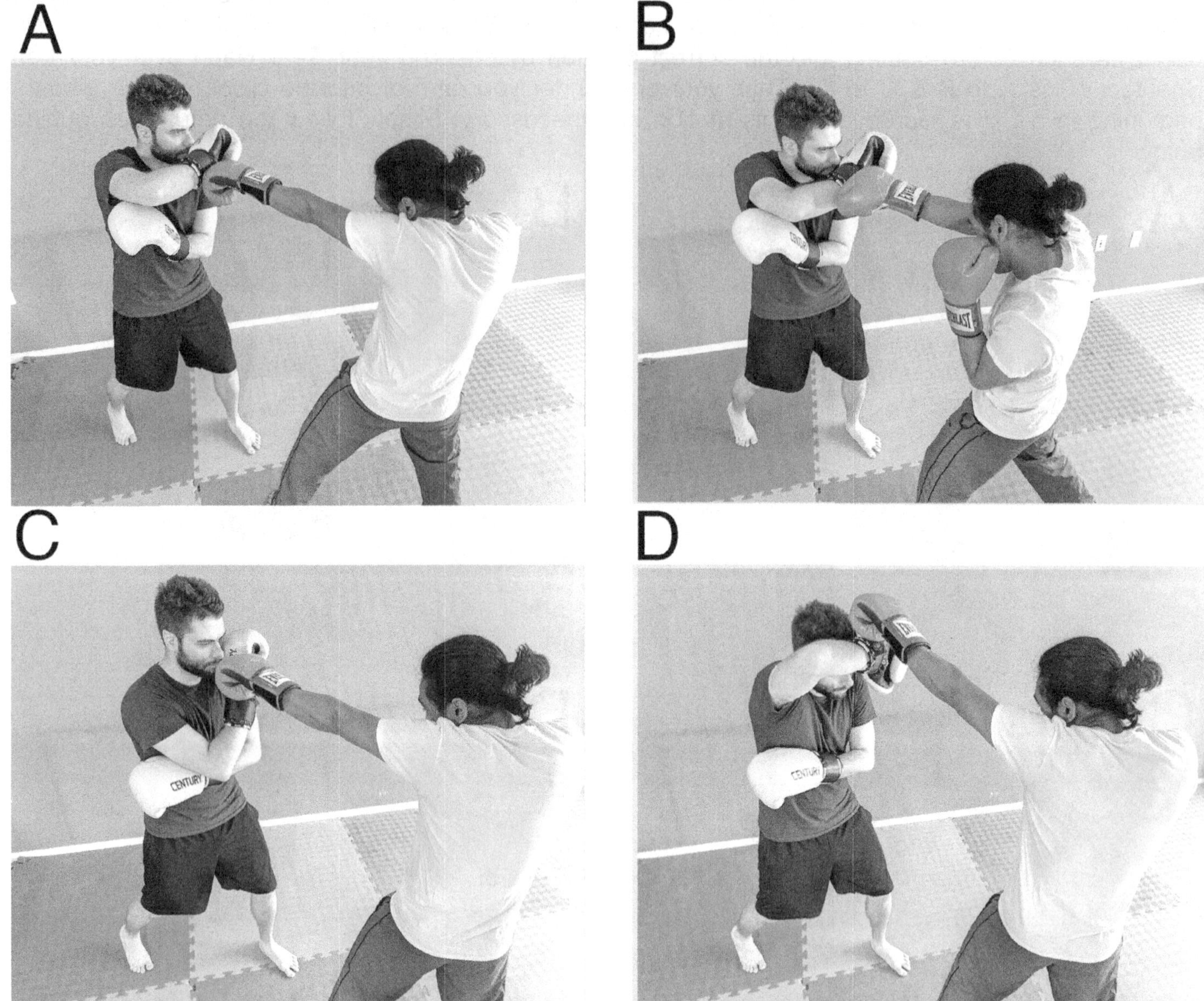

For Lateral Strikes such as Hooks and Roundhouse Kicks to the Rear Side, flair your elbow to block the strike (Pics A to B). Be sure to tuck your chin. Once again, this movement may connect directly or deflect the strike upwards by connecting underneath of it. You can also change your Rear Hand into a Cover Block fairly easily to Block shots to the body (Pic C). You can do the same for a Roundhouse Kick and use your other hand to Cross Parry (Pic D).

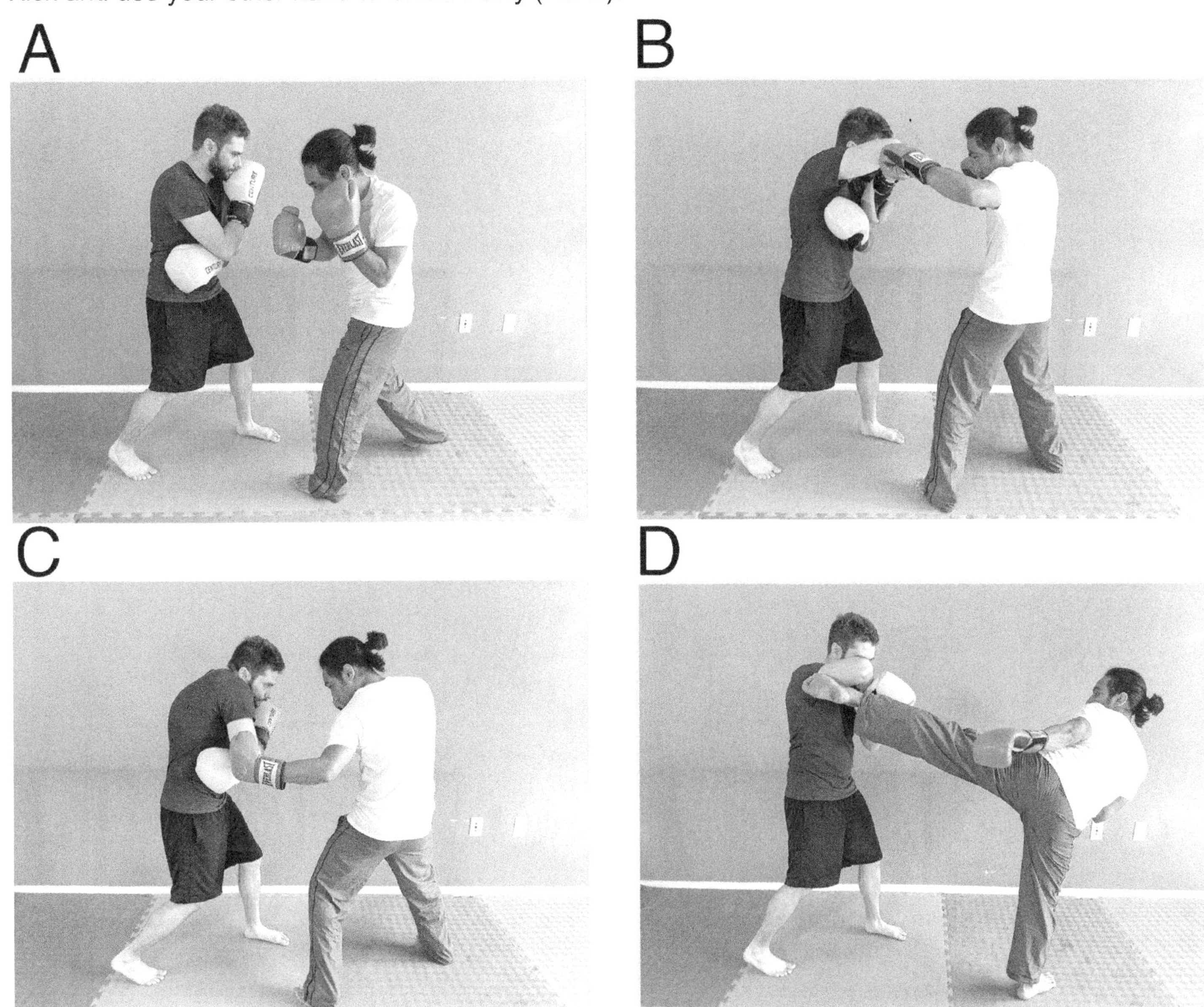

For lateral strikes to the Lead Side, use your Rear Hand to Cross Catch/Parry, and Cross Block your head. At the same time, hunch your Lead Shoulder to add support (Pic A). You may also use a Cross Parry to reinforce a Shoulder Roll (Pic B). To defend against Roundhouses to the body or head, continue with your Cross Parry to sweep the kick away (Pics C & D).

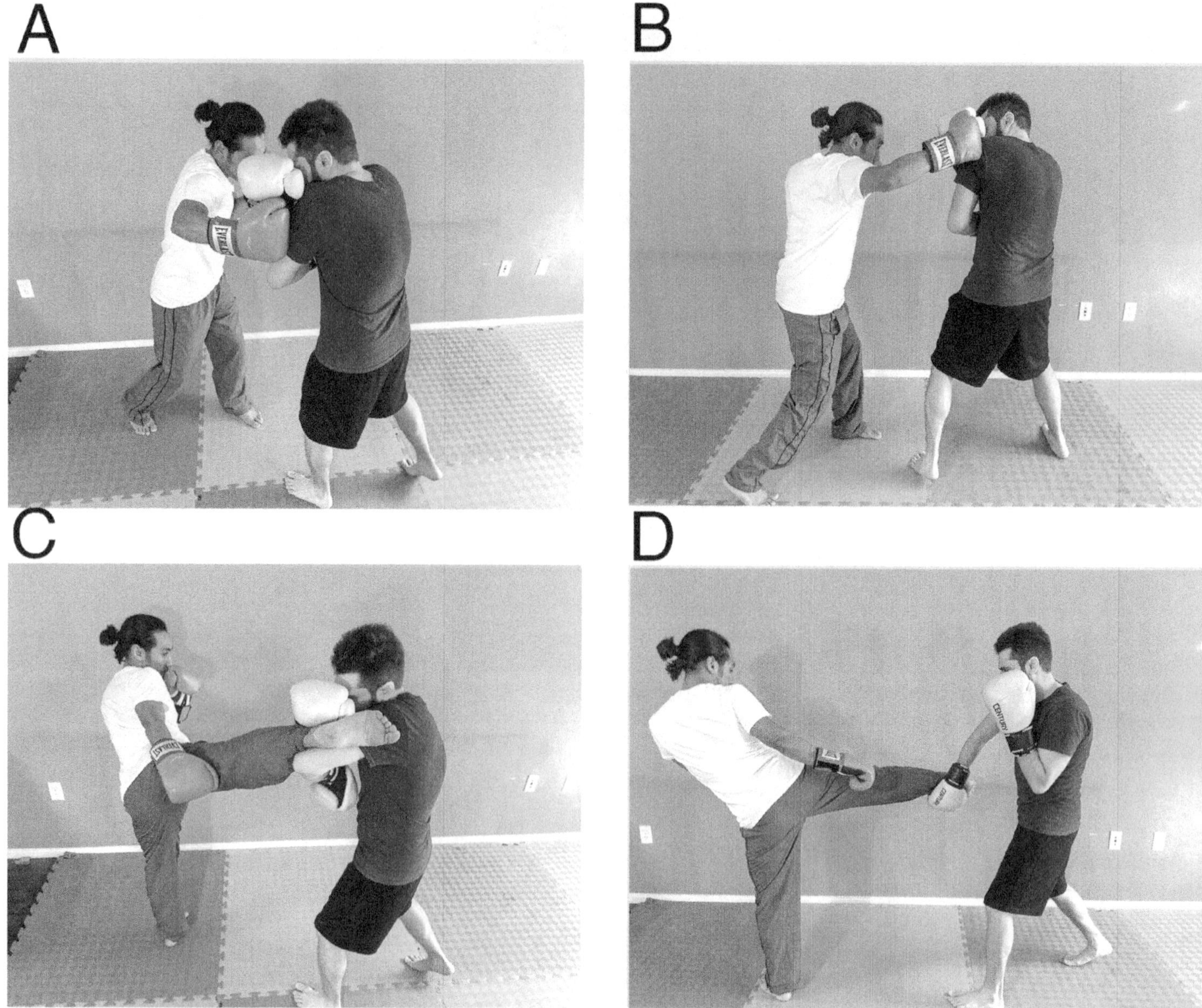

A major benefit of the Cross Guard is that is defends against uppercuts, knees and vertical elbows that would normally travel through the middle of other Guards (Pics A, B, C & D).

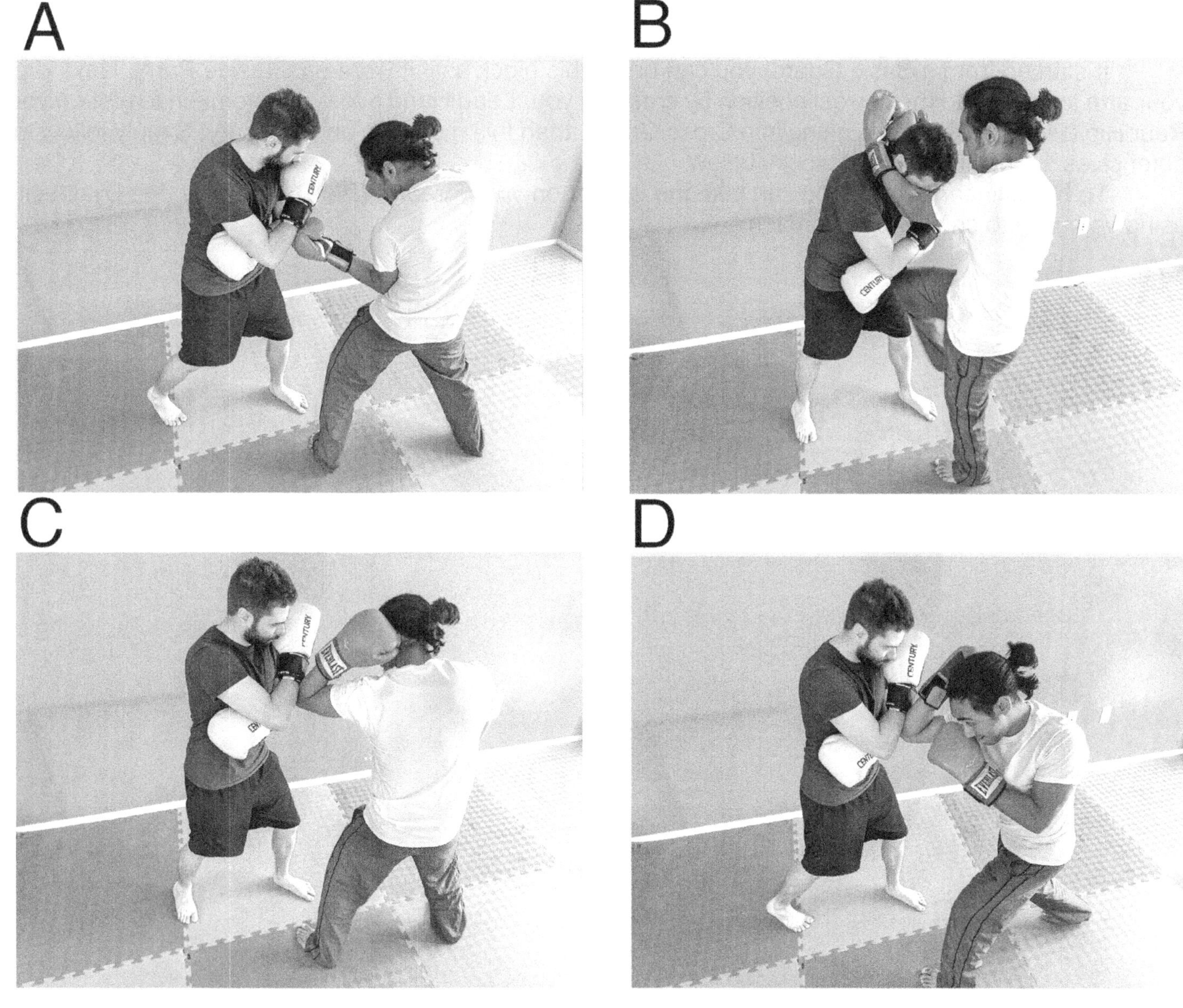

Lead Hand Defenses In Cross Guard

If starting from a Basic Guard, you can begin this block as if it were an Outside Parry. Next, drop your arm to settle into the correct position by crossing your Lead Hand over your stomach to rest on your Rear Hip (Pics A to B). If beginning in a Cross Guard, then this motion is unnecessary. Simply follow the defensives to specific kinds of blocks below.

To block linear strikes, you can take the impact on your forearm (Pic C) or elbow (Pic D) directly, using your arm to shield your stomach.

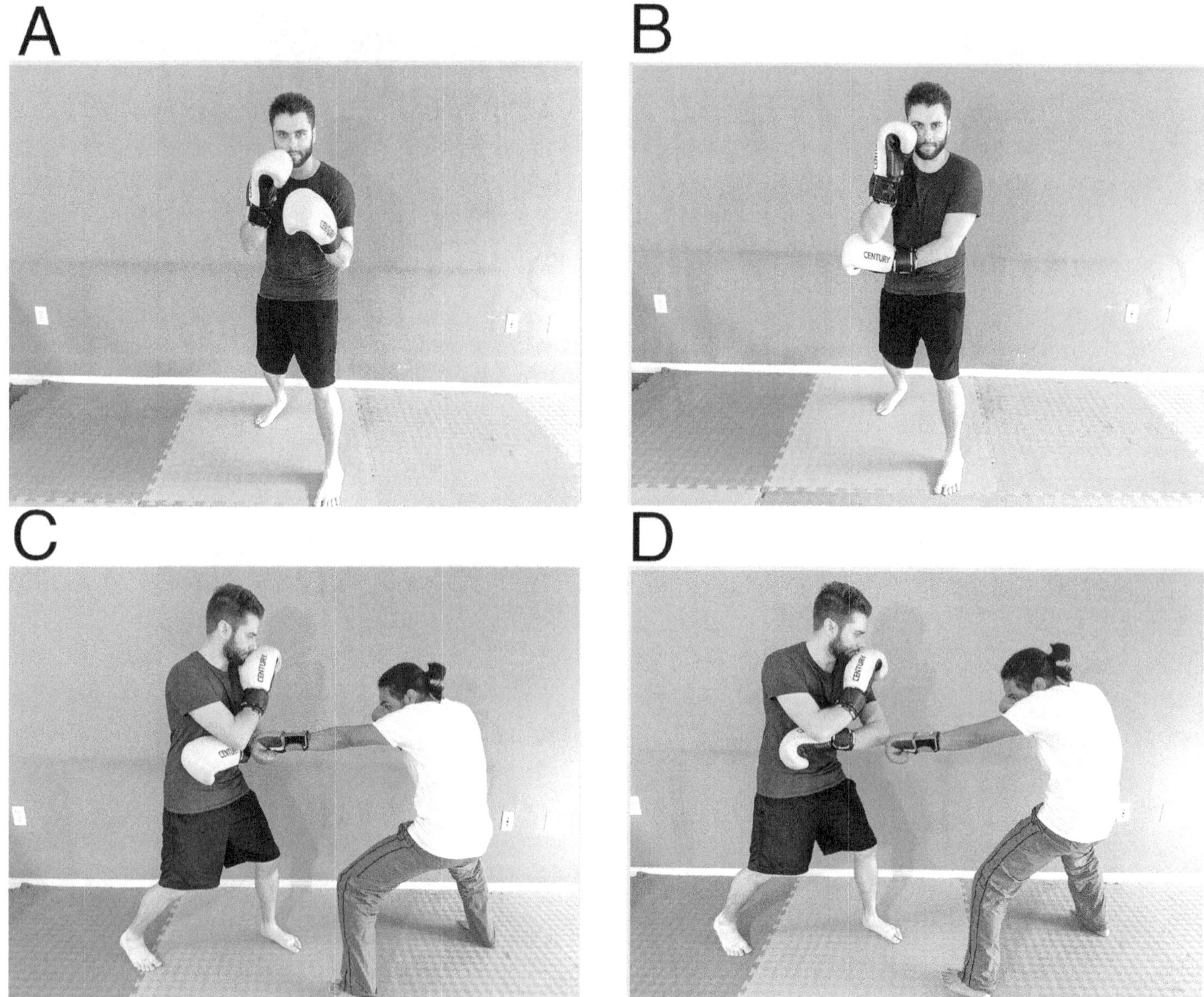

For lateral strikes to the Lead Side such as Hooks and Roundhouse Kicks, use your Lead Elbow to take the impact (Pics A, B & C). You may also pivot and Shoulder Roll, as shown earlier.

For Lateral Strikes to the Rear Side, such as a Lead Body Hook, slide your Lead Hand across your ribs to block the strike with your palm. At the same time, lower your Rear Elbow to help reinforce your defense (Pic D). To protect against kicks to your Rear Side, Cross Parry the kick (Pics E to F). You may also reinforce with a Rear Cover or Forearm Block.

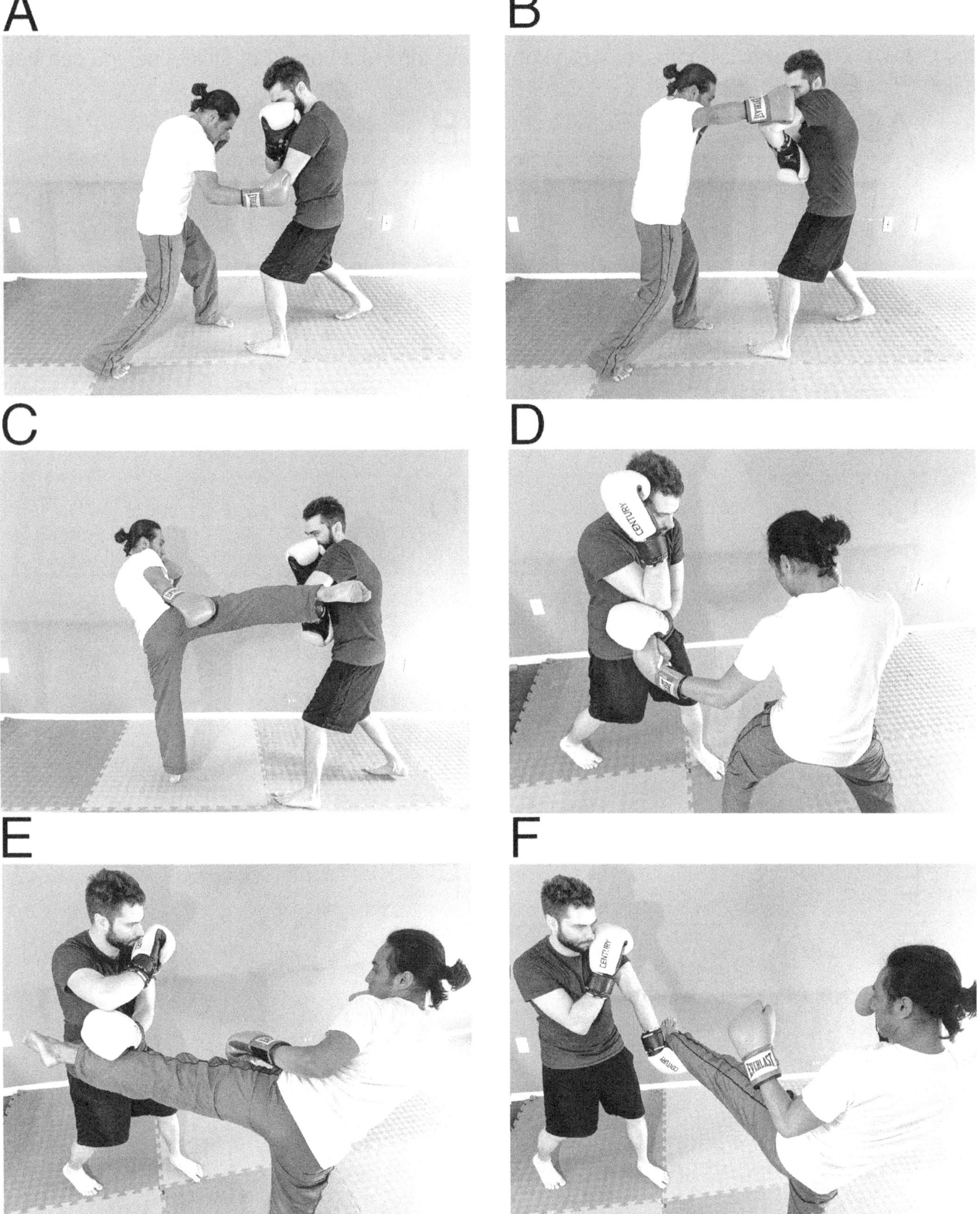

Cross Shell

Cross your Rear Hand over your Lead Shoulder. At the same time, quickly bring up your Lead Hand to touch the tip of your Rear Elbow. Bring your forearms together and brace them hard. Tuck your chin but keep your eyes over your arms to maintain vision (Pics A to B).

This defense works well for all linear strikes, and can defend well against lateral strikes from Mid to Long Range You can raise or lower your arms to place them in the path of head shots or body blows, or you can crouch forward to protect your stomach and bring your Cross Shell up to defend your head (Pics C & D). When practicing, make sure your partner throws a variety of strikes so you can become familiar (Pics E to F).

Open Stance Considerations

The Cross Guard is a fine idea in an Open Stance, as your arms can better protect more of the openings inherent in this position (Pics A through D). However, the weakness inherent in the Guard will be even more vulnerable from an Open Stance, so consider carefully.

A big consideration is that the Cross Guard does not lend itself well to controlling your opponent's Lead Hand, as your arm is low and folded. You may remember that Lead Hand control is a crucial factor in an Open Stance. The Lead Side of your head is also more vulnerable to attack from your opponent's uninhibited Lead Hand (Pic A).

While Shoulder Rolling Lead Hand attacks is a viable option (Pic B), what you may want to do instead is switch your arms, putting the Lead Arm on top (Pics C to D). This way you can defend against your opponent's Jab or Lead Hook with your forearm. You may also Cross Parry any Rear Leg Round House Kicks to your head more easily (since the Lead Leg is not as big a concern in an Open Stance but the Rear Leg is killer.)

There is a page covering the concept of switching which hand is on top at the end of this section. Gene Fulmer used this version of a Cross Guard with great success, as has Yoel Romero in MMA. Romero has even done so in Southpaw (in an Open Stance) many times. You may alter your hand positions and Stance for all of the drills below and see which methods work best for you.

Vulnerabilities

The Cross Guard works particularly well for fighters with long arms. However, even if you have a decent wing span you should be aware of certain vulnerabilities that are inherent in the Cross Guard (Pic A). Mainly, the high arm will tend to leave your body more open on that same side (Pic B), while the low arm will leave your head more open on the same side (Pic C). The body opening from the high arm will might entice opponent's to target your liver (depending on if you are in Orthodox or Southpaw and which arm is the high arm). It is very possible to protect both of these spots, as outlined in this chapter. Still, it is important to be aware of them.

A

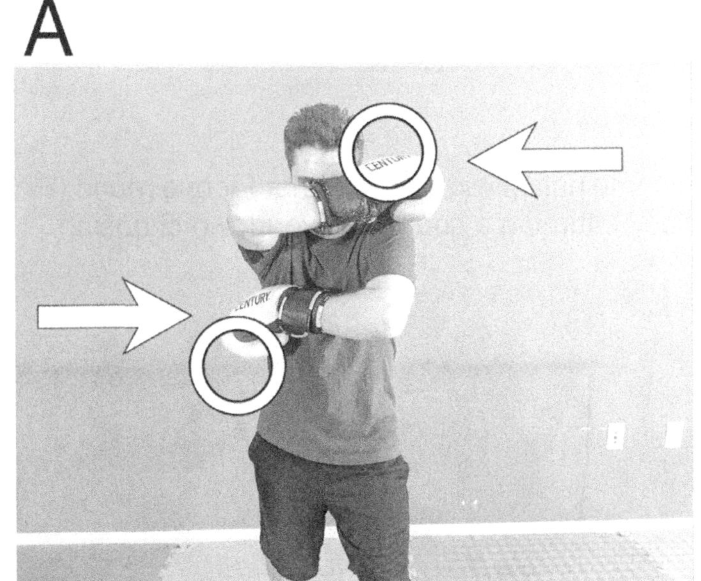

B

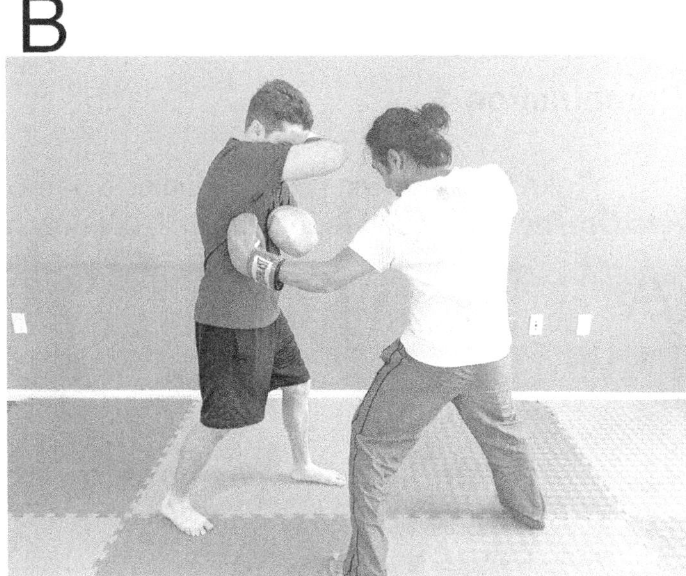

C

Drills/ Combinations

The Cross Guard will be so alien to many that it is best to simply work through combinations to get the feel of it. Remember that either arm may block either side or both arms can work together. That extra reliability and versatility is a major strength of the Cross Guard. Experiment with finding which techniques require which tactics as you go through these combinations.

The last thing to take into account is the movement of your body as you block. Because your arms are crossed, it can take longer to throw punches. However, turning your posture more sideways or more squared up can help to load and align certain punches. This is similar to the Twisting motion learned in the High Guard section. This will be explored more in the Drills section after these combinations.

Combination 1

Take turns throwing and defending a Jab-Cross combination with your partner for one round (Pics A to C). The next round repeat the drill, but now practice Returning a counter of your own choosing.

A

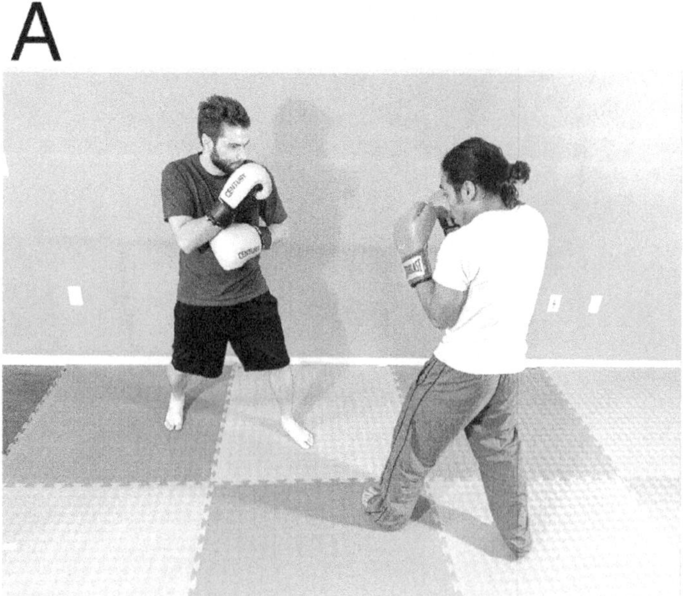

B

C

Combination 2

Take turns throwing and defending a Jab-Lead Hook-Rear Hook combination with your partner for one round (Pics A to E). The next round repeat the drill, but now practice Returning a counter of your own choosing.

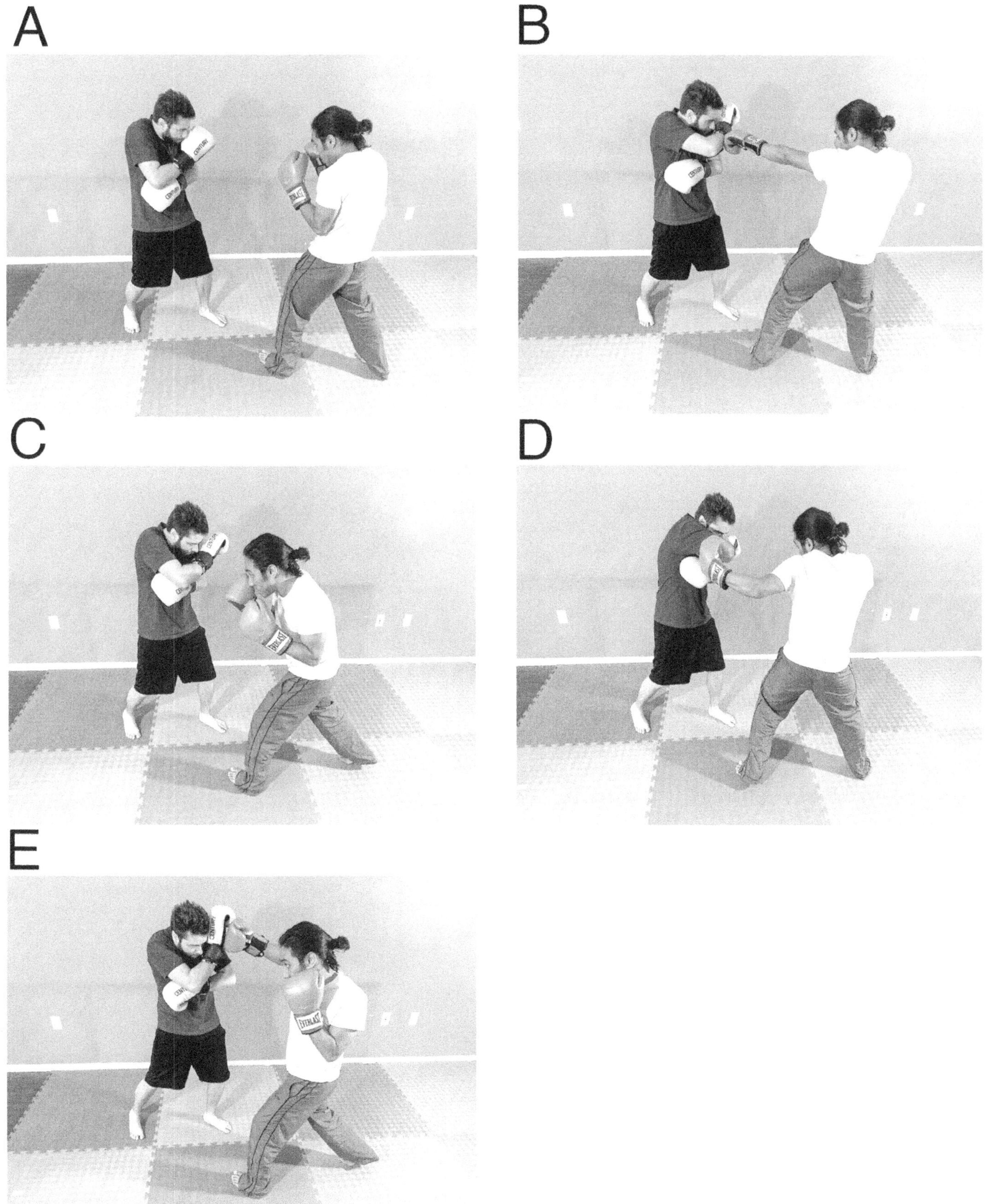

Combination 3

Take turns throwing and defending a Jab-Uppercut combination with your partner for one round (Pics A to D). The next round repeat the drill, but now practice Returning a counter of your own choosing.

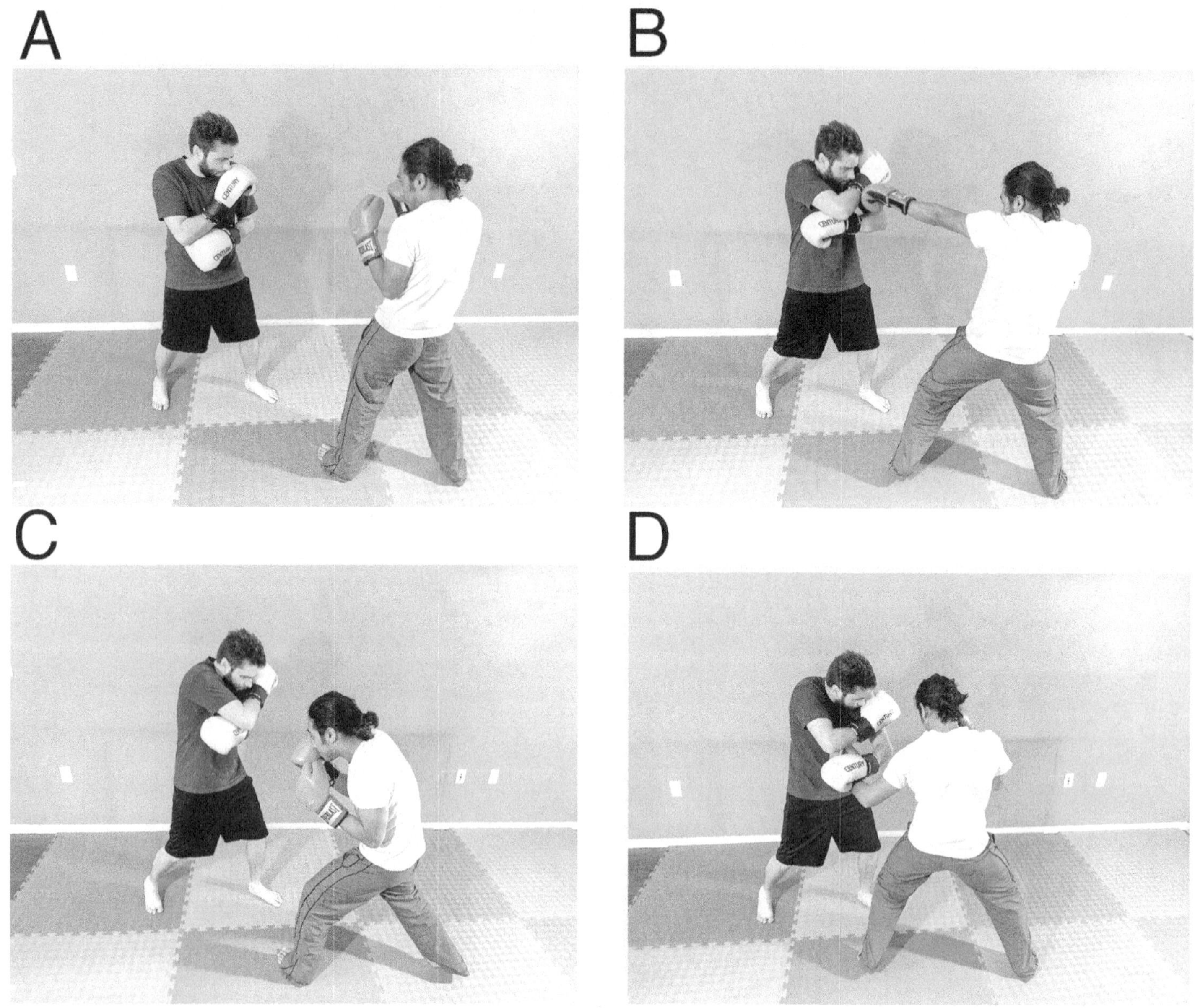

Combination 4 & 5

Take turns throwing and defending a Jab-Rear Leg Roundhouse (Pics A to B) or Jab-Cross-Lead Leg Roundhouse combination (Pics C to E) with your partner for one round. Your partner may alternate between the two in no particular order. The next round repeat the drill, but now practice Returning a counter of your own choosing.

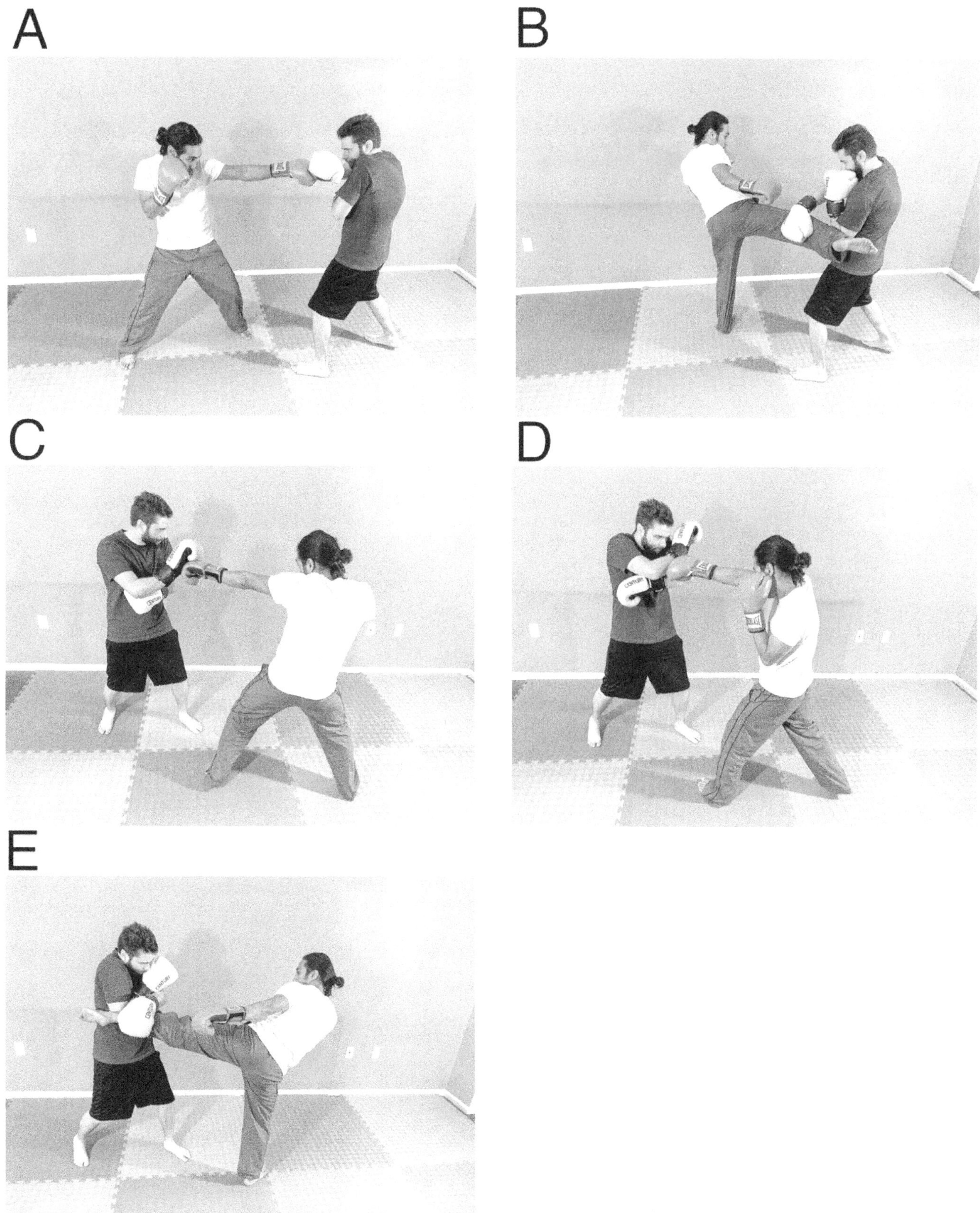

Drill 1 A

Have your partner throw multiple combinations at random. Focus on trying to block in such a way that your Lead Arm in pulled back (Pics A to B) at the correct moment to throw a loaded Hook (Pics C to D).

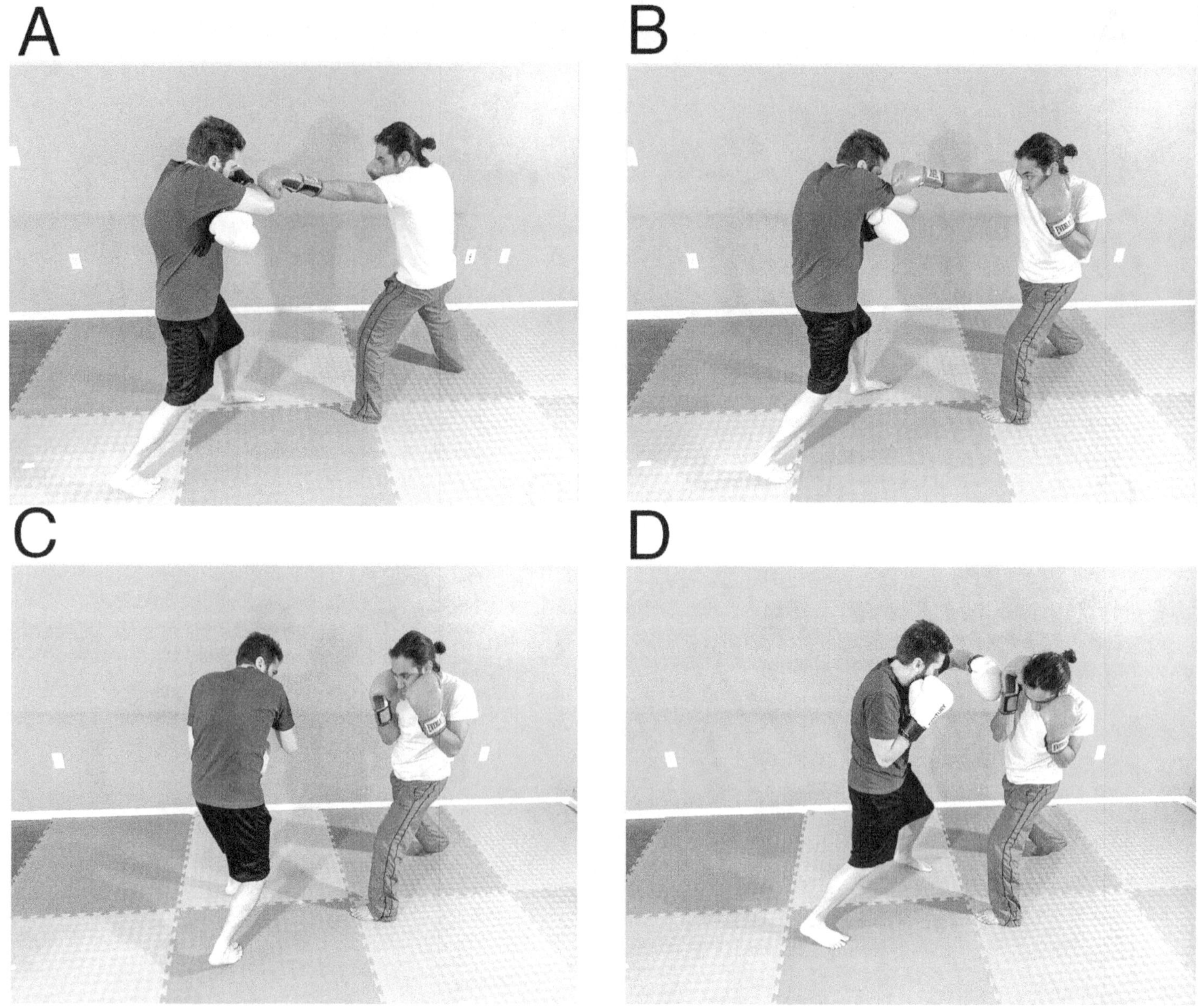

Drill 1 B

Have your partner throw multiple combinations at random. Focus on trying to block in such a way that your Rear Arm is pulled back (Pics A to B) at the correct moment to throw a loaded Cross (Pic C). The next round, try to combine this drill and the last, finding moments to align your Lead and Rear Arm to punch by turning your body as you Block.

A

B

C

Drill 2

A common tactic in fighting is to circle Inside as you Jab to try to square up your opponent. This opens up your opponent to more attacks. However, the Cross Guard provides so much protection that becoming squared up to your opponent is not as big a problem. Have your partner Jab and circle Inside. Rather than Pivot to try and remain narrow, stay where you are and practice Blocking their attacks from a more forward position (Pics A to C). When ready attack from Southpaw (Pics E to F) and then regain your original stance. Go back and forth attacking and defending this technique with your partner. Go light! In the pictures Emon had just said that Jin would have beat Mugen if they had finished their fight so he deserved it.

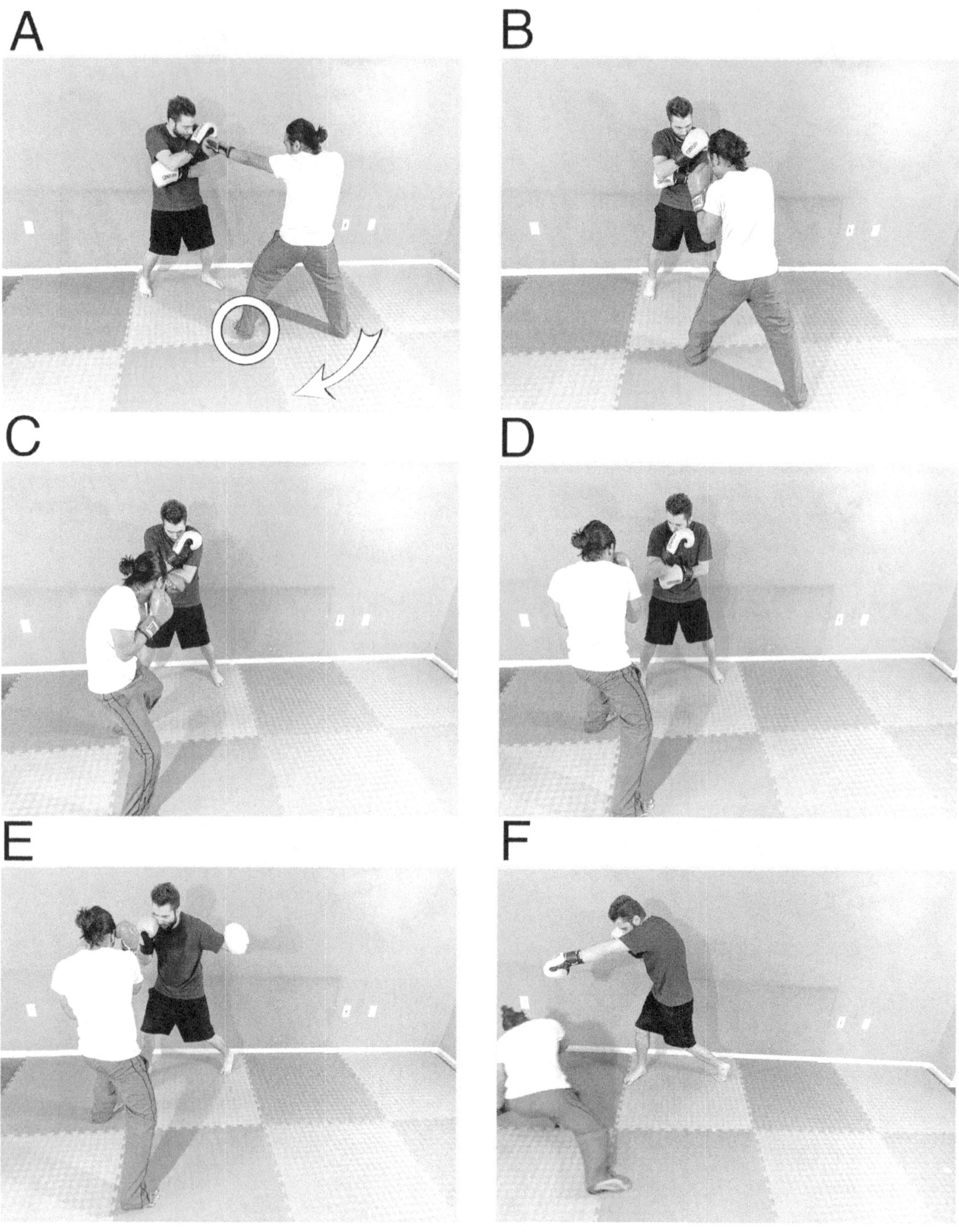

Drill 3

Another great component of the Cross Guard is that it is easier to establish a Cross Frame. Have your partner throw combinations and practice setting up Knees and Roundhouse Kicks. Alternate attacker and defender each round.

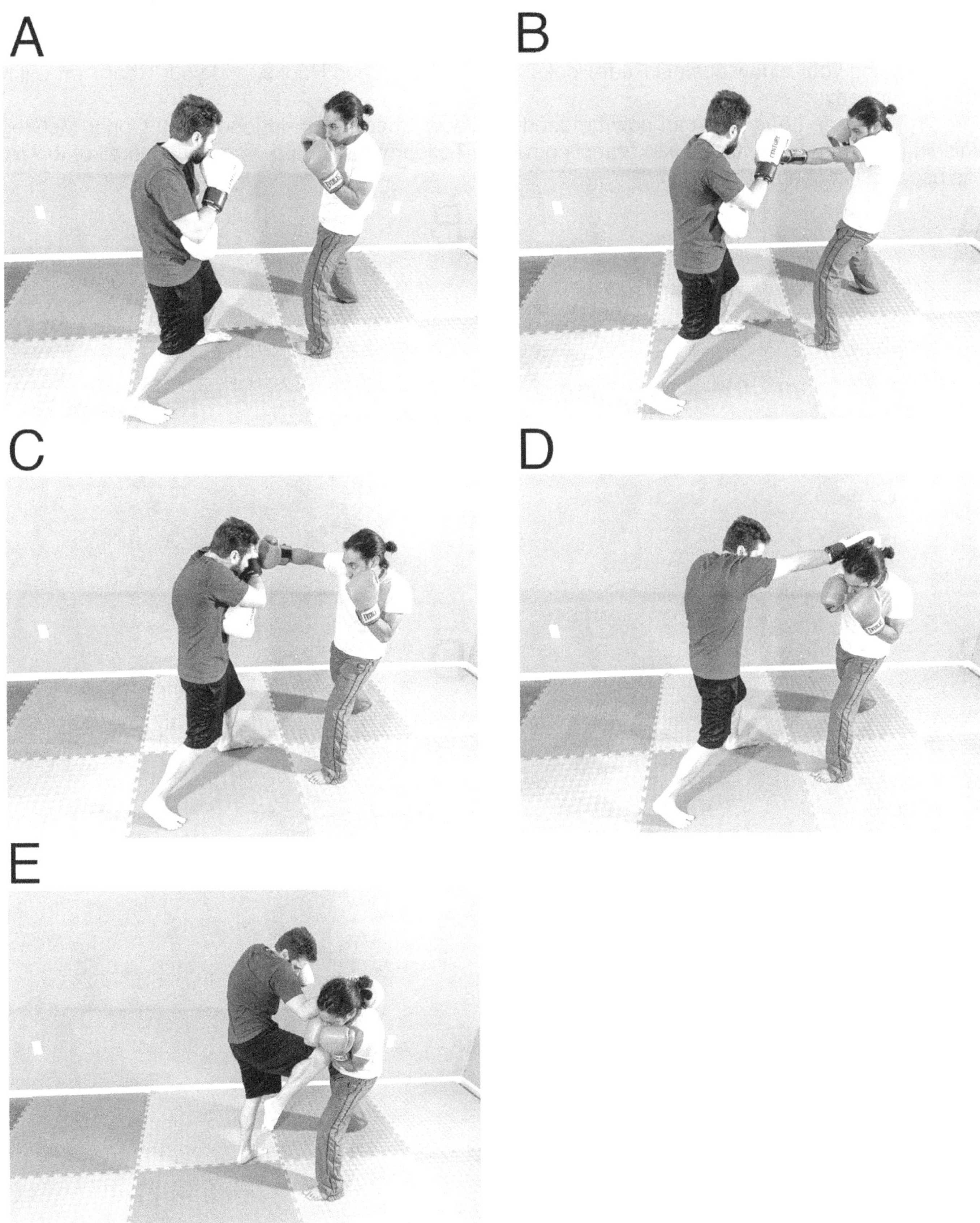

Reverse Cross Guard Considerations (Gene Fulmer)

This variation is much, much rarer, but was used successfully by Gene Fulmer throughout his career and was instrumental in his defeat of one of the greatest boxers of all time, Sugar Ray Robinson. Yoel Romero, one of the top fighters in his division, has also used this variation at times with great success in MMA.

Everything works practically the same, only in reverse. It will now be the Lead Arm defending your head by flaring your elbow against Rear Hooks and Catching Lead Hooks, and your Rear Arm will now protect your body.

In MMA the Lead Arm can now be used to Elbow Check your opponent like Conor McGregor, punishing them for trying to get into grappling range. To learn this Guard, you may use all of the same drills used in this chapter.

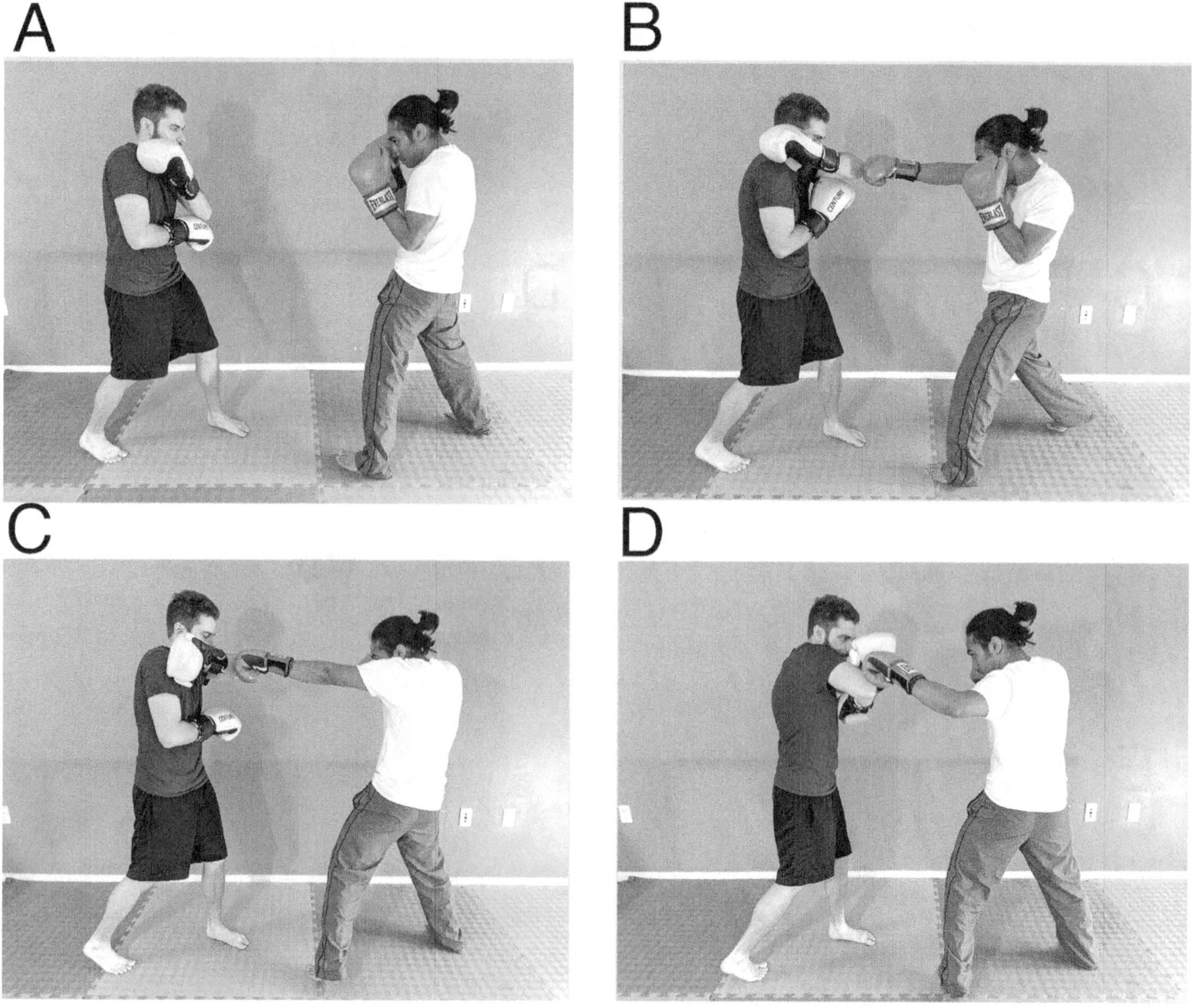

Pairing The Cross Guard With The Philly Shell

We've already gone over how strikes can be set up off your Rear Side by Shoulder Rolling in the Cross Guard, so it should be evident that the Cross Guard pairs very well with the Philly Shell. In fact, they're practically related. Archie Moore used both a Basic Guard, Philly Shell (Pic A) and Cross Guard (Pic B) to earn his record of most knock outs ever recorded. As you may have guessed, many of these knockouts came about when Moore used his Guards to set up hard counters.

The Philly Shell section is next. If you want to use the Cross Guard, I would recommend thinking about how the two might work together as you read. Moore tended to mostly use the Philly Shell and Basic Guard at mid to long range (Pic C) and the Cross Guard at close to mid-range (Pic D). But you can experiment to find what works best for you.

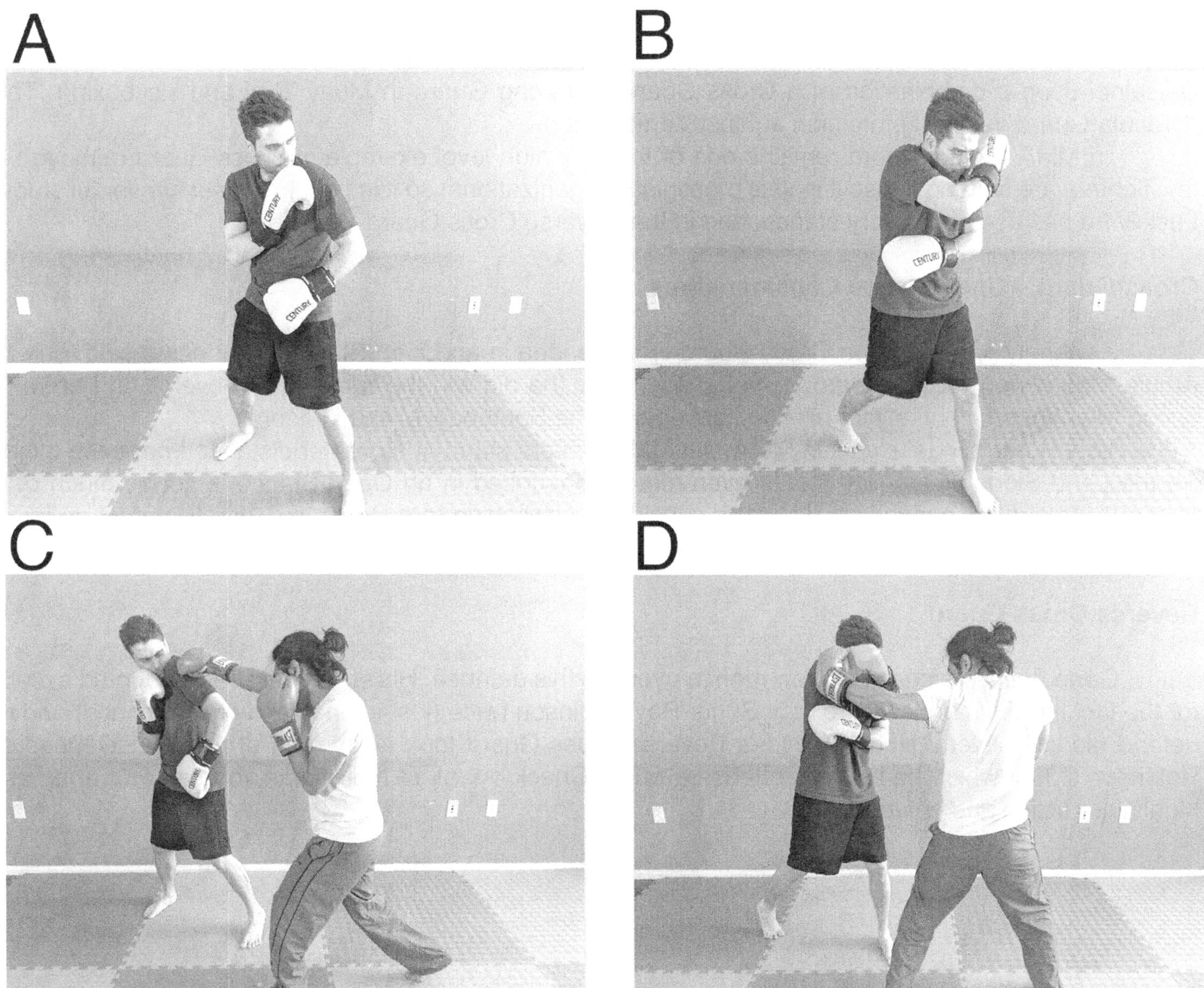

References – Cross Guard

Cross Guard

Archie Moore is the go-to fighter to watch for the Cross Guard. While Foreman used it purely defensively (staying safe as he closed distance) Moore used the motion of his body to block and Load up Return Counters. Ken Norton was another great fighter who used the Cross Arm defense, even using it effectively against Muhammad Ali. Norton tended to turn his Rear Catch or Rear Parry into a Cross Block for extra protection against Jabs and Lead Hooks. Joe Frazier also used the Cross Guard while Weaving and Crouching to help protect himself from Uppercuts. Rising up out of his Crouch gave him more than enough time to bring his arm around to deliver his legendary Lead Hook.

Manson Gibson used a Cross Guard in kickboxing while his opponents tried to clinch. It protected him from knees, but it's not a great idea to use in the clinch in MMA for obvious reason. Buakaw and Deisalnoi used a combination of a Cross Guard and Long Guard in Muay Thai and kickboxing. The "Dracula Guard" is great protection against Vertical Elbows.

In MMA, Yoel Romero remains one of the only high level example of Cross Guard (although a few fighters are starting to use it in less prestigious organizations) so it is best to look at him for all study. Luckily he has used it in every stance, and in the Reverse Cross Guard Variation.

Cross Guard – Open Stance Considerations

Generally speaking, the Cross Guard is a fine idea in an Open Stance. That being said, one of Archie Moore's only losses was against a Southpaw (he did win the rematch however) and Foreman chose to abandon it entirely for his title fight against the Southpaw Michael Moorer.

Yoel Romero has used it in MMA, but MMA fighters stand at a greater distance from each other. So the Lead Side vulnerability that is even more pronounced in an Open Stance is not as much of a concern. As already suggested, it's worth considering switching to a Reverse Cross Guard when in an Open Stance if you are reluctant to give it up altogether.

Reverse Cross Guard

Gene Fulmer is one of the few men to ever use this defense. His style could be discounted except for the fact that Fulmer used it to beat Sugar Ray Robinson twice (losing once and drawing once) and to defend his title several times. Fulmer's Reverse Cross Guard took away a lot of the effectiveness of Robinson's Jab, which he built his offense around. Check out all of their fights you can find, they are highly instructive and entertaining.

Philly Shell – Fighting On The Centerline

One of the great advantages of the Philly Shell is that it naturally places your Rear Hand and Lead Shoulder right on the Centerline, guaranteed to be on the inside of your opponent's hands if they are in a Standard Guard. Why does this matter? Because you now have the straighter path to defend (Pics A, B & C) and attack (Pick D). This means that if both you and your opponent moved at the exact same speed, your Block would always connect and your Rear Hand would always land first (Pics C to D).

Another huge benefit is that, combined with a sideways, narrow stance, there are very few openings for your opponent to exploit.

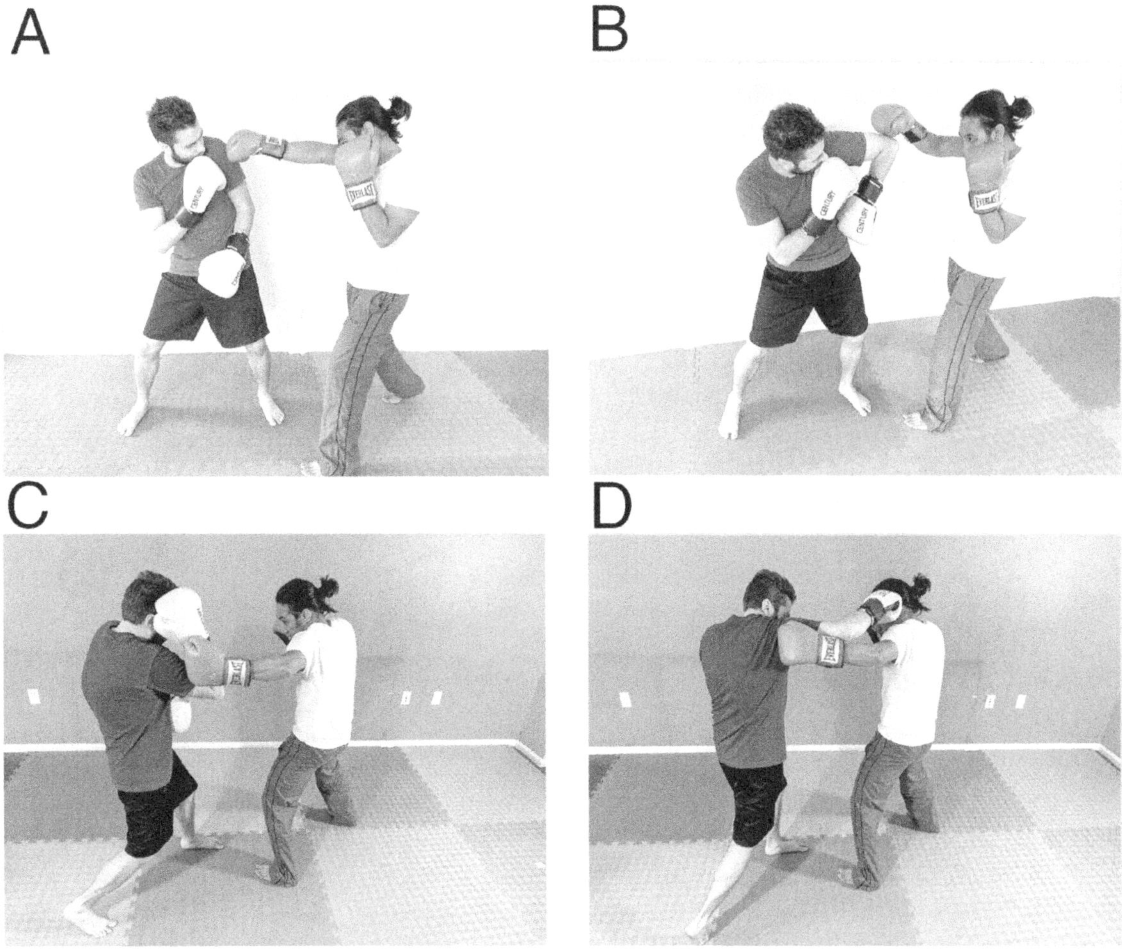

Advanced Shoulder Rolls

There's a reason very few fighters can Shoulder Roll effectively, let alone rely on it as their primary method of defense. Although it may look simple and straightforward, shoulder rolls require a very high level of nuance and careful judgement.

The simplest and most well-known version has already been covered in the Basics section; simply turn and pop your shoulder to deflect a punch before countering with your own. But this movement alone is only enough to protect against straights to the chin. Read on to learn how to defend against additional punches.

Against Straight Punches To The Temple

To defend shots to the temple you must Pull, forcing your opponent to aim down towards the protection of your popped shoulder (Pics A & B). Fighters like Floyd Mayweather and James Tony at times leaned beyond 45 degrees to let punches slide off the slant of their Lead Arm and shoulder.

A

B

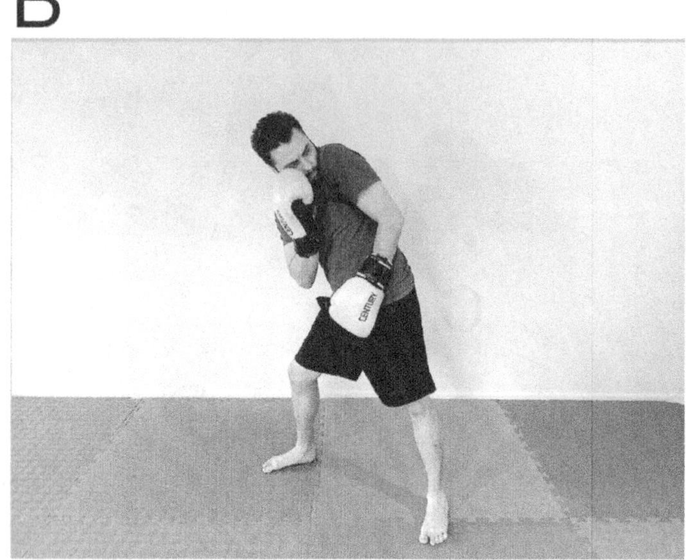

Without Pulling, your opponent may still clip your temple or catch you behind your ear (Pics A to B). By leaning back just out of range and using the angle of your arm and shoulder to let the punch slide off of you, you can frustrate your opponent as they continue to miss shots while appearing to be in range (Pics C & D). If you keep stepping back as well, you can condition your opponent to over reach (Pics C to E), something all great counter punchers hope for (Pic F).

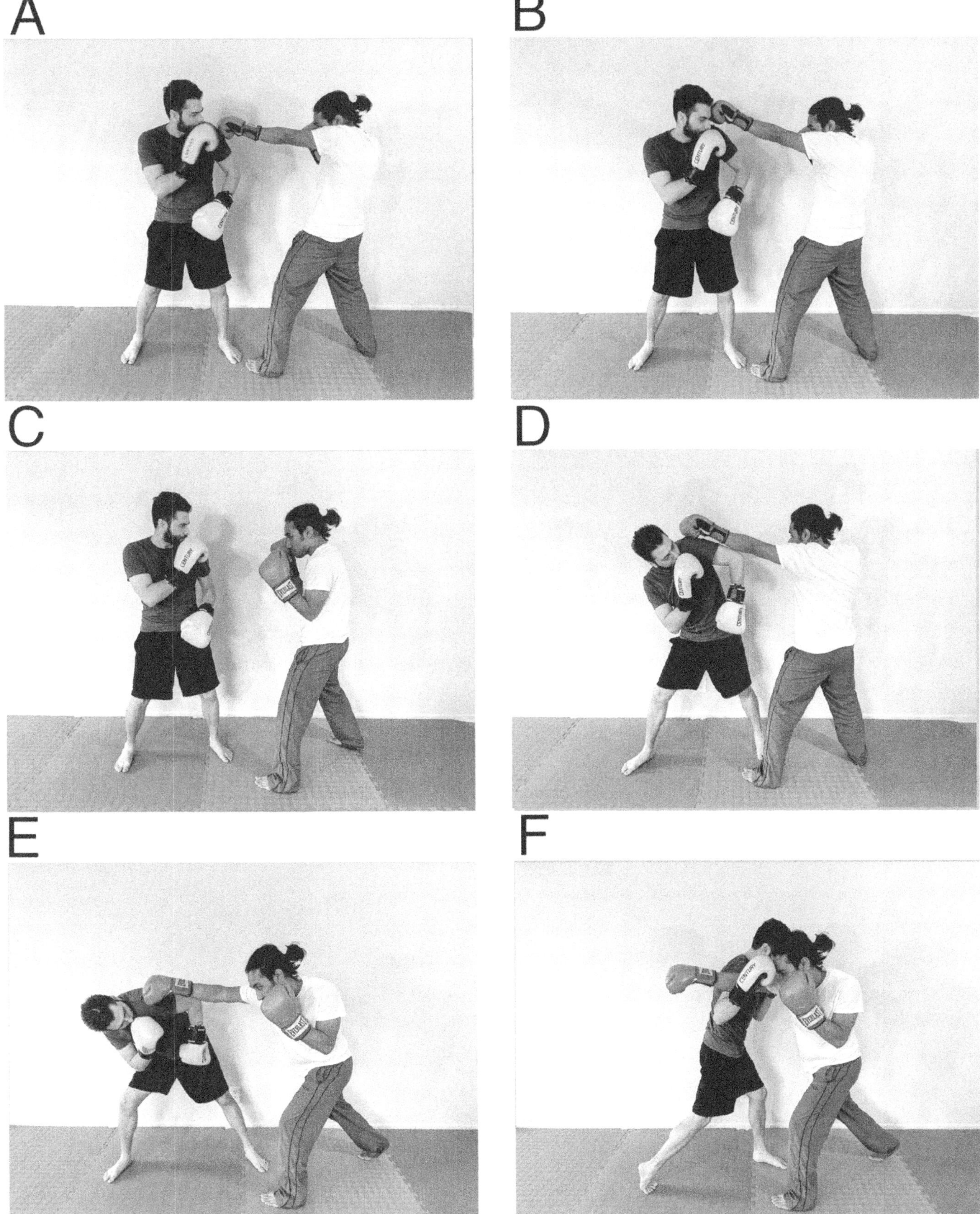

You can also Pull back as you step forward (Pics A to B & C to D). Mayweather does this a great deal, as it keeps his weight back even as he moves forward, allowing for an easy retreat. Daniel Cormier does this as well as it allows him to dodge punches as he moves into position to Clinch or try for a Takedown.

Against Rear Hooks & Overhands

Against Rear hooks and Overhands, you will need to tuck your chin, hunch your back and lean down (Pic A). Think of moving your body along the same trajectory as the punch. The way you are hunching your back and popping your Lead Shoulder should keep your chin safe, but your temple and the sensitive spot behind your ear will still be open if you do not tuck your chin and duck. If you make this shape and time it correctly, your opponent's Hook should skid off your back or shoulder (Pics B to F). The motion should be similar to a Weave, with the Twist quickly blending into a small Duck.

Overhands are particularly devastating to those who do not know the nuances of the Philly Shell. Overhands have a way of sneaking over Shoulder Rolls, so stay alert and remember that a simple Twist is not enough. Obviously it is crucial to be able to quickly tell exactly which kind of punch is coming. At times you may need to adjust mid movement, which is why this kind of reactive Guard is not for everybody. Play to your own strengths.

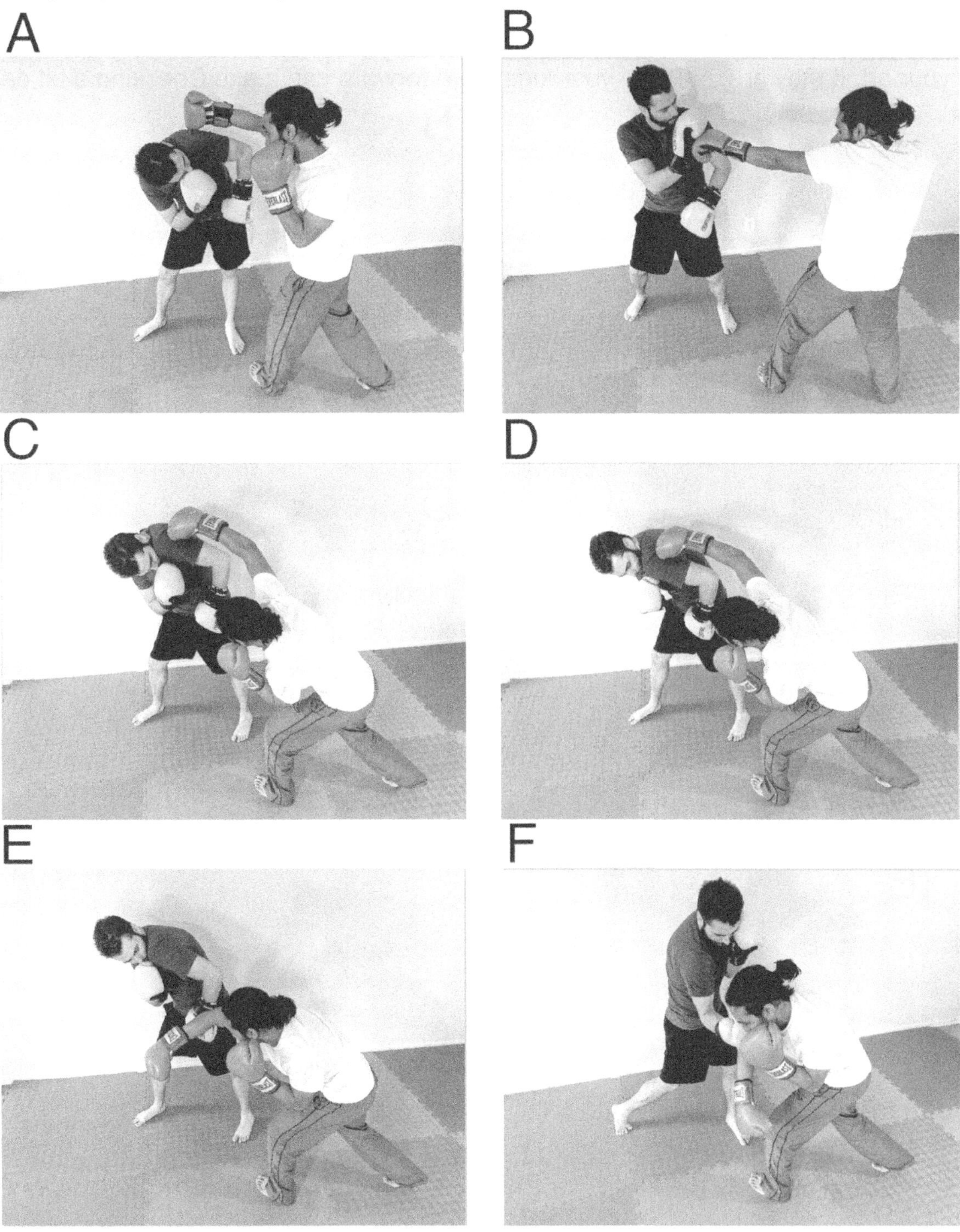

Principle - Lead Foot Placement

If you truly want to fight like Mayweather, then you should be sure to keep your Lead Foot right next to your opponent's, or slightly to the outside of it (Pic A). This will leave as few openings as possible, especially in conjunction with a sideways Stance and Posture. If you opponent wants to attack they will be forced to step Inside (Pic B). Because you know what your opponent will do, it will be easier to set up counters.

However, placing your foot like this will also limit your own ability to attack (Pic C). Notice in Pic C how the fighter has few angles to land his Jab because his hand is blocked by his opponent's Guard.

As such, it's important to note that it is very possible to use the Philly Shell in a more aggressive manner, placing your Lead Foot further Inside. This will let you to step in deeper, which will help you land shots down the middle (Pic D). Although you lose your closed off position with your foot deeper Inside, you can still Roll effectively by Pivoting (Pic E). Or you can Shoulder Block by stepping Outside (Pic F). Lead Foot position is important to the Philly Shell, but should be a consideration no matter what Guard or style you practice. As mentioned before, be wary of using a sideways stance if leg kicks are allowed in your art. If they are, pointing your toes more forward can make Checking a bit easier.

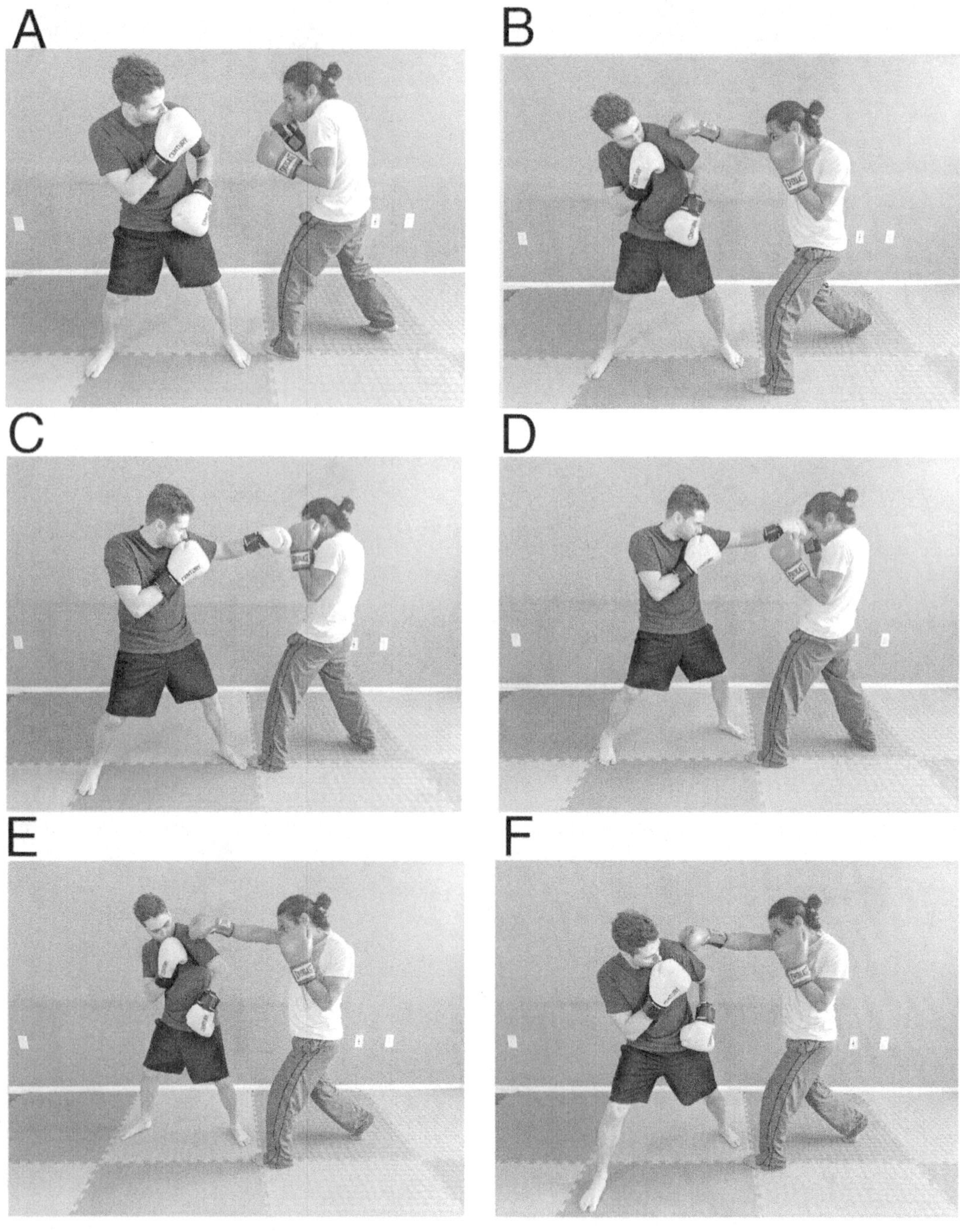

Vulnerabilities

Shoulder Rolling against Hooks or Overhands require some amount of Crouching (Pic A). This will leave you very vulnerable to Uppercuts and angled Hooks (Pic B). To protect against this, you can either duck down below the waist (Pics C to D), as Mayweather and James Tony did (this is also a possibility in MMA as it threatens a takedown, Stipe does this on occasion). Or you may block the punch as you straighten up. Because the position is so vulnerable, you may wish to use an Elbow Block rather than a Cover Block, as Mayweather tends to do (Pics E to F).

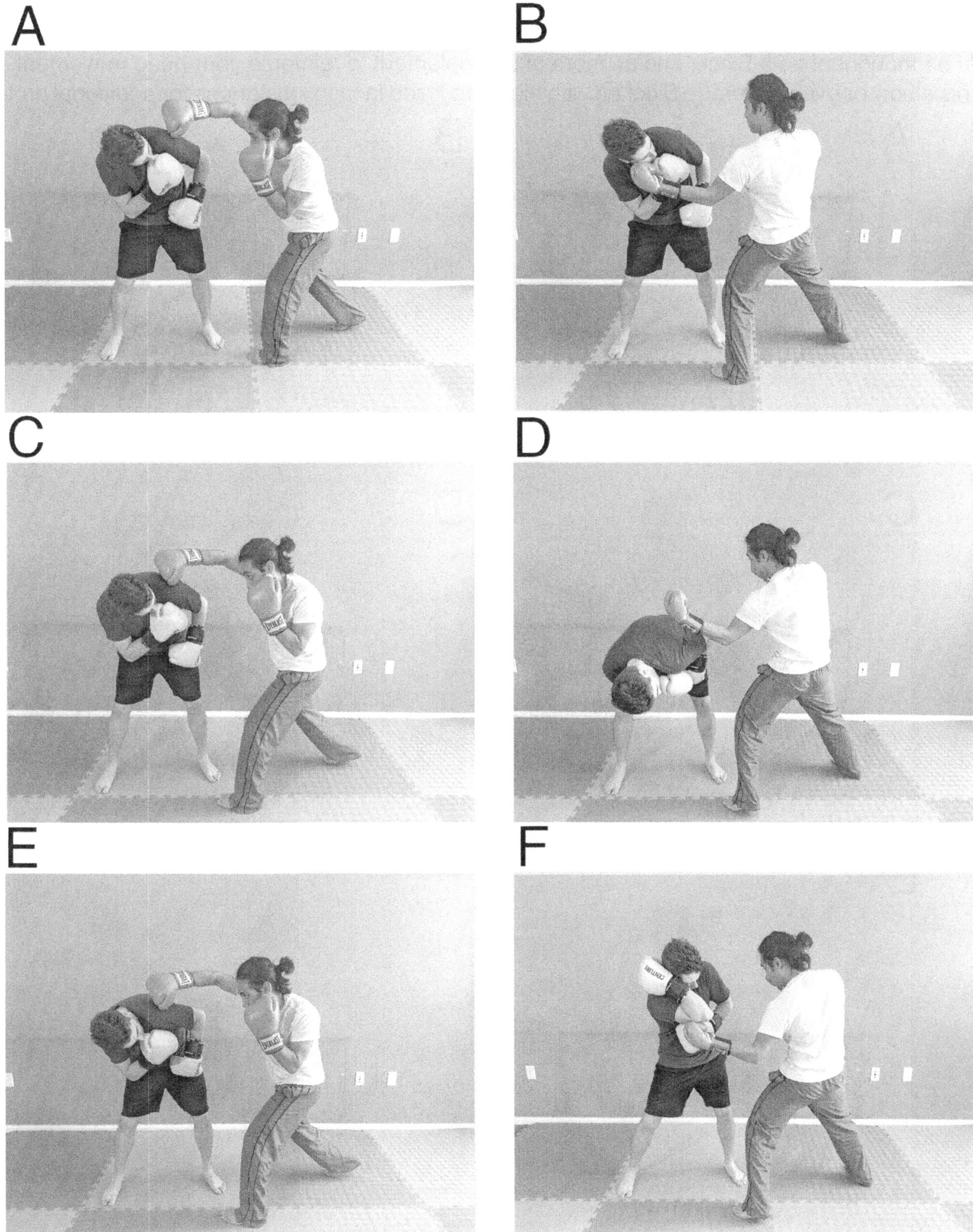

Open Stance Considerations

In an Open Stance you will instead Roll against your opponent's Lead Side attacks rather than their Rear Side attacks (Pics A to B). This can be done in the exact same way as outlined above, and can provide even more effective counters off your Rear Side since your opponent will be more vulnerable in an Open Stance. Of course, you will be more vulnerable as well.

Can you still use your shoulder to Block your opponent's Rear Side attacks? Yes. Should you? Probably not. That said, this book seeks to cover all successful defenses, and James Toney Shoulder Rolled his opponent's Rear Side attacks in an Open Stance very effectively. This technique requires that you step Inside and Crouch deep at the same time (Pics C to F). The Shoulder Roll in this instance should be thought of as a Block, and as more of a supplement to reinforce your head movement. Toney used his elbow or even Leverage Blocked with his Lead Hand in many instances for additional protection.

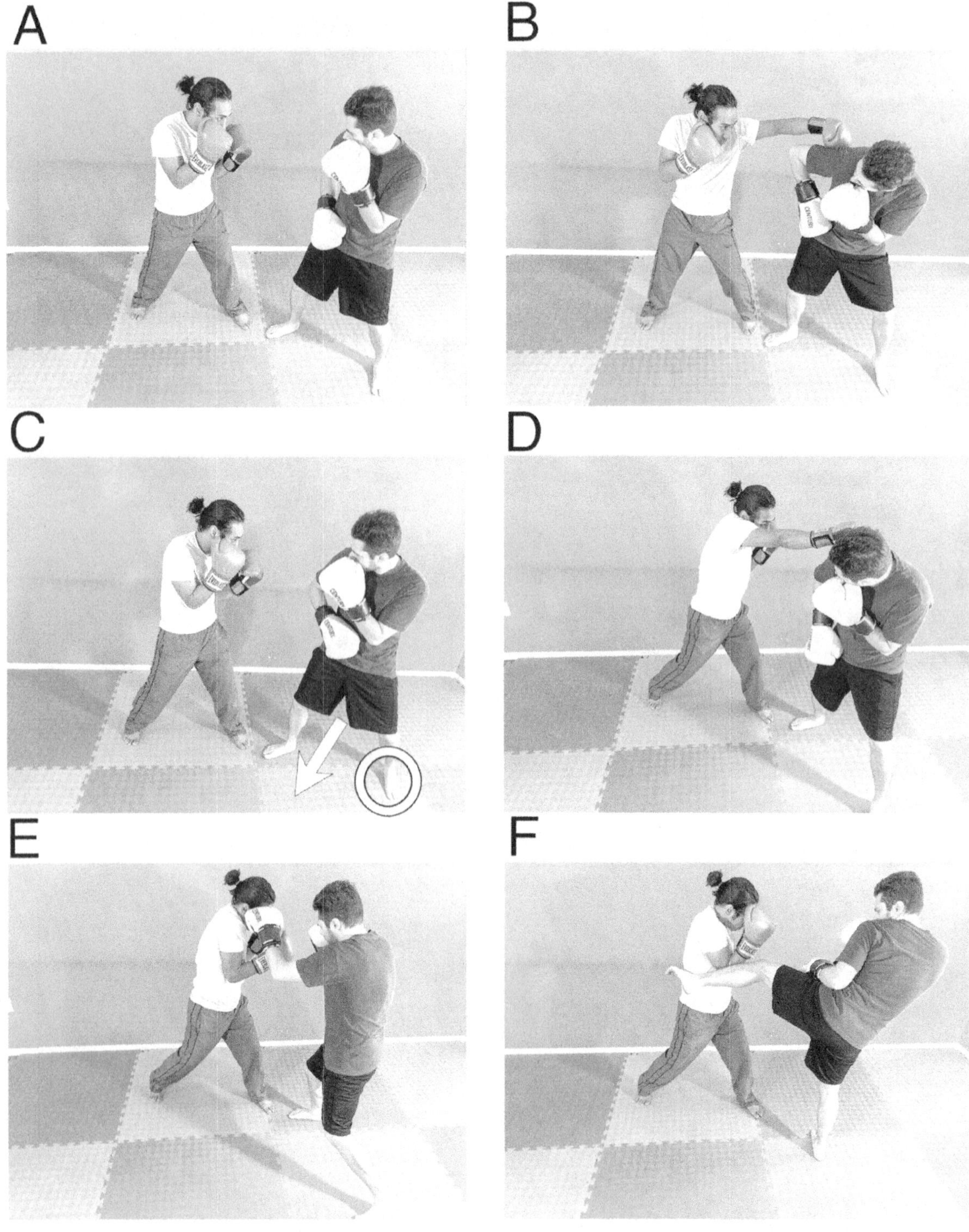

Drill

Have your partner throw a number of Jabs (Pics A to B), and then every once in a while surprise you by throwing with their Rear Hand. Have them alternate between throwing Rear Straights, Hooks and Overhands(C Pics). Try to gauge which attack is coming and use the correct response. If your style involves kicks, have your partner follow up some of their attacks with a Rear Leg Roundhouse to your Lead Leg to remind you not to leave yourself vulnerable by over rotating (Pics D to E). Switch who is attacking and defending each round.

If in an Open Stance, have your opponent throw Lead Hooks instead of Crosses.

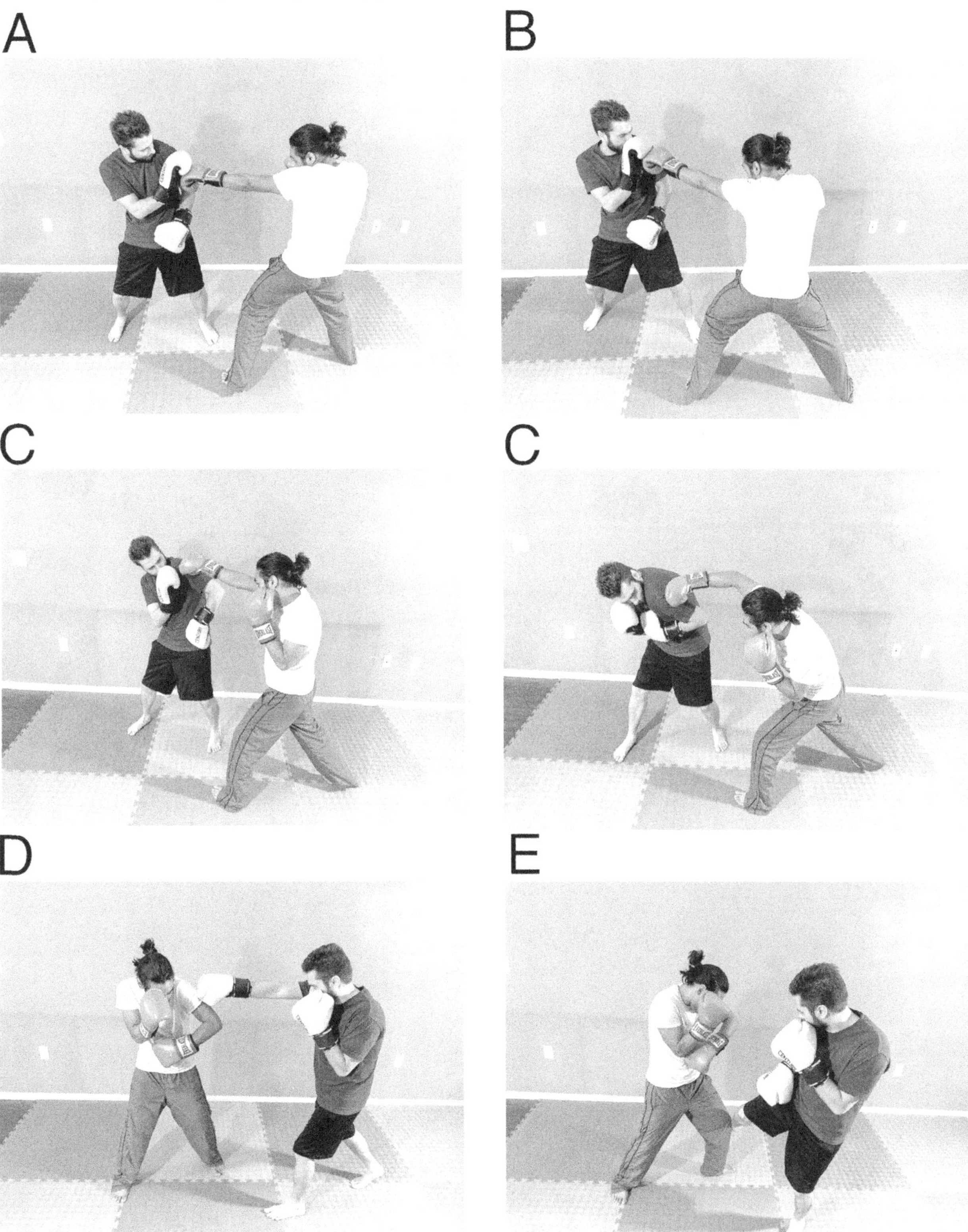

Forearm Shield

Lift your Lead Arm to create a horizontal shield against incoming strikes (Pics A to B). Because you are fighting on the Centerline, with a narrow opening in your defense, you need only use your Lead Forearm for defense at Long Range if you so choose. It can also easily turn into a Jab or Frame (Pics C to D).

You can also use this technique to close distance by moving in off of your opponent's strike and smothering their Guard (Pics A to B). At Close Range, this technique can be used to gain distance. You can ruin your opponent's Guard and Posture by tilting their head up, and shoving your forearm underneath their chin (Pics C to F). Floyd Mayweather used this technique all the time. However, if boxing this must be done at a slow enough speed to not elicit a warning for elbowing from the referee.

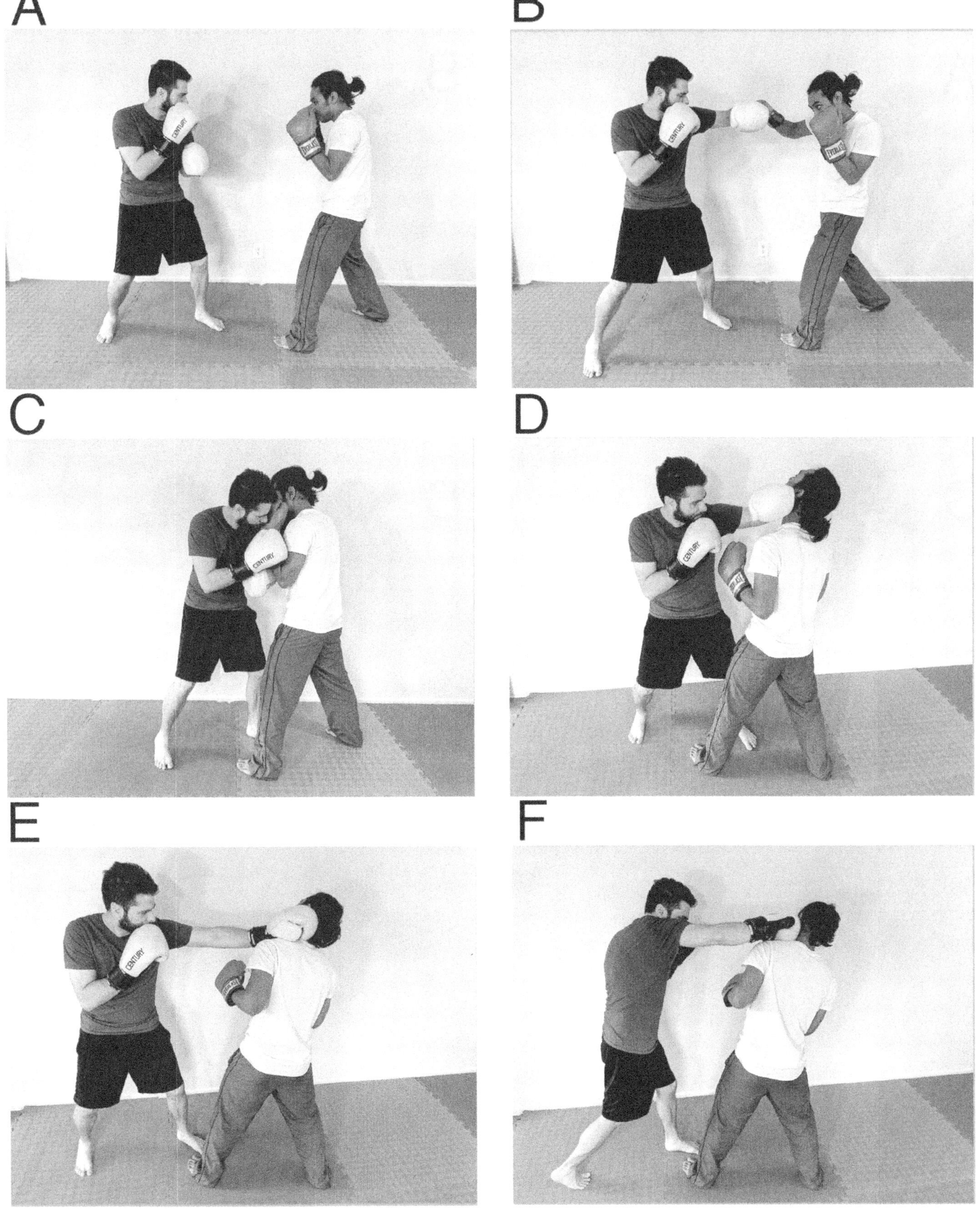

Open Stance Considerations

This defense is extremely effective in an Open Stance due to Lead Hand control. Rigondeaux has used it to great effect. Not only is it a useful and energy efficient way to defend a Jab, but it also allows you to Return a Jab from that same position immediately (Pics A to C). As you are Blocking your opponent's peripheral vision on their Rear Side, it is the perfect time to throw a Rear Side attack (Pic D).

Inverse Elbow Block

Raise your Elbow to Block or Parry an opponent's strike (Pics A to B & C to D). The Inverse Elbow Block can be used to supplement Shoulder Roll mechanics or on its own. When Shoulder Rolling, this block can help to throw an opponent's strike off course, unbalancing them and making a follow up attack more difficult. Or it can be used on its own on either side.

Ali used this block extensively in his early career, and Tyson Fury has used it many times.

Dustin Poirier will use these Blocks on their own as well. He will even remain squared up as he does so, rather than try to Roll. To pull this off he positions his hand on the middle of his stomach, giving his elbow room to travel to his centerline without rotating his body (Pic F).

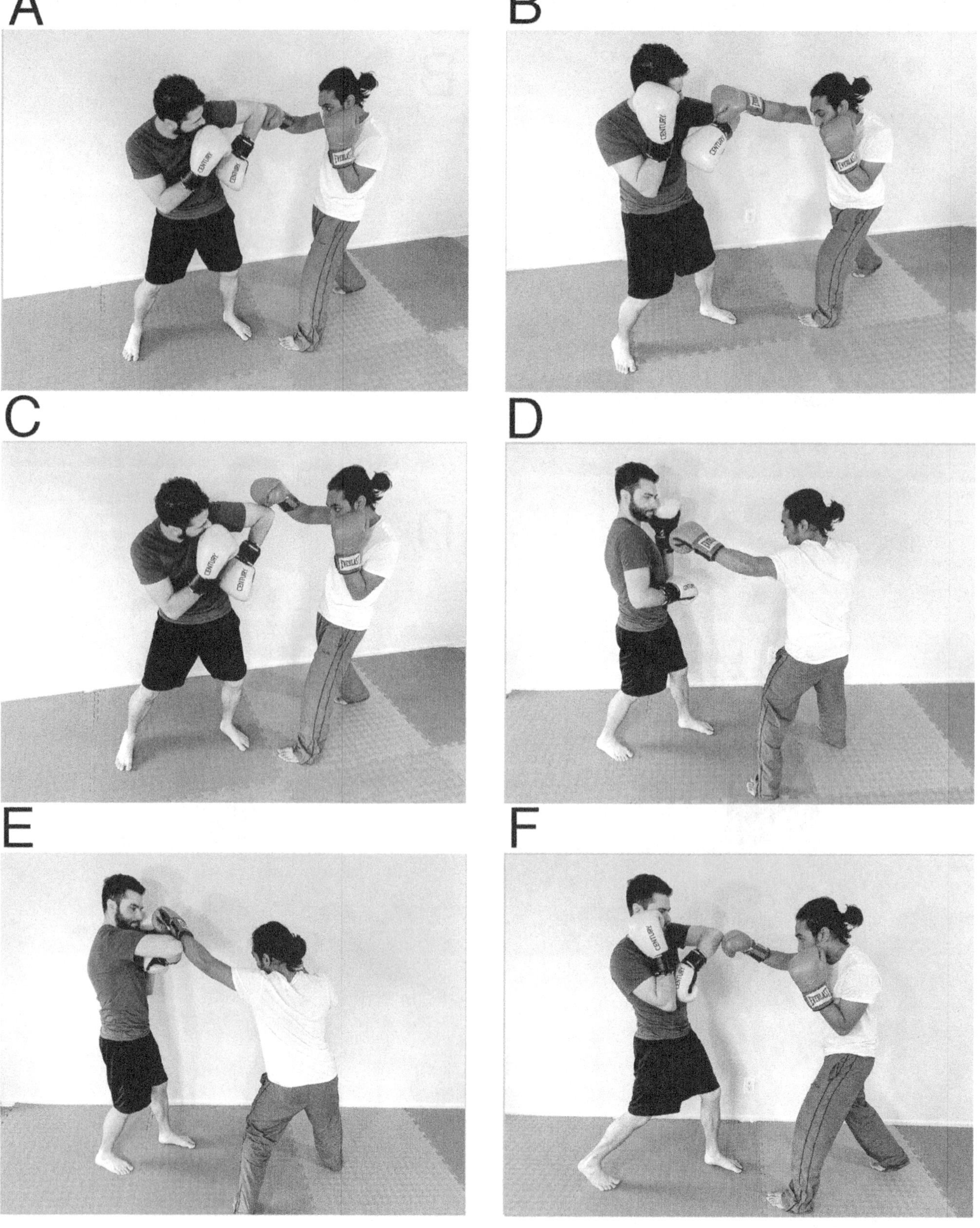

Open Stance Considerations – Specialty Counter

In an Open Stance, an Inverse Elbow Block is a great way to stay safe right after you throw your Jab. Rather than retract your Jab normally, turn it into an Inverse Elbow Block to turn away your opponent's Lead Hand counter (Pics A to C).

A common sequence used by Lomachenko is to Jab, then Inverse Elbow Block his opponent's counter Hook as he steps in deeper, as stated before. Next, he continues the motion of his Block to come down with a raking Lead Hook (Pic D).

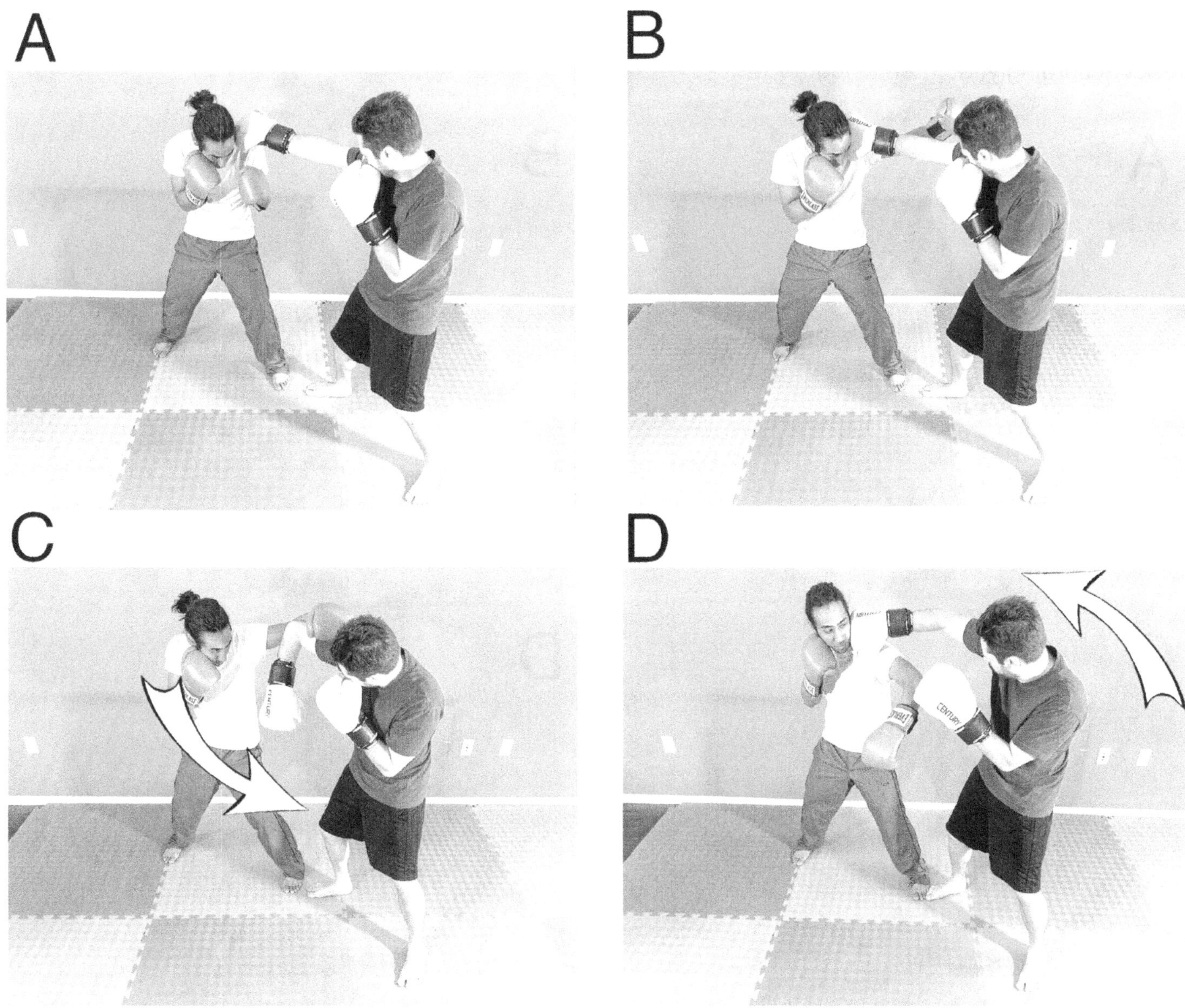

The Yin Yang Defense

One of the most powerful aspects about the Philly Shell is that you can block the majority of your opponent's strikes by simply standing in place and Twisting. Your Rear Arm Cover Block will catch most of the punches thrown to your Read Side so long as you square up your stance, and the same can be said for your Lead Side due to the Shoulder Roll. This not only puts you into the correct position with very little movement, it also dispels the impact of the punches being thrown at you (as discussed in the High Guard section). This leads to great moments where Mayweather defends against a torrent of punches by swiveling back and forth, something both hilarious to watch and highly discouraging to opponents. Keep in mind that to do this, you must be able to read which kind of punch is coming and react accordingly, as mentioned above.

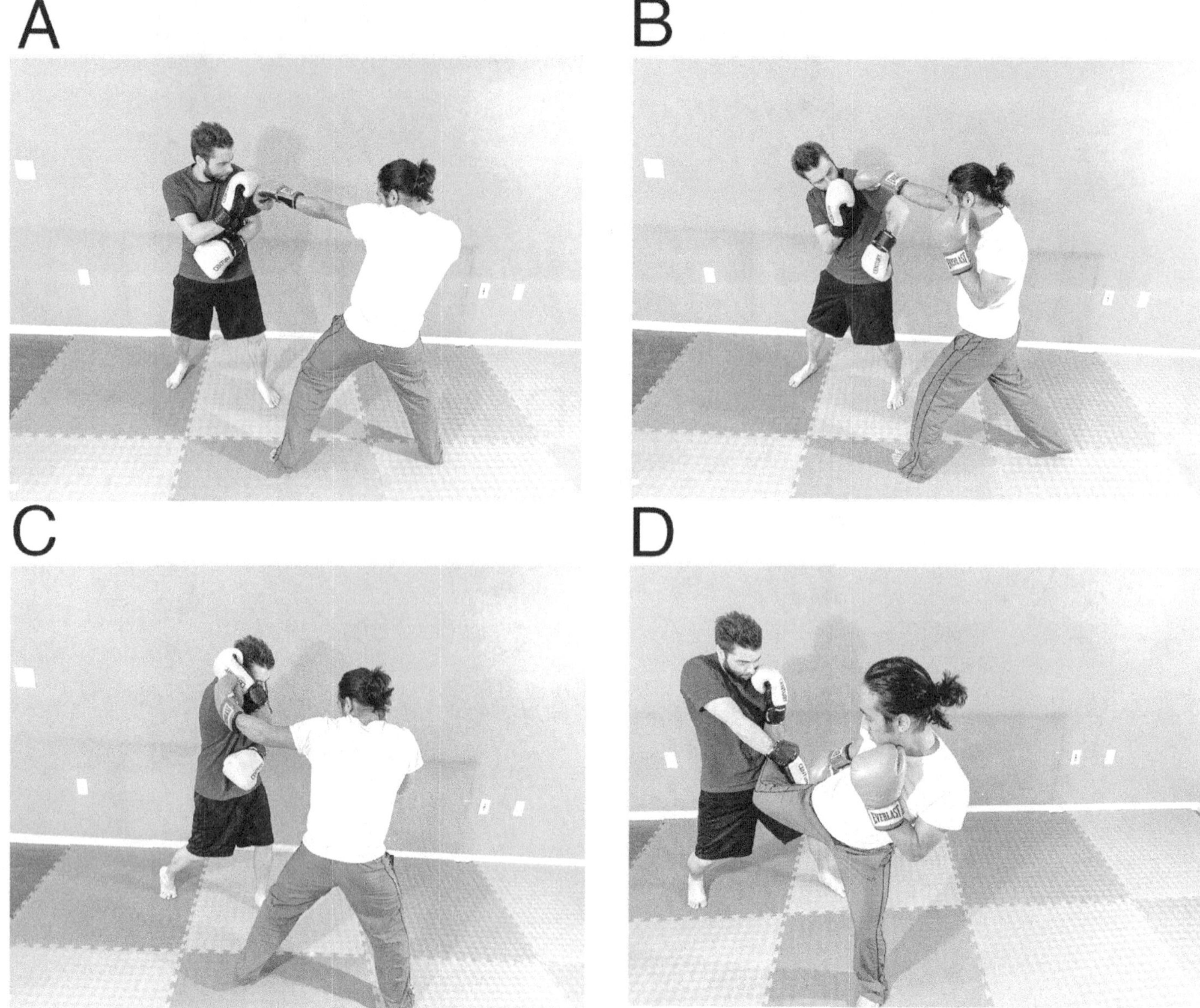

Drills

Drill 1

Have your partner throw combinations at you, never once doubling up on the same side. This drill is to teach the Yin Yang principle explained above, and happens to be how most people throw combinations anyways. We will incorporate doubling up later. For now, have your partner throw Left-Right-Left-Right combinations (Pics A to C), never Left-Left or Right-Right. Go one round and then switch which partner is attacking and which is defending.

Use kicks as well if they are part of your sport/style. You may find that, just like the Cross Guard, Cross Parrying kicks may actually be easier (Pic D). Although in this case, you may find it harder to pull off a Cross Parry with your Lead Side due to your lower Lead Hand. However it may help against wrestling by making it easier for you to Frame against your opponent's hip or secure an Under Hook.

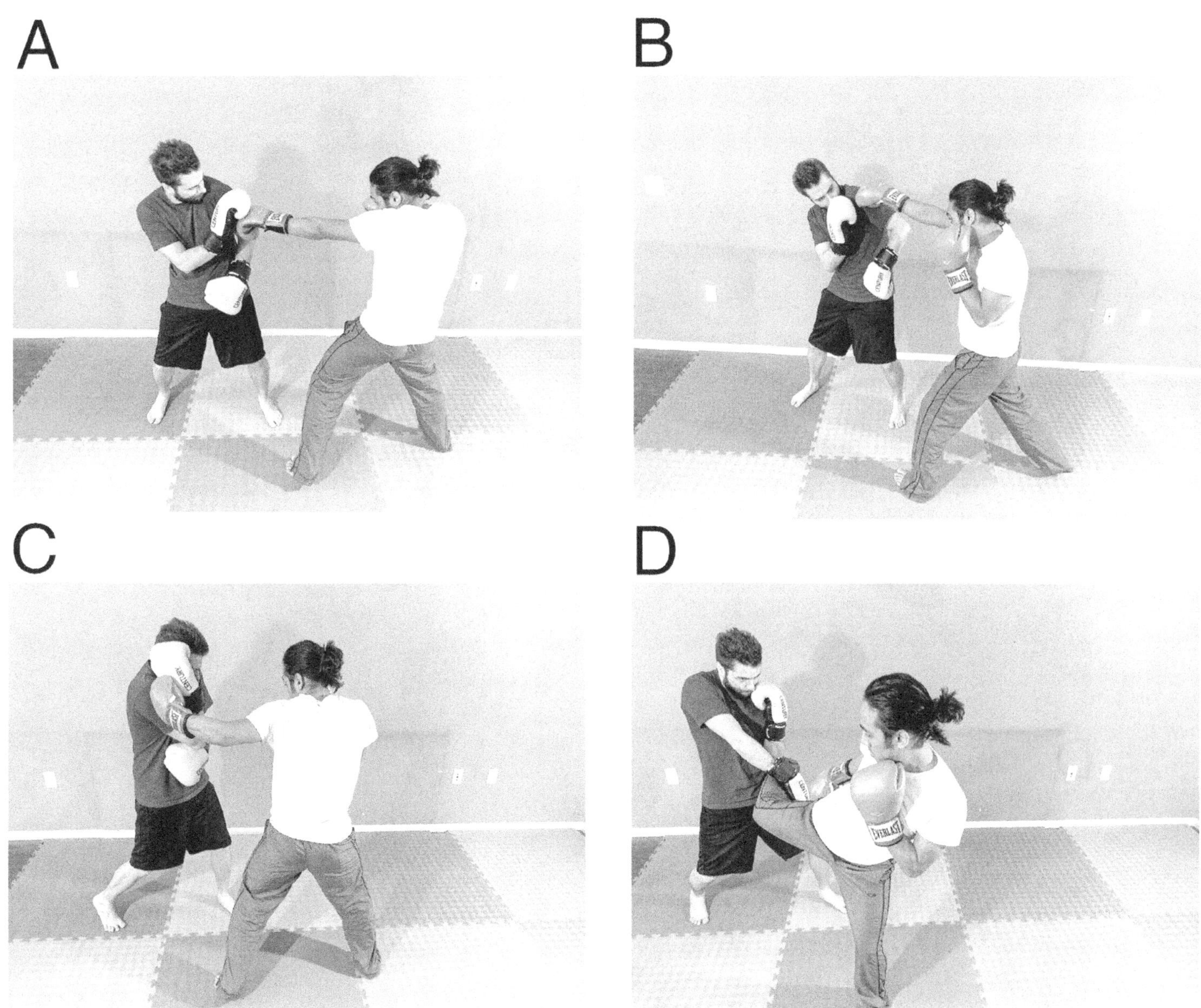

Drill 2

Now repeat the last drill, but have your partner only throw combinations where they double up on their attacks (Pics A to B). You may find this more difficult than usual to defend, and it is in fact a great way to disturb an opponent who uses the Philly Shell. This is because so much of the Philly Shell's ability to dispel the force of blows comes from Twisting, Pulling and Smothering. If you have already performed one of these movements and another shot is coming from the same side, you have no motion left to help absorb the impact.

One way you can defend against this is to Pivot away from the second strike (Pics C & D). This won't work as well if you're caught against the ropes, but it's a nice trick to have up your sleeve nonetheless.

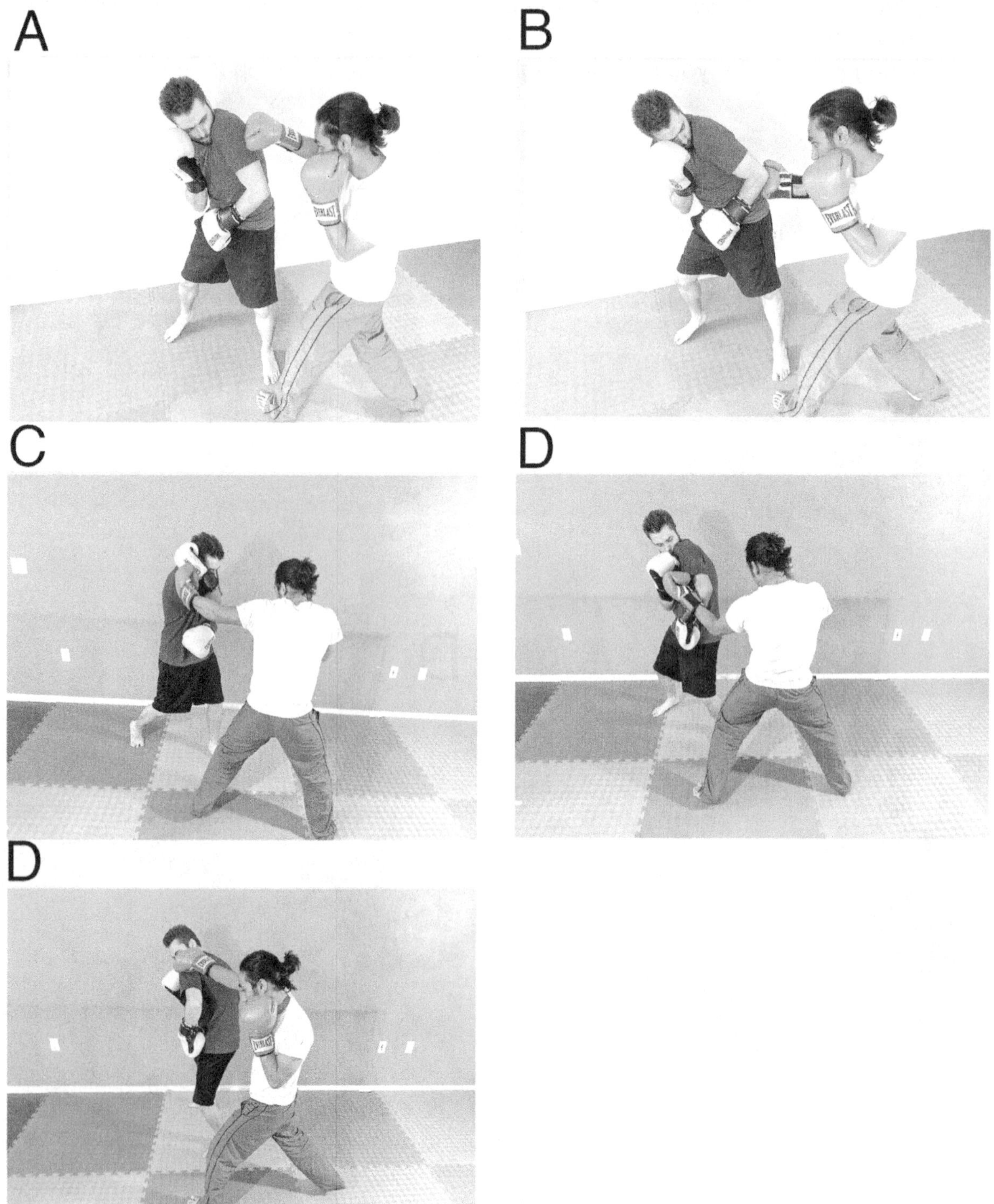

References – Philly Shell

Advanced Shoulder Rolls

In boxing, there is obviously no one better to study for the Philly Shell than Floyd Mayweather or James Toney. Mayweather's fight against Canelo and Toney's fight against Iran Barkley are great examples of how to defend multiple punches from multiple angles. Mayweather tends to use his Shell to keep at Mid to Long-Range while Toney prefers to use it to move in close and throw flurries. In MMA Dustin Poirier is the most high level fighter (and one of the only fighters) to use the Philly Shell. His fight against Max Holloway has plenty of Closed Stance and Open Stance examples.

Advanced Shoulder Rolls – Open Stance Considerations

James Toney vs Jason Robinson contains an incredible amount of quality examples. Toney Shoulder Rolls or Blocks against every kind of punch imaginable and ends the fight with a knockout. In MMA, Dustin Poirier's fight against Justin Gaethje has a lot of examples and is a great juxtaposition between High Guard and Philly Shell in MMA. Poirier tends to fight in an Open Stance, which may actually be a better choice in MMA. While using a Philly Shell in boxing is more effective in a Closed Stance since you can Roll against your opponent's Rear Hand attacks, in MMA this can put your Lead Leg in major danger of taking hard Rear Leg Roundhouse Kicks. By staying in an Open Stance in MMA, you can still Roll and have your shin pointed in the correct direction to immediately Check Rear Leg Roundhouses.

Lead Foot Placement

Mayweather vs Juan Manuel Marquez is a great fight to study the concept of keeping your Lead Foot aligned with your opponent's. Notice how Mayweather keeps himself closed off with his foot placement, forcing Marquez to step Inside to attack. When Marquez steps in, Mayweather uses Rolls or head movement and Pivots to regain his closed off position. Or he uses his new angle to counter with a sharp Overhand or Lead Hook.

When Mayweather attacks first, he takes the shortest step Inside possible. Notice the small step he uses to knock Marquez down with a Shovel Hook in round 2. He then immediately regains his safe Lead Foot position.

Vulnerabilities

Watch Adrien Broner's more recent fights to see a fighter who grasps many of the concepts of the Philly Shell but does not know some of the subtleties and therefore struggles against the highest level fighters. To see how the Philly Shell practitioner can struggle against multiple punches thrown from the same side, watch Mayweather vs Miguel Cotto. In the middle rounds, Cotto's tactic of doubling up his punches on the same side gave Mayweather a lot of trouble. Cotto also did a great job mixing up body and head shots.

Forearm Shield

Mayweather has used this technique to help control his opponent's Jab and used it as a feint to set up his Jab and Lead Hook (you may have noticed him doing so in his fight against Canelo). However, at Mid to Long-Range it is mostly useful in an Open Stance. That being said, Mayweather has used it successfully at Close-Range to gain space, lift his opponent's chin and set up punches.

Check out Mayweather vs Maidana to see how this one technique can change the course of a fight. Maidana smothered Mayweather, drove his head into his chin and doubled up on the same side. Mayweather eventually figured out he could use a Forearm Shield to keep distance. Because Maidana led with his head, Mayweather using a Forearm Shield was not considered an Elbow. Essentially, Maidana was driving himself into Mayweather's Guard. Mayweather also used Collar Ties and Overhooks, countering Maidana's wrestling with his own. All the same, it was the Forearm Shield that made the most difference by denying Maidana the Close-Range fight he wanted. Ali also used Forearm Shields to block body shots. You can see him do this a few times in his brief second bout against Liston.

Forearm Shield – Open Stance Considerations

Rigondeaux uses this technique to help control his opponent's Lead Hand so he can set up his tremendous Overhand Left. Pacquiao (though he does not fight from a Philly Shell) uses this technique in a different, sneakier way. Similar to how Mayweather will feint with this motion into a Jab, Pacman will throw his Jab elbow first, with a bent arm. This blocks any Counter-Jab that his opponent may throw. From there he will throw with more of a Backfist motion to the Rear Side of his opponent's face. This is pretty much the definition of Aggressive Defense, as Pacman's own punch protects him from his opponent's. You can watch any of his fights in the last 10 years to see this, but his knockdown of Thurman is a dramatic example.

While Mayweather will often choose to use a High Guard against Southpaws to better protect his Rear Side (since Open stances come with a more open Rear Side), he has also stuck with his Philly Shell defense on occasion. Check out Mayweather vs Sharmba Mitchell to see Mayweather use a Forearm Shield repeatedly to control his opponent's Lead Hand. Mayweather really starts exploiting this technique in round 2.

Inverse Elbow Block

James Toney used his elbow to block punches that would have otherwise sneaked over his shoulder when he Rolled. You can see examples in the fights recommended so far. In MMA, you can see Brian Ortega use this technique to defend against Frankie Edgar's Hooks before knocking him out into the first round with an Uppercut. Ortega used a Leverage Block (explained in the next section) to keep distance, and when that failed turned his elbow up to Inverse Elbow Block Edgars punches.

Inverse Elbow Block – Open Stance

Pernell Whitaker preferred to block punches with his elbow rather than Shoulder roll. Apparently he didn't want to risk a bruised shoulder ruining the force of his punches, while figuring that his forearm or elbow may hurt his opponent's hand. Manny Pacquiao will use this technique without the Rolling motion. Watch his fight vs Broner for examples.

Specialty Counter

Lomachenko uses this block in a different way. After throwing a Jab, he will roll his opponent's Return Hook off his elbow and then turn that same motion into a Lead Hook. Watch nearly any of his fights to see this, but you will probably need to slow the footage down to catch it.

Yin Yang Principle (Alternating Blocks)

Mayweather vs Oscar De La Hoya contains a lot of great examples of this principle. Oscar is skilled enough to get some good punches through, but Mayweather's defense holds up, and he's able to Roll and Block multi-punch combinations several times.

Long/Extended Guard

Long Guard is highly versatile. It can be used to move in quickly to clinch, or to stay at Long-Range and keep distance. The Long Guard leaves you more open and in exchange creates more offensive and defensive opportunities. The idea is to control distance through contact.

Manipulations, Frames & Redirects

An Extended Guard is all about establishing contact with your opponent as early and as often as possible. The plan is to disturb your opponent's balance, timing, and defense every step of the way. In doing so you will drain their energy by forcing them to constantly readjust and place them into compromising positions where it is easy to land strikes or takedowns. It's a good Guard for defensive and offensive styles alike.

Leverage Block

To Leverage Block, straighten your arm to intercept your opponent's strike (Pic A). Shoot your arm Inside of your opponent's strike in order to Block their attack (Pics B to D). Tighten your muscles and fully lock out your arm in order to create a strong barrier. The space in between your opponent's shoulder and head is usually the ideal spot to shoot for.

While you should aim to get your glove through you opponent's Guard (Pics A to B), sometimes your aim will be off. This is not a problem. If your glove hits your opponent's glove straight on or from the Outside, just continue locking out your arm to push your opponent's strike off course (Pics C to F).

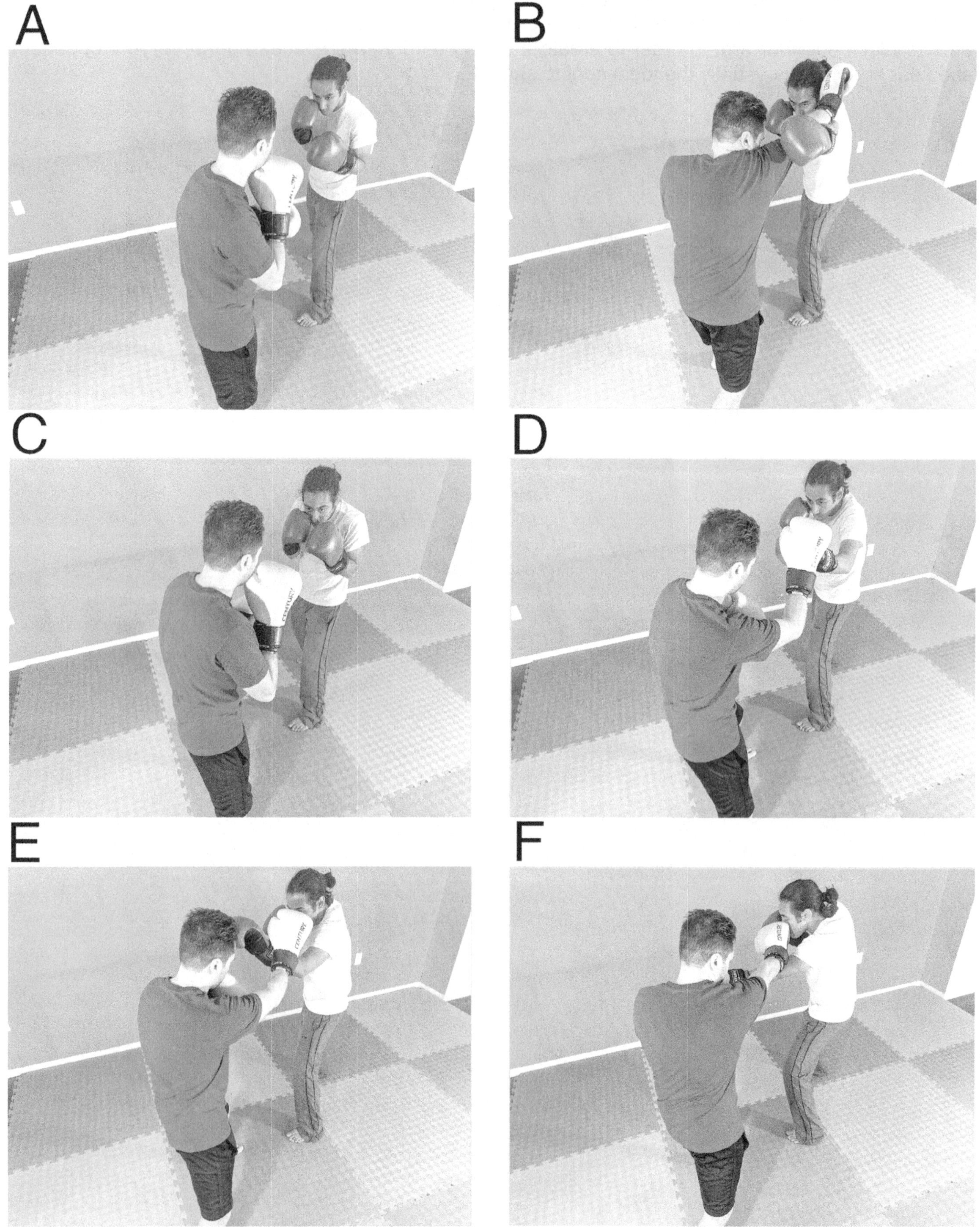

Sometimes your opponent's Hook Punch can threaten to sneak around your Leverage Block (Pics A to B). If for whatever reason your Leverage Block fails, you can still evade the punch. You may either Shoulder Roll by hunching your shoulder and leaning towards the side (Pic C), turn your elbow over to Vertical Elbow Block (Pic D), or push down to Frame against your opponent's chin (Pic E). Rear Leverage Blocks may require you to step back while doing so (Pics C & E) while Lead Leverage Blocks work best with a Pivot (shown on the next page as an example of how to use Leverage Blocks to Control your opponent's posture).

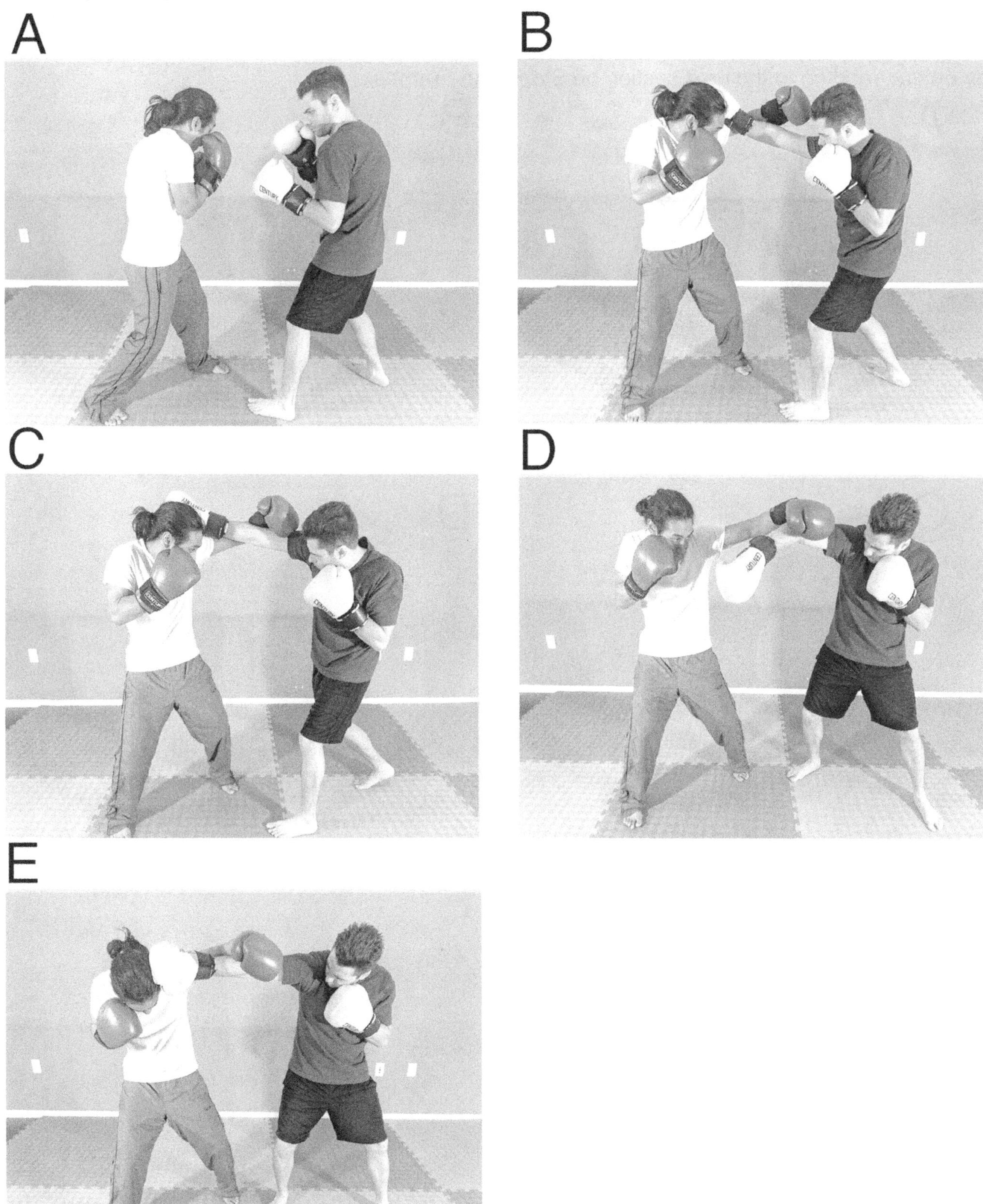

To Control

A successful Leverage Block can be used to either Frame or secure a hold. Frames can be used to control an opponent's posture while changing angles (note how the fighter Frames against his opponent's head and Pivots out in Pics A to C). To establish a hold, you may either turn your Leverage Block into a Collar Tie (D to F), or pull down on your opponent's Bicep near the crook of their elbow. Ali used a Leverage Block to Collar Tie several times in his famous fight against George Foreman, tiring him to the point of exhaustion. To learn even more clinching tactics that Ali used during that fight and many others, read on to the next section on Stops and Frames.

Drills

Drill 1A

Have your partner throw Jabs at you, and defend with an Inside Parry (Pics A). Each time, try to extend your Parry a little bit further up your partners Jab. Eventually, try for a full Leverage Block (Pics B to C). Once you are comfortable, have your partner counter your Leverage Block with a Hook or Body Hook, taking advantage of the openings that this block creates. Use footwork and Cover Blocks to defend yourself. This will teach you how to use the Leverage Block safely, without allowing an opponent to exploit the openings that it creates. Go one round and then switch which partner is attacking and defending. You may also throw Roundhouse Kicks along with Hooks if applicable.

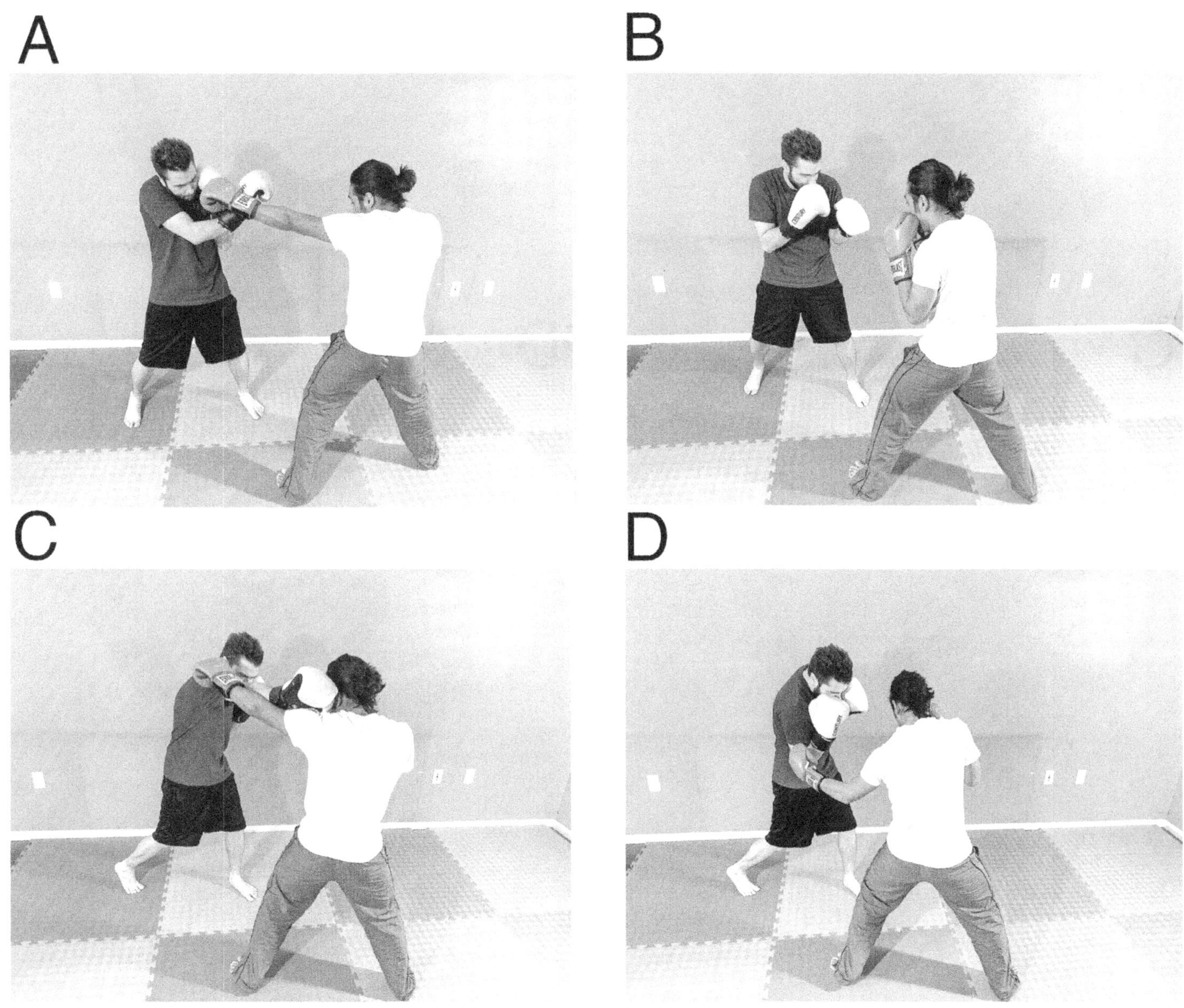

Drill 1B

Repeat the last drill, but now have your partner throw Jab-Cross combinations and Leverage Block his Cross (Pics A to C). Rather than Block his Return Hook, you can try to circle out with your arm still locked out (Pic D). Read on to the section on Stops and Frames to earn more about this technique.

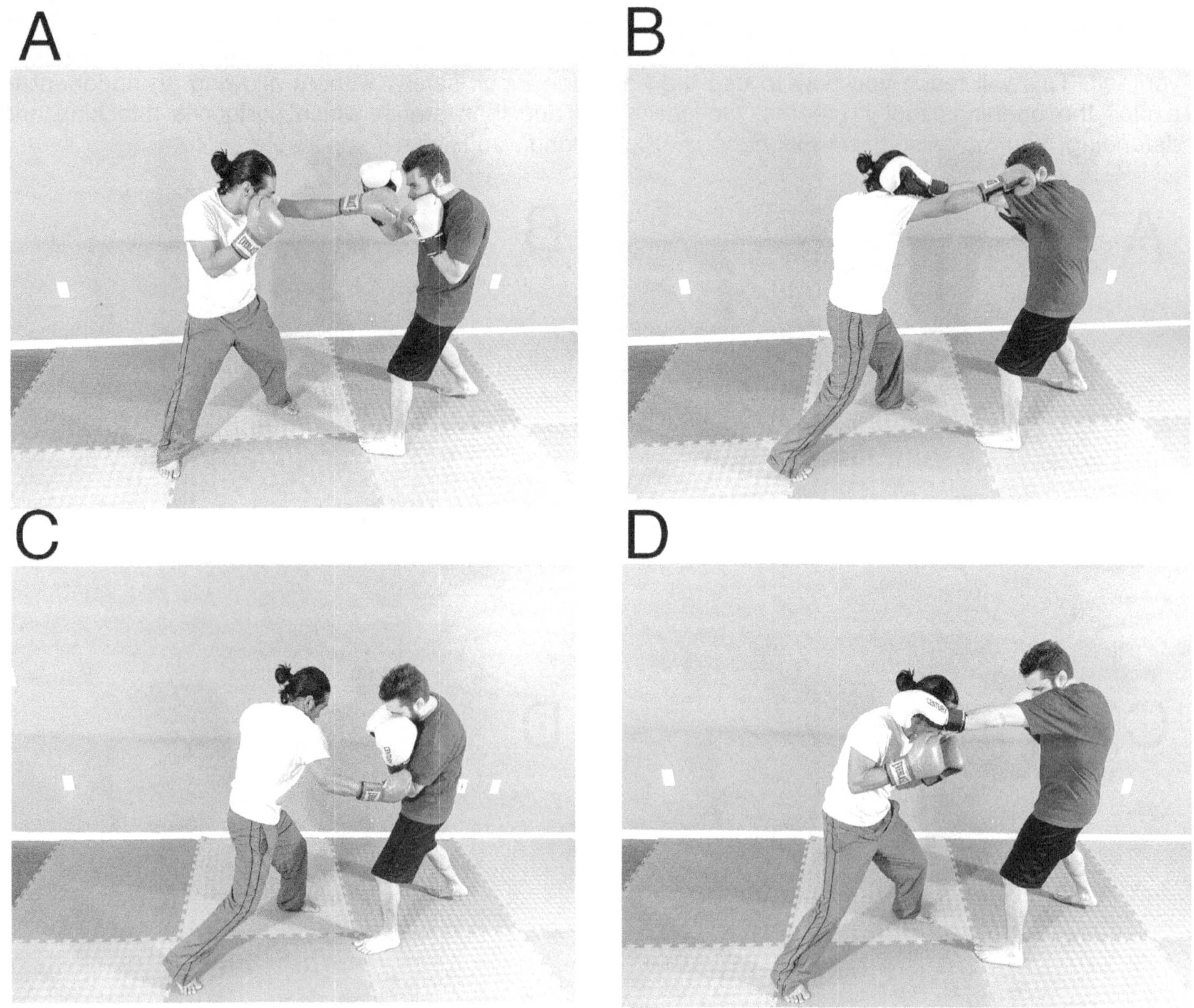

Drill 1C

Now have your partner throw Jabs and Crosses until he surprises you with a high or low Lead or Rear Hook (Pics A to B & C to D). Use your preferred defense against Straights but Leverage Block your partners Hooks. Make sure to hunch your shoulder and tuck your chin for an extra layer of protection. Pay attention to how using this technique against Hooks feels different than using it against Straights. Go one round and then switch which partner is attacking and defending.

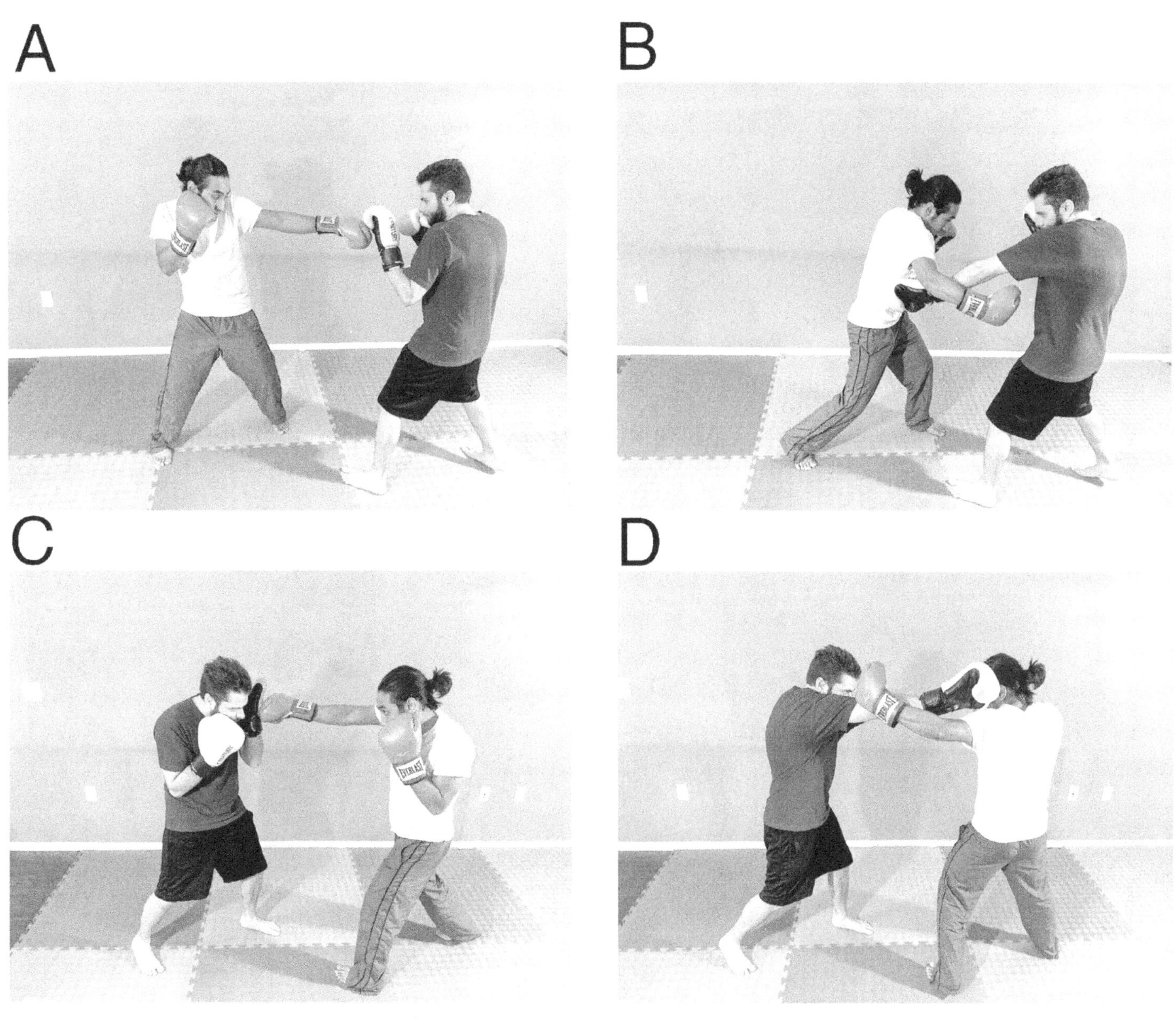

Stopping

To Stop an opponent's punch or takedown entry, forcefully push against their hand, bicep (Pic A), chest (Pic B), hip (Pic C), stomach (Pic D), head (Pic E) or shoulder (Pic F). From here, either reestablish your Guard or tie them up and control them. Pressing against your opponent's head or shoulder is particularly effective, as it usually destroys their balance, creating opportunities to counter.

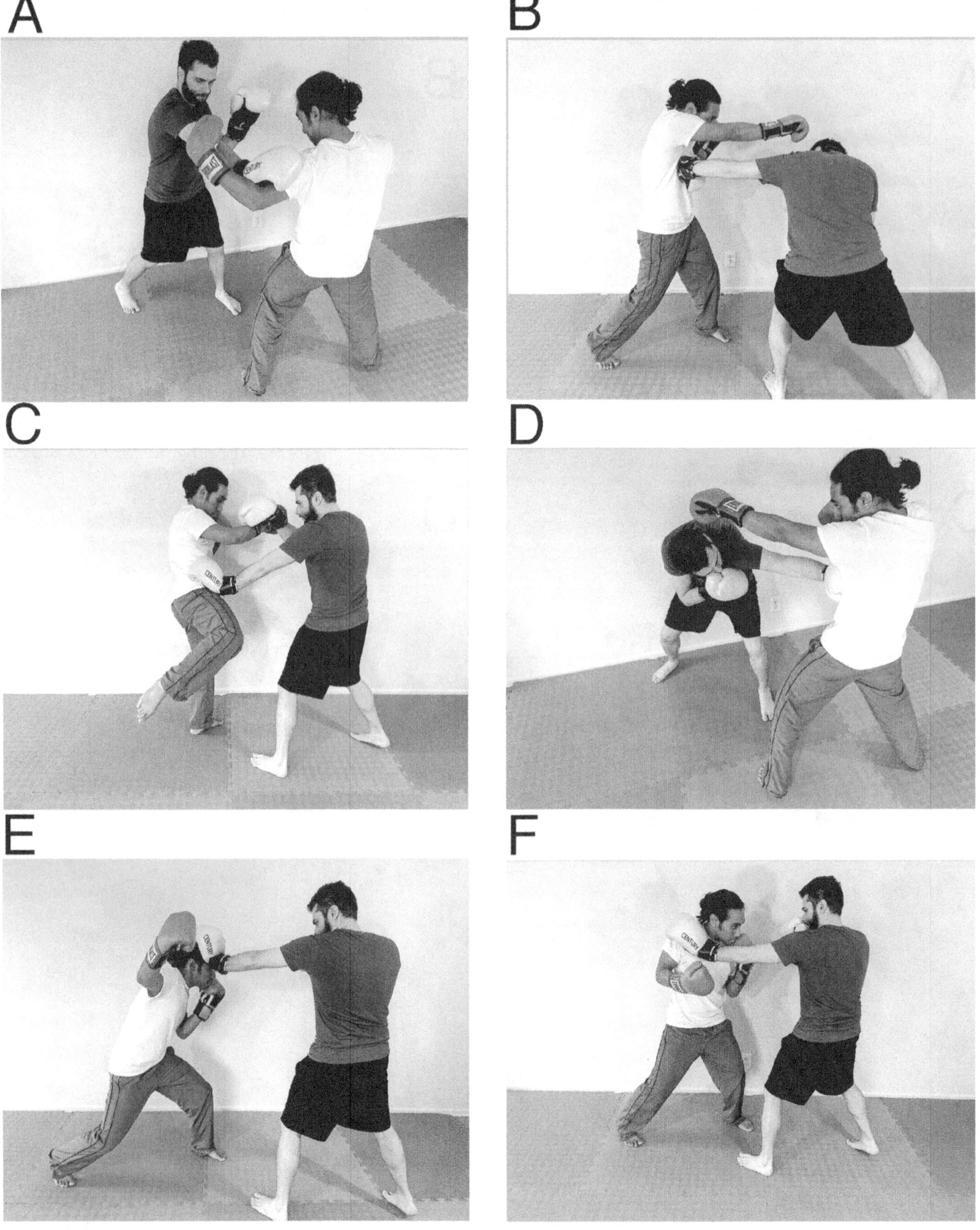

Drill

Drill 1

Have your partner throw single punches, and practice Stopping your partner's attack in its tracks (A to B). Immediately move away off angle to avoid a follow up attack. If you miss or your partner gets past your Stop, then turn it into a Leverage Guard (Pics B to C).

A

B

C

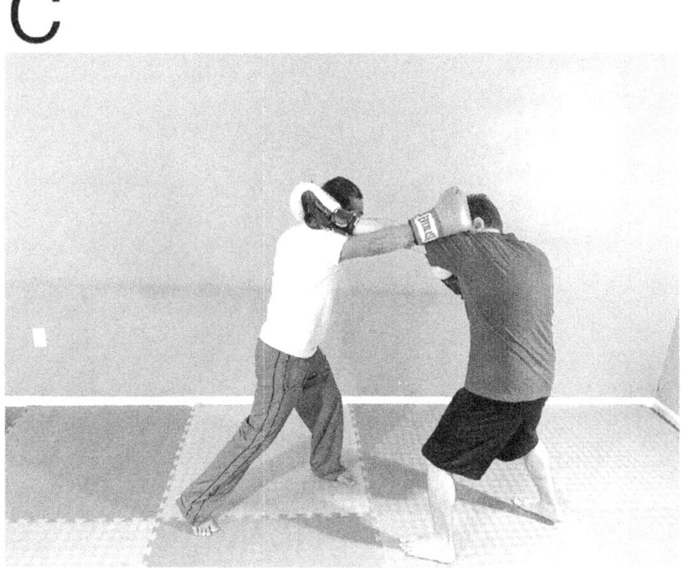

Drill 2

Have your partner throw Double Jabs and Jab-Cross combinations at you. At the opportune time, Leverage Block their attack and drive them into a knee. Just a reminder, drills are there to get the feel of technique so watch your power!

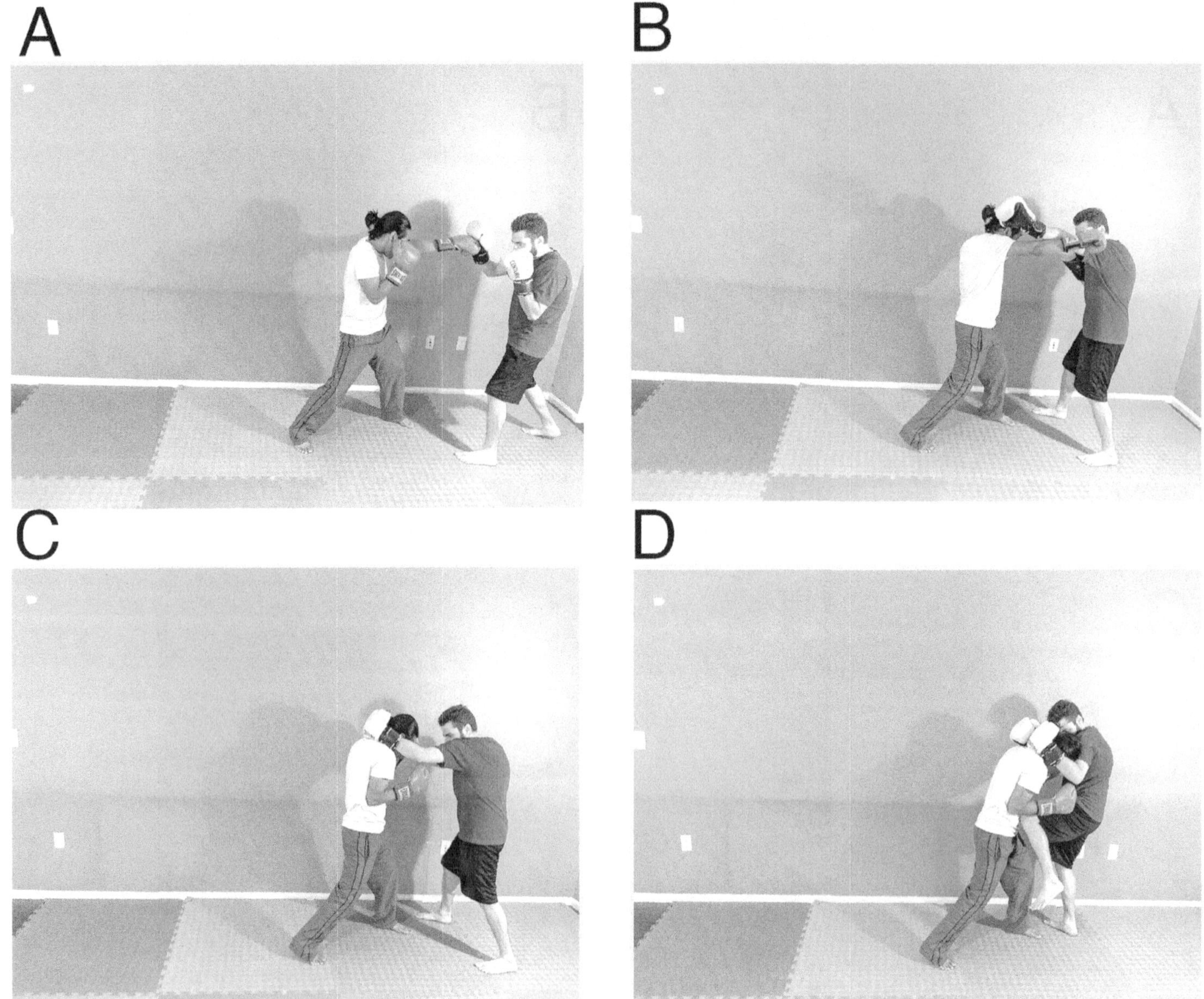

Framing

Once you have Stopped an opponent's attack or made contact in some other way, you may now take advantage of the contact you are making to manipulate their balance in order to create distance. This will set up new angles and move them into counters. You may be surprised at just how powerful Frames actually are. They have been used extensively in boxing, kickboxing, wrestling, BJJ and MMA.

Framing The Head

Framing against your opponent's head may not stop their strike, but it will undoubtable send it wildly off course. Pressing down while they try to crouch is a great way to stop their attempt as they try to work their way in. If you can turn their chin, then you have not only greatly disrupted their balance, but ruined their vision as well (Pic A).

There are several ways to Frame against an opponent's head. One of the most effective is to press against their temple or chin as you Pivot away (Pics B to D). This not only moves you off line from your opponent's attack, but also disturbs their balance and inhibits their vision. You can also push their head down as you do so, creating a great set up to deliver an Uppercut or Roundhouse. Or you can transition to clinching tactics via a Collar Tie.

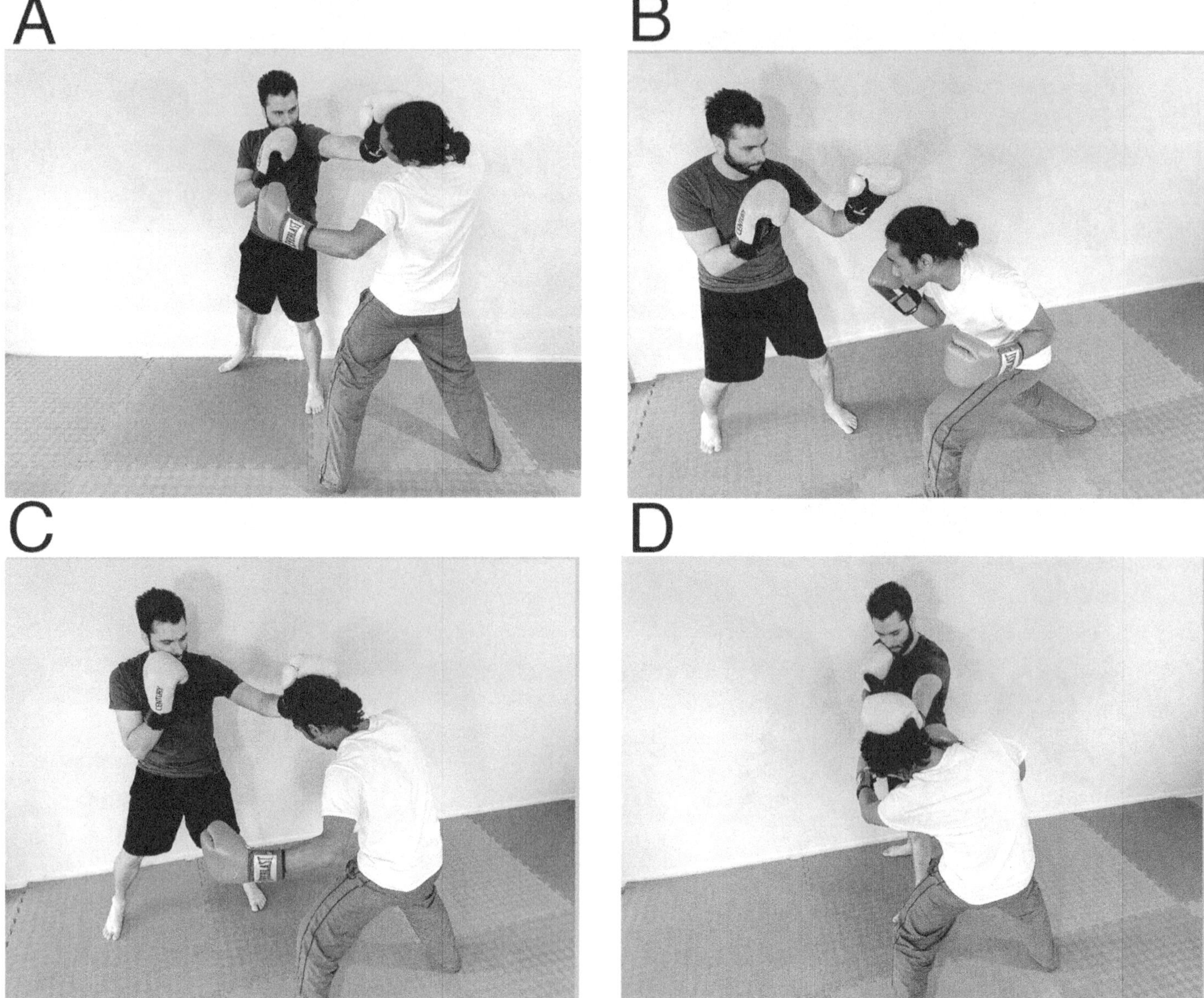

Framing is possible with your Rear Side as well, stepping Outside with your Back Foot and then stepping back or pivoting into Southpaw to set up a counter off of your new side. Or you may simply Duck under your opponent's Lead Hand, using your Rear Arm as a Leverage Block and Shoulder Rolling against any of your opponent's Lead Side Attacks (Pics A to E). This can also be useful in an Open Stance without the need to first Shift back.

Framing The Shoulder

The major benefit of Framing against your opponent's shoulder is that it can turn them, opening new lines of attack. Rather than using footwork or head movement to create angles from which you can penetrate your opponent's guard, you can simply turn them into the right position.

This technique set up one of the coolest knockdowns of all time; Thomas the Hitman Hearns' knock down of Sugar Ray Leonard in their second fight. Hearns let his Jab linger and then dragged it down to push against Leonard, turning him into his Rear Hand.

To set up a similar attack, turn your Jab or Leverage Guard into a Frame against your opponent's Rear Shoulder (Pics A to B). Step in hard, turning them and opening up their Lead Side (Pic C). Then take advantage of their newly sideways posture, hammering your Rear Hand into their Lead Side (Pic D).

Cross Framing The Head & Shoulder

This is a great tactic to stay safe while creating a superior angle. Boxers like Muhammad Ali used it to remain defensive while circling deep to the Inside, and Muay Thai fighters use it to set up kicks and knees. The mechanics work near the same as Framing off the same side, but you can now take a large step to the side rather than Pivot. Step off-angle towards your opponent's Rear Side (Pics A to B) and either pull to drive your opponent into an attack (Pic C) or push to create distance and attack off angle (Pics D to F).

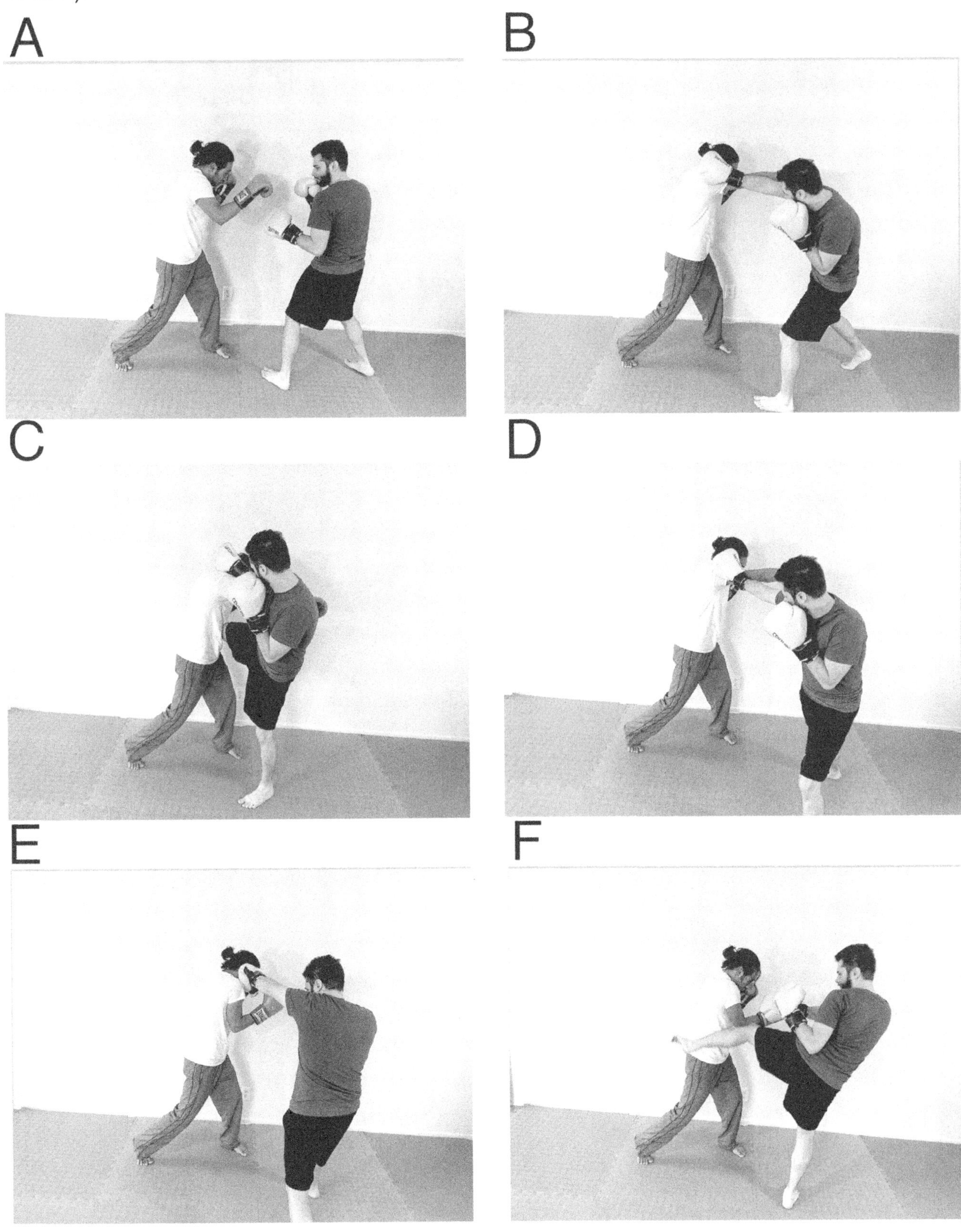

Open Stance Considerations

In an Open Stance, Frames can be used with footwork to defend against both hands. You can either Cross Frame with your Lead Hand and step Inside (Pics A to B) or Cross Frame with your Rear Hand and step Outside (Pics C to D). Look out for body shots! This technique works well but should not be used too regularly. Likewise, if your opponent tries this on you, body blows should convince them to give up on the tactic.

Framing The Guard

Sometimes your opponent will try to eat a few shots in order to close the distance, keeping their Guard tight and offering few openings. Luckily, Framing against their Guard will work whether they are attacking or not. If they're throwing a punch or trying to clinch, then you can Frame against their Guarding Arm as you defend their attack (Pics A to B). Once their attack is Stopped, you can Frame off of their Guarding Hand to change angles (Pic C). If they are just coming forward, then you can Frame against either arm or both.

A

B

C

The tactics outlined earlier on Framing the head and shoulder mostly all hold true to Framing against the Guard as well.

Open Stance Considerations

Another great technique is to throw a Jab at your opponent's Rear Hand, and then Frame against their Guard as you move in to close range (Pics A to C). From here, you can move Inside to throw a Rear Body Cross to Lead Hook combination like Pacman (Pic D), or move Outside to throw a Rear Uppercut like Lomachenko (Pics E to F).

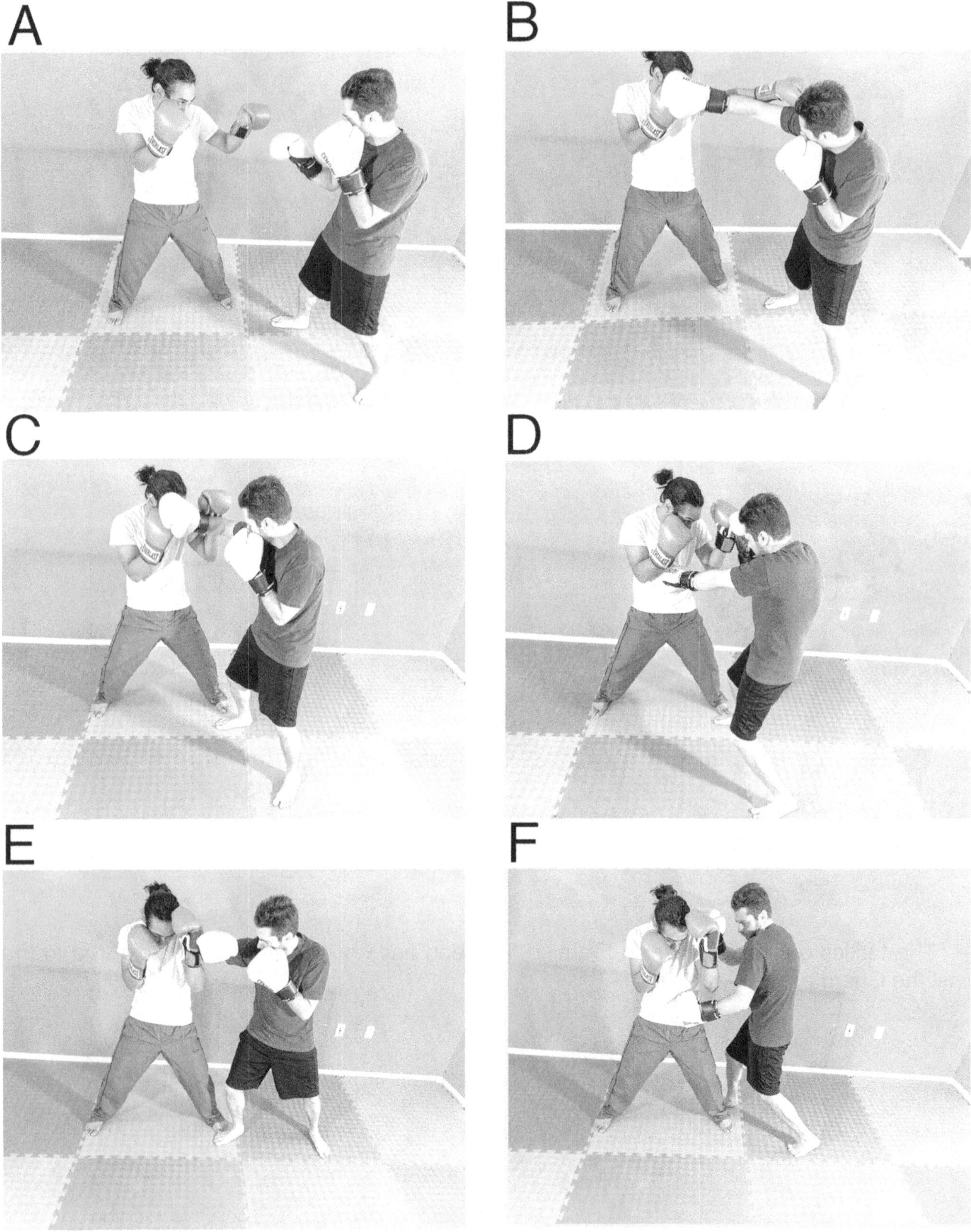

Framing With A Cross Block (Dracula Guard)

It's worth mentioning that some popular fighters use a hybrid of the Long Guard and the Cross Guard (Pics A & B). Buakaw is a big proponent of this. He Lead Hand Leverage Blocks and Frames to enter clinching range while his Rear Arm Cross Blocks. This is beneficial because it protects him from Uppercuts, Knees and Vertical Elbows (Pics C to D) in a way that Cover Blocks cannot. With this Guard it will be easier for the Rear Hand to Cross Frame but harder to establish a Frame on the same side (Pics E to F).

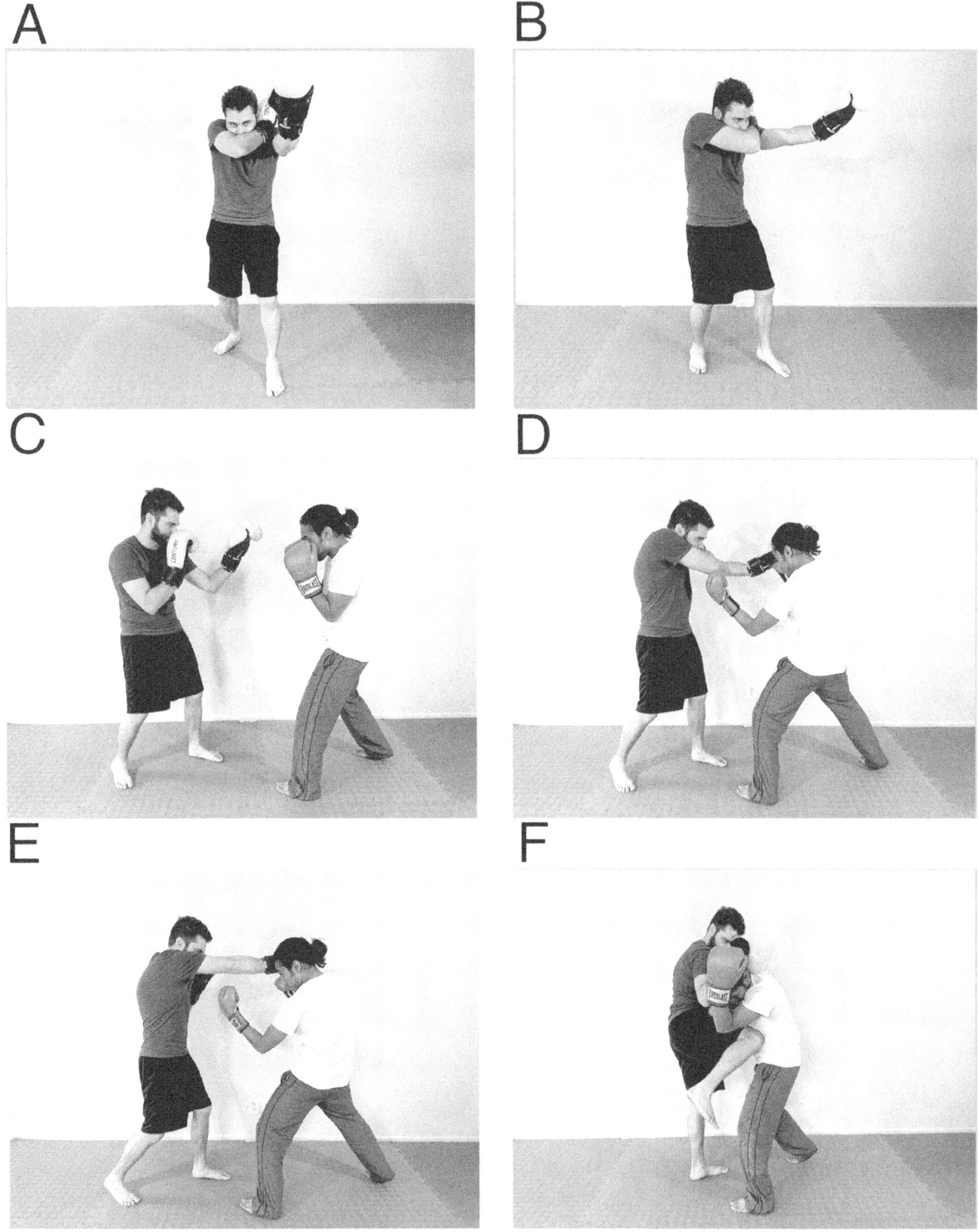

Framing With A Missed Punch

If your opponent Ducks under your Hook, you can use the retraction of your punch to Frame off of his head (Pics A to D). Lomachenko does this all the time, taking it one step further by leaning on his opponent and shuffling off angle (Pics D to E).

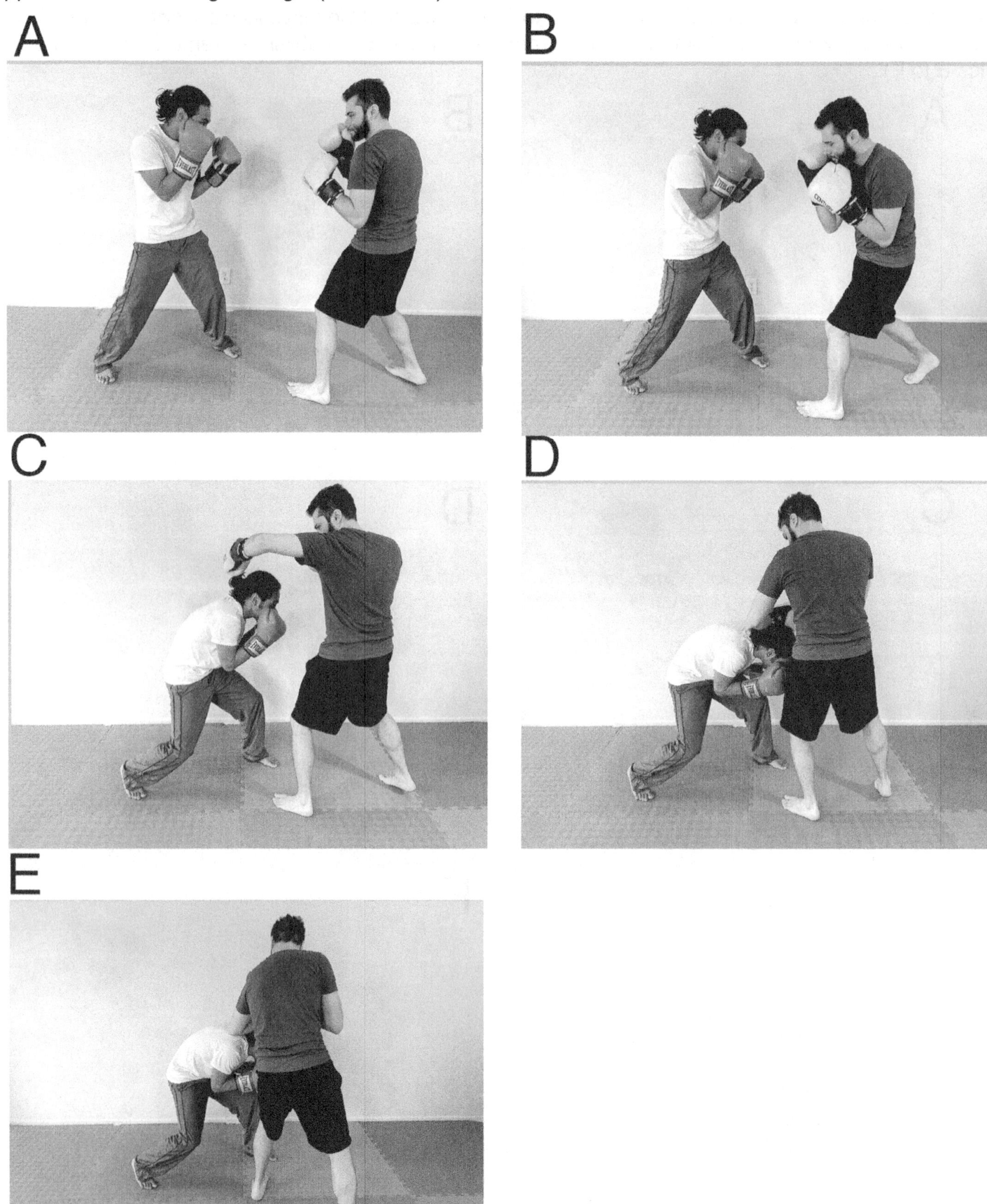

Open Stance Considerations

This technique works even better in an Open Stance, as it allows you to take a superior Outside Foot Position (Pics A to F). This is truly using your opponent's own defense against them.

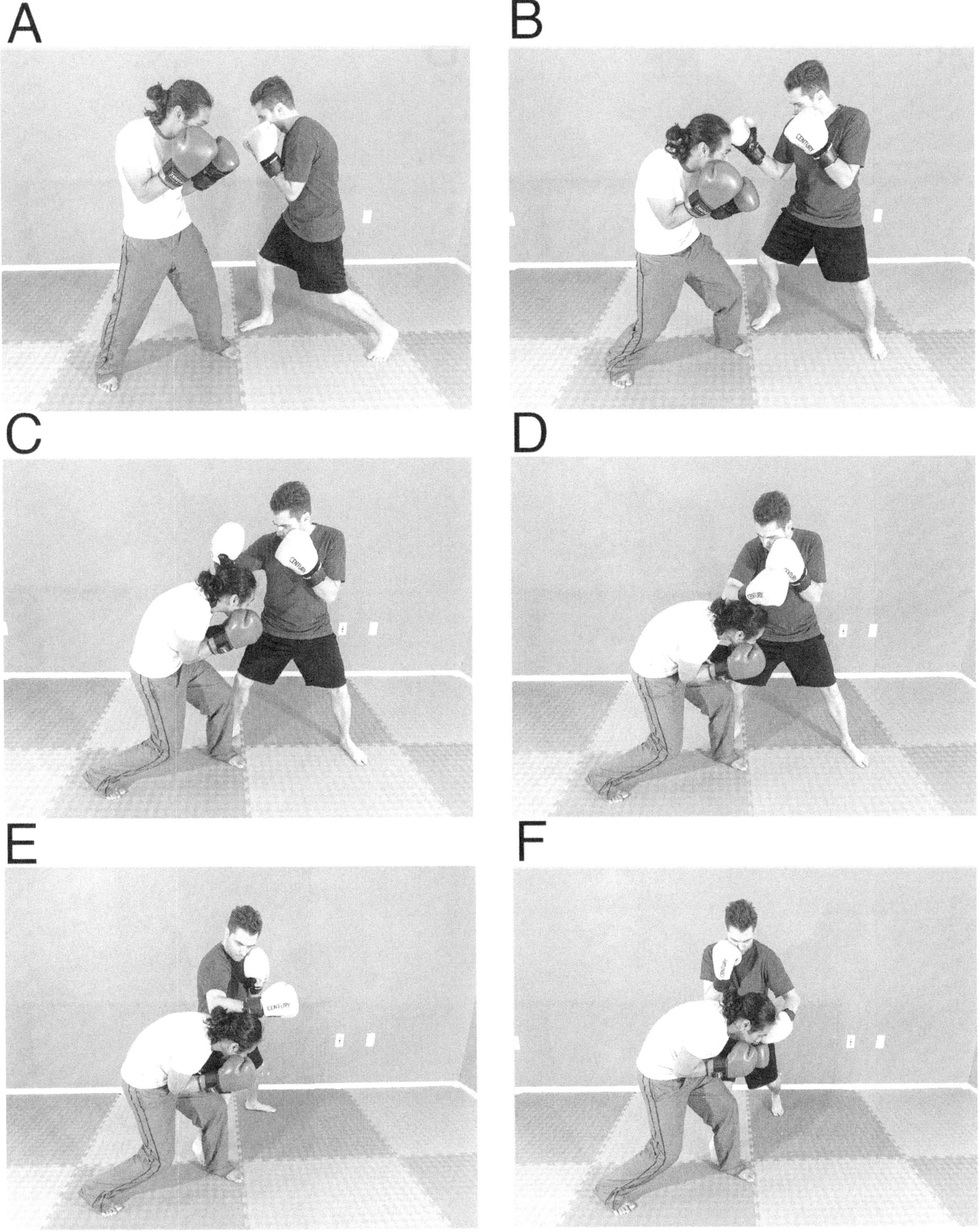

Knee Frame

Pin your knee across your opponent's legs, stifling their ability to throw kicks (Pics A to C). This one is Muay Thai or Kickboxing specific, and pretty specialized even then as you are still open to throws. This is a temporary measure but may be good to know if no other option presents itself. It's undoubtedly better than getting Kneed.

A

B

C

Drills

Drill 1

Have your partner keep a tight Guard and try to get close enough to touch their head to you. Keep him away by Framing (A to D). You may back up, but you may not circle or angle out unless your hand is Framing against your partner. As soon as your Frame is broken you are only allowed to go backwards. Go one round and then switch who is attacking and who is defending.

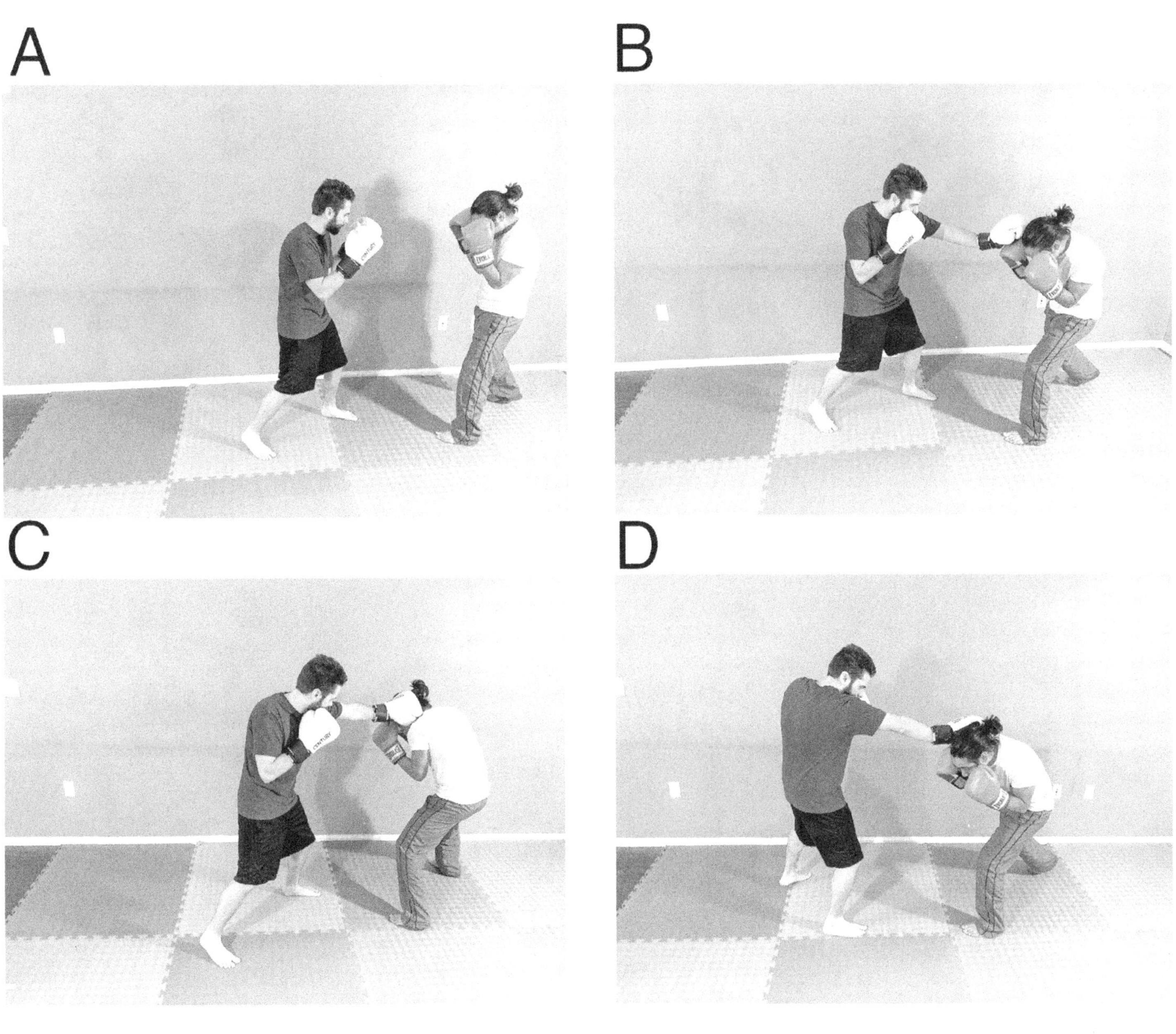

Drill 2

Have your partner throw straight punches at you. When you feel the time is right, Leverage Block and then Frame against your partner to move off angle before Returning a counter (Pics A to D). Remember that you can both push, as shown in the pictures below, or pull, as shown previously. Go one round and then switch who is attacking and who is defending.

Drill 3

Repeat the last drill using Cross Frames (Pics A to D). Go one round and then switch who is attacking and who is defending.

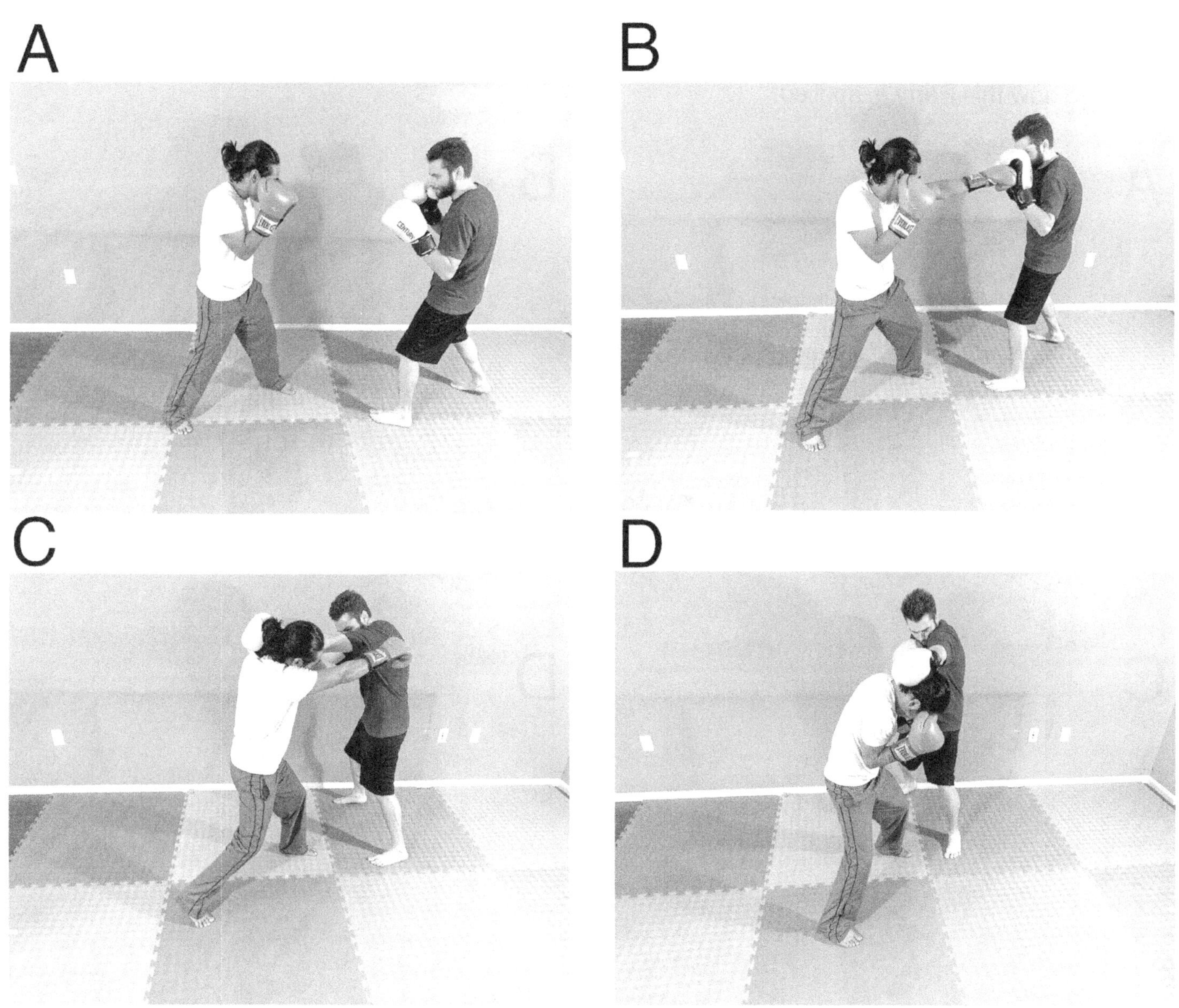

Circular Parry

Stop or Leverage Guard your opponent's attack (Pics A to B). Now, circle your extended arm to the Inside and then complete the circle, coming back to Guard (Pics C to D). In a closed stance, you may Parry Lead Side attacks.

Now that you know all of the places to aim when Framing and the techniques and counters that come with them, you can experiment with a highly advanced technique used by Vasyl Lomachenko. One of the greatest Muay Thai fighters of the Golden Age, Samart Payakaroon, also used this tactic. Read on to see how this Parry is applied.

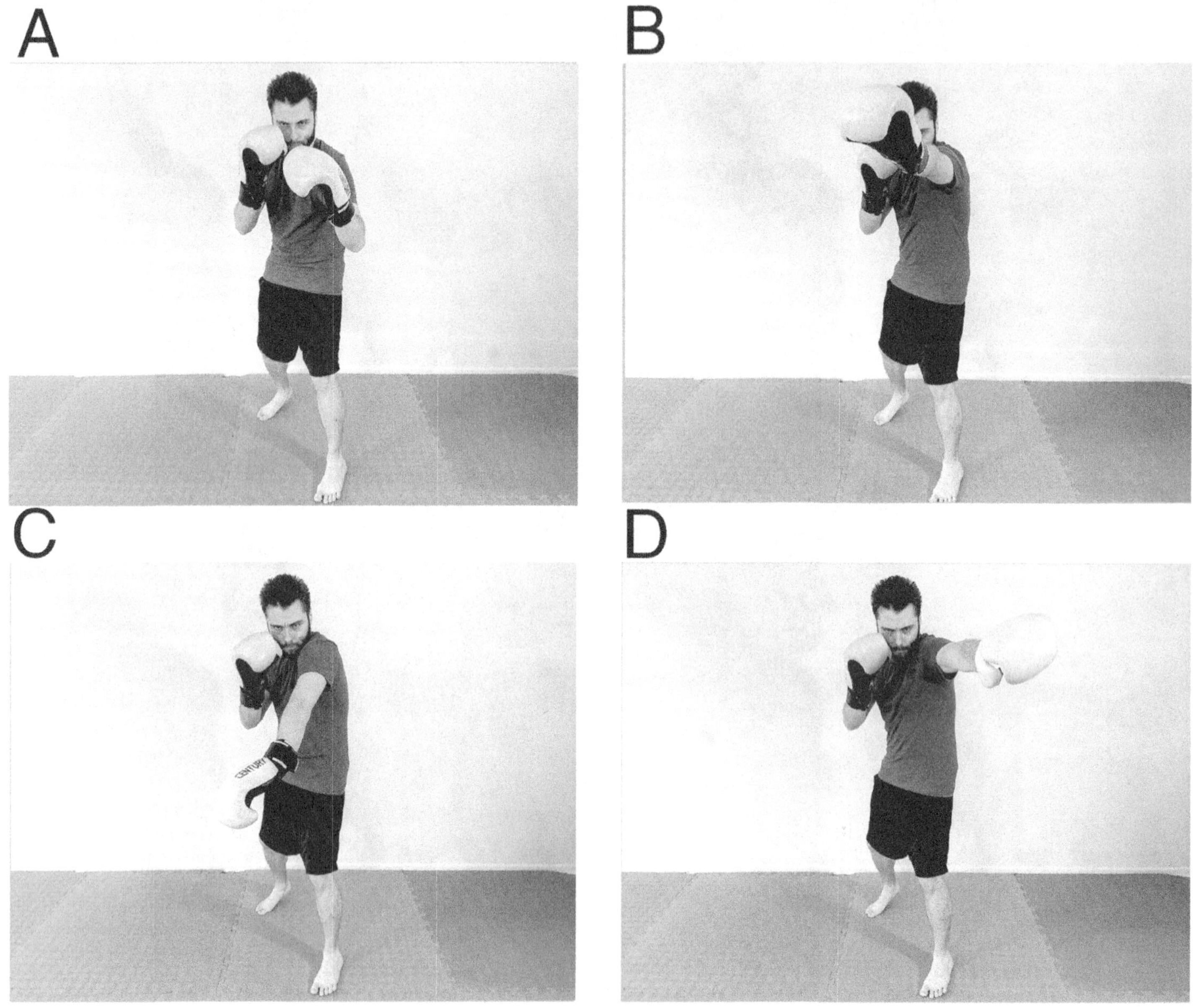

***Disengage To Cross Parry**

This works best in an Open Stance (shown on next page), but you can try it out in a Closed position if you like. After throwing out a successful Leverage Block against your opponent's Lead Hook or Jab (Pic A), your opponent next tries to throw an attack off their Rear Side (Pic B). Use the extension of your arm to reach across and Parry the strike (Pics C to D). You may wish to step back or Shift back into Southpaw to clear space for your Circular Parry (Pics E to F).

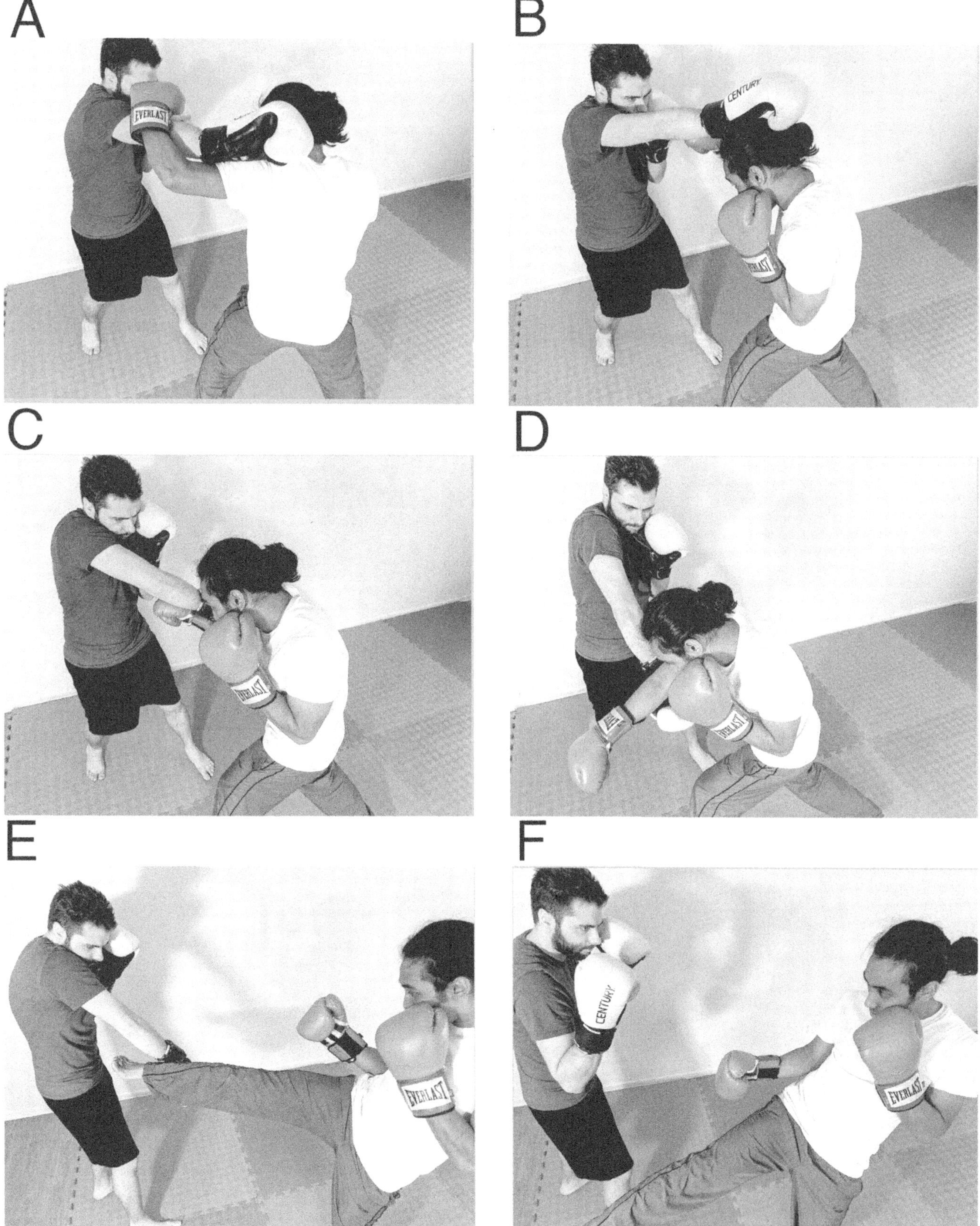

Open Stance Considerations

Circular Parries are best used in an Open Stance with your Lead arm. Lomachenko has used it many times to Parry his opponent's Crosses off of his Jab (Pics A to D), and Samart has done the same to Cross Parry kicks off of his Frames and Jab (Pics E to F).

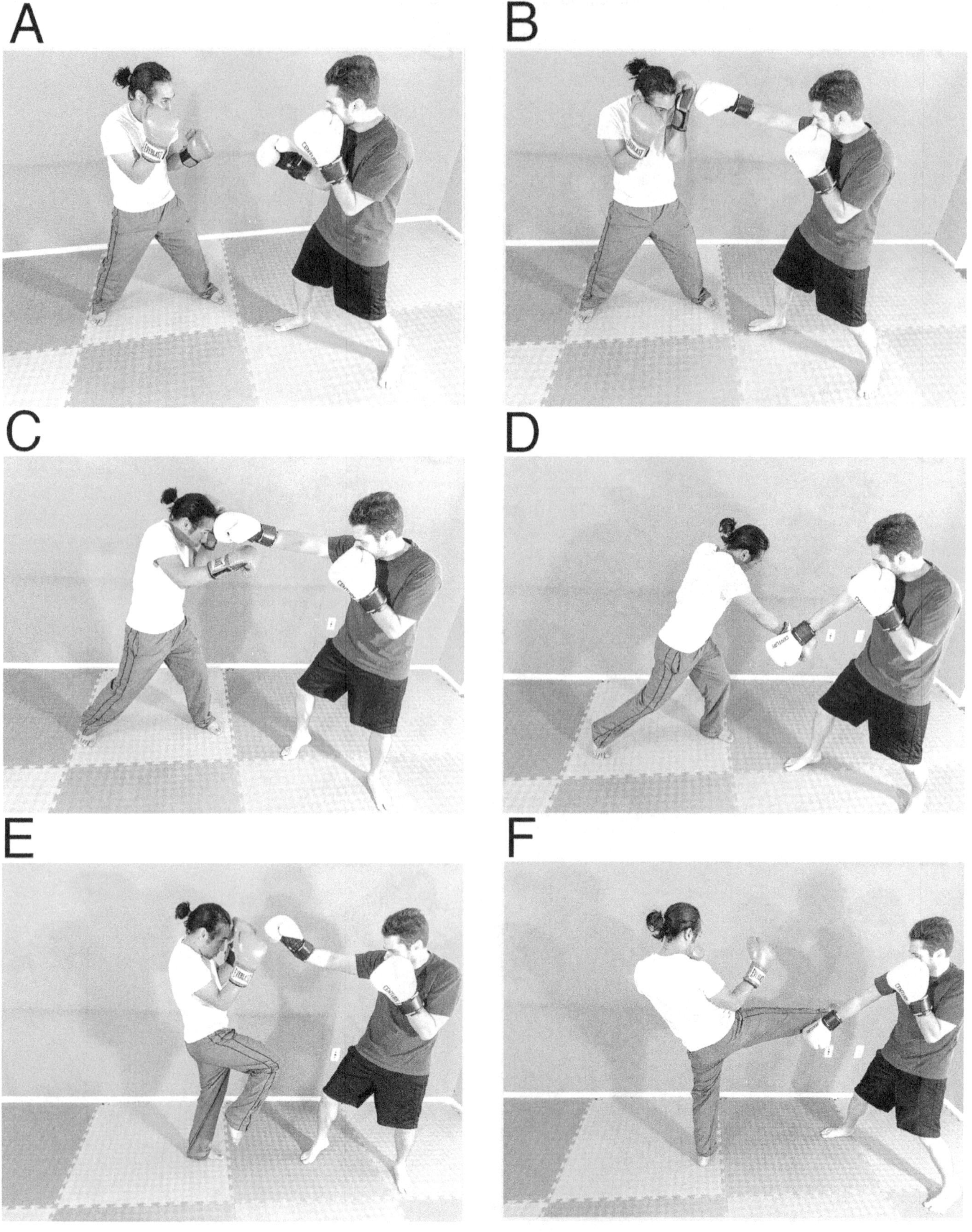

Concept: Hand Fighting

Hand Fighting, the concept of constantly pestering your opponent's hands with your own in order to gain a superior position from which to attack, is used today by such fighters as Daniel Cormier. But it has also long been prevalent in boxing, by fighters such as Jack Johnson and George Foreman. Hand fighting is an important element of wrestling. In striking sports, especially those that encourage dirty boxing or wrestling, it can be used in a number of unique and creative ways. Some of the techniques are listed below, along with many other Guard manipulations. Most if not all of these techniques can be used in boxing, kickboxing and MMA. If a Knee, Round Kick or Elbow is shown in the demonstrations below, it should be possible to substitute those in for punches and vice versa. Of course the boxing gloves will always make these techniques more difficult to pull off.

Take Inside Position To Clinch

As your opponent reaches out to Trap, punch, Frame or secure a hold, take the opportunity to glide a hand Inside of theirs to secure a hold on the back of his neck. At the same time, Parry your opponent's other hand so that it is not a threat (Pics A to B). Now pull your opponent into a Collar Tie, making sure to control their arm on the opposite side (Pic C).

A

B

C

Cross Frame & Parry

As your opponent reaches out to Trap, punch, Frame or secure a hold, take the opportunity to Parry one of his outstretched hands. At near the same time, take advantage of your opponent's inability to defend themselves on that side by Cross Framing and then moving off angle to attack (Pics A to C & D to F).

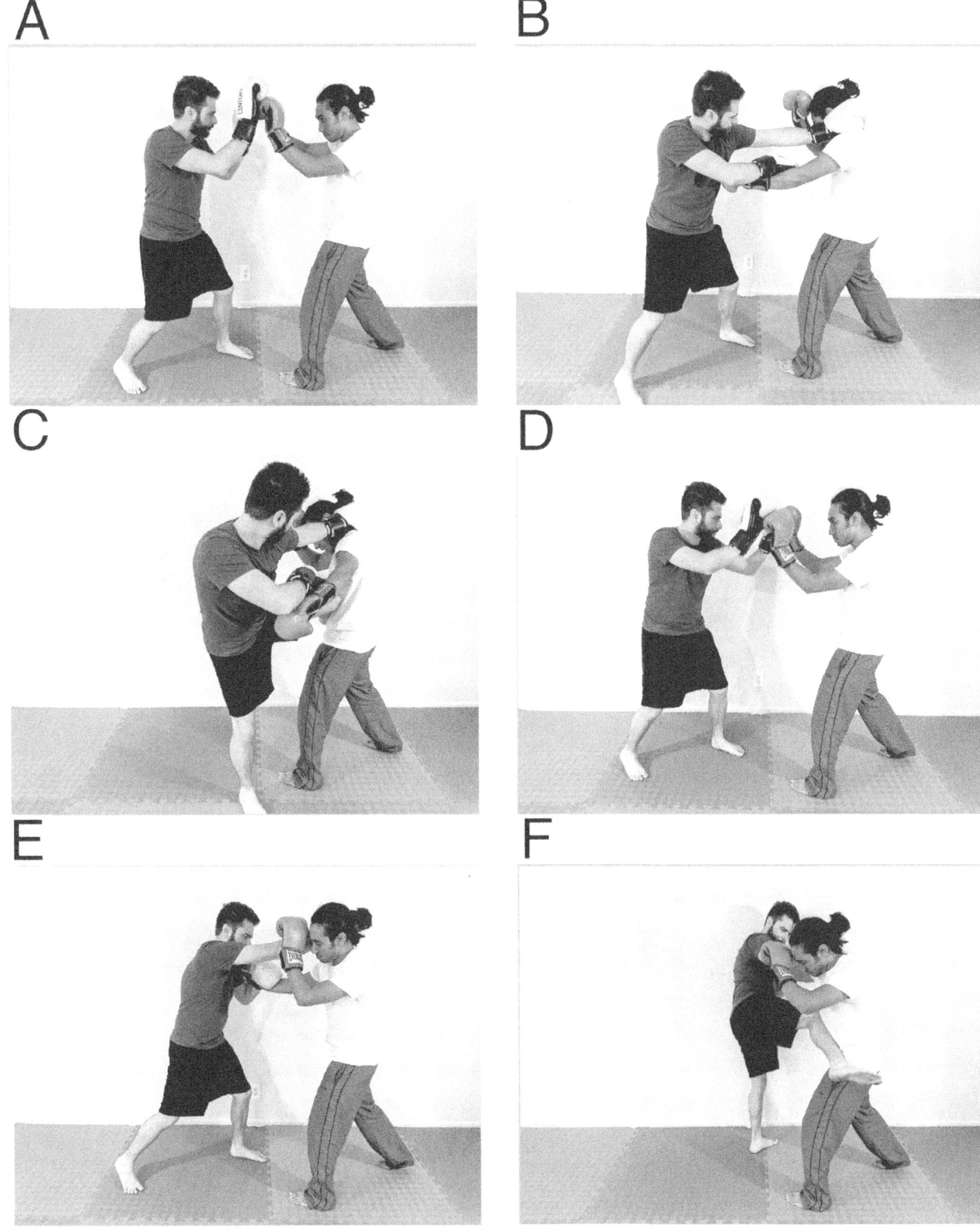

Parry/Trap & Attack Off The Same Side & Opposite Side

As your opponent reaches out to Trap, Frame or secure a hold, take the opportunity to Parry or Trap one of their arms and throw an Elbow off the same side (Pics A to C). Alternatively, you can Parry or Trap with one arm and then use it to pull your opponent into an Elbow with the other (Pics D to F). If you want to drill these techniques, it will be far safer to practice with Hooks or Uppercuts instead. Or you can stop your Elbows before they land. Whichever you choose, remember to respect your partner by going light.

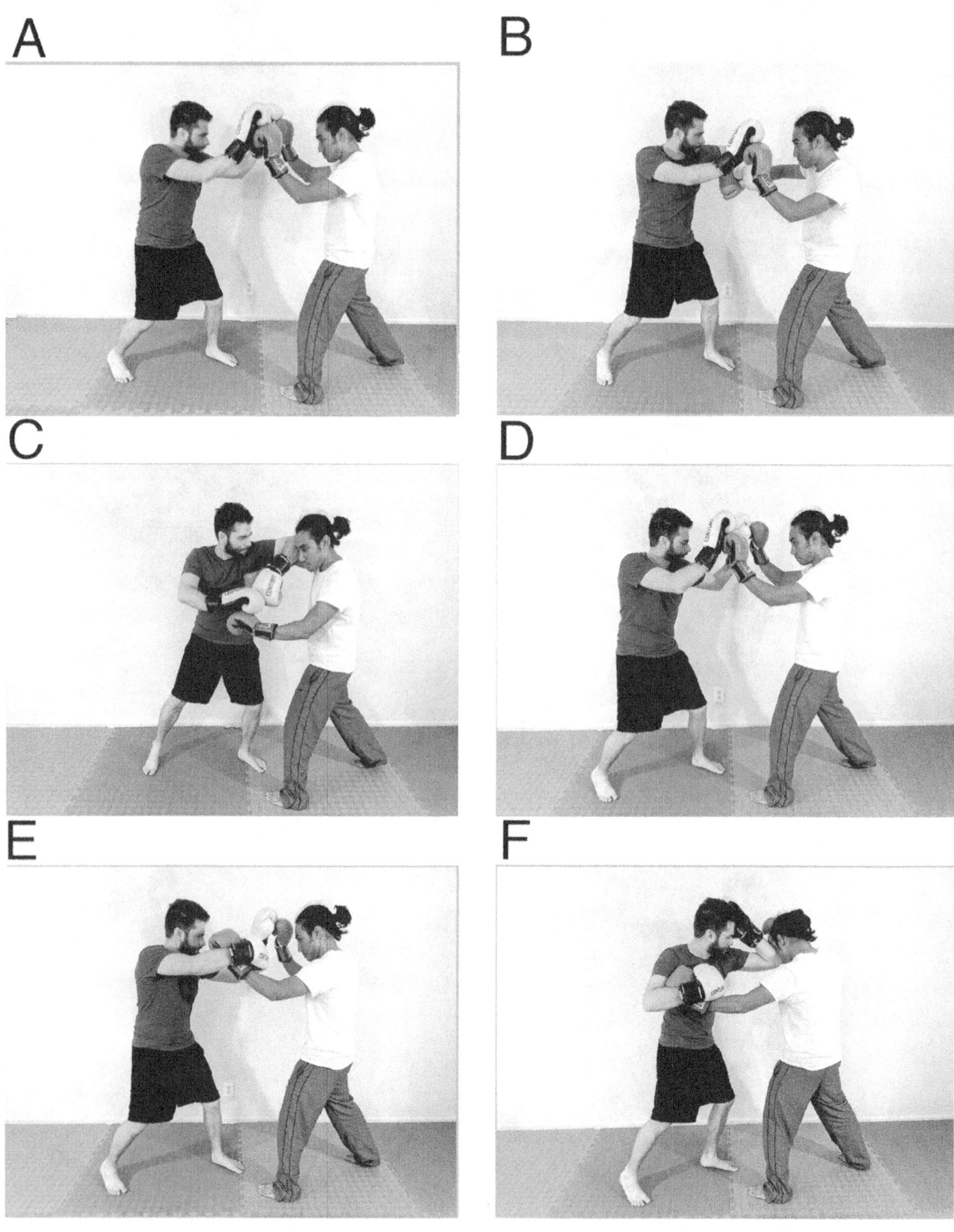

Open Stance Considerations – Lead Hand Traps

In an Open Stance most of your attention will be directed towards controlling your opponent's Lead Arm. There are definitely instances where you will hand fight with both hands, and all of the techniques shown before should still work well. However, at Mid to Long-Range your opponent's Lead Hand will be the main obstacle that stops you from clinching, securing dominant foot positions and landing strikes to their Lead Side.

One tactic is to use the techniques shown so far on your opponent's Lead Hand, and move Outside as you do so (Pics A to D). This angle should make their Rear Hand a now issue. From this position you can move Outside to strike, takedown, or lock your opponent in several kinds of holds).

Another tactic is to move Inside and square up your stance, often Shifting into Orthodox from Southpaw or vice versa. In this case you have reached basically the same position as being at close range in a Closed Stance. Make sure to control your opponent's hands as you step in (Pics E to F).

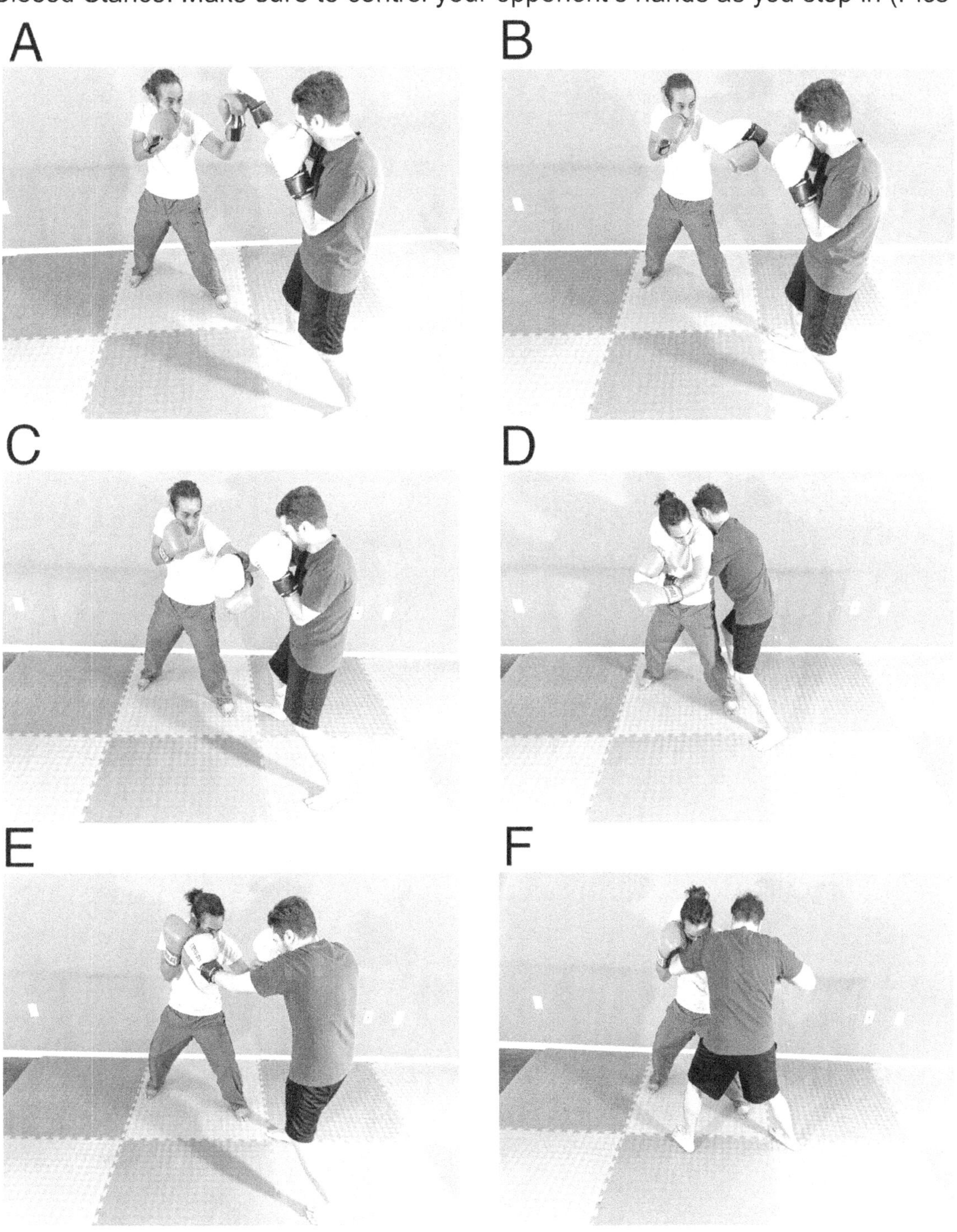

Ankle Catch

Open your Guard and wrap your arm around your opponent's incoming kick. You may place either hand on top. If your opponent's kick is not entirely extended by the time you Catch it, turn your body and step away to move the kick past you rather than take the impact. It is more important than normal to breath out and tense your muscles upon contact. Some talented fighters can also Ankle Catch with one hand and throw an Intercepting Counter with the other. Check the References section for examples.

A

B

C

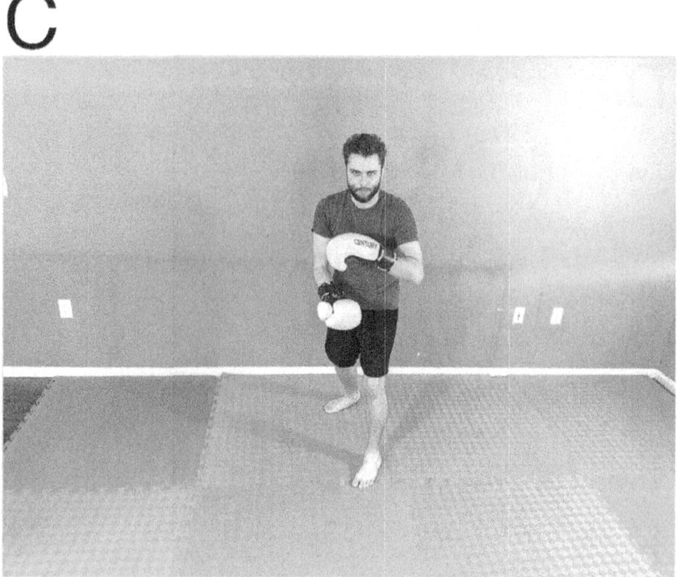

This is one of the best ways to discourage kicks. In MMA and many kickboxing organizations, you can punch, trip, throw or sweep you opponent after catching the kick (Pics A to D) .

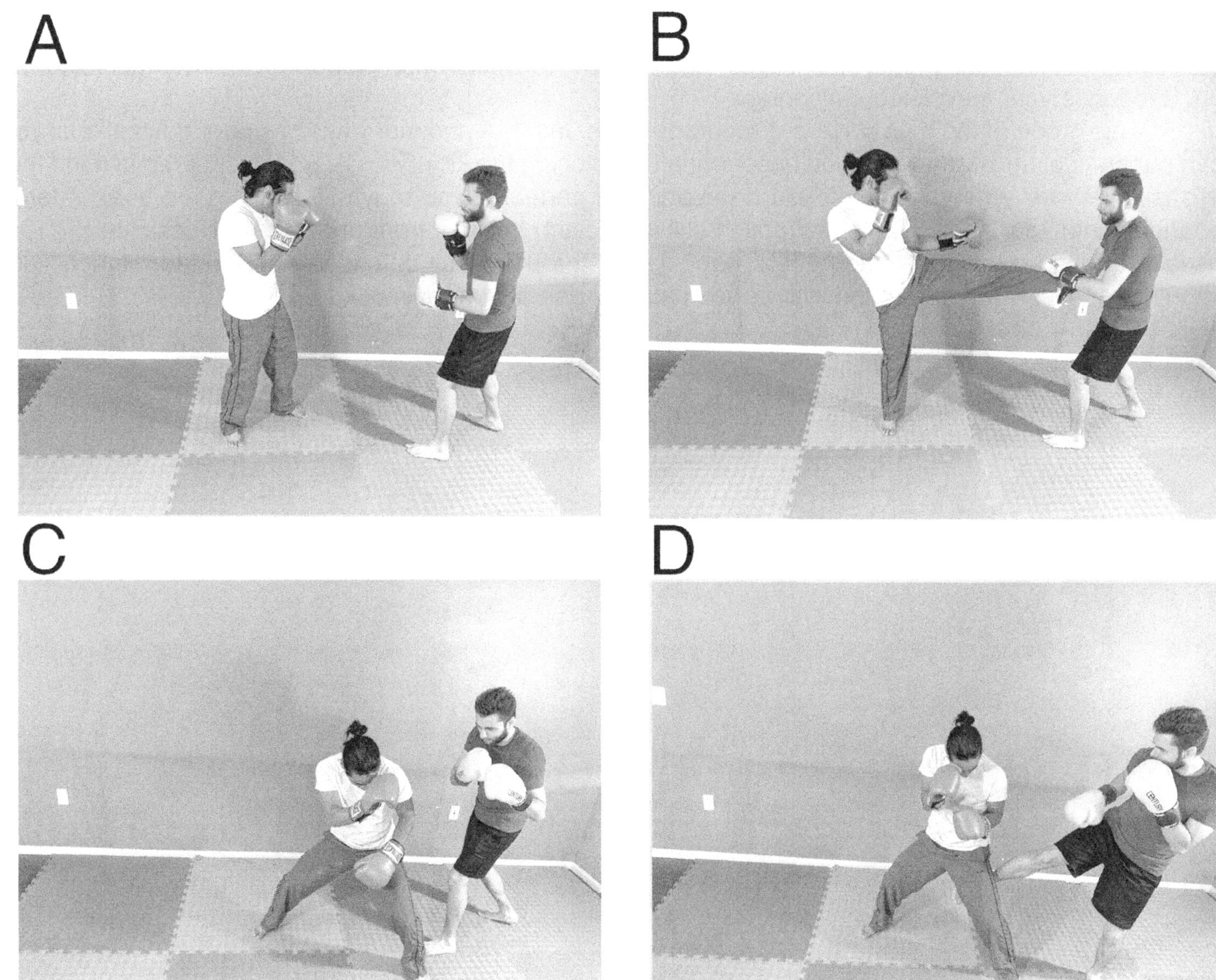

Leg Catch

Open your Guard and wrap your arm around your opponent's incoming kick. Turn your body and step away to soften the impact against your body (Pics A to B). It is more important than normal to breath out and tense your muscles upon contact.

This is one of the best ways to discourage kicks. In MMA and many kickboxing organizations, you can punch, trip, throw or sweep you opponent after catching the kick (Pic C). However, keep in mind that this is a very risky move. Even if you do everything perfectly, you may still feel a good deal of force pounding into your ribs. A far riskier option still is to catch the kick from underneath (Pics E to F). This usually only ever happens after a kick has slipped through your defenses and landed. Hunch your shoulder and lean away from the kick as you catch it. Use at your own risk.

Specialty Counter

Lerdsila, one of the slickest kickboxers to ever live, evades sweeps and kicks in this compromised position by hopping over them (Pics A to D). He then brings his weight down on his opponent as he lands to get out of the Ankle Catch (Pic D). From there, he takes advantage of his opponent's confusion to attack. If you use this technique, it's best to secure a Collar Tie before-hand. This will help you jump and help you bring your weight down as well.

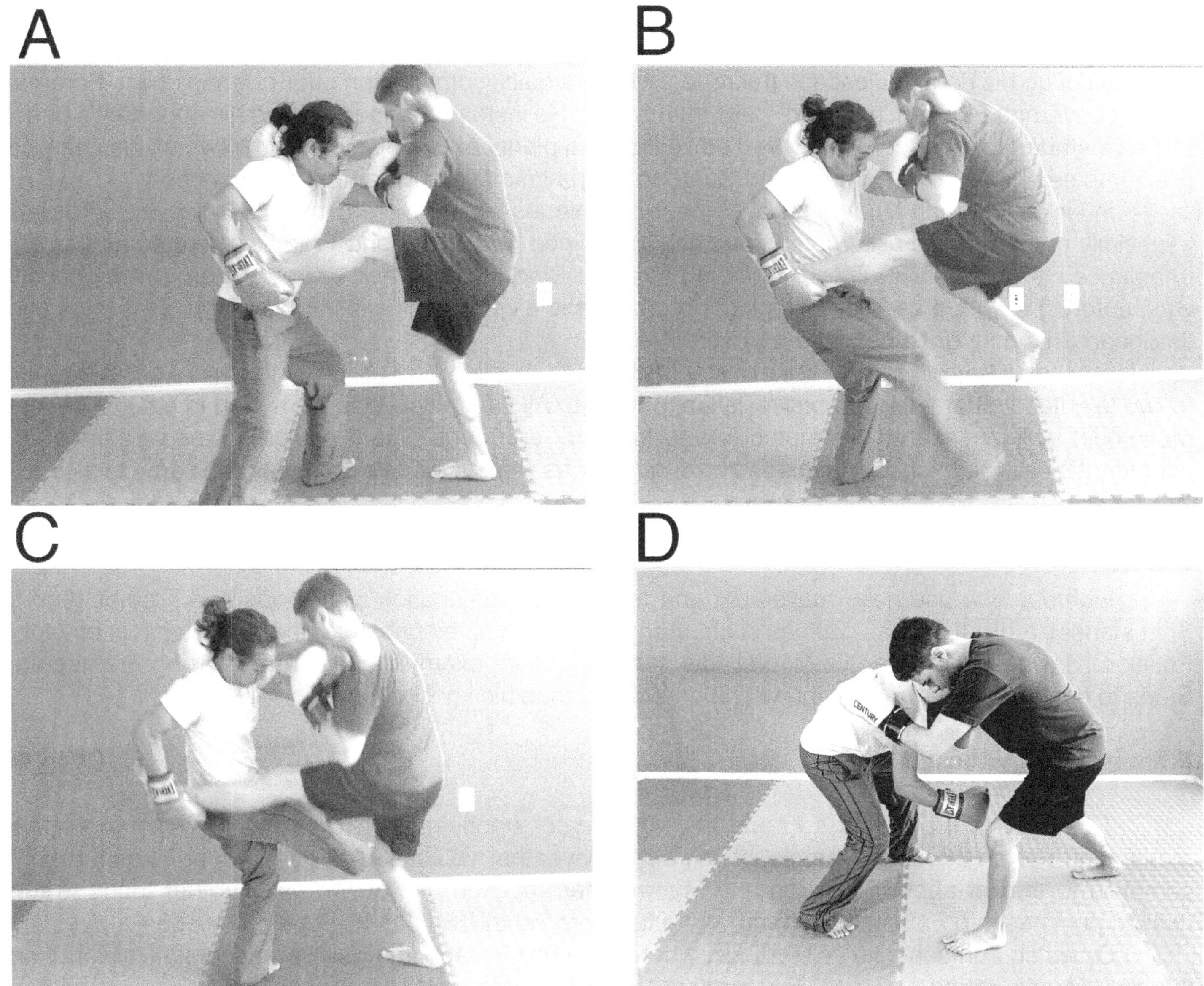

References – Long Guard

Leverage Blocks, Stops & Frames

While it's not commonly talked about, most Long-Range boxers use Frames in some fashion. The same cannot be said for Leverage Blocks or Stops however. Boxers who use Leverage Blocks and Stops include Muhammad Ali and Tyson Furry. Watch Fury vs Klitschko or Ali vs Foreman for reference. Ali would often turn his Leverage Blocks into Collar Ties against Foreman, although it was a Cross Frame that set up the famous knockdown in the 8th. Ali used it to lower Foreman's head and position himself off angle to set up his right and escape the ropes, where a quick combination put Foreman down. Foreman himself Leverage Blocked, but used it less than Ali did. He instead Stopped, stifling his opponent's punch just as it started to extend. His fight vs Ted Gullick has plenty of examples. You can watch his fight with Frazier to see him Frame his head and Guard to keep him off balance and set up punches.

In kickboxing and Muay Thai all of these techniques are far more common. However, Lerdsila is especially good at it. He uses head movement combined with Stops and Frames to create angles and unbalance his opponent's. Dieselnoi used Leverage Blocks, Stops and Frames in the exact opposite way, entering in with a Leverage Block to clinch. This is a common tactic in Muay Thai. Watch his fight vs Shogo Shimazu for some text book examples.

In MMA, it is very worth it to study Israel Adesanya. His fight vs Kelvin Gastelum is a great example of two talented fighters using opposite styles. Similar to Ali vs Frazier, Gastelum tried to enter with head movement while Adesanya attempted to use footwork and Long Guard tactics to keep distance and counter. It's worth it to check out his kickboxing fights as well, as he uses many of the same tactics.

Leverage Blocks, Stops & Frames – Open Stance Considerations

Fighters who use head movement and footwork in conjunction with Stops and Frames tend to Shift stances a great deal as well. As such, many of the examples provided above will work in an Open Position. However, Foreman vs Moorer has some excellent examples of Foreman using Frames and Stops to control Moorer up until the very moment he lands his knockout punch.

Framing With A Missed Punch

Turning your Hook into a Frame to lean on your opponent is a great way to stop their head movement. For an extreme example, check out Mayweather vs Gatti. In the first round Gatti turned to complain to the ref about this tactic and Mayweather knocked him down. Mayweather tends to turn missed punches into Frames in general, using far more variations than this one technique.

Or watch Lomachenko vs Martinez, where Martinez collapsed under Lomachenko's weight from this technique in round 1. Usually this tactic should be used to stop an opponent from rising up, without too much pressure. It's up to the ref how much he will let you get away with, but at the same time a boxer technically should not be allowed to drop his head below waist level and you are allowed to keep you elbow where you want to. If you watch any early Lomachenko fight you can see him use this technique with lightning fast footwork to gain a dominant angle. Of course there are many other ways to Frame off of a missed punch. In MMA, TJ Dillashaw has Framed off of missed punches to stay safe and set up strikes in most of his fights.

Knee Frame

Singdam, a Muay Thai fighter, should provide plenty of examples of this technique. There's even a compilation on YouTube of him using this tactic. However, the Muay Thai legend Samrak used it in perhaps an even more useful way. Samrak would only half-way retract his kick, keeping it at an angle to

Check his opponent's Return Counter or Knee Frame to stop him from closing distance. He used this technique often enough that you can see it in most any of his fights.

Circular Parry

Lomachenko uses this tactic heavily in boxing, while Samart used it in Muay Thai. You can see Lomachenko pull this off against Roman Martinez multiple times. Look at round 4 with 2 minutes left and round 5 with 2 minutes 35 seconds left for some clear examples. Samart's fight vs Panomtoanlek has an example come up fairly quickly.

Hand Fighting

George Foreman uses a lot of principles explained in the Hand Fighting section in boxing, although his opponents usually don't know how to respond.

In Muay Thai, check out Sak Kaopon Lek, who set up many of his vicious kicks and legendary elbows with Hand Fighting. His fight vs Visanupon (available on YouTube for free upon writing this sentence) has great examples of both, and a cut from a nasty elbow ends the fight.

In MMA, Toney Ferguson will hand fight to set up his signature Spinning Elbows. Jon Jones vs Daniel Cormier 1 and 2 contain some incredible examples as well. At times you would be forgiven for thinking you were watching the opening moments of a wrestling match, except that the two are fairly upright and of course their hand fighting can be used to set up strikes. There is also an ample number of examples of Lead Hand fighting in an Open Stance.

Lead Hand Battle

Watch Roy Jones Jr. vs Reggie Johnson for some great Lead Hand battles that lead to several knockdowns for Jones.

Ankle Catch

Tenshin Nasukana's fight vs Federico Roma contains an astonishing amount of picture perfect Ankle Catches and Counters. Tenshin uses one hand for these, something harder to pull off. Saenchai is another fighter who has amazing Ankle Catches, although he tends to use two hands to throw or sweep his opponent.

Leg Catch

GSP is amazing at Catching kicks. Once he's got a hold of the leg, he'll either Intercept with a Cross, take the opponent down in a similar fashion to running the pipe on a Single Leg, or both. You can see an example of a knockout by Leg Catch and Intercepting Cross by watching Anderson Silva vs James Irvine. To see the dangerous version where the leg is caught from underneath, watch Dominick Cruz vs TJ Dillashaw. Cruz Catches Dillashaw's leg in round 1 with 3:29 left on the clock and dumps him on his back.

Specialty Counter – Jump Over Sweep

Lerdsila vs Sok Thy contains a high definition example of this technique at round 2 with 0:22 left on the clock and is available for free on YouTube as of the moment I write this.

Part 2 – Head Movement & Footwork

Basic Head Movement

Slip

To Slip, twist slightly as if throwing a punch. This will naturally move your head off line (Pics A to B). If you wish to add more distance, lean or crouch slightly. This is a subtle movement and not much effort is needed. It is perfectly normal and often preferred to feel your opponent's punch graze your head or shoulder (Pics C to D). It is a testament to the skill of a great fighter that they can move just enough to stay close. This preserves their ability to quickly counter.

The slip is the simplest form of head movement but perhaps the hardest to master. The big conundrum with the Slip is exactly how far to go. If you go too far you run the risk of becoming stuck in place by sinking your weight down (Pics A to B). But if you do not Slip far enough you may get hit. It is often a personal preference based on the style of the practitioner (Pic C vs D.)

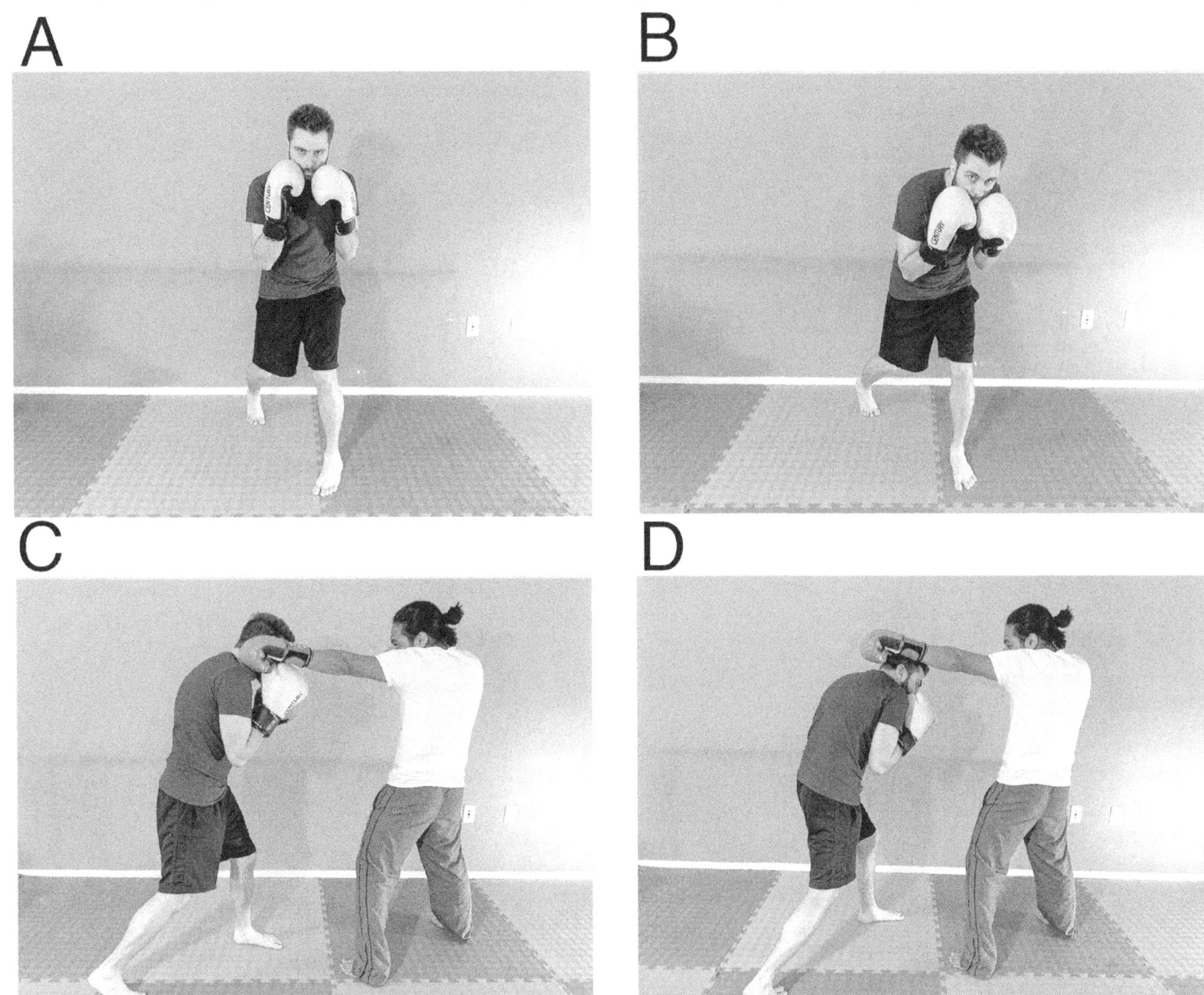

Think of the available space in which you can Slip your head from one side to the other as the numbers on a clock. For instance, 11 or 1 would be a slight Slip (Pics A to B) while 10 or 2 would be more of a Crouch (C to D), which is covered in the Armstrong Style section. You can see the major difference in the potential for footwork and counters (Pic E vs Pic F). Neither is “right”, it all depends.

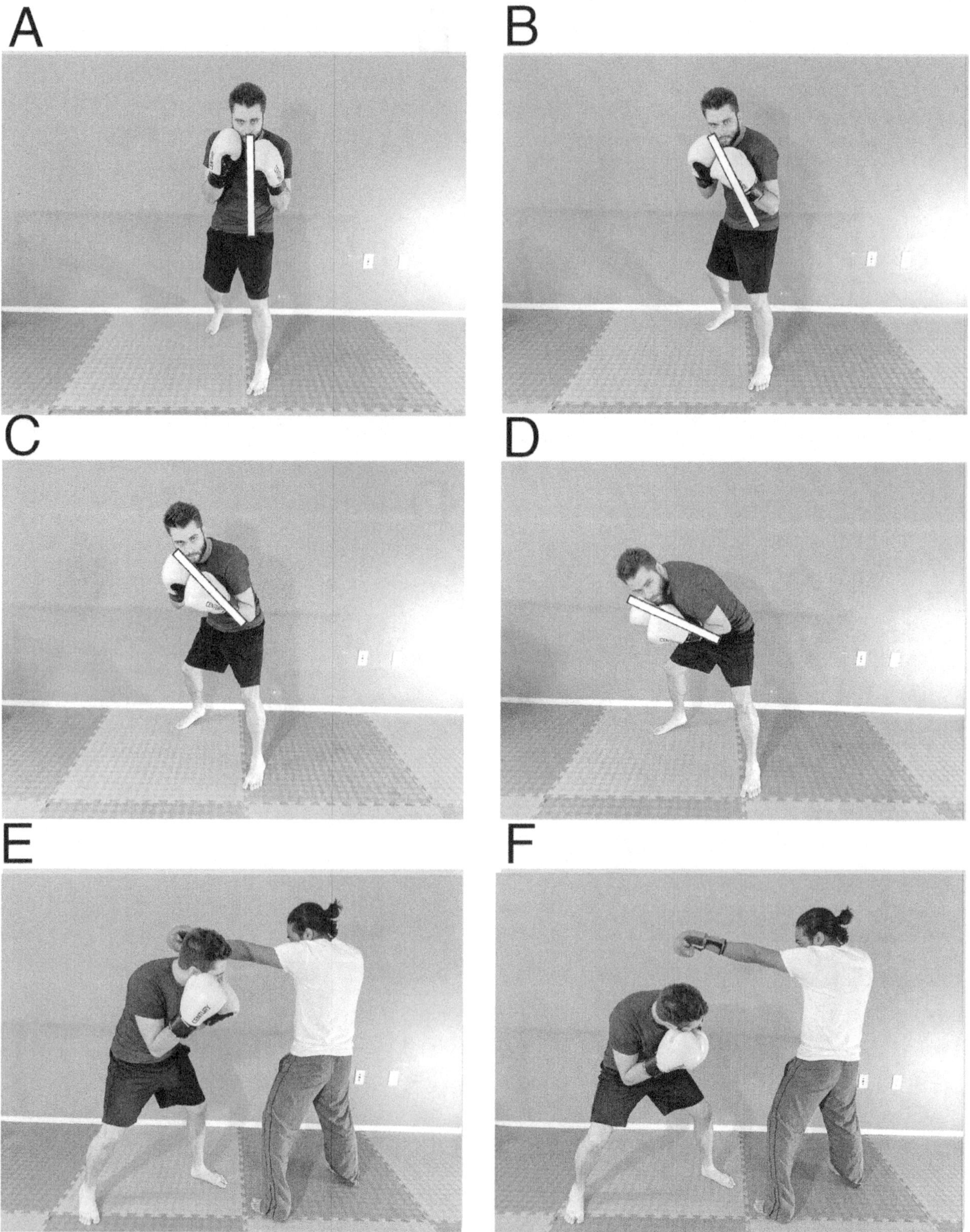

Keep in mind for now that Boxers and mixed martial artists will be able to Crouch fairly low, while kickboxers will not want to go too far beyond 1 or 11 O Clock.

This is because kickboxers must worry about dipping into a kick or knee. Mixed martial artists must worry about this as well, but changing levels provides the threat of a takedown in MMA. Also, kicking at an opponent who has just changed levels is extra risky, as you will be even more unstable on one leg. In the end it is all about risk versus rewards.

Slipping Outside

Successfully Slipping Outside is one of the best positions you can attain in fighting. The great opportunity in this position comes after you have slipped your opponent's Jab. In most instances, they have just spent their Lead Hand (which you have successfully Slipped) and their Rear Hand is now very far away (Pics A to C). You can help ensure that you hold a superior angle by stepping in the direction in which you Slip (Pics D to F). While your opponent is retracting their Lead Hand or trying to reposition, now is the time to shoot off a counter to their exposed side.

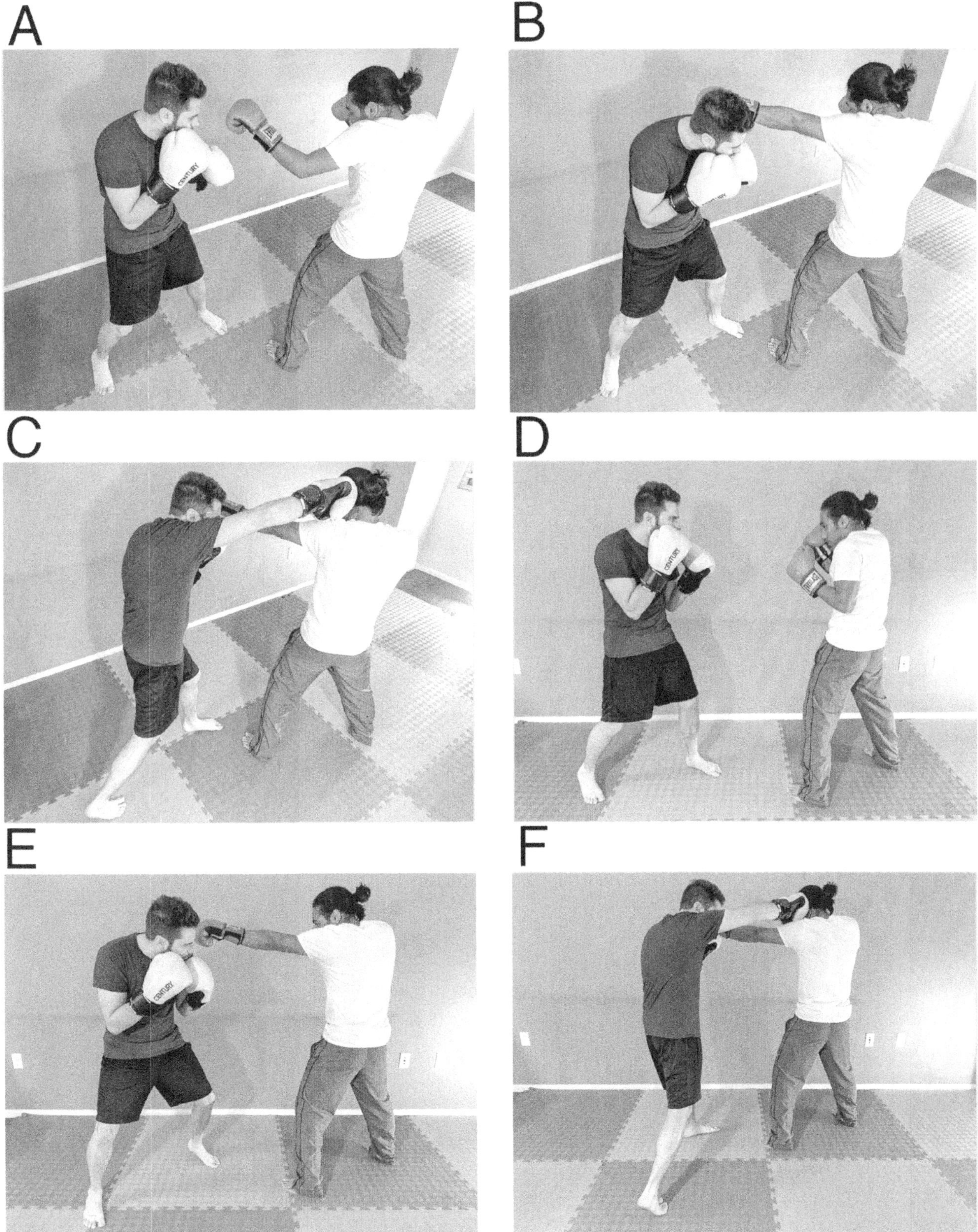

Alternatively, you can intercept their Lead Hand with your own Lead Hand the way Frazier did repeatedly to Ali (A to B). Or you can Slip a Jab to the Outside as you throw a Lead Leg Roundhouse (C to D). Make sure to step as you do so to load your Lead Leg with more power.

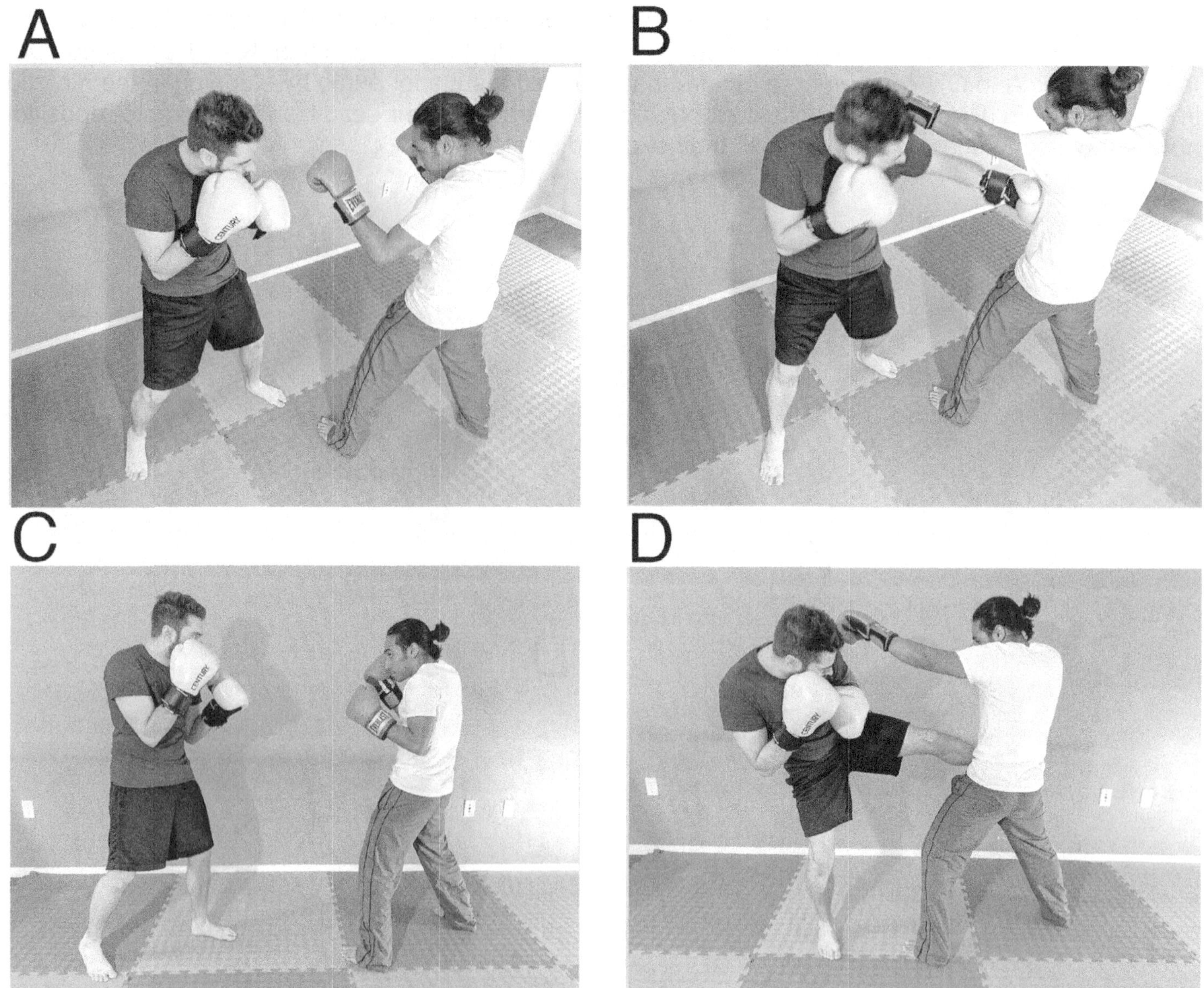

Slipping Inside

Slipping to the Inside is more high risk/high reward than Slipping to the Outside. This holds especially true for Southpaw fighters. Slipping Inside leaves you much more vulnerable to attack, especially from your opponent's Rear Side. If you are not careful, you will have just lined your head up with your opponent's Cross for them. However, Slipping Inside will open up your opponent to attacks as well.

A staple Intercepting Counter is to Slip very slightly and "cross over" your opponent's Jab with a Cross (Pics A to C). This is where the term Cross actually originated from. But you may in fact be driving yourself into an opponent's Cross at the same time, so be ready to Slip further than you had initially intended to stay safe (Pics D to F)

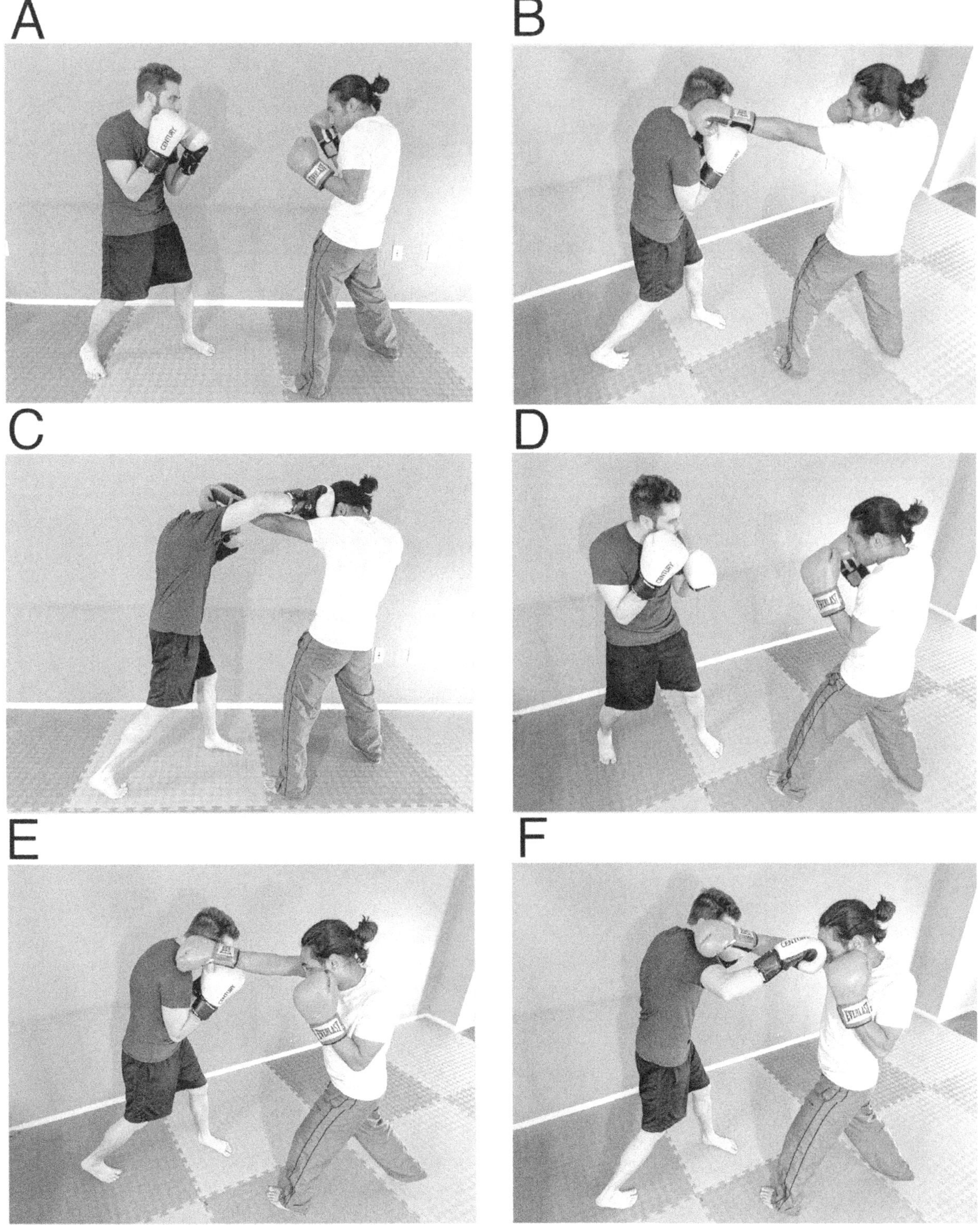

In kickboxing, you can take advantage when your opponent throws a Jab or a Cross by Slipping Inside and slamming their Lead Leg with a Rear Leg Roundhouse (Pics A to B). Stepping Inside as you Slip will not only create more distance, but help to load your Rear Leg attack with more power.

A

B

Open Stance Considerations

In an Open Stance, Slipping to the Outside is a far safer option most of the time (Pics A to B). This lines up your Rear Hand to Intercept your opponent's attack (Pic C) and helps protect you from your opponent's Rear Hand. This position will also put your opponent at a bad angle to evade Lead Side attacks (Pic D) and move your Rear Leg closer to your opponent (Pic E).

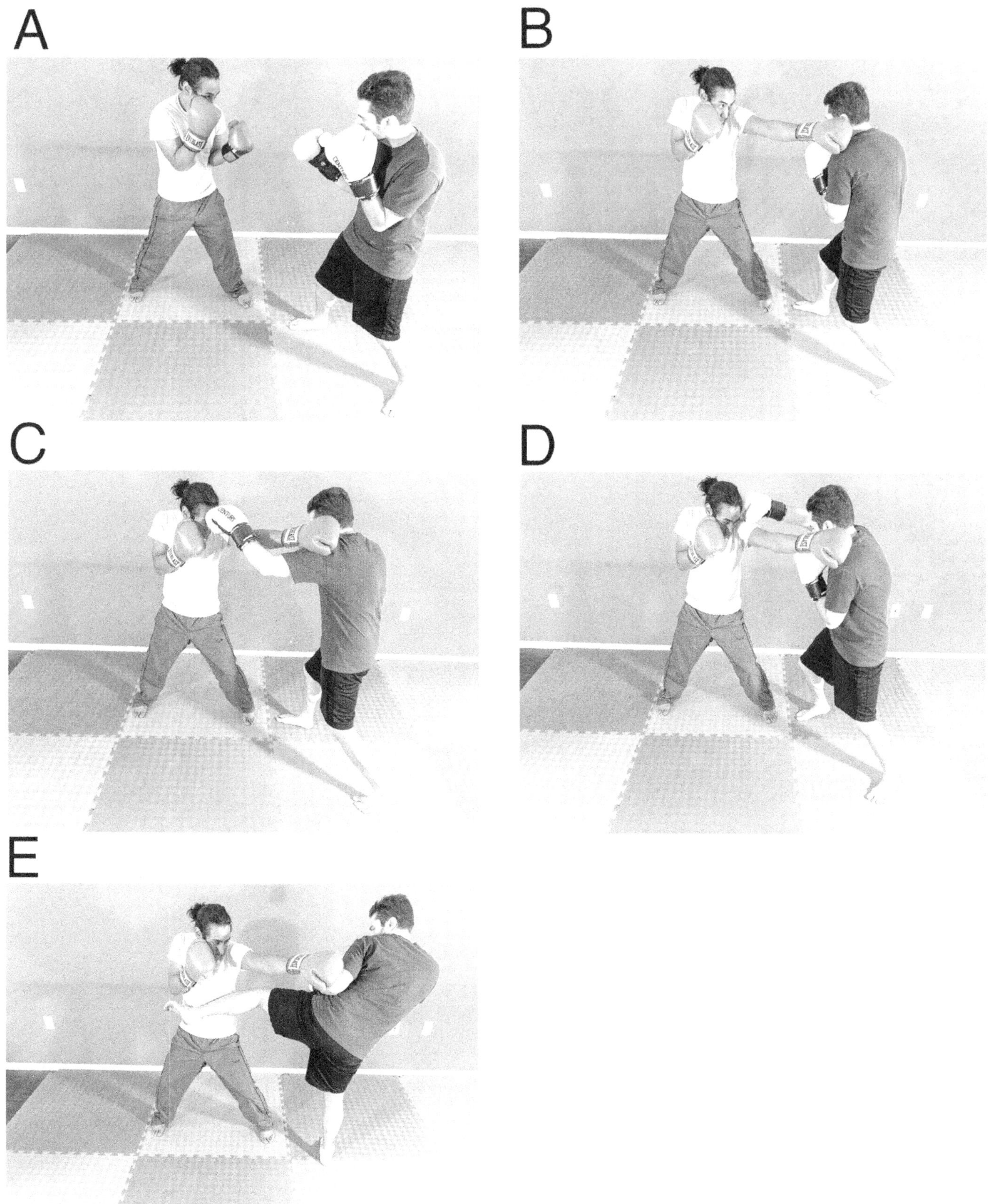

If you Slip Inside of your opponent's Lead Hand attack (Pics A to B), you may be aligning yourself with your opponent's Rear Hand. If in this position, be prepared to Slip Inside even deeper to avoid a Cross or Duck to avoid a Rear Hook (Pics C to D).

Duck/Level Change

To Duck, bend your knees to lower yourself in a balanced position (A to C). Your head may dip down very slightly, but most of the work should be done by your legs. Do not bend too much at the waist. There are fighters who do Duck this way, but this should be seen as a specialty style and will be covered in a later chapter. Although you do not want to bend at the waist, you may wish to tuck your chin and hunch your shoulders for additional protection (Pic D).

Ducking works well for setting up body shots (Pics E to F) or level changing for takedowns. It can also help to load up power into your strikes by setting your weight low. Rising up into Hooks, Knees or Uppercuts works particularly well.

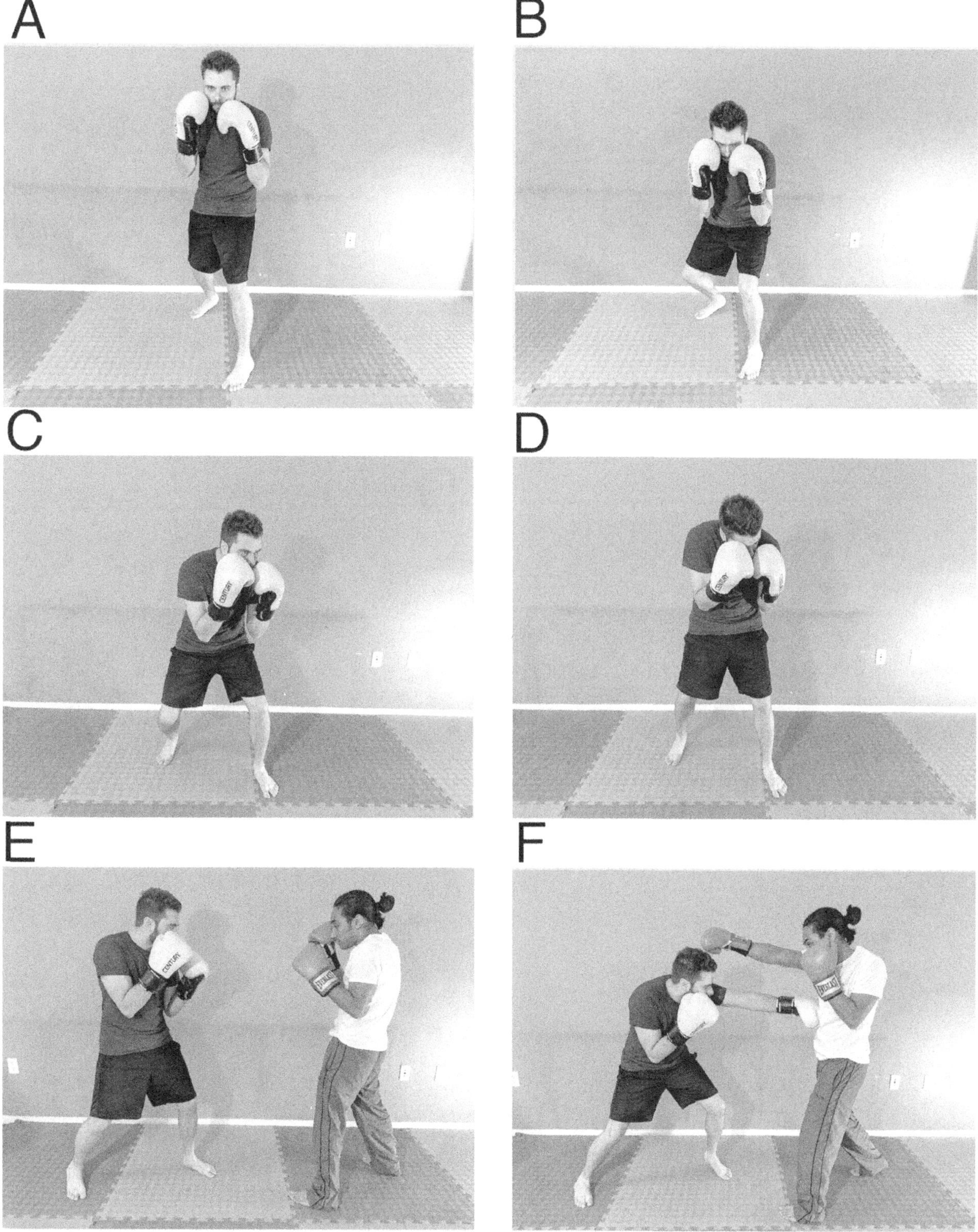

Drills

Drill 1A

Standing in place, have your opponent throw Jabs, Crosses and Hooks at your head. Slip and Duck to stay safe, paying close attention to your timing and balance (Pics A to D). You head movement should never make you feel as if you need to take a step to stay balanced. Go for one round and then switch who is defending and who is attacking.

Drills

Drill 1B

Repeat the last drill, but this time move forward, steadily advancing on your partner (Pics A to D). Pay close attention that you do not place too much weight forward as you advance. You should be able to quickly straighten up and step back at any moment. To help ensure this, have your partner occasionally throw light uppercuts when they feel you may be off balance. When they do so, you can step back, straighten up or Slip them.

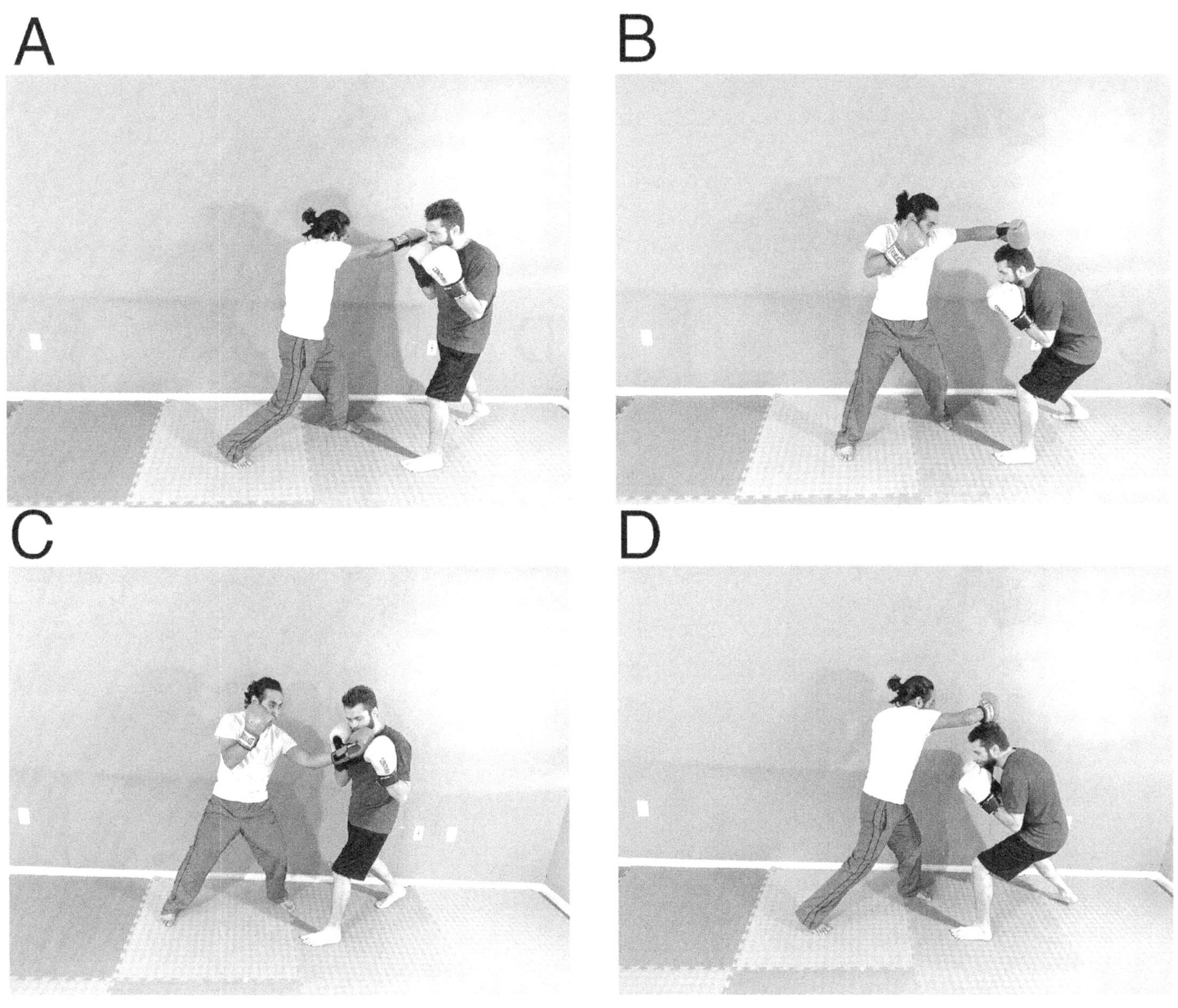

Drill 1C

Repeat the above drill, but now focus on circling to the Inside or Outside. See how far you can flank your opponent as they throw a punch (Pics A to D). You should be able to stop circling and be still at any moment. Once you feel that you are comfortable, try quickly reversing direction as your partner punches, stepping and Slipping Inside after circling Outside and vice versa.

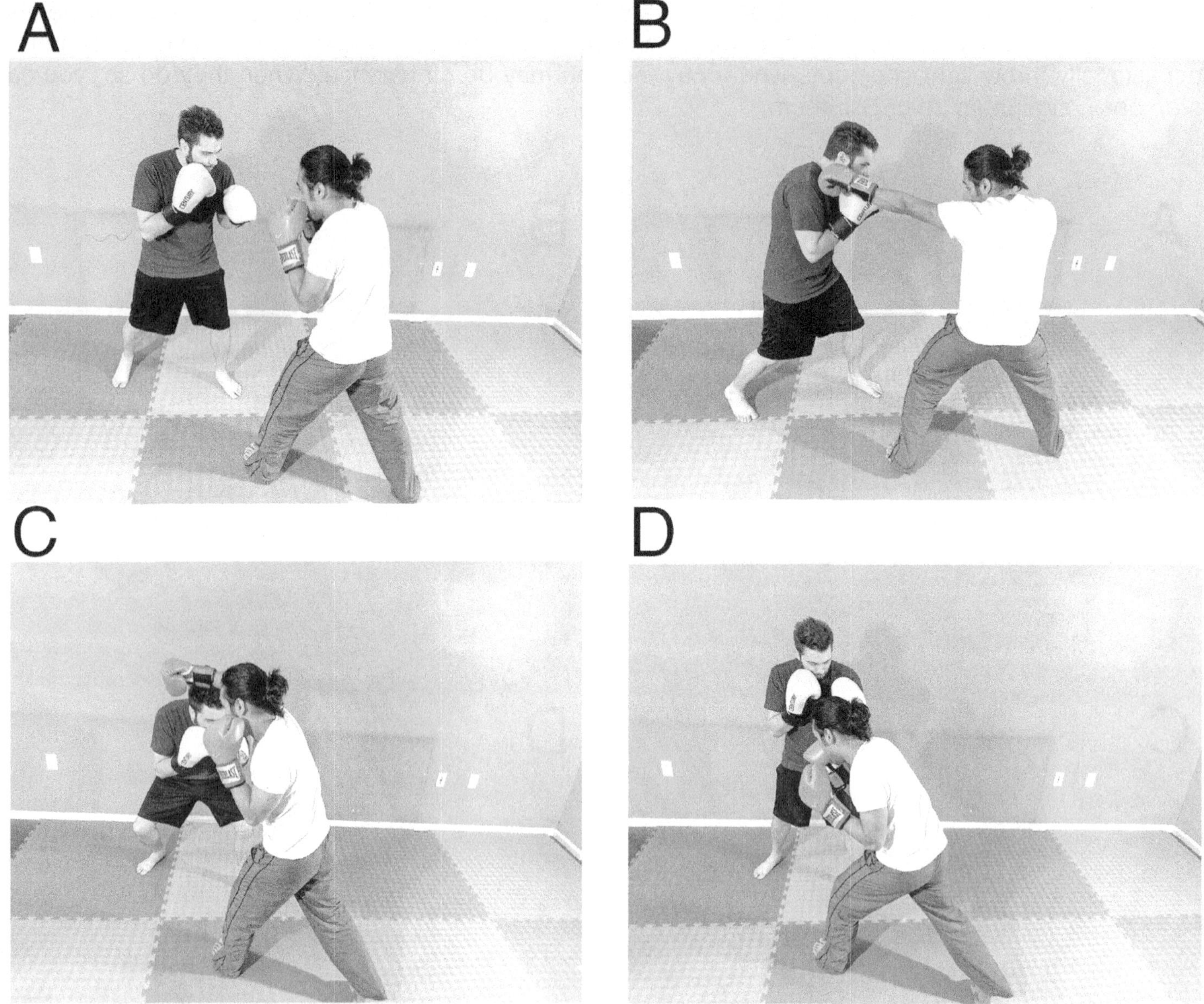

Drill 2A

Now that you have the correct timing and balance and know how to react well to punches, it's time to practice counters. Have your opponent throw Jabs, Crosses, Hooks and Uppercuts to the head. Wait for the right time and then Return a counter off the same side that you Slipped to. You may Slip right and Return a counter with your Rear Hand (Pics A to C) or Slip left and Return a counter with your left (Pics D to F). Go for one round and then switch which partner is defending and which is attacking. Feel free to add on the kicking counters learned in previous sections if your style allows them.

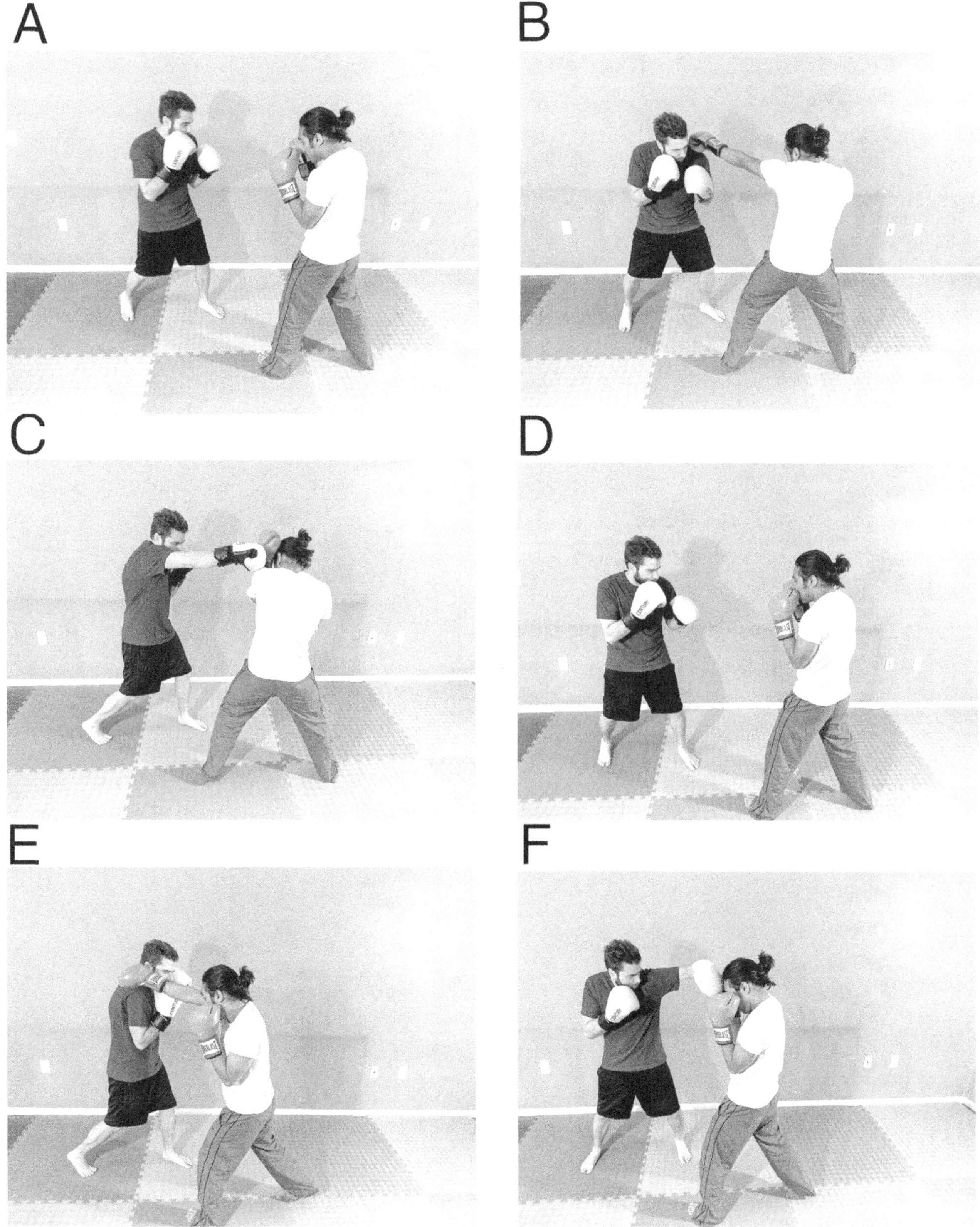

Drill 2B

Now perform the same drill but use Intercepting counters (Pics A to B, C to D, E to F). It is perfectly fine for you and your partner to add on to your head movement by Catching, Parrying or blocking. This is a good idea anyways, and as you progress you will find yourself naturally pairing certain blocks with certain head movement patterns. A Catch paired with a Slip, and a Cover Block with a Duck are probably the most popular. Go for one round and then switch which partner is defending and which is attacking.

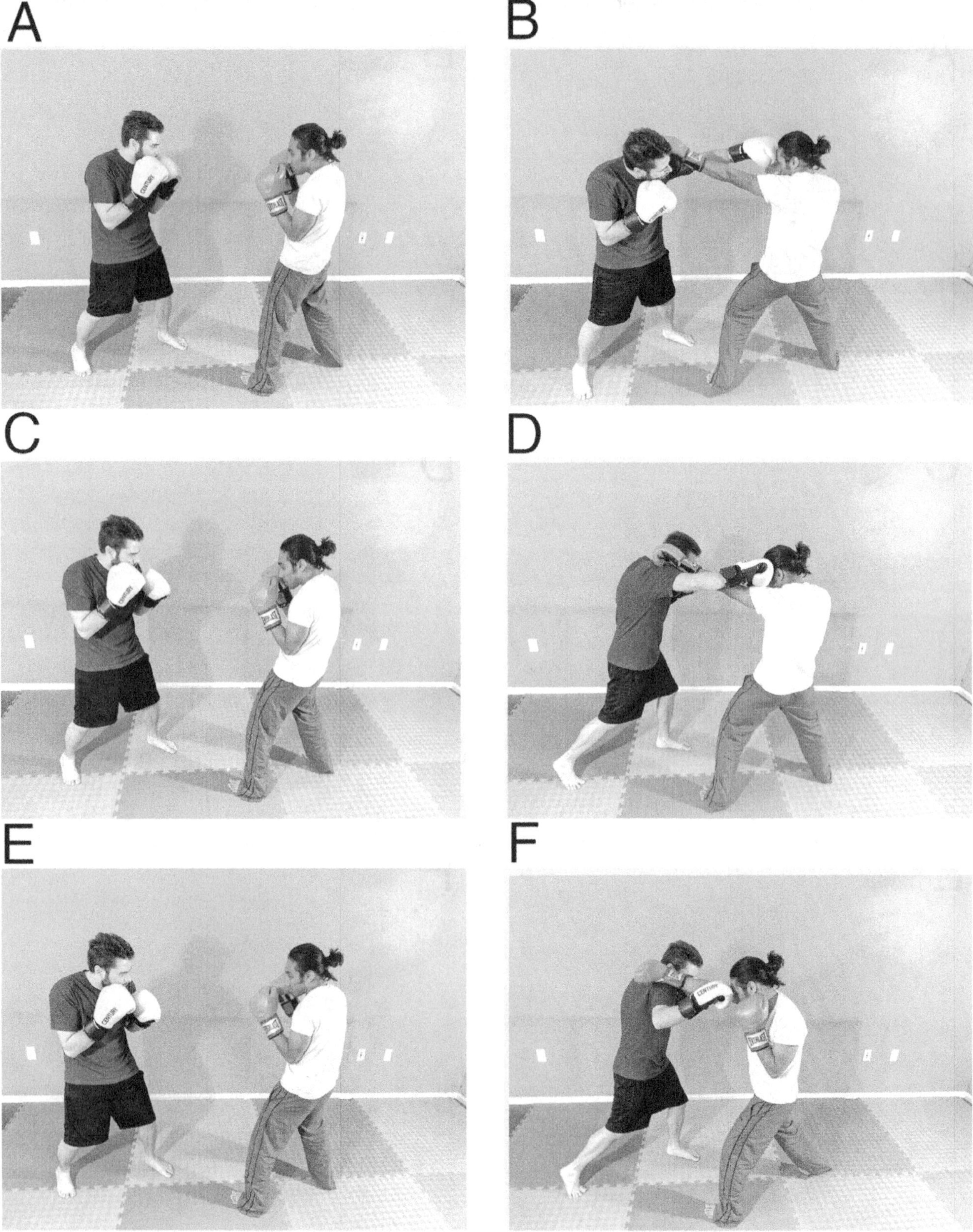

In an Open Stance, it is best to Intercept your partners Jab by Slipping Inside to throw one of your own (Pics A to B). Otherwise, you can Slip Outside to Land a Cross (Pics C to D). Refer to the prior Open Stance Considerations in this section for more ideas.

Similarly, you can Slip to the Outside when your opponent throws a Cross to land your own (Pics A to B). Slipping to the Inside against an opponent's Cross is more dangerous, but you can try it if you like (Pics C to D). Now is the time to get your timing down and see what you can pull off, since you and your partner will of course be lightly tapping each other to get used to these patterns. Keep in mind that Ducking to Intercept with a body Jab or Cross can also be effective and fairly safe options.

Drop Slip

A Drop Slip is the definition we will use for Ducking/Level Changing and Slipping at the same time. To Drop Slip, shift your weight to the leg on the side you are Slipping to and then squat down to Duck as well (Pics A to B, C to D & E to F). Do not move your head past your Lead Foot. If you are Drop Slipping to your Rear Side, do not move your head past your Rear Knee. Although you should bend very little at the waist, you can further protect yourself by putting your chin to your collar bone or hunching your shoulders.

Besides moving your head further away from your opponent's attack, the main benefit of a Drop Slip is how well it loads power into your counters.

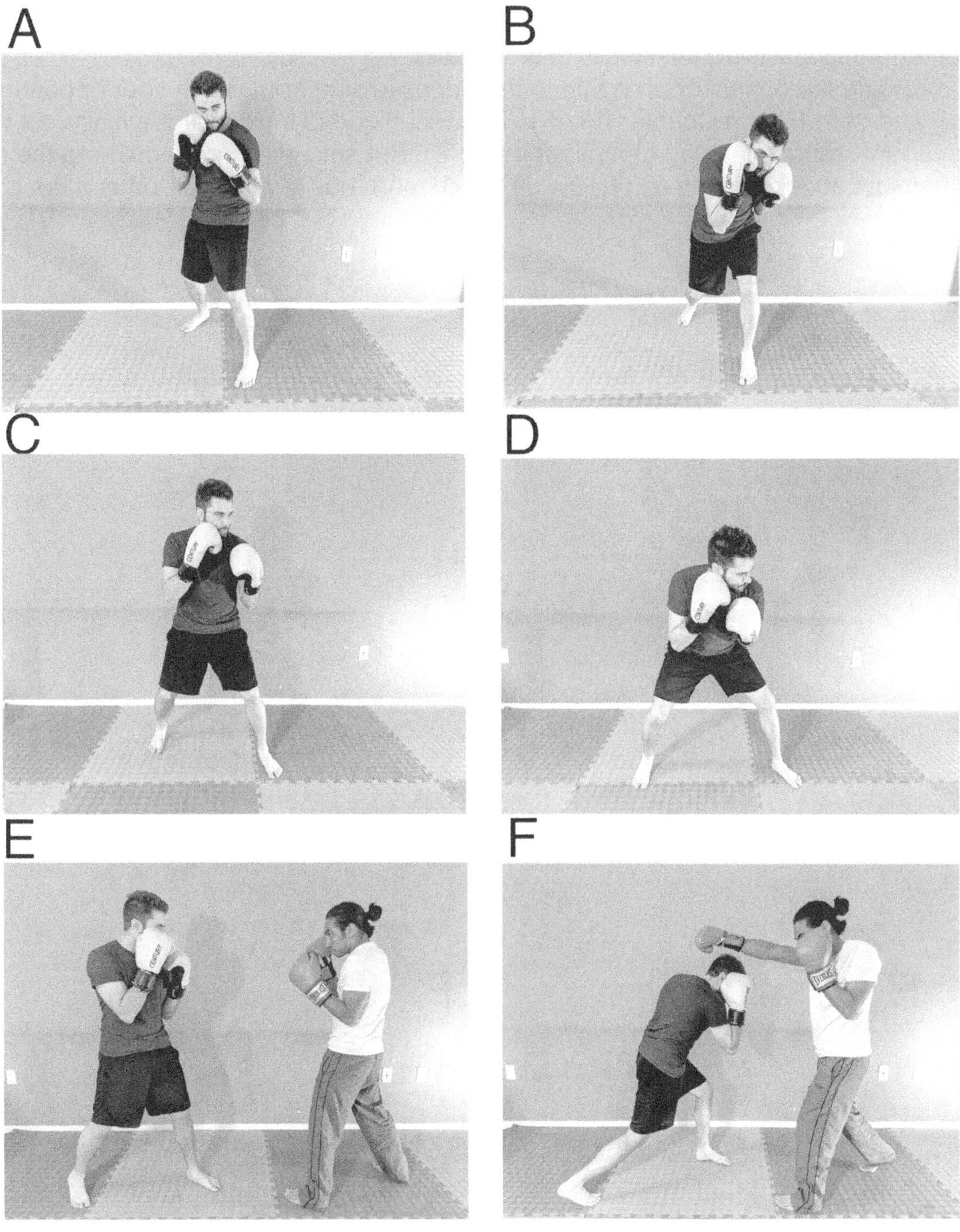

For Return Counters, this movement loads power on the same side to which you are Drop Slipping. For instance, Drop Slipping to the Inside in Orthodox can help to load up an explosive Gazelle Hook. For Intercepting Counters, it loads power on the opposite side. We will go into this in depth later, so don't worry about it too much for now.

Drills

Drill 1A

Have your partner throw Straights and Hooks to your head from either side. Drop Slip to the same side as your partner's punch. For instance, if they throw with their left, Drop Slip to their left (your right) and vice versa (Pics A to B). Return a counter off the same side you Drop Slipped to (Pic C). Start off going very slow. Getting caught by a Hook while Drop Slipping will feel much worse than if you were simply Ducking, because you will be moving your head towards their punch. However, the trade-off is that it is near impossible for them to land an immediate attack afterwards. Notice in Pic B that the fighter is too far away for the opponent to land with attacks thrown off his right side, and it will be difficult for him to throw another attack off of his left side with any power.

Next round try the opposite. Drop Slip to the opposite side from which your opponent is punching (Pics D to E), and then Return Counter (Pic F). This technique is much safer initially, as you are going with your opponent's punch instead of against it (Pic E). But since you are moving to the opposite side from which they just attacked, they can follow up much more easily with their other side; so look out!

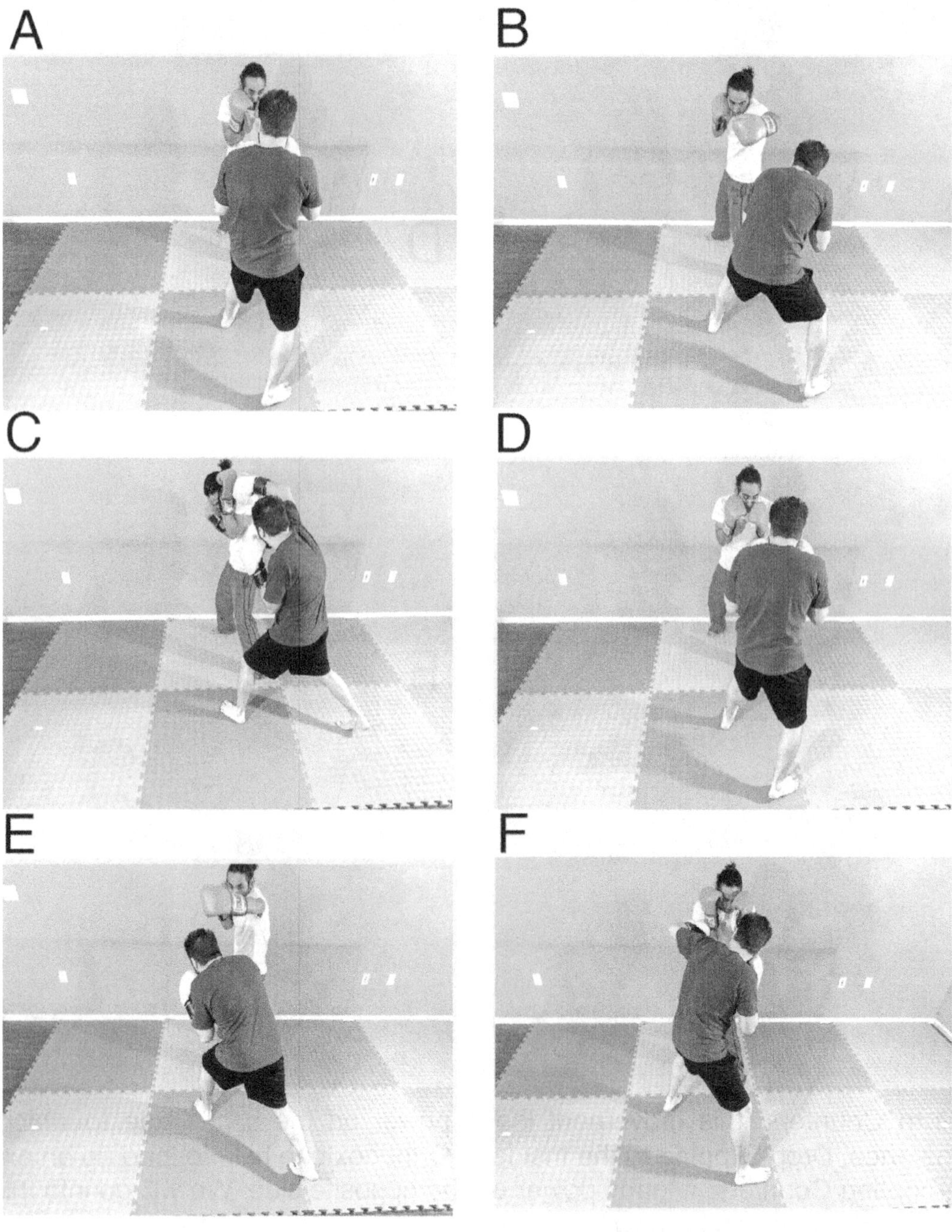

Drill 1B

Repeat the last drill, but this time use Intercepting counters (A to B & C to D). Take note of which counters work well when going both with and against the direction of your partner's punch. Go light, and have your partner be prepared to block.

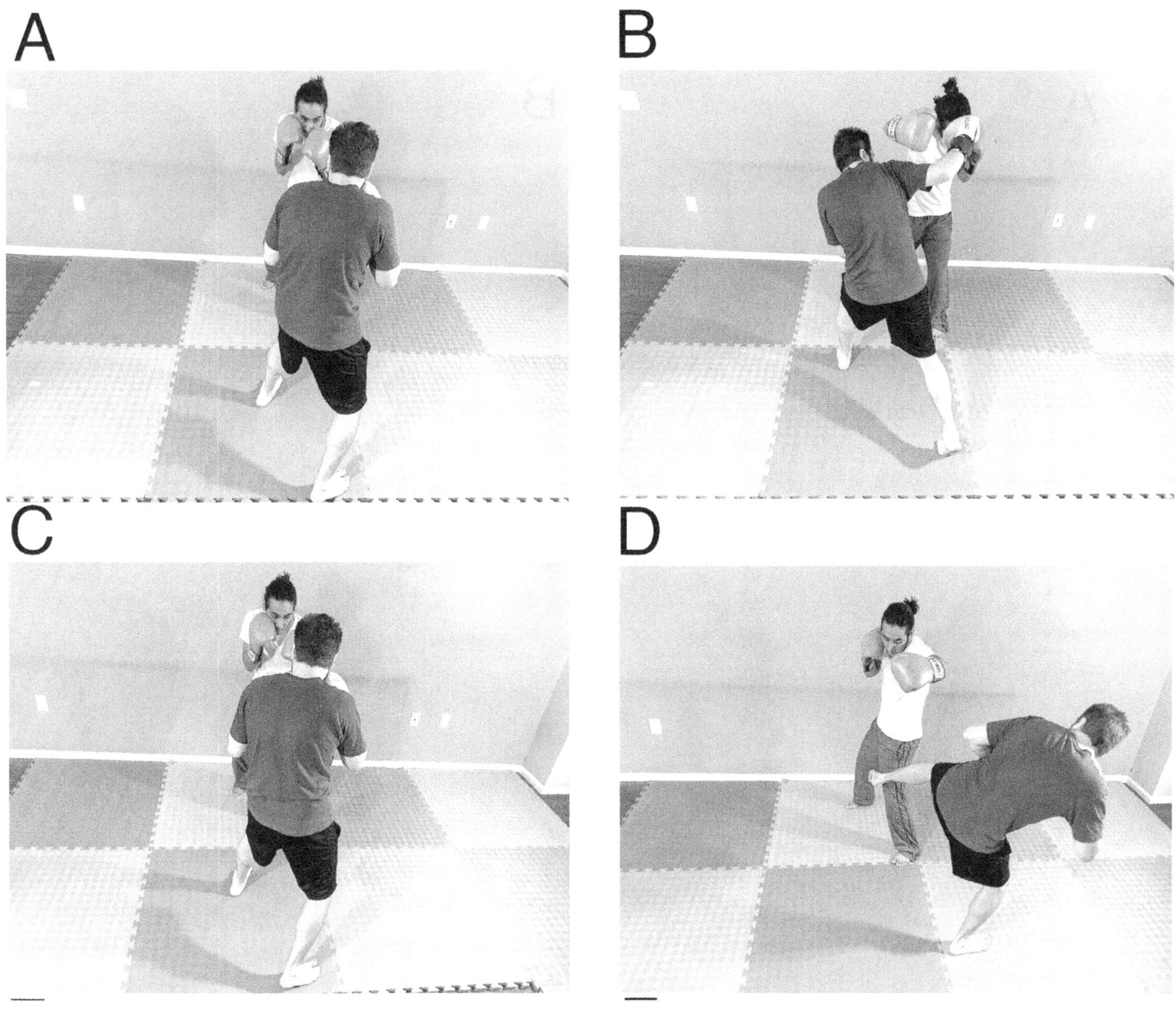

Return

Returning to your normal Stance and Posture is seen by many as just a normal part of head movement (Pics A to B), but in fact you can use this Return in order to dodge punches (Pics C to D). For instance, if you Slip to the Outside to dodge a Jab (Pic E), then it is entirely possible to use a Return to dodge your opponent's follow up Cross (Pick F). Oddly enough this is rarely ever talked about. But it is one of the most potent forms of defense, as it puts you right back into your ideal position to follow up with well-balanced attacks.

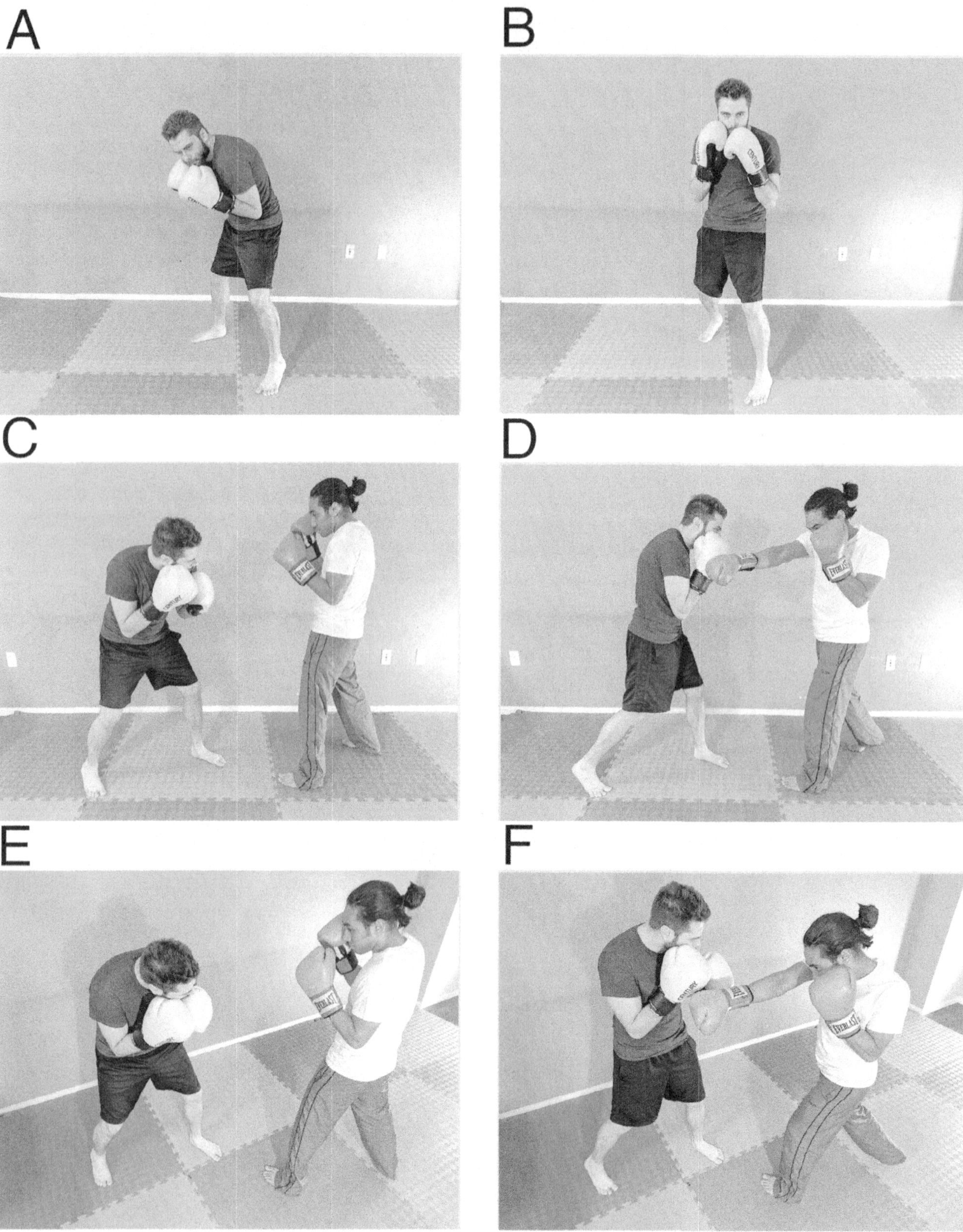

Pull

To Pull, smartly snap your head back (They say smartly in old-timey boxing books and I don't know why, who's trying to do it stupidly?). Move back just far enough to avoid your opponent's strike. Never lean your head further back than your Rear Foot. That is the maximum, but in actuality you should aim to only pull a few inches to half a foot (Pics A to B). While most Pulls use a bit of a lean back, it is not necessary. If you are keeping your body over your Lead Foot, then simply moving your body back so that your head is now in the middle of both of your feet will work (Pics C to D). An exception would be if you were leaning back to try and get your opponent to overreach and punch down (Pics E to F). In this case, widen your stance to keep your feet under you.

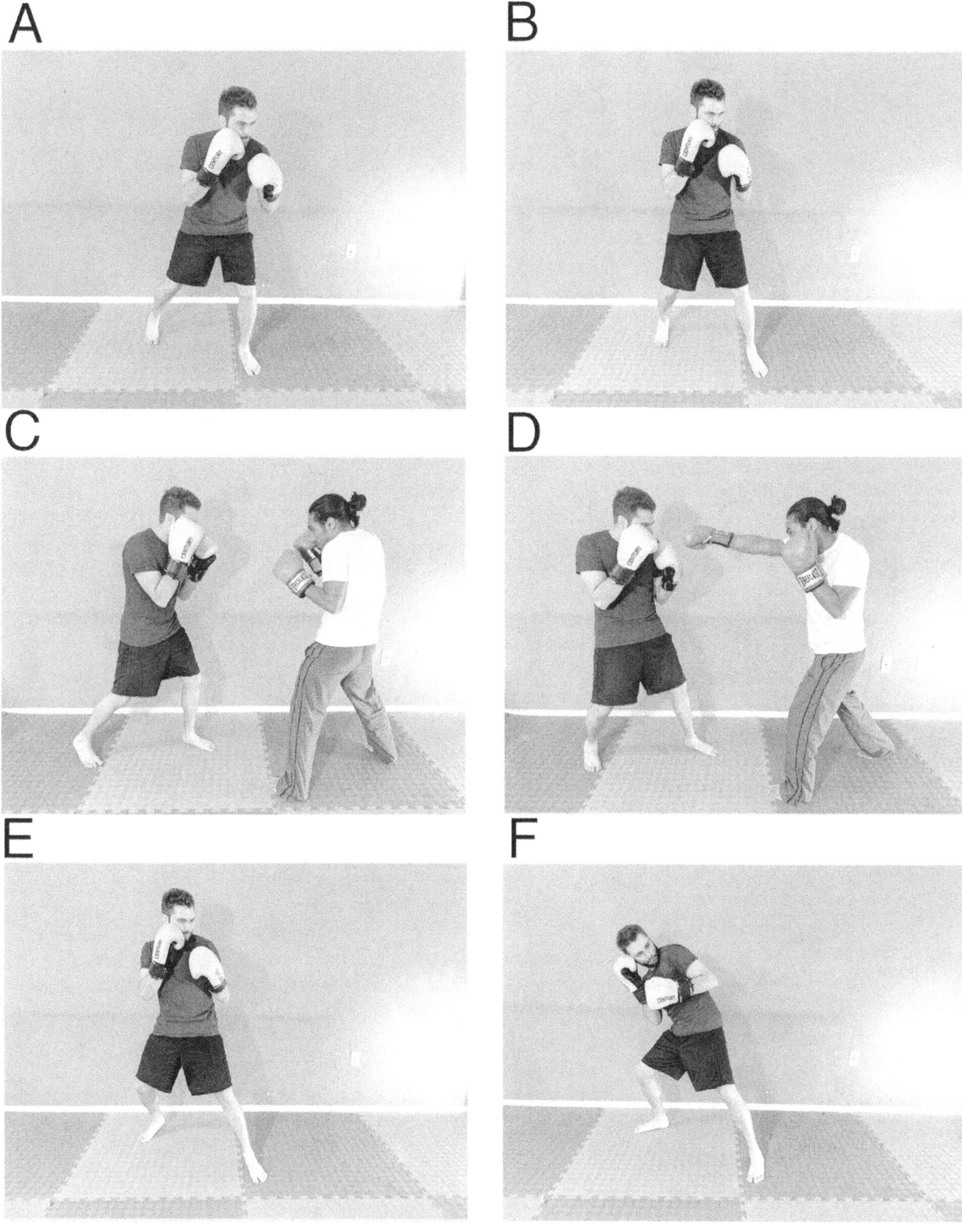

Drill

Follow your partner around the ring, Ducking or Drop Slipping under Hooks. The moment they fire off a Jab, Pull back and fire off a Jab or Cross (Pics A to C). If you happen to be Ducking or Drop Slipping, then you may simply Return to your normal position and do the same (Pics D to F). A small step backwards may be necessary at times. Go a full round and then switch which partner is attacking and which is defending and countering.

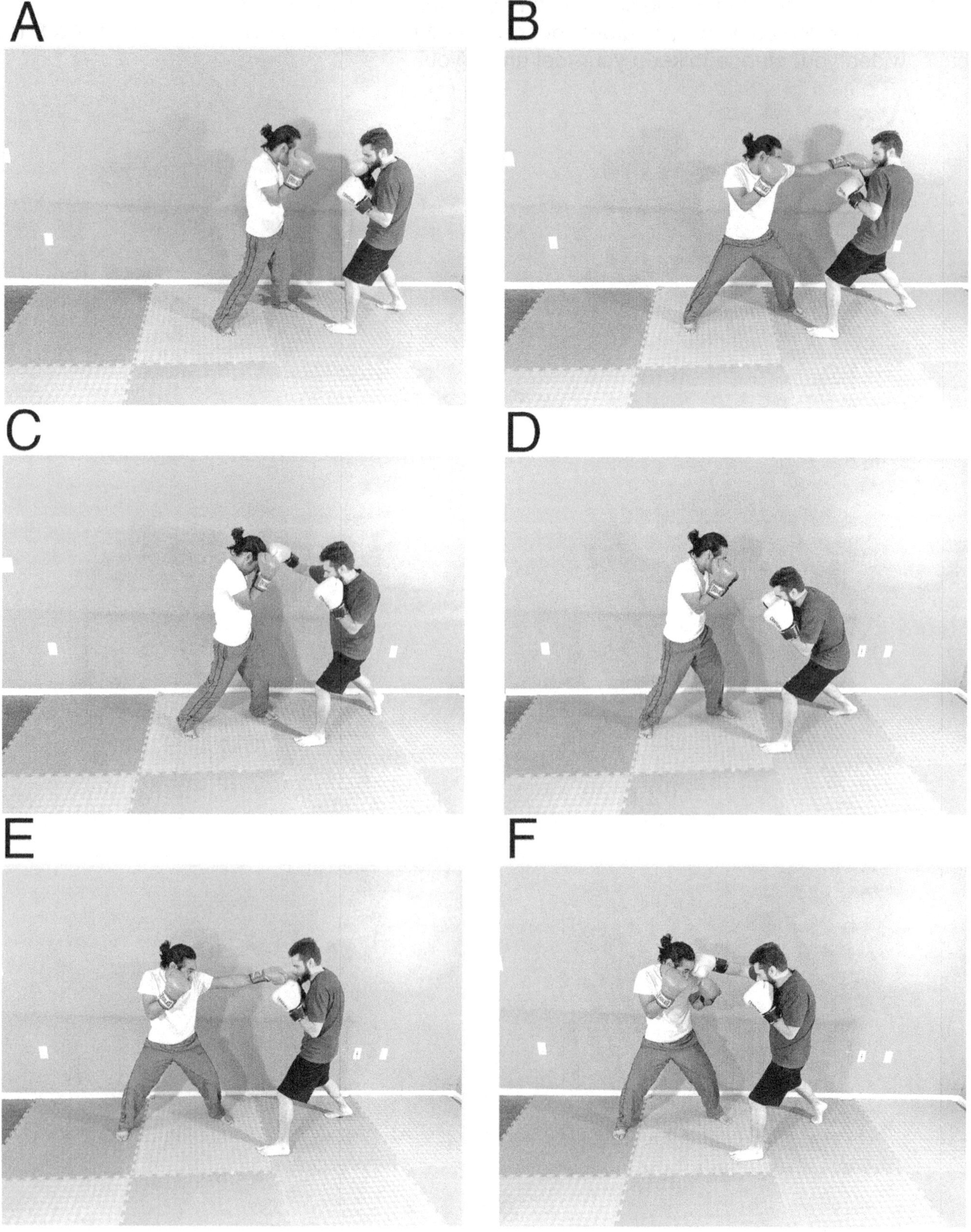

Pull Slip

Rather than pulling straight back, move your head back and to one side (Pics A to B). Slipping your head to the side as you Pull can help to load up your shots and create new angles of attack. The benefits, as opposed to a Drop Slip, is that you can load more weight into your Return Counters by shifting your weight backwards. A Pull Slip can also provide additional protection if your opponent is aiming for your head right after you have already Slipped or Drop Slipped (Pics C to D).

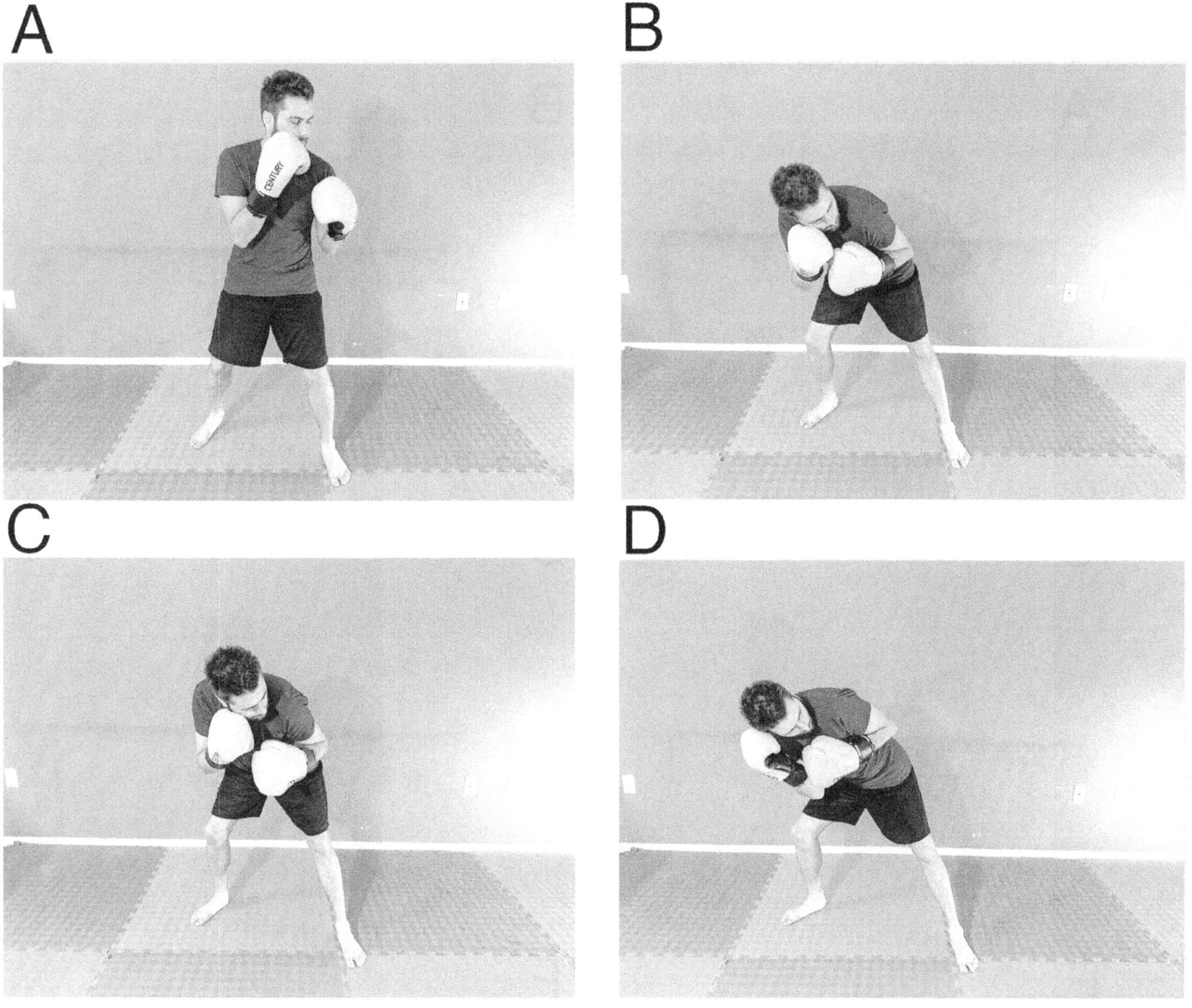

The majority of your Pull Slips should be to the Outside (Pics A to B). This maintains a safe narrow posture from which you can Shoulder Roll if necessary, and loads up your Rear Side for a powerful counter. Watch the great heavyweight boxer Rocky Marciano. Rocky would step forward while Pull Slipping an opponent's punch by leaning far back and dipping his shoulders Outside. This loaded his right with a tremendous amount of power (Pics C to D).

An Inside Pull Slip is a fairly dangerous idea. You will have to square your posture up to both Pull and Slip Inside (Pics E to F). If you are in a narrow, bladed stance then your balance will be highly compromised. That said, certain fighters like Ali used to pull this off all the time. The Greatest would even use it to evade Hooks. Check out the Low Guard section for more on this. Obviously, this is not something that everyone will want to do.

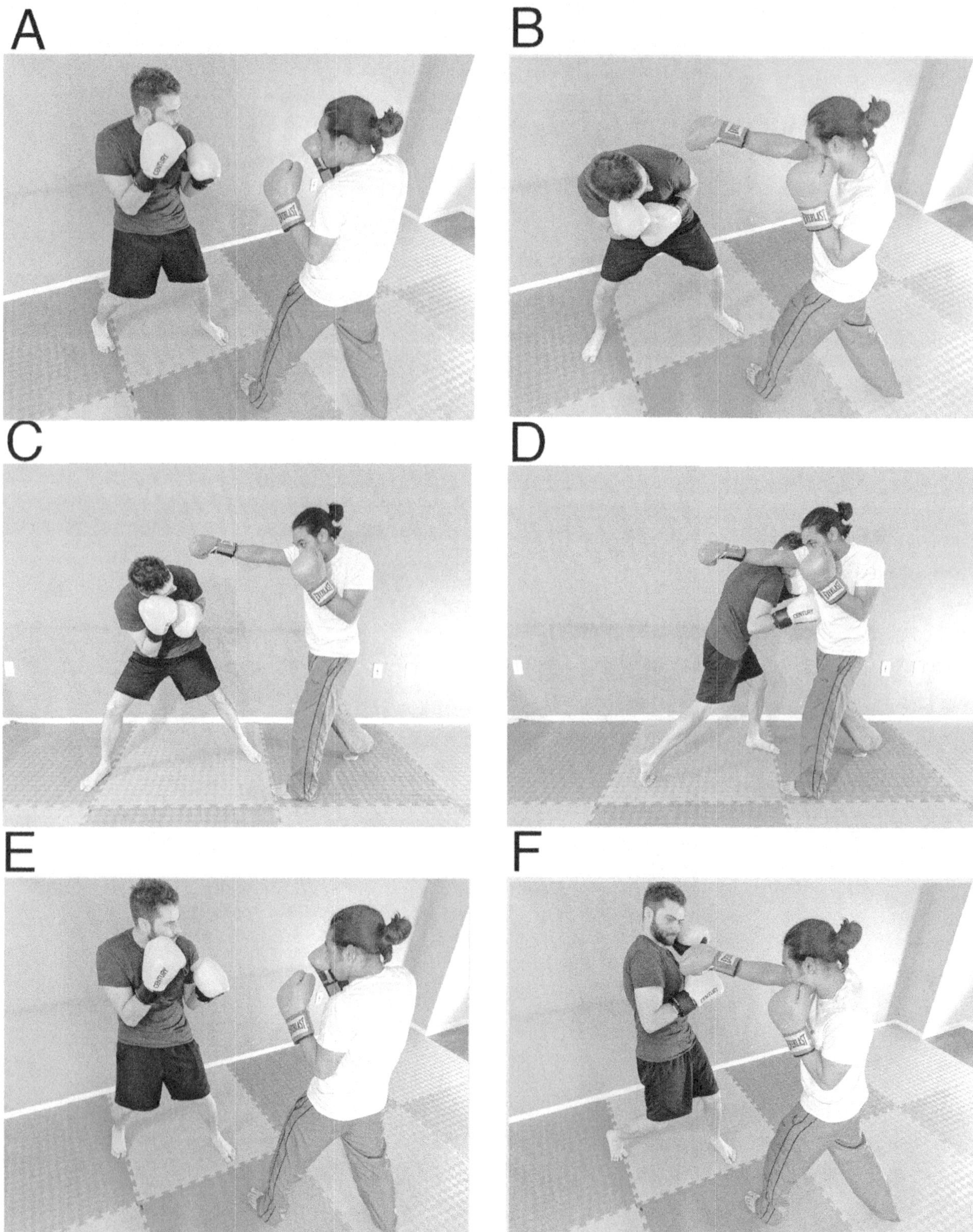

Drill

Go back and forth with your partner attacking and then defending. One partner will throw a Jab-Cross combination and the other will Pull Slip and then Return either a Cross or Rear Uppercut. Experiment with just how far you like to lean back on your Pulls and how deep Inside you like to Slip. Find an angle that is both safe and works well for counters.

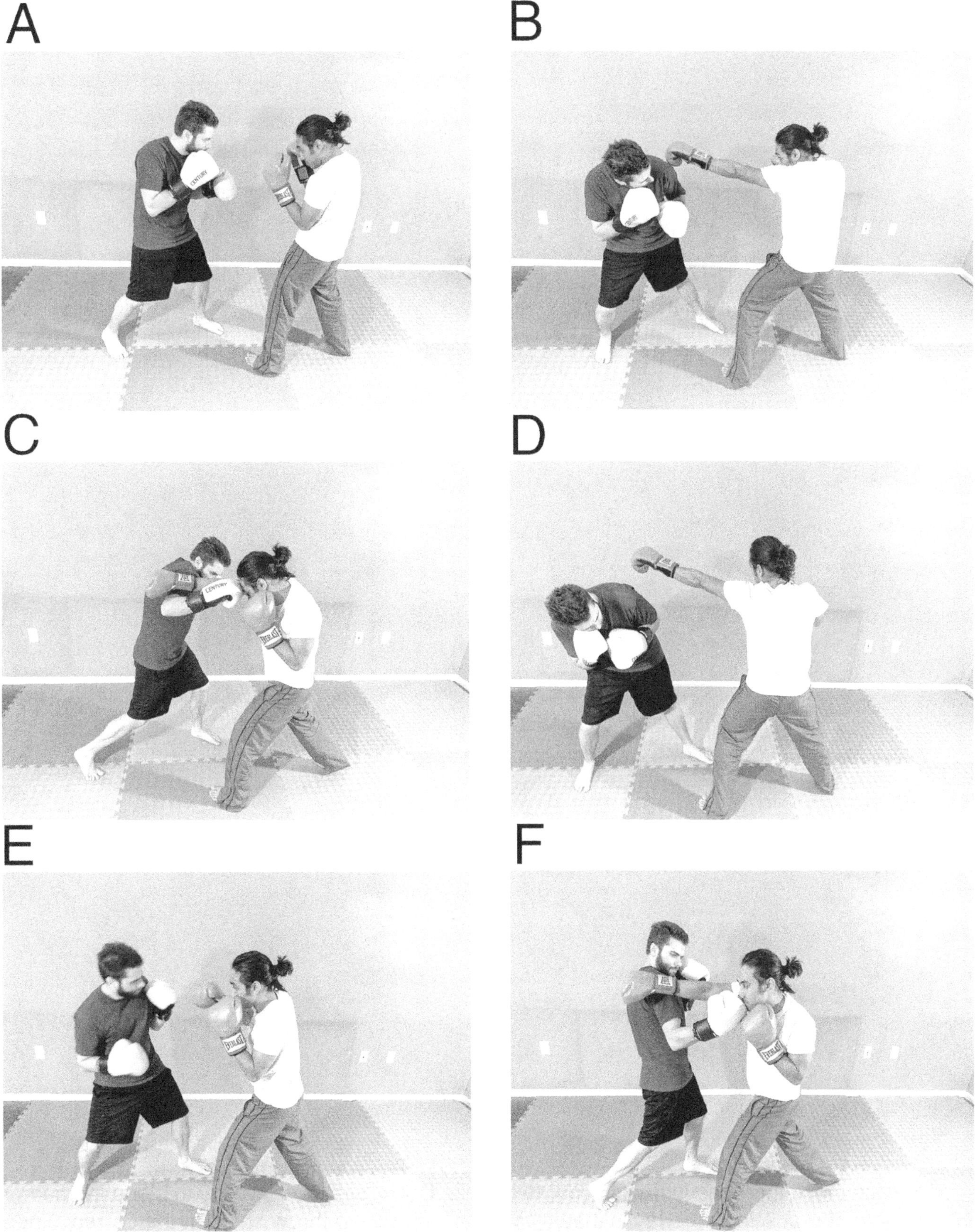

Weave (Basic)

When learning the Weave, it is best to break it into separate movements that you are already familiar with. Generally, Weaves can be used to evade combinations as well as a single punch. They will usually begin as a Slip that follows the same direction as your opponent's punch (Pics A to B) or as a Duck. Slipping first means that you can Roll with the punch if it still connects, but is not strictly necessary. Once you have Slipped and Ducked, move your head to the opposite side (Pics C to D). Return to come back to a balanced stance (Pic E).

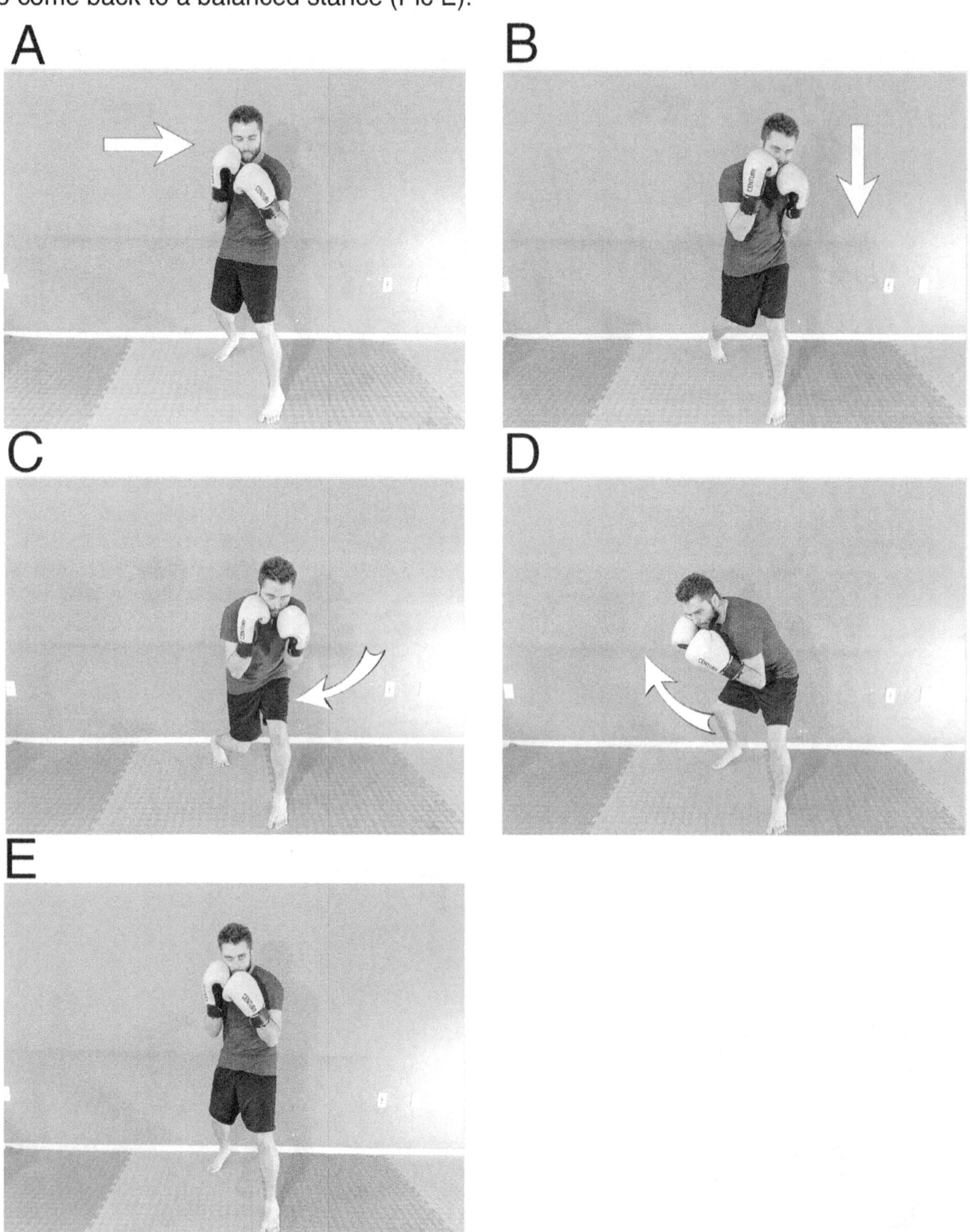

Practice these three movements separately (Slip, Duck, Slip) and then try to blend them together. A huge benefit of practicing this way is that it will later help you to throw shots at the correct times and in the correct manner, off of movement patterns that you are already familiar with.

Drill

Drill 1A

Stand in place and have your partner throw Lead Hooks at your head. Evade them by Weaving Clockwise. (Pics A to F). Over the course of the drill, try to gradually shorten the arc of your Weave. Focus on staying balanced. You should be able to Weave without taking a step. After the round, switch which partner is attacking and which is defending.

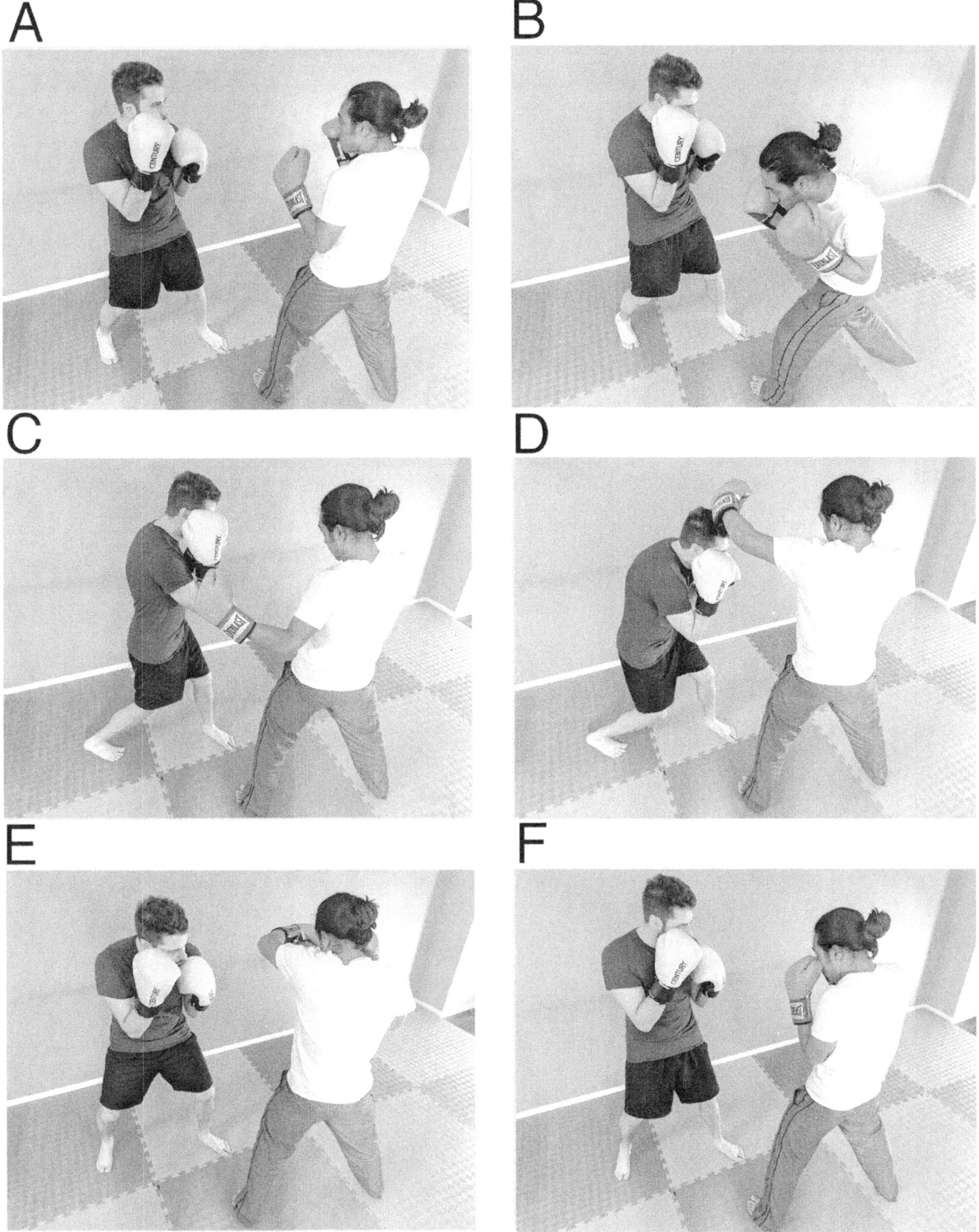

Drill 1B

Stand in place and have your partner throw Rear Hooks at your head. Evade them by Weaving Counter-Clockwise. (Pics A to F). Over the course of the drill, try to gradually shorten the arc of your Weave. Focus on staying balanced. You should be able to Weave without taking a step. After the round, switch which partner is attacking and which is defending.

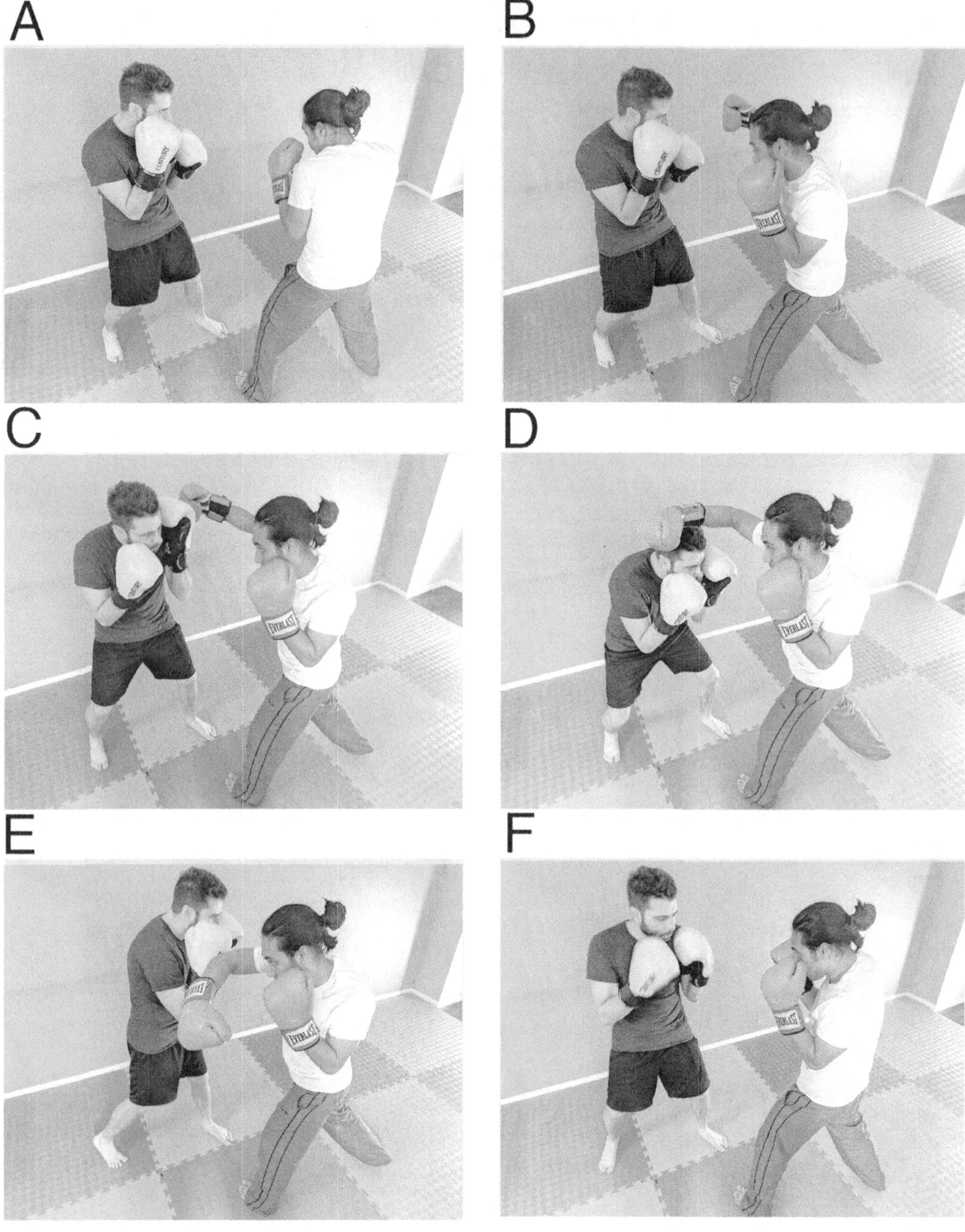

Drill 2

Have your partner throw mostly Straights, and then try to surprise you with a Lead or Rear Hook every so often. Slip their Straights (Pics A & B) and Weave underneath their Hooks (Pics C to E). After Weaving, throw a Return or Intercepting counter (Pic F). After the round, switch which partner is attacking and which is defending.

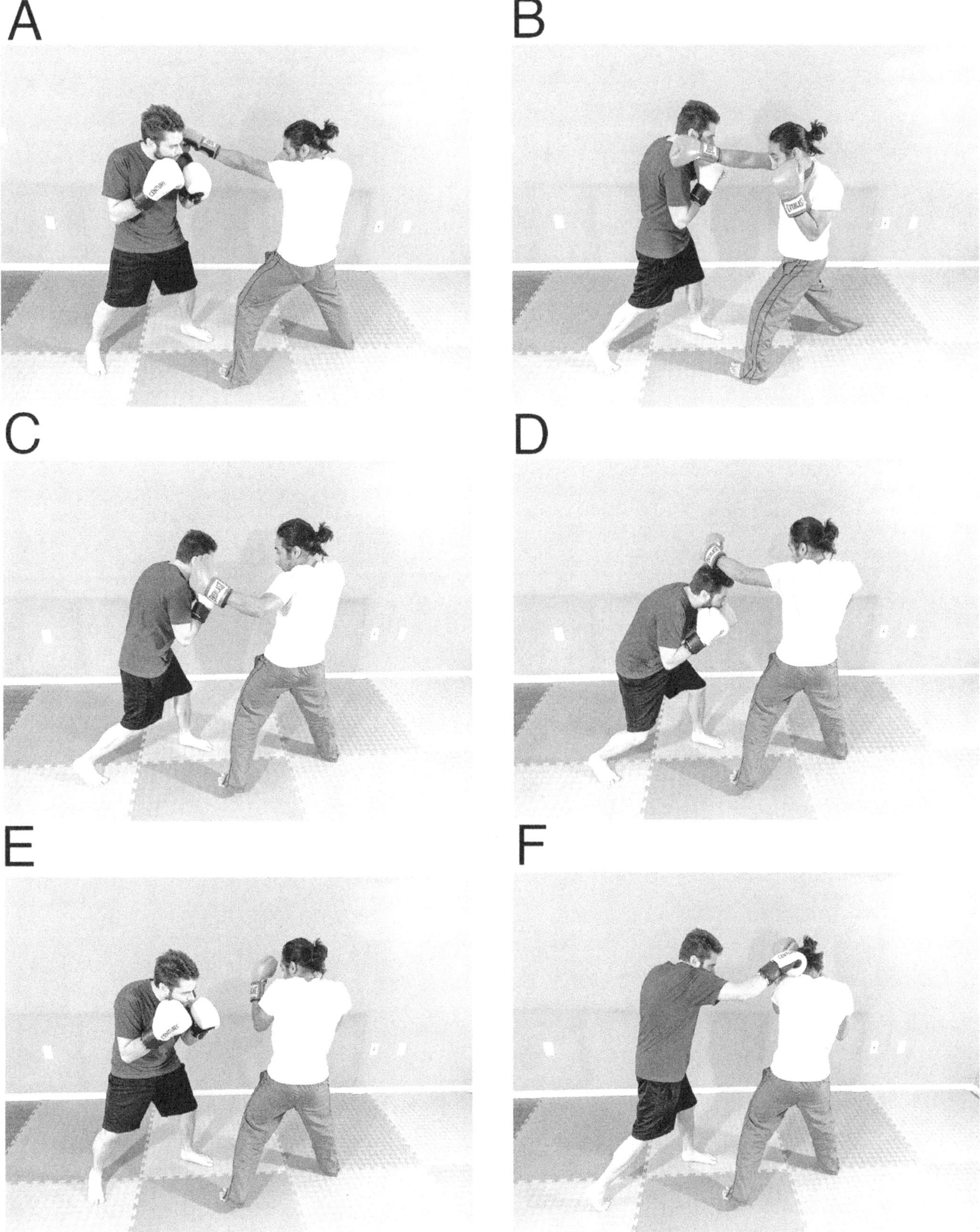

Drill 3

Have your partner throw punches at your head. Practice circling, stepping out and Pivoting away to take a superior angle (Pics A to C). Pivoting out of a Weave is one of the best ways to put an opponent in a vulnerable position. You may add on Return counters after you feel you get the hang of it (Pic D). After the round, switch which partner is attacking and which is defending.

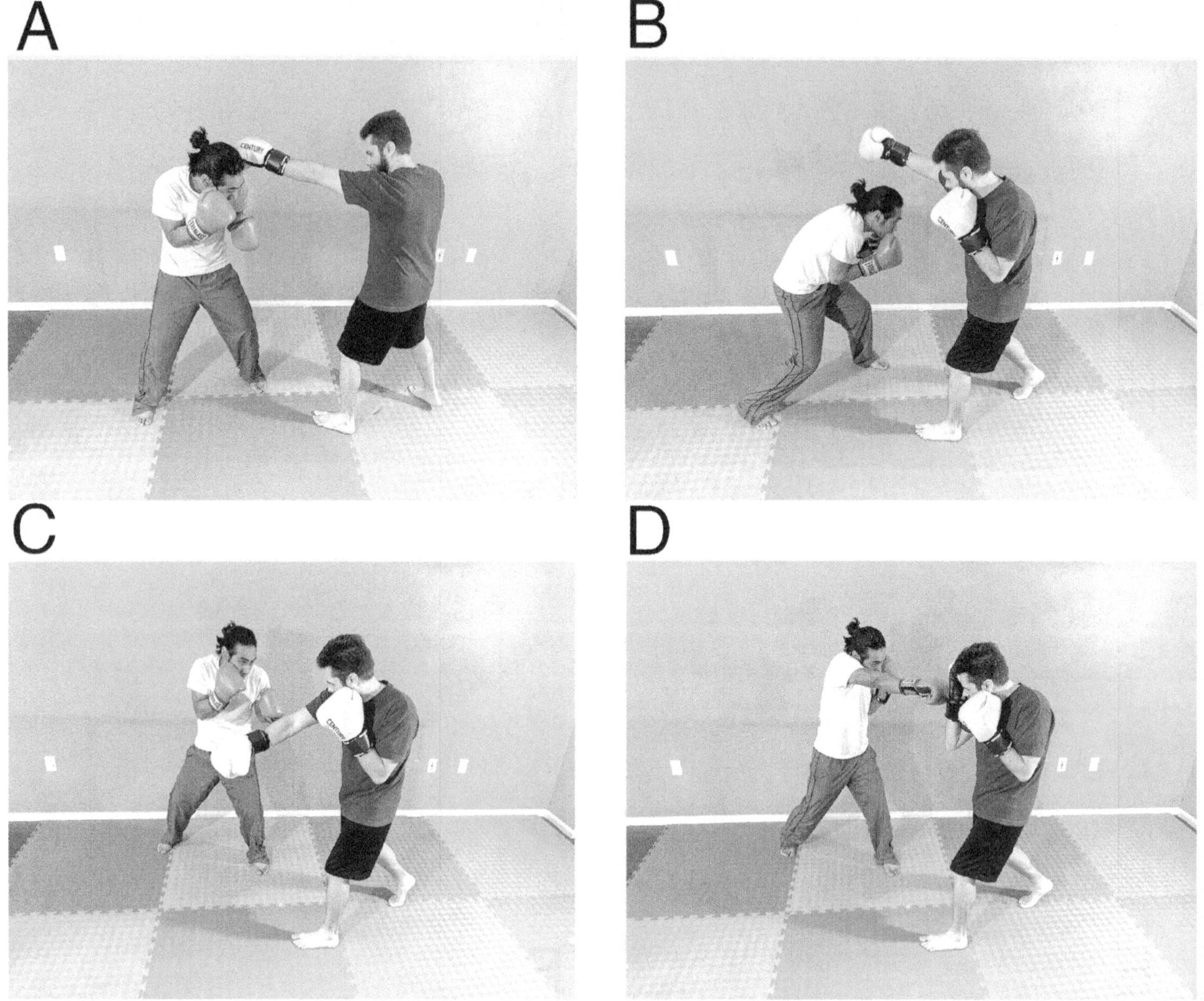

Drop Slip vs Rolls vs Weaves

It's important to note the differences between Drop Slips and Weaves. While Weaving means that your head is moving in a circular motion (like the letter U), Drop Slips are straight diagonal lines that moves towards (and hopefully under) your opponent's punch. They look like a slash /. The pics below illustrate a Weave (Pics A to F). Note how the fighters head first moves straight down (Pics A to C) before moving towards the punch (Pics D to E) and then finally straightening up (Pic F). You may also begin by Slipping in the same direction as the punch (Pic B). This will help you Roll in case the punch connects before you can Duck underneath. Rolls were covered in the High Guard section.

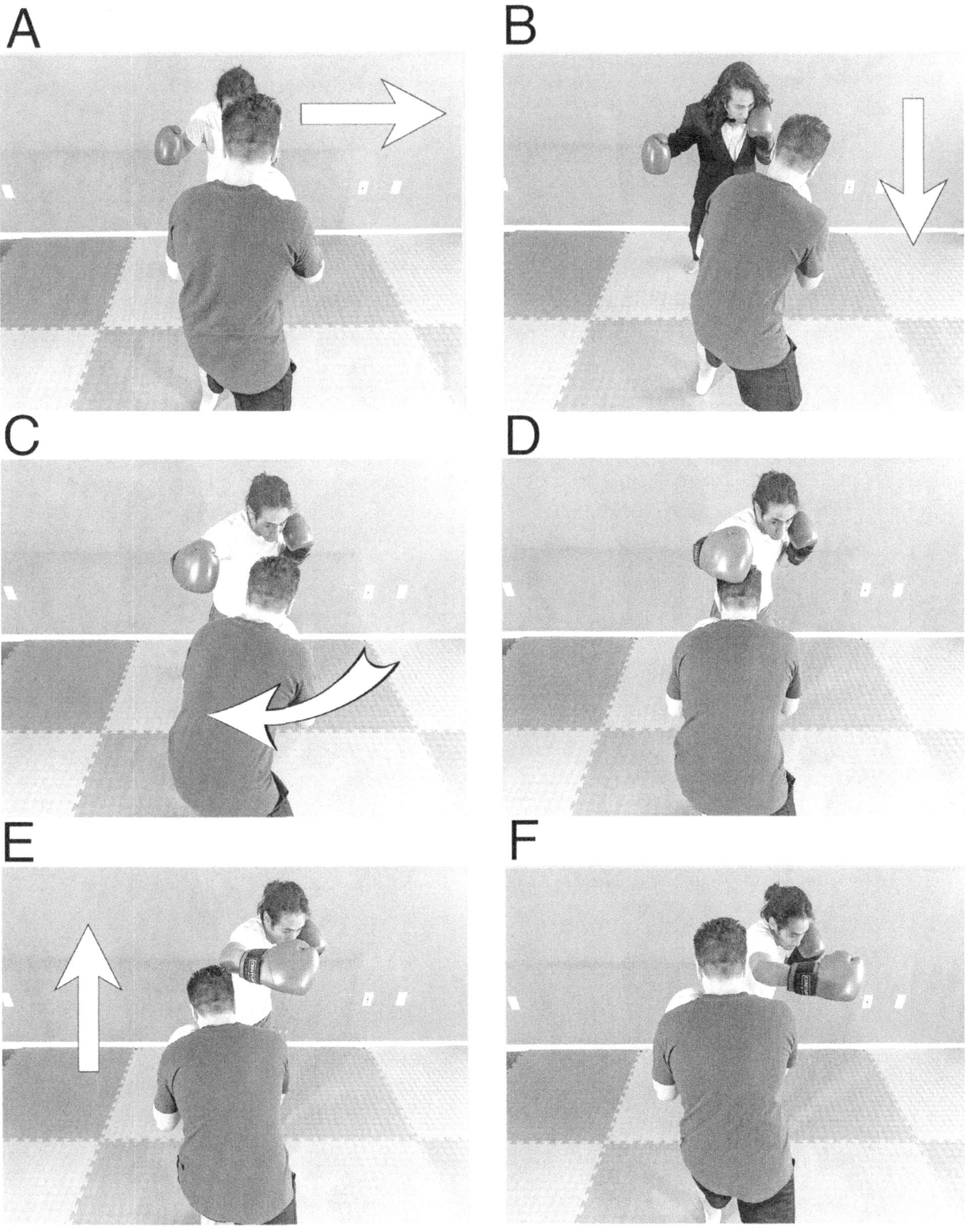

In contrast, Drop Slips move in a near straight line (Pics A to D). As such, they get you to your destination quicker for potentially faster counters. It should be apparent that while this may be faster, it is also more dangerous. As such, if you fear your opponent may be throwing lower than anticipated, you can supplement the Drop Slip with an Elbow Block (Pics E to F). You may also turn your Drop Slip into a Roll, provided you were moving in the same direction of your opponent's punch (moving with or against a strike was covered on page 224, and Rolls were covered in the High Guard chapter).

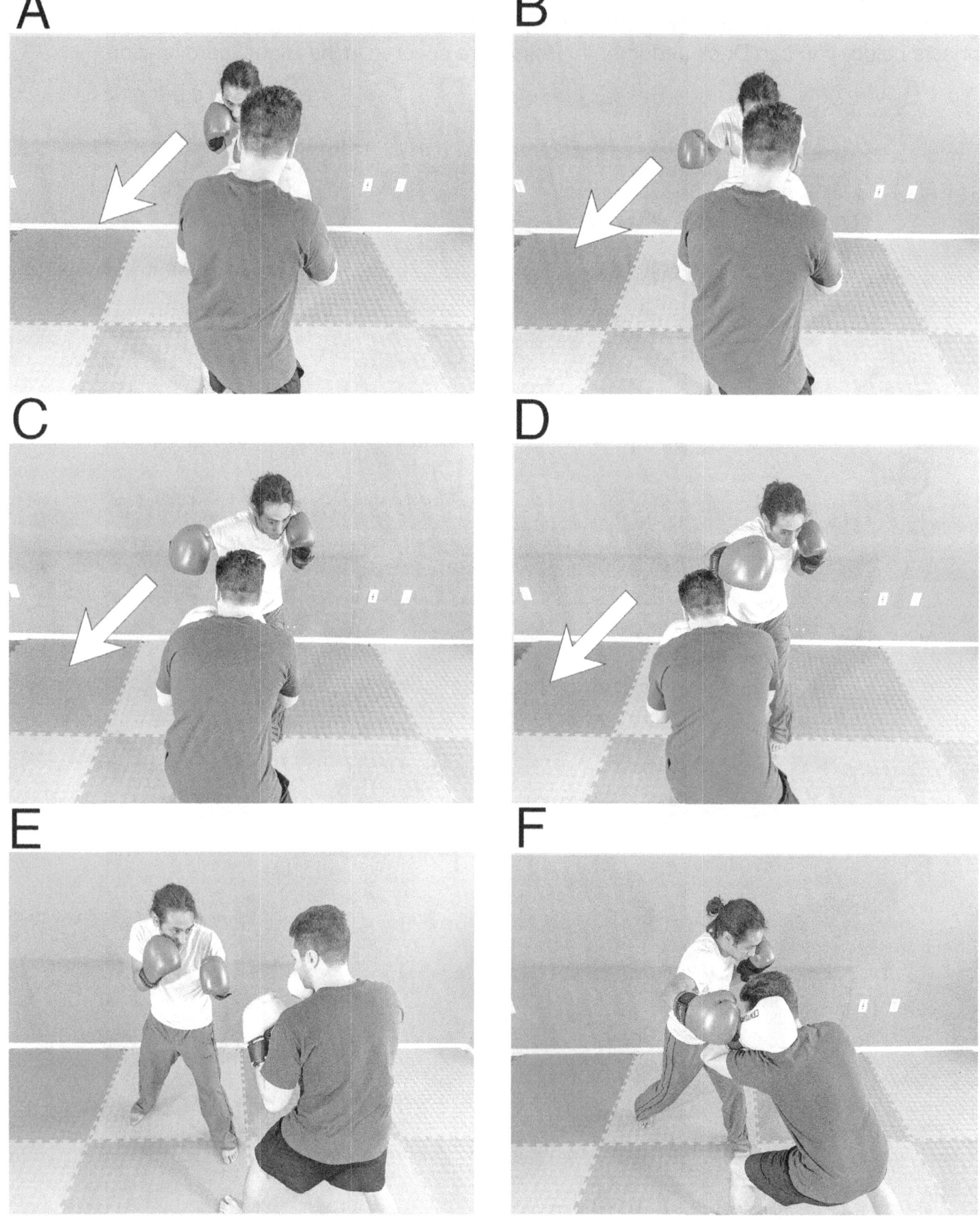

Concept - Head Slots & Draws

It is crucial to be ready to counter from any head slot that you use on a regular basis. In fact, some fighters keep their head well off the center line as part of their normal Posture and Stance. Whether you keep your head off line as part of your regular style or just like to Slip or Duck into a few favorite positions, it is crucial to have counters ready. I am going to repeat this because I have recently seen a number of fighters with decent head movement lose because they used it purely defensively: HEAD MOVEMENT IS COMPLETELY USELESS IF YOU CANNOT FOLLOW IT UP WITH COUNTERS. Let's look at a few popular head positions before exploring some effective counters from those positions.

In picture A the fighter's head is directly on the center line. His high posture and straight legs will keep him mobile, and his defense will most likely be based on footwork. In picture B the fighter's head is leaning to his Lead Side. This is a rarer head position, but was used by the likes of Ali and Sugar Ray Leonard. The idea is usually to Cross Step and Jab, but you may also step out to land a Cross. In picture C the fighter is leaning his head to his right. This is a very common head position. It helps to Load your Rear Side attacks with more power, and positions your head in a way that forces opponents to over reach with their own Rear Side attacks. Picture D is another common head position. The fighter leans far forward. His Guard protect his head and his stomach is far away, with his elbows providing additional defense. This position can be used to Pull back to an upright posture to counter, or to Duck under to close the distance. Read on to see examples of counters from each of these positions. Keep in mind these are not the only counters available. There are many more shown throughout the book.

The important thing is to understand the concept of setting traps. Because you know what your opponent is likely to throw while in any given position, you can try to goad your opponent into throwing that attack on purpose so that you can counter them. This is known as a Draw.

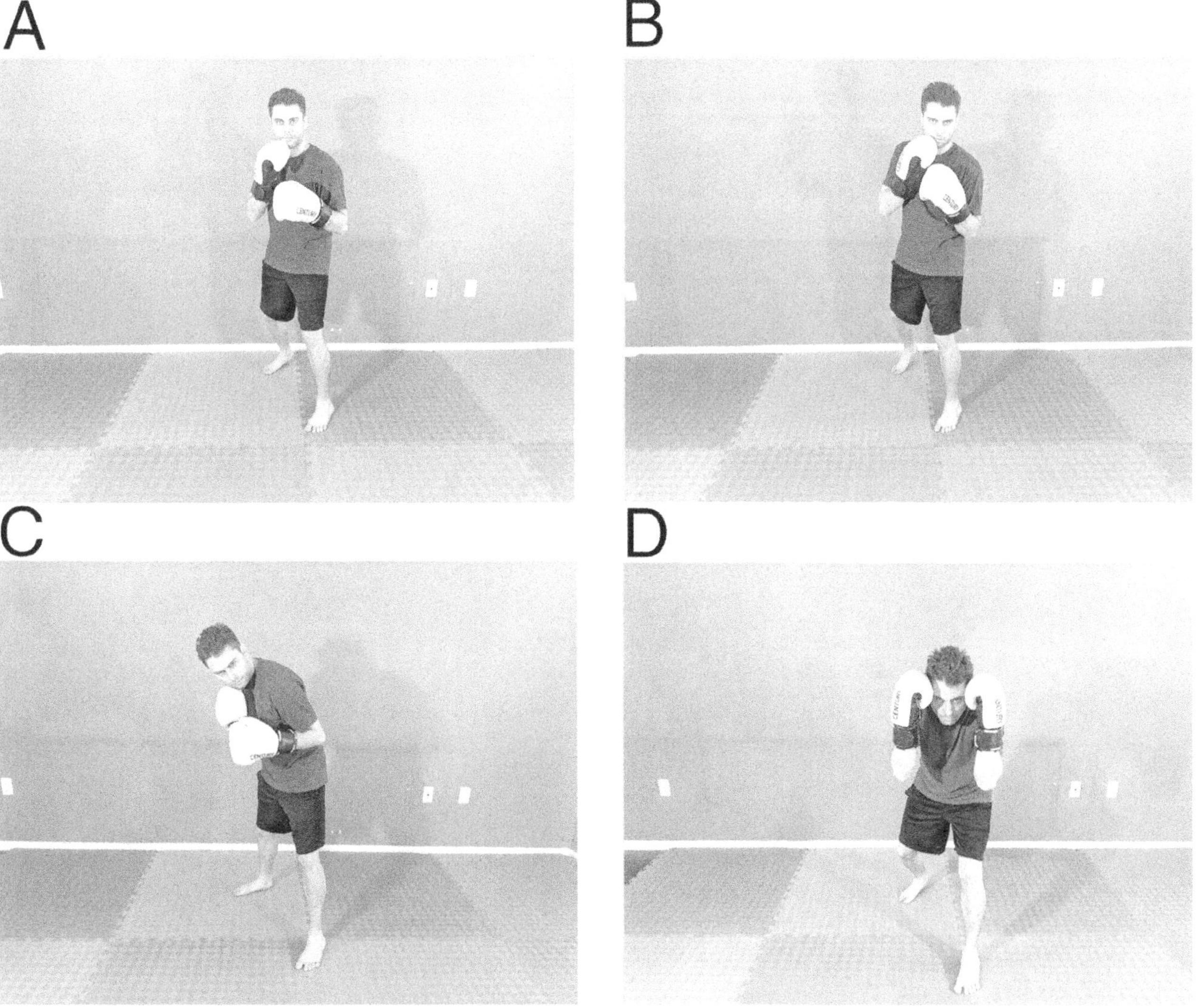

Here the fighter keeps their posture far forward, inviting the opponent to attack his head (Pic A). When his opponent takes the bait, he Returns to an upright posture, and Side Steps or Pivots to Intercept his opponent's Cross with a Lead Hook (Pic B).

Below, the fighter Crouches down, goading the opponent to punch down (Pics A to B). When the opponent takes the bait, the fighter Slips his opponent's Cross to connect with an Overhand (Pics C to D).

A B

C  D

In Pics A to B, the fighter leans to the Inside. This unstable position invites his opponent to throw Jabs at his open head. The fighter then Cross Steps (breaking a fundamental rule by crossing his own feet) to move his head offline and Returns with a Jab of his own (Pics C to D). This was a favorite of Ali, who would also counter by stepping Inside and throwing his right over his opponent's Jab. Check out Ali's knockout of Zora Folley for a real life example. Prince Naseem Hamed would also use this head position to Pull Slip and land a Lead Uppercut underneath his opponent's Jab or Cross.

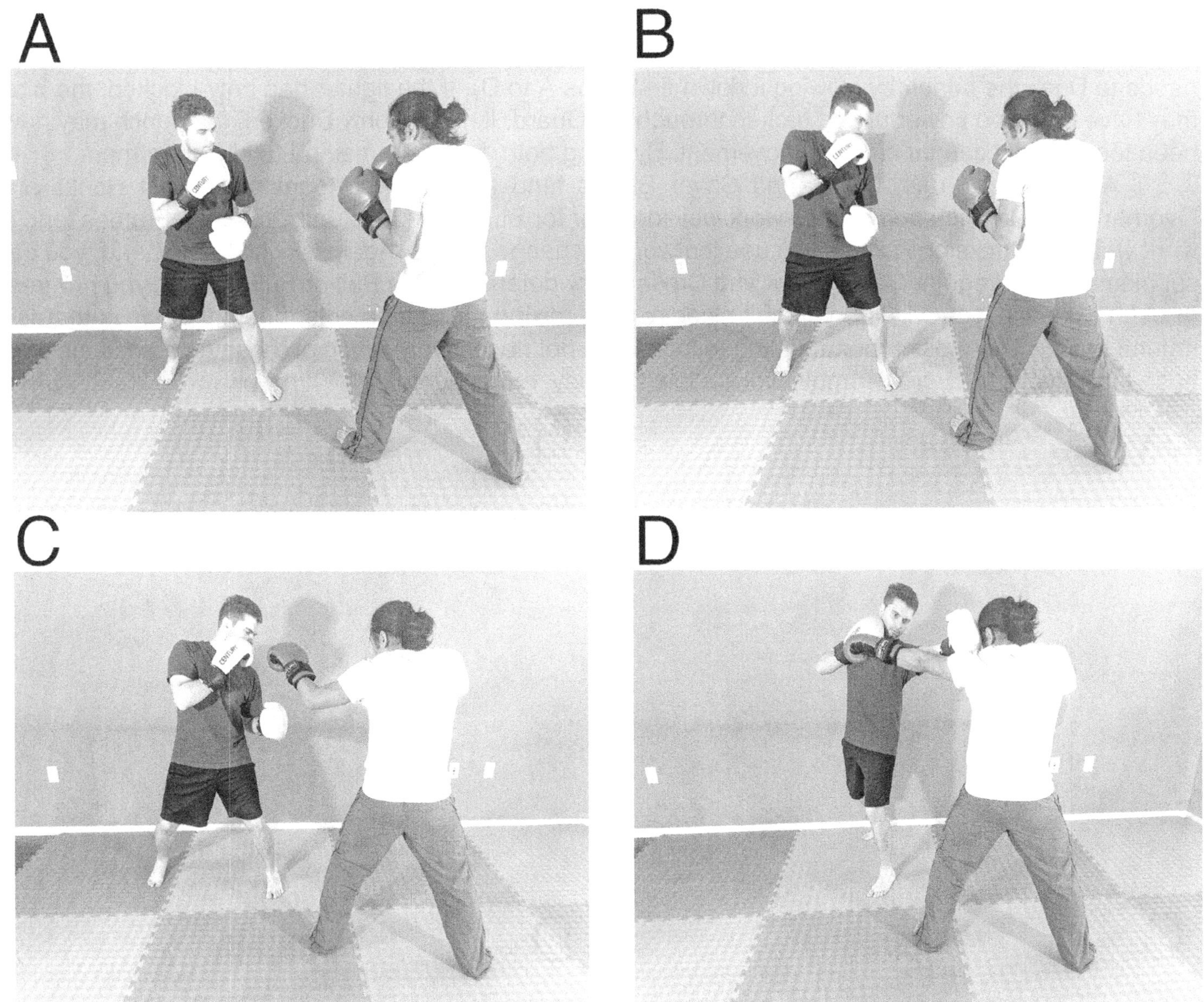

Concept – Supplementing Head Movement With Blocks & Parries

While it looks impressive to keep your hands low and rely solely on head movement for defense, it is not always the most practical idea, to say the least. Supplementing head movement with blocks and Parries may take away the odds of landing some counters, but it will also keep you more safe. Furthermore, adding Parries or Frames to your head movement can greatly disturb your opponent's balance and timing by knocking their strike off course.

Below is a simple example. The fighter Blocks as he Ducks, giving himself the extra time he needs to Duck the punch by slowing it down first (Pics A to D). If the fighter had only blocked, the blow may have been too powerful and broken through his Guard. If he had only Ducked, the punch may have been too fast and caught him mid movement. By using both, he has remained totally unharmed.

As a general rule, Ducks and Cover Blocks tend to work well together against Hooks and Overhands, while Slips and Parries work well together for Straights (Jabs and Crosses). Frames tend to work well with Ducks or Pulls as you use footwork to change angles. Against kicks to the head, you can supplement your regular Cover Block and Cross Parry defense with a Pull or Pull Slip. As you progress through the drills, you will find yourself blending and mixing these elements together in ways that feel natural to you. The most important thing to look for is not necessarily which of these combinations work best defensively, but which combinations allow for easy, hard counters.

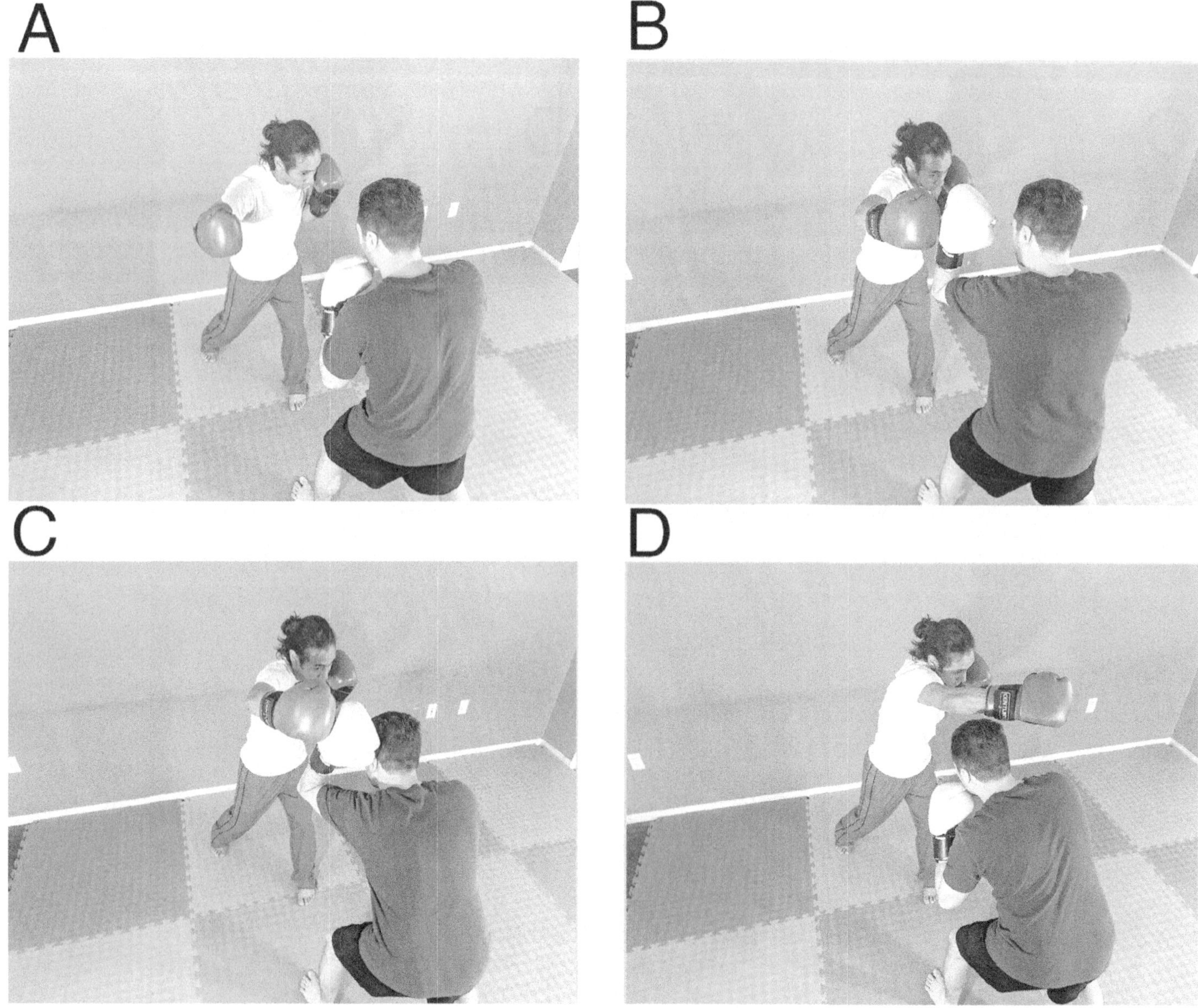

Concept – Mixing A Tight Guard With Head Movement

A fighter who knows how to take impact behind a tight Guard *and* has great head movement is a very dangerous fighter. One of the best at this is Canelo Alvarez. Alvarez will get his opponents used to beating on his High Guard, conditioning them to expect resistance. This has the same affect that punching the heavy bag too often does in some people. Over time, Canelo's opponent will become so used to resistance that they begin to lean into their punches. If your opponent does this (Pics A to B), it is an opportune moment to suddenly Duck, Slip or Pull instead. With any luck your opponent, expecting more of the same resistance, will over reach and teeter off balance, hurling themselves right into your counter (Pics C to F). Hooks work great (Pic F) but Canelo has also used a Rear Upper to great effect.

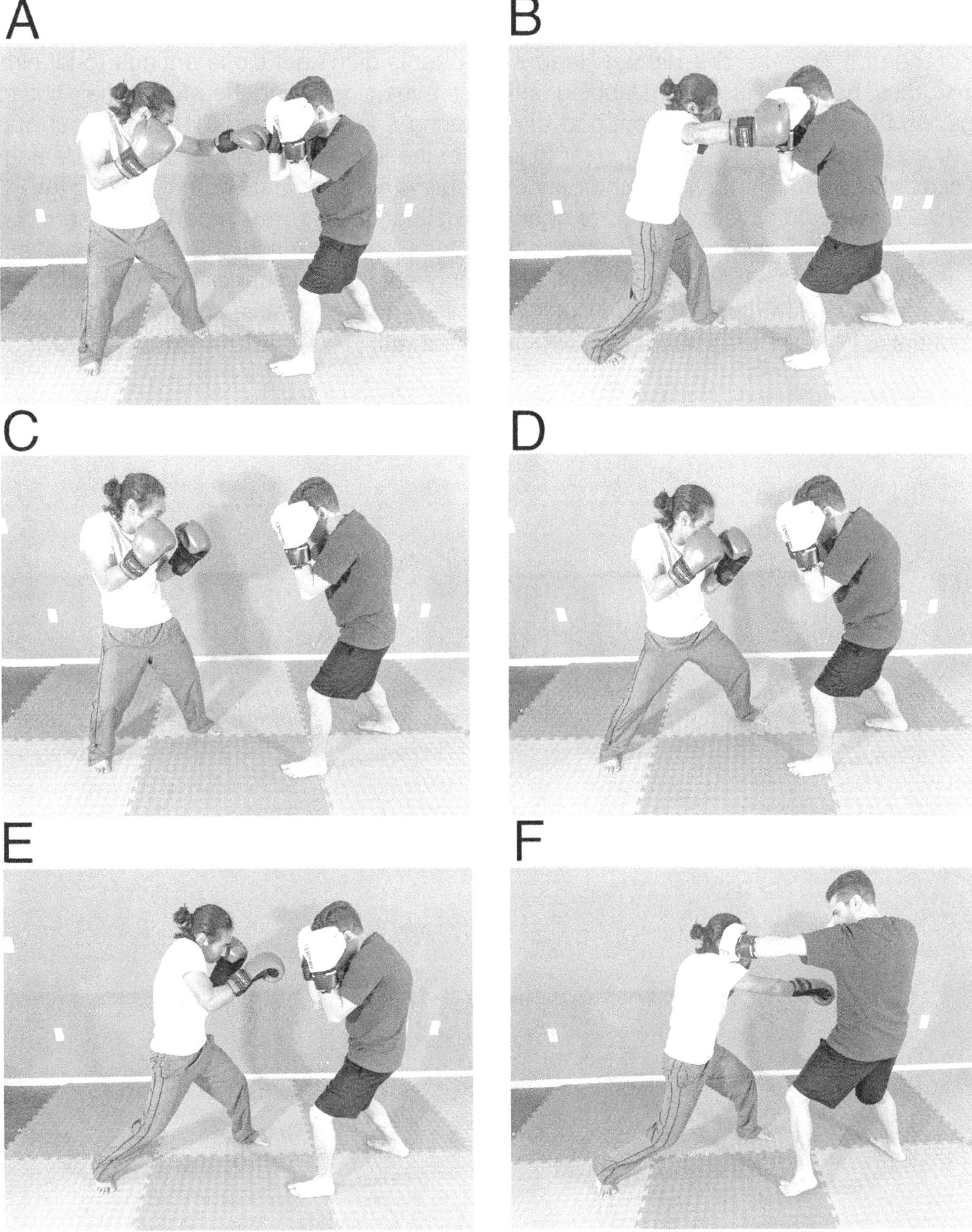

Concept – Drawing With Low Risk Attacks

There is often nothing more boring than a fight between two counter strikers. This is because both are waiting for the other to lead, and when no attack is forthcoming they are at a total loss about what to do. If you are a counter striker you should not rely on your opponent to take the lead. Instead, master a low risk attack to keep the action going. The Jab is the go-to in Boxing, and works fairly well in kickboxing and MMA as well. Teeps and Sidekicks to the Thigh and Roundhouse Kicks to the Calf are also great options for Kickboxing and MMA.

If you take this one simple piece of advice your game will improve dramatically for a number of reasons. First, you will be racking up points. Even if your attacks aren't doing much damage, the score cards will show the difference.

Second, it is actually very possible to damage an opponent with weaker attacks if you just throw enough of them. If Thomas The Hitman Hearns opponents didn't get close enough to let him land his signature Cross, he would just keep Jabbing until their eyes closed and the pain in their ribs took away their legs. And that gets us to the best part of mastering a low risk attack: it forces your opponent to engage or accept defeat. If he doesn't want to lose on the score cards or keep taking damage, he will have to commit to something. As a counter puncher, this is exactly what you are looking for.

While you should have a counter for nearly any situation, it is very important to learn counters off of your low risk attack. For instance, if your opponent tries to counter your Jab with a Jab of his own, be ready to throw a Cross over his Jab like Ali. If your opponent learns to check your Roundhouse Kicks to the leg, be ready to follow up with a Lead Hook like Jose Aldo. Be creative and try to use something that your opponent is not expecting and not equipped to deal with. This is what crafting your own style is all about.

Concept – Using The Weakness In Your Guard or Stance To Draw & Counter

Each Guard, Posture, or Stance comes with different strengths and weaknesses. Turning your weakness into a positive is a powerful concept. Look at it this way; Your opponent will target you where you're most vulnerable anyways, so why not capitalize on it?

We'll look at how keeping your head open can help Draw attacks to counter in the Low Guard section, but there are a lot of different ways to use this concept that have nothing to do with leaving your hands down.

One great example of using a weakness to bait your opponent comes from the kickboxer Manson Gibson. Gibson kept a bladed, sideways stance. In kickboxing or MMA, this is just asking for a Rear Leg Roundhouse to your Lead Leg. Knowing this full well but preferring his sideways stance, Gibson would dispel the force of his opponent's kick by spinning with it, countering with a Spinning Back Fist or Back Kick.

Try your best to analyze your own Stance, Posture and Guard. If there is an inherent weakness or a few attacks you notice keep getting through your defenses, try coming up with a powerful counter that takes advantage of these "weaknesses". You may be surprised at what you can pull off. Intellect and creativity are a fighter's greatest assets, so put them to good use.

References – Basic Head Movement

Slips, Ducks & Pulls

Wilfred Benitez had legendary defense. It comprised mostly of very slight movements that caused his opponents to miss by an inch or less. Check out any of his fights in his prime to see it on display. His fight vs Roberto Duran is a great example of how to use head movement to deal with head shots so you can leave your arms free to protect your body. Sugar Ray Leonard had amazing head movement and actually out-boxed Benitez. You can watch Salvador Sanchez for Returns so great they sent his opponents swinging wildly off balance. In Muay Thai, Samrak Khamsing judiciously used boxing-like head movement and incorporated it into his already stellar Muay Thai defenses. In MMA, Jose Aldo and Max Holloway are great fighters to study for masterful use of basic head movement in mostly Closed Stance positions.

Slips, Ducks, & Pulls – Open Stance Considerations

Watch Pernell Whitaker vs Oscar De Le Hoya to see some otherworldly head movement by Whitaker. Whitaker was robbed (in my opinion, some disagree) but both fighters put on a great performance and are well worth studying for Open Stance head movement. Terence Crawford is a multi-stanced fighter with great head movement. He's particularly good at Pull Slipping away from an opponent's Jab to come over his shoulder with a Lead Hook. He will also Slip a Cross to land with a Rear Hook or Uppercut. He's a great example of countering in an Open Stance while circling or going backwards (although he does get aggressive depending on the situation and opponent).

Lomachenko is a great fighter to watch for aggressive head movement. Blame it on the rarity of Southpaws in boxing or acknowledge his incredible skills, but Lomachenko is once again a prime example of Open Stance tactics. Watch how he stays at Mid-Range, Ducking or Slipping punches as he closes the distance. In Muay Thai, Saenchai, Samart and Lerdsila have phenomenal head movement from an Open Position. Saenchai and Lerdsila use flashy Pulls against kicks. Samart is adept at Slipping strikes to counter. In MMA, there is no better fighter to study than a prime Anderson Silva. His head movement ranges from precise and subtle to ridiculous and flashy. His fight vs Forrest Griffin is legendary. Another great option is Connor McGregor, who built a career off of Pull Slipping to Return Counter with a hard left.

Drop Slips

Although Tyson was excellent at Weaving, he would often go for the more dangerous method of Drop Slipping (Ducking while Slipping off line) underneath his opponent's punches to Return Counter with a Gazelle Hook. Check out his fight vs Donnie Long for very quick examples of these counters. Tyson knocks down Long by Drop Slipping under his Jab and shuffling into a Lead Hook in the first round and then finishes him off soon after. Canelo vs Khan is an example of a fighter using a Drop Slip to knock out an opponent with an Intercepting Counter. His fight vs Kovelev contains several examples of Return Counters as well. Finally, Floyd Patterson used Drop Slips to knock out opponents with his flashy Gazelle Hook.

In MMA, GSP Drop Slipped to set up punches and takedowns. Check out any of his fights to see this in action multiple times. TJ Dillashaw is another great example. Dillashaw would even Shift stances as he Drop Slipped. Sometimes this would turn into a Hook or Overhand, and sometimes he would use his new Lead Foot to Trip his opponent. Watch his fight vs Issei Tamura to see Tamura react to a Drop Shift by Sprawling for a takedown and instead receive a shin to the face, ending the fight.

Drop Slips – Open Stance Considerations

Watch Manny Pacquiao vs Chris Algieri for a master class in Drop Slipping. Pacman Drop Slipped Outside to Intercept Algieri's Jab with hard Crosses and Overhands and Drop Slipped Inside to Load Return Counters all night long, resulting in several knockdowns. You can also see present the same Pull Slips and Return Lead Hooks you saw Terence Crawford execute earlier.

Weaves

There are so many legendary boxers who made Weaves a primary method of defense. Julio Cesar Chavez Sr. used it very aggressively to cut off the ring. Nicolino Locche is an old school example. Known as a defensive genius, Locche shows how small and tight it's possible to keep the motion of your Weave and still be effective. Mike Tyson is an obvious example, check out any videos of him during his rise to the championship. In MMA, Stipe Miocic is a talented champion who uses Weaves not only to stay safe, but also to threaten and score takedowns. Watch his fight vs Francis Ngannou to see these tactics put into action multiple times. There is also a good deal of Slips, Pulls and Ducks followed up with hard counters.

Drawing

Prince Naseem Hamed provides both subtle and extreme variations of Drawing to counter. Jersey Joe Walcott vs Ezzard Charles 3 has one of the most beautiful examples of a draw and counter ever. Walcott Slips Outside to Draw Charles Jab, and then Slips Inside to KO Charles with an Uppercut that seems to come out of nowhere. In kickboxing and Muay Thai, Saenchai is one of the best at baiting attacks to counter. In MMA, Wonderboy Thompson baits his opponent's into Leg Kicks with a forward Lead Leg and then Intercepts with a Sidekick to the body or head.

Drawing With A Low Risk Attack

Great counter punchers irritate their opponents with a low risk attack. When their opponent tries to counter this low risk annoyance, the counter puncher is ready to counter their counter. Watch Thomas Hearns in nearly any fight. His bout vs Pipino Cuevas provides some obvious, quick examples. Hearns throws almost nothing but his Jab until Cuevas tries to counter. Then Hearns counters the counter. You can see Hearns Jab and then counter Cuevas's Return Hook with an Intercepting Hook several times, and eventually end the fight with an Intercepting Cross over Cuevas's Return Jab.

Using The Weaknesses In Your Guard To Draw Attacks

Manson Gibson's stance basically screamed "Leg kick me!" at his opponent's. Gibson spun with the attack to land a Spinning Back Kick or Spinning Back Fist. Watch his fight vs Hoost for some great examples, or any highlight reel of him.

Using A Tight Guard With Head Movement

Canelo vs Kovalev once again provides a number of examples. Justin Gaethje's more recent fights also have great examples of this principle.

Supplementing Head Movement With Blocks & Parries

Most fighters do this. Pick a few of your favorites or some previous recommendations from this book and look at how they use head movement in combination with blocks, Parries and Frames.

Crouching – Armstrong Style

Crouching really is an extreme and specialized form of head movement. Like the Low Guard, fighters that attempt it either give up or develop excellent defense. By Crouching, you open up new angles of evasion. You also make your strikes unpredictable and Load them with a lot of power. But although you enhance the range of your head movement, you may also limit your footwork mobility. As such, Crouching may work best for shorter fighters who lack reach and distance anyways. In fact, Crouching is one of the best ways to quickly cover distance and move into Mid or Close-Range.

Crouch

Rather than bend at the knees, hunch your back and bend at the waist to lower your trunk and extend your torso over your feet. Never dip your head down lower than waist level. Crouching fighters choose to forego the "proper" technique and bend at the waist to Duck, Slip and Weave to close distance more quickly (Pics B to D).

There are a number of benefits to this idea, but a lot of potential pitfalls as well. Crouching can leave you more vulnerable to uppercuts and knees. Lowering your center of gravity can also limit mobility, making it difficult to quickly change directions.

However, if done properly Crouching can be a highly effective technique for boxers and, believe it or not, mixed martial artists as well. Boxers who crouched low include Jack Dempsey, Rocky Marciano, Henry Armstrong (who this section is named after) and Joe Frazier. Mixed Martial Artists who Crouch include Khabib and Daniel Cormier.

When Crouching, you can keep your torso more square; like Joe Frazier or Julio Cesar Chavez, or more sideways; like Daniel Cormier. Or you can alternate between the two, like Rocky Marciano. Keep in mind that if you keep a narrow stance, you may need to step your Lead Foot out to square up in order to obtain the full range of head movement from side to side.

Forwards Crouch

When Crouching forward, you can fully utilize lateral head movement, Weaving or Slipping left and right. This is a great boon when it comes to cutting off the ring and pressuring your opponent. In Boxing, you can unbalance your opponent by turning these Crouching Weaves into active pressure by driving your head and shoulders into your opponent's hip, chest or shoulder (Pics A to C). This can move them into inferior positions which you can then capitalize on (Pic D) or help to drive them to the ropes. In MMA, you can use this form of head movement to set up takedowns and drive your opponent to the cage (Pics E to F).

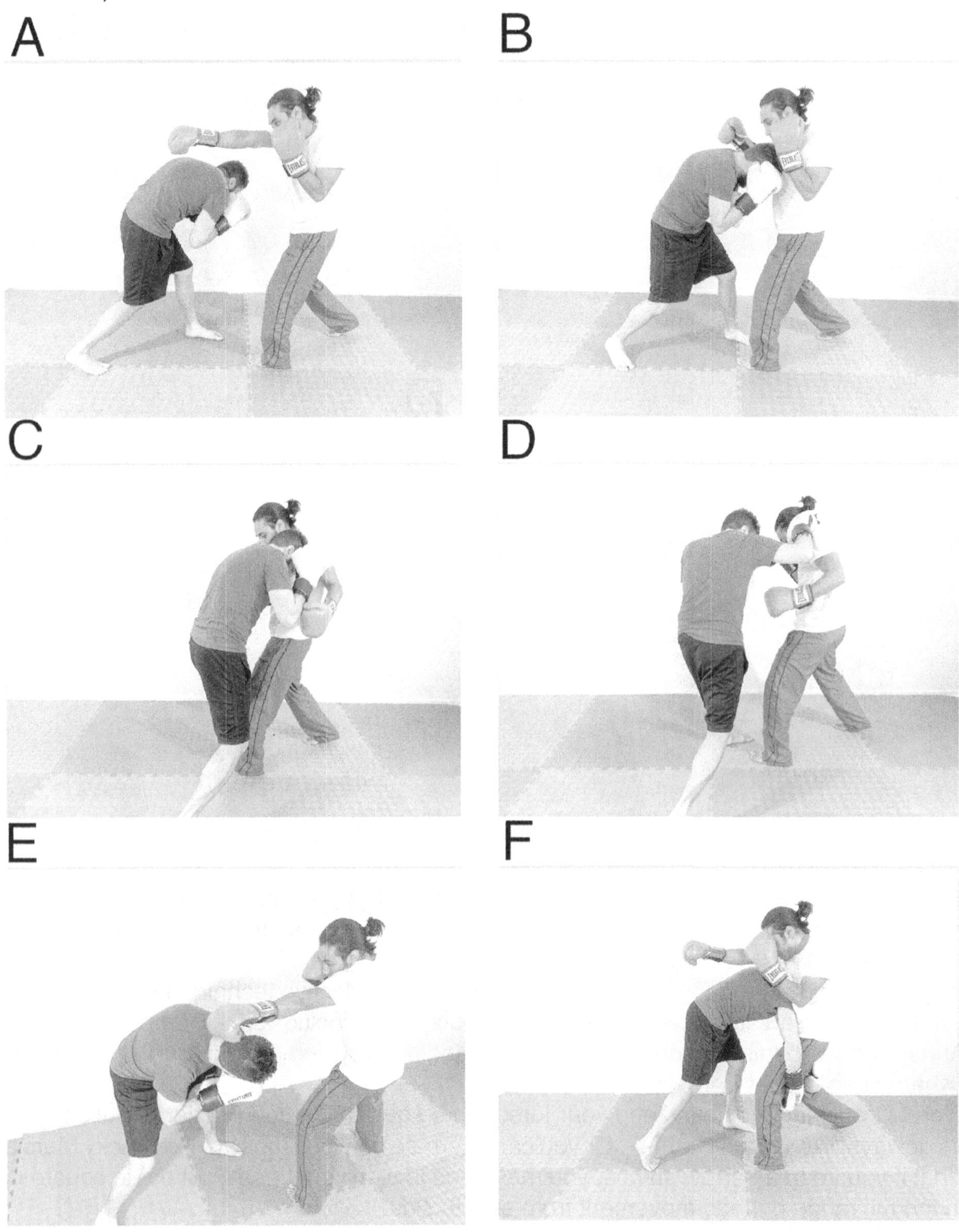

While Knees and Uppercuts are a major concern, Weaving in a low Crouch has proven a surprisingly effective method of evading them (Pics A to C & D to F). Watch the difference between Ben Askren, who simply jumps into his takedowns like an Olympic diver, and Khabib, who throws Hooks and Overhands while Weaving into close range.

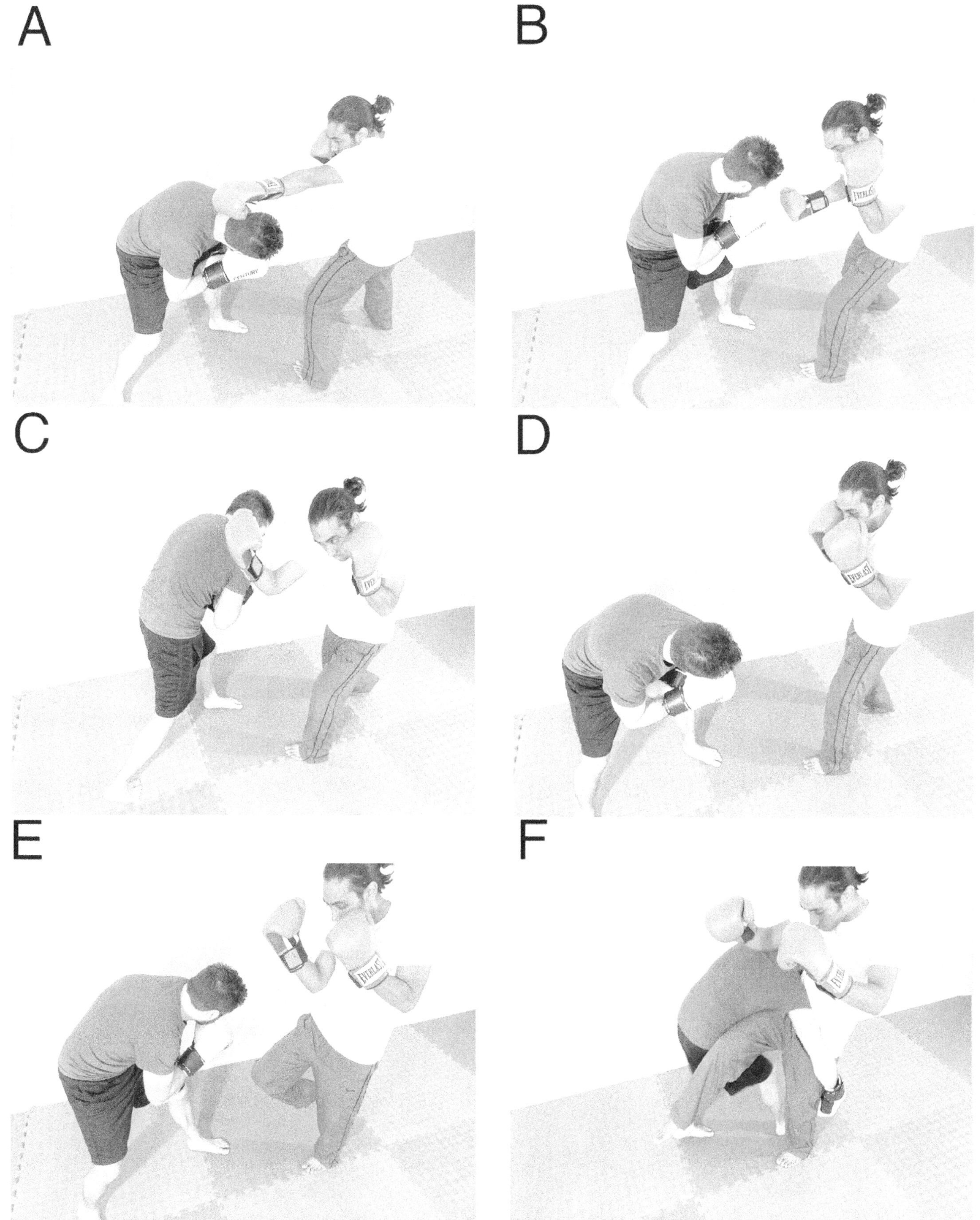

Sideways Crouch

When Crouching sideways, you can fully utilize linear movement, Pulling far back. This not only keeps you a small target, it also puts you in an ideal position to load up your Rear Hand. Watch Rocky Marciano, who stayed safely sideways until he chose to throw one of his insane Overhands.

In MMA, Daniel Cormier has used this Sideways Crouch in all of his fights, Weaving in low to secure a Collar Tie (Pics A to D) and then dirty boxing (Pic E) or wrestling (Pic F) from there. In this way Cormier blends head movement and head control. Read on to learn more about this type of Weave.

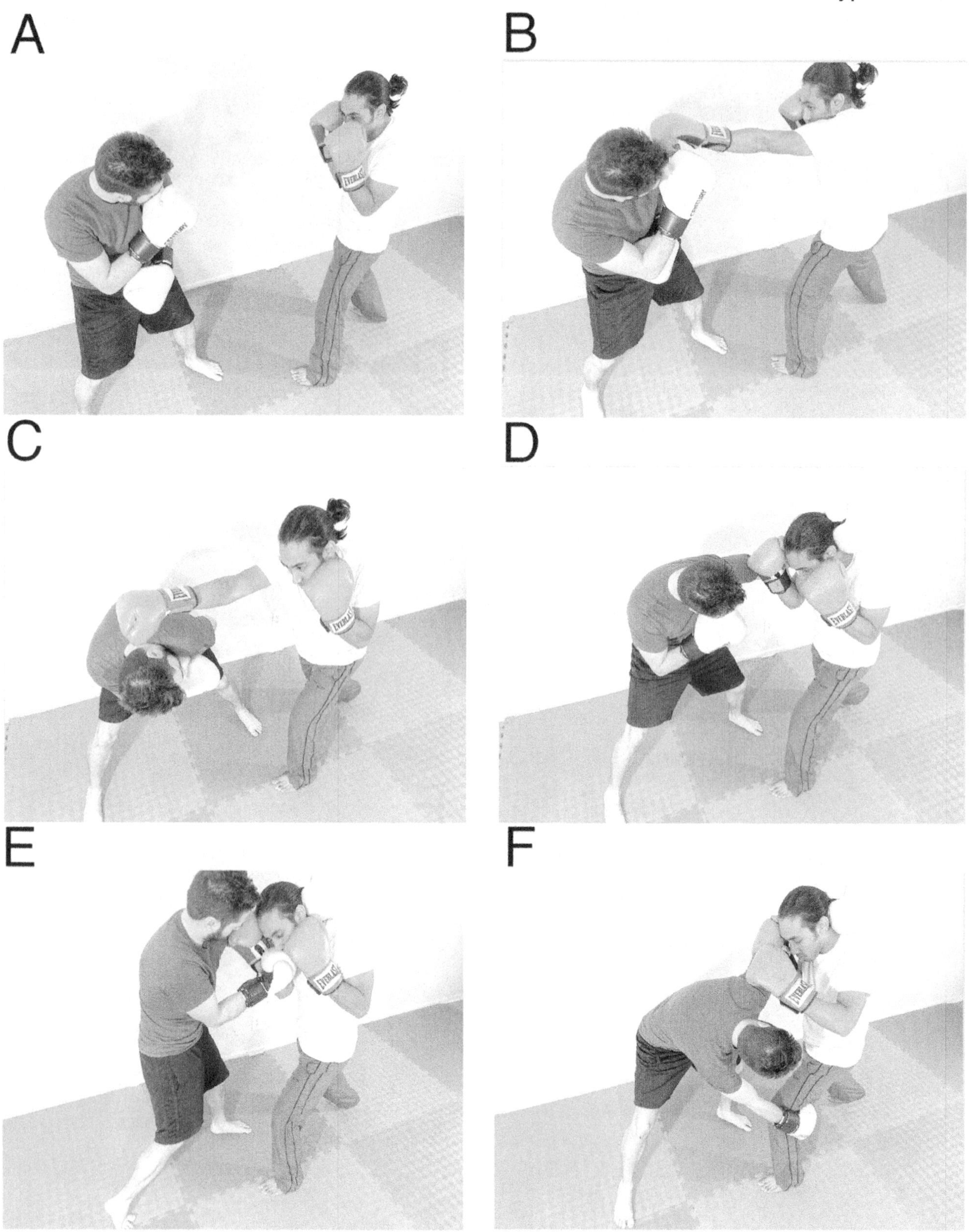

Open Stance Considerations

In an Open Stance, Overhands are highly effective in striking and Single Legs are best for grappling. Believe it or not, both of these work well with an Outside head position in MMA. This is because headlocks are not as big of a threat as taking a Knee. A tactic used by Khabib is to feint with your head to the Inside and then Weave Outside to pin your head to your opponent's (Pics A to D).

You may also use an Overhand to Shift forward into an Orthodox Stance and attempt a takedown from a Closed Position. This can be better for certain kinds of takedowns or to follow up with a Hook off your new Lead Hand.

Linear Weave

A Linear Weave is what we will call the movement pattern where a fighter first Pulls or Pull Slips, then goes into a deep Sideways Crouch before Returning to their regular posture (Pics A to F). This works well with a Shoulder Roll. Mayweather has Weaved like this after Rolling to evade a ridiculous amount of punches while staying in place. Mainly though, it is used to press in close.

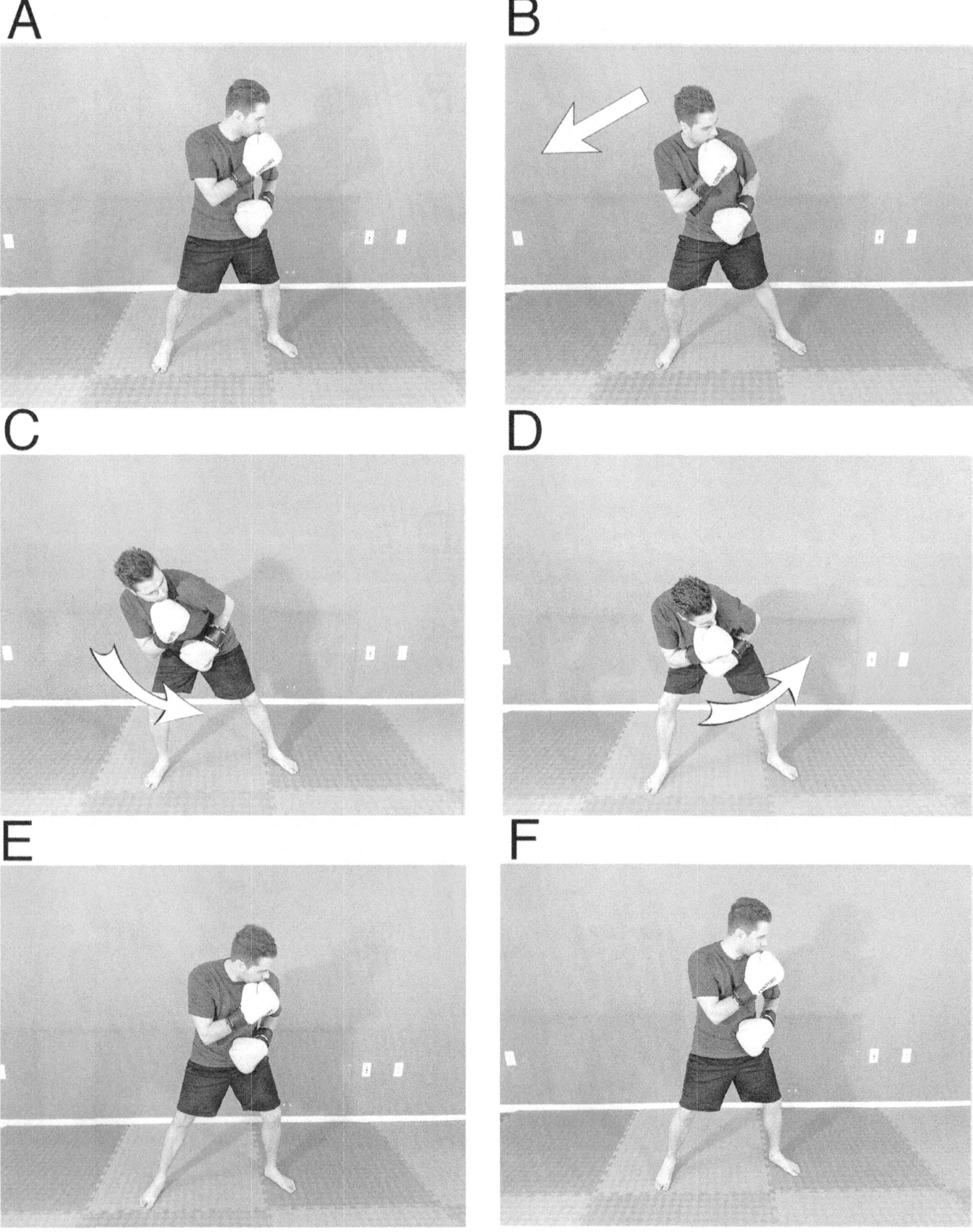

The truly bizarre thing about this head movement pattern is that it is mostly used to enter into Close Range, meaning that your head will be moving far back at the same time you are stepping forward towards your opponent's attack (Pics A to F). This Weave was used by Roberto Duran and many others throughout boxing history. It is now used by MMA Champion Daniel Cormier to enter into close range.

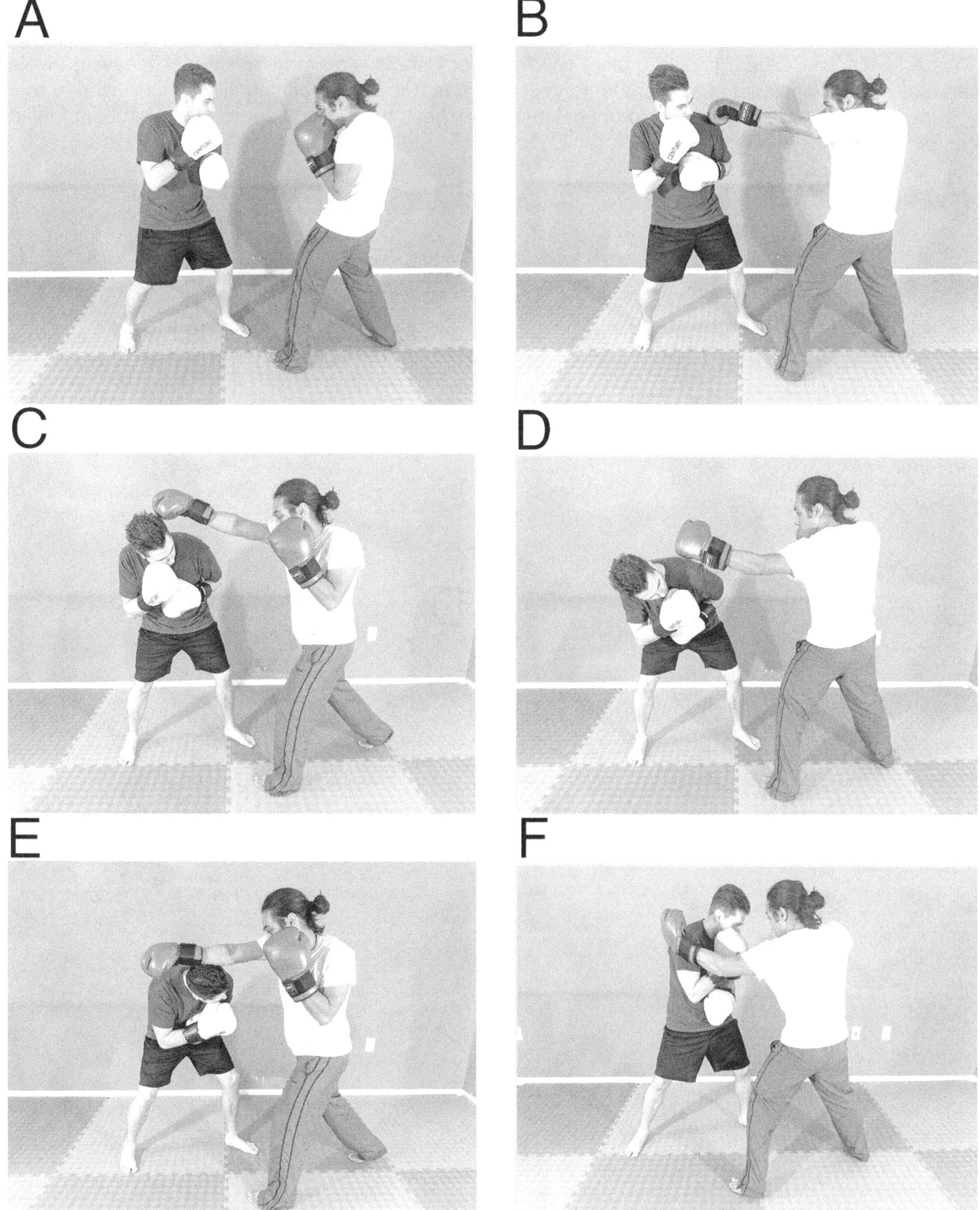

Drills

Drill 1A

In a Forward Crouch, chase your partner around the ring as they try to catch you with Straights and Hooks. Use the skills you have attained from previous drills to Slip, Duck and Weave to stay safe (Pics A to C). Your Guard should protect you from body shots. You may notice that Weaving this low can really add a whole lot of momentum to your punches (Pic D). Crouching allows your head to reach your opponent much faster, so try to drive it into their chest, hip or shoulder to pressure them towards the ropes or knock them off balance.

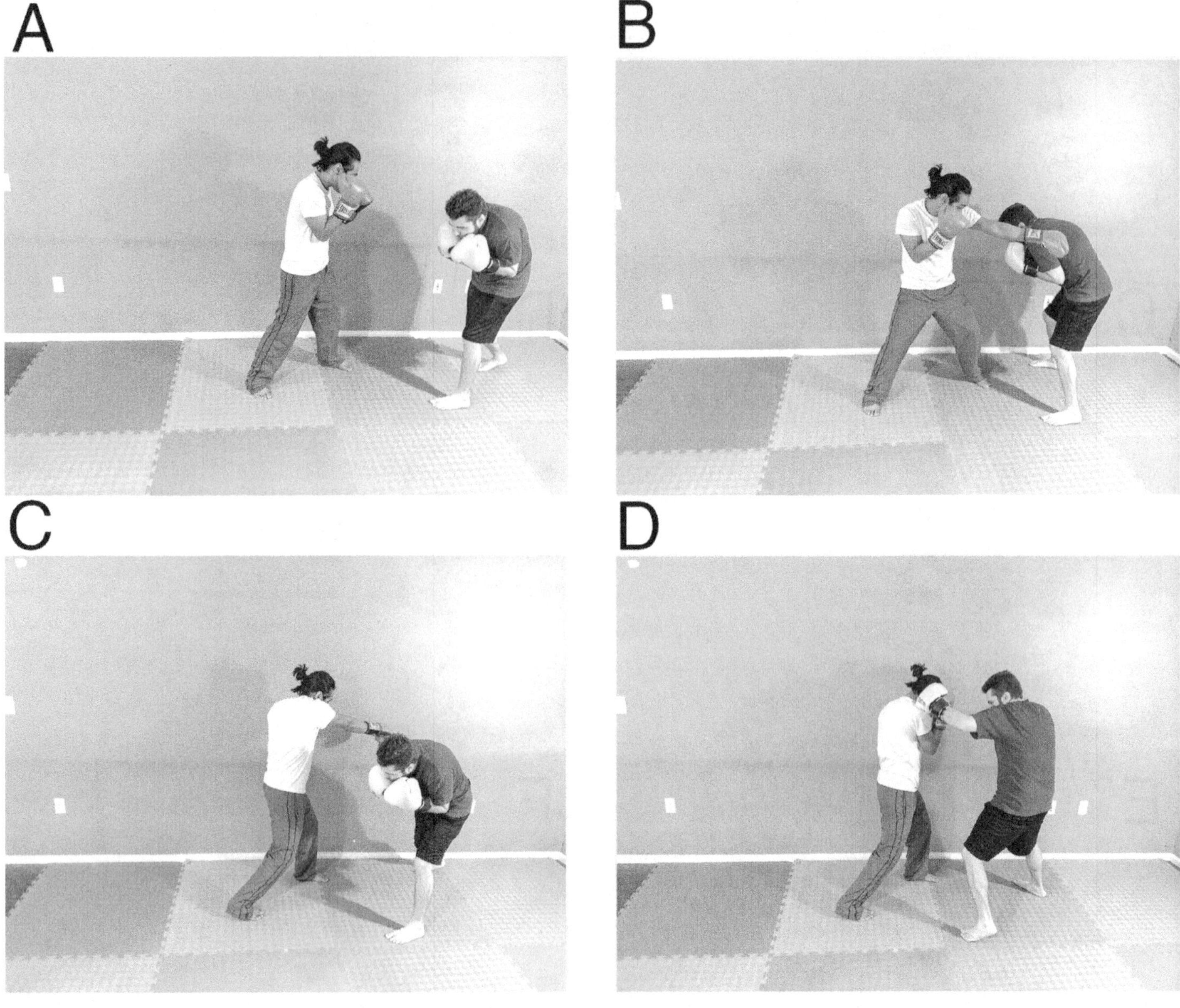

Drill 1B

Repeat the previous drill, but now have your partner throw Uppercuts, Knees and Roundhouse Kicks as well. Rather than trying to Return to a more upright posture, Slipping far to the side will probably prove a more effective technique as well as keep your forward momentum (Pics A to E). Stepping in the direction you are Slipping or Weaving will not only keep you safe, but can be used to cut off the ring as well. You may also be able to Leg Catch your partner's Knees or Roundhouses (Pic F).

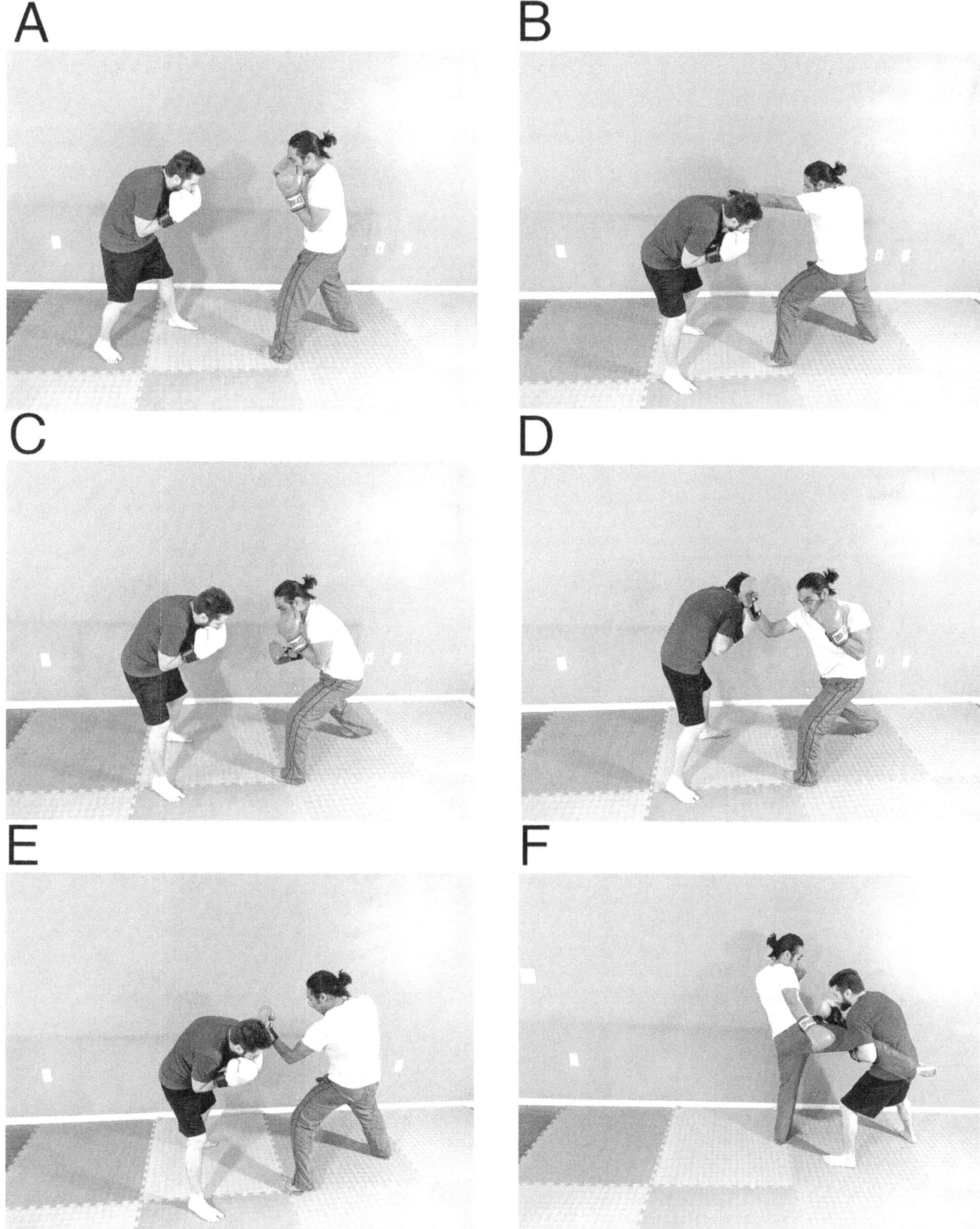

Drill 2

Repeat the previous drill with a Sideways Crouch. Try to pin your head to your partner's chest of Lead Shoulder to knock them off balance and drive them to the ropes (Pics A to B). If your partner starts to punch down, a simple Return will work well to unbalance them and put you in a prime position to counter (Pics C to D). Returns and Linear Weaves work very well together, as Mayweather has proven countless times.

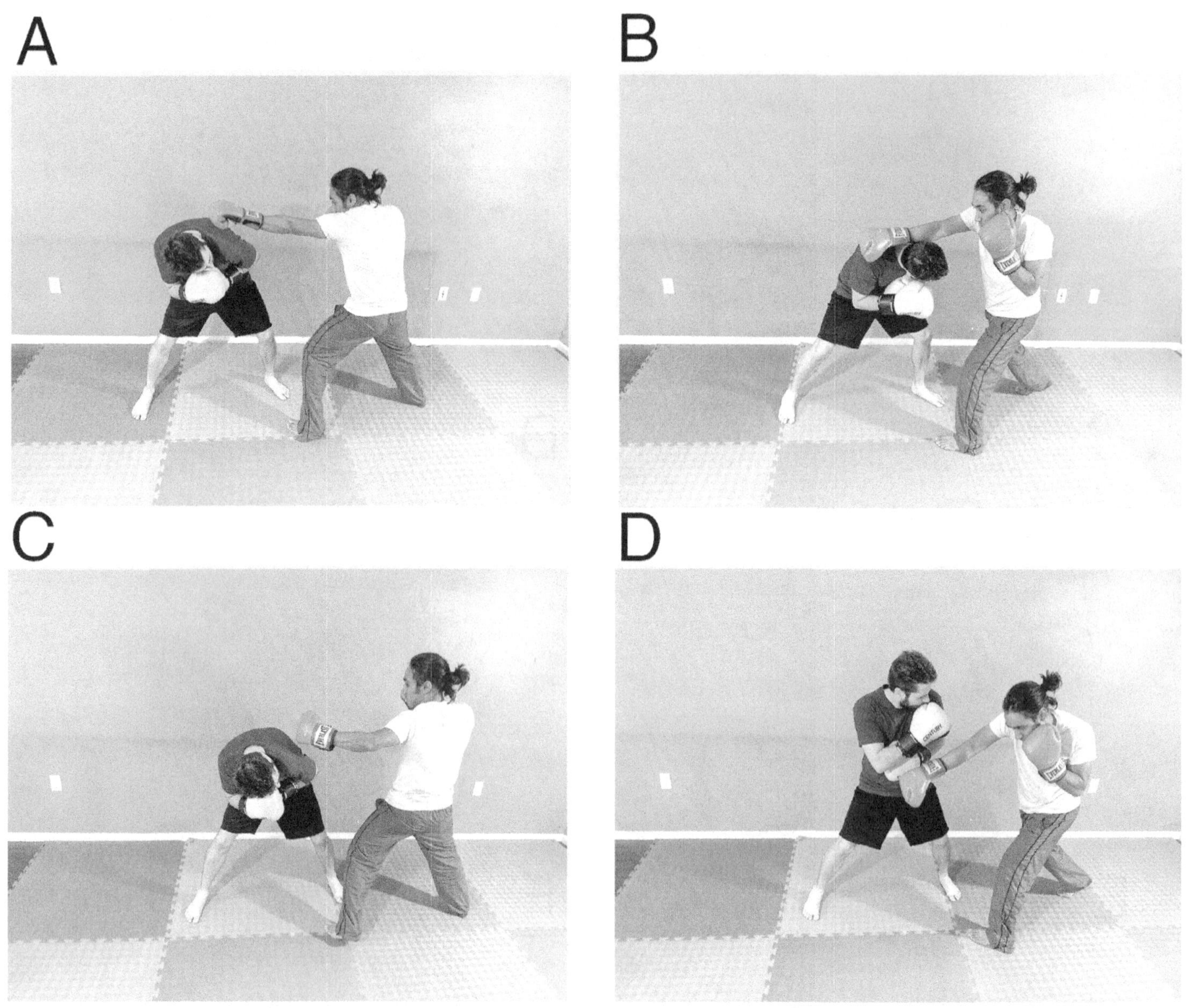

Drill 3

Repeat the previous drill, but now combine Forward and Sideways Crouching techniques by picking your moments to step out to a wider, more forwards stance. A good way to do this is to get your partner to commit to punching low as you perform a Linear Weave (Pics A to C), and then step deep Inside to continue Weaving into a big Overhand or Lead Hook (Pics D to E).

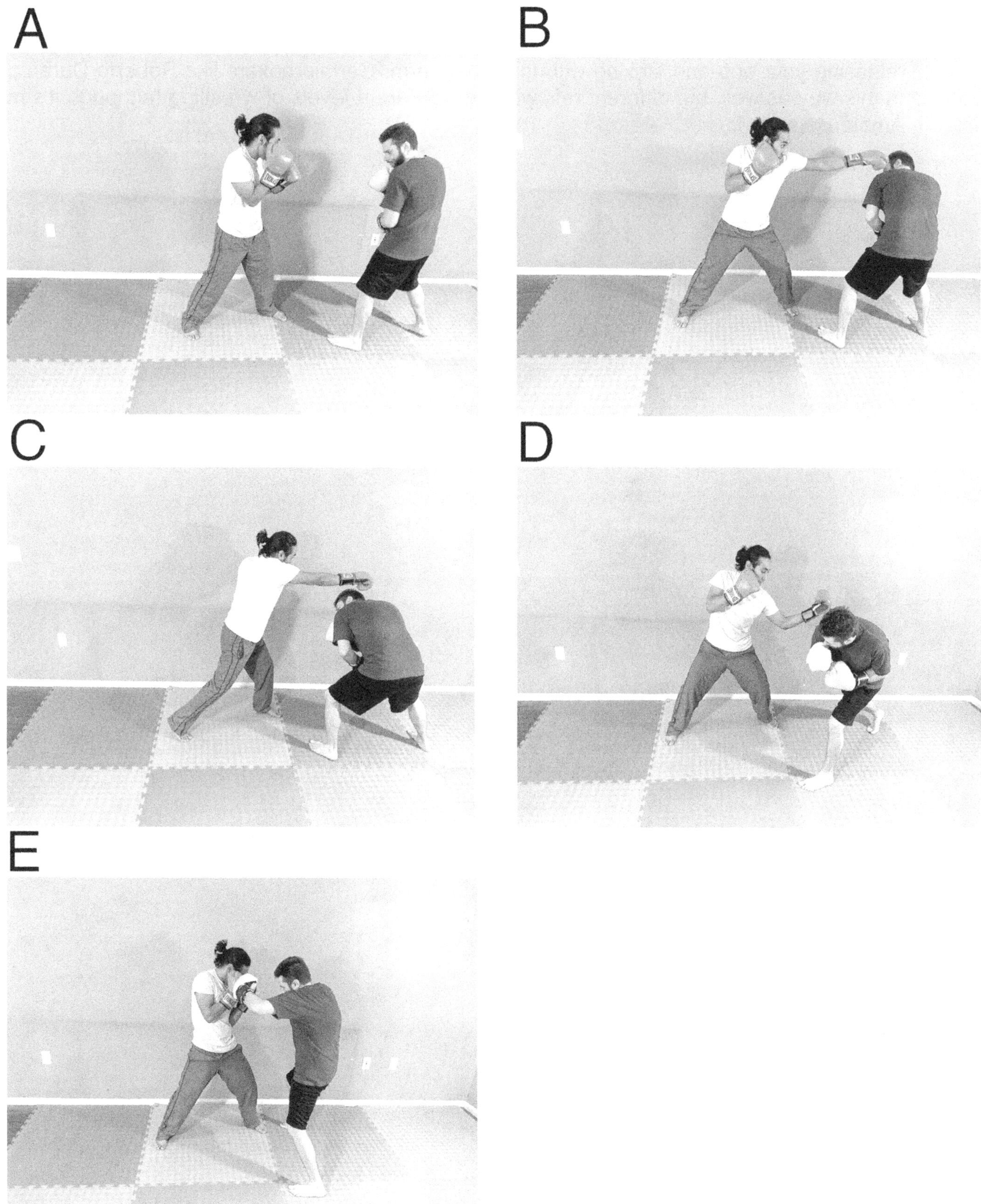

Head On Shoulder – Close Range Fighting

If you've never fought at extremely close range than it will be a nasty surprise when you happen to encounter someone skilled at it. The principles outlined in this section will teach you how to defend yourself or even gain an advantage. The techniques shown will be without grappling, for clarity. If you practice kickboxing or MMA, these same principles can still be applied to supplement your clinch-work. If you have control of just one of your opponent's arms (to the point where you can easily disentangle yourself just by letting go), then you can use these head movement principles to set up strikes by suddenly releasing your grip and striking with that same arm. Certain boxers like Roberto Duran used grappling in this way as well, but different refs will allow different levels of wrestling (although it's much stricter in Amateur Boxing).

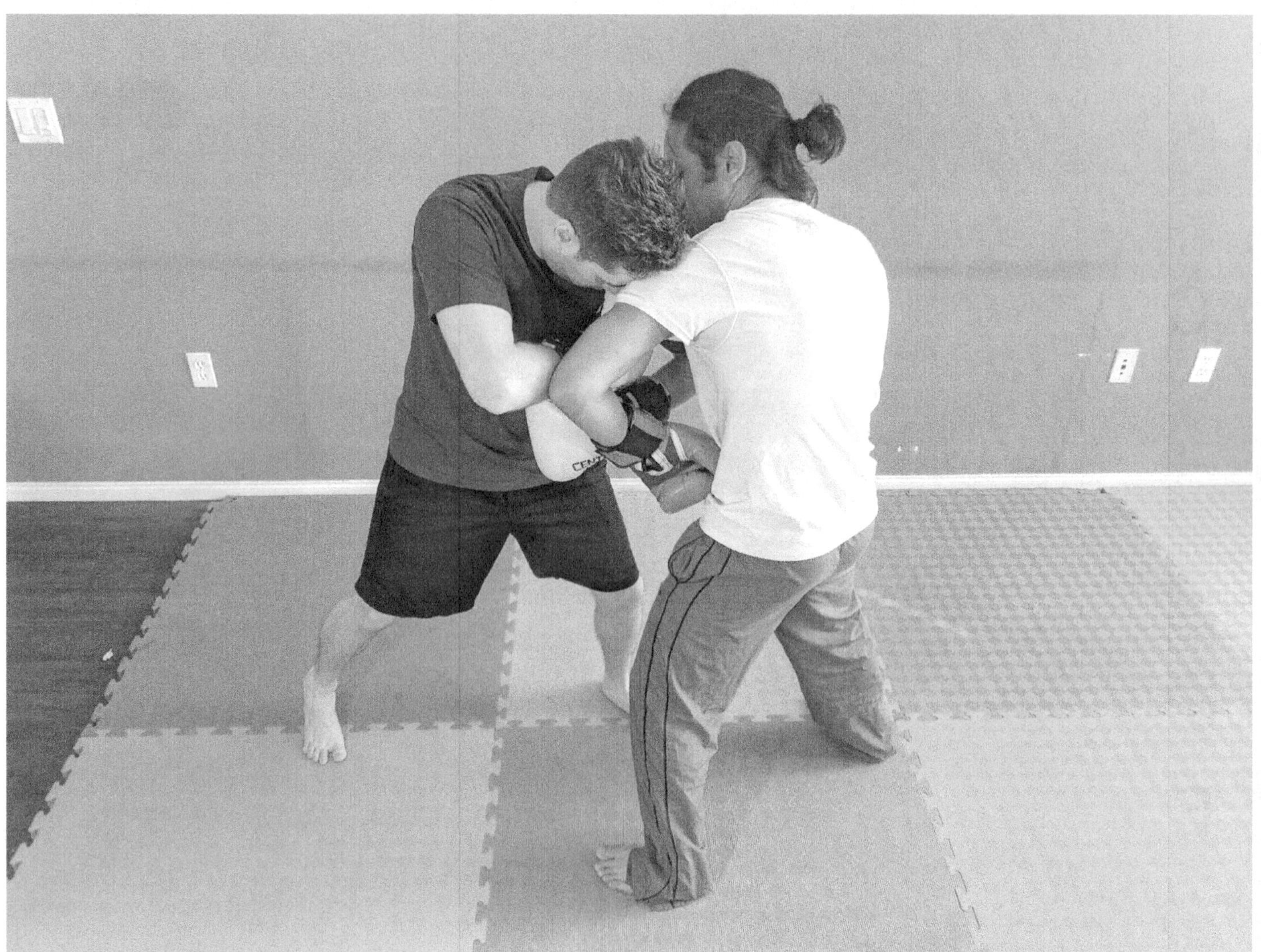

Putting your head on your opponent's shoulder (Pics A to B) does three things: First, it helps protect you from your opponent's hand on the opposite side. In other words, if your head is on their left shoulder, then you will be shielded from their right hand (Pic C). Alternatively, if your head is on their right shoulder, then you will be shielded from the left hand.

The second thing to note in this position is that one hand has much more room to punch, and this effectively turns it into you Power Hand. For instance, if your head is on your opponent's left shoulder, then your right hand has much more room to punch (Pic D). However, while your opponent's body is open to Hooks and Uppers (Pic D) you will have to take your head off of their shoulder to punch their head (Pic E to F). Doing this will leave you open as well, and your opponent will try to use this brief opening to Intercept your attack. For these reasons and a few others, controlling your head position is crucial to infighting.

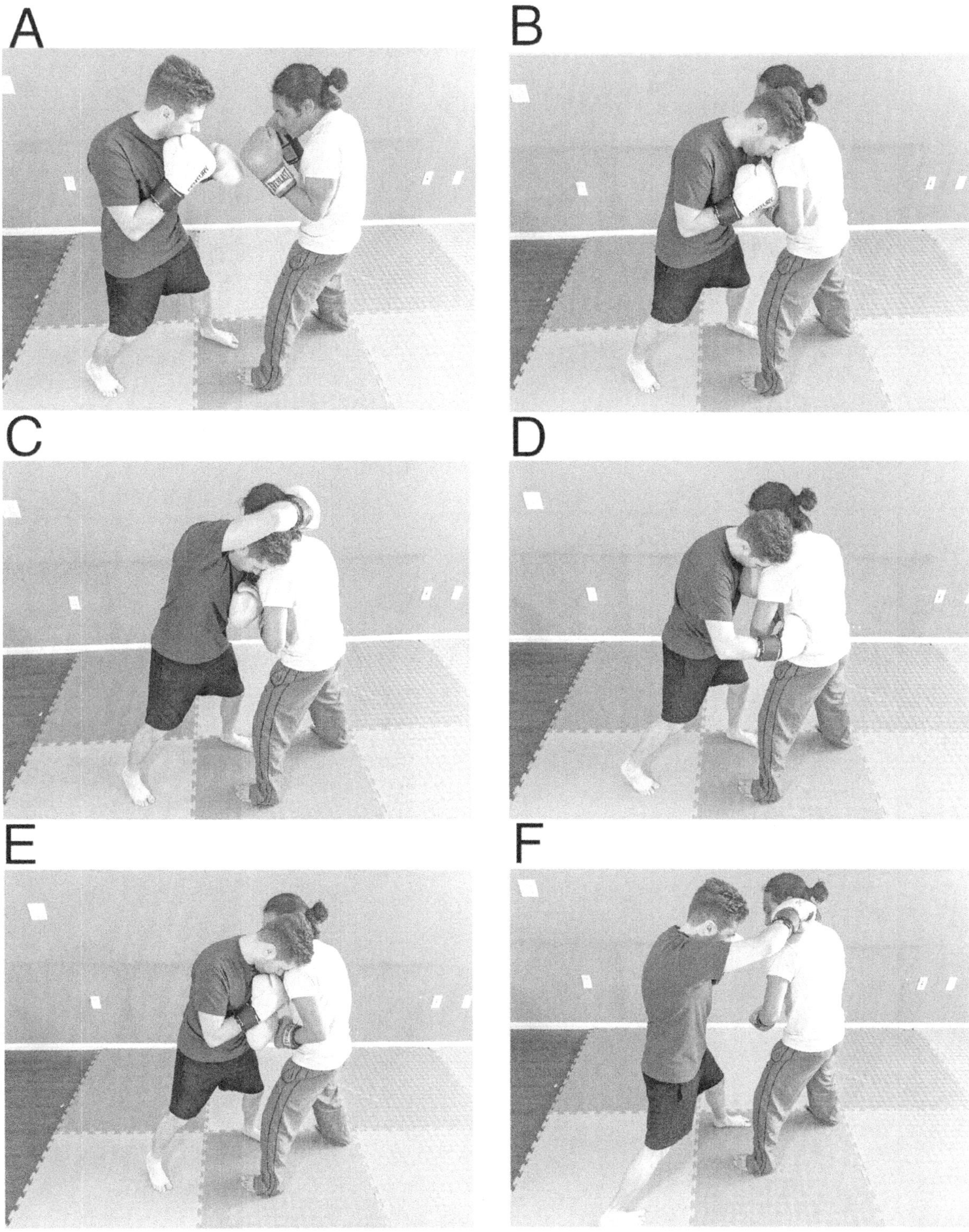

The last consideration in the head-to-shoulder position is what to do with your Lead Arm. This will be your left arm if your head is on your opponent's right shoulder, and vice versa. It is essentially the weaker arm, as it is pressed too tight against your opponent to throw with as much power. However, it can still do major damage. You can use it to smother your opponent's far arm, using a Vertical Elbow Frame (Pics A to B), or to land short Uppercuts or Hooks to your opponent's body (Pic C) or head (Pic D). When doing this, move your head away as little as possible to stay safe, and return it to your opponent's shoulder as soon as possible.

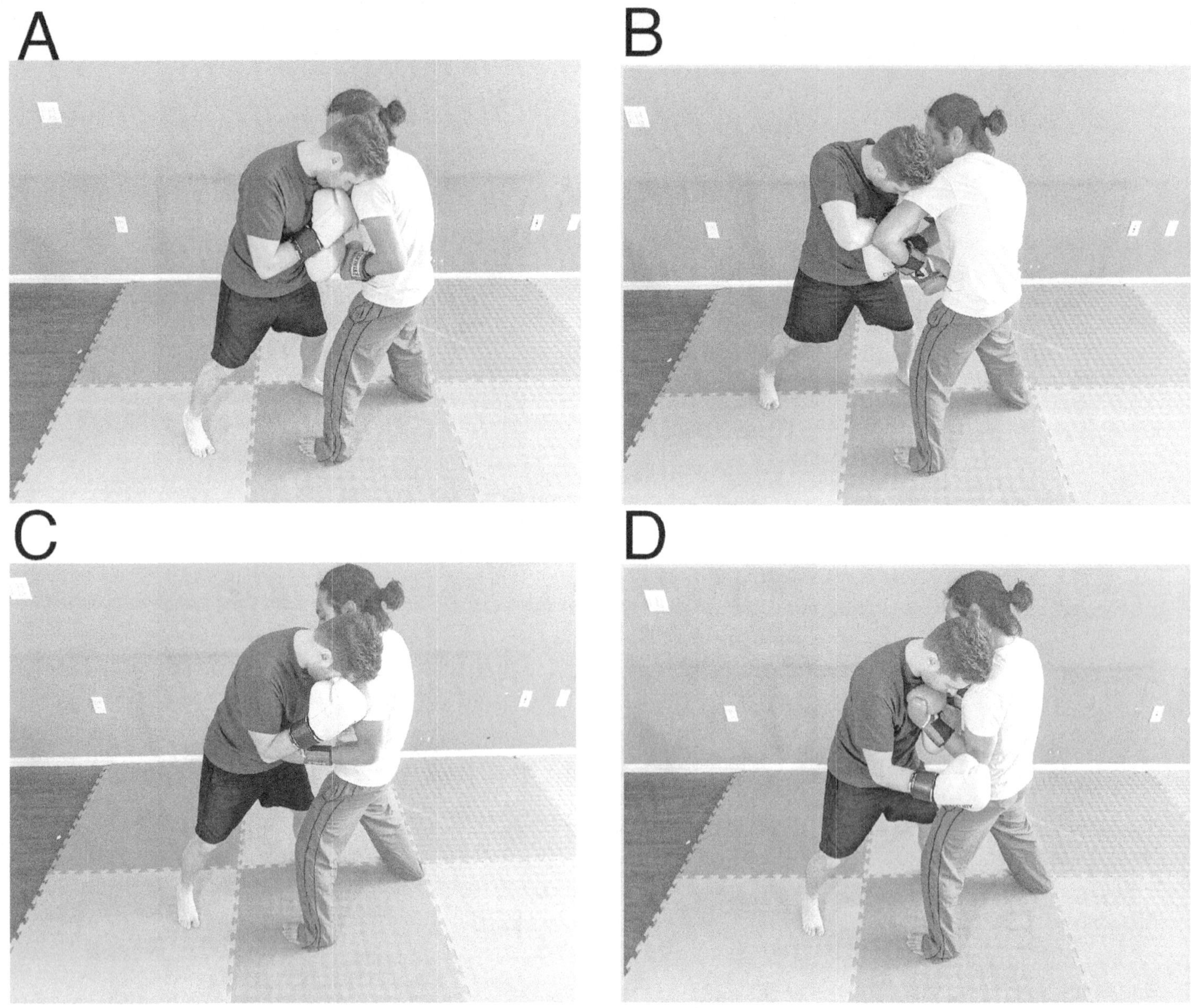

Usually, it's best to put your head on your opponent's Lead Shoulder in both an Open Stance (Pics A to B) and a Closed Stance (Pic C). This will shield you from their dominant hand, and it's an easier position to get in general. There are exceptions, which we will cover below.

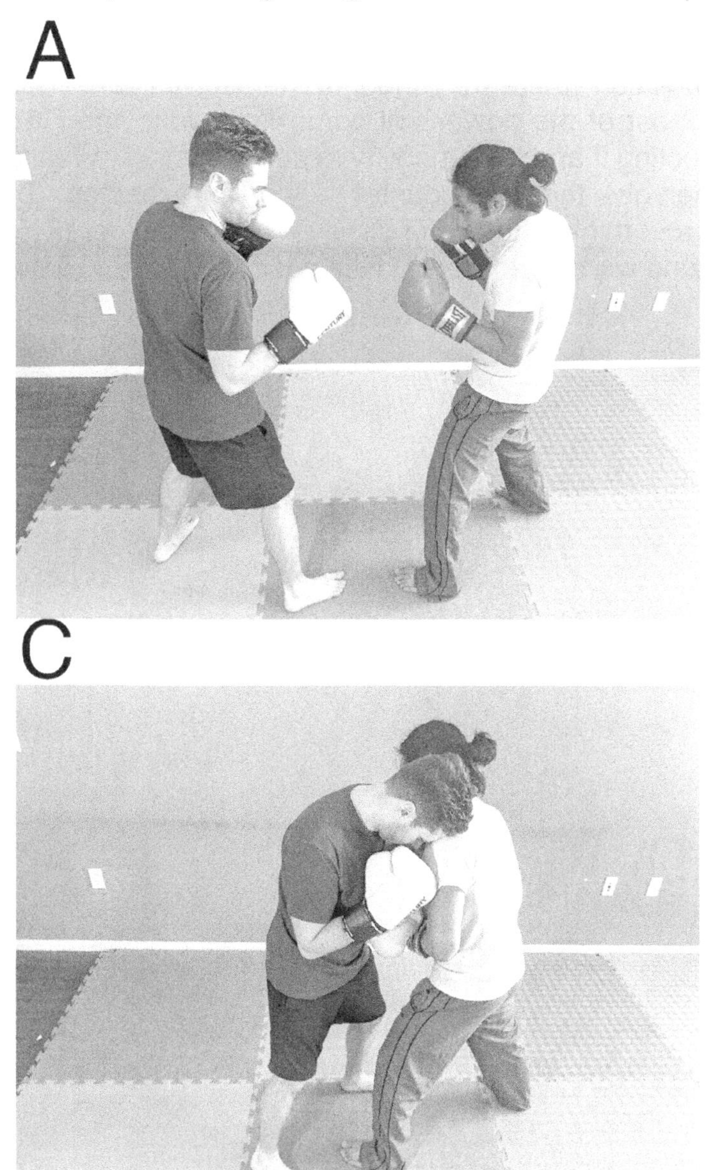

The Duran Uppercut

Believe it or not, it is possible to throw an extremely short Uppercut with your Rear Hand to your opponent's chin while still keeping your head on your opponent's shoulder. Roberto Duran used this technique to absolutely decimate opponents from a position where they thought themselves safe. This punch is very tight. There is little hip rotation and most of the power will come from your arm. It's effectiveness is mostly due to your opponent not expecting it and their inability to see it coming. Wait to feel your opponent retract their hand to punch, and then give them the counter they never expected. To throw it correctly, keep your arm touching your body and think of throwing dirt over your shoulder (Pics A to C). A small Shoulder Bump or Vertical Elbow Frame will help to clear a little space (Pics D to F) but is not necessary.

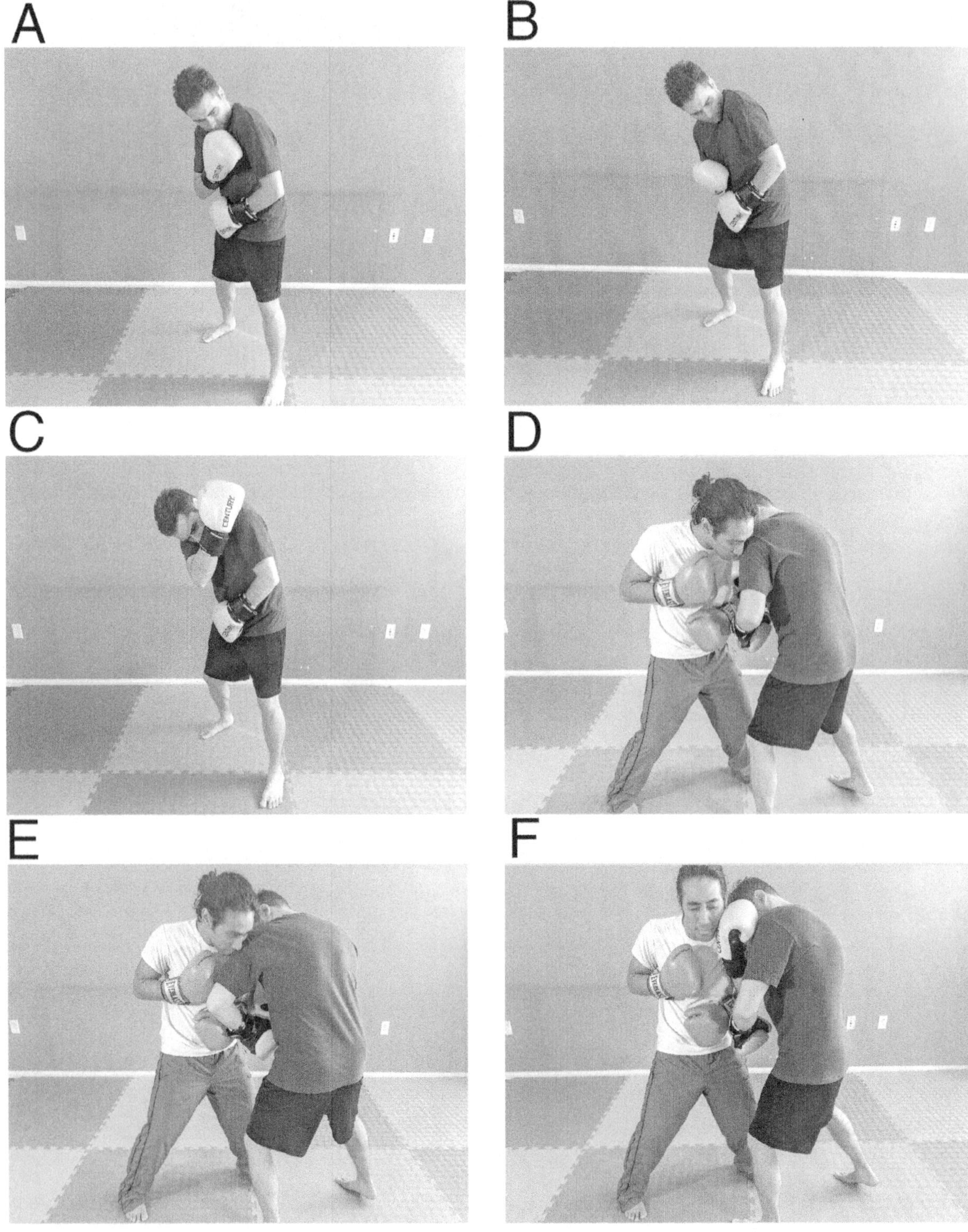

Head Shift

When you change which shoulder your head is on, you also effectively change which hand is your power hand. In this way, changing head positions can be thought of like Shifting stances. Putting your head on your opponent's left shoulder (Pic A) puts your right hand further away and gives it more room to throw, so it is closer to an Orthodox Stance. But if you reposition your head on your opponent's right shoulder (Pic C), you free up your left hand to throw (Pic D).

Since your left hand is now the Power Hand, it is similar to being in a Southpaw position. If you adopt this mentality and think of changing head positions as switching stances, infighting becomes far easier to comprehend. The reasons for changing head positions become very clear. If your opponent Shifts to your right shoulder, you know that they are most likely trying to clear space to land a big shot with their left hand. Or, they may be trying to reposition to land an Uppercut with their right hand through your Guard. One way to change head positions is to Reverse Weave. Simply lift your head up and then drop back down to their opposite shoulder, where you have a clear path for your new power hand to land (Pics A to D).

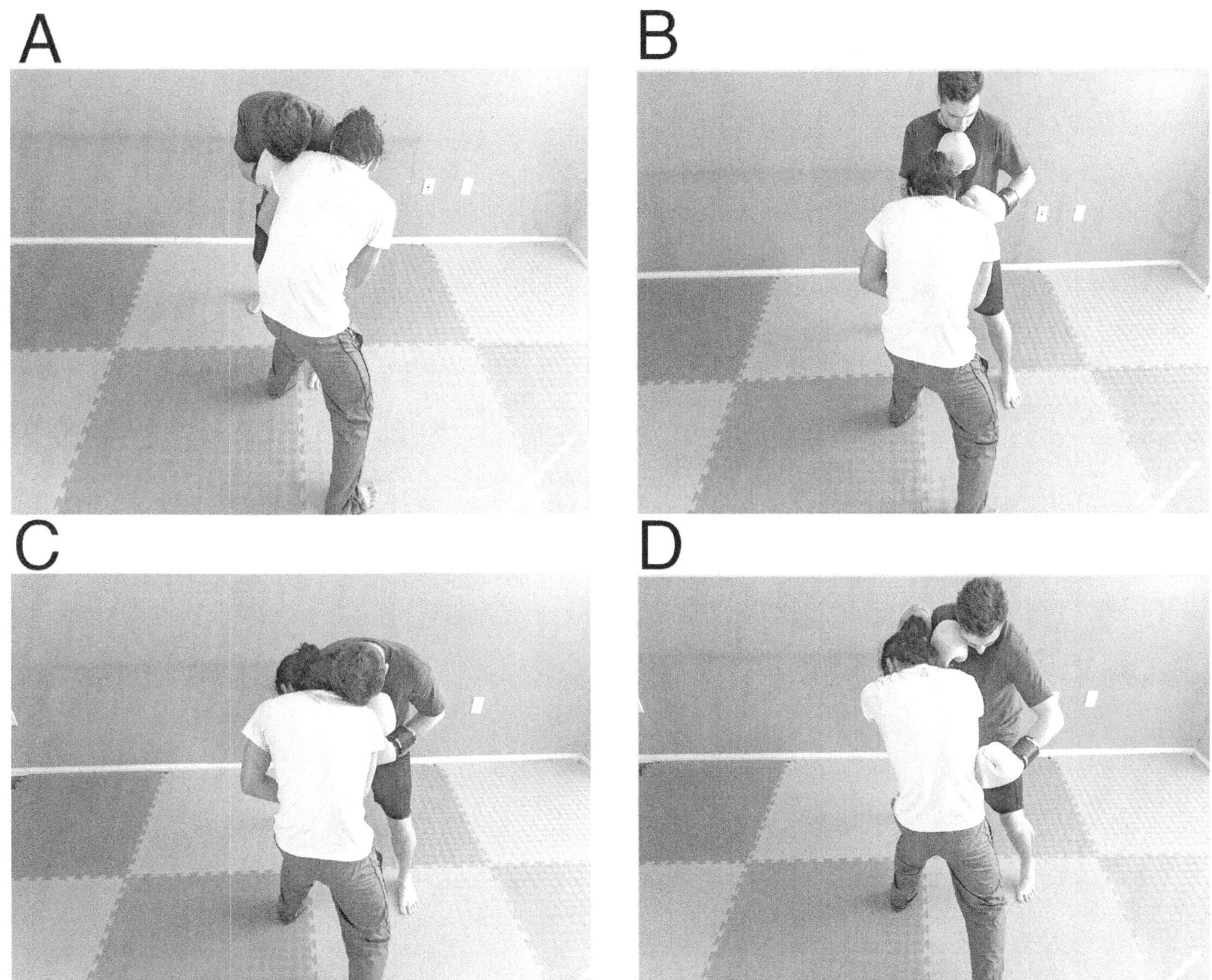

You can use your Head Shift defensively and offensively at the same time, evading an opponent's punch and setting up a Return Counter simultaneously (Pics A to D). It is also possible to land an Intercepting Counter as you Head Shift. This is highly advanced, but if you are going to try it you should know it is best to counter Uppercuts with Hooks and Hooks with Uppercuts. For instance, in Pic B the fighter could Intercept his opponent's Uppercut with a right hand Hook as he Head Shifts.

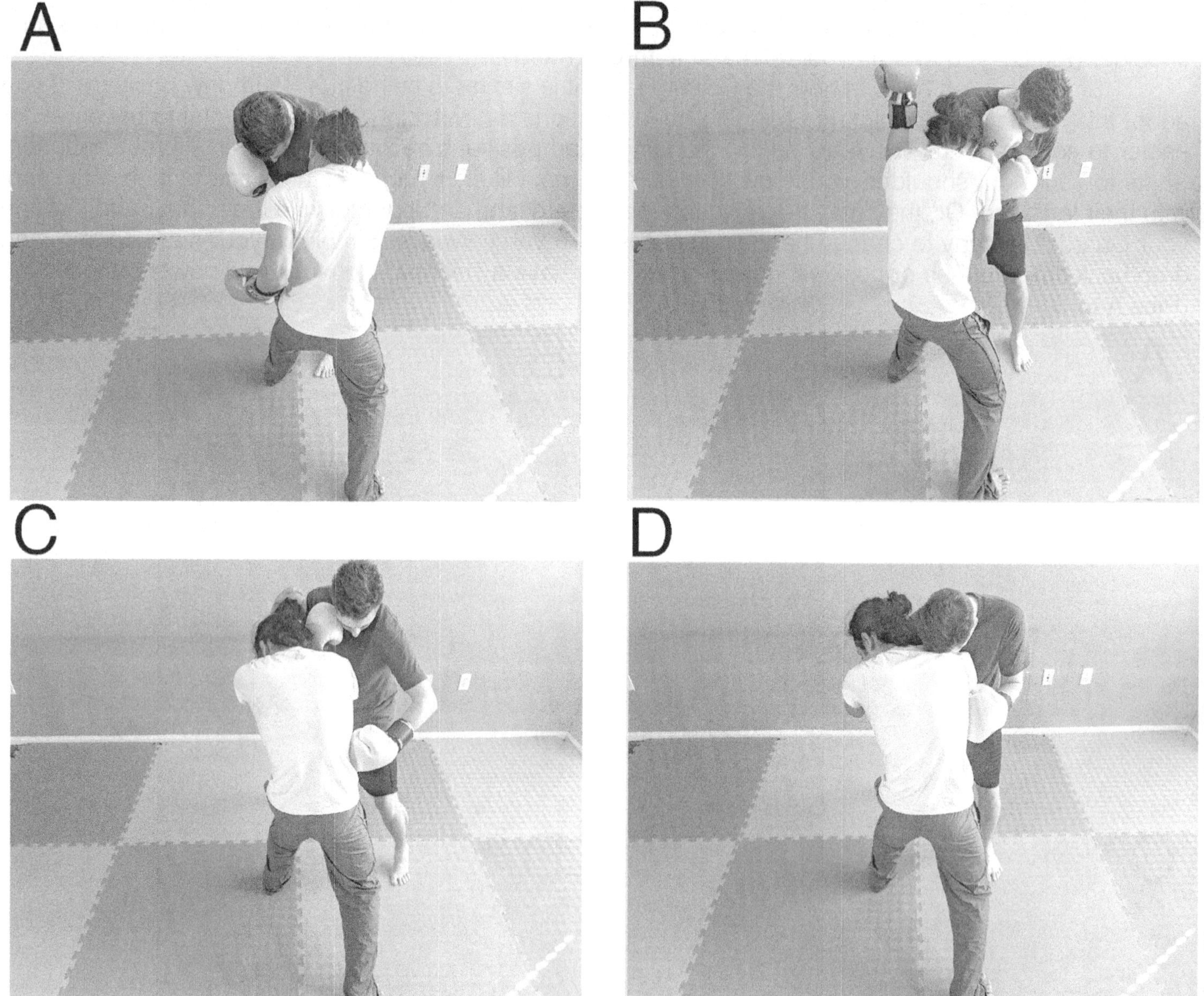

Another way to Head Shift is to Weave from one shoulder to the other. To maintain control of your opponent's posture, it is best to keep your head tightly pressed to their chest as you Weave. While doing so, you must make sure not to Weave in such a way that would get you warned for head butts. Head gear is always a good idea to avoid cuts and protect your eyes, but it is an even better idea when practicing this technique. It will be more difficult, but it's a worthwhile procaution to take to protect both yourself and your partner from cuts or broken noses. Go slow, go light, and practice in front of a qualified coach.

One of the best times to change shoulder positions is when your opponent throws a Hook (Pics A to D). This is a great time to throw a Return Counter to your opponent's liver or an Intercepting Counter to their body.

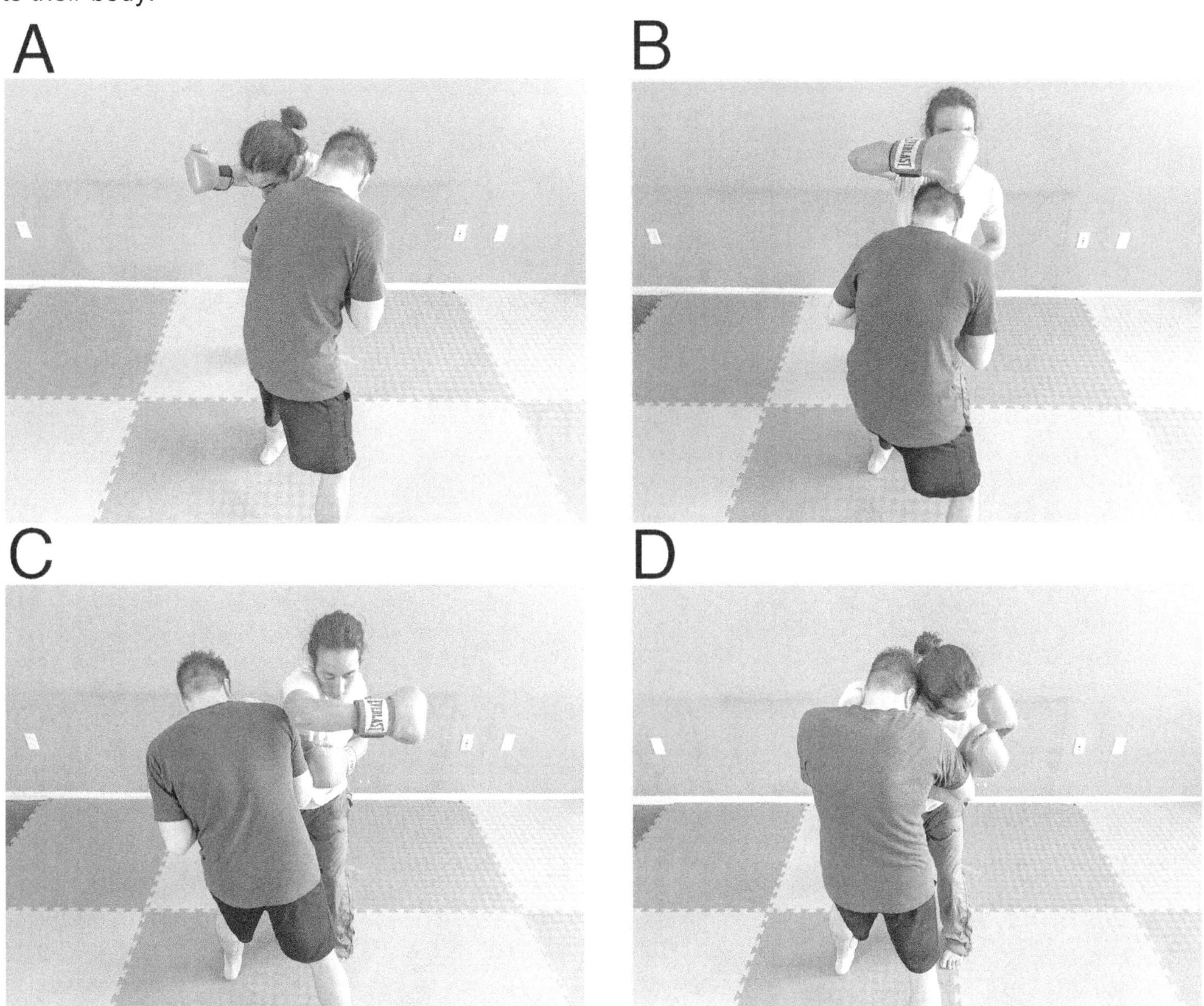

Head Drive

A quick way to disturb your opponent's balance is to drive your head into their shoulder. This can be done as you enter in from a Crouch (Pics A to B) as Armstrong used to do. Or you can simply drop your head and push forward, knocking your opponent off balance and following up with a hard shot (Pics C to F). Once again, go light and use head gear if you practice this. As always, get a qualified coach to lead you through it.

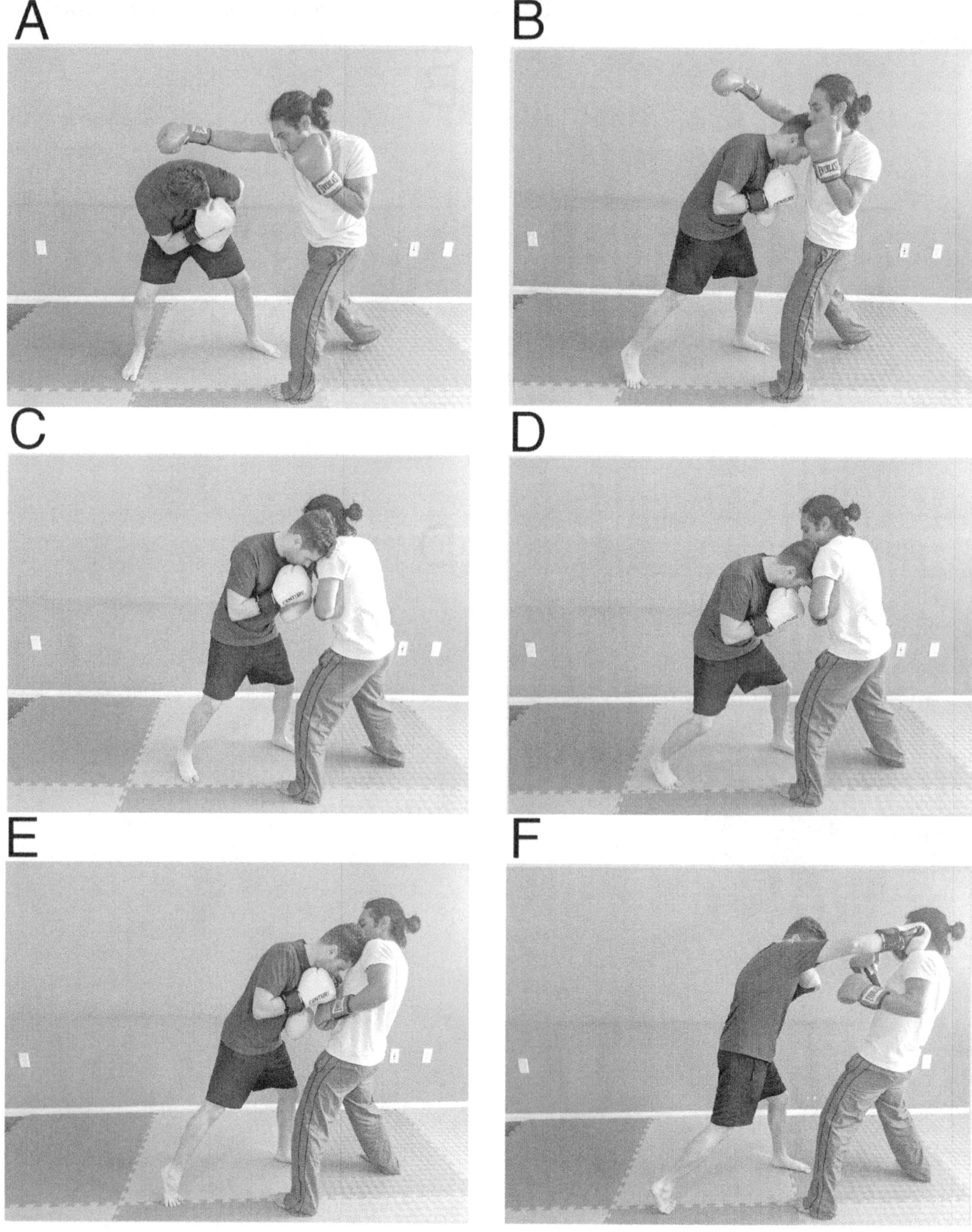

Shoulder Bump

When you sense that your opponent is trying to create space to punch (Pic A), use the space they have created to drive your shoulder into their chest (Pic B). Once they are knocked off balance (Pic C), follow up with a hard shot (Pic D).

While Shoulder Bumps can be used in a more wrestling like manner without getting called as a foul in boxing (although it all depends on the ref as always) it can be used as a blatant strike in MMA. Jon Jones has used this technique for years, as have many others before him. Recently McGregor used it against Cowboy to break his nose. What was unusual about that exchange was that Cowboy was not stuck up against the cage at the time, but right in the center of the ring. Obviously, it is a move worth exploring.

A

B

C

D

Drills

Drill 1

Infighting is complex and taking more hits than usual comes with the territory. As such, it's best to start practicing with one side of your body at a time. Take turns trying to strike your partner with your right hand, while they try to block with their left (Pics A to C). Now it's their turn to throw with their left. Try your best to block (Pics D to C) and then repeat the drill. Go for one round and then switch sides.

If your art allows grappling, you can practice pummeling your arm or securing ties and holds to gain a favorable position from which to strike. The great boxer Roberto Duran liked to use wrist control (even though he had boxing gloves on!) to clear away his opponent's Guard. Nowadays many MMA fighters use these same techniques.

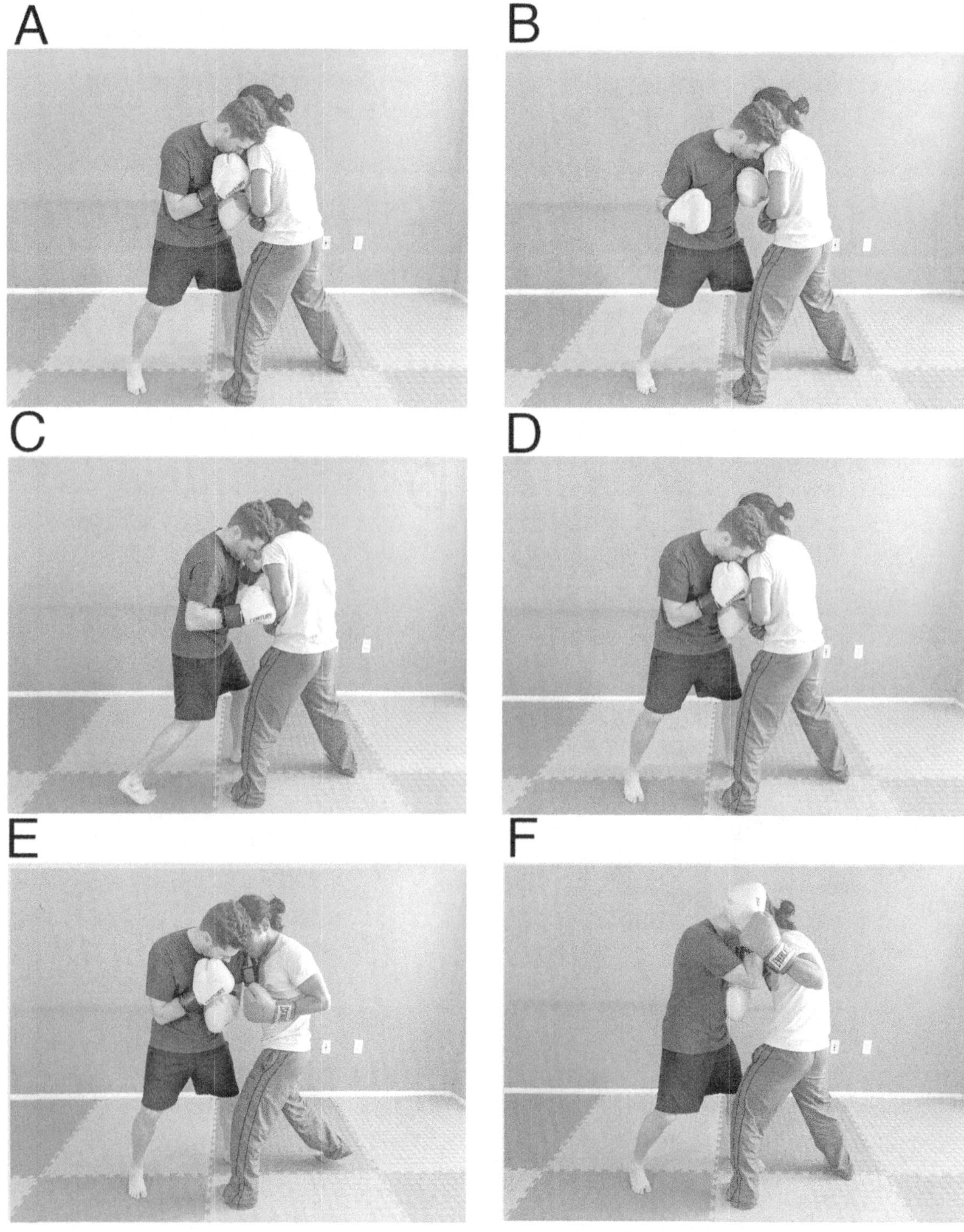

Drill 2

As your opponent throws an attack with either hand, Weave underneath or Reverse Weave to Head Shift to their other shoulder (Pics A to C). Once you've evaded their attack, throw one of your own and have your partner Head Shift away and throw a counter. Once again, it is best to wear head gear and go light and slow. Head Butts, even accidental Head Butts, are serious business. Once you have the hang of both of these drills, you can begin to combine them until you are essentially sparring.

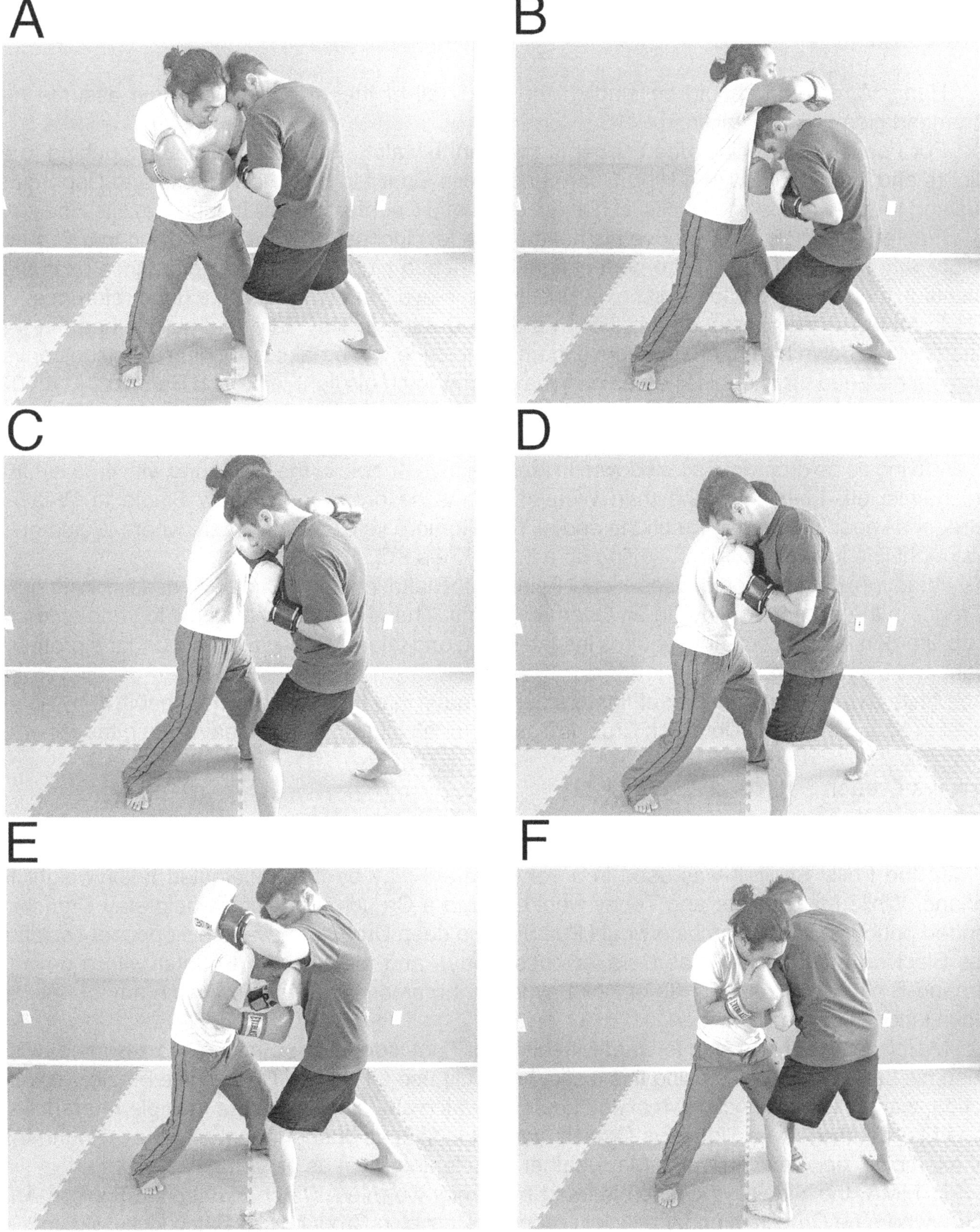

References – Crouching (Armstrong Style)

Note:

There will be no kickboxing or Muay Thai examples given, as Crouching is generally not done. This is largely due to kicks and knees being a major threat. This holds true in MMA as well, but the threat of takedowns balances out the risk, allowing much lower head movement than even boxing.

Forward Crouch

Henry Armstrong should be studied for nearly all of these techniques. Just assume he is a recommendation on every tactic.

For Forward Crouching, Joe Frazier is the man to watch. Frazier combined Crouching to evade Straights and high Hooks with a High Guard and Cross Guard to block low Hooks and Uppercuts. His Crouching Weaves, Slips and Ducks let him get close and Counter with his insane Gazelle Hook. As you watch Frazier, note how he will move his head only a few inches to Slip while staying in a Crouch. His first fight with Muhammad Ali is the perfect fight to watch to study these concepts. Since examples are so plentiful, there's little reason to list exact instances. Floyd Patterson is also a good reference.

In MMA, Khabib has used Weaves in a deep Crouch to stay safe and put his head in a prime position to take down his opponent or drive them to the cage. He breaks traditional wrestling convention by placing his head far over his knee as he Weaves in. Watch his fight vs Edson Barboza. At 4:10 left in the second round, Khabib Crouches and Weaves under two Hooks, pinning his head to Borboza's hip to take him down. He pulls this off against Poirier in the second round with 3:48 left, Drawing a Jab and then Weaving as he drops into a takedown. In McGregor vs Khabib in the first round with 4:45 left, Khabib Head Feints left, then right, and then Weaves left as he drops into a Low Single to Weave past McGregor's knee. In contrast, watch the end of Yoel Romero vs Chris Weidman, where Weidman drops in a straight line towards Romero, setting up a brutal Knee KO.

Although Khabib mostly uses Head Feinting for takedowns, he actually used it to knockdown McGregor in the second round with an Overhand Right. These principles are how to keep safe and not end up like Ben Askren, but they requires insane timing and talent. As always, train under a professional, go light and use caution.

While a depressing number of fighters don't Weave into their takedowns, Khabib is by no means the first to do it. Check out Dominick Cruz vs Takeya for a picture perfect Weave into a takedown.

Sideways Crouch

In boxing, the Sideways Crouch is used often by Floyd Mayweather and James Toney, as it pairs well with the Philly Shell. It was used in a very different way by the undefeated heavyweight Rocky Marciano. While Mayweather and Toney would go into a Crouch, Marciano would stay Crouching for extended periods of time. Marciano would Pull Slip in a deep Crouch to evade his opponent's Jab (Rear Cross Blocking against Hooks as Cormier does today), and then Return Counter with a devastating Overhand Right. Check out his KO of Rex Layne for a dramatic example, or watch any of his fights to see him land it multiple times.

Marciano would also step forward with his Rear Foot, sometimes Shifting into a Southpaw stance to Load his Lead Hook. While using this tactic, he would use a Forward Crouch like Frazier. To see this in action, watch his first knockdown of Joe Louis (or watch any of his fights for multiple references).

To see Mayweather use a Sideways Crouch, watch his fight vs Juan Manuel Marquez. Round 4 has a lot of examples, and you can watch Mayweather Shuffle and Pivot as he Crouches.

In MMA, the Sideways Crouch is used by Daniel Cormier. Watch his second fight vs Anthony Joshua, where he Crouches under a kick in round 1. He's also Crouched to Catch kicks, like in his fight vs Josh Barnett to score a takedown near the end of the 4th. Of course this technique comes with danger, as his KO by Jon Jones Roundhouse shows. Cormier might have done better to keep at least one arm blocking as he usually does rather than try to Parry or Catch with both.

Crouching – Open Stance Considerations

Rigondeaux is the king of Crouching in an Open Stance. Watch his fight vs Donaire for some beautiful examples of him Crouching and Pivoting to create defensive angles and set up shots.
For an example of Shifting forward from an Open Stance to a Closed Stance to try for a Double Leg, check out Khabib vs McGregor. In round 4 with 4 minutes left, Khabib feinted a Jab, then Slipped and Weaved under McGregor's outstretched Lead Hand, Shifting forward as he did so from an Open Stance into a Closed Stance. This put him in position to grab a hold of both legs, drive McGregor to the cage and take him down. It was this takedown that lead to the submission that won the fight.

Linear Weaves

Roberto Duran Linear Weaved to evade Ray Leonard's Jab several times in their first fight. He would step forward as he did so, wrapping his Lead Arm around Leonard's waist and placing his head into his shoulder as he came up. This kept Duran safe as he entered the clinch, where he brutalized Leonard for much of the fight.

In MMA, Daniel Cormier performs Linear Weaves with a Rear Cross Block and Lead Leverage Guard to stay safe and set up strikes and takedowns. Watch the first minute of Cormier's fight vs Volkan Oezdemir for several examples of Cormier Linear Weaving forwards and backwards. This kept him both safe and threatened takedowns. Oezdemir did a much better job defending than most, but Cormier did a great job dodging strikes and you can check out the rest of Cormier's fights for examples that lead to takedowns or counter strikes.

The Duran Uppercut

Duran vs Buchanan has several examples of these sneaky Uppercuts that cross over the Center Line in the clinch. You can also see Cormier land several of these in his first fight with Jones in the time suggested below in the Head Shifting reference.

Head Shifting

I said it before, but watch any Henry Armstrong fight to see the Grandmaster of infighting at work. Armstrong would place his head on his opponent's shoulder for safety, then Weave away to punch and dodge. He would then return his head to their shoulder in one seamless motion.

Roberto Duran vs. Carlos Palimino is a fight where two amazing infighters show off their skills. The infighting starts getting intense around the middle or round 2.

James Toney vs. Iran Barkley is one of the best beat downs from Close Range in boxing history. Toney's fight vs Jirov also has a lot of examples form an Open Stance. His ability to stay safe and land shots from Close Range is brilliant.

Jon Jones vs Daniel Cormier 1 has an insane amount of similarities to the boxing fights recommended, but with Elbows, Knees, and takedowns allowed. Watch round 2 with 2:05 left for plenty of examples on and off the cage. There are lots of Head Shifts in the later rounds as well.
Watch Khabib vs Poirier round 2 at 2:55 to see Khabib use these tactics against a downed opponent to set up punches against the cage.

Head Drive

Henry Armstrong moved his opponents around the ring with his head. Watch any of his fights to see these techniques used multiple times.

Shoulder Bump

Any of the James Toney fights recommended should have plenty of examples. Conor McGregor vs Cowboy is the most recent, most dramatic example, but Shoulder Bumps against the cage have been a common tactic in MMA for a very long time.

Peek-A-Boo

Aggressive Shifting Head Movement

The major benefit of the Peek-A-Boo style is that it gives the practitioner the ability to quickly and easily transition from Inside to Outside and from Orthodox to Southpaw. The style is built around the concept of being able to use each side in the exact same way. This allows for total access to all angles and positions at all times.

Tilt Slips

To Tilt Slip like Mike Tyson or any of the other great fighters that Cus D'Amato taught, simply lean to one side while keeping your posture facing mostly forward (Pics A to C). Do not twist, turn or dip as you might in the more traditional way of Slipping. To pull this off, you will require a slightly wider, more forward stance than you may be used to.

Like the rest of the Peek-A-Boo style, this modification is meant to ease the angled footwork. From a more forward position, it will be easier to cut off the ring, Shift forward, or angle off to either side. For this same reason, Peek-A-Boo practitioners do not turn their heel out when they throw a Lead Hook (Pic D). Everything is tailored to be able to quickly move to either side, so any kind of movement that freezes you in place is avoided. This type of head movement may be helpful for kickboxers, who often stand more forward to negate leg kicks.

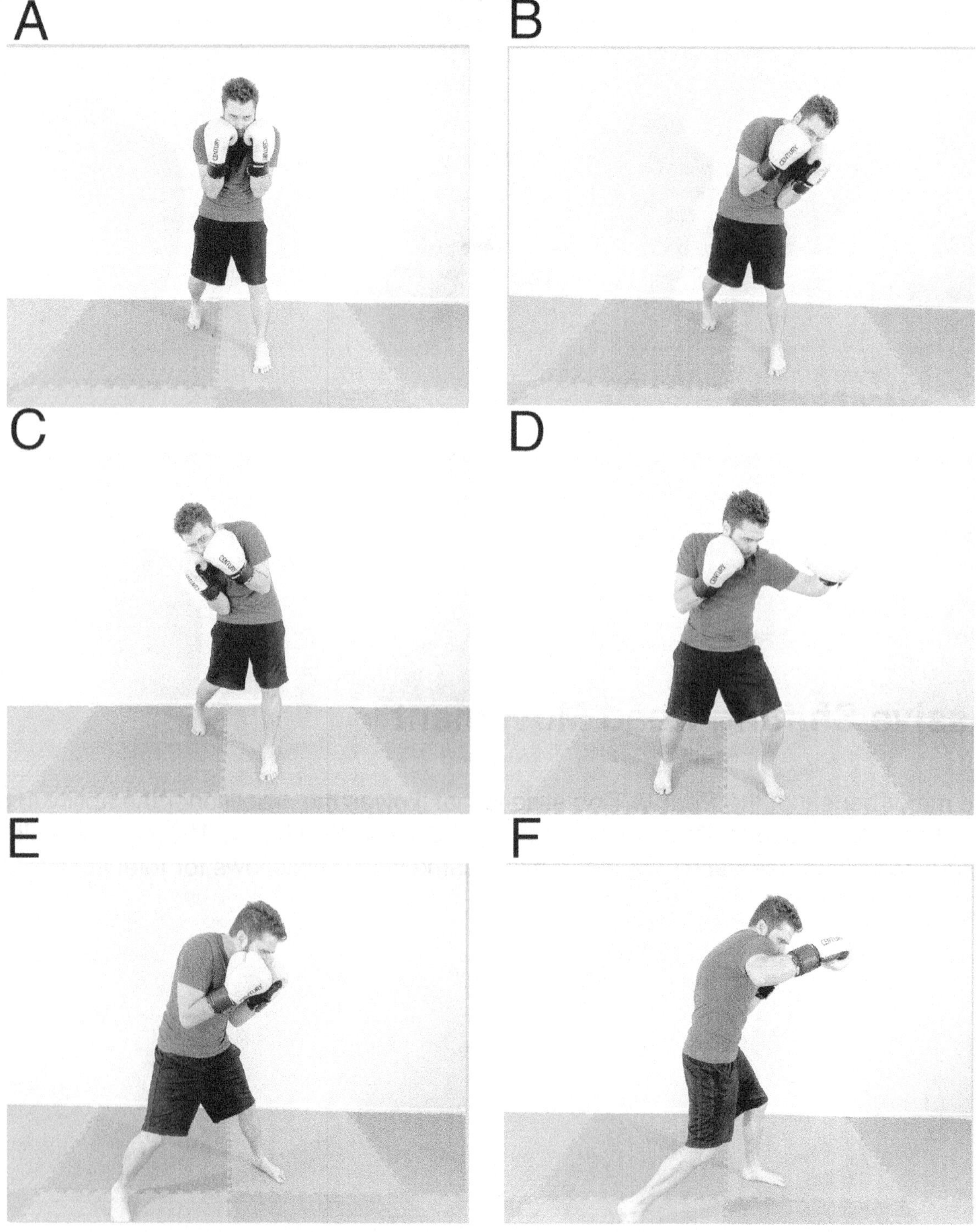

Double Slip Same Side

You may Tilt Slip your opponent's Jab to the Outside as you would a regular Slip (Pics A to B). But when Tilt Slipping to the Inside you may need to continue leaning even further to to Slip their Cross (Pics C to F). This is something less common in other styles, but it's a great tool if you wish to counter your opponent's 1-2 with a Return Lead Hook (Pic F).

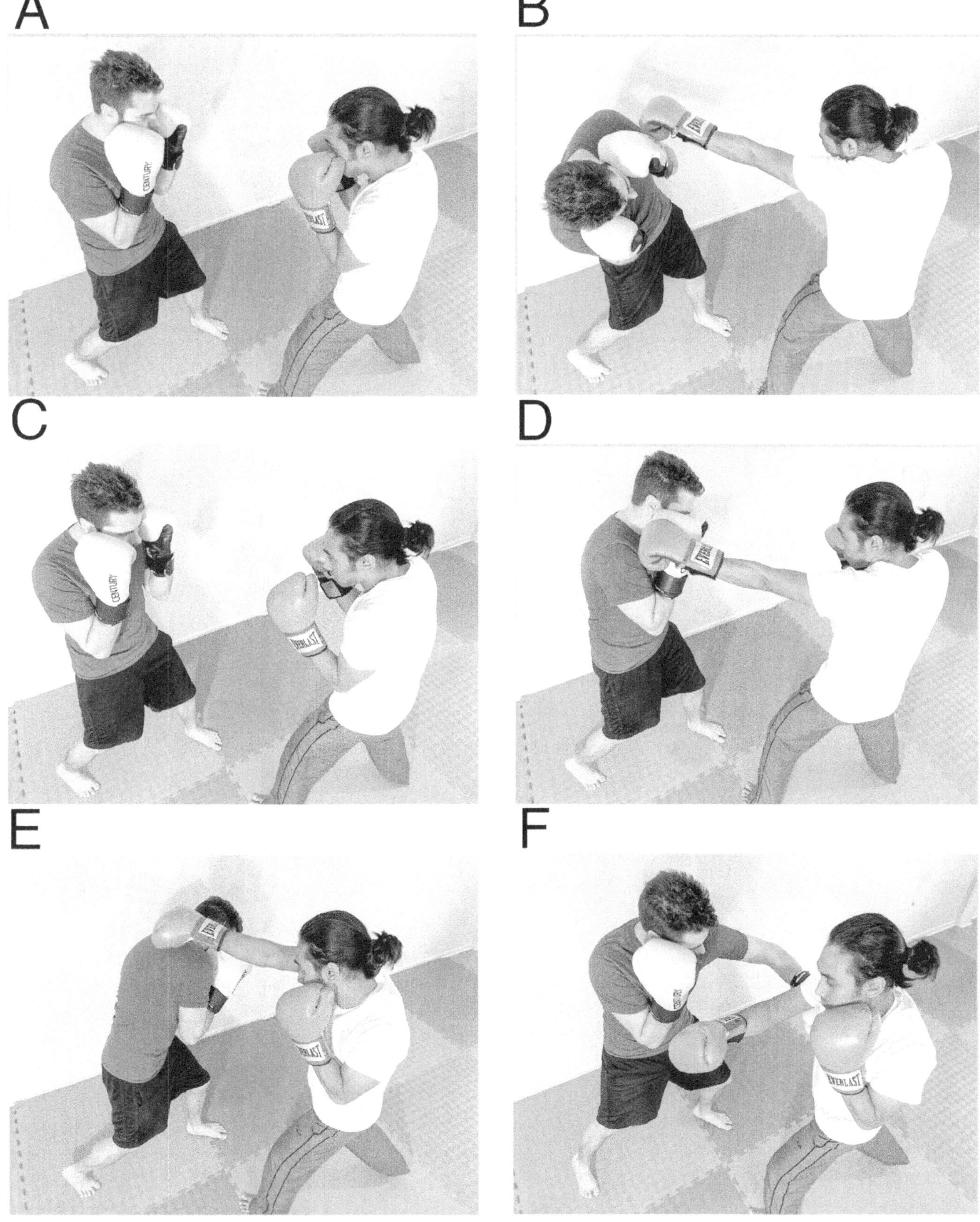

Reverse Weave

Slip or Drop Slip to the Inside, then Return to your basic posture before Slipping or Drop Slipping to the Outside (Pic A to C). Another way to think of it is to Tilt to one side and then the other. Your head should make an upside-down U. Repeat this motion, setting up a predictable rhythm to try and Draw a punch to counter (Pics D to F). This is a great way to keep your head moving offline and tempt opponents into firing off shots. Once you see a punch coming, suddenly up the pace to Slip and Intercept. In Pic E the fighter throws a Cross over his opponent's Jab, and in Pic F he Intercepts his opponent's Cross with his own.

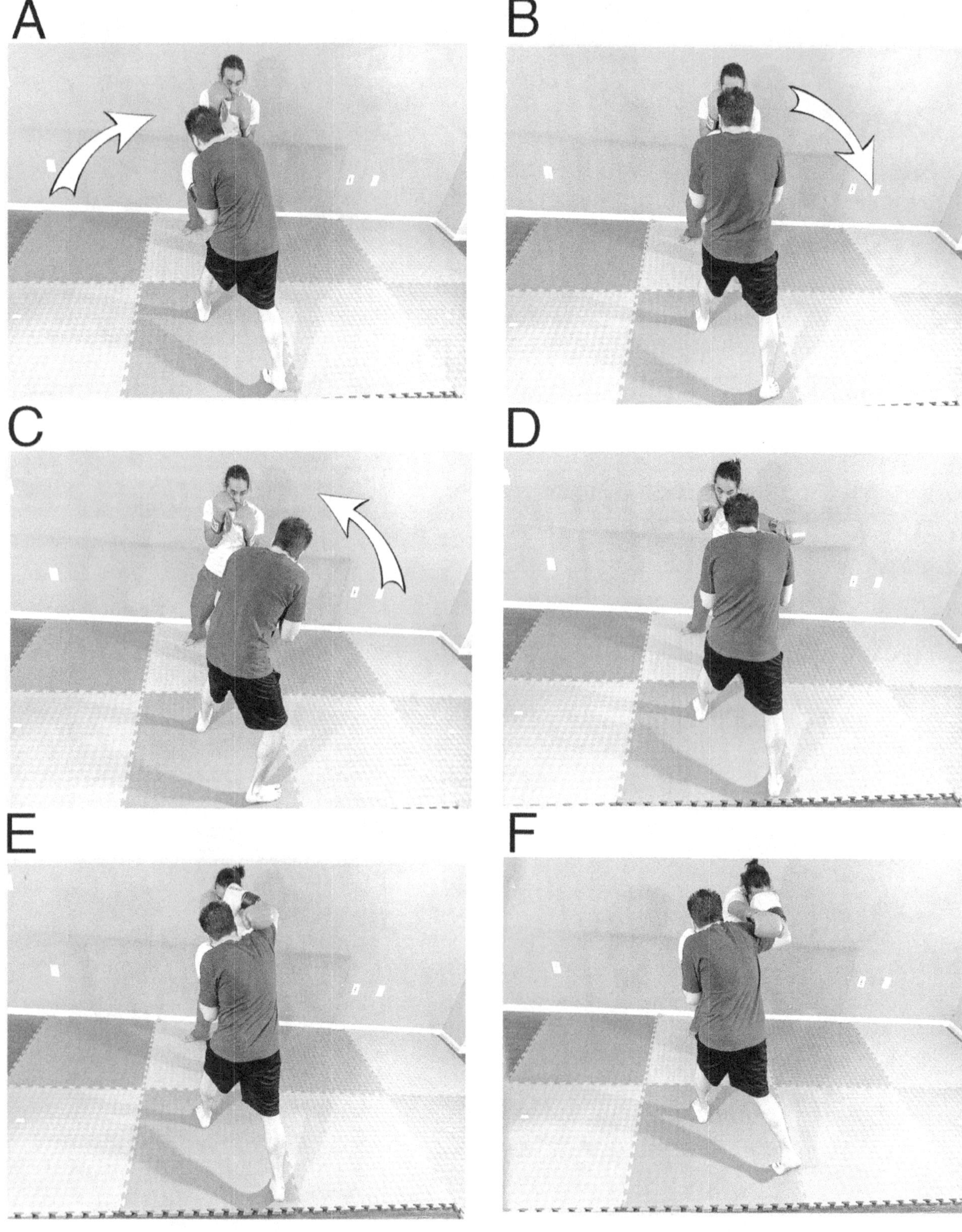

Open Stance Considerations

This technique works even better in an Open Stance because you can more easily counter with your Power Side. Manny Pacquiao uses this technique all of the time. When his opponent fires off a Jab while he is moving his head Outside, Pac fires off a left Cross (Pics A to D).

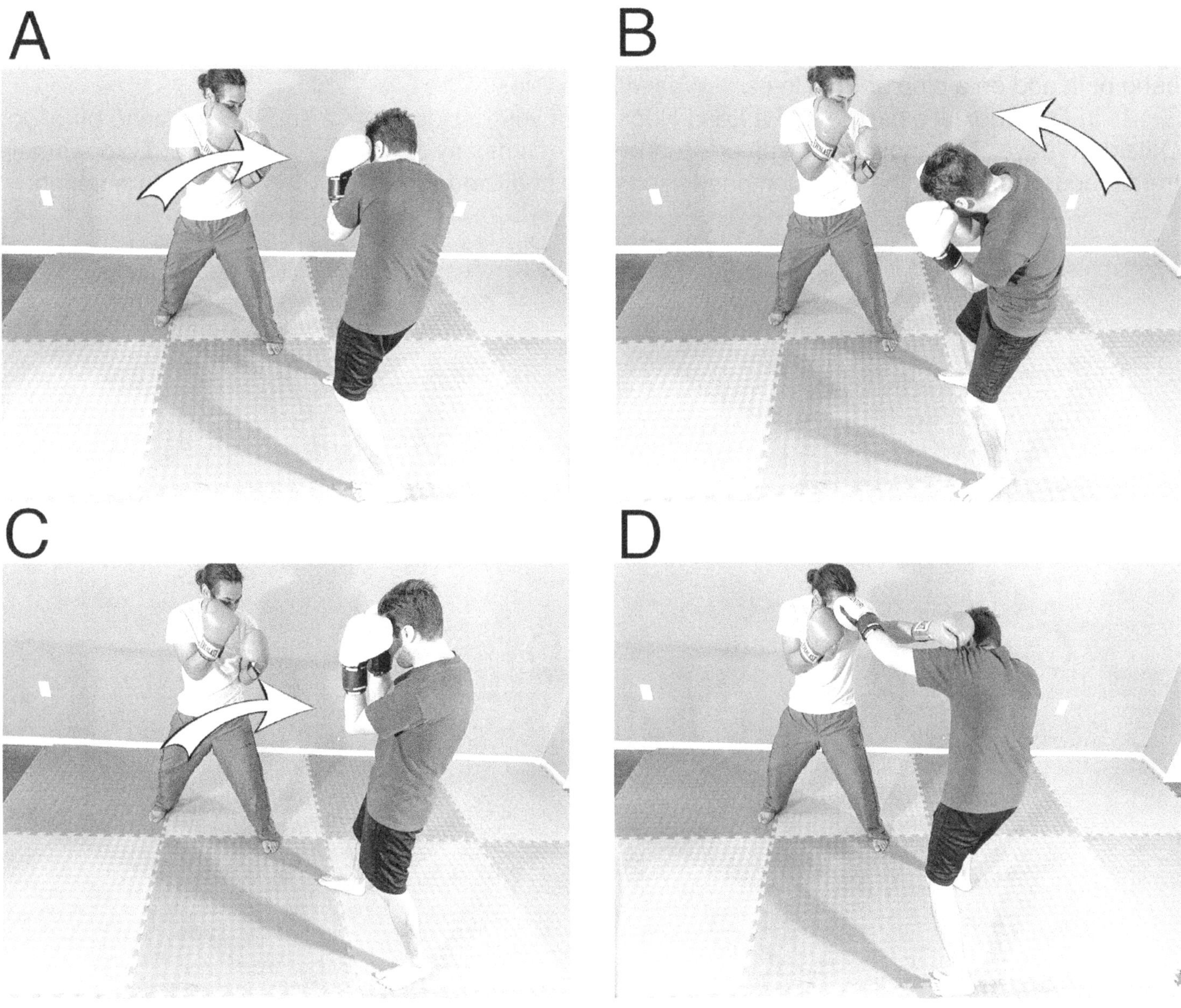

Figure 8/Dempsey Roll

The Dempsey Roll is essentially what happens when you blend a Clockwise and Counter-Clockwise Weave, alternating between the two. Doing so allows you to come in underneath your opponent's strikes and throw power shots at the same time. Once you have completed one Weave (Pics A to D), smoothly rise up and drop down to Weave the opposite direction (Pics D to F). This same idea can be used with Inside and Outside Drop Slips. Your head will make a figure 8. Once you have the hang of it, add on a step or Shift to each Weave/Drop Slip.

In Orthodox, It's best to add a Lead Hook off of your Inside Weave and an Overhand off of your Outside Weave. This movement was created by Jack Dempsey and perfected by Mike Tyson. It helps tremendously to cut off the ring. Dempsey used more of a Crouch, while Tyson stayed more upright.

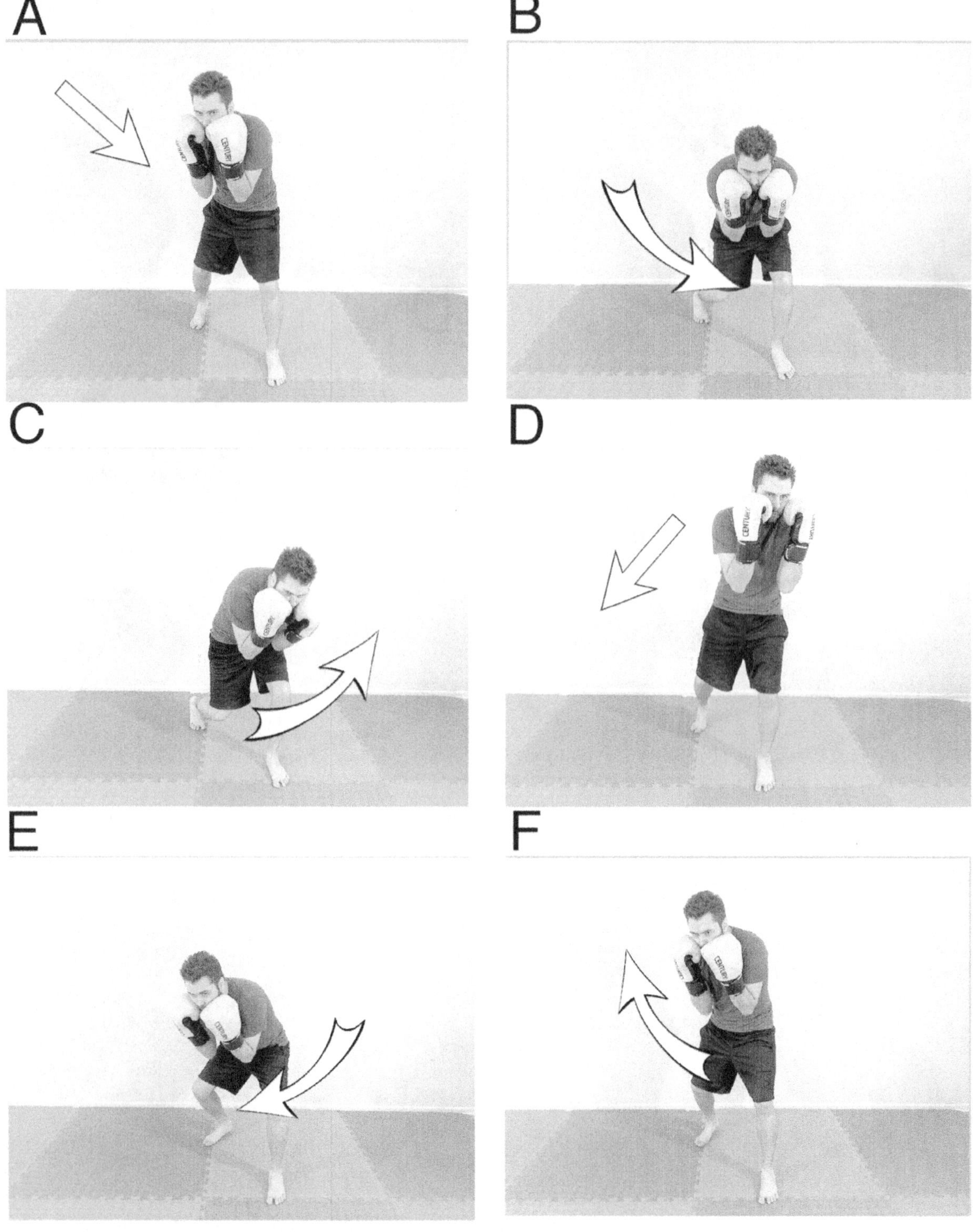

Turn Shift Counter

Drop Slip to the Inside (Pics A to B). As your opponent looks to Pivot away to the Outside (Pic C), do not attempt to Pivot with them. Instead, keep your feet in place and simply turn towards them. You will find yourself in more of a Southpaw position (Pic D). From there, you can attack with a Left Hook, Cross, or Right Hook from Southpaw (Pic E).

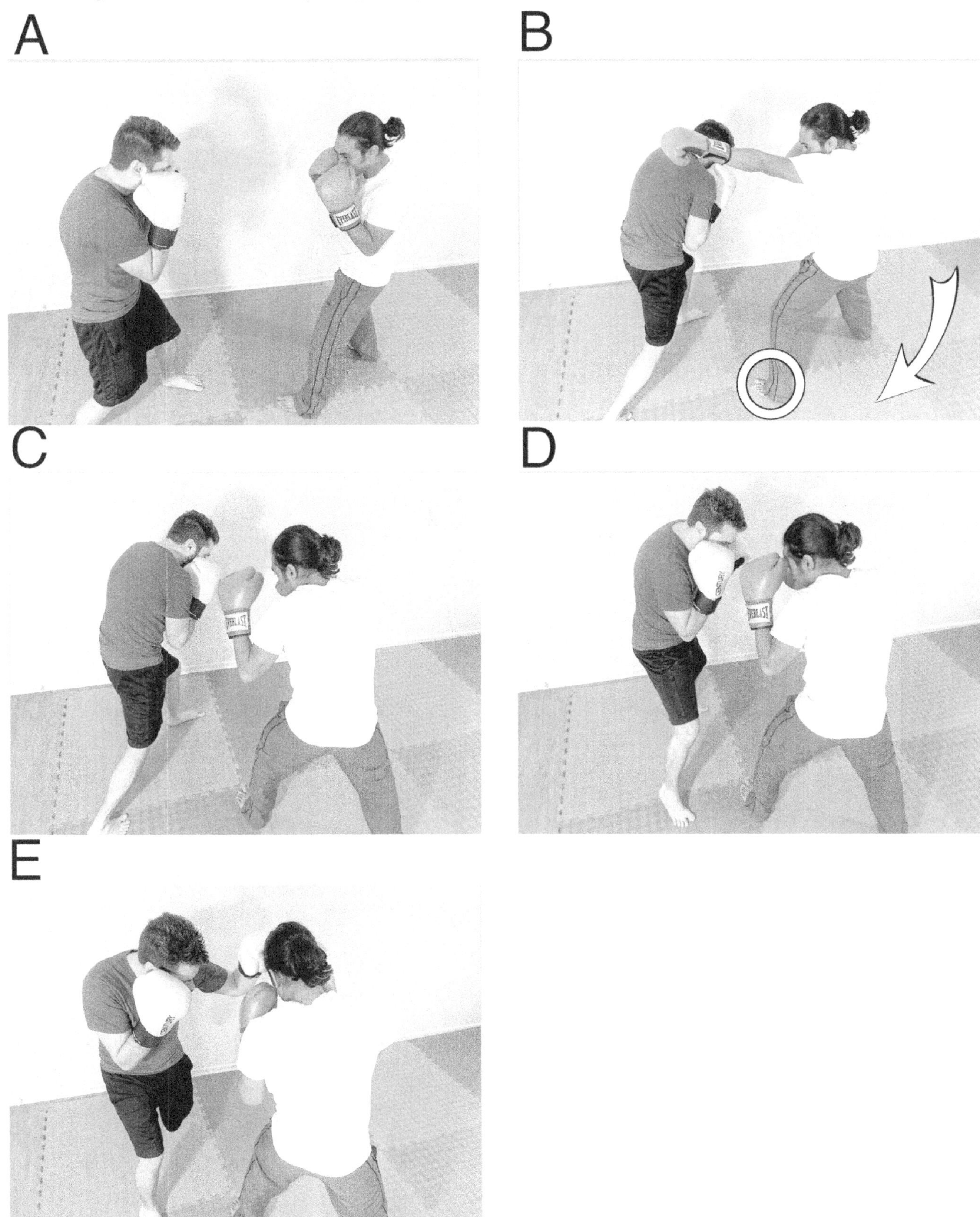

Open Stance Considerations

Turn Shifts work well in Open Stance as well. An opponent against the ropes may try to move Inside and Jab or Hook to escape (Pic B). Simply Slip and Turn Shift to counter with a Cross or Lead Hook from Orthodox (Pics A to D). A small step with your Left Foot may help close the distance and adjust your angle.

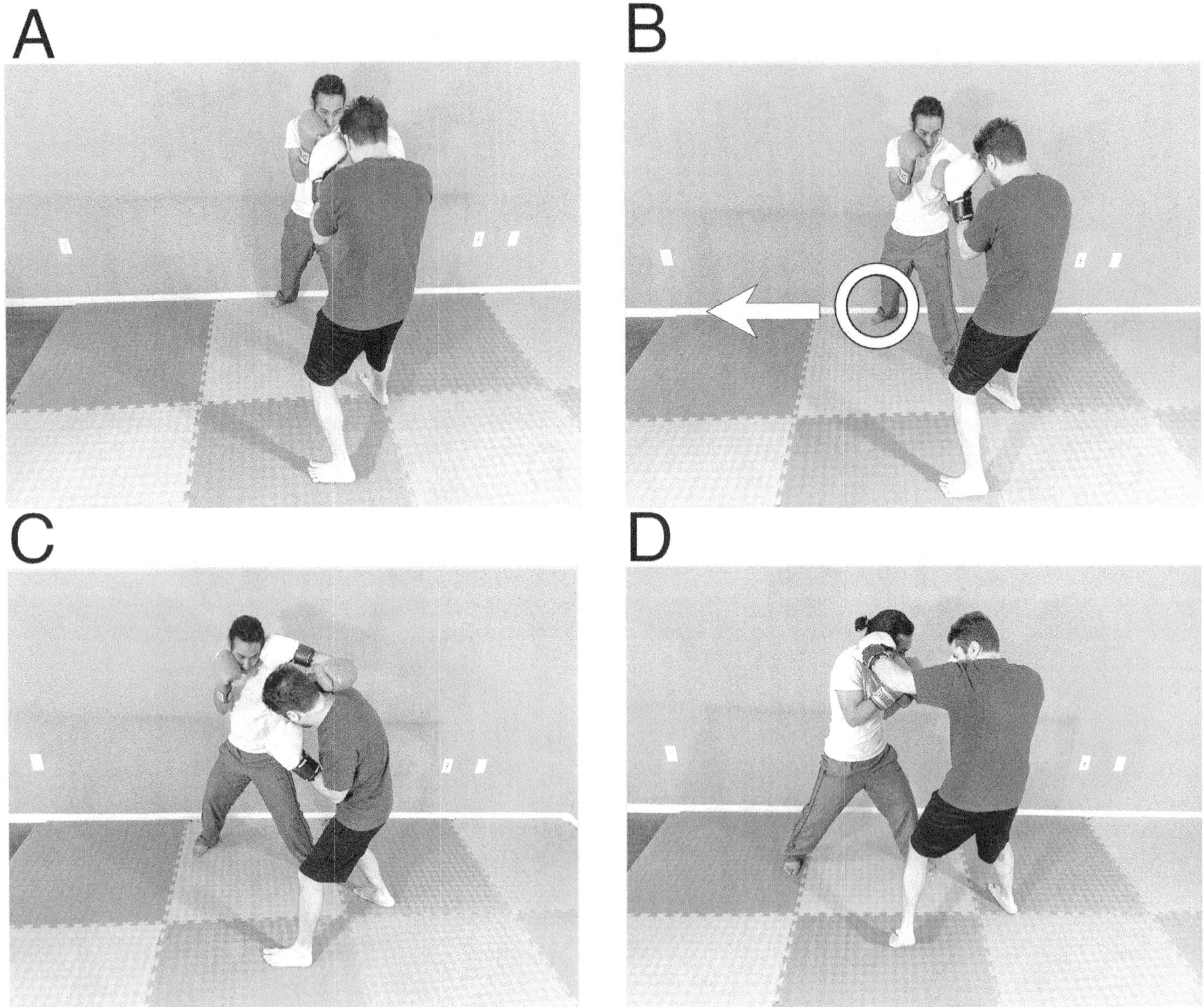

Open Stance Considerations – Specialty Counter

This counter is another one from Pacman. This technique is for opponents trying to circle and Jab. In an Open Stance, opponents are more likely to circle and Jab to the Outside. As they do so, Drop Slip Inside (Pics A to B) and then Return a Rear Cross or Hook, Pivoting hard off your Lead Foot (Pics C to D) The load up of the Hook in Pic C is exaggerated for clarity.

This technique requires a great deal of agility. It is very difficult to Slip Inside with an Inside foot position and then catch your opponent as they pivot Outside. But if you can pull this off, it is a tremendous way to counter your opponent's Jab while moving forward.

Lateral Shift/Shuffle Weave

As your opponent throws a punch, Weave to the Inside (Pics A to B) and simultaneously step or shuffle so far to the Inside that you switch to a Southpaw Stance (Pics C to D). From there, Counter off of your new Rear Hand (Pic E) or throw a Lead Hook with your new Lead Hand (Pic F). This can often work in tandem with a Turn Shift, with both yourself and your opponent contributing to the stance switch.

Once again, Peek-A-Boo allows the practitioner to angle off to either side with either Stance.

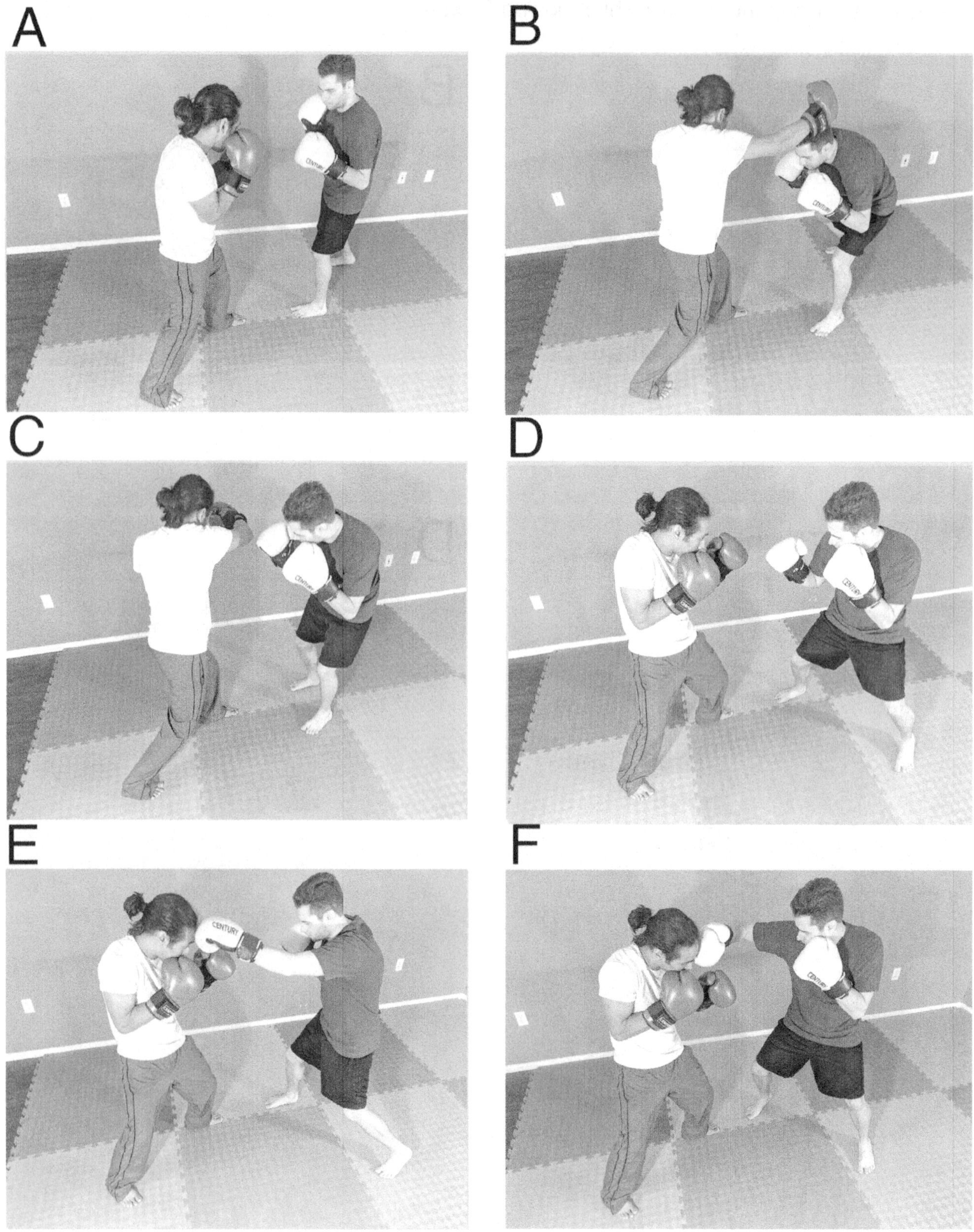

Drills

Drill 1A

Have your partner throw punches at you as you chase them to the ropes. Use the head movement of your choice to stay safe (Pics A to C). You may wish to try out the Reverse Weaves or Dempsey Roll outlined earlier in this chapter.

If you get caught, then start the drill over. However, if you manage to get their back to the ropes/cage, then have them try to Pivot Inside to get away. As they do so, step out with your Rear Foot to Lateral Shift into Southpaw and then attack with either side (Pics D to F).

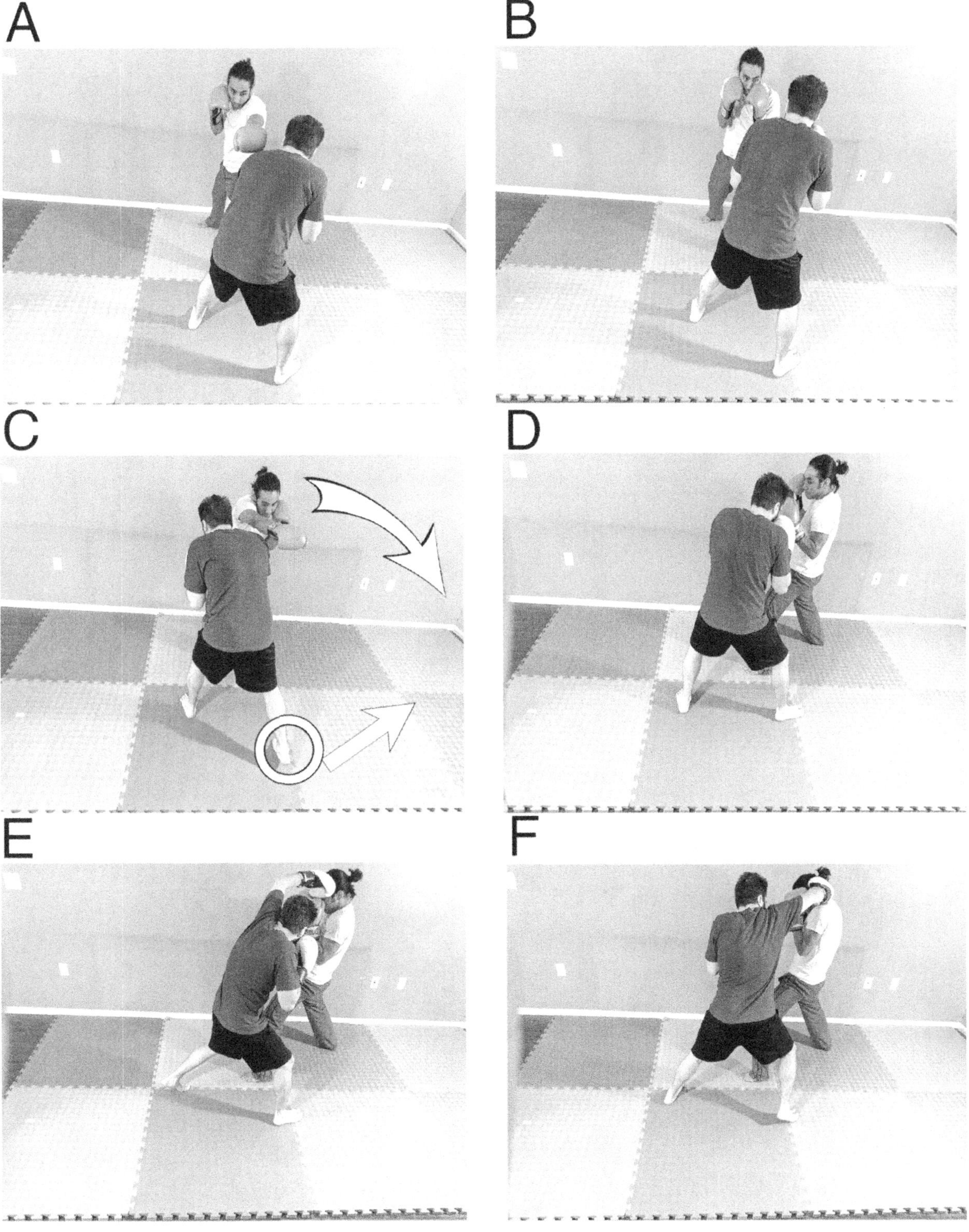

Drill 1B

Repeat the previous drill (Pics A to D), but this time have your partner try to escape to the Outside. As they do so, step out with your Lead Foot to cut them off and catch them with an overhand or Gazelle Hook (Pics D to F). Once you have the hang of both this drill and the last, have your partner vary which way they attempt to escape and try to react correctly each time.

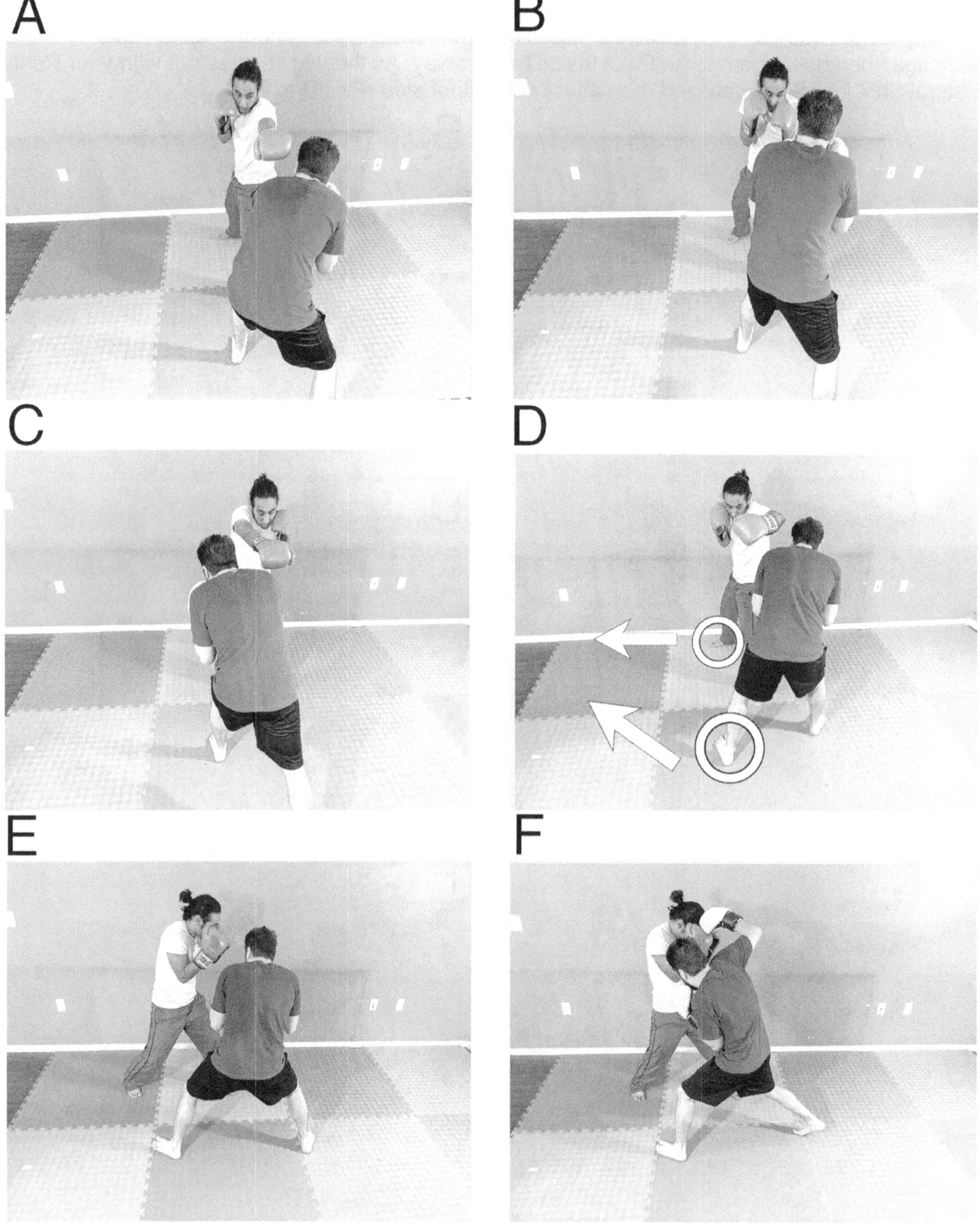

Drill 2A

Repeat the previous drill, but this time have your partner stay put and try to hold their ground, fending you off with punches (Pics A to D). As they do so, Weave under their punches to take an angle and counter from there (Pics E to F). You may use either angle from the previous two drills. The pics on this page show a deep Inside Position.

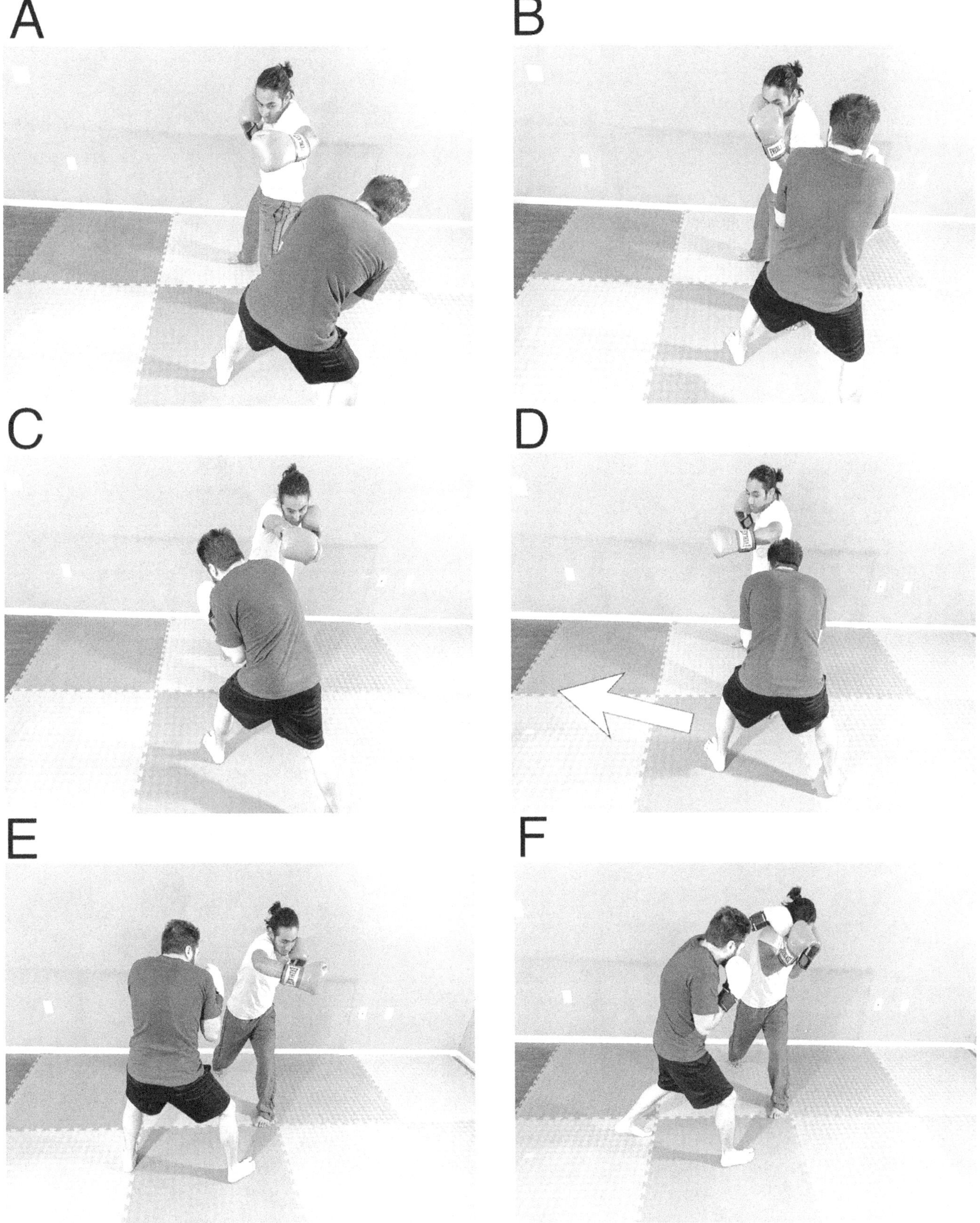

Try to vary which side you choose to attack (Pics A to E). The pics on this page show the fighter taking a deep Outside position.

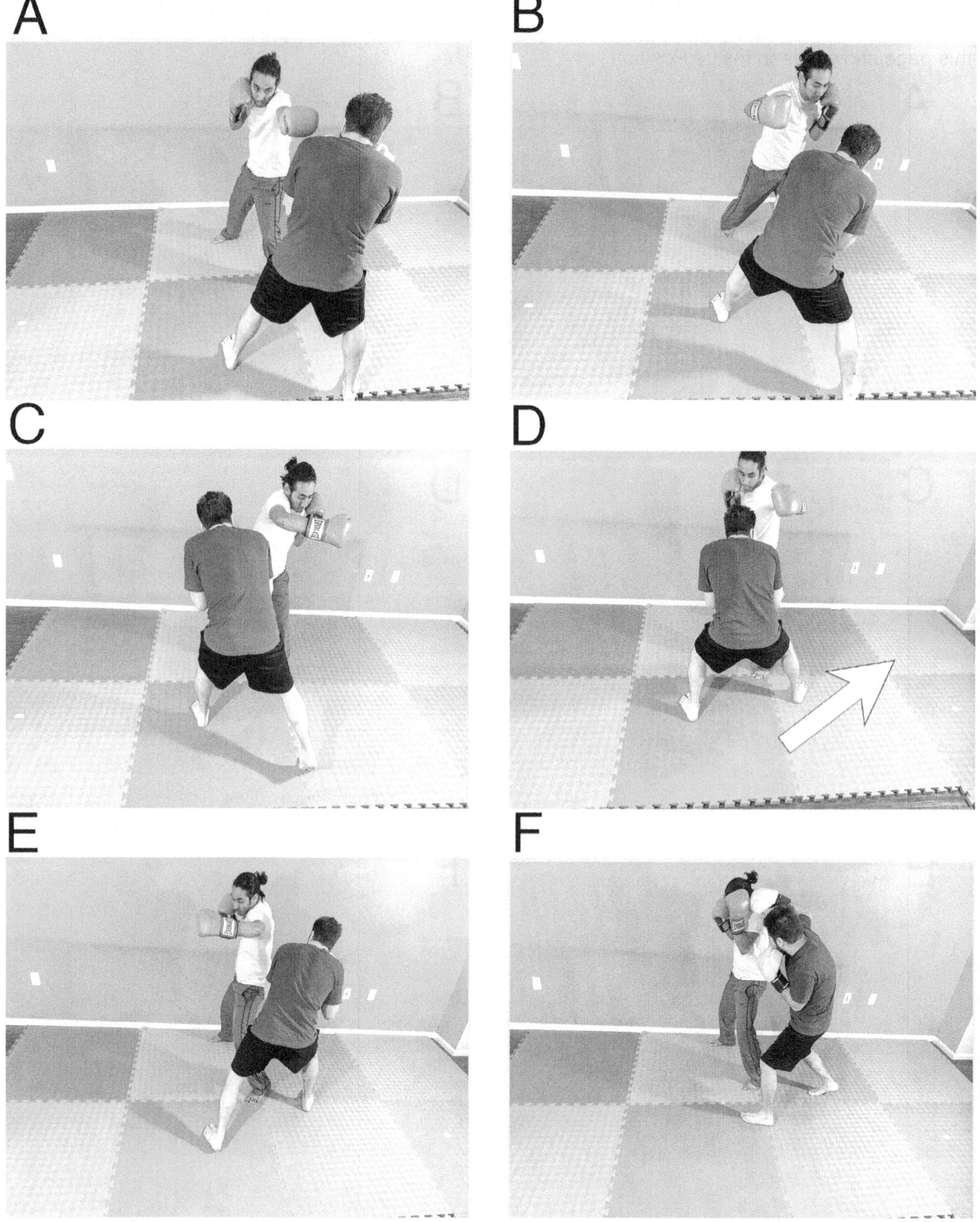

Linear Shift (D'Amato Shift) Weave

I first heard the term D'Amato Shift on the excellent YouTube Boxing channel Lee Wylie. It refers to the way that D'Amato's fighters would often move past an opponent's Center Line, transitioning both fighters from Orthodox to Southpaw. This will of course be beneficial for the fighter used to fighting in either stance, and startling and uncomfortable for the fighter who isn't.

To perform a Linear Shift Weave, Duck as you step in deep, well past the middle of your opponent's stance (Pics A to B). Now stay low and Shuffle past your opponent, turning to face them as you do so (Pics C to D). Rise up back to your regular posture as you complete the movement, firing off a counter if possible (Pics D to E). You should now both be in Southpaw (Pic F). Henry Cejudo pulled off this move against Demetrious Johnson to obtain a single leg on Johnson's Rear Leg.

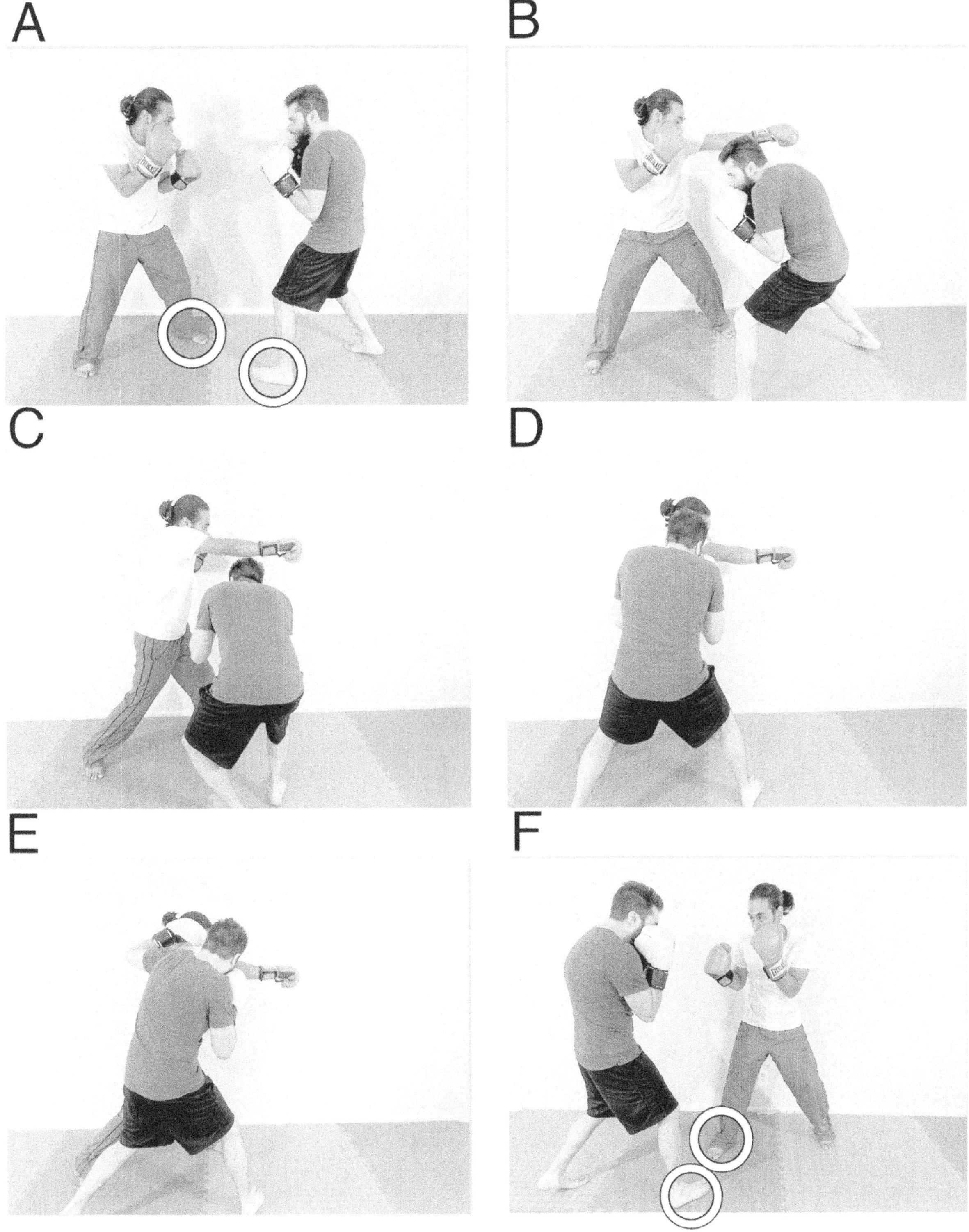

Jump Turn Counter

Get into Close or Mid-Range. As your opponent throws a Hook or Uppercut, Jump Turn to the Inside or Outside to take a superior angle (A to B). Practice countering off of both sides (Pics C to F). This movement is a quick turn, similar to the drills you see football players use for footwork. It is difficult to illustrate with pictures, so it may be best to look up the Tyson knockouts recommended in the Reference section to see it in action. Plus, then you get to watch Tyson knockouts.

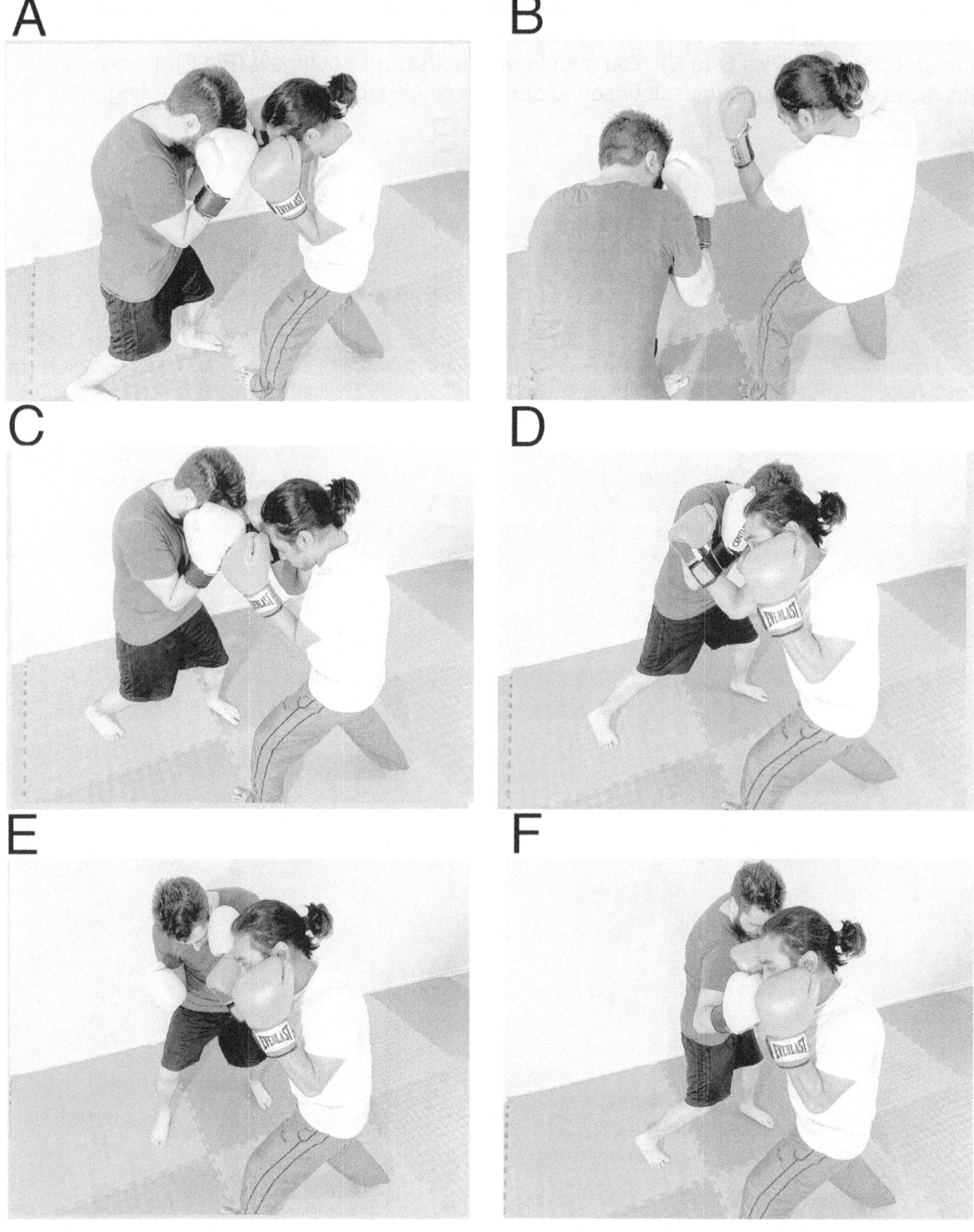

References – Peek-A-Boo

Tilt Slips:

Tyson vs anyone will show plenty of these, but there's a great example in Tyson vs Mitch Green. Green had been holding for 4 rounds. In the 5th with 1:25 left, Green illegally pulls Tyson into an Uppercut and starts throwing flurries. Tyson took the opportunity to taunt him, evading twenty-two punches in a row.

Justin Gaethje uses Tilt Slips in a very pronounced way in MMA. Chad Mendes also tended to Tilt Slip, though nowhere near as far as Tyson. Check out his fight vs McGregor. Although he lost in the end, he gave McGregor a run for his money and showed great head movement to set up both strikes and takedowns.

Reverse Weave:

Pacman vs De Le Hoya has plenty of examples of these. Julio Cesar Chavez Sr. used this motion to set up counters a great deal as well.

Figure 8 (Dempsey Roll):

You can check out Jack Dempsey vs Jess Willard for plenty of these. Or check out the end of Tyson vs Reggie Gross to see it done in place. Chaves Sr. also used these a great deal as he chased his competitors to cut off the ring.

In MMA you can watch Cody Garbrandt Dempsey roll against Dominick Cruz in round 3 with 40 seconds left.

Turn Shift Counter:

Watch Mike Tyson's knock out of Robert Colay. For an Open Stance example, watch Hagler's knockout of Willie Monroe in round 3.

Slip & Pivot Inside Counter - Open Stance:

Watch Pacman vs Chris Algieri to see Pacquiao pull off the maneuver over and over again, even knocking Algieri down with it. Rigondeaux vs Landeros is another good fight to watch to see this concept in action.

Lateral Shift/Shuffle Weave:

Tyson used this all the way back in the amateurs to knock out Joe Cortez within the first few seconds of the fight. You can see him use the exact same sequence in his first knockdown of Michael Johnson. Willie Pep used it many times to rebound back and counter.

Wonderboy Thompson, Anderson Silva, Dominick Cruz and Cody Garbrandt are all great MMA fighters to study for this technique. Wonderboy pulled off this technique vs Masvidal to land a Sidekick with his new Lead Leg.

Linear Shift (D'Amato Shift):

Tyson vs Mark Young has Tyson pulling off this move to land a terrific KO. Cody Garbrandt also landed using this footwork pattern against Dominic Cruz in the first round of their fight with 33 seconds left. Cruz attacks, and Garbrandt Weaves and Linear Shifts underneath, then quickly reverses directly to land a Reactive Takedown.

Jump Turn Counter:

Watch Tyson's evade a punch with this tactic and Return Counter to knockdown Tillman in the 4th.

Low Guard

The Low Guard works well for taller fighters with fast reflexes and good head movement. It is primarily a Long-Range counter-striking style. There is a lot of Drawing involved as the practitioner moves their open head into different positions to try and tempt their opponent into throwing shots. It pairs well with the Long Guard and requires excellent footwork. In MMA, the lower hands can help with takedown defense.

Inside Pull Slip With Cross Step

Take a narrow stance. As your opponent throws an attack, Slip to the Inside. But do not step Inside with your Lead Foot. Instead, Cross Step your Rear Foot to the Inside as you Slip (Pics A to B). Now step or hop off of your Lead Foot to fire off a Jab (Pic C).

This is a dangerous technique that requires a lot of skill to pull off. The benefit is that it permits lateral head movement (an Inside Pull Slip) to your Lead Side even with a safer narrow stance. It essentially sacrifices stability (a crossed leg position is not ideal for balance) for mobility. Muhammad Ali used this set up all the time as he danced around the ring. It has also been used extensively by Sugar Ray Leonard, Thomas The Hitman Hearns and many others. You may also step out to throw a Cross, something Ali used to knockout several opponents (Pics D to F).

Pull Weave

As your opponent throws a long Lead Hook or looping Jab, Pull Slip back and Inside (Pics A to B), and then move your head Outside to the position used for an Outside Pull Slip (Pic C). Return back to your regular posture as your opponent's Hook retracts, completing the Pull Weave. This may be done from Outside to Inside as well (Pics D to F).

This is perhaps the most dangerous technique shown so far. It allows you to stay in range of your opponent with both hands free, but requires insane precision and an impeccable sense of distance. Ali could do it consistently, but not everyone can fight like Ali. If this is confusing, it is demonstrated with a partner on the next page.

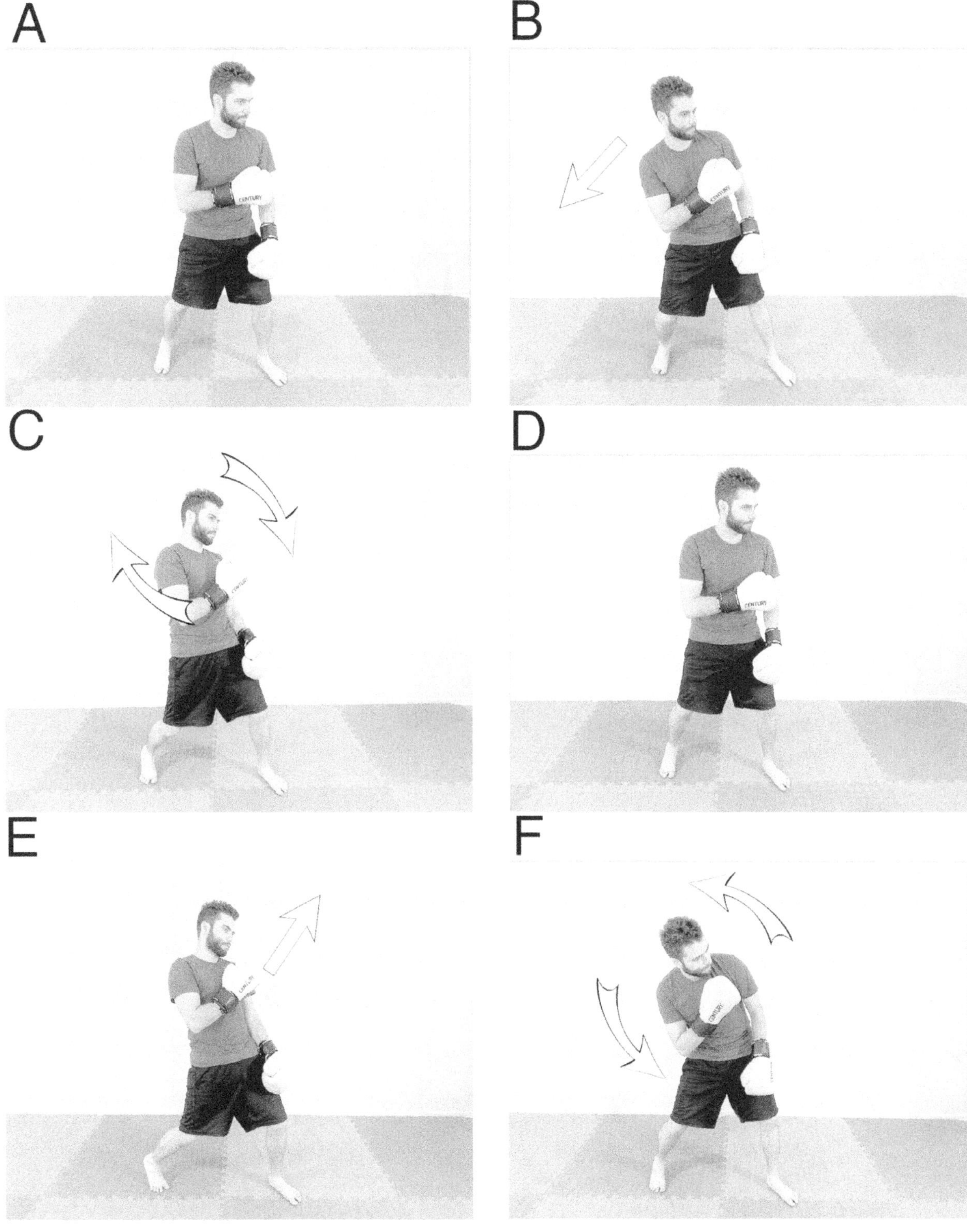

Like all other Weaves, this may be used to defend against one strike or many. After Slipping Inside to avoid a Jab (Pics A to B), Pull (Pic C) to Weave to an Inside Slip (Pic D), avoiding any follow up punches (Pic D to E).

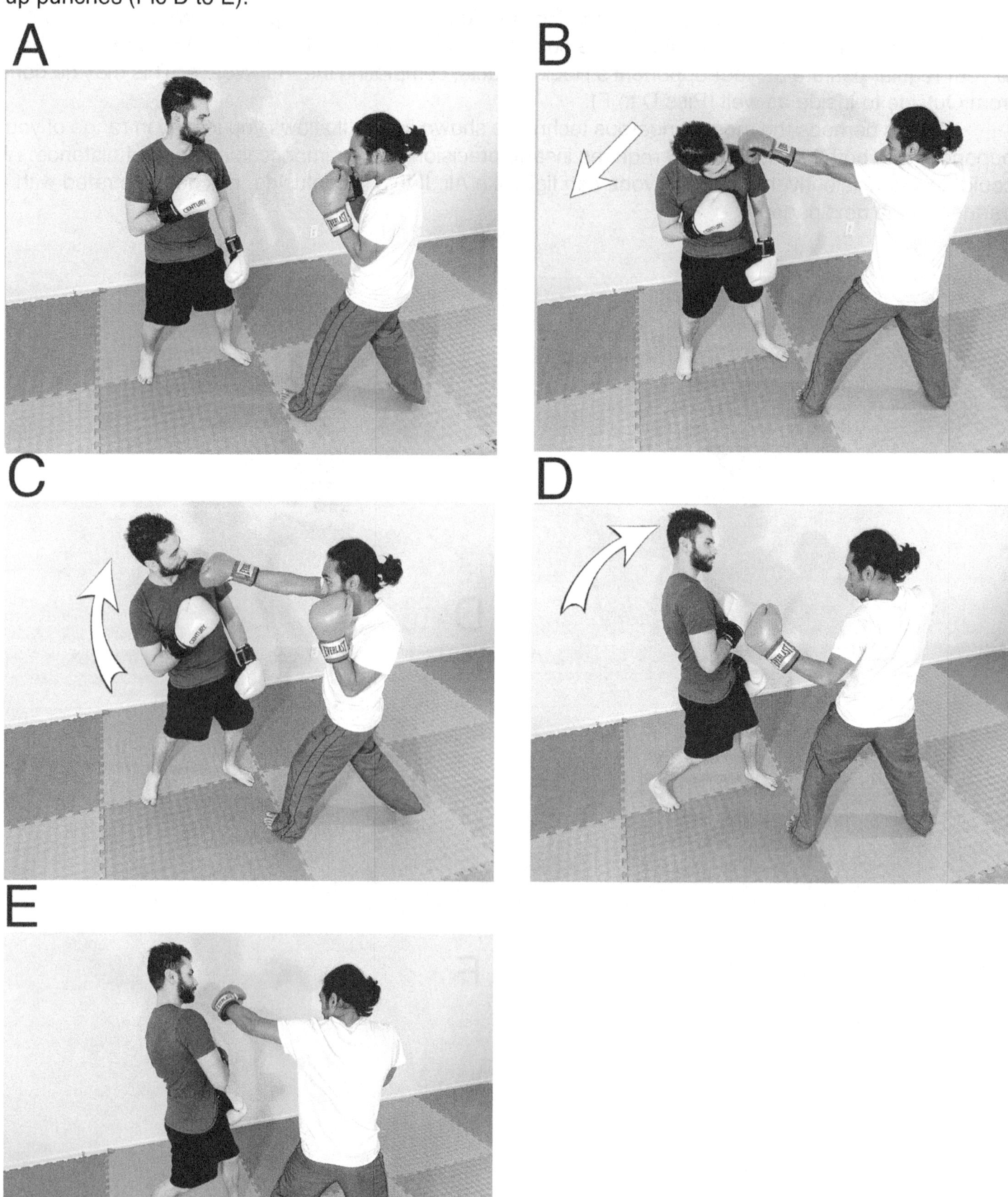

With Head Turn

Remember one page before when I said this was the most dangerous technique shown so far? Well, now this is (Pic A). Ali would turn his head at the same time to let his opponent's punch sail past a mere inch away (Pics B to E). He would then counter with a Lead Hook or Cross. Look up Ali's knockouts to see multiple examples of this technique. This is not advised, but it is of course up to you if you would like to attempt it. It's best to think of it as an extra precaution and count on your Pull Weave and shoulder to protect you. Recently Israel Adesanya used this same tactic to become a champion in the UFC.

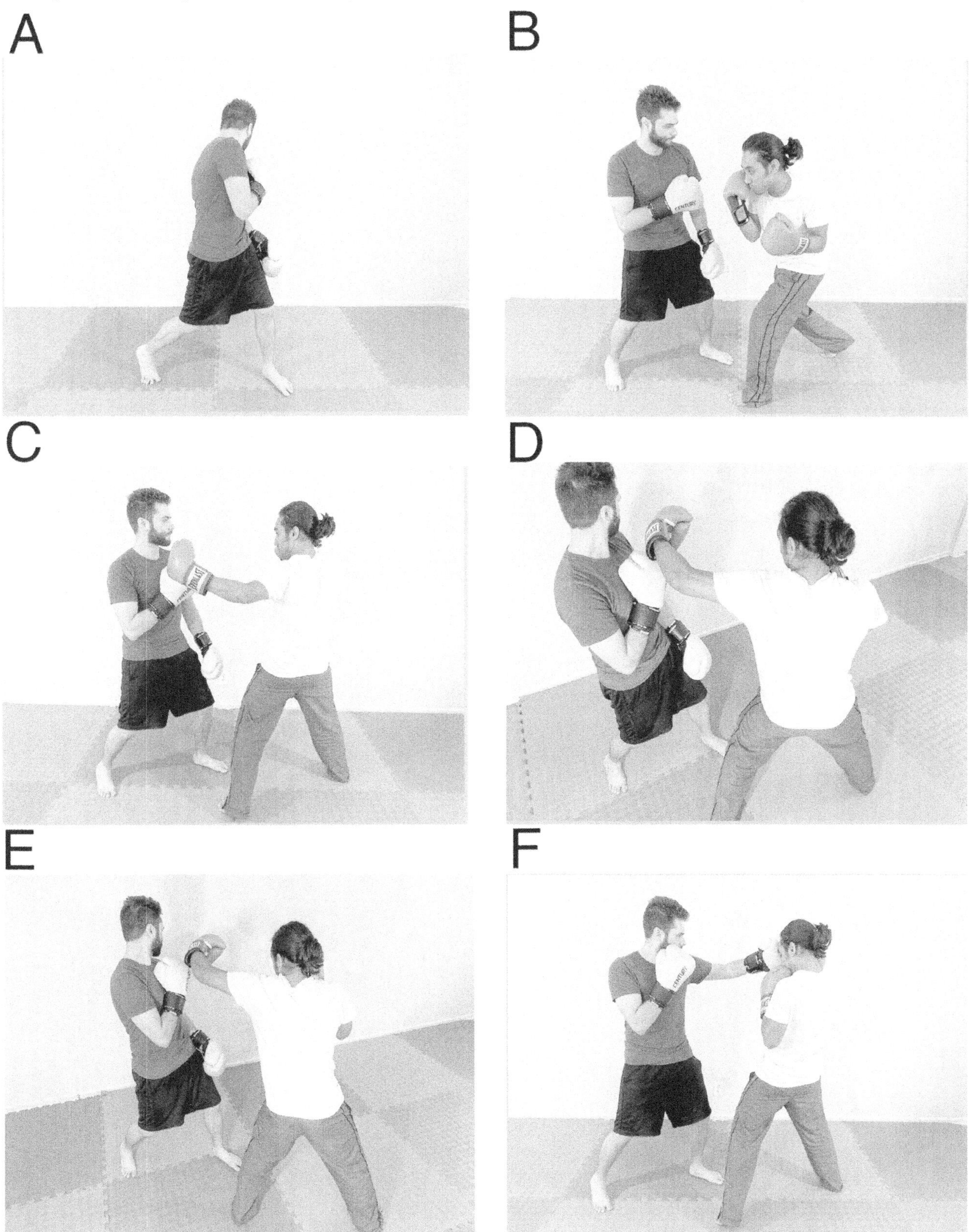

Pivot With Head Turn

As your opponent throws a Rear Hook or Cross, Pivot away and turn your head back to let the punch pass you (Pics A to B & C to F). Raise your Lead Shoulder high for extra protection. You may also step back with your Rear Foot to add some distance to avoid follow up punches.

This is another very dangerous technique. An example of a fighter consistently using it effectively today would be Canelo Alvarez. If you want to attempt it, think of the head turn as extra insurance rather than your primary form of defense. Be careful of counters as you turn your head back and try your best to not lose sight of your competitor.

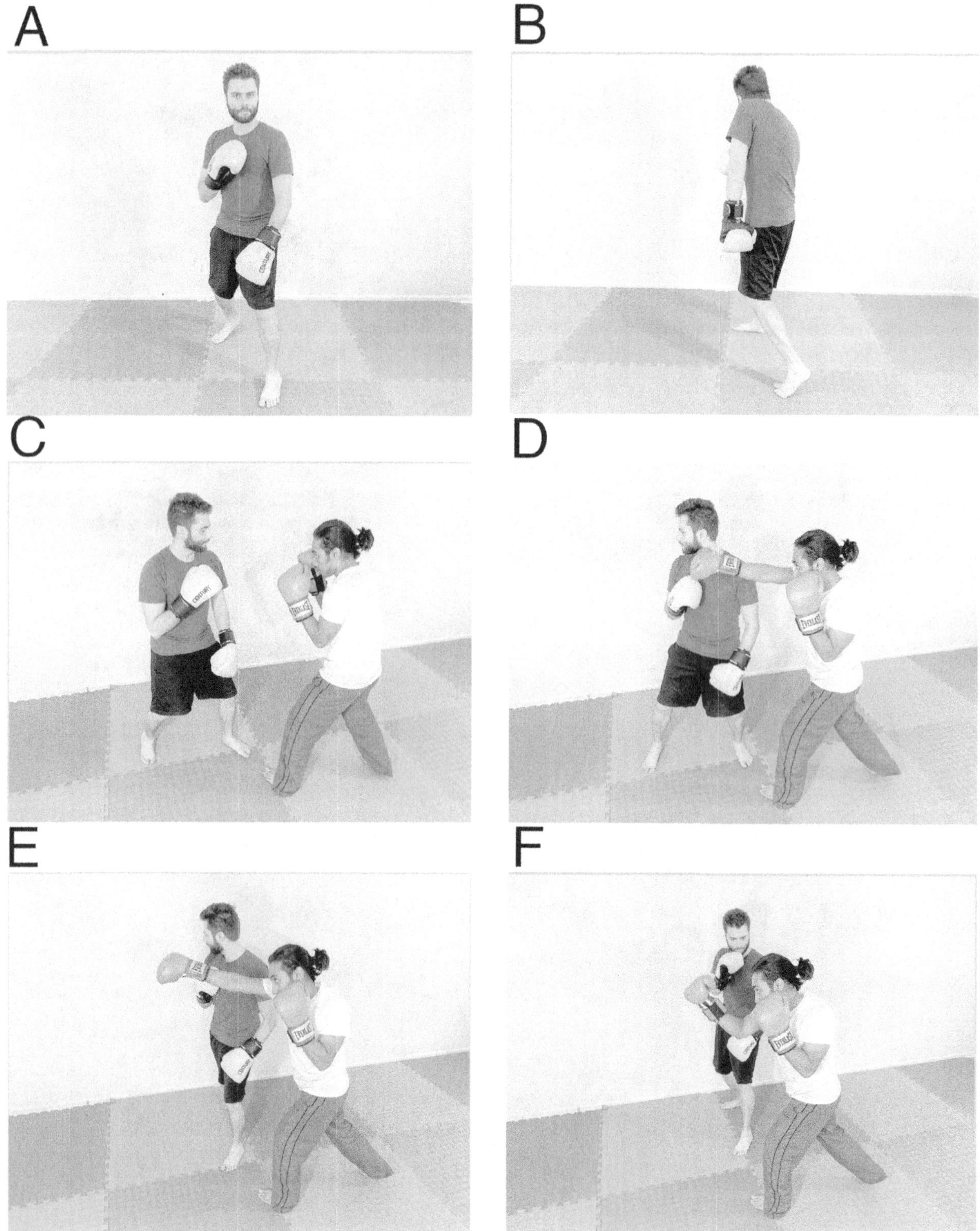

Butterfly Weave

This is a combination of a Weave and Pull Weave, once used by Ali to dodge 20 punches in a row. You can also think of it as Drop Slipping from one side to the other (Pics A to C), and then leaning back to Pull Slip from one to the other, completing the circle (Pics D to F). This technique was used by Ali and Anderson Silva and a few other highly skilled individuals.

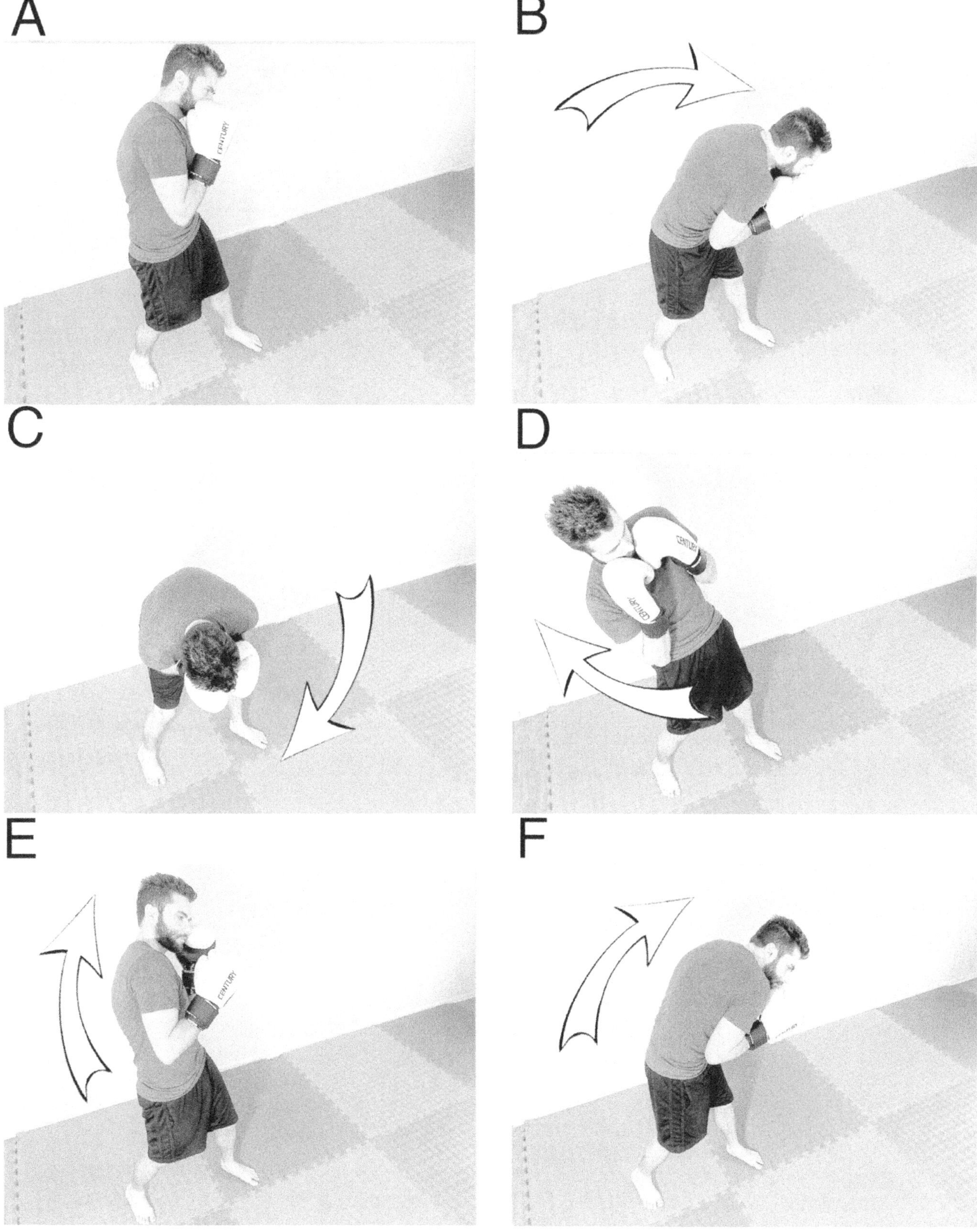

Do I even need to say that it's dangerous? Still, if your intention is to irritate your opponent and trick them into head hunting, this is a great way to do it (Pics A to D). You may reverse direction at any point to remain unpredictable.

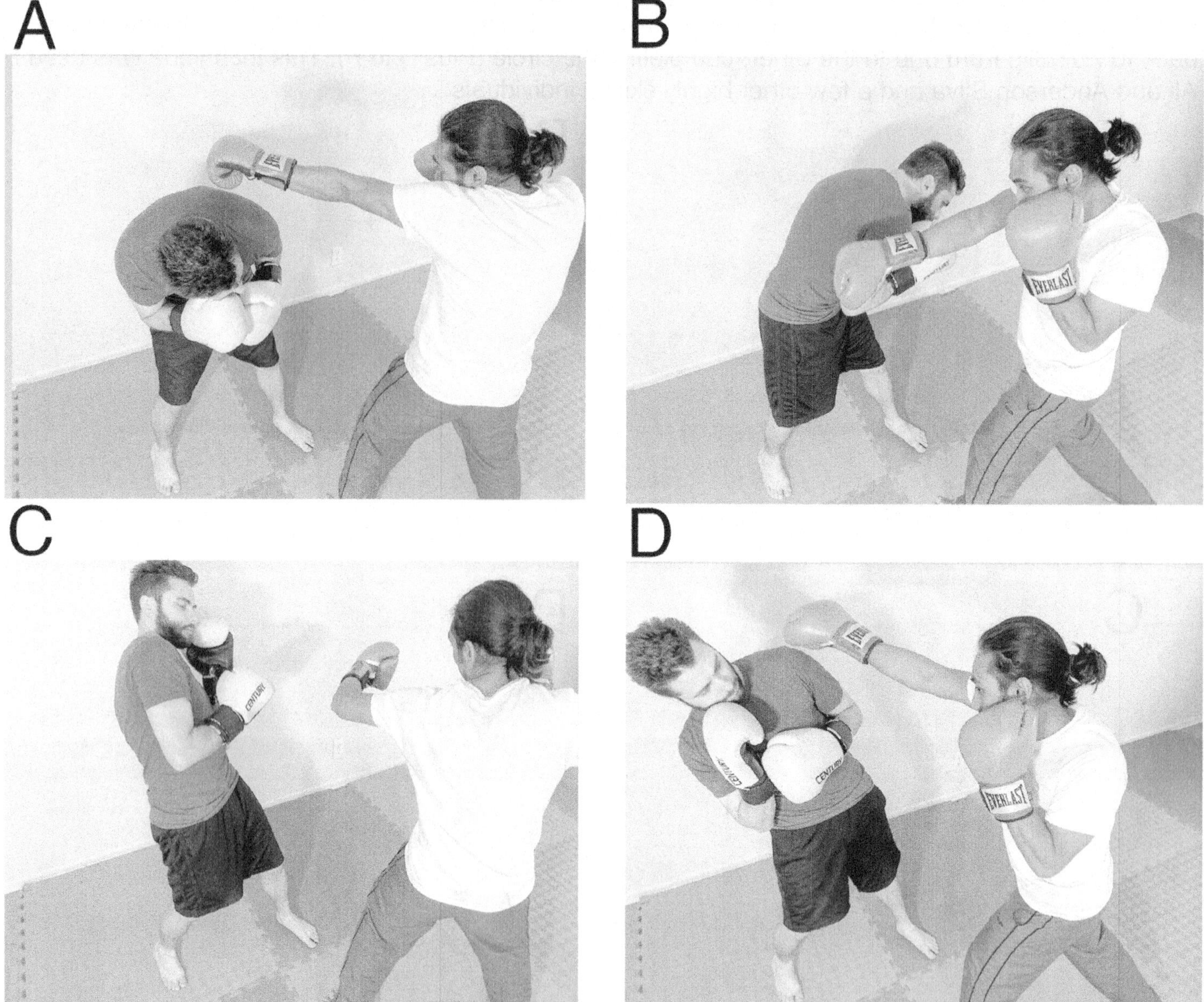

Drill

Stay in place and have your opponent throw very, very light strikes at your head. See how many punches you can evade before getting hit. Now switch which partner is attacking, and have them try to beat your score. Go back and forth until you've beaten them thoroughly.

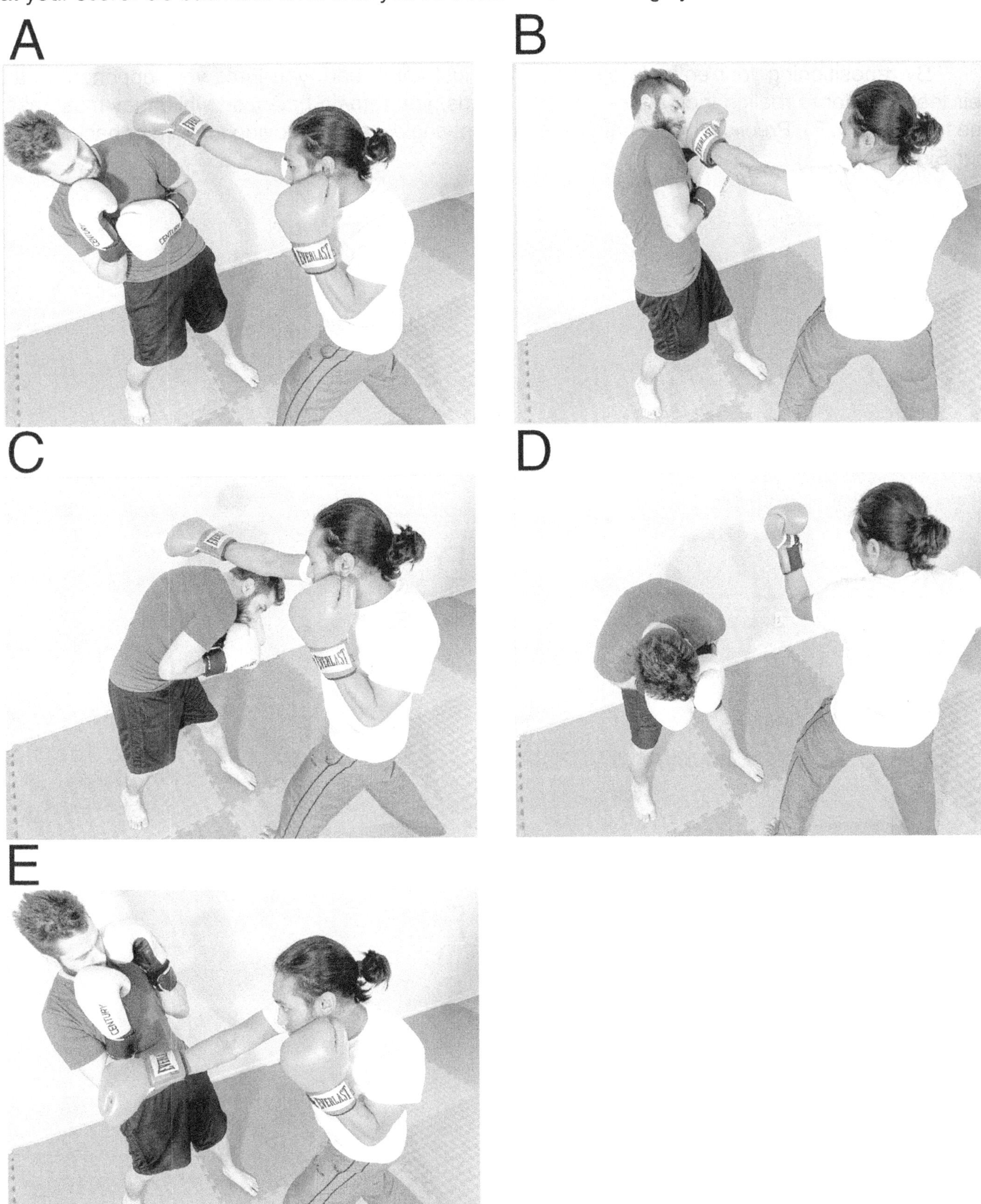

Side Step

To Side Step an opponent's attack, first move the foot that corresponds to the direction you would like to go. If you want to Side Step Left then move your left foot first (Pics A to B), and vice versa. Your other foot then follows, putting you back into your usual stance (Pic C).

Fighters who master the Side Step can use it like a Slip without moving their head at all (Pics D to F). However, you may wish to begin learning the movement by adding on a Slip or Duck.

By repositioning your entire body rather than just your head, you force your opponent to adjust their feet in order to realign their attack. In other words, you remain balanced while they must take the time to reset (Pic F). Practice this technique at different angles, either moving forward or backwards with your Side Step.

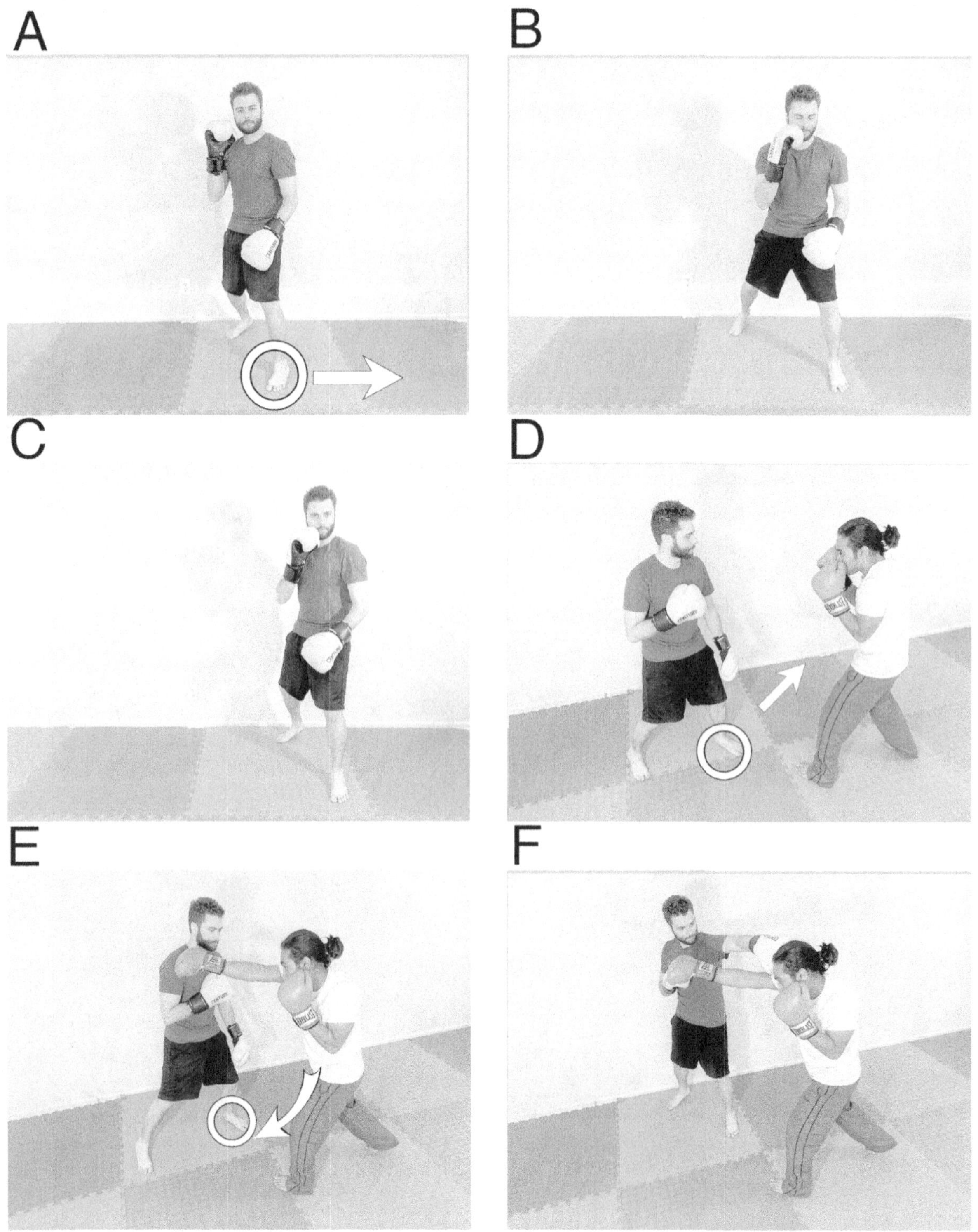

An interesting variation used by Willie Pep and Dominick Cruz is to Side Step Inside but Drop Slip to the Outside, or vice versa (Pics A to C). What this does is it help aligns your posture to throw shots with the opposite hand. For instance, by stepping Inside but Drop Slipping Outside, your Rear Hand is still aligned to throw an Intercepting Counter (Pic C).

A

B

C

Slide/Step Back

Simply slide your Lead Foot back towards your Rear Foot to move out of the way of your opponent's kick (Pics A to B). If your midsection may be in danger, then move your hips back as well. Make sure to never completely lock or straighten your leg.

Combined with good footwork, this is one of the most high-level and effective defenses. With good balance, you can have your opponent swinging at air and then quickly rebound to move back in and take advantage of the tempo you have gained against them (Pics C to F).

This movement also blends well with L Steps and V Steps, making it a good choice for footwork based fighters.

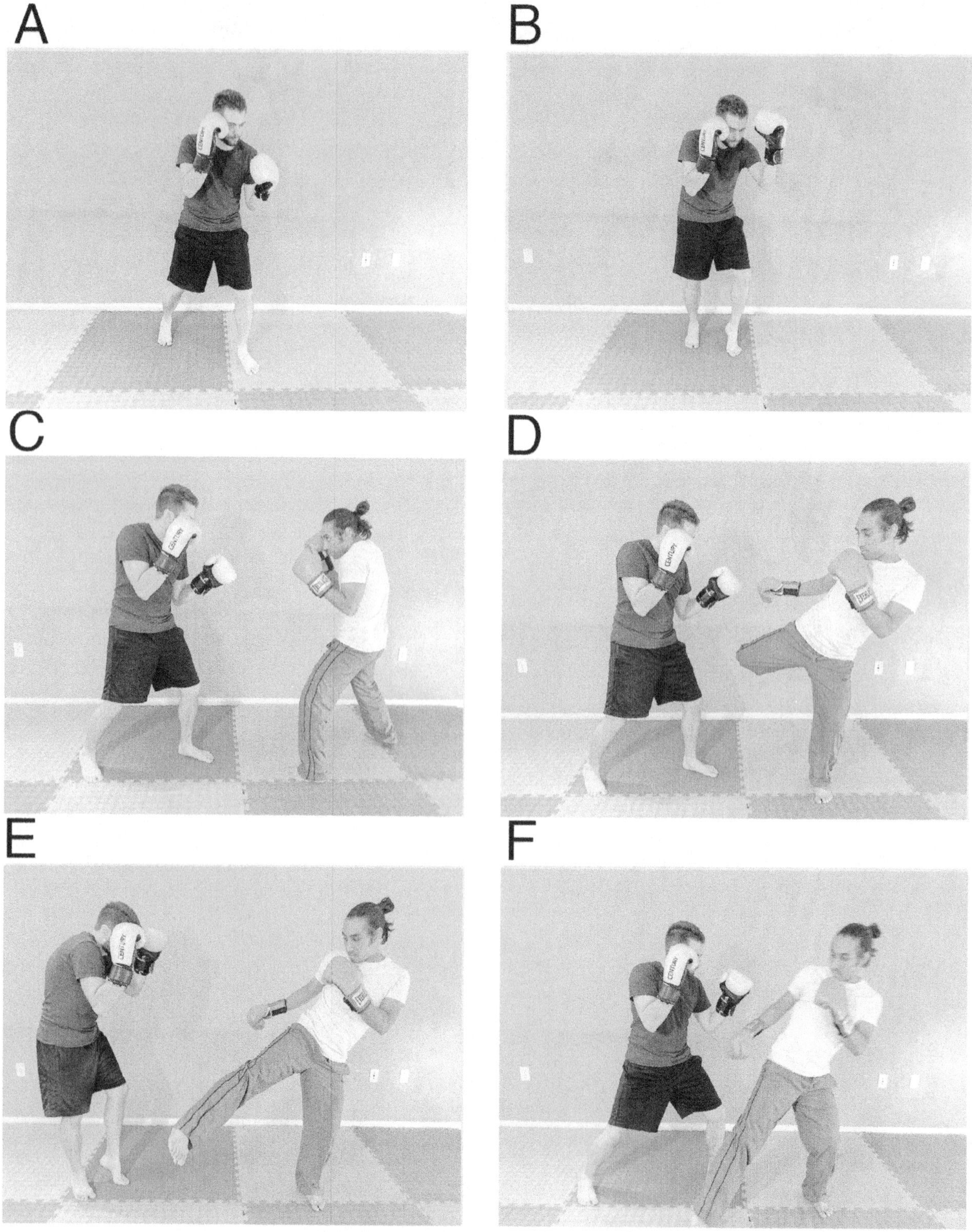

L – Step

To L-Step, slide your Lead Foot back close to your Rear Foot (Pics A to B), and then step out laterally with your Rear Foot to move off angle (Pic C), making the shape of an L. Reestablish your stance (Pic D). Watch Max Holloway, Willie Pep, Dominick Cruz and Mighty Mouse to get a feel of how to counter off of these movements.

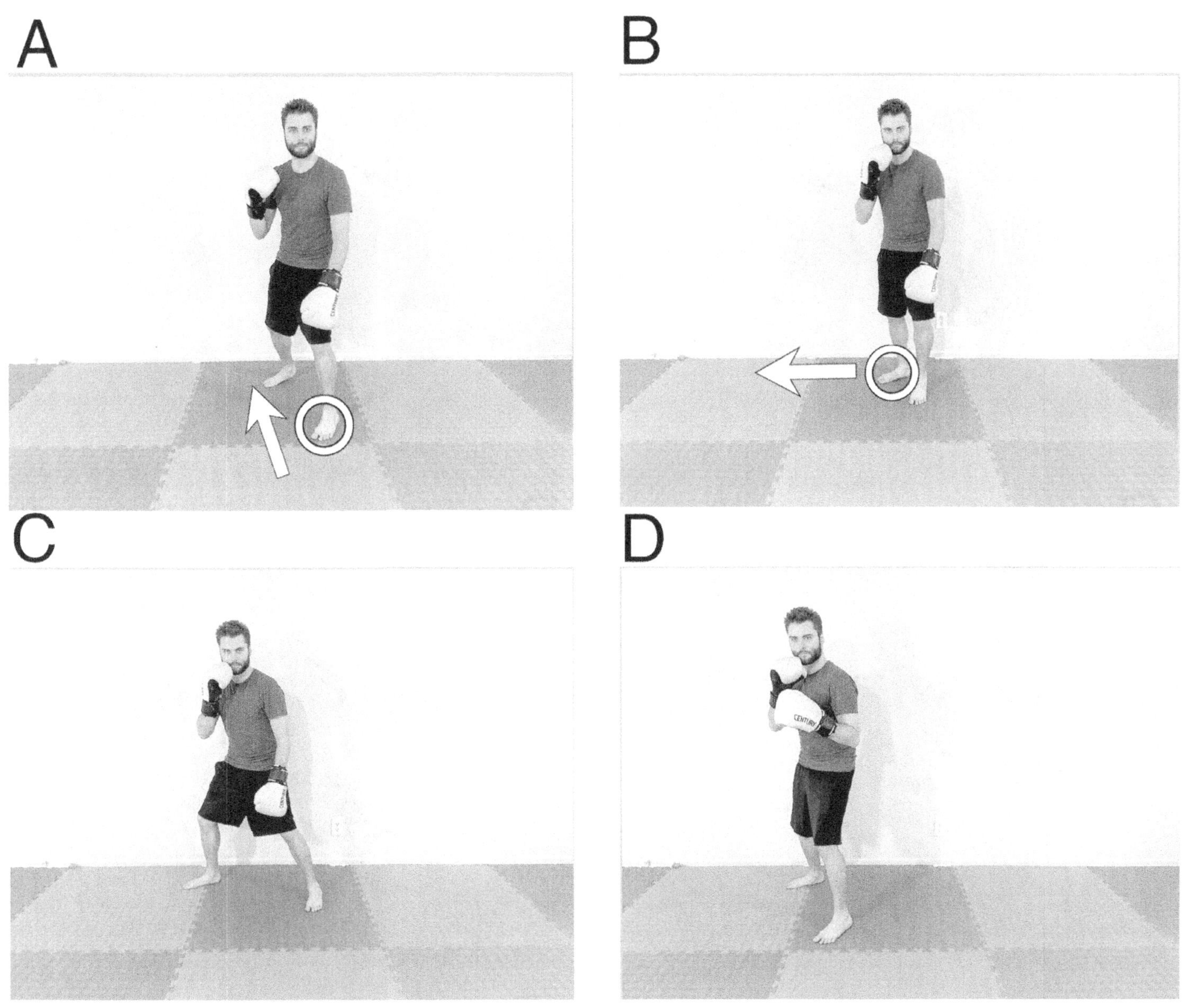

This can cover much more distance than a Side Step and moves you backwards or off angle at the same time.

The L-Step may be used like a Side Step to counter off angle, but it has even more potential in kickboxing and MMA. You can use a Slide Back as the first part of your L-Step to defend a kick (Pics A to B), and then continue the movement to strike from off angle while you opponent is still trying to recover their balance from kicking (Pics C to D). Holloway and Mighty Mouse have used this technique repeatedly to stay mobile while still defending kicks.

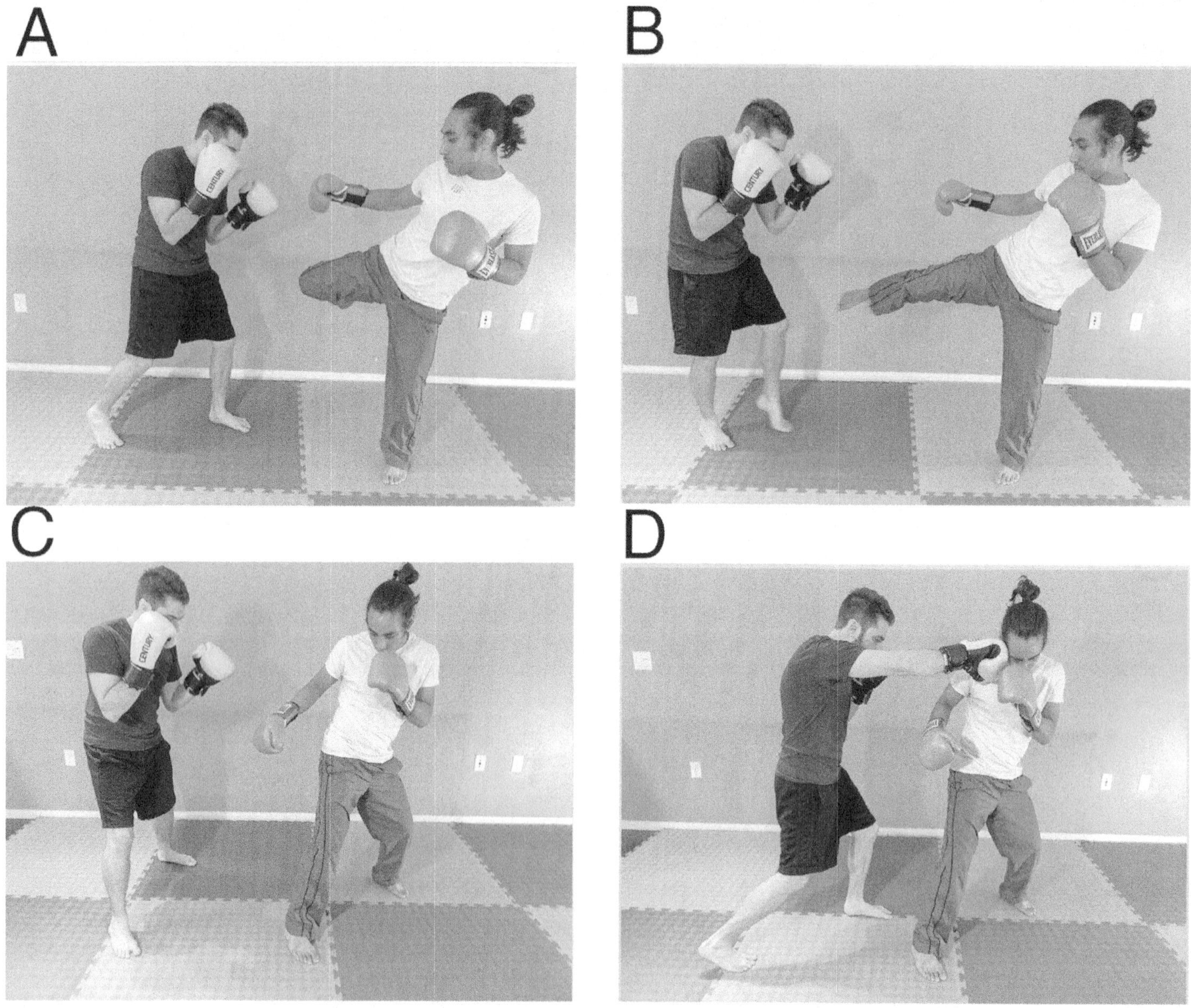

V-Shift

The V-Step is similar, except you Shift Forward with your Rear Leg to gain a new angle, making the shape of a V (Pics A to D). You can watch the same fighters mentioned above to get a better feel for this advanced movement, or check out Footwork Wins Fights for more aggressive options. From this position it is also possible to counter with your new Rear Leg.

Open Stance Considerations

The Step Back, L-Step and V-Step all work very well in an Open Stance. The L-Step works well for countering both kicks (Pics A to C) and punches (Pics D to F). Ali actually preferred to move Inside when in an Open Stance fighting Southpaws, so L-Steps were a great help to him.

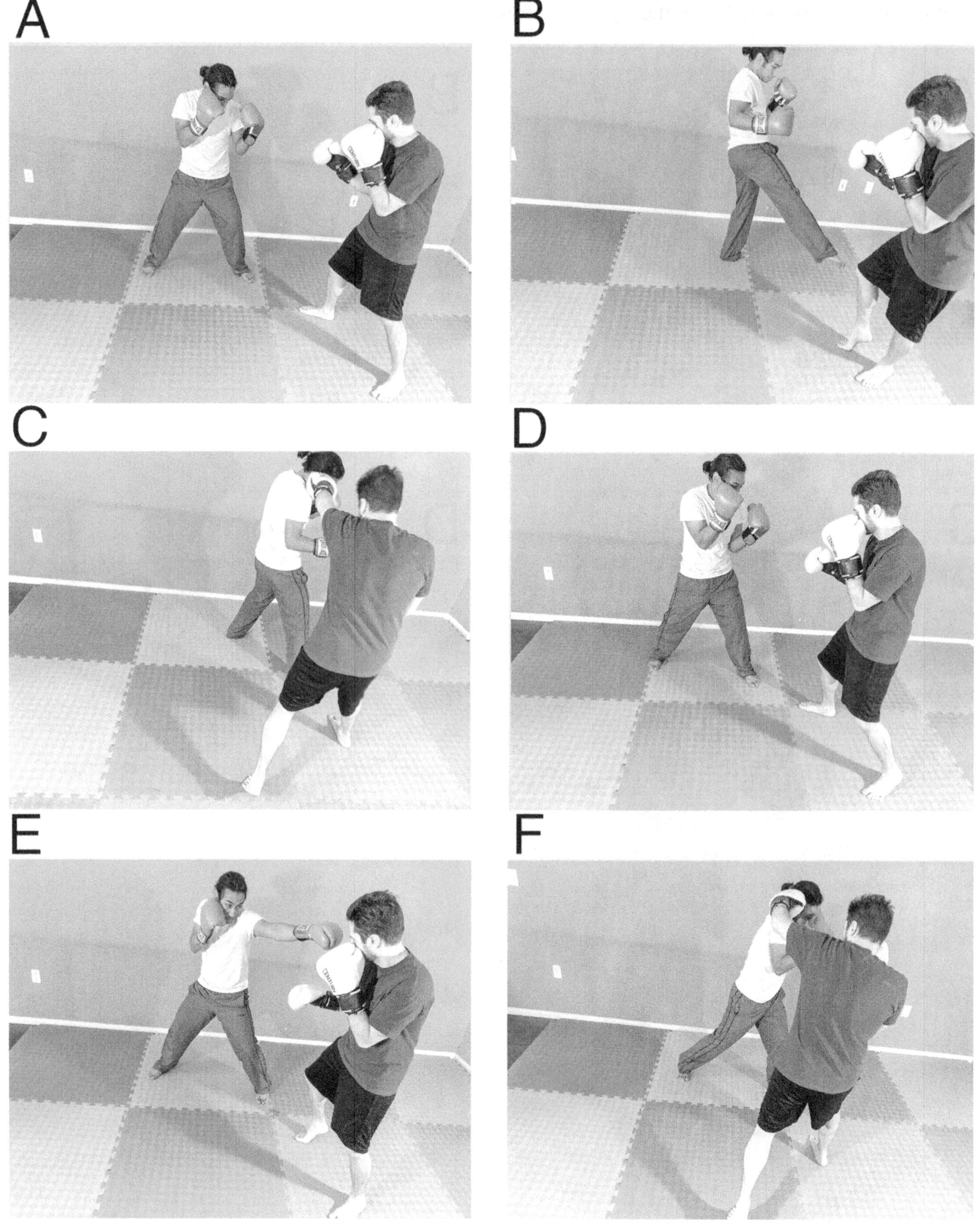

Shift Back Roll/Crouch

This is essentially a Rear Shoulder Roll. Step out and back with your Lead Foot to Shift back into a Southpaw stance, popping your new Lead Shoulder while Slipping Inside (Pics A to B). The beauty of this technique is that the Roll protects you from your opponent's Lead Side attacks and the Slip protects you from their Rear Side attacks (Pics C to D).

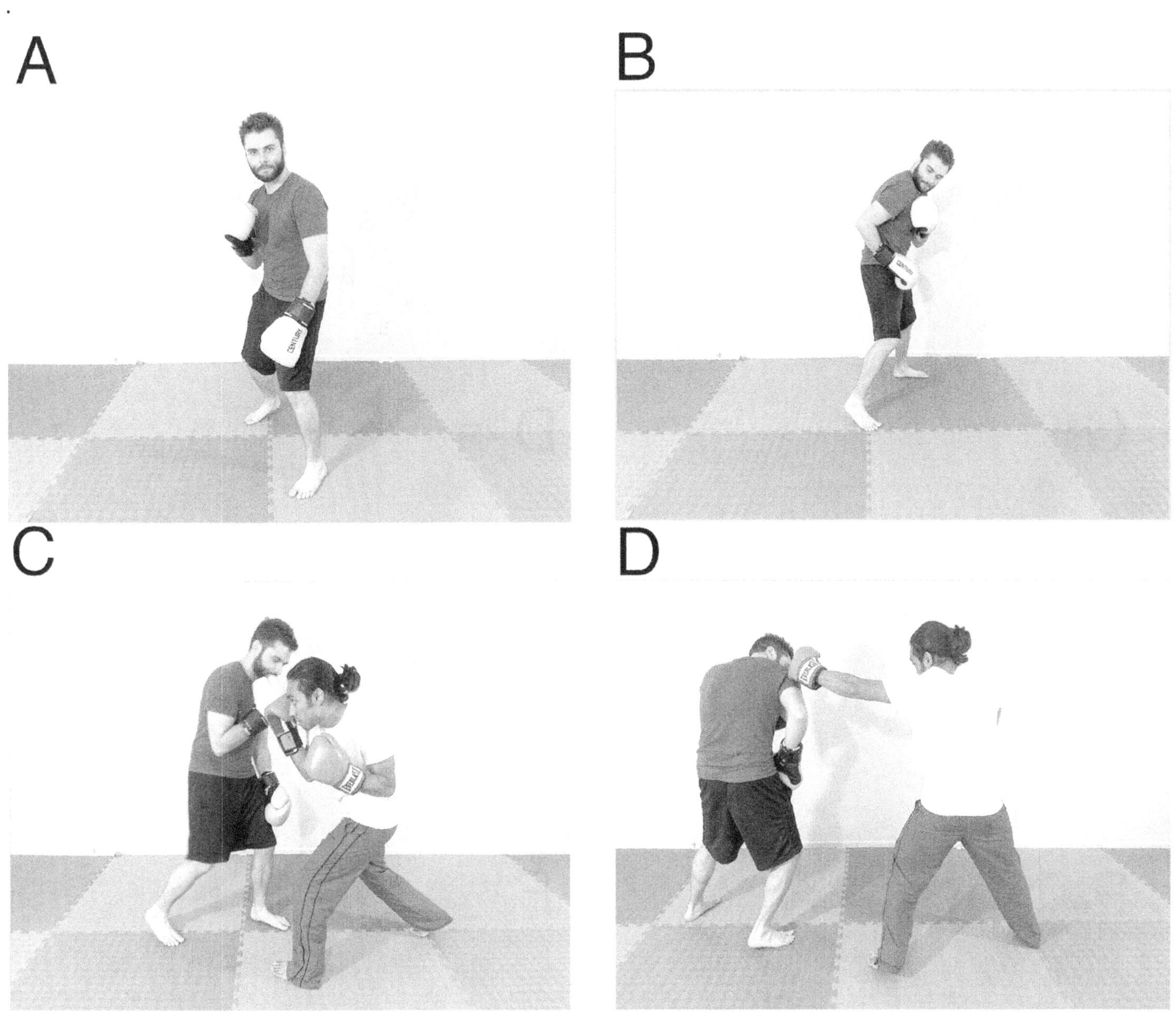

Shift Back Weave

Begin by Slipping or Drop Slipping your opponent's punch (Pics A to B). Now Shift back, Weaving under their follow up punches (Pics C to D). From here you can counter or repeat the pattern again (Pics E to F). Watch James Toney or Willie Pep for examples of this technique in the ring.

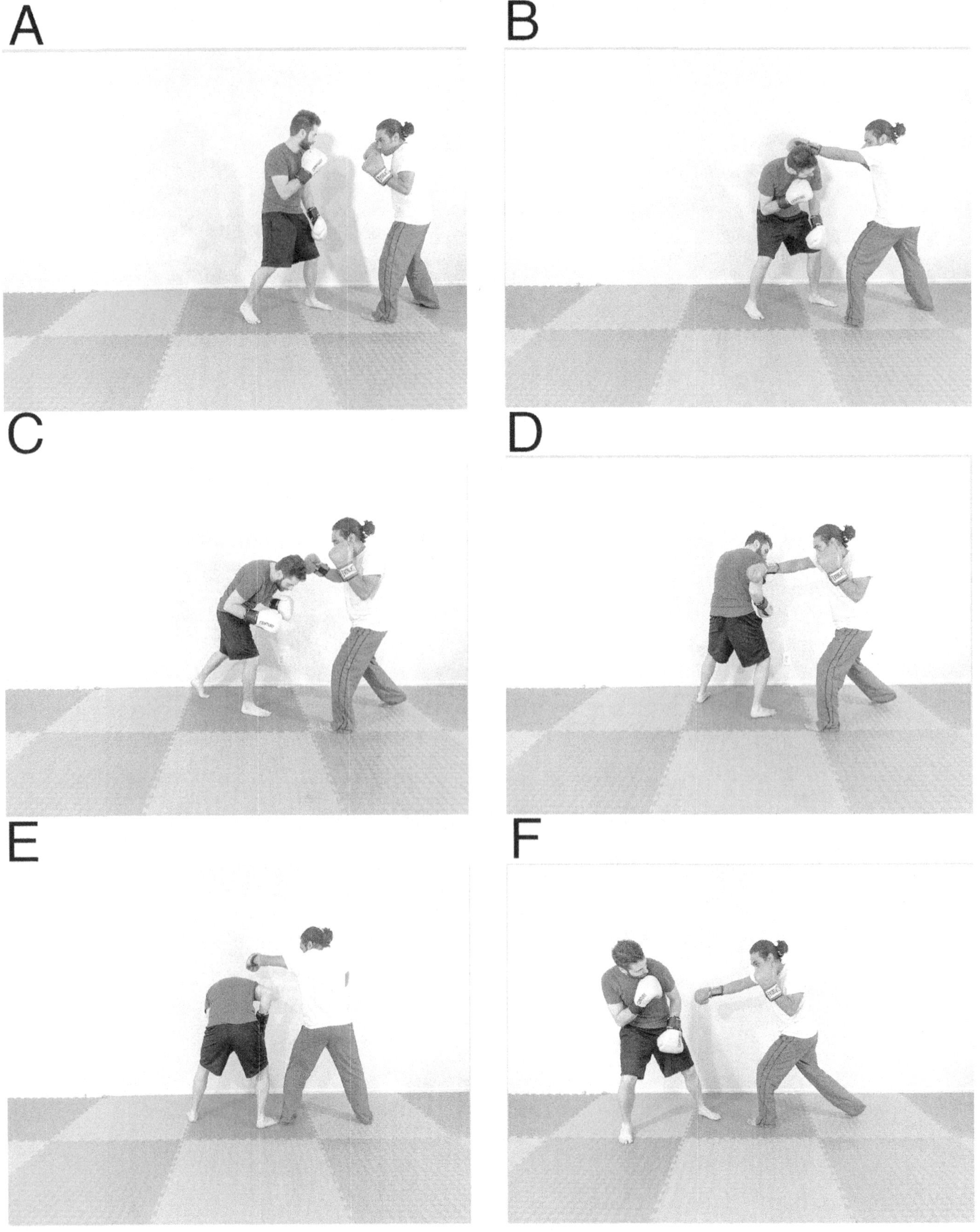

Shift Back Weave & Roll

Begin by using a Shift Back Shoulder Roll (Pics A to B). Now Shift Back Weave(Pics C to D). Now Shoulder Roll again off your new Lead Side (Pic E). You can now repeat this technique indefinitely, Shoulder Rolling then Shifting back with a Weave then Shoulder Rolling again. Check out the Drunken Master Emanuel Augustus or James Lights Out Toney to see examples of pros setting up shots off of this technique (Pic F).

A

B

C

D

E

F

Ali's Footwork & Head Movement Patterns

In Boxing

Stand in front of your partner, bouncing lightly on the balls of your feet. When they fire off a Jab-Cross, Side-Step their jab (Pics A to B). Then you may either Cross Step and Inside Pull to Return a Jab (Pics C to D) or Head Turn and Pivot to Return a Jab (Pics E to F). Once you are comfortable, try it out in free sparring.

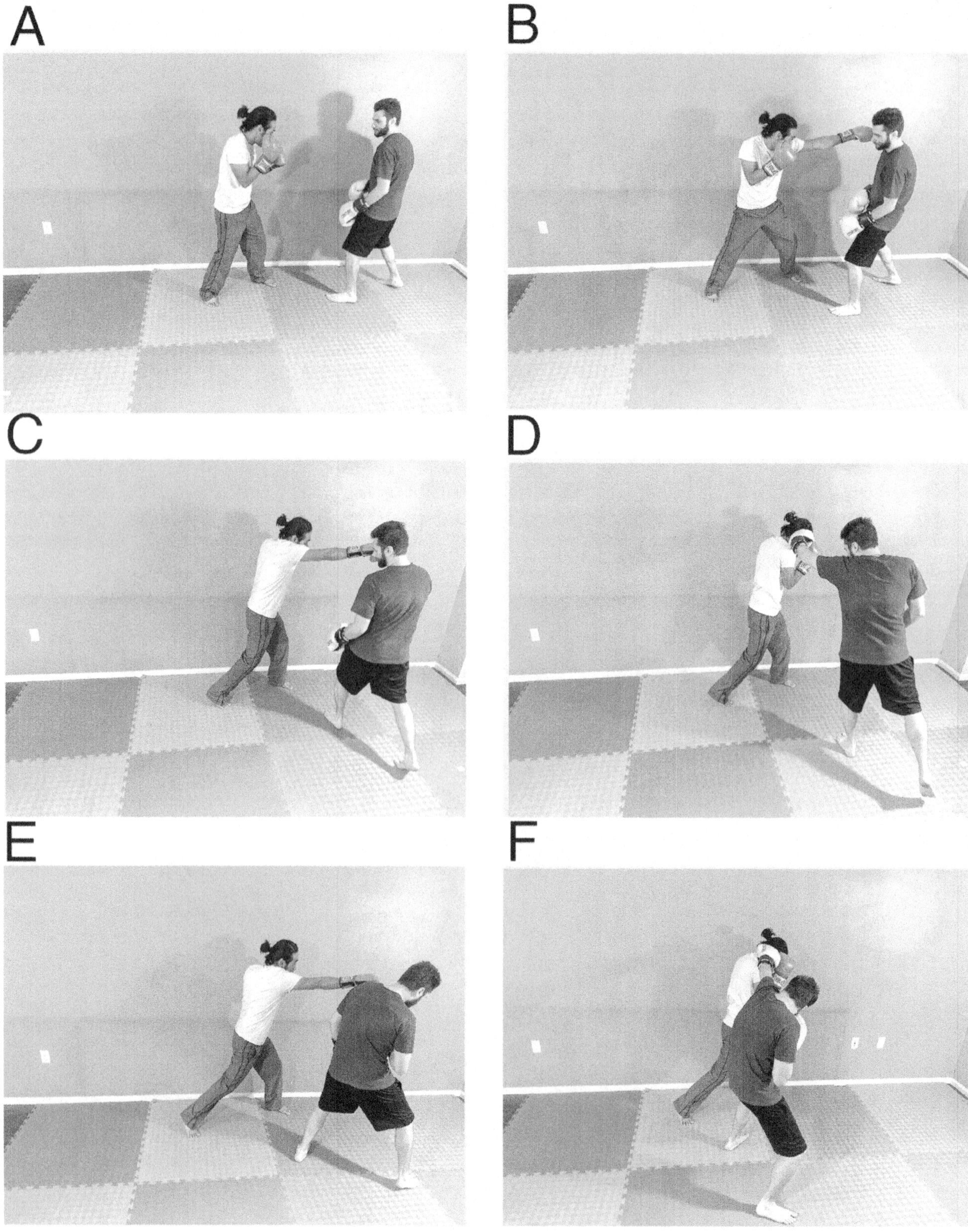

Open Stance Considerations

If in an Open Stance, you can attempt these techniques while circling Outside instead. Pernell Whitaker is perhaps the only fighter to ever really master the Open Stance version of Ali's techniques. So to dance as he did, stand in front of your partner in an Open Stance, bouncing lightly on the balls of your feet. When they step Outside to fire off a Jab or Cross, Cross Step your Rear Foot Outside. At the same time, either Pull Slip Outside, Crouch Inside, or Shoulder Roll and fire off a Jab of your own (Pics A to B).

Now Step Back with your Lead Foot and then Step Outside to get the dominant foot position (Pics C to D). At the same time, throw a counter from your new position. If this seems complicated, that's because it is. There's a reason only one man ever fought this way successfully, while several Orthodox fighters like Leonard and Hearns were able to add Ali's footwork and head movement to their style. The important thing to take away is that you must step back after your Cross Step so you have room to step Outside of your opponent's Lead Foot.

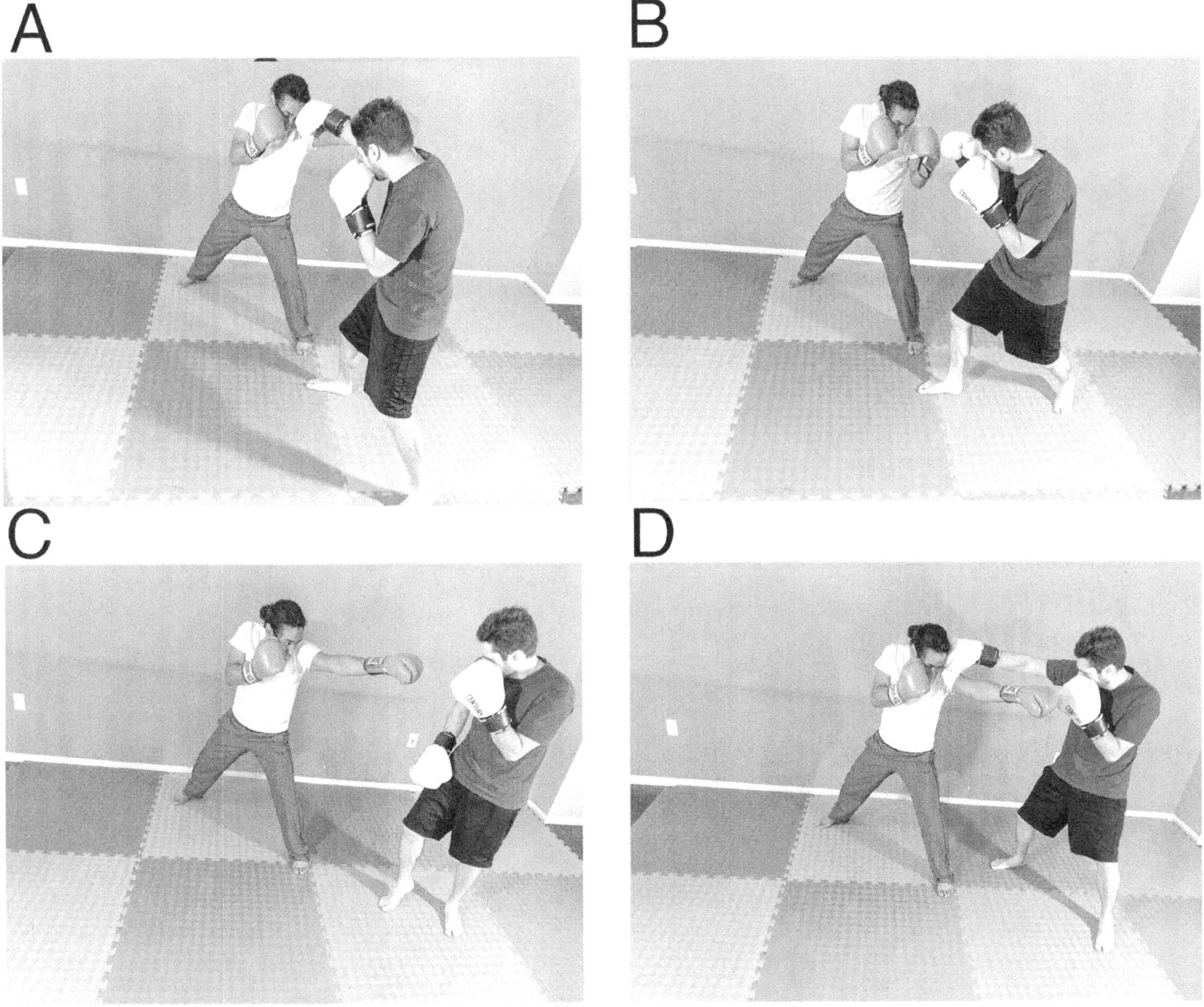

In Kickboxing

Few have used this sequence in MMA. Wonderboy Thompson and TJ Dillashaw have used Cross Steps to circle Inside at times, but it is by no means staples of their styles. However, in Muay Thai and Kickboxing, Samart Payakaroon (also a champion boxer) was able to modify Ali's footwork with great success. Samart fought in both an Orthodox and Southpaw Stance, meaning we have examples in both a Closed and an Open Stance. To perform Samart's footwork in a Closed position, lift your Lead Leg to Check after you have Cross Stepped (Pics A to F).

Open Stance Considerations

To perform Samart's footwork from an Open Stance, Shift Back after your Cross Step. This essentially works as a Pull Back to protect your Lead Leg and repositions you off angle (Pics A to D). If your opponent is closer or attacks after you have Shifted back, use your new Lead Leg (your left leg in Pic D) to Check. Whether you Check or not, Pivot out to regain your Southpaw Stance and put yourself and your opponent back into an Open Stance. Samart would use this footwork and head movement pattern to land Intercepting Jabs and Lead Teeps to the stomach.

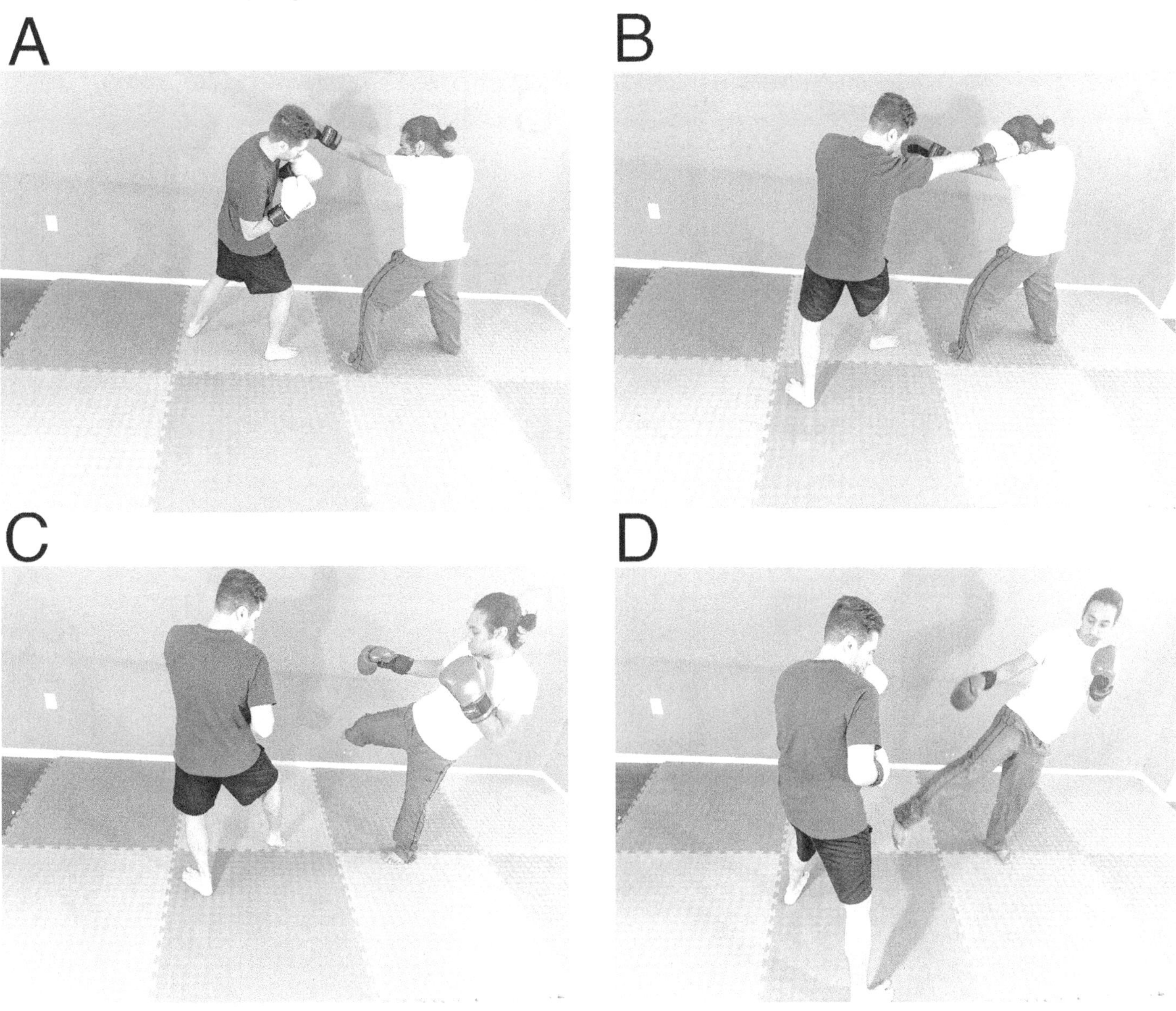

Drills

Drill 1

Have your partner chase you around the ring attempting to hit your head. Use Pulls and Pull Weaves to evade them (Pics A to B). When you feel that they may be overreaching, step your Lead Foot back and out and drive them into your Rear Hand (Pics C to D). Once again, Ali scored numerous KO's with this tactic. As always, your partner should try to defend your Counter. If they cannot, tap lightly or stop before contact.

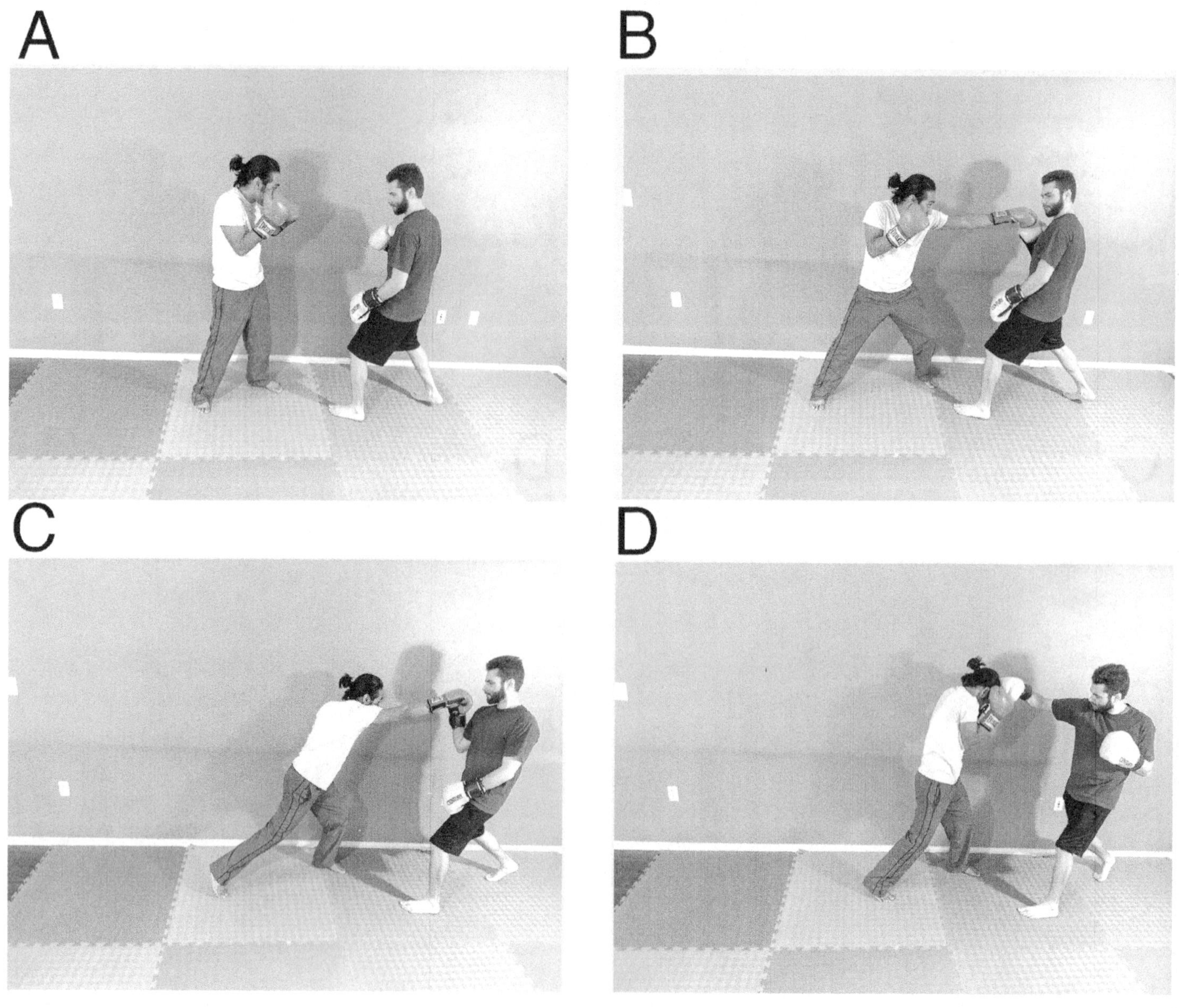

This works very well in an Open Stance as well. Conor McGregor has made a career of it. It's usually best to step your Rear Foot slightly Inside to stay safe and load up your strike before throwing (Pics A to D).

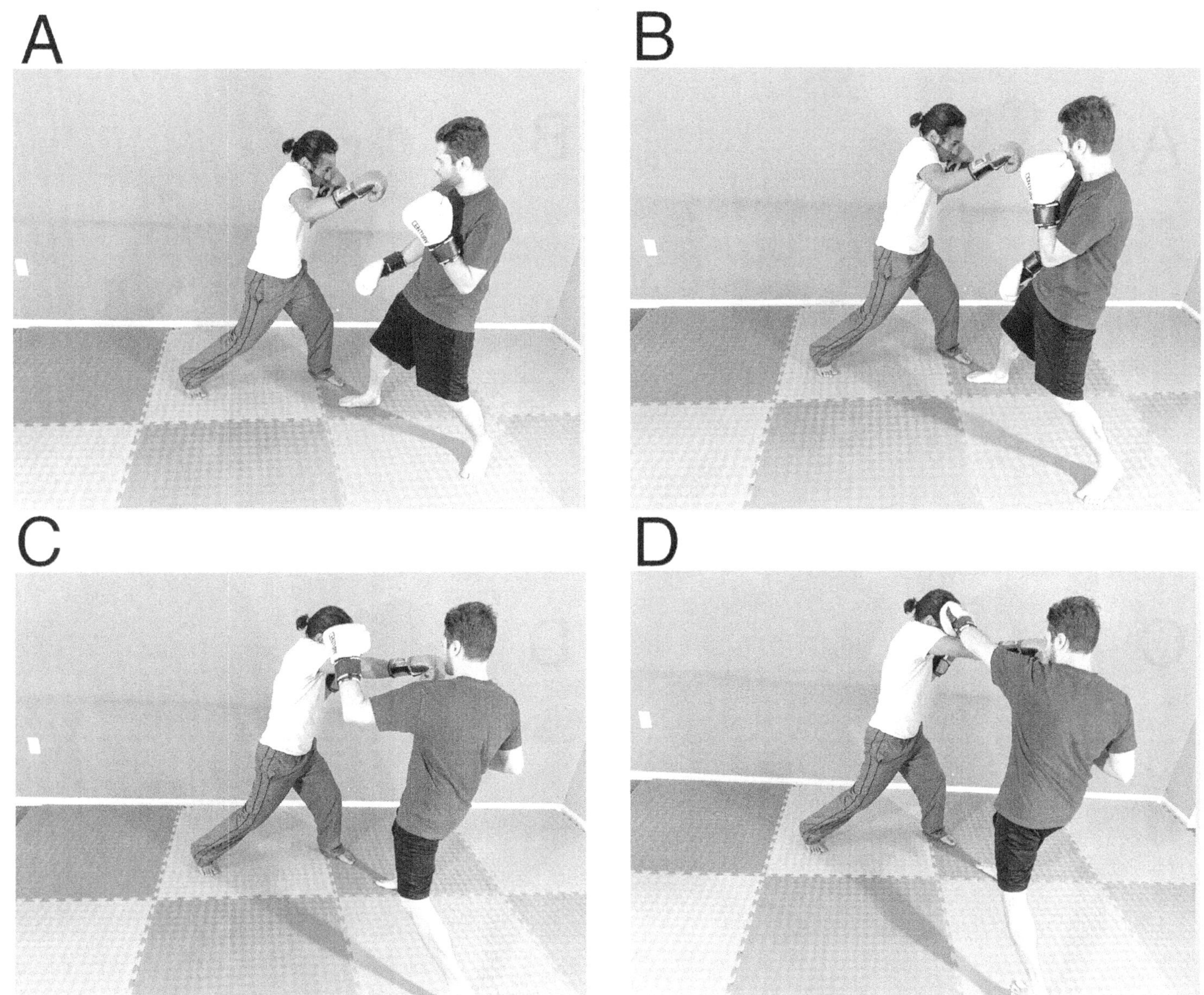

Drill 2

Have your partner throw strikes at your head. Shift Back Roll and Shift Back Weave to evade their punches (Pics A to D). For an advanced version, try to drive them into light Close-Range Hooks and Uppercuts, which they in turn will try to defend.

A

B

C

D

Drill 3

Have your partner attack your head. L-Step Outside while Drop Slipping Inside, leaving you off angle with your Rear Side lined up to throw (Pics A to D). You can also V-Step (Pics E to F). If in an Open Stance, you will be moving Inside and using the counters demonstrated earlier.

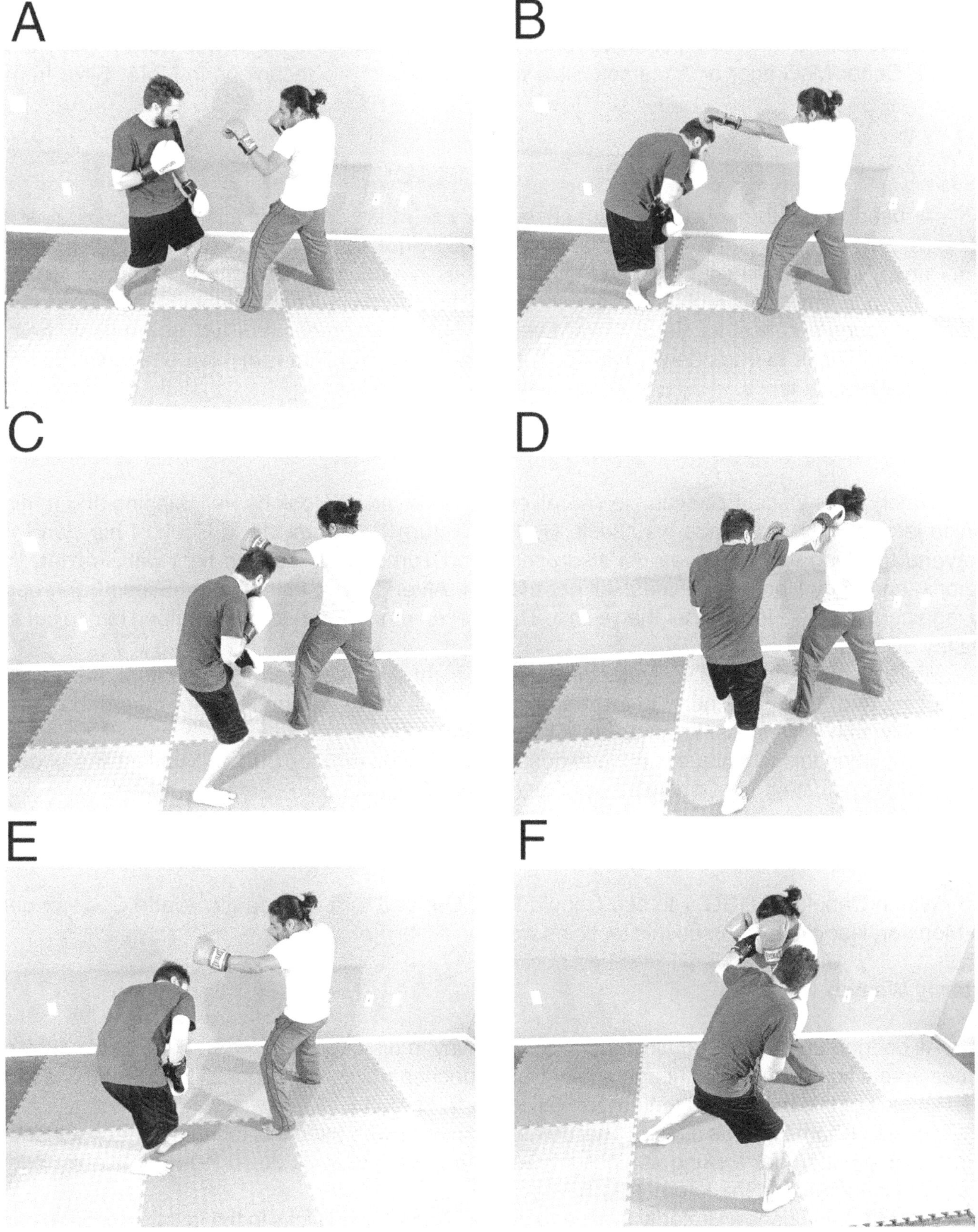

References – Low Guard

Lead Side Pull Slip:

Ali vs Ernie Terell has many great examples of this technique. Watch the 7th for plenty of demonstrations, as well as Ali screaming "What's my name!?" at the end of the round. Or watch round 3 of Ali vs Williams to see this technique result in a knockdown, or his fight with Zorah Folley to see a knockout. Conor McGregor or Anderson Silva really mastered this technique in MMA, Silva from both stances.

Pull Weave:

Ali used these throughout his career, but they're most evident in his first fight against Floyd Patterson. Patterson was known for his leaping Gazelle Hooks, and Ali Pull Weaved to evade most of them. Prince Naseem Hamed also used them frequently in a much more extreme way than Ali, and you can see them in any of his highlight reels. In Muay Thai, Lerdsila Chumpairtour uses them frequently against the ropes and against Head Kicks. Even crazier, he'll sometimes Pivot as he uses them. The fights can be difficult to track down, but YouTube has a few highlight reels that show him pull off this technique dozens of times.

Head Turn:

Watch Ali vs Oscar Bonavena to see Ali evade Bonavena's Hook by Pull Slipping and turning his head to let the Hook just graze his cheek. He then Return Counters with a Hook of his own to send Bonavena tumbling to the canvas. Ali also used Head Turns in his second fight with Frazier, though Frazier's legendary Hook sometimes still got through. Ali ended up actually Pull-Slipping the opposite way, against Frazier's Hook rather than with it. This is even more dangerous but helped him to cut angles and stay off the ropes.

Watch Israel Adesanya vs Anderson Silva for plenty of these from both fighters, including Silva Pull Slipping and turning his head to just barely evade Adesanya's Head Kick near the end of round 1. Or you can watch Silva's final knockdown of Forest Griffin.

Sometimes this technique is done in desperation to Roll with the punch, as a last line of defense. GGG did this against one of Canelo's bombs and seemed to take zero damage.

Pivot & Head Turn:

Watch Canelo vs GGG 1 to see Canelo Pivot Out and turn his head to evade GGG's punches. The Monster, Naoya Inoya, uses this tactic as well.

Butterfly Weave:

Ali dodged 20 punches against the ropes this way in his exhibition vs. Dokes, but he did it plenty of times in real fights as well (although against less punches obviously). Leonard vs Davey Green has a few examples of this movement pattern as well in the third round.

Somrak Khamsing was a Muay Thai defensive master who used this technique often. Once again, you may have better luck looking at highlight reels than trying to track down individual fights, but there are a few floating around the internet.

In MMA, Silva uses a Butterfly Weave to evade punches and kicks in the last 20 seconds of round 1 in his second fight against Rich Franklin, right before knocking him down.

Side Step:

Tyson Fury vs Klitschko or his first fight vs Wilder have several good examples. The move itself is something everyone learns, it's the way it's used and the timing that can turn it into a powerful tool.

Step Outside & Slip Inside (And Vice Versa):

Willie Pep was a boxing genius who used this move frequently. Inspired by him, Dominick Cruz has used it to land several counters in his impressive MMA career. Check out his fight vs TJ Dillashaw in the first round with 2:12 left for an example of the technique followed by a hard counter.

Slide/Step Back

Saenchai, Wonderboy Thompson and Mighty Mouse Johnson are good fighters to watch for this one.

L–Step & V–Shift

Willie Pep, Samart, Dominick Cruz and Mighty Mouse are good fighters to watch for L–Steps and V-Shifts. Check out Dominick Cruz vs Uriah Faber for plenty of examples.

The Ali Footwork & Head Movement Pattern

Watch any early Ali fight to see this in action. Ali modified it from Sugar Ray Robinson, and Leonard and Hearns imitated Ali. In kickboxing, Samart (a champion boxer himself) was able to use this system to set up Jabs and Teeps. In MMA, TJ Dillashaw has used a similar pattern. It's very noticeable in his championship fight vs Renan Barao. He even used the footwork to knock him down in the first. Wonderboy Thompson also likes to use the pattern from an Open Stance in Orthodox to Jab.

Shift Back & Roll/Crouch/Weave

Emanuel Augustus fights can be hard to find, but you can watch him pull off these tactics and many others in highlight reels on YouTube. Or watch James Toney Shift Back twice in round 2 with 1:21 left in his fight against Ricky Thomas, and again a few more times in the same round. Or watch his fight vs Freddie Delgado to see him counter off of a Shift Back Roll to end the fight. For an MMA version, you can see Cody Gardbrandt pull this off against none other than Dominick Cruz in round 3 with 1:24 left.

Thanks for reading.

Please feel free to email me with any questions at: TheMMArts@gmail.com.

Or follow me on Twitter: @MMArtist

You can see full video breakdowns of techniques, fights and fighters at:

https://www.youtube.com/c/TheModernMartialartist.

If you enjoyed this book, please leave a positive review! If you have any suggestions for more defensive techniques, please email me at the email provided above. It is actually fairly easy to alter the book and reupload it, and if your suggestion helps improve the book I can send you the new version in an E-Book format to show my appreciation.

Happy training,

David

Made in the USA
Las Vegas, NV
04 December 2023